CHILD
DEVELOPMENT

Sara Miller McCune founded SAGE Publishing in 1965 to support the dissemination of usable knowledge and educate a global community. SAGE publishes more than 1000 journals and over 800 new books each year, spanning a wide range of subject areas. Our growing selection of library products includes archives, data, case studies and video. SAGE remains majority owned by our founder and after her lifetime will become owned by a charitable trust that secures the company's continued independence.

Los Angeles | London | New Delhi | Singapore | Washington DC | Melbourne

CHILD DEVELOPMENT

MARTIN J. PACKER

DEVELOPMENT

UNDERSTANDING A CULTURAL PERSPECTIVE

⑤SAGE

Los Angeles | London | New Delhi
Singapore | Washington DC | Melbourne

Los Angeles | London | New Delhi
Singapore | Washington DC | Melbourne

SAGE Publications Ltd
1 Oliver's Yard
55 City Road
London EC1Y 1SP

SAGE Publications Inc.
2455 Teller Road
Thousand Oaks, California 91320

SAGE Publications India Pvt Ltd
B 1/I 1 Mohan Cooperative Industrial Area
Mathura Road
New Delhi 110 044

SAGE Publications Asia-Pacific Pte Ltd
3 Church Street
#10-04 Samsung Hub
Singapore 049483

Editor: Luke Block
Editorial assistant: Lucy Dang
Production editor: Imogen Roome
Copyeditor: Audrey Scriven
Proofreader: Neil Dowden
Indexer: Elske Janssen
Marketing manager: Lucia Sweet
Cover design: Wendy Scott
Typeset by: C&M Digitals (P) Ltd, Chennai, India
Printed in the UK by Ashford Colour Press Ltd,
Gosport, Hampshire.

Library of Congress Control Number: 2016950445

British Library Cataloguing in Publication data

A catalogue record for this book is available from
the British Library

ISBN 978-1-4739-9336-5
ISBN 978-1-4739-9337-2 (pbk)

At SAGE we take sustainability seriously. Most of our products are printed in the UK using FSC papers and boards.
When we print overseas we ensure sustainable papers are used as measured by the PREPS grading system.
We undertake an annual audit to monitor our sustainability.

CONTENTS

ABOUT THE AUTHOR

Martin Packer is Associate Professor of Psychology at the University of the Andes in Bogotá, Colombia. He received his BA in Natural Sciences at Cambridge University, United Kingdom, and his PhD in Psychology at the University of California, Berkeley. He was a research psychologist at Bedford College, University of London, and St Mary's Hospital Perinatal Research Unit. He has taught at the University of California, Berkeley, the University of Michigan, and Duquesne University. He has been visiting professor at Univérsidad de las Américas, in Puebla, Mexico, and at Univérsidad Autónoma Metropolitana, in Xochimilco, Mexico City. His research has explored interactions between neonates and their mothers, early childhood–peer relations, conflict among adolescents, and the way schools change the kind of person a child becomes. Packer is co-editor of *Entering the Circle: Hermeneutic Investigation in Psychology* (with Ritch Addison), *Cultural and Critical Perspectives on Human Development* (with Mark Tappan), and *Reflections on the Learning Sciences* (with Michael Evans and Keith Sawyer). He is author of *The Structure of Moral Action*, of *Changing Classes: School Reform and the New* Economy, and of *The Science of Qualitative Research* (translated into Spanish). He was one of the founding co-editors of the journal *Qualitative Research in Psychology*, has been editor of *Mind, Culture, and Activity*, and has published articles in *American Psychologist, Educational Psychologist, The Journal of the Learning Sciences, Revista Colombiana de Psicología,* and *Mind, Culture & Activity.* He is currently an editorial board member of *The Humanistic Psychologist, Qualitative Research in Psychology,* and *Mind, Culture, and Activity.*

THE SAGE COMPANION WEBSITE

Visit the SAGE companion website at **https://study.sagepub.com/packer** to find a range of free tools and resources that will enhance your learning experience.

For students:

- **Multiple Choice Questions** allow you to test your knowledge and give you feedback to help you prepare for assignments and exams.

- **Read more widely!** A selection of *free* SAGE journal articles supports the book to help deepen your knowledge and reinforce your learning of key topics.

- Watch author-selected **videos** to give you deeper insight into select concepts and to build on context to foster understanding and facilitate learning.

- **Weblinks** direct you to relevant resources to broaden your understanding of chapter topics and expand your knowledge on Child Development.

- **Group and individual tasks** are designed to help you think critically and check your understanding.

CHAPTER 1

INTRODUCTION

Human beings do not grow up, and adults do not parent, in isolation, but always in physical and social contexts. Children, parents, and cultures are, therefore, intimately bundled because children must learn and adapt to their culture to survive and thrive; a major goal of parenting is to successfully embed the next generation into the existing culture … Culture plays an overarching role in organizing and directing the ecology of childhood and parenthood … It has been observed that perhaps the most significant factor in determining the overall course of a person's life is the culture into which that person was born. (Bornstein, 2010, p. ix)

1. A CULTURAL PERSPECTIVE ON CHILDREN'S DEVELOPMENT

Every human child is born into a community, a society with a culture, in which she will live, grow, and develop. This community is essential for her survival, and in time she will become able not only to participate in it, but also to help reproduce and even transform her community. How this happens is a mystery that developmental research is beginning to unravel. It can be argued that the most important characteristic that defines human beings is our ability to arrange a culturally organized environment. Indeed, all humans need to live in such an environment; without it we would not survive. For much of the history of developmental psychology, however, the role of culture has been ignored, or reduced to a simple influence such as shaping behavior or socialization. For example, one of the most influential theorists of children's development, Jean Piaget, focused on the child's interaction with the physical environment, and largely ignored the fact that the child lives with other people in a complex cultural world of artifacts, practices, and institutions. When one reads Piaget's books on infancy, which are based on case studies of his own three children, one wonders who changed their diapers!

The field of developmental research is currently in an important and exciting transition, with growing recognition of the significance of culture in children's development. There is a pressing need for a fundamental change in the organization of textbooks in this field, for very few currently place culture at the center. The challenge is to appreciate cultural differences and cross-cultural variation but at the same time to recognize that the role of culture goes beyond this.

The central question that this text sets out to answer is this: how does a child, who at birth knows nothing of how her culture works, develop the psychological skills and abilities to participate in that culture and contribute to its reproduction and transformation? The book explores what we now know about the answer to this question, and what we do not yet know. My goal is that students understand a cultural perspective on children's development.

The book has a chronological organization, because I consider it essential to trace the process of ontogenesis through time. In addition, social, cognitive, emotional, and physical aspects of development are interwoven in each chapter, since showing their interconnections is, in my view, indispensable. The psychological functions form a dynamic system, and separating their components, as most textbooks do, is misleading.

In addition, while some developmental textbooks have begun to pay attention to culture, this has generally taken the form of cross-cultural comparisons, reflecting the assumption that the influence of culture only leads to differences in children's development. However, this is only half the story: human beings need to live in culture, and culture is an essential component of every child's psychological development. In my view, a child development text that attends to culture has to seek to achieve two goals. The first goal is to represent the variety of cultures, plural, in which children live. The second goal, equally important, is to explore the ubiquity of culture, singular. Culture is a characteristic of the way that all human beings live, and we shall see that culture, in the singular, plays a *constitutive* role in children's development.

Adopting a cultural perspective on the development of children means paying attention to the artifacts that people have created in order to survive and thrive, and that they then pass down to their children. It requires abandoning the assumption, central to Piaget's account of development as well as many others, that there is a sequence of stages universal to all children. It means being skeptical about measurements and evaluations of children's abilities and performance when these are created in one culture but then used in another.

What has started to emerge over the past decade or so is an interdisciplinary approach to the study of children's development, one that does not restrict itself to the limited techniques of traditional experimental research design. The fruits of this approach, and this way of thinking, are what I hope to share in this text.

The text, then, adopts the perspective of "cultural psychology." This is not simply a specialized area within psychology, it is a fresh approach to all areas of psychology, whether developmental, cognitive, clinical, or even neurological. Cultural psychology pays attention to the undeniable fact that human beings are cultural animals. We live in culture, we create culture, and we are created by culture. This is not say that biology plays no part: on the contrary, the chapters of this text explore how culture and biology are woven together so tightly that it is difficult to distinguish one from the other.

A cultural perspective on children's development is, then, a fresh approach that helps us understand how human children develop uniquely human abilities without drawing a rigid boundary between ourselves and other animals (by claiming that humans have unique biologically based capacities, for example), and without dividing research in two (insisting that neurobiology has nothing to say about the study of culture and social interactions, for example).

One psychologist who was critical of the lack of attention given to culture in the study of children's development wrote: "it can be said that much of contemporary developmental psychology is the science of the strange behavior of children in strange situations with strange adults for the briefest possible periods of time" (Bronfenbrenner, 1977, p. 513). A cultural perspective on children's development calls for us to look at children in situations that are aspects of their everyday lives, and in their relations with significant people.

Developmental psychology is the scientific study of the development of human psychological functions, including perception, knowledge, thinking, memory, emotion, and language. It is principally the study of **ontogenesis**, the development of the individual human organism from childhood to adulthood and beyond. (Note: the term "genesis" here does not refer to the genes, the biological carriers of inherited characteristics. Genesis here means the origins of something, or its mode of formation.) One of the central themes of this book, however, will be that the individual child should not be studied in isolation, abstracted from her social relationships or her cultural circumstances. If we are to adequately understand ontogenesis, the development of the child, we must take into account not only her current circumstances, but also the origins of these, in the sense both of **phylogenesis**, the evolution of the human species, and of **sociocultural evolution**, the historical changes in human societies and human culture.

Developmental psychology is often assumed to be just one branch or specialty within psychology, alongside clinical psychology, cognitive psychology, social psychology, and so on. But it is more appropriate to think of developmental psychology as a specific approach to *all* psychological phenomena. Developmental researchers are interested in clinical phenomena, such as autism and aggression, and in cognitive phenomena, such as reasoning and memory, and in social phenomena, such as attachment and communication. Developmental psychology is also increasingly a cross-disciplinary or interdisciplinary enterprise; that is to say, it involves researchers and investigative techniques not only from psychology, but also from biology, neuroscience, linguistics, anthropology, and cultural studies. Some have proposed the term **developmental science** for this collaborative work.

The following points highlight core features of the chapters that follow:

Children's development (ontogenesis) is an aspect of evolution, both biological and societal. It has become clear that the development of a child from conception to maturity and ultimately death is not a process distinct from biological evolution, or the evolution of human societies, but an essential component of the process of evolution. Society is the kind of ecological niche that humans construct, and children inherit it along with their parents' genes. The human life cycle has evolved, with each hominid showing a different balance of developmental stages. Societies have also evolved, and made a variety of arrangements for the raising and education of their children. Children's development must be studied, and understood, in the context of these other temporal processes.

Cultures change over time, and so does development. A cultural perspective, then, requires taking into account not just different human communities but also the historical changes in those communities. Many theories of the development of children, whether in psychology, anthropology, or sociology, have been ahistorical, assuming that children simply will become what adults already are. We know now that children do not simply acquire the competence of the adults around them, they transform it into something new.

Cognition is inherently social. A cultural perspective on children's development means adopting a new theoretical framework that rethinks the relationship between social and cognitive aspects of development. Developmental psychologists have often assumed that the child is a biological creature, who only becomes social and/or cultural as a consequence of the influence of other people. This division is perpetuated by textbooks that deal only with cognitive development, or those that deal only with social development, or those that deal with both but divide them into separate chapters. A cultural perspective on children's development avoids an artificial separation of the child into two components, the intellectual and the social.

The child is always social. This separation into components is inappropriate because the human child is always social. I emphasize in this text that the child, even as an infant—especially as an infant—always acts in and through relations with other people. It is only with time that the child may become an "individual"—the kind of abstract person with rights and responsibilities that is recognized by modern society. Of course, development is necessary—an infant is considerably different from an adult—but this development does not take the form of "socialization," in the sense of training the child to become social. Only as an adult, and then only in certain societies, can the child become the freely choosing, autonomous, and independent agent that we in the West take an adult to be. Even when an adult, other people are essential for the survival of an individual.

The child is active in her own development. It is these other people, especially caregivers, who organize the conditions in which a child lives, grows, and develops. But they do not, and cannot, determine what the child makes of those conditions. Culture is not something the child "acquires" as she might a collection of colored pencils. Culture is the basis for, the condition for the possibility of, the child becoming an adult. Indeed, it is the basis upon which the human child can live at all. But the child is always actively involved in the interactions that provide the local impetus for her psychological development. This text repeatedly emphasizes the active character of the child, at every stage of development.

Culture is not simply context. Culture is not simply "context," any more than the body is a mere context for the development of the brain. Culture weaves together the people who have woven it, and a culture is inextricably interconnected with the psychology of its people. Culture does not simply "influence" development, or "impact" development. Certainly culture doesn't "cause" development, either alone or with the help of biology. As I have already suggested, we need to rethink the relationships among biology, culture, and ontogenesis. If we think of ontogenesis not as a process that occurs "in" the child, or as a process that occurs "to" the child, but as a dynamically unfolding process in which the child, as a material organism, is actively engaged with the environment as a humanly organized material setting, we will be on the right track.

Children become normative animals. Developmental researchers are paying increasing attention to the "normativity" of human action, and of the societies in which we live. For example, a recent book is titled *The Normative Animal?* (Bayertz & Roughley, in press), and other books and several dozen research articles on this theme have been published in the past few years. Humans create, and live in, social realities in which we permit that our actions are regulated by customs, conventions, agreements, rules, contracts, and laws. It has been proposed that it is principally this normativity—this shared sense of what is considered the normal or correct way of doing things—that distinguishes us from our primate cousins. It has become clear than any discussion of moral development and moral reasoning has to be part of this larger consideration of the normativity of human life. The analysis by philosopher John Searle of the way that every society is built from "institutional facts" that define rights and responsibilities (*The Construction of Social Reality*, Simon & Schuster, 1995) is one of the influences on this textbook.

This normative dimension is central to this book. I have been following this area of research with great interest, and at each stage of development it is a central theme. For example, it has been proposed that alongside the "intentional stance" that is often known as "theory of mind," children also develop or acquire a "normative stance." Children understand a person's actions not only in terms of beliefs and desires (individual psychological states) but also in terms of roles and responsibilities (aspects of normativity). Without doubt, children need to come to understand the various kinds of normativity of the society in which they live, and researchers are now beginning to understand how this happens. There is increasing evidence that they pass through a series of levels in their comprehension of normativity. Clearly, this is an area of research that is central if we are to grasp how children become fully competent members of the society into which they are born. The explosion of research on normativity is another indication of a dramatic change in developmental psychology, one which to my knowledge no other textbook discusses.

In conclusion, then, a cultural perspective on children's development means thinking about culture not as a causal variable or as a factor that simply has an influence on psychological processes and that consequently produces differences among children who grow up in different cultures, but instead as playing a constitutive role in children's development: culture (along with biology, of course) is what makes possible the complexity and sophistication of human psychological functioning.

2. ORGANIZATION OF THE BOOK

The chapters of this text unpack the ways in which children's psychological capabilities develop within the conditions provided by the culture of a society.

CHAPTER 2: THEORETICAL PERSPECTIVES

This chapter offers a brief history of developmental psychology in terms of its major theoretical perspectives. For most of this history a pendulum has swung between a focus on nature and a focus on nurture. Now there is a growing appreciation that nature and nurture, biology and culture, are two sides of the same coin. We shall see that the theoretical perspective of cultural psychology emphasizes that human beings enjoy more than one form of inheritance: parents pass genetic material to their children, but in addition each generation passes to the next the artifacts they have created to accomplish the tasks of everyday life, from growing crops to studying distant stars.

CHAPTER 3: INTERWOVEN LINES OF DEVELOPMENT

A child is born with a body and brain that are her biological inheritance from billions of years of evolution of life on our planet. At the same time she is born into a world that has been shaped both by that same process of evolution and by the labor of her community, who have transformed their material conditions over the course of their history. This chapter aims to locate children's development within the context of biological evolution and societal evolution. Reconceptualization of biological evolution in the light of niche construction theory, and reconceptualization of societal evolution— to avoid the nineteenth-century notions of a historical progression towards "civilization"—enable us to see that there is a single process of evolution and that ontogenesis—the development of an organism from conception to maturity and finally death—is an aspect of this process. We should not think of biological or societal evolution as having an "impact" on children's development, because development is a *component* of evolution.

CHAPTER 4: PRENATAL DEVELOPMENT, BIRTH, AND THE NEWBORN (CONCEPTION TO 6 WEEKS OF AGE)

Birth is the moment from which we begin to count the days, months, and years of a child's life. But birth itself is the culmination of a process which in one respect began 9 months earlier and in another respect, when we consider homo sapiens as an animal species, has roots that can be traced back billions of years. This chapter explores the processes of conception and prenatal development, with an emphasis on the formation and growth of the human nervous system, including the brain, which is of course an organ of central importance. The moment of birth is a dramatic transition not only for the neonate but also for the mother and the other people who are involved: a transition in which one biological unit becomes two. Although birth might seem a solely biological process, it is culturally organized and filled with cultural significance. Paradoxically, a newborn human can do far fewer things for herself than the newborn of other species. This dependence has evolved, and this chapter considers its possible evolutionary value and implications for the infant's further development. But, at the same time, the newborn is by no means helpless and the chapter also explores the capabilities of the newborn child.

CHAPTER 5: INFANCY—A PRACTICAL UNDERSTANDING OF THE WORLD (6 WEEKS–12 MONTHS)

It has been recognized for some time that infancy is a stage in which the child learns about her immediate environment in a direct, practical manner. Chapter 5 explores how, dependent on others and exquisitely tuned to them, the infant explores in an embodied manner a world that is completely social, a world that Vygotsky called the "Great-We." The infant understands this world on a simple level, in terms of its contingencies.

CHAPTER 6: INFANCY—TOWARDS BIOLOGICAL DIFFERENTIATION (6 WEEKS–12 MONTHS)

Chapter 6 continues with a discussion of the primary emotions, for this is an age, and a stage, at which there is as yet no clear differentiation between the social and the intellectual, the cognitive and the emotional, between physical movement and planning. This chapter concludes with a discussion of the three aspects of the transition at around 12 months of age: starting to walk, starting to talk, and the biological differentiation that prompts the emotional bond called attachment.

CHAPTER 7: TODDLERHOOD—A WORLD OF IRRESISTIBLE INVITATIONS (1 YEAR–30 MONTHS)

The ability to walk independently and to speak recognizable words are aspects of a biological separation from significant others that provides new strengths as well as new anxieties.

Toddlerhood is a stage of mastering the simple skills of daily life, such as feeding and dressing, and in doing so coming to understand the customary uses of everyday artifacts—their functions, and the norms for using them. Chapter 7 explores first the world of the toddler, then turns to the character of caregiving at this stage, contrasting attachment theory with the proposal that caregiving is guided participation. As the toddler participates in a widening range of activities with other people she shows a growing ability to understand the intentions in their actions, and also begins to recognize the tacit social norms and customs that her family lives by and to hold other people accountable to these.

CHAPTER 8: TODDLERHOOD—TOWARDS PSYCHOLOGICAL DIFFERENTIATION (1 YEAR–30 MONTHS)

Chapter 8 describes the character of speech during the second year of life, and explores the impact of oral language on the toddler's perception, including her growing ability to recognize and use material representations. Finally, it describes the dramatic transition that marks the end of toddlerhood, as a form of self-consciousness begins to appear in which the toddler starts to understand that she too is held accountable to these norms, along with a dawning understanding of the distinction between males and females (though it is far too early to speak of "gender identity").

CHAPTER 9: EARLY CHILDHOOD—HOW THINGS APPEAR, AND HOW THEY ARE (2.5–6 YEARS)

Early childhood is the stage for creating representations. In fantasy play with peers the young child turns one thing into another, exercises imagination, and develops initiative and self-control. Her spoken language becomes increasingly sophisticated, and she is now able to talk both to act on other people and to share information. During this stage, with the help of language, the young child breaks away from the lure of how things appear, and starts to grasp how they really are. In this, however, the "cosmology" of her culture has a central role.

CHAPTER 10: EARLY CHILDHOOD—TOWARDS INNER AND OUTER (2.5–6 YEARS)

In Chapter 10, we will see how the young child becomes able to understand other people's prior intentions, and also the scenarios in which people act, as conventional characters. We consider debates about the value and consequences of different styles of caregiving, and then turn to the origins of verbal thinking at this stage. The young child begins to recognize that she herself is a kind of person, a "girl," for example, while her brother is not. Finally, we consider the biological changes that occur during this stage.

CHAPTER 11: MIDDLE CHILDHOOD—UNDERSTANDING INSTITUTIONAL REALITY (6–12 YEARS)

In the crisis around 6 years of age, the child applies the distinction between appearance and reality to herself. The 5-to-7 transition is marked by physical changes, and changes too in the child's position in family and community, as new responsibilities are placed on her shoulders. She learns new skills and knowledge, through participation, apprenticeship, or formal schooling. She can now infer other people's underlying beliefs and desires, and also recognize the institutional roles that people occupy, including herself.

CHAPTER 12: MIDDLE CHILDHOOD—TOWARDS THE ACTUAL AND THE POSSIBLE (6–12 YEARS)

Chapter 12 focuses on the institution of school, and the psychological consequences of schooling. We discuss the influence of schooling on concrete operational reasoning, its role in the higher psychological functions, and the psychological consequences of literacy. Finally, we examine what children are doing outside school and work, in organizations such as the girl scouts, and in interactions and games with peers.

CHAPTER 13: THE TEENAGE YEARS—ADOLESCENT OR ADULT? (12 YEARS AND UP)

We hear and read so much about the character and challenges of adolescence that it is hard to imagine that this is not a universal stage of development. In fact, however, adolescence emerged very recently in human history, though perhaps not for the first time. It is not culturally universal, even today. Adolescence, then, is a stage in which the role of culture in ontogenesis is very clear. Evolution has produced a growth spurt following puberty, and such plasticity to the human brain that the key frontal areas are still forming and linking with complex networks. Both brain changes and cultural arrangements facilitate greater conscious control of thoughts, feelings, and actions. The adolescent lives in a world of possibilities, both empowering and frustrating.

CHAPTER 14: THE TEENAGE YEARS—TOWARDS ADULTHOOD (12 YEARS AND UP)

The teenager becomes aware of who she might be as well as who she is, and compares her own view of herself with other people's views of her. Identity is a matter of self as self-conscious subject, self as known by self and by other people. The self-awareness and self-control that emerge in the teenager involve a new psychological center, a new form and source of agency.

In the teenage years relations with adults are renegotiated, and peers become even more important. The circumstances of these changes vary widely from culture to culture, however. Finally, research on moral judgments opens a window onto the ways that adolescents understand other people. Many adolescents, at least among the advantaged groups that have been studied, pass through a stance of epistemological relativism, in which they consider a person's knowledge to be their personal opinion. All opinions are valid and should be listened to, but debate is pointless in the sense that it cannot decide between conflicting opinions.

Many adolescents also pass through a stance of ethical relativism, in which they conclude that social conventions do not have the societal functions that they are claimed to have, so that morality is no more than what seems right to an individual in a specific position and context.

These two forms of relativism have been interpreted as a problem and even a failure, but they can also be seen as a critical response to authorities who are seen as insincere and inadequate.

CHAPTER 15: SUMMING UP

The final chapter reflects on the concepts that have emerged as key in this exploration of children's development from a cultural perspective. The first section reviews what we have learned about stages and transitions, and developmental trajectories. The second section reflects on the two sequences of stances that children adopt as they understand other people. One sequence involves theory of mind, but not only this. The other sequence involves what has been called the normative stance. The third section considers the ways that a cultural perspective attends to both "lower" and "higher" psychological functions: those that we share with other animals, and those that make humans unique.

Finally, a note on terminology: I have adopted the convention of calling the stage from birth to 1 year of age *infancy*, and the child during this stage an *infant*. During the stage from 1 year to around 30 months the child is a *toddler* and I call this stage, rather awkwardly, *toddlerhood*. The stage from 30 months to around 6 years I call *early childhood*, and use the term *young child* rather than preschooler, because children do not attend school in every culture. The stage from 6 to around 11 years is *middle childhood*, and I simply use the term *child*, rather than school age child, for the same reason. The stage from around 11 years up is generally called *adolescence*, but I will often use the more culturally neutral term *teenager*.

CHAPTER 2
THEORETICAL PERSPECTIVES IN DEVELOPMENTAL PSYCHOLOGY

Development is not simply a function which can be determined entirely by X units of heredity and Y units of environment. It is an historical complex, which at any stage reflects its past content. In other words, the artificial dualism of heredity and environment points us in a fallacious direction; it obscures the fact that development is an uninterrupted process which feeds upon itself; that it is not a puppet which can be controlled by jerking two strings. (Vygotsky, 1993, p. 253)

LEARNING OBJECTIVES

In this chapter we will reflect on the history of the scientific study of children's development. We will summarize a series of theoretical perspectives and meet some of the key people whose work will appear in later chapters:

- The Genetic Psychology of G. Stanley Hall and Arnold Gesell.
- The Behaviorism of John Watson and B. F. Skinner.
- Cognitive Developmental Psychology, with its central assumption that the human mind functions like a digital computer.
- The Constructivism of Jean Piaget, proposing that the child constructs knowledge as she actively explores her environment.
- The Cultural Psychology that draws from the writings of Lev Vygotsky.
- This will enable us to see how developmental psychology has struggled with key conceptual issues, centrally the relationship between nature and nurture.

FRAMING QUESTIONS

- Which do you consider more important in your own development: nature or nurture?
- A psychologist tells you that biology is the cause of what is common to humans across the world, while culture is the cause of the differences. Do you agree?

INTRODUCTION

Every developmental psychologist works within a theoretical perspective, which provides a lens through which to look at the child. At times the perspective is explicitly stated, at other times it is implicit and

the changes that make men aggressive and prepare women for maternity. Adolescence is the time of a "reconstruction" and a changing of the relations among "psychic functions." Sex now "asserts its mastery" and "works its havoc" (1904, p. xv). The adolescent "craves more knowledge of body and mind"; he "wakes to a new world and understands neither it nor himself." These new powers must be "husbanded and directed," for at this age "everything is plastic" (1904, p. xv).

1.2 ARNOLD GESELL

Another significant figure in the genetic perspective, a generation later than G. Stanley Hall, was Arnold Gesell (1880–1961), who worked at the Yale University Clinic for Child Development. Where Hall was a Romantic, Gesell, in contrast, was interested in the rational, ordered, and self-disciplined aspects of human nature. For him, the scientific study of children's development should be based on empirical facts, not on images of a distant life of the soul.

Despite their differences, Gesell, like Hall, emphasized the role of biological maturation in children's development. In an article written for the *Encyclopaedia of the Social Sciences* Gesell equated "development" with growth: "Growth is itself a unifying concept which removes undue distinctions between mind and body, between heredity and environment, between health and disease and also between separate scientific disciplines" (Gesell, 1930, pp. 392–393). He also stated that "like the heavenly bodies the human life cycle is governed by natural laws. In surety and precision the laws of development are comparable to those of gravitation" (1930, p. 59), and that the phenomena of growth "are subject to general and unifying laws which can be formulated only by coordinated contributions from several scientific domains" (1930, p. 392).

Gesell believed that the scientific disciplines of psychology and biology are linked, in a scientific division of labor. He envisioned psychology becoming psychobiology, and producing a "psychotechnology" of testing and assessment. In time, he predicted, "the early span of human growth will come more fully under social control," and "this is only the beginning of a policy of health supervision ... ." In his view, then, the goal of scientific developmental psychology was to discover laws of growth to achieve "a constructive and preventive supervision of human infancy" (1930, p. 393). He also argued that, "With the employment of scientific method, however, errors are being steadily reduced and the manifold problems of child development are approached in a new spirit of rationalism" (1930, p. 391).

Although Gesell emphasized that the infant "is a biological fragment of nature," he saw that "he is also meshed in a web of human relationships," and reasoned that "the system of child psychology which any culture achieves is an index of that culture." He proposed that child psychology leads to "a deeper comprehension of the process of social organization itself." Gesell himself undertook a series of highly detailed studies of children's development and put children under the microscope—or at least under the film camera. His laboratory housed a dome under which children of different ages were observed objectively and filmed for detailed analysis of their behavior.

Gesell viewed development as a movement through distinct stages, but he insisted that it proceeds not "in a staircase manner or by installments. It is always fluent and continuous" (Gesell et al., 1943, p. 61). He saw development as the result of an interaction between child and environment; however, the basic characteristics of each developmental stage are, in his view, the products of an evolutionary process in which new qualities are acquired and then handed down.

1.3 ERIK ERIKSON

Another key figure whose work had its roots in the genetic perspective, though it moved beyond this perspective, was Erik Erikson (1902–1994), who trained as a Freudian psychoanalyst at the Vienna Psychoanalytic Institute. After moving from Europe to the USA he worked to articulate a "psychosocial" model of development, which expanded Freud's psychosexual account of children's development to include attending to the culture in which a child develops. He wanted to create a psychoanalysis that was "sophisticated enough to include the environment" (Erikson, 1994 [1968], p. 24).

Erikson viewed the human life cycle as a passing through distinct stages. Each of these stages has its own dynamics, the result of "the laws of individual development and of social organization" (Erikson, 1994 [1959], p. 7), and each stage involves a distinct kind of **crisis**. By "crisis" Erikson meant not an impending catastrophe but "a necessary turning point, a crucial moment, when development must move one way or another, marshaling resources of growth, recovery, and further differentiation" (Erikson, 1994 [1968], p. 16). He proposed that each stage involves a culturally defined moratorium (a temporary delay) during which the individual is given time to master the challenges of that stage, and during which structured institutional contexts provide guidance. The moratorium is a period during which the potential crisis of the stage can be resolved. If the crisis is not resolved, there will be challenges for future development.

Erikson's account of development represents an early and important attempt to understand the role of culture in the formation of the personality and the dynamics of psychological processes. We shall return to Erikson's ideas in later chapters, in particular in Chapter 14.

Stage	Crisis	Positive Outcome
Infancy 0–1 year	Basic trust v. mistrust	Hope
Toddler 1–3 years	Autonomy v. shame & doubt	Will
Play age 3–6 years	Initiative v. guilt	Purpose
School age 6–12 years	Industry v. inferiority	Competence
Adolescence 12–19 years	Identity v. confusion	Fidelity
Early adulthood 20–25 years	Intimacy v. isolation	Love
Adulthood 26–64 years	Generativity v. stagnation	Care
Maturity 65–death	Integrity v. despair	Wisdom

Figure 2.2 Erik Erikson's stages of psychosocial development

The genetic perspective assumed that as a child develops she passes through a series of invariant stages, and that endogenous factors—internal to the child—dominate development. Each of these stages is characterized by a qualitatively distinctive structure of the organism, and a qualitatively distinct pattern of interaction between organism and environment. Gesell wrote, for example:

Environment … determines the occasion, the intensity, and the correlation of many aspects of behavior, but it does not engender the basic progressions of behavior development. These are determined by inherent, maturational mechanisms. (Gesell, 1940, p. 13)

The metaphor that Gesell used to explain the relationship between culture and the developing organism was that of a glove on a hand. Culture is a mere covering for development, an addition which is shaped rather than shaping, external to the mechanisms of development:

Neither physical nor cultural environment contains any architectonic arrangements like the mechanisms of growth. Culture accumulates; it does not grow. The glove goes on the hand; the hand determines the glove. (Gesell, 1945, p. 358)

1.4 THE CHILD STUDY MOVEMENT

An important element in the genetic perspective was the Child Study Movement. Around the start of the twentieth century many societies and associations for child study were formed both in the United States and in other countries, such as England, Germany, and France. One was founded by G. Stanley Hall himself in 1893: *The National Association for the Study of Children*. Large numbers of children were assessed and measured, using questionnaires, observations, and tests of various kinds. Emphasis was placed on the educational value of the research; its aim was the improvement of both the child and society.

As part of this movement, Child Study Institutes were funded, with nursery schools attached for research purposes. For example, the *Institute of Child Welfare* at the University of California, Berkeley, was created in 1927 (it later became the *Institute of Human Development*). A few years later the Oakland Guidance Study began, a long-term study that repeatedly examined and tested babies for 18 years, and then contacted them again when they were 30 and 40 years of age.

Significant methodological advances were made by the psychologists who worked in the genetic perspective. G. Stanley Hall conducted laboratory research early in his career, though his studies employed little, if any, statistical analyses. When he turned to child development his approach was considered by many people to be impressionistic, even literary. He used **questionnaires** to, for example, make an inventory of the "contents of children's minds" when they entered school for the first time. His questionnaires were, however, rather simple, and lacked clear validity and reliability.

Arnold Gesell was concerned that the study of children and their development should be scrupulously scientific. He championed the use of the new technology of filming, writing that "The cinema sees with an all-seeing, impartial eye and it records with an infallible memory" (Gesell, 1932, p. 266). In his laboratory, children were observed and filmed at regular intervals in the controlled conditions of a special crib within a hemispherical photographic dome fitted with a **one-way mirror** (which Gesell pioneered). He insisted that it was crucial to collect permanent, systematic records to document the form of children's behavior and how it transformed as they grew older. The films were projected on a viewing glass to permit measurement and charting of "the patterns of behavior which express the laws and norms of early mental growth" (1932, p. 266). Much of Gesell's research was focused on "individual deviations from the normal," with the goal of designing appropriate **interventions** for those children who lagged behind the norm, and providing special educational opportunities for those "gifted" children who were ahead of the norm.

Much of Gesell's research had a **cross-sectional design**, comparing different children of different ages, but he also conducted other kinds of research design. In addition, he carried out **twin studies**, comparing identical and dissimilar twins, raised together or raised apart.

The Child Study Movement made much use of **standardized tests**, such as the Bayley Scale. It also set up projects with a **longitudinal design** with large numbers of participants, such as the Berkeley Growth Study (Jones, 1938). Longitudinal research involves repeated observations of participants over long periods of time—often many decades. Since longitudinal studies track the same people, the differences observed are less likely to be due to **confounds** such as differences across generations, cultural changes, or historical changes in health or material well-being.

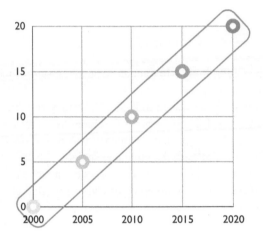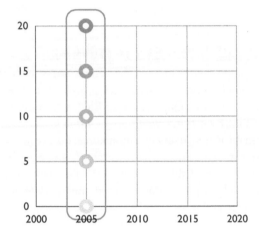

Figure 2.3

2. BEHAVIORISM

The second perspective in the history of developmental psychology rejected innate factors and instead emphasized the role of the environment. Exogenous factors, influences that come from the outside, were seen as primary. In this perspective, development or learning (for these two were often not distinguished) was viewed as "shaping" behavior, often through reward and punishment. Development was assumed to be a gradual, continuous process, in which there are no qualitatively distinct stages.

The behaviorists' critical opinion of the genetic perspective can be summed up in the terse comment made by J. B. Watson to Yerkes in 1909 (cited in O'Donnell, 1985, p. 159): "Damn Darwin!"

Skinner (1953, p. 91) described the basic position of behaviorism in the following way:

Operant conditioning shapes behavior as a sculptor shapes a lump of clay. Although at some point the sculptor seems to have produced an entirely novel object, we can always follow the process back to the original undifferentiated lump, and we can make the successive stages by which we return to this condition as small as we wish. At no point does anything emerge which is very different from what preceded it. The final product seems to have a special unity or integrity of design, but we cannot find a point at which this suddenly appears. In the same sense, an operant is not something which appears full grown in the behavior of the organism. It is the result of a continuous shaping process. (Skinner, 1953, p. 91)

2.1 JOHN B. WATSON

From the 1920s to the 1940s, John B. Watson (1878–1958) developed a highly descriptive and objective approach to the study of human behavior which he called "behaviorism." In his manifesto, *Psychology as the Behaviorist Views It* (Watson, 1913), behaviorism was defined as a purely objective science—a branch of the natural sciences, whose goal was the prediction and control of behavior. Behaviorism studied both humans and animals, seeing no rigid line between the two.

Watson considered speculation about the evolutionary origins of children's thoughts and feelings to be mere pseudoscience. Scientific psychology should only study what could be directly observed, and since consciousness and mental states were unobservable they could not be part of psychology:

> Let us limit ourselves to things that can be observed, and formulate laws concerning only those things. Now what can we observe? We can observe behavior – what the organism does or says. (Watson, 1925, p. 6)

The result of this scientific psychology, Watson believed, would be expert and scientific guidance for parents in how to raise their children. Parents were hungry for advice from child-rearing experts, and Watson insisted that they should treat their children in an objective and unsentimental manner:

> Treat them as though they were young adults. Dress them, bathe them with care and circumspection. Let your behavior always be objective and kindly firm. Never hug and kiss them, never let them sit on your lap … If you must, kiss them once on the forehead when they say good night. Shake hands with them in the morning. Give them a pat on the head if they have made an extraordinarily good job on a difficult task. Try it out. In a week's time you will find how easy it is to be perfectly objective with your child and at the same time kindly. You will be utterly ashamed of the mawkish, sentimental way you have been handling it. (Watson, 1928, pp. 81–82)

Raised using the appropriate techniques, any child could become a well-adjusted, successful adult:

> Give me a dozen healthy infants, well-formed, and my own specified world to bring them up in and I'll guarantee to take any one at random and train him to become any type of specialist I might select—doctor, lawyer, artist, merchant-chief and, yes, even beggar-man and thief, regardless of his talents, penchants, tendencies, abilities, vocations and race of his ancestors. (Watson, 1928, p. 82)

One of the central concepts of behaviorism was that of **conditioning**. Watson conducted research on the phenomena of classical conditioning before he had read of the work of Russian psychologist **Ivan Pavlov** (see below), but there are clear resemblances. In **classical conditioning**, an organism's reflex responses are changed when one environmental stimulus, that previously elicited no response, comes to signal the occurrence of a second stimulus. In his 1916 presidential address to the American Psychological Association, Watson emphasized the importance of the "conditioned reflex" (Watson, 1916).

In 1920, Watson conducted conditioning research that was to become highly controversial. His "Little Albert" experiment aimed to show how classical conditioning could be used to shape infant behavior. Albert, an 8-month-old, was first tested for his emotional reaction to a white rat, a rabbit, a dog, a monkey, various masks, and other materials. He showed no fear of any of these stimuli. Then the white rat was repeatedly placed near Albert and each time a loud sound was made behind his back. The sound disturbed Albert and he began to cry. After several such pairings, the rat was presented without the sound. Albert now showed fear when the rat appeared: he cried and tried to avoid the animal. Watson concluded that pairing the loud sound (the unconditioned stimulus) with the rat (the neutral stimulus) had led to the response to the first (the unconditioned response) being transferred to the second (the conditioned response). He considered this to be evidence that fear was a learned response, not innate. In addition, Albert now showed fear not only to the rat, but also to other furry objects: Watson considered this as evidence for the **generalization** of the learned association.

Watson left Johns Hopkins University around this time and began a new career in advertising. There he applied his scientific techniques of behavior modification to the marketing of products such as tobacco and soap.

2.2 IVAN PAVLOV

Behaviorism is often associated with the work of the Russian psychologist Ivan Pavlov (1849–1936), though Watson came to learn of Pavlov's research only after having founded behaviorism. Pavlov trained as a physiologist, and his early research involved the nerves of the heart. In the 1890s he studied the gastric functions of dogs, observing that the animals began to secrete saliva before they actually received food, and he focused his investigations on this phenomenon.

Pavlov's concept of the **conditioned reflex** refers to a kind of conditioning that he demonstrated in 1927. A neutral stimulus is presented along with a second, unconditioned, stimulus which has significance to the animal or human. The innate reflex reaction to the unconditioned stimulus becomes produced in response to the new stimulus. For example, the salivation produced when food is presented begins to occur in the presence of the person who delivers the food. Pavlov paired a bell with the presentation of food, and showed that the dogs began to salivate in response to the bell.

As we shall describe later in this chapter, Vygotsky's first statements in the 1920s about a cultural psychology were framed in Pavlovian terms; this was by far the dominant kind of psychology in Soviet Russia at that time.

2.3 B. F. SKINNER

Another well-known figure in the history of psychology is Burhuss F. Skinner (1904–1990), who developed what has been called **radical behaviorism**. Skinner studied and taught at Harvard University

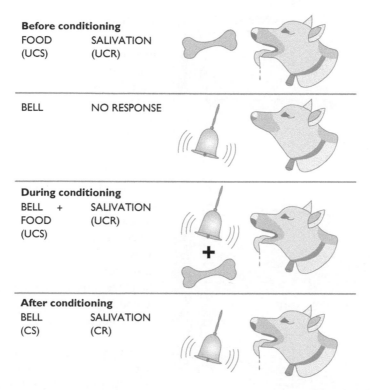

Figure 2.4 A conditioned reflex

for many years. His aim was to understand all human and animal behavior in terms of the organism's history of environmental reinforcement, both positive and negative. Skinner's views differed from Watson's in that he accepted that feelings and mental states existed and could be studied by a scientific psychology once they were identified with bodily states or behaviors. This proposal was what he considered "radical." Skinner argued that attempts to explain what someone does in terms of what is going on inside them are fruitless; on the contrary, feelings and thinking are kinds of behavior, and so should be explained in terms of the environment.

Skinner also moved away from the focus on reflexes that characterized earlier behaviorism. His work dealt with **operant conditioning**, in contrast to classical conditioning, which he called "respondent conditioning." *Respondents* are reflex reactions, such as salivation. *Operants*, in contrast, are emitted responses, behaviors that may be structurally distinct but are functionally equivalent. For example, the bar-pressing behavior of a rat is an operant; the rat may press the bar in a variety of different ways, but all will have the same consequence.

Skinner's research explored the trial-and-error learning that other psychologists had demonstrated in various animals. Rather than explaining this kind of problem-solving in terms of a learned association, Skinner explained it as a **shaping** of operants as a result of a history of **reinforcement**. He studied in detail

Figure 2.5 Skinner's daughter in her air crib

the effects of different rates and schedules of positive and negative reinforcement, aiming to identify universal laws of learning. Skinner was able to successfully modify animal operant behavior in multiple and systematic ways, and his work led to the founding of the *Society for Quantitative Analysis of Behavior*.

Skinner built what he called an "air crib" for his own daughter Deborah, and this became a topic of many rumors. The crib was designed to eliminate what Skinner considered the worst aspects of a baby's typical sleeping arrangements: the clothes, sheets, and blankets. These not only had to be washed, they also restricted arm and leg movement in an undesirable way. Skinner's daughter looked back on her experience as something very positive, in an article titled "I was not a lab rat":

I was very happy, too, though I must report at this stage that I remember nothing of those first two and a half years. I am told that I never once objected to being put back inside. I had a clear view through the glass front and, instead of being semi-swaddled and covered with blankets, I luxuriated semi-naked in warm, humidified air. The air was filtered but not germ-free, and when the glass front was lowered into place, the noise from me and from my parents and sister was dampened, not silenced. (Skinner Buzan, 2004)

In 1957 Skinner published the book *Verbal Behavior*, in which he attempted to extend his analysis of behavior to include human speech (Skinner, 1957). He argued that spoken language is no different in character from any other kind of behavior, so that it is subject to the same controlling variables in the environment as other operants. Speech is a function of the speaker's current environment and her past behavioral history; there is no need to invoke a special "language capacity" to explain speech. Nor do we need to refer to mental states such as intentions or beliefs in order to explain speech behavior.

Skinner distinguished several classes of verbal behavior, including "mands" and "tacts." Mands are acts of speech that are controlled by a state of deprivation or satiation, such as calling "water!" when one is thirsty. Tacts are acts of speech that "make contact" with the environment, such as saying "It is hot today." As we shall see, this book became the focus of key criticism from proponents of a new theoretical perspective.

2.4 ALBERT BANDURA

A third representative of the behaviorist perspective is Albert Bandura (born 1925). A survey in 2002 found that Bandura was the fourth most cited psychologist, after Skinner, Freud, and Piaget. Bandura began his career as a learning theorist with beliefs very similar to those of Watson and Skinner, but over time he has come to emphasize the importance of learning through imitation or **modeling**.

Bandura accepted that the environment has an important influence on a child's behavior, but he also proposed that in addition the child's behavior influences the environment, in what he has called "reciprocal determinism." Later he would add that mental imagery and language must also be considered. In these respects Bandura has moved away from the behaviorism in which he was trained. He is often given credit for being influential in psychology's movement away from behaviorism towards cognitive psychology.

In a series of studies in the 1960s Bandura explored the phenomenon of **observational learning**. He noted that children can learn new behavior without being reinforced for it, if they observe someone performing, or modeling, that behavior. A child can apparently learn from vicarious experience, watching other people's behavior. Bandura also called this **social learning**. In the famous "Bobo doll" studies, Bandura showed young children a film of a woman acting aggressively towards an inflatable clown figure. The children were then allowed to play freely with a variety of toys, including another Bobo doll. The children not only behaved towards the doll as they had seen the woman do, they also invented novel forms of aggressive behavior, such as shooting a toy gun at the doll.

Bandura explored what happened if the model was rewarded or punished, if the children were rewarded for their imitation, and if the model differed in their attractiveness or their gender. He also explored the difference between observing a live model and watching a film. He concluded that a child observing adult aggressive behavior will come to think that this behavior is acceptable and her own inhibitions against aggression will be weakened, with the result that she is more likely to respond in an aggressive manner in future situations. In the following decade Bandura published *Aggression: A Social Learning Analysis* (Bandura, 1973) and *Social Learning Theory* (Bandura & McClelland, 1977).

Bandura also explored the phenomenon of **self-regulation**. In his view, a child controls her own behavior through a process with three steps. First is self-observation, in which the child monitors her own behavior. Second is judgment, in which the child compares what she has done to a standard. Third is self-response, in which the child rewards or punishes herself on the basis of this evaluation. The self-responses can be overt (such as eating a candy) or covert (such as feeling shame or pride). Over the long term, a child establishes a level of **self-esteem** on the basis of her history of self-punishment and self-reward.

Social modeling enables the child to learn from the experiences of other people; Bandura included instruction and guidance as forms of social modeling. He defined **self-efficacy** as a person's belief in their ability to succeed in specific tasks. A child develops skills through social learning, and her self-efficacy reflects her understanding of her own skills. On the basis of their perception of her successes and failures, a child organizes her self-concept. Self-concept is learning, organized, and dynamic. In 1986 Bandura published *Social Foundations of Thought and Action: A Social Cognitive Theory* (Bandura, 1986).

Forms of clinical intervention based on Bandura's research and theories, for example to cure phobias, have proved effective. So have educational efforts such as the use of telenovelas ("soap operas") to model appropriate behavior, for example in the use of contraceptives.

Increasingly, Bandura came to view humans as self-organizing and self-regulating, rather than as solely governed by external, environmental influences. He called this **social cognitive theory**. In his view, experience, whether personal or vicarious, was important, but the way people *think* about their experience is equally important. This provides us with a link to the third theoretical perspective.

2.5 THE CONCEPT OF DEVELOPMENT IN THE BEHAVIORIST PERSPECTIVE

In the behaviorist framework, development is viewed as a process in which biology provides "the clay," and the environment "shapes" it, though processes of reward and punishment or providing models. Development, in at least the classic form of this framework, is a matter of learning. However, learning is defined in quite narrow terms, as the shaping, conditioning, or training of behavior. In social learning theory, the concept of learning is expanded to include observational learning and imitation.

In this view, the environment, the "sculptor," is the active agent in development, while what has been encoded in the genes plays only a passive role. Moreover, new forms emerge from this process in a continuous manner, rather than in discontinuous stages. In this framework, development is assumed to be gradual; child and adult don't differ qualitatively. Skinner's emphasis on the dominant role of the environment in shaping development continues to have many adherents.

2.6 RESEARCH METHODS IN THE BEHAVIORIST FRAMEWORK

With the rise of behaviorism, researchers' interest turned away from the observation of the "natural occurrences" of children's behavior towards the experimental manipulation of their behavior, since they viewed development as something that needed to be directed and controlled. The behaviorists were very concerned that psychology should become a rigorous science, and at that time this meant adopting the rigid model of scientific inquiry promoted by philosophers of science known as "logical positivists." According to **logical positivism**, scientific research requires the design of experiments with dependent and independent variables which are defined explicitly in terms of operations of measurement and manipulation (this is called "operational definition"). It requires the random assignment of participants to control and experimental treatment groups. It also requires the statistical testing of hypotheses. We now know that while randomized clinical trials are important, scientists use many other kinds of research design. Observations in non-laboratory settings can be very informative. In addition, psychologists increasingly use various kinds of qualitative methodology, such as ethnographic fieldwork, analyses of interactions, and open-ended interviews (Packer, 2011).

3. COGNITIVE DEVELOPMENTAL PSYCHOLOGY

Some say that the cognitive framework has a specific birth date, in September 1948 (Gardner, 1985). This was the date of a conference at the California Institute of Technology on "cerebral mechanisms in behavior," which has been considered the start of the "cognitive revolution" in psychology. The speakers at this conference all emphasized a new approach to the study of mental phenomena: thoughts and beliefs, which behaviorism had rejected as being outside science because they are unobservable, or as being behaviors that can be shaped by the environment, were now open for investigation as forms of "information processing." The brain was seen as a version of the new electronic computer. Mechanical devices could perform "logically." The "serial order" of behavior—the way activities such as playing tennis or a musical instrument show advance planning and organization—was now explained as a consequence of this type of computational logic.

In 1956 another important symposium on "information theory" was held at the Massachusetts Institute of Technology. Allen Newell and Herbert Simon presented their Logic Theory Machine, a computer program designed to model human problem-solving skills (Newell & Simon, 1958). This was one of the first explorations of "artificial intelligence," though the term was not used until a few years later. George Miller spoke on the "magical number seven, plus or minus two," arguing that human reasoning was constrained by the limited capacity of memory (Miller, 2003). The linguist Noam Chomsky spoke on "three models of language," and suggested that language should be treated as made up of computational procedures (Chomsky, 1956) Meanwhile, Norbert Wiener was writing on "cybernetics": the science of control and communication in animals and machines (Wiener, 1965[1948]).

3.1 THE COMPUTER METAPHOR: THE INFORMATION-PROCESSING MODEL

This cognitivist counter-revolution to behaviorism approached human functioning in general, and children's development in particular, on the basis that the mind (and/or the brain) is like a computer. At the time of the 1948 and 1956 meetings the computer was a brand-new invention. This incredible new machine's ability to process information, and seemingly to reason and infer, offered the irresistible suggestion that there might also be "human information processing." Where the behaviorists had insisted that the only data for a science of psychology came from observable behavior, the early forms of electronic computing device which where built in the 1950s seemed to show that unobservable "internal" processes could also be topics for science. The casual observer cannot see the operations of binary addition and subtraction that form the heart of a computer, but no one doubts that these are real processes, and that they can be studied scientifically using appropriate techniques, so why cannot "internal" psychologically processes be studied in the same way?

The result was the **information-processing model** of human functioning. A human seems to be in some ways like a computer, collecting information and processing it. In this metaphor, the senses—sight, hearing, touch, etc.—are input devices. Long-term memory is a storage device, like a hard drive. Short-term memory is like random-access memory. The other psychological processes are modules which are programmed to perform various functions, such as coding data, storing and retrieving these, and making decisions.

A computer is often said to be made up of hardware—the integrated circuits and mechanical connections—and software—the programs which provide the instructions in how to manipulate information. In an analogous fashion, humans are said to have "wetware" (hardware and software) which is provided by biology, while the environment provides the information.

Computer programs operate on formal representations. For example, a spreadsheet program contains a data structure which includes variables that represent the information that is important for the

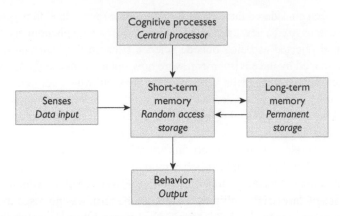

Figure 2.6 Psychological functions in the computer model

user, such as prices and dates. Cognitive psychologists believe that in a similar way the human mind constructs and operates on mental representations of the world around us. These representations are often said to be "theories" about the world; they are assumed to be **mental models** that the organism builds. In this view, individuals differ because each one of us constructs a different theory, as a consequence of our different experiences. This has been called the "theory theory."

In the cognitive perspective, development is assumed to be a process of constructing these cognitive representations. From this point of view, even the youngest infants must be able to form representations about the world, because this is the only way that a human can know anything about the environment.

3.2 NOAM CHOMSKY

A key figure in the formation of the cognitivist perspective was the linguist Noam Chomsky (born 1928). Chomsky's work has had a great deal of influence outside his own discipline of linguistics, in psychology, including in developmental research. In 1959 he published a devastating critique of Skinner's (1957) book *Verbal Behavior* (see above). Chomsky had himself just published an influential book titled *Syntactic Structures* (1957), where he argued that there was a deeper organization to sentence structure than linguists had generally noted, and consequently deeper processes that had to be taken into account.

Why, for example, does (1) seem grammatical, while (2) does not?

(1) friendly young dogs seem harmless

(2) furiously sleep ideas green colorless

Observable speech behavior is the data that linguists work with, but Chomsky argued that from this observed speech a **grammar** "must be inferred," and this "grammar" must be assumed to be "a component in the behavior of the speaker and listener" (Chomsky, 1957, p. 57). He drew a distinction between linguistic **competence** and linguistic **performance**. Competence is the person's knowledge of a language; performance is the actual use of language in concrete situations. Chomsky proposed that in actual use people make errors in what they say, change direction, and deviate from grammatical rules. The task for the linguist, according to Chomsky, is to infer or reconstruct the "underlying system of rules" that is being put to use, a system which, in Chomsky's words, amounts to "a mental reality underlying actual behavior" (1957, p. 2).

A grammar, from Chomsky's point of view, is an information-processing system. This system builds hypotheses about a language on the basis of the samples of speech that are heard by a child as she develops, and the system builds a representation of the language that can then generate new grammatical sentences. The task of a researcher is to figure out the grammar that someone is using when they produce and recognize sentences of their native language.

The enthusiastic reception of Chomsky's work, and its impact on the new field of **developmental psycholinguistics**, were part of the broader shift in thinking that the cognitive revolution led to. We will consider in later chapters some of the details—and problems—of Chomsky's approach to linguistics, and to the question of how children learn to speak and understand the language of their community.

3.3 THE CONCEPT OF DEVELOPMENT IN THE COGNITIVE PERSPECTIVE

The cognitive perspective considers the interaction between a child and her environment to be a process of gathering information and constructing mental models. Within this general view a range of positions is possible on the issue of whether nature or nurture plays the major role in a child's development. Some cognitivists are **nativists**: that is, they believe that a child's information-processing capabilities are largely innate and do not change significantly during development. Other cognitivists believe that as information is gathered from the environment the way it is processed changes: learning can transform the computer's programming.

Chomsky and those who have followed his lead fall into the nativist group. Chomsky has always insisted that the capacity to learn language must be biologically based and innate. Of course, the particular language that a child learns to speak will depend on the social environment in which she lives, but the capacity to learn any language at all is evidently innate. For Chomsky, this innate capacity has the form of a **universal grammar**—a language-specific mental module. This **modular** approach to mental processes has been popular (Chomsky, 1984; Pinker, 1988). The assumption is that each module can be studied independent of the others.

Cognitive psychologists who believe that the environment plays the major role in a child's development tend to emphasize that the sensory information that is available to a child has a great deal of structure and redundancy. For example, they suggest that a child can learn language without having a biologically based language-specific module because the speech she hears around her is simplified and directed towards her in highly predictable ways.

What is central to the cognitive perspective in developmental psychology, then, is not an emphasis on one factor, nature or nurture, over the other, but the central presumption that a child deals with the world by forming mental representations. These representations are variously called "concepts," "schemas," "models," "theories," or "data structures," but in every case the assumption is that a child knows the world only by constructing mental representations of it. We will see in the next section that the constructivist perspective shares a very similar assumption. We shall also see later in this chapter that cultural psychology offers an alternative to this assumption.

3.4 METHODS OF RESEARCH IN COGNITIVE DEVELOPMENTAL PSYCHOLOGY

Cognitive developmental psychologists have often been involved in laboratory experimentation. However, their approach differed from that of lab research in the behaviorist perspective: rather than providing positive and negative reinforcements they used the laboratory to present information to the child in specific, highly organized ways. For example, objects would be presented to an infant in a specific arrangement, or moving in a particular way.

The goal was also different: it was not to control and observe a child's behavior, but to **reconstruct** what was assumed to be the child's underlying cognitive competence. To return to the example of language, in the cognitive perspective a child is assumed to have the competence to understand and produce sentences of a certain degree of grammatical complexity. But this competence is hidden, because it is mental, or internal to the brain, or both; all that can be observed is the child's performance. This distinction between **competence** and **performance**, which as we have seen Chomsky insisted on, has been central to cognitivism. The researcher observes performance and has to infer or reconstruct what must be the underlying competence, which is assumed to be a formal information-processing system, a set of rules. Laboratory research is designed in order to assist this goal of reconstruction. Often the reconstruction involves the creation of **simulations**, usually in the form of computer programs which are capable of producing the same performance output as a human; they "simulate" the behavior that has been observed in a laboratory or natural setting.

4. CONSTRUCTIVISM

The fourth theoretical perspective is associated centrally with the work of the Swiss psychologist Jean Piaget (1896–1980). Piaget was undoubtedly the most influential developmental theorist of the twentieth century. Many people have viewed his approach to children's development as part of the cognitive perspective, and it is true that it has much in common with that perspective, but it is different in important ways. Like the cognitivists, Piaget assumed that a child is always building knowledge about her environment. Piaget, however, did not believe that the capacity to form mental representations is the only way to know the world, or that it is present from birth.

He also disagreed with Chomsky's view that the mind has a fixed structure of innate and unchanging modules (Piattelli-Palmarini, 1980, 1994). Instead, he proposed that as a consequence of her active interaction with the environment, the child **constructs knowledge structures** about the world. Piaget was a **constructivist**, and his theoretical approach is known as **constructivism**.

As a result of this emphasis on the ongoing interaction between child and environment, constructivists do not consider either endogenous and exogenous factors to have primary importance. Rather, they consider *both* the child's biology and the environment to be equally necessary for development. On the one hand, Piaget asserted that "Mental growth is inseparable from physical growth; maturation of the nervous and endocrine systems, in particular, continue until the age of sixteen" (Piaget & Inhelder, 1966/2008, p. viii). On the other hand, he argued that the structure of the environment plays an equally important role. However, he focused his attention primarily on the *physical* environment, because his central interest was in children's developing knowledge of physics and mathematics.

Piaget's emphasis on the child's active construction of knowledge has been very influential in educational research, and has been the basis for designing school curricula and strategies of teaching. His research on children's development was rooted in his interest in the link between biology and **epistemology**. What makes it possible for the human organism, the newborn child, to come to use logic and abstract, conceptual knowledge? The newborn seems an entirely biological entity; however, she will become an adult who is capable of logical reasoning. What transforms the biological into the logical? Piaget's answer, put very briefly, was that logic arises from the spontaneous organization of the human organism's actions. Actions in the world have a logical organization, and when the child grasps this, her thinking about the world starts to become logical.

The speed and extent of the reception of Piaget's work in the USA are shown by the fact that in 1936, when he was aged only 40, Harvard University awarded him an honorary doctorate. It was the first of a total of 60 he would receive.

Piaget insisted that he was not a psychologist but a "genetic epistemologist." Here, again, "genetic" means the study of origins, not genes or genetics. Piaget was interested in the origins and growth of children's knowledge and reasoning about the world. He had worked with Théodore Simon, a colleague of Alfred Binet, the inventor of the intelligence test, and he came to believe that the children whom he tested made "errors" on the test questions for good reasons, not because they lacked intelligence. Children at different ages, he came to see, think about and know the world in qualitatively different ways. He set out to map and describe those qualitative differences. When Piaget writes about "intelligence" he is not referring to a capability that differs from child to child, so that one child might be judged more intelligent than another, but an active involvement with the world that every child possesses, and that changes qualitatively as the child develops. He is reputed to have said, "Intelligence is what you use when you don't know what to do."

4.1 PIAGET'S CONCEPTION OF DEVELOPMENT

Piaget viewed the child's psychological development as a process of **adaptation** to the environment. He was influenced here by the evolutionary theory of his time, and he drew a parallel between evolutionary change and psychological change. (We shall see in the next chapter that evolutionary theory now recognizes that organisms do not only adapt to their environment, they also transform that environment.) The interaction between a child and her environment, he proposed, has two sides to it: the child applies her patterns of action, and she modifies those patterns. Piaget called the first side **assimilation**; the second he called **accommodation**. Assimilation and accommodation are the unchanging *functions* in the process of development.

In addition, Piaget described development in terms of constantly changing *structures*. These structures he called **schemas**. He defined a schema as "a cohesive, repeatable action sequence possessing component actions that are tightly interconnected and governed by a core meaning" (Piaget, 1952b, p. 240). A schema is the basic unit or building block of knowledge. A child adapts to the environment by modifying her schemas, and so these become more and more complex as development proceeds. At first, during the first two or three years, the schemas are patterns of physical action (in the sensory-motor stage, see below). After that, according to Piaget, they are patterns of mental action, of increasing sophistication (from the pre-operational stage onwards).

In *assimilation*, existing schemas are applied to objects and situations that may be familiar or may be new. For example, the very first schemas are the reflexes of a newborn baby, one of which is the sucking reflex. This schema assimilates all objects to itself: an infant will suck on anything and everything.

When a schema is modified, on the other hand, this is *accommodation*. The infant discovers that it is necessary to suck differently on a pacifier than she does on a bottle. The schema accommodates; the action pattern is changed.

You can see that assimilation is essentially conservative: the status quo is maintained. Accommodation, on the other hand, involves change. Together these two functions make up the child's continual interaction with her environment. In practice assimilation and accommodation always go hand in hand; both occur at the same time. But the balance between the two varies. Sometimes there is a primacy of accommodation, sometimes a primacy of assimilation. When there is a balance, this is **equilibrium**, and Piaget saw equilibrium as defining the optimal path of adaptation, and of intelligence: "Intelligent adaptation is the equilibrium between assimilation and accommodation" (Piaget, 1951, p. 84). Assimilation and accommodation have been called the "Batman and Robin" of developmental psychology: all-powerful yet somewhat mysterious, this duo pops up on every page of Piaget's writing (Klahr, 1982).

Piaget described a series of developmental stages, which he proposed are universal and follow an **invariant sequence**. The sequence of stages is not the result of age, or of biological maturation, it is the result of adaptation. Piaget was not a maturationist (though he is sometimes mistakenly described this way). Each stage is a more logically adequate way of thinking; each is better adapted psychologically, so that each stage builds on the previous stage. The transition from one stage to another is the result of the child's efforts to move from disequilibrium to equilibrium. Each stage is qualitatively different from the others, and it functions as an integrated whole. In Piaget's account of development, the *form* of reasoning at one stage of cognition becomes the *content* at the next stage. So, for example, the perception-action schemas of sensory-motor intelligence provide mental images for preoperational thinking. The relations about membership of "classes" (sets and subsets of entities) that a child can organize using concrete operational reasoning become the contents that the teenager reasons about.

4.2 PIAGET'S STAGES OF COGNITIVE DEVELOPMENT

In later chapters we will discuss in detail each of the stages of development that Piaget identified and investigated in his research. However, it will be helpful to have available an overview that summarizes the most important characteristics of each stage. That is what we provide here.

INFANT AND TODDLER: SENSORY-MOTOR INTELLIGENCE (0–2.5 YEARS)

Piaget believed that a child's perception and knowledge of the world are an active product of what she brings to the task of knowing the world. In this belief he was influenced by the philosopher Immanuel Kant (1724–1804), who considered space, time, causality, and object to be innate "*a priori* categories," built into the structure of the mind, although they seem to be objective properties of the world. Piaget generally agreed with Kant, but he thought the latter had gone too far in assuming that these categories are innate. In his books about infancy—*The Origins of Intelligence* (Piaget, 1952a[1936]) and *The Construction of Reality in the Child* (1954[1937])—Piaget argued that during the first two and a half years of life the infant and then the toddler is gradually constructing a practical understanding of space, time, causality, and object. This **construction of reality** is the central outcome of **sensory-motor intelligence**.

EARLY CHILDHOOD: PREOPERATIONAL THINKING (2.5–7 YEARS)

At the end of the sensory-motor stage the toddler acquires the capacity to understand and use representations, in what Piaget called the **semiotic function**. This involves, in his view, her ability to "internalize" action, that is, to act mentally on internal **signifiers** rather than act physically on objects. This **mental action** is at first simple and not fully logical, but nonetheless it is an important step forward. The young child's mental actions are not yet true operations—they are **preoperational**.

In Piaget's view, the first mental signifiers are internal images of objects, the results of imitation. For example, when Piaget describes how his young daughter Lucienne opened and closed her mouth in imitation of the opening and closing of a box of matches, and then opened the box to retrieve a hidden object, we are witnessing the formation of a signifier that is not yet fully internalized and mental but will soon become so.

The semiotic function makes four things possible. First, the child can grasp a series of events simultaneously, all at the same time. Second, she can engage not only in action but also in contemplation and reflection. Third, she can deal with non-tangible elements, ones that are abstract or hypothetical. Fourth, she can be influenced by the public medium of symbols and signs—she can be **socialized**. For Piaget, the child is at first individual and only slowly becomes social. We shall see that Vygotsky had the opposite view—that the child is first social and only slowly becomes an individual.

In the preoperational stage the young child takes only the first steps towards these four possibilities. Considering the fourth, for example, the first signifiers are, in Piaget's view, private symbols, not public signs. For him verbal signs such as words are not the basis of thought, but are acquired after the young child has already acquired the ability for thinking. This too was a point of debate and key disagreement between Piaget and Vygotsky, as we shall see later.

As Piaget viewed it, the major limitation of preoperational thought is that the balance between assimilation and accommodation is not yet stable. We see this in the vacillations in early childhood between play (assimilation) and logical reasoning (adaptation). This absence of a stable equilibrium is the source of various deficits that Piaget identified in preoperational thought.

MIDDLE CHILDHOOD: CONCRETE OPERATIONAL THINKING (7–11 YEARS)

In middle childhood, ages 7 through 11, a child's reasoning forms a coherent and integrated system of thought. Assimilation and accommodation are now in balance. Her mental actions are now true **operations**: each is part of an organized system of related acts, and the system has logical properties such as **reversibility**. This coherence can now be seen in her ability to perform intellectual tasks successfully, such as adding, subtracting and classifying.

Yet still the child can reason only about **concrete** things and events. She cannot reason about verbal statements. The child, according to Piaget, can still think only about the real and concrete, not about the possible and abstract.

ADOLESCENCE: FORMAL OPERATIONAL THINKING (11 YEARS ...)

A fundamental reorganization and reorientation leads to what Piaget considered the final stage of intellectual development, **formal operations**, in early adolescence. What is *real* is now subordinate to what is *possible*. This involves a reversal of what has gone before: now the empirical—what is actually the case—comes to be seen as merely one possibility among many. The real becomes a subset, albeit a special one, of what is possible.

This change permits new kinds of reasoning. First, the teenager's reasoning is now hypothetico-deductive: it can deal with hypothetical entities and states of affairs. Second, reasoning is now combinatorial, able to explore all the possibilities, all the combinations of factors, that are implicit in a situation. Third, reasoning now operates not on representations of objects and events, or on representations of the properties of those objects, but on representations of *propositions*—that's to say, on statements or assertions—that are about objects and events. If we state that such propositions were the results of concrete operational reasoning, this illustrates the point I made earlier, namely that reasoning in each stage operates on the results, the products, of reasoning in an earlier stage.

The adolescent is now able to solve tasks in which several factors are varied at once (such as the four liquids task and the pizza problem that we shall explore in Chapter 13). She can now reason about such matters as proportions, probability, and mechanical equilibrium.

Stage	Structures of Knowledge
Infancy & toddlerhood	Sensory-motor intelligence
Early childhood	Preoperational intelligence
Middle childhood	Concrete operational intelligence
Adolescence	Formal operational intelligence

Figure 2.7 Piaget's stages of cognitive development

4.3 THE CONCEPT OF DEVELOPMENT IN THE CONSTRUCTIVIST PERSPECTIVE

It will be evident that central to Piaget's account of development is the view that intelligence moves through a universal sequence of qualitatively distinct stages of cognition, from physical intelligence (sensory-motor) to mental intelligence (operational). Many people think that because Piaget described universal stages he considered development to be a matter of maturation, but this is far from the case. Piaget believed that the stages are universal because progress through them is *logically necessary*. The precursors of thinking and language lie in the elementary actions, perceptions and imitations of babies, but even here what is important is the logic that is implicit in these actions.

In the theoretical perspective of constructivism, nature and nurture are considered to play equal roles, though by "nurture" here we are referring to the physical environment. We have seen that for Piaget the child and the environment are in continuous interaction, and development is a process of adaptation, the active construction of increasingly adequate ways of knowing. Individual differences in cognitive ability are explained by the proposal that individuals pass at different speeds through the universal sequence of stages.

Culture plays a very limited role in Piaget's theory. It is restricted in the main to providing differing amounts of raw material for the processes of assimilation and accommodation to "feed upon" in given social circumstances.

4.4 RESEARCH METHODS IN THE CONSTRUCTIVIST PERSPECTIVE

Piaget is famous for conducting **clinical interviews**, in which he questioned individual children about some aspect of the world, and for the **Piagetian tasks** that he used to assess the quality of children's reasoning. "Clinical" here means that these interviews explored what children actually knew and were interested in. In Piagetian tasks such as those exploring **conservation** (see Chapters 9 and 12), Piaget would show a child concrete situations such as liquid poured from one beaker to another. As we mentioned earlier, Piaget assumed that the "errors" a child made were in fact positive evidence for the kind of reasoning she was using.

5. CULTURAL PSYCHOLOGY

The fifth theoretical perspective explicitly includes culture as a constituent of children's development. Cultural artifacts provide the means with which people interact with the world around them and with one another. For example, I eat food with the help of a knife and fork. You may use chopsticks. We communicate with one another through speech, which is also a cultural artifact. The material artifacts we use on a daily basis greatly extend our physical powers and capabilities, and cultural psychology proposes that they also provide the basis for dramatic developments in our psychological powers and capabilities.

In the cultural psychology perspective, human development is viewed as a process in which biology and culture are interwoven so that increasingly complex psychological functions emerge. In this process none of the constituents alone is sufficient for development to occur, and none is reducible to the others.

Cultural artifacts were first created to **mediate** between people and the natural world. A digging stick made planting easier in hard ground. A spear made the hunting of wild animals more successful. In this sense, culture can be viewed as the way that human biology and the natural world are linked, as the mediation between the child as a biological organism and the environment in which she lives. Increasingly, today, we use artifacts to interact with other artifacts. We use a hammer to drive a nail into a planed and mass-produced plank of wood. We use glasses to see the TV screen. In fact, humans have modified our planet to such a degree that our environment has itself become largely artifactual, no longer "natural" in the sense of being uninfluenced by humans. (It has been suggested that the Earth has now entered an epoch called the Anthropocene in which human activity has altered many geological conditions and processes; see Steffen et al., 2007.)

This is not to say that biology is unimportant. It is a puzzle that although as humans we share 99 percent of our DNA with our closest primate cousin the chimpanzee, and primates also show a simple culture in the sense of learning how to use simple tools and copying one another (McGrew, 2004), human cognition is clearly dramatically different from that of the chimpanzee. How can this be? Clearly the difference is not due to biology alone. In the following chapter we will explore what is now known about the divergence between humans and apes.

One of the important origins of the cultural psychology perspective is the "cultural-historical psychology" of Lev Vygotsky and his colleagues.

5.1 LEV VYGOTSKY

Lev Semyonovich Vygotsky (1896–1934) is considered the founder of cultural-historical psychology. Born in what is now Belarus in Eastern Europe, he was by all accounts a very gifted child who read widely and showed great intelligence. As a young man, he was a student at the same time at both the Moscow State University and the Moscow Public University, studying law, philology (the history of how languages change), history, and literary analysis. After graduating in 1917—the year of the Russian Revolution, when World War I was still raging—Vygotsky worked for several years as a teacher and teacher trainer, work which led to his first book *Educational Psychology* (1997b[1926]). After presenting an impressive paper at a national conference, Vygotsky was invited to work at the Moscow Institute of Psychology, where he began to collaborate with Alexander Luria and Aleksei Leontiev. Around this time he wrote an important analysis of the history of psychology, *The Historical Meaning of the Crisis in Psychology* (2004b[1997]). This text included a diagnosis of what Vygotsky considered to be the major conceptual problem in psychology, **dualism**, and a statement of the need for a new, general psychology.

Vygotsky pointed out that psychology tends to rely upon a series of paired concepts: mind and body, knowledge and world, thought and action, subject and object. In his diagnosis, all these pairs stem from a persistent underlying dualism.

What is dualism? Dualism is the assumption or claim that, as the name suggests, *two* kinds of entities exist: mental (or ideal) entities and material entities. **Idealism** is the philosophical position that the basic constituents of reality are mental entities, such as ideas or forms. **Materialism** is the counter-position that the basic constituents are types of matter, material objects.

Put this way, you will see that much of psychology today continues to be dualist: many psychologists assume that their task is to study "mental states," such as beliefs, desires and intentions, which have a kind of existence that is distinct from that of chairs, tables, and other material entities. Psychology tends to oscillate between idealism or materialism, or struggles to combine or connect them.

Many psychologists maintain some version of dualism, even though it has often been pointed out that the separation between mind and matter leads to all sorts of conceptual problems, and a vast literature exists that has defined and explored these problems, in philosophy and elsewhere. To pick just one example, how can one know whether a belief about some object in the world is accurate or not? How could we possibly compare the belief with the object to see whether or not they correspond? To do so would require some kind of direct access to the object, when all we have is our perceptions, our beliefs, and our concepts of it.

To overcome this dualism, Vygotsky argued, we need to cut out the idealist side of psychology in order to have a thoroughly materialist science. Vygotsky argued that the new psychology must study consciousness, but he considered consciousness to be a *material* phenomenon. If that seems a strange proposal, consider that barely a hundred years ago people insisted that a mysterious "vital force" was essential to all living organisms. However, it is now accepted that life is a material, chemical, and biological process. Consciousness, in Vygotsky's view, is not something mysterious, it is an aspect of our way of living in the world. Consciousness, also, is made up of a **system of psychological functions**: memory, perception, emotion, conceptualization, and so on. Vygotsky argued that it is not necessary to use introspection (personal reflection on one's own individual experience) to study consciousness: instead, psychology can reconstruct a person's psychological functioning from the traces that their consciousness leaves. This was a provocative conclusion, and we shall see below that it prompted disagreement from Leontiev and some of his followers.

Why is this psychology cultural and historical? Vygotsky viewed human development as a process driven by the child's need to live in a social world: "[T]he fundamental definitive necessity of all human life," he wrote, is "the necessity to live in a historical, social environment and to reconstruct all organic function in agreement with the demands set forth by the environment" (Vygotsky, 1993, p. 155). In particular, he argued that psychology needs to recognize an important difference between **lower psychological functions** and **higher psychological functions**. The latter, he argued, develop only because the child lives within a culture, and employs the artifacts that this culture makes available. This enables the child, he proposed, to gain mastery of her own lower psychological functions, and transform these in her relations with significant other people.

As part of his project for a cultural-historical psychology, a project in which Luria and Leontiev joined him, Vygotsky conducted research on many topics, including children's play, concept formation, and adult reasoning, and he worked with children with disabilities, in the field known at the time as "defectology," but which we would now call children with special needs. Vygotsky made the proposal, radical for his time and still so today, that a child who is blind or deaf is not handicapped, except insofar as she has to live in a world organized for the hearing and seeing. In other words, the child's deficit is produced by society, and this means the treatment of her condition should take the form of a redesign of her environment. Experimental schools for the blind/deaf based on these ideas were tremendously successful.

Vygotsky emphasized the importance of language in children's development. Both oral speech and written language are material artifacts which mediate interactions among people. Vygotsky argued that in addition they provide the opportunity for a person to act on herself. In the chapters that follow we will explore the role of language in children's perception of the world, in self-control, in thinking, and more.

Vygotsky was a prolific writer, despite his ongoing struggle with tuberculosis, which he contracted while caring for his older brother, who died of the disease in 1918. His major works include *The History of the Development of the Higher Psychological Functions* (1997[1931]) and *Thinking and Speech* (1987[1934]) (the title has also been translated as *Thought & Language*). A selection from his writings was first translated into English in the 1970s, as *Mind in Society*. A six-volume collection of his writings was published in Russian in 1982, and in English in 1987. Vygotsky died in 1934, aged 38, as he was finishing *Thinking and Speech*. With Stalin in power in Soviet Russia, his work was banned after his death, and it was only in the 1960s that his writing started to become available again in Russian.

5.2 ALEXANDER LURIA

Alexander Luria (1902–1977) became a world-famous neurophysiologist. As a student, he founded a local Psychoanalytic Association and exchanged letters with Sigmund Freud. In 1923 he began to work at the Institute of Psychology in Moscow, and carried out a research project which provided the basis for the lie-detector test that is used today. In 1924 Luria met Vygotsky, and together with Leontiev they began the project of creating a radically new psychology, one which would combine cultural, historical, and experimental approaches. In collaboration with Vygotsky, Luria carried out psychological expeditions to the central Asian states of the Soviet Union to study the influence of cultural development on the perception, memory, and cognition of unschooled peoples. Later he explored the study of identical and fraternal twins to examine the relationship between cultural and genetic influences on development.

During World War II, Luria worked with soldiers with neurological injuries, and helped create the modern discipline of neuropsychology. He published two well-known case studies—one of a man with a traumatic brain injury, *The Man with a Shattered World* (1972), and one of a journalist with a prodigous memory, *The Mind of a Mnemonist* (1987).

Luria proposed that psychological functions are not localized in specific specialized regions of the brain, but are the results of many regions working together to create what he called "functional systems." This proposal has recently been confirmed by neuroscience researchers.

5.3 ALEKSEI LEONTIEV

The sociohistorical nature of the child psyche is determined, consequently, not by the fact that she communicates, but by the fact that her relationship to reality is socially and objectively mediated—that is, by the fact that his reality takes shape under specific sociohistorical conditions (Leontiev, 2005, p. 24)

Aleksei N. Leontiev (1903–1979) worked with Luria and Vgotsky from 1924 to 1930, collaborating with them on the project for a cultural-historical psychology. He studied the mediation of memory in children and adults and wrote *The Development of Higher Forms of Memory* (1981[1931]). He left Moscow in 1931 and moved to Kharkov. Together with colleagues there he developed the approach known as **activity theory**. As we have noted, Vygotsky focused on consciousness, which he considered to be a system of psychological functions, but to Leontiev, Vygotsky's approach to psychology seemed to involve the very idealism that Vygotsky had set out to avoid. Leontiev argued that the proper object of study in psychology is human activity: "The activity of man makes up the substance of his consciousness" (Leontiev, 1978, p. 95). There was something of a split between the two men, although they continued to communicate. Leontiev returned to Moscow in 1934 and became head of the Psychology Department of Moscow State University, and then in 1966 the first dean of the new Faculty of Psychology there. Activity theory became a widely practiced approach during these years, and today is still very influential. Leontiev distinguished three different levels of analysis of an **activity system**. The first is that of "activity," the most general level, and the level at which motivations operate. The second level of analysis is that of the component "actions" and "goals." The lowest level of analysis is of the "operations" that are means to the achievement of those goals.

5.4 CULTURAL PSYCHOLOGY OUTSIDE RUSSIA

No one person can take the credit for modern cultural psychology, nor is there a single event than can be considered the moment of its birth. Calls for attention to be given to culture in psychology, and criticisms of the cognitive paradigm, began in the 1960s and 1970s.

Jerome Bruner is often considered to be one of the founders of the *cognitive* perspective in psychology, but already in a 1964 paper titled *The Course of Cognitive Growth* Bruner proposed that "the development of human intellectual functioning from infancy to such perfection as it may reach is shaped by a series of technological advances in the use of mind" (1964, p. 1). These technological advances, he suggested, include **cultural amplifiers** of human motor capacities (tools, the lever, the wheel, various modern devices), amplifiers of human sensory abilities (the microscope, the microphone), and amplifiers of human reasoning capacities ("from language systems to myth and theory and explanation"). In *Acts of Meaning* (1990), Bruner argued that while cognitive psychology had focused on what he called "mindless" computation, we should pay attention to folk psychology, the culturally constituted cognitive systems that people use to "organize their experience in, knowledge about, and transactions with the social world" (Bruner, 1990, p. 35). He proposed that the organizing principle of such systems is narrative: we make sense of the world by telling stories which link events in terms of the elements of agent, actions, scene, goals, instruments, and trouble.

Richard Shweder, a cultural anthropologist, has also been a proponent of cultural psychology (though he might call it psychological anthropology). His books include *Cultural Psychology: Essays on Comparative Human Development* (Stigler et al., 1990). Shweder views cultural psychology as an interdisciplinary field that investigates the fact that "there are distinctive psychologies associated with alternative ways of life" (Shweder, 1999, p. 64). Cultural psychology, in Shweder's view, is attentive to "local conceptions of what is true, good, beautiful, and efficient" (1999, p. 66), along with the ways people face up to universal "existential questions." Shweder concludes that "Cultural psychology is thus the study of the way the human mind can be transformed, given shape and definition, and made functional in a number of different ways that are not uniformly distributed across communities around the world" (1999, p. 68).

Both Bruner and Shweder argue that the cognitive revolution of the 1950s and 1960s failed because it replaced meaning with information. The computer model turned out to be nothing more than another kind of **reductionism**. What is needed, consequently, is a return to the phenomena of meaning: to the semantics and pragmatics of language, to the significance that humans find in their worlds, to the symbolic mediation of human action, the **intentionality** (object-directedness) of human consciousness, and the constitution of mind by culture (Cole, 1991).

Michael Cole's interest in cultural psychology as a basis for studying children's development grew out of his involvement in cross-cultural research. His work conducting psychological experiments in eastern Africa led him to become suspicious of the ability of the technical apparatus of standard scientific psychology to reveal how minds are constituted in culture. Cole studied with Alexandra Luria in Moscow, and in this way he came into contact with Vygotsky's work. He arranged the first translations of Vygotsky's writing, in *Mind in Society* (Vygotsky, 1978), and is the founding editor of the journal *Mind, Culture and Activity*. He has explored the way different cultures define distinct developmental pathways for children, and has written widely on the ways that human nature is constituted in culture.

5.5 VYGOTSKY'S ACCOUNT OF DEVELOPMENT

Like Piaget, Vygotsky insisted that every child actively makes sense of the world. Unlike Piaget, however, he also insisted that there is always a **social moment** in development: the child develops because other people interpret and respond to what she does and says. Vygotsky described this social moment in several ways. One was in terms of what he called the **general law of cultural development**, which states that every psychological function appears twice—first on a social and interpersonal level, and second on an individual and intrapersonal level:

> every function in the cultural development of the child appears on the stage twice, in two forms. First it appears as social, then as psychological; first as a form of cooperation among people, as a group, as an interpsychical category, and then as a means of individual behavior, as an intrapsychical category (Vygotsky, 1987) [Vygotsky, 1987, #3198]

This is often read as an account of **internalization**—a move "into the mind"—but, as we shall see in Chapter 10, the process is both more complex and more simple than this!

It is sometimes said that Vygotsky offered an account of development without stages (see for example Papalia et al., 2004, p. 31), but this is not the case: Vygotsky wrote of "crises," "transformations," and even "revolutions" in a child's development. He referred to these transitions as "a very profound process interwoven into the course of the child's development" (Vygotsky, 1998c [1932–1934], p. 296). He strongly criticized psychological theories that consider transitions to be solely biological or "natural" in origin, and wrote that one can see in the child's development:

an ordered picture … [in which] critical periods alternate with stable periods and are turning points in development, once again confirming that the development of the child is a dialectical process in which a transition from one stage to another is accomplished not along an evolutionary, but along a revolutionary path. (Vygotsky, 1998c [1932–1934])

In Vygotsky's account of development, during each stage *the child's world is slowly transformed* as she learns and adapts. During each transition, in contrast, *the child is transformed*, so that she approaches the world with new motives and needs, or one might say that in a sense she is entering a different world. More specifically, a transition is a fundamental *differentiation or division* for the child. At birth, for example, the newborn is literally physically and physiologically separated from the mother. In the crisis at age 13 the change is qualitatively quite different, but it is still a differentiation, this time between the young person's actual self and her possible selves. In both of these transitions the developing child experiences a differentiation in which she is directly involved: between self and other people, or within self:

[T]he process of cultural development may be characterized as development of the personality and world view of the child … The essence of cultural development, as we have seen, consists of man mastering processes of his own behavior. (Vygotsky, 1997a, pp. 242–243)

The differentiation that happens during a transition opens up a field of action that previously did not exist for the child. For example, birth opens up the field of the world outside the womb. The transition at 12 years of age, in contrast, opens up a field of imaginative possibilities. In the stage that follows each transition, the new field is explored and progressively mastered. In the course of mastery, contradictions grow which build towards a new transition. It is important to recognize that none of these transformations is accomplished by the child alone. All of these transformations stem from the child's relations with significant others. Each transformation arises from the child's efforts to overcome the challenges and demands of living a social existence.

5.6 RESEARCH METHODS IN CULTURAL PSYCHOLOGY

It might seem that psychology already has the methodology needed for research on the role of culture in children's development, namely the methodology of **cross-cultural** research.

Cross-cultural investigations use a type of research design called **quasi-experimental**: two or more groups, to which the research participants have *not* been randomly assigned, are compared on measures or tasks. The participants cannot be randomly assigned for both practical and ethical reasons: if a researcher is comparing Japanese and American culture, for example, they cannot assign a person to either group. Quasi-experiments have limited validity because the independent variable is not being manipulated by the researcher.

Notice that in cross-cultural research culture is being treated as something that "belongs to" the individual. When a Japanese person is studied it is assumed that this is a way to study Japanese culture, or at least the influence of Japanese culture, even when that person is studied outside Japan.

Furthermore, to equate culture with nationality introduces problems: a nation is a political unit; each nation contains many cultures; nations differ on characteristics such as geography, wealth, and resources that have nothing to do with culture. When people from two different nations are compared there is usually no way of knowing which of these differences produces the observed outcomes. In short, when culture is treated as an independent variable severe methodological difficulties can arise, and these make it difficult for researchers to draw clear inferences about causation.

Most importantly, in this approach to the investigation of culture, culture is treated as a causal factor, and evidence for a cultural influence is assumed to take the form of *differences* between groups. It might appear that biology has defined a universal human nature while culture creates differences among peoples, but things are not in fact this simple. Sometimes culture is responsible for human universals, and sometimes biology is responsible for human differences. For example, the universal ability to speak a language requires participation in a speech community. On the other hand, genetic differences—such as lactose tolerance—have evolved in different cultural groups. It would be a mistake, then, to look for the influence of culture in children's development only in the *differences* among children from different parts of the world.

In the theoretical perspective of cultural psychology, however, culture is considered to play a *constitutive* role in human development, so that psychological processes are in a real sense *aspects* of culture. This book explores the premise that culture is the medium in which children develop uniquely human characteristics.

I do not mean to suggest, though, that looking at how children develop in different cultures is not important—on the contrary! As one cultural psychologist who studies children's relationships with peers has put it:

> The value of looking at friendship and peer interactions in children in other cultures thus goes beyond "seeing how others live." Although it is fascinating to consider the scope of variation in social interaction provided for our species through different patterns of cultural learning, it serves an additional purpose of allowing European American researchers to recognize that the patterns they study within their own culture are also culturally structured and need to be understood not as "natural" but as contributing to specific goals we have for our children's development and socialization. If they fail to recognize this, they will fail to understand the full complexity of children's social worlds. (Gaskins, 2006, p. 306)

A cultural perspective on the development of children explores new methodologies and new research designs. There are methodological opportunities and problems associated with the study of the cultural constituents of development, whether this study is conducted intra-culturally or cross-culturally. If culture plays a constitutive rather than a causal role, research designs need to reflect this. Researchers working in the perspective cultural of psychology use a variety of methods when they carry out their investigations. They do use laboratory methods, but they are likely to combine these with **naturalistic observations**—observation in real-life, everyday situations. They may conduct design research (Cole & Packer, 2016). Figure 2.8 illustrates some of the important differences between cross-cultural psychology and cultural psychology.

Cross-cultural Psychology	Cultural Psychology
Culture is viewed as an independent variable	Culture is viewed as a contribution to the constitution of the child
Generally compares people from different cultural groups	Generally studies people in their cultural context
Uses tests and other measures in quasi-experimental designs	Uses ethnographic methods. If tasks and tests are used they are derived from local practices

Figure 2.8 Cross-cultural psychology and cultural psychology compared

Source: modified from Cole (1996)

CONCLUSION

Despite the fact that psychologists constantly talk about interaction or relationship—between self and others, between person and environment—the language of psychology is filled with static, visual images of separation (Gilligan, 1987, p. 2)

Every developmental psychologist views children through the spectacles that are provided by a specific theoretical perspective. During the 100-year lifetime of developmental psychology it has passed through five distinct theoretical perspectives. In the chapter I have briefly summarized each of these.

In this brief history we can see the *dualism* that Vygotsky considered to be the central problem in psychology. An emphasis on biology and nature first alternated with an emphasis on the environment and nurture: as Sameroff (2009) noted, "The history of developmental psychology has been characterized by pendulum swings between a majority opinion that the determinants of an individual's behavior could be found in his or her irreducible fundamental units or in his or her irreducible fundamental experiences." Then developmental science explored various ways of granting that *both* play a role, such as Piaget's insistence that nature and nurture are in interaction. However, this approach has continued to assume that they are distinct factors.

What the cultural perspective tries to do is overcome this dualism. Biology and culture are interwoven so that we cannot distinguish nature from nurture. In Chapter 3 I shall describe news of thinking in evolutionary theory that support this proposal that biology and culture are constituents in a single evolutionary process. In a sense, biology and culture are two perspectives on a single phenomenon.

In addition, biology and culture are constituents of children's development, not causes. Development is viewed as a process of constitution, an assembly of components or constituents. Cultural psychology grants that children are both biological and cultural, while avoiding dualism. In this respect, cultural psychology is a fresh perspective on *all* of psychology. In particular, cultural psychology is not *cross*-cultural psychology; the latter is one branch of psychology, an area of investigation in which psychological characteristics or processes are compared for people from different cultures. Figure 2.9 represents the emphasis that each of the five theoretical perspectives places on the contributions from biology (nature) and the environment (nurture) to children's development. The perspective of cultural psychology is in my view unique in its efforts to transcend this dualism.

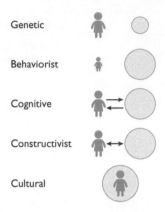

Figure 2.9 The role of endogenous (internal) and exogenous (external) factors in each of the theoretical perspectives

Researchers in a range of disciplines are currently working together to give us a subtle and more complete picture of how phylogenesis, cultural change, and ontogenesis are woven together —or more accurately, how they are all aspects of a single temporal process of human life on this planet. The theme of the next chapter will be these interwoven lines of development.

As we shall see in the chapters that follow, key aspects of Vygotsky's project for a new psychology resonate with, and sometimes have influenced, current trends in developmental psychology today. The following four aspects play a central role in the account of development that is offered in this book.

1. Vygotsky's advice to *avoid dualism* resonates with:

    - theories of embodiment, which envision cognition not as forming mental representations, but as how the body responds to challenges in the environment (Chapter 4, section 1.4);

    - new ideas in neuroscience, such as the proposal that the brain and body are components in a "perception–action cycle" that also includes the environment (Chapter 4, section 1.4);

    - dynamic field theory, which focuses on the ongoing formation among neurons in the brain of changing fields of electrical activation (Chapter 5, section 1.3);

    - efforts in anthropology to rethink the distinction between biology and culture (Chapter 3, Conclusion);

    - new research and conceptualization about evolution, which has led to notions such as 'biocultural coevolution' (Chapter 3);

    - the distinction between 'cosmovision' and 'cosmology' in cultural anthropology (Chapter 9, section 3.4).

2. Vygotsky's emphasis on the *cultural character of artifacts*, such as tools and signs, resonates with:

    - moves to define culture in terms of assemblies of artifacts, rather than in terms of people's subjective beliefs and values (Chapter 2, section 5);
    - proposals that psychological processes are "situated" and "distributed" (Chapter 2, section 5; Chapter 6, section 1);
    - views of evolution that highlight the importance of "niche construction" (Chapter 3, section 1);
    - the way that "institutional facts" provide the basic components of social reality (Chapter 11).

3. Vygotsky's insistence that the *psychological functions form a system*, and also that there is a "social moment" in the ontogenesis of these functions (stated, as we have seen, in the General Genetic Law), resonates with:

    - the insight that a child's development is not divided into separate domains and should be studied as "a highly complex system in which biological, cognitive, emotional, and social elements are powerfully intertwined" (Bronfenbrenner et al., 1986, p. 1223). (The entire organization of this book reflects this insight.)
    - proposals that culture is not a "causal factor" in children's development, but plays a "constitutive" role (Chapter 1; Chapter 2, section 5) (Packer, 2010);
    - proposals that a child's ability to regulate emotions has its origins in social interaction with caregivers (Chapter 6, section 1);
    - new ways of thinking about the origins of thinking (Chapter 10, section 3), and the origins of the experience of "mind" (Chapter 10, section 3, and Chapter 11, section 1).

4. Vygotsky's emphasis on the importance of the *distinction* between the lower psychological functions and the higher psychological functions resonates with:

    - the proposal that the fundamental way that people know the world is by living in it, so that in ontogenesis "residence" in the world is prior to "representation" of the world (Chapter 5, section 1.3);
    - research on "dual systems theory" (Chapter 5, section 1.4);
    - the proposal that living in the world is a process of constant interpretation, a "semiotic process" (Chapter 5, section 1);
    - that this interpretation passes through a series of levels, which are evident in how children understand other people (Chapter 5, section 2; Chapter 7, section 3; Chapter 10, section 1; Chapter 11, section 3; Chapter 14, section 3);
    - the proposal in neuroscience that a perception–action cycle with a hierarchical series of levels emerges in the course of ontogenesis (Chapter 4, section 1.4.3; Chapter 13, section 1);
    - new ways of thinking about the psychological consequences of schooling (Chapter 12, section 1);
    - new ways of thinking about the psychological strengths and vulnerabilities of adolescence (Chapter 13, section 3).

SUMMARY

Developmental psychology has moved through five broad theoretical perspectives since its inception more than one hundred years ago.

GENETIC PSYCHOLOGY: HALL AND GESELL

When psychology first became a scientific discipline, the theoretical perspective of developmental psychology was focused on the biology of its time, and viewed development as a process of recapitulation and maturation, which environments could either foster or corrupt. The characteristics of each developmental stage were viewed as products of an evolutionary process.

BEHAVIORISM: WATSON AND SKINNER

Behaviorism was intended as a truly scientific approach to psychology, focused only on what is observable. Development, in this perspective, was view as a result of environmental conditioning. Children were viewed as malleable clay, molded by their circumstances.

COGNITIVE DEVELOPMENTAL PSYCHOLOGY: CHOMSKY AND OTHERS

With the cognitive revolution, attention shifted to invisible cognitive processes, which were assumed to be a form of "information processing" similar to that of the new computers. Knowledge was held to be composed of formal representations, mental models or concepts. Some cognitivists emphasize innate hardware, others emphasize how new information can lead to change.

CONSTRUCTIVISM: PIAGET

Constructivism views the child as actively involved in the environment, adapting and constructing knowledge through processes of assimilation and accommodation. Development is the result of an interaction between child and environment, so that nature and nurture are equally important.

CULTURAL PSYCHOLOGY: VYGOTSKY, LURIA, AND LEONTIEV

Cultural psychology emphasizes the role of material artifacts in human psychology and children's development. Biology and culture are interwoven so that we cannot distinguish nature from nurture. Both are constituents of children's development which is viewed as a process of constitution not causation.

CHAPTER 3
INTERWOVEN LINES OF CHANGE

[T]here is a peculiar methodological approach [that considers human psychological functions] as if they were innate, natural categories of psychology. Everything is taken outside the historical aspect. The concepts of the world and of causality of a modern European child from an educated milieu and the same concepts of a child of any primitive tribe, the world view of a child of the stone age, the middle ages and the 20th century, all of these are [considered as though] basically the same, identical, equivalent to each other. Cultural development is as if isolated from history and considered as a self-satisfying process governed by internal, self-contained forces, subject to its own immanent logic. Cultural development is considered self-development. This is the source of the immovable, static, absolute character of all the laws governing the development of the child's thinking and world view. (Lev Vygotsky, *Collected Works*, vol 4. p. 9)

In arguing for a 'wider concept of evolution' … my intent was not to reinforce the boundary between the biological and the cultural but to break it down – to find a way of talking about evolutionary processes that would not require us to interject an unfathomable quantum leap from an animal to a human level of being. (Ingold, 2008, p. 25)

LEARNING OBJECTIVES

The central topics of this chapter are the two lines of change, biological evolution and sociocultural evolution:

- We first outline the process of evolution in general terms and summarize the broad outlines of the evolution of life on Earth.
- We then summarize what is known about hominid evolution.
- Within that topic we consider two subtopics in more detail: the evolution of language and the evolution of the human lifespan.
- We then turn to look at how humans have created societies that have changed in specific ways over prehistorical and historical time, that is to say over the past 50,000–70,000 years.
- Finally, we explore whether these seemingly distinct lines of change can be viewed as products of a single process.

FRAMING QUESTIONS

- In your opinion, have humans changed biologically in the past 10,000 years? In the past 1,000 years? If so, in what ways?
- Were you born in a city? What proportion of children around the world are born in cities, in your estimation?

INTRODUCTION

A child is born with a body and brain that are her biological inheritance from billions of years of evolution of life on our planet. At the same time she is born into a world that has been shaped both by that same process of evolution and by the labor of her community, who have transformed their material conditions over the course of their history.

A distinction is often drawn between two forms of inheritance, though one of the main points of this chapter is that in fact these are not truly separate. The first inheritance is genetic, the fact that each individual organism inherits genes and other cellular material from their parents. This has been viewed as central to the process of biological evolution, in which humans emerged from other animal species and became physically and physiologically what we are today. The second inheritance is environmental, the fact that organisms in many species live in environments that have been transformed by previous generations. This transformation is called "niche construction."

In the case of humans, this niche takes the form of different societies, each of which has its own culture. As she develops, the child will come to understand the organization of her specific family and community. One community may use spoons to handle food while another uses chopsticks, for example. One community uses cash currency while another uses credit cards. As a child learns about these, she is transformed into a specific kind of person.

It has been proposed that in the case of humans a second evolutionary process is occurring, "cultural evolution," which is parallel to but distinct from biological evolution. In this chapter I will explore the evidence and arguments for a different view: that human "sociocultural evolution" is an extension and continuation of biological evolution.

As the child grows and develops, her species' biological inheritance and her community's cultural inheritance become woven into her ontogenesis. These three lines—ontogenesis, sociocultural history, genetic evolution—are mutually constitutive and mutually dependent in complex ways which we shall try to understand. Indeed, the distinction among them is really no more than one of convenience.

1. WHAT IS EVOLUTION?

The many species of animal, plant, and microorganisms that we can find around us today are products of the process of evolution operating over a very long time. Figure 3.1 represents this time as a spiral, wound up to take up less space. You will see that human beings are a very recent arrival.

The planet we call Earth was formed about 4.6 billion years ago (bya). For many long years it was a turbulent, volcanic globe. The origins of life are unclear, but scientists have shown in the laboratory that some organic molecules can make copies of themselves, and this is probably what happened on Earth, perhaps in the deep ocean. The origins of cellular life are also unclear, but the first living cells—simple bacteria (known as **prokaryotic** because they lack a cell nucleus)—date back to 3.5 bya. (We know this because even single cells leave fossils.) Cells using oxygen (**eukaryotic** cells) had evolved by 1.5 bya, and the first multicellular organisms appeared around 1 bya.

Earth scientists divide the history of our planet into periods of time called "eons," "eras," and "epochs." In what is known as the Paleozoic era, starting around 542 million years ago (mya), a great variety of complex organisms evolved, in what has been called the "Cambrian explosion," named for

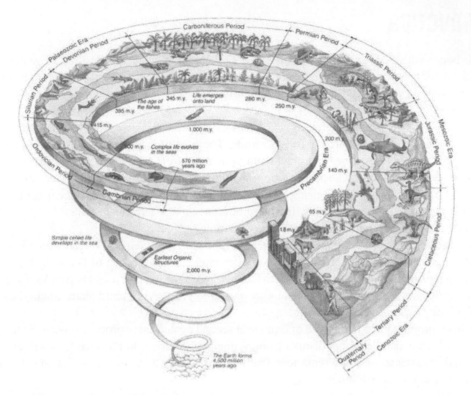

Figure 3.1 The spiral of evolutionary time

the era in which it occurred and the rapid and dramatic evolutionary changes. Some of these complex organisms are alive today; others became extinct quite rapidly. The first vertebrates, animals with backbones, were fish with bony jaws and an external tough protection, dating from 488 mya. Around 416 mya the first amphibious fish had begun to spend time out of the water on dry land, and they would have found simple plants growing there. Fossils have been found of these amphibious fish—a step between two modes of living (see Figure 3.1). Amphibians today include frogs and toads, salamanders and newts.

By 360 mya the first trees—conifers, like pine trees today—had evolved, along with reptiles and insects. Around 250 mya the appearance of the first flowering plants marked the start of what is known as the Mesozoic era (this contains the famous Triassic, Jurassic, and Cretaceous periods). The color and smell of their blossoms enticed insects to unknowingly take pollen from the male to the female plant. The dinosaurs appeared, along with the first birds and mammals. Whereas other animals lay eggs, mammals give birth to live young and they are warm-blooded with specialized teeth and body hair. The first mammals lacked placentas, and they gave birth to underdeveloped young probably protected in a pouch (kangaroos and other marsupials in Australia today still give birth in this way). Placental mammals evolved around 145 mya; they nourish their infants with milk.

A massive extinction of many species, including the dinosaurs, occurred at the boundary between the Mesozoic and Cenozoic eras, around 65 mya. It was probably caused by a large meteor or by massive volcanic eruptions throwing dust into the atmosphere, which cut off the sun's light and killed the plants which provided food to animals. The Cenozoic is the era we are still in today (as we have seen, some have proposed that the Anthropocene is a new epoch within this era). The first recognizable primate species, early **prosimians**, evolved around this time.

Biologists disagree on the exact categorization of mammals, but **primates** are generally considered to be an order of intelligent mammal that evolved around 65 mya. Primates have good eyesight because the visual fields of their two eyes overlap extensively. They have grasping hands and feet with flat nails rather than claws. They have a large brain relative to their body size, and they show a long **gestation** period and slow postnatal growth. That is to say, the time between fertilization and birth is relatively long, and so is the time during which the young primate grows to adult size and status. Many primates live in trees. There are currently about 200 species of primates, in three main groups: tree shrews, prosimians (such as lemurs and tarsiers), and **anthropoids**. The anthropoid group includes marmosets and tamarins, monkeys, and the great apes. Within this group are the great apes, also called **hominoids**, made up of gorillas, orangutans, chimpanzees, and humans. The first hominoids had evolved by 23 mya, and they began to spread out of Africa at a time when planetary temperatures were warm and tropical forests covered the central latitudes. Further adaptations led to the absence of a tail, to modified shoulders and arms, and to a larger body and brain. The details of how humans, known as **hominins**, separated from the great apes are the topic of the next section.

What kind of process is evolution? Are there more than one kind of evolution; biological evolution and cultural evolution, perhaps? These are questions in a debate that is very active today.

The fundamental task that faces every living organism—since immortality is impossible—is how to reproduce itself. The fact that organisms are alive today, many millions if not billions of years after they first appeared, is clear evidence that they have been successful in this task. Their solutions to the problem of reproduction have been diverse and complex. Generally reproduction is not perfect: offspring do not completely resemble their parents. Indeed, the imperfections of reproduction appear to be part of the strategy of reproduction itself; there is benefit to be derived from reproduction that introduces variation. From this perspective, evolution—the development and diversification of different kinds of organism— is a reflection of the fact that reproduction is essential, and that it introduces variation.

Our understanding of biological evolution is changing dramatically. We now see that evolution is not merely a process of filtering, or **selecting**, those individual organisms which are best adapted to the specific conditions of a particular environment. Organisms actively choose where they live and they modify their surroundings to construct an **environmental niche**.

Among the variety of organisms in a species it is those that can find adequate food and shelter that will survive longer, and that will be more likely to reproduce and pass along their genes to the next generation. Characteristics that are genetically based will be inherited and are more likely to appear again in the young of these organisms. This is as true of a bacterium as it is of a human being.

But an organism does not pass along only its genes. Its offspring also inherit its environmental niche. Although it is common to think of evolution as a process of adaptation of organisms to the natural environment, the fact that organisms change the environment means that we ought to think of a dynamic relationship, or a system, in which both organisms and environment are altered. The intimate relation between organism and environment that is evident in niche construction has led some biologists to propose that if we insist on a distinction between nature (the organism) and nurture (the environment) we risk failing to observe how the two form an indivisible whole, an "extended organism" (Palmer, 2004; Turner, 2009). Constructed niches "outsource" important physiological functions, so that "animal-built structures are properly considered *organs of physiology*" (Turner, 2009, p. 2, original emphasis). For example, the earthworm, whose ancestors lived in fresh water, transforms its environment by constructing tunnels which play the role of accessory kidneys, and in doing so alters the chemical composition of the soil. Physiological processes such as respiration, ingestion, and many others entangle organism and environment to such an extent that drawing a boundary between the two becomes very hard.

The clearest example of this mutual modification is the way that 2.5 billion years ago the bacteria that evolved photosynthesis, the ability to collect the energy of sunlight and use it to synthesize foods (eukaryotic cells), produced oxygen in such quantities that the composition of the earth's atmosphere was transformed, changing the environment for all living species. Subsequently, bacteria and multicellular organisms evolved which relied on oxygen, just as humans do. As we shall see later in this chapter, it makes sense to see the societies that human beings create as advanced forms of niche construction.

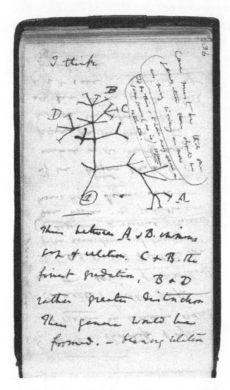

Figure 3.2 Diagram in Darwin's notebook

2. EVOLUTION OF HUMAN BEINGS

Humans, then, are products of this process of reproduction with variation—evolution—going on for a very long time, namely between 3 and 4 billion years. Much of our basic physiology is the same as that of other organisms. However, humans of the kind we are today have been on planet Earth for a very, very short time compared with other species—around 200,000 years. Yet in that time we have greatly changed how we live, and we have also changed the planet itself in significant ways. Opinions differ on how it is that we have changed much more quickly than any other animal species.

It is now clear that the evolution of human beings has not been a single, straight line of progressive improvement. Although the image of a "tree of life" was printed in Darwin's *On the Origin of Species*, the diagram in his notebook (see Figure 3.2) portrayed evolution as more like a bush than a tree, and human evolution is no exception (see Roberts, 2015). Archeologists have identified numerous branches of different geni homo, related more like cousins and uncles in a large extended family than in a single line of descent, as Figure 3.3 illustrates (it focuses on the discovery

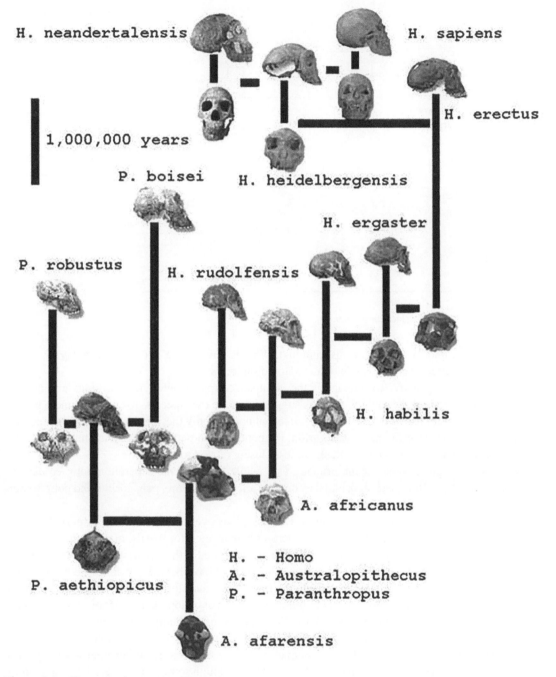

Figure 3.3 The multiple species of hominin

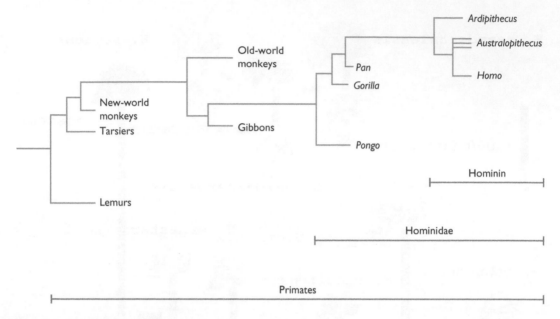

Figure 3.4 All the primates, including humans

of a new early hominid, Australopithecus ramidus). What is remarkable, then, is that today all human beings on Earth are members of a single branch, Homo sapiens sapiens.

The closest animal relative to humans is the chimpanzee (pan troglodytes). Chimps and humans share nearly 99 per cent of their DNA, and this suggests that the two species diverged around 6 million years ago. Chimpanzees have evolved too, of course, but undoubtedly they have not changed as much as hominins have. The other great apes—the gorilla, the bonobo (pan paniscus) and orangutan (pongo)—and lesser apes, such as gibbons (hylobates), are less closely related to humans.

Figure 3.4 is a representation of the primates as a whole, showing the separation between pan and genus homo around 6 million years ago, and the common ancestry of homo, pan, gorilla, and pongo dating back to around 8 to 9 mya.

Much of the evidence about the evolution of Homo sapiens over this 6 million-year period is in the form of fossils. There are now hundreds of specimens of human ancestor fossils, many from east Africa, in the rift valleys caused by movement of the tectonic plates of the Earth's crust, which is exposing deep strata from periods in the distant past. This region also seems to have been a dry area where early hominids chose to life, in contrast to the rain forests favored by the ancestors of chimpanzees and gorillas. We will meet four of these early hominids, our main relatives: **Australopithecus**, **Homo habilis**, **Homo ergaster**, and **Homo neanderthalis**. (Sixteen extinct species of hominin have now been identified.) Comparing these different members of genus homo will help us understand how humans are different from other animals alive today, but also how humans today are different from our relatives in the past. Each of these ancestors of modern humans evolved in Africa, though some of them left that continent for other parts of the world, and of course humans today occupy virtually every corner of the globe.

2.1 AUSTRALOPITHECUS (4–3 MYA)

Some time between 6 mya and 4 mya the genus Homo branched from their shared ancestor with the genus pan, the chimpanzee. This earliest kind of hominin after the division between the chimp and human lines is known as Australopithecus. Australopithecus had many primate features including a small brain and a protruding face, but they walked upright on two feet. Their fossilized skeletons show several adaptations to this **bipedality**. There were several different genera of Australopithecus. One of the earliest, around 4.2 to 3.9 mya, was *Australopithecus anamensis*, partially adapted to bipedality but with an upper body still suited for climbing and swinging in trees. Australopithecus anamensis were short and squat, about 4 to 4.5 feet tall (1.2 to 1.4 meters), with proportions like apes. Their brains were around 450 cc in size, about that of a chimpanzee—the size of a modern human fist and about 35 percent the size of a modern human brain: an EQ of roughly 3.5. (EQ or Encephalization Quotient is the ratio of an animal's brain size to its body size. An EQ of 1 indicates that the brain is the size that would be expected for that mammalian body size. The modern human EQ is 7.4.) These early ancestors had large teeth, a strong jaw, and a low receding skull. There was also considerable **sexual dimorphism**, that is, the males were considerably larger than the females.

Another genus was *Australopithecus afarensis*, dating from 3.9 to 3.0 mya. Afarensis seems to have been bipedal but probably still also spent time in trees. Their diet was varied but mainly vegetarian. Their EQ was around 2.2. One famous example of Australopithecus afarensis is the fossil named Lucy.

Australopithecus have been found in both what are known as robust and gracile body forms—that is to say, some were beefy and other more slender. Some researchers consider these to be two distinct genera. The gracile kind of Australopithecus lived throughout Eastern and Northern Africa.

Australopithecus probably lived in social groups with multiple adults and young. Their social organization might have been like that of chimpanzees today, with a sexual division of labor.

2.1.1 OLDOWAN TOOLS

Did Australopithecus use tools? Afarensis probably used wood and other natural objects as tools, but made only minimal modifications to them. The only tool that has been associated with Lucy's species is an antelope horn that seems to have been used for digging. If they used other naturally occurring material as tools, such as sticks (as do Capuchin monkeys, for example), we would be unlikely to find these today. However, a species of Australopithecus about 400,000 years later than Lucy, *Australopithecus garhi*, has been associated with stone tools and animal bones that show signs of having been scraped to take off the meat. We know these marks are not from teeth, because magnification shows the multiple scratches that are characteristic of stone edges. These are the earliest stone tools found in the fossil record and are known as Oldowan tools. They appear in the fossil record around 2.4 mya, and continued to be made for over a million years. They appear to have been made by cracking a round stone on two sides to create an edge. It is thought that Australopithecus probably ate crude vegetable food such as shoots and roots, but they would have found the carcasses of large hoofed animals abandoned by carnivores. The long bones of such animals are too thick and heavy to be cracked with the teeth alone, but they contain nutritious marrow and so there would have been motivation to open them. These first simple stone tools with a sharp edge would have done the job.

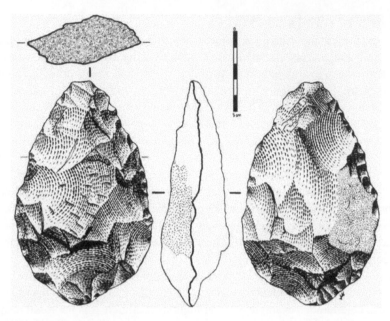

Figure 3.5   Oldowan tools

To make such a tool requires a type of rock that chips well (many do), which is then hit multiple times on two sides of the stone. Half a dozen strikes can produce an adequate edge, so such a tool can be made when it is needed, rather than being made in advance and transported to where it will be used.

On the basis of the analysis of the geometry of these 2-million-year-old artifacts, it has been suggested that the hominids who made the Olduvai Gorge tools possessed the kind of intelligence that Piaget called "pre-operational" (see Chapter 7): that they were are able to learn through trial-and-error but not to anticipate errors and so avoid them, and that they were able to classify along a single dimension but not in terms of two or more dimensions (Wynn, 1981). However, this remains a somewhat speculative inference.

2.2 TRANSITIONAL FORMS: HOMO HABILIS AND HOMO RUDOLFENSIS

Around 2.5 mya two new species of hominid evolved, the first to be named Homo. It is not clear whether they split off from the earliest species of Australopithecus or developed from an earlier common ancestor. These two species mark the transition from genus Australopithecus (with reduced canines, large molars, and sexual dimorphism) to the genus Homo (hominins that were fully bipedal, no longer with skeletal adaptations to climbing in trees, with smaller molars and small canines, larger brains and reduced dimorphism that approaches modern levels). They are called *Homo habilis* and *Homo rudolfensis* by some researchers, though other researchers view them as continuous with Australopithecus and have named them *Australopithecus habilis* and *Australopithecus rudolfensis*. I will use the first of these nomenclatures.

The two species are transitional in different ways. Each one retained features of the previous lineage but combined these with features found also in subsequent lineages. Homo habilis are first found around 1.8 mya. They were short with long arms. They had lost skeletal features such as grasping toes and curling fingers, and the pelvis had changed to be more suited to walking. There was less sexual dimorphism, suggesting a smaller division of labor between the two sexes, perhaps a consequence of tool use. The name Homo habilis ("handy man") reflects the fact that fossils of this species (but rudolfensis also) are found with stones modified to use as simple tools, such as scrapers and choppers. These were at first Oldowan-type tools, though later they changed.

The face of Homo habilis was reduced, with less protrusive teeth and jaws. The entire organization of the mouth had changed: they had small molars, with thin enamel (like ours in both structure and size), a smaller jaw, and larger incisors, with the flat teeth at the front of the mouth. This may have meant they were eating fewer crude vegetables due to the use of tools to prepare meat. The skull was also rounder, with a shorter jaw muscle.

All this is very consistent with features found in later hominins such as Homo ergaster, but at the same time the brain cavity remained small, like Australopithecus. The cranium of Homo habilis was slightly larger and rounded and smooth, with no ridge. The brain was still relatively small (the size of some apes' brains today). Skin color and hair color are unknown, though dark skin would have been likely if body hair had been lost.

Homo rudolfensis, in contrast, although living around the same time, had a larger brain like later hominins such as H. erectus and H. ergaster, but had a face and mouth much more like Australopithecus. The cranium was large and vaulted, and the brain much larger, well above the size of the brain of modern apes or that of Australopithecus. Their body was larger than that of Homo habilis. But the upper face was heavy and the upper jaw was large, like Australopithecus, probably with large teeth.

These two species produce a dilemma. Modern humans have both a large brain and a small jaw. Jaw reduction and brain increase would both be adaptations likely to be associated with tool use. One of these transitional species has a reduced jaw but a smaller brain; the other has a larger jaw and face, but also a larger brain. Each has features of both the previous and the subsequent lineages. The obvious question is, which one of these two separate lineages led to us? We cannot tell. We don't know which one of these was the ancestor of Homo sapiens. Perhaps neither, or perhaps both—maybe they could interbreed. They may not have been separate species in the sense that they could have produced viable offspring (just as breeds of dog can be very different and still interbreed). We see clearly here that there was no direct and simple line of evolution that led to modern humans.

2.3 OUT OF AFRICA: HOMO ERGASTER (1.8–1.4 MYA)

We start to find hominins outside Africa for the first time from 1.8 to 1.4 mya. This was the time when genus Homo began to spread around Europe and Asia. They apparently walked around the perimeter of the Indian Ocean, which was lower then due to the enlarged polar ice masses. What led to this dramatic event?

The hominin we first find outside Africa has been named both *Homo erectus* and *Homo ergaster* (for "workman"). (Sometimes H. erectus is used to describe the later groups of this species, or only the Asian group, while the name H. ergaster is used for the earliest African members. Many researchers use the terms "erectus" and "ergaster" interchangeably. I will call them H. ergaster.)

Homo ergaster are first found *within* Africa from 1.8 mya. They were anatomically very different from their predecessors, very tall and thin with body proportions much more like modern humans. The arms were shorter, and the legs longer. They stood about 6.2 feet (1.9 meters) tall, and their bodies were larger than their predecessors, with a more lineal skeleton below the neck. The rib cage was no longer shaped like a cone, wider at the bottom than the top, like earlier hominins. These were the first exclusively bipedal hominin. Fossil footprints show that they had feet very much like our own. Their bones were a little heavier than ours, probably due to a harder lifestyle with more exercise. Sexual dimorphism was further reduced.

2.3 OUT OF AFRICA: HOMO ERGASTER (1.8–1.4 MYA)

Homo ergaster had an elongated brain case, longer from front to back rather than with a high forehead, with a reduced face and smaller teeth. They had the largest brain so far: the earliest fossils had brains of around 900cc and over time brain size increased to around 1200cc. The modern human has a brain in the range 950–2000 cc, with an average of 1350cc, but brain size in modern humans does not correlate with intelligence, and people alive today with the smallest brains are still able to function adequately, learning language, and so on. Homo ergaster's brain was large enough.

Although the earliest examples of Homo ergaster were found in Africa, it is clear they were able to explore and thrive in many different kinds of environment. Fossils have been found all over the world, dating to 1.7 mya in northwest Africa, Europe, central and east Asia, and even in Java, an island off east Asia. It is possible there was a large migration out of Africa around 1.8 mya. At that time glaciers extended down into Europe and the sea level was much lower all over the world, so that the continental shelves (which are now 300 feet below sea level) were exposed. These shelves formed extended, flat planes where game animals would have roamed. It was possible at that time to walk along these planes from Africa to Indonesia, so the migration from Africa may have been the result of hunting large hoofed animals along these planes.

2.3.1 ACHEULEAN TOOLS

Homo ergaster continued to use the Oldowan tools that had been developed in Africa, but around 1.5 mya a new type of tool appeared in addition, Acheulean tools, different from the crude Oldowan choppers. These were fabricated from carefully selected kinds of rock, often volcanic glasses such as obsidian, which can carry a very sharp edge. These tools were transported, in contrast with the Oldowan tools, which were simply made on the spot when they were needed. Such sophisticated and precise tools required several stages of preparation: first the removal of several large chips to prepare the core, then the removal of smaller chips, and perhaps the use of bones to prepare the final edge. This Acheulean toolkit (see Figure 3.6) has been found all over Africa and in some parts of Europe. Fewer such tools have been found in Indonesia and China, and it is possible that sharpened and fire-hardened bamboo was utilized here instead, since volcanic rock was less available. It has been proposed that fabricating Acheulean tools required patterns of flake removal that could only have been organized with an understanding, to use Piagetian terms, of reversibility and/or conservation—that is, operational intelligence (Wynn, 1979).

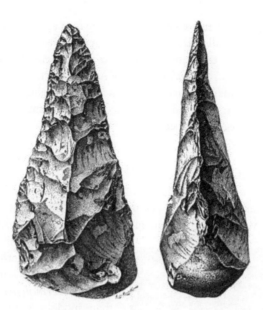

Figure 3.6 Examples of the Acheulean tool kit

Homo ergaster probably lived in **cooperative social groups**, gathering food and hunting together. There is evidence to suggest that by 500,000 ya fire was controlled and by 300,000 ya shelters were constructed. However, Homo ergaster shows nothing like writing, or art, or other symbolism.

At the time of the first migration from Africa, robust Australopithecus were still living there, in territory similar to that favored by Homo ergaster. The two may have been competing for the same foods and Australopithecus may have been pushed into extreme adaptation and eventually extinction. At the same time, this competition may have pushed Homo ergaster further towards the use of animal foods.

A number of subsequent migrations occurred from 1.8 mya until 300,000 ya, into central China, Asia, and Europe, then into Europe and northern China, and finally into northern Europe as the glaciers declined. There were also returns back south into Africa. It is possible that Homo ergaster in different parts of the world developed different characteristics due to geographical separation of the different populations. As we shall see shortly, the differences among modern humans evolved in only tens of thousands of years, and if that same process had occurred with Homo ergaster for a million years it could have produced significant variations.

2.4 ARCHAIC HOMO SAPIENS: HOMO HEIDELBURGENSIS (800,000–300,000 YA)

Not many hominin fossils are found dating from the period between 1.5 and 1.0 mya, perhaps because populations were very small during that time, and the few fossils that have been discovered show little evolutionary change taking place. Then transitional forms began to appear, with a brain size in the modern range or larger: 1200cc or more. Called **Homo heidelburgensis**, these fossils have been found in many parts of the world, including Africa, dated to different times in different places: 800,000 ya in Spain, from 500,000 ya in other parts of Europe, from 250,000 ya in Asia. Importantly, they have also been found in Australia, which required that heidelburgensis crossed the open sea using boats or rafts around 80,000 to 60,000 years ago. Homo heidelburgensis had a flatter face, a larger brain, and an arched cranium, but they still had the large face and big noses of predecessors.

2.5 HOMO NEANDERTHALENSIS (300,000–27,000 YA)

Homo neanderthalensis was a special and very prolific subgroup of archaic Homo, living from around 300,000 to around 27,000 years ago in Europe and much of the Middle East. In popular culture they have often been viewed as primitive and only half human, but in fact they were an advanced people, very close

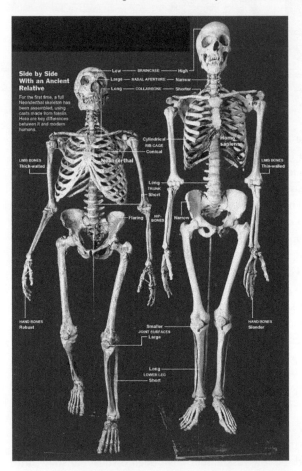

to home sapiens in evolutionary terms. Their similarity to modern humans is reflected in the fact that they are sometimes called *Homo sapiens neanderthalensis*. They were a little shorter than modern humans, stockier and stronger, with robust features. A comparison between a Neanderthal and a modern human skeleton (see Figure 3.7) reveals some differences, such as a more conical rib cage and a slightly more flaring pelvis, but Neanderthal hips, arms, and hands were similar to ours. They were sturdy, with larger, stronger bones than we have. As the figure shows, Neanderthal faces had stronger features than ours: the face was large with a pronounced brow ridge, a large mouth and jaw, and a big nose, which was perhaps an adaptation to the cold, dry subarctic climates in which they lived. Their brain case also extended backwards rather than upwards. Notably, Neanderthals had brains somewhat larger than modern humans, on average 1500 cc.

The Neanderthals were a very successful species, surviving for almost 300,000 years, while in comparison we modern humans have survived so far for only around 200,000 years. The range of territory that they occupied extended across Europe into the British Islands (much of what is now the North Sea was then land) and into the Middle East.

Figure 3.7 Neanderthal and modern human skeletons

2.5.1 MOUSTERIAN TOOLS

Neanderthal tools included spears, and they probably hunted large animals in organized groups. They continued to use the Acheulean tools, largely unchanged. But they also used what are called Mousterian tools, which included carving, scraping, and penetrating instruments, as well as projectiles. Neanderthals were able to produce at least 60 types of tool made from wood, stone, and bone, and the patterns of their tools varied regionally (see Figure 3.8). They controlled fire and were perhaps able to create it. They constructed functional living spaces within caves and rock shelters, with hearths surrounded by seating and with sleeping areas made of grass that might have been covered with animal fur. They seem to have

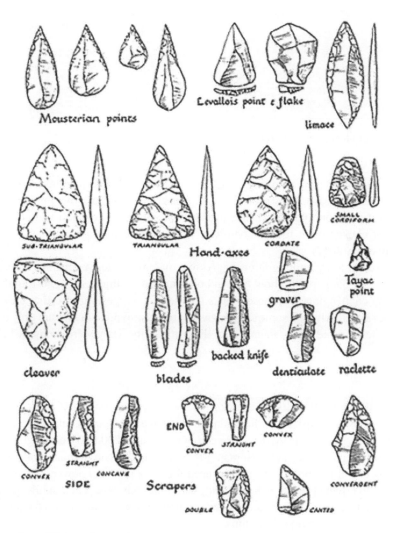

Figure 3.8 Examples of Mousterian tools

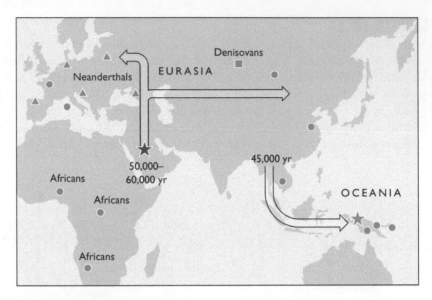

Figure 3.9   Routes of Neanderthal migration

cooked, eaten, and slept near the warming fires. They lived and worked in communities, and may have buried their dead (Balter, 2012). They probably used items of personal adornment, and there are suggestions that they created decorative and artistic artifacts. Recent studies of their teeth debris suggest they also ate a range of cooked plant foods, along with yarrow and camomile, perhaps for their medicinal properties (Hardy et al., 2012).

Neanderthals survived by hunting large, aggressive mammals such as mammoth, bear, and elk in a cold climate. Many of their fossils show broken bones and other injuries, suggesting that their way of life was tough and challenging. But these breaks had healed, suggesting also that they cared for each other. Some fossils are elderly, and some show signs of arthritis, so presumably not only the wounded but also the old were being cared for by members of the community. They were doing just fine until Homo sapiens arrived.

2.6 HOMO SAPIENS (200,000–TODAY)

As is the case with the other species of hominin that we have considered, anatomically modern *Homo sapiens* seems to have evolved in Africa, between 300,000 and 700,000 years ago. Physically, modern Homo sapiens (the name means "wise man") is more gracile than archaic Homo sapiens, perhaps because increasing use of technology meant less need for brute physical power. The first Homo sapiens stood on average 5 to 6 feet (1.5 to 1.8 meters) tall, with thin body hair. Their skulls had a high rounded cranium and a distinct chin, a consequence of changes in the muscles that operate the jaw. The teeth were much smaller than those of previous hominins.

When we look around at our fellow human beings we are likely to be struck by how different we all are. In contrast, when we look at a group of chimpanzees or gorillas they all seem very similar. In fact, however, humans are much more similar genetically than even a small group of chimpanzees. Nucleotide diversity between humans is about 0.1 percent, meaning there is 99.9 percent similarity. In addition, there is as much genetic variation *within* a human community (for example, within the Aborigines in Australia) as there is variation *among* communities. This relative lack of variation suggests that at some point in the evolution of modern humans—presumably some time before 100,000 years ago—there was a **genetic bottleneck**, a point at which only a small number of individuals, perhaps 10,000, survived. Indeed, the size of the population of which "Mitochondrial Eve" was a member is estimated to have been only about 10,000 individuals (Hawkes et al., 2000). Every human alive today is descended from this relatively small population, hence the genetic similarity among modern humans, despite superficial differences. Furthermore, as humans travel around the globe today and intermarry the human genome is becoming increasing homogeneous.

This similarity is strong evidence that Homo sapiens evolved in one place. It is also clear that Neanderthals were not our direct ancestor; in fact over time Neanderthal evolution took the form of specializations in which they increasingly differed from Homo sapiens.

Around 125,000 years ago, Homo sapiens migrated for the first time out of Africa. They quickly spread to inhabit virtually all parts of the globe, due in part to their ability to develop new forms of transportation, such as boats. Of all the hominins, only H. sapiens reached the Americas. This series of migrations has been reconstructed through analysis of **mitochondrial DNA** (inherited from the mother by both male and female children) and **Y-chromosome DNA** (inherited from the father by male children). In 1987, a team at the University of California, Berkeley, compared the mitochondrial DNA (mtDNA) of several groups of people from different geographic locations. Unlike DNA in the nucleus of the cell (called "nuclear DNA"), which is mixed when sperm meets ovum in the process known as recombination, mtDNA is inherited directly from the mother within the ovum, and so it is unchanged except for random mutations. These mutations occur at a steady rate, and this enables samples of mtDNA to be dated. These studies showed that the most recent common ancestor to all humans alive today lived in Africa between 200,000 and 100,000 ya (see Figure 3.10). Perhaps confusingly, the team named her "Mitochondrial Eve." It might appear surprising that all the mitochondrial DNA in modern humans was inherited from a single individual, but because maternal lineages die out whenever there is no daughter to carry on it is statistically probable that all but one lineage will eventually disappear. The research merely took advantage of this fact to pinpoint the region of origin for modern humans (Africa) and estimate the time at which they arose.

Studies like this can also be used to trace the migrations of modern humans (see Figure 13.11). As humans moved away from the tropics the need for protection from solar ultraviolet radiation became less, and mutations started to accumulate in the genes responsible for the production of melanin, the pigment that gives color to the skin (when a fair person gets a suntan, the color is due to melanin). As a result, humans acquired a variety of different hair, eye, and skin colors. Such characteristics have often been taken to define distinct **races**, but in fact they represent only very superficial differences. These differences, however, can be used to estimate how long ago a group of people arrived in a particular location.

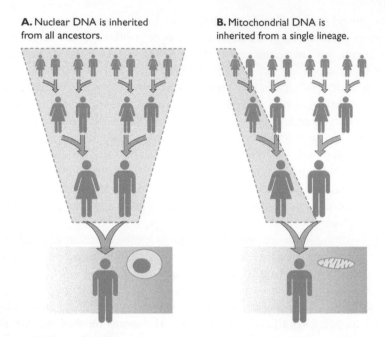

A. Nuclear DNA is inherited from all ancestors.

B. Mitochondrial DNA is inherited from a single lineage.

Figure 3.10   How mtDNA is inherited

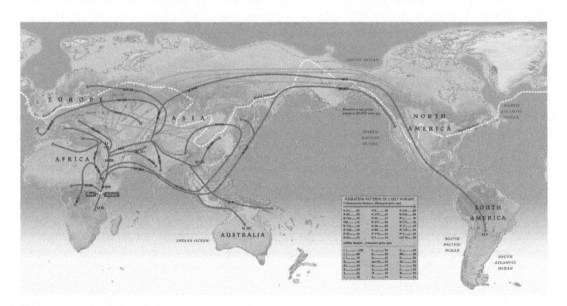

Figure 3.11   The migration routes of Homo sapiens

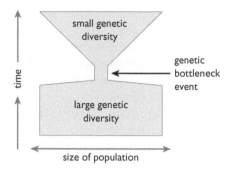

Figure 3.12 Genetic bottleneck

At first, Homo sapiens used Mousterian tools. But around 40,000 years ago, just before the Neanderthals disappeared, in the period known as the Upper Paleolithic (Paleolithic means "old stone age"), many new and diverse tools appeared, varying by region. This transition between toolkits seems to have occurred first in Africa. These complex new tools included blades, long pointed weapons with wood or bone handles, carved tools including hooks and needles, spears and spear throwers, barbed harpoons, and bows and arrows. These were evidently tools for specialized functions, but they were also tools suited to diverse cultural practices. Around this time, the diet of Homo sapiens expanded around, to include fish, shellfish, and food which had been prepared by being crushed, chopped, and cooked.

Some researchers see this new toolkit as evidence of a growing ability for advanced planning, and consequently of a new awareness of time. However, an equally significant adaptation of Homo sapiens,

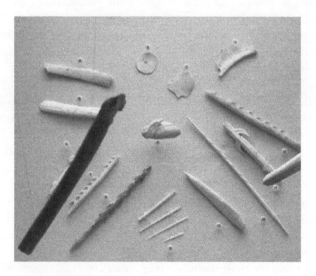

Figure 3.13 Early Homo sapiens tools

from our point of view, was the appearance of symbolic artifacts. Biologically there are few differences between humans alive today and Homo sapiens of 200,000 years ago. For example, there has been no apparent increase in brain size. But when Homo sapiens first emerged we believe that there was no language, and no evidence has been found for the production of symbolic artifacts. It is not easy to date the appearance of these adaptations, but when they appeared they marked a new qualitative distinct phase of evolution, in which one generation learns from its elders not only through observation, or through person-to-person learning, but also through symbolic communication.

Clear evidence has been found that material representations were made around 40,000 years ago in the Upper Palaeolithic—carving in bone and ivory, paintings, and burials with grave goods such as beads and other adornments. This was a time of an explosion of such representations. For a period of around 15,000 years cave paintings were the vogue, with dramatic depictions of animals, such as horses, mammoths, reindeer, goats, lions, and more. Venus figures date from that period too.

There is great debate about what these findings tell us about the psychology of these early modern humans. Surely it shows the power of their imagination? One possibility is that "the newly emerging artifacts have much the same function as props in children's games of make believe" (Harris, 2000, p. x) and that for the first time human beings became able to live in an **imagined world**. Ritualized burial, for example, implies that the dead person was treated both as a corpse and as preparing for a journey to some kind of after-life. Did this practice mark, then, the start of symbolic thinking? There is a tendency to assume that the capacity to think symbolically must have come first and was then expressed in these paintings and practices. But the opposite seems equally likely to be true: that these material representations may have provided the first step towards symbolic cognition. It is important to remember that other possible kinds of symbolism—such as body markings, dancing, or music—left no traces and have been lost in the mists of time, so we have no way of knowing when they first appeared.

Homo sapiens arrived in Europe and parts of Asia while Neanderthals were still living there, and the two must have lived side by side for tens of thousands of years (Callaway, 2014). A much debated topic has been how the two interacted, and in particular whether there was interbreeding. Svante Pääbo, of Germany's Max Planck Institute for Evolutionary Anthropology, led a team that sequenced the Neanderthal genome. Neanderthal fossils are sufficiently recent that not all the organic material in the bones has leached away, and DNA can be extracted from this. The comparisons of Neanderthal and modern human DNA identified portions of Neanderthal DNA in modern humans: the genomes are more than 99.5 percent identical. Pääbo found that modern human genomes share 1 to 4 percent of genomic material with that of Neanderthals. However, the genes appear to offer no benefit and are randomly located. Additionally, the transfer appears to be only one way, namely from Neanderthals to humans. Evidently modern humans interbred not only with Neanderthals but also with Denisovans (another recently discovered hominin) shortly after leaving Africa. About 2 percent of the modern genome is made up of Neanderthal genes. They are associated with diabetes in Latin Americans, for example. (Pääbo's DNA comparisons also provide an estimate for the time when Neanderthals and modern Homo sapiens had a common ancestor: around 400,000 ya.) There is no evidence, however, that modern humans exchanged genes with older species such as Homo erectus (Green et al., 2010).

There is also evidence that the most recently living Neanderthals, between 42,000 and 27,000 years ago, were becoming more delicate in their features than "classic" Neanderthals. One possible explanation

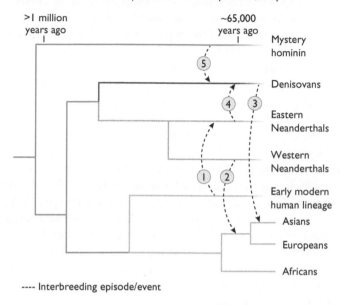

A HISTORY OF INTERBREEDING

Early modern humans, Denisovans, and Neanderthals all interbred with each other on multiple occasions in the past 100,000 years.

Figure 3.14   Interbreeding between humans, Denisovans, and Neanderthals

for this is their interbreeding with modern humans. Excavations also show that they started to make stone tools using chert rather than quartz, something that mirrored the tool production of the modern Homo sapiens who were living alongside them. In other words, contact between the two hominins was leading to changes that were both physiological and behavioral. In addition, Neanderthals seem to have died out very quickly, around 27,000 ya, and their extinction may have been a result of competition with modern humans. Figure 3.14 shows a simulation, based on mtDNA data, of modern human expansion into Europe, starting 1600 generations ago. The Neanderthal range is shown in light gray, and it is evident how Homo sapiens increasingly occupied this territory.

3. TRACING THE ORIGINS OF LANGUAGE

Something we really would like to know is at what time in human evolution, and with what species of hominin, language evolved or was invented. Since oral language leaves virtually no traces this is a difficult topic to study. What we know comes from tracing the origin of modern humans, from fossil features, and from comparison of languages around the world today. It turns out that we can learn a lot.

Babies all over the world are born with the ability to learn language. This fact might mean that the ability was possessed by the most recent common ancestor of all the diverse peoples of the

Earth, who lived as we have seen about 100,000 years ago. (Though having the capacity does not mean it was necessarily put into practice of course.) Or this could mean that once language was invented—a simple protolanguage, presumably—it soon became so necessary for human existence that infants who could not learn to speak and understand were simply not able to thrive and reproduce. There would have been selection for the ability to learn language, in what is called "genetic accommodation" (Dor & Jablonka, 2010).

It is important to recognize that the capacity to learn language does not necessarily mean the capacity to speak. Deaf children learn sign language at about the same rate as hearing children learn oral language (see Chapter 6). The capacity for language does not dictate what medium is used: language can be heard, or seen, or even felt, in the case of braille. This is a really remarkable ability.

Did Neanderthals speak? Opinions have changed over the years. At first it was assumed that they lacked both the physiological and the intellectual capacity for spoken language. But in 1983 a Neanderthal hyoid bone was found that was virtually identical to that of modern humans. The hyoid is a small bone which connects the muscles of the tongue with the larynx, allowing subtle movements of these two organs, movements which are necessary for speech (Laitman et al., 1990). The Neanderthal brain also has a large hypoglossal canal, which in humans today carries the nerve which controls the tongue muscles. However, studies have found that the size of this canal is not correlated with speech potential. Then, studies of the ear structure of Homo heidelbergensis indicated that they had an auditory sensitivity equal to that of modern humans and much better than that of chimpanzees, which suggests that these earlier hominins might have had the capacity to differentiate the sounds of spoken language.

Neanderthals lacked the point at the tip of the chin where one of the muscles that move the lower lip is attached in Homo sapiens. However, they shared with modern humans a version of the FOXP2 gene, which is known to play a role in human language. On the one hand it has been argued that even Homo habilis had Broca's area 43, while on the other hand it has been suggested that Neanderthals never developed a descended larynx like modern humans.

Another proposal has been that the Neanderthals had a system of prelinguistic communication which predated the separation of language and music into two separate modes of communication, and which was based on variations of tone, rhythm, the timbre of voice, and body language (Mithen, 2005).

An analysis of the phonemic diversity of the more than 500 different languages on Earth today has found that the number of phonemes in each language diminishes the further its speakers are from southern Africa (Atkinson, 2011). (I will explain the character of phonemes in Chapter 5.) The theory is that the distribution of languages today is the result of a succession of events in which a small group of people left a larger population and their language lost phonemes as a consequence. It is known that smaller, close-knit communities have languages with fewer phonemes, presumably because a small group of people can tolerate reduced linguistic contrast. Previous reconstructions of the history of language have focused on words, not phonemes, and have been able to trace this history back only about 9,000 years. Tracing phonemes, in contrast, enables a much older reconstruction. Several languages in Africa today have more than 100 phonemes, including click-sounds—smacks of the lips and flaps of the tongue against the roof of the mouth. At the other extreme Hawaiian, the language that is the furthest from Africa in terms of human migration, has only 13 phonemes. These findings have several important

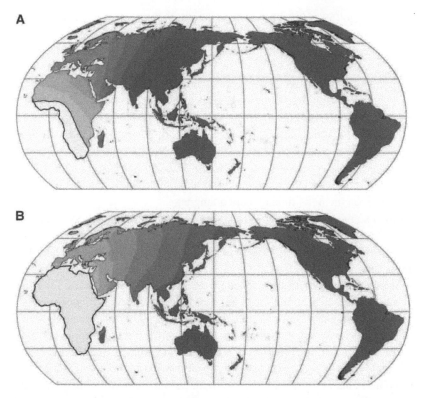

Figure 3.15 Lighter shading indicates greater phonemic diversity among the languages in that area

Source: Atkinson (2011)

implications: (1) language was invented only once, so that the languages that exist today, and those that no longer exist, are derived from a single protolanguage; (2) the place of this invention was southern Africa; and (3) the protolanguage dates to around 50,000 to 70,000 years ago. This coincides with the time of the earliest archaeological evidence of the creation of material representations, which we have seen was about 80,000 to 160,000 years ago.

If this timing is correct, it would mean that among the hominins only Homo sapiens actually spoke phonemic language. It is possible that other hominins such as Neanderthals also had the biological capacity to do so, but were never given the opportunity. If so, this achievement would have been something that Homo sapiens took with them when they migrated from Africa to other parts of the planet. Perhaps phonemic language was another advantage that Homo sapiens had over the Neanderthals whose territory they entered. Or perhaps Homo sapiens taught language to the Neanderthals with whom they interbred.

There is another proposal, however: that spoken language predates the common ancestor of modern humans and Neanderthals. This would place the origins of language not 50,000 to 100,000 years ago, but half a million years ago (500,000). The claim is that "speech and language are ancient, being present in a modern-like form over half a million years ago in the common ancestor of Neandertal and modern humans, the result of evolution in the prior one million years or so as H. heidelbergensis evolved from H. erectus" (Dediu & Levinson, 2013, p. 9).

Part of this argument is that, as we have seen, Neanderthals and Homo sapiens interbred, and probably Denisovans too, suggesting that Homo sapiens was not dramatically different from Neanderthal, either genetically or psychologically. Neanderthals shared with us the FOXP2 gene, as I mentioned, and apparently had a descended larynx and a hyoid bone. In short, Neanderthals had the anatomical prerequisites for speech. Moreover, making and using the Neanderthals' complex tools would have required an ability for complex motor control—as does speech. In addition, Neanderthal infants seem to have matured slowly (as we shall see in the next section), although probably not as slowly as human infants, and this would have given them the time to learn a language.

These similarities suggest that the ancestor common to Neanderthals and modern humans already had the capacities that were crucial for spoken language more than 400,000 years ago. This argues against the proposal that a "modern package" of skills suddenly appeared around 40,000 years ago, unique to Homo sapiens.

What, then, might have been the sequence of building the foundations for modern language? First would have been the interactional and motivational infrastructure: cooperation, passing along tool-making skills, recognizing intentions, all of which were likely characteristics of Homo erectus. Gesture would have been important, and spoken language, once it was invented, would have accompanied and supplemented gesture, not replaced it. Phonology, syntax, and lexicon would have come last. We know now that syntax changes relatively slowly in the history of a language, much more slowly than sound change and change in word meaning, with perhaps a major change in a structure such as word order every ten thousand years. This suggests that the syntactical diversity of the 7,000 or so languages that exist today must have taken far longer than 50,000 years to develop.

If this proposal regarding the antiquity of language is correct, it is likely that when the Homo sapiens who left Africa 50,000 years ago came into contact with Neanderthals who had evolved in Europe, these groups would both have been speaking languages with very ancient origins. The languages that exist today may be products of the two hominids mixing not only their genes but also their languages.

4. EVOLUTION OF THE LIFE CYCLE

Another aspect of hominin existence that we would like to know about is the form their **life cycle** took. How long did they live? How long did their childhood last? Did they pass through the same developmental stages as modern humans?

The stages of childhood and adolescence in humans today differ significantly from those of other mammals and our primate cousins. Primates, like many mammals, have just three stages in their life cycle: infant, juvenile, and adult. Infants are completely dependent on adults for food and shelter. Juveniles are more independent, able to obtain their own food and fend for themselves, but they are sexually immature, incapable of having babies themselves. As we shall see in detail in the chapters that follow, modern humans have three additional developmental stages to the life cycle: childhood, adolescence, and the post-menopausal period for adult women.

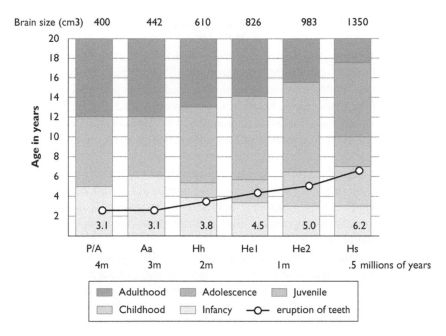

Figure 3.16 Evolution of the human life cycle

Source: Author, based on Bogin & Smith (2000)

Surprisingly, we now know quite a lot about the developmental stages of our ancestors. Fossils have now been discovered of individuals from various species of hominin who died at different ages. Characteristics of the skeleton and teeth enable us to estimate the age at death. For example, a brief interruption of tissue formation that occurs at birth is visible in the teeth. Weaning is indicated by enamel defects. Patterns of teeth emergence and root growth, and incremental growth lines (like tree rings) in bones and teeth, can show age and also developmental stage. Computed tomography (CT) scanning can show the status of tooth development. There is also microanatomical evidence of age at death.

Studies of these fossils suggest that the life cycle has evolved over the course of human evolution. The human newborn has become increasingly immature, childhood has become extended, adolescence has also extended, and the lifespan extends much further past the reproductive years than in the other hominin species. The duration of childhood has increased with each new kind of hominin, while both infancy and the juvenile stage have become shorter.

Austalopithecus, the earliest hominins at around 4 mya, had an infancy that lasted until around 5 years of age, like their primate cousins. This was followed by a juvenile stage lasting until 12 years, at which point adulthood began. Their relatively long infancy would have allowed plenty of time for learning, through observation, imitation, and some independent exploration. The first permanent teeth (the molar teeth) erupted around 3 years of age, so older infants were able to eat solid food. During the juvenile stage the young Australopithecus would presumably have learned additional skills that were necessary for survival in the local environment, and so become better adapted. Juveniles were independent from adults in the sense that they could survive if they were separated, but they probably didn't have either adult status or adult responsibilities.

By the time of Homo habilis, at around 2 mya, a new distinct stage of childhood had evolved. During this stage, from around 4 to 5 years of age, children were still dependent on adults. This was when the permanent teeth appeared—children would have been weaned, but their continued brain growth would have required special food which adults obtained or prepared for them. As we have seen, during this period of evolution adult brain size increased to around 800 cc. Homo habilis children had a relatively large brain, but their small body size meant that their food requirements were not large, so their burden on adults was not great.

The emergence of childhood for Homo habilis would also have reduced the energy costs for a mother, because other people could help her by feeding and taking care of the children. Homo habilis of both genders had larger bodies than Austalopithecus, and reduced dimorphism. The larger body would have required more energy input, but changes in the strategy for gestation, lactation, and weaning would have provided some compensation for this.

By the time of the evolution of Homo ergaster, around 1 million years ago, childhood had become even longer, with infancy ending around age 3 and the juvenile stage (what in this book we call "middle childhood") starting at 6 and ending around 14 years of age. Permanent teeth now appeared in the middle of the stage of childhood. New social arrangements probably gave children increased opportunities for cultural learning and transmission. The time needed for these evolutionary changes may explain why the Acheulean toolkit didn't appear for half a million years, but the increased opportunity for cultural learning explains why this toolkit was stable—transmitted and reproduced—for so long.

In the past million years a number of changes to the life cycle have evolved. Modern Homo sapiens continue to have an infancy about the same length as that of Homo ergaster, lasting around 2.5 years. Childhood is somewhat longer, lasting around 3 years and ending around 6 or 7 years of age. The appearance of permanent teeth is now delayed until the end of childhood, and this means that during this stage young children remain dependent on adults to prepare special food for them. This is a stage of significant brain growth, while the body grows more slowly.

The juvenile stage is shorter for modern humans than it was for Homo ergaster, lasting only 4 years and ending around 10 years of age. During this stage children are more independent and can eat adult food, but they continue to learn important survival skills. Then a developmental stage begins, that of adolescence, which seems to be unique to Homo sapiens. During this stage important biological changes occur which are not evident in other primates, and apparently did not occur in earlier hominins. Most notable is a spurt of rapid physical growth, in which young people add perhaps 10 percent to their adult height and weight. In contrast, a juvenile Homo ergaster, known as "Turkana boy," died about 1.5 million years ago, when he was aged around 8. He was already 154 cm tall (5 feet), and it is estimated he would have grown only 5 to 14 cm more, reaching hia adult status of 5 feet 4 inches (163 cm) at age 12 (Graves et al., 2010).

In modern humans adolescence ends at around 17 years of age, and it is the longest of the developmental stages before adulthood, lasting about 6 years.

This reconstruction of the life cycle is based, of course, on fossil evidence, and so the definitions of the stages of development are drawn from what is visible in bones and teeth. However, there is no reason to think that these anatomical changes were the products of biological change alone. On the contrary, they undoubtedly reflected changed cultural practices, including the control of fire, shared responsibility for feeding and protecting younger members of the community, innovation in tools and other technology, and migration to new settings. Overall we can see a general tendency in the changes in the life-cycle strategies of hominins, so that modern humans grow more slowly and die older than our hominin ancestors. Australopithecines probably lived at a rate twice as fast as that of modern humans: they grew fast and died young. We shall see in the next section that cultural practices continue to alter human genes and human biology. It is quite possible that human neurobiology has changed dramatically over this time, and that biologically based behavior has changed as well.

I just said that Australopithecines grew fast and died young. But how young? Recent studies have been able to reconstruct the length of the lifespan for different hominins. It turns out that from Australopithecus through Homo erectus and Homo ergaster to Neanderthals, virtually no one survived beyond the age of 30 (Caspari & Lee, 2004, 2006). As we have seen, the ability to reproduce was apparently reached around age 12 or 13. Almost no child would have had a grandparent.

Only around 30,000 to 20,000 years ago did the lifespan of modern humans start to increase (Caspari & Lee, 2004). (See Figure 3.17.) Among Neanderthals, for every 10 individuals who died between 15 and 30 years of age there were 4 others who survived beyond 30. In contrast, among early modern humans for every 10 young adults there were 20 individuals old enough to be their grandparents. Clearly this was not only a dramatic change in the length of the average human lifespan, it was also a dramatic change in the circumstances in which children lived. Now they could spend time with, and learn from, older adults who had lived long enough to learn a thing or two.

So what caused this change? Examination of fossils of older modern humans, dating to around 100,000 years ago, showed that they too died young. The difference must have been cultural, because the biology could not have been substantially different. We don't know exactly what people started to do differently, but it must have produced positive feedback: longevity was the result of some change in lifestyle, and then having older people around proved to be a valuable resource for rearing and educating children. This in turn supported more complex cultural practices and societal organization, and this in turn provided greater support for a longer life, so that communities grew even larger and formed more intricate kinship systems and networks for trade, cooperation, and production. This reconstruction has been called "the grandmother hypothesis": humans started to live longer not because the young took care of older members of the community, but because these older people took care of the young, enabling parents to attend to other necessary tasks (Hawkes, 2003, 2004). Human life changed for the better in several ways.

In conclusion, it is evident that we should think of evolution as a process that shapes not the adult, but the entire course of the development to adulthood. We now appreciate that "the adult individual is not the end product of evolution; rather, the whole life span and its patterning is a result of selective forces and thus evolutionarily shaped" (Keller & Kärtner, 2013, p. 79). This is not to say that ontogenesis has been genetically programmed; on the contrary, it means that human evolution has prepared the newborn child to interact with her environment and learn accordingly.

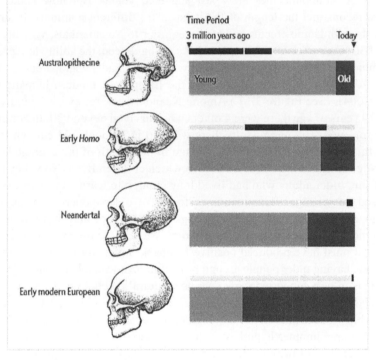

FINDINGS

Growing Older

Analyses of the fossilized teeth of hundreds of individuals spanning three million years ago indicate that living long enough to reach grandparenthood became common relatively late in human evolution. The author and her colleague assessed the proportion of older (grandparent-aged) adults relative to younger adults in four groups of human ancestors—australopithecines, early members of the genus *Homo,* Neandertals and early modern Europeans—and found that the ratio increased only modestly over the course of human evolution until around 30,000 years ago, when it skyrocketed.

Time Period

3 million years ago — Today

Australopithecine — Young / Old

Early *Homo*

Neandertal

Early modern European

Figure 3.17 Changes in hominin longevity

Source: Caspari (2011)

5. SOCIOCULTURAL EVOLUTION

At the time of the Upper Paleolithic, around 40,000 years ago, humans lived in **hunter-gatherer** societies. They continued to do so until around 10,000 years ago. Since then, however, extraordinary changes have taken place in how humans live, the technology we use, the size of our communities, and how they are organized. Today, many humans live in large cities with as many as 10 million people, using complex technology, dealing with elaborate economic and political institutions.

How to understand and explain this change in human communities? Social scientists have struggled over this question. One approach has been to place cultures on a single line of "cultural evolution," a process whereby communities advance from a state of "savagery" through "barbarism" to more adequate "civilized" forms. This proposal has been controversial to say the least, because it assumes that societies can be arranged along a single line (Schultz, 2009).

Many anthropologists continue to be skeptical about evolutionary accounts of societies and cultures. However, an analysis by anthropologists Allen Johnson and Timothy Earle (2000) is interesting in the way it combines an account of linear stages with an appreciation that societies change in different ways due to their specific environmental and historical conditions.

Johnson and Earle propose a sequence of scales of societal organization which I shall illustrate through concrete examples:

- The family-level group, which may be foragers or have domesticated animals and plants.
- The local group or clan, living in a village or hamlet, generally practicing agriculture.
- The chiefdom or a state, with a ruler and elite governing institutions.
- The global society, with international economic and political institutions.

5.1 THE FAMILY GROUP: THE !KUNG

The !Kung, who we shall meet several times in the chapters that follow, provide an example of a society organized at the family level. A total of 15,000 !Kung range over what are now Botswana, Namibia, and Angola in Southern Africa, chiefly on the high, flat Kalahari desert and scrub land, with a population density around one person per 25 square kilometers.The conditions in this wide region are unsuitable for agriculture or grazing animals, and so the !Kung survive as hunter-gatherers by gathering plants and hunting a few animals when they are available (though some !Kung are becoming settled pastoralists as a result of contact with other communities). Seventy percent of their diet is plant food. The population density remains low—as we shall see in Chapter 8, fertility is low among the !Kung and births are spaced roughly every four years. The !Kung are also physically small, an average of 5 ft 3 in tall, weighing 110 lbs.

The central !Kung social unit is the family household, with its own simple, temporary shelter and hearth. Each family is occupied primarily with obtaining enough food and avoiding danger. Their daily life tends to be calm: warfare and disputes over territory are rare, and conflict among individuals is unusual and discouraged. The family group is able to be flexible and self-sufficient because it has the necessary land, labor, and technology to sustain itself. Life is not hard: hunting is necessary only three days each week, and children, adolescents, and old people do not need to work. Relations are personal and intimate—those of husband–wife, parent–child, and among siblings—and people's conduct is organized by common understanding rather than by formal rules or principles. Their commitments to one another are based on personal attachments and affection, rather than being rule-governed or institutionalized. They have no social hierarchy, nor social positions with a recognized status: "Duty is, as it were, owed between people rather than between their positions" (Wilson, 1988, p. 34). There is a taken-for-granted division of labor by gender: women gather, care for the children, and make simple utensils. Men hunt and manufacture tools. The interdependence among husbands and wives leads to mutual respect, and in general family members expect equality and reciprocity from one another.

Two other scales of organization are at times important for the !Kung. The first is the *camp*. For part of each year the !Kung live in groups of several families, ranging in size from 20 to 60 people, though families and individuals can move freely from one camp to another. A camp has no established leader; instead decisions are made through long discussions to reach consensus. The camp also enables the teamwork that is essential for the !Kung's survival, and when someone kills an animal the food is shared not only with their family but also throughout the camp. This custom spreads the risk of obtaining food and ensures that a family that is unlucky in hunting will not go hungry.

The camps across a wide region are linked into networks of exchange and communication, and this forms the third scale of organization: the *regional network*. The camps come together when cooperation is needed; for example the !Kung congregate during each dry season around permanent water sources, and members of different camps gather for rituals of trance dancing and curing. However, when the rains come and there is competition for resources, the camps disperse again. These regional networks are able to respond flexibly when conditions change.

The !Kung way of life is typical of gatherer communities, with the family being the most important level of organization. As I noted, this way of life has existed for hundreds of thousands of years, and it continues to be viable except when imposed upon from outside. The !Kung have complex knowledge of their environment, and quite sophisticated technology. There is ritual and some shamanism in their society, but no ceremony. Their way of life certainly cannot be called primitive, and they are highly intelligent and creative people, who live in harsh and difficult circumstances which they have exploited skillfully, and to which they have adapted biologically and culturally. Their population has remained low and their technology adequate to their way of life. They evidently feel there would be no benefit in settling in one location.

5.2 THE LOCAL GROUP: THE GUSII

The second scale of societal organization is as a tribe with a settled village or hamlet, composed of 100 to 500 members. Often, but not always, this settlement involves agriculture. Domestication of plants and animals occurred for the first time in the Neolithic period, around 15,000 years ago, and it usually required settling in one resource-rich location which became a territory to be defended.

Such communities have an economic organization that extends beyond the family, although they contain embedded families, each of which is a clan, house, or lineage with a clear sense of identity and tradition. Descent and ancestry within the clan become important matters, for they define key rights and obligations, including who has legitimate claims to land and labor. Interactions and conflicts among these clans have to handled by the community, usually through the linked institutions of leadership and ceremony.

Groups organized in this way are represented by leaders, in meetings and in warfare with other groups. Leaders manage collective technology and they arrange community work. Complex and expensive ceremonial events, with displays, dancing, and games, demonstrate the prestige and vitality of the community, bind together its members, and impress outsiders. They invoke ancestral spirits, cement marriages and exchanges, and mark status with symbolic artifacts. The result is that members become loyal towards the community as a whole rather than only to the family clan.

An example of a community organized on this scale is the Gusii, who live in western Kenya, not far from Lake Victoria. We shall meet them again from time to time. Their land is very productive, with rich soil and plenty of rain, and the Gusii population is far denser than that of the !Kung—as much as 600 people per square kilometer. On average a woman will have nine children, and infant mortality is relatively low at about 80 per 1,000 live births.

The traditional Gusii clan is a polygynous family (in which each husband has several wives) living in a homestead that includes a series of houses, one for each wife and her children, and other buildings surrounded by farmland. The family grows millet, maize, and other crops such as beans and sweet potatoes, they gather wild vegetables, and they tend livestock—cattle, goats, sheep, and chickens—that provide meat and milk. In addition, local ore is smelted to manufacture iron tools, weapons, and decorations, which are then exchanged among the homesteads and with neighboring communities.

Each Gusii tribe is composed of several such clans. Disputes are resolved by elders, who appeal to traditional rules about issues such as the inheritance of land and appropriate behavior, which generally amounts to being a hard worker who respects kinship obligations and raises children with similar values. Strong emotion is avoided among the Gusii, and interactions between the genders or across generations are especially regulated, and often require avoiding looking at the other person's face since this could risk the "evil eye." Eye contact is also avoided between parents and children, though infants are held for much of the time. Young children help with the care of infants.

The Gusii arrange elaborate and important ceremonies around initiation and marriage. Girls are initiated at the age of 7 or 8, and boys a few years later. Initiation, which involves a clitoridectomy for girls and circumcision for boys, prepares them to be mature beings who know the rules of shame (*chinsoni*) and respect (*ogosika*).

The settled local group not only domesticates plants and animals, it also domesticates its members. Built spaces, enduring over generations, divide public from private spaces, and they define customs and traditions whose origins have disappeared into the mists of time. Spatial settlement provides evidence of an extended past, and a sense that the individual is beholden to, and a representative of, past generations. A child born into such a society must discover not only who her parents and siblings are, but also the clan and tribe to which she belongs, and the ancestors who must be respected. Children must also respect their leaders, and a boy may perhaps aspire to become a leader himself in time.

5.3 THE CHIEFDOM OR STATE: THE NSO

The Nso community lives in the Central African country of Cameroon, in land that is largely savannah with patches of forest. Their economy is based on subsistence agriculture, growing corn, beans, potatoes, yam, and fruits and other vegetables. Most of the 217,000 Nso live in villages, similar to those of the Gusii, in multi-building compounds that each house a lineage, an extended family of at least three generations. Each family is headed by the father, and the lineage as a whole has a head. The Nso value children, who are raised by the whole complex family network.

The family must collaborate to grow crops. Women work in the fields, raise the children, and perform household chores. They also sell some of the produce at local markets. Cash comes from selling produce and crafts rather than from wages. Adults are often helped in their work by children and youth of the same sex. However, today more and more children are attending school.

Unlike the Gusii, however, the Nso have become organized as a highly stratified and hierarchical kingdom, with a traditional political and religious ruler, the *Fon*, who appoints the head of each lineage, and who speaks to ordinary people only through a spokesperson. The government also includes various fellowship organizations. The *Ngwerong* is a political organization that enforces the law, arranges public works, and implements the Fon's orders. The *Ngiri* has a more ceremonial role, arranging festivals. Other titles are appointed by the Fon, with important ceremonial and military roles. Children assume some of these roles: the *Shunghaiy* is a girl aged between 3 and 6 who is enthroned at the Fon's side. The *Asheey ver ntoh* are boys who from age 5 become custodians in the *Nwerong* and *Ngiri*.

In this scale of organization, local homesteads produce a surplus that is used to support a governing elite, which in turn exerts control on the homesteads but also offers prestige and invests in the infrastructure, thereby increasing production. Such settled communities have a much higher population density and a more complex division of labor than societies organized around the family, and increasingly they develop political and bureaucratic institutions and linkages through trade with other societies. The production of surplus food enables a growth in population, which ironically undercuts some of the initial benefits that agriculture offers. Instead of a small group enjoying a varied diet obtained by foraging and hunting, now larger groups make do with a more restricted diet, high in grains. Tending to crops and herds is assigned to a class of laborers, while an elite enjoys free time to do other kinds of work.

In some regions of the world these settled communities grew into cities, dense habitations with specialized occupations, including professional administrators, a system of interlinked legal and economic institutions, some kind of taxation, and a governing elite whose legitimacy might be based on family, religion, or military power. This "Neolithic complex" of characteristics was clearly evident in the Sumerian cities in Mesopotamia (now Southern Iraq), around 5,300 BC.

Imagine the daily life of a child growing up in such a city. This would depend greatly on the social class they were born into; they would have to learn the customs and practices of city life; and with time they would have to respect the rules and laws of economic and legal institutions or face the consequences of breaking them. In addition, they would have had the advantage of the availability of new kinds of cognitive tool: writing and arithmetic.

5.4 THE GLOBAL SOCIETY: WEIRD PEOPLE

Most of the children who have been studied by developmental scientists, however, have lived in urban areas, or at least in nation states that are components of a global economic system that has again enabled rapid population growth. In later chapters we shall review research with children from Japan, Germany, the United States, and the United Kingdom. These children are "WEIRD" people—**W**estern, **e**ducated, **i**ndustrialized, **r**ich, and **d**emocratic—and in these respects very unrepresentative of the world as a whole. In this scale of societal organization, the extraction of new resources and the exploitation of new forms of power (steam, electrical, nuclear) have gone hand in hand with the construction of new social technologies, including the liberal state, financial markets, and complex chains of production and consumption. Increasingly people live in cities, the growing, raising, and processing of food is the job of a minority, work is done far from home, and bureaucracy has become international and ubiquitous. Children living in such societies—still the minority in terms of their number—will surely develop in ways very different from those that have been typical for much of human history.

It would be tempting to think of the changes I have described in the organization of human societies as "progress." However, there is no reason to think that a larger or technologically more complex society is more successful, or more civilized, than a smaller or simpler one. In particular, a more complex society does not necessarily mean a better life for its members.

Early attempts to line up human cultures in a progression from "primitive" to "civilized" made the mistake of assuming what they needed to demonstrate. People have tended to assume, for example, that agriculture is more advanced than hunting and gathering. But the adoption of agriculture often meant shorter lifespans and poorer health. It permitted population growth, but the life of each individual was often marked by more and harder labor, times of hunger and even famine, work-related illness and infirmity, and an early death.

Similarly, industrialization brought many benefits, but it also brought pollution and unhealthy working conditions. Today, so-called "developed" or "advanced" nations consume far more than their share of the world's resources and they contribute far more to the planet's pollution than their "developing" or "underdeveloped" neighbors. We have to be very careful before we jump to the conclusion that one way of life is better than another. In addition, we have to avoid thinking that one single measure—such as technological sophistication—can be used to arrange societies in a line. It is nice to have an iPad, but to live in a society where this kind of technology is available does not by itself mean that we are more civilized than the ancient Greeks, or more sophisticated than hunter-gatherers in the Amazon basin. It seems more appropriate that we should view different cultures as neither better nor worse than one another, but as diverse ways of solving the common problems of how to live on this planet.

In the analysis I have illustrated here, change in human societies is linear to the extent that there is a common process: improved technology enables people to transform and make more efficient use of the local environment and so feed more people. This larger population generates various kinds of problems, such as strains on resources, issues of coordination, raids, and wars with neighbors. To address these problems, political and economic institutions are created or transformed. This "institutionalization" aims to integrate the society, organize how people work, and control and develop the community's resources. Institutions manage risk, build alliances with other groups, and regulate trade. Institutions also generate social stratification: they define categories of people which are ranked in a hierarchy. If institutionalization is effective, population will increase further and once again there will be pressure for innovative technology and more complex institutions, in a "spiral" of development (see Figure 3.18). Complex societies grow bureaucracies, and these require technologies of material representation. People then need to be trained to use them, and so schools are necessary, as we shall see in Chapter 12.

At the same time, societies do not all change in the same way, because each community has to solve the problems of daily life that confront it in specific environmental circumstances. In fact, there is no necessity for a society to change at all.

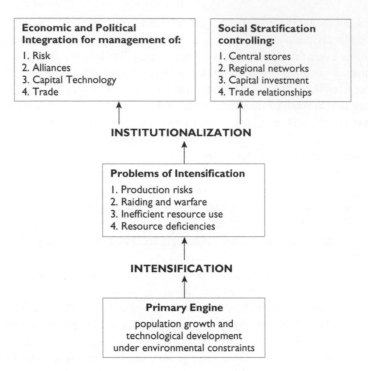

Figure 3.18 Evolution of human societies

Source: Johnson & Earle (2000)

CONCLUSION

EVOLUTION, HISTORY, AND ONTOGENESIS

It seems that speculations on human prehistory often deny cultural elaboration itself the causal role it so clearly deserves. Greater cultural elaboration must, the arguments seem to imply, depend on something else: greater intelligence, a speciation event, or some biological basis for an independent demographic spurt. But human culture is a spiral which under the right conditions will simply ratchet up. The right conditions are time left over from subsistence activities, strong norms of parental investment in the young, relative health, sufficient peer competition, ecological wealth for conspicuous consumption, etc. These enabling conditions have to be met, and then incremental cultural transmission will do the rest (Dediu & Levinson, 2013, p. 9).

How is the history of human societies related to biological evolution? Are they two separate and distinct processes of change? It is popular to think of biology and culture as though they are two completely separate sources of human capabilities—two distinct origins for human capabilities. For example, walking and playing the cello seem quite different. One seems an innate, biologically based ability, universal to all humans (except for cases of mutation or accident). The other seems to be a skill acquired by a select few. One appears to have its origins in the genes, the other in education.

But in fact the two are not as different as they seem. Walking is something that infants have to figure out how to do, usually with a good deal of adult help and guidance. And, as Marcel Mauss observed, there is no single "natural" way of walking: people in different countries walk in different ways (Mauss, 1973). The Japanese traditionally walked from the knees, in a shuffle that made sense when one wore sandals. And learning the cello also requires figuring things out, with support and guidance from an expert. Both are bodily skills whose acquisition is part of human development. At the same time, they are equally biological: in each it is the case that what the body can do becomes transformed. Of course, in neither case have the genes been changed, but it would be a very narrow definition of biology that included the DNA of the genome but excluded the rest of the body.

One of the interesting consequences of looking at sociocultural evolution in the way we have in this chapter is that it suggests that there are not two separate kinds of evolution. The creation of human societies is a continuation of the niche construction that is key to biological evolution. As humans have evolved they have repeatedly and increasingly transformed their environments. Hominins were apparently using and even making tools hundreds of thousands of years prior to the emergence of Homo sapiens, and consequently transforming their environmental niche, albeit in simple ways. This undoubtedly played a role in the evolution of Homo sapiens (Ingold, 2004).

Similarly, the larger and more complex societies that have emerged since then have also depended on reworking the environment. Clearing forests, preparing fields and pastures, building systems for irrigation, constructing paths and then roads ... all of these can be viewed as aspects of niche construction by human communities. The positive feedback between population and technology that drives societal evolution depends centrally on the use and transformation of the community's environment.

Human societies have also constructed a social technology, of elaborate kinship systems, economic instruments of credit and debt, political roles and functions, systems of law and control. These, too, are aspects of the human environmental niche. We shall see later, in Chapter 11, that the philosopher John Searle has proposed that the basic constituents of human social reality are these "institutional facts" (Searle, 1995, 2009).

It is sometimes suggested that biological evolution has stopped in the modern world, and there is no longer selection of the fittest individuals. Research shows, however, that selection of DNA mutations continues in modern societies, and some evidence suggests that the rate has actually increased (Laland et al., 2010). Biology and culture are working together, because when humans alter their environment this changes the challenges and selective pressures of that environment. Our biology has been, and continues to be, adapting hand in hand with changes in the ways we live (Li, 2003; Quartz & Senjowski, 2002).

This complex process is called **biocultural evolution**. One example is lactose tolerance. Until the innovation of farming cattle for their milk, very few humans were able to digest lactose (the natural sugar in cows' milk) beyond infancy. The genetic mutation that enabled a life-long digestion of lactose conveyed the advantage of making a good source of protein available, and lactose tolerance spread rapidly, but only in communities who practiced dairy farming. This example shows that "culturally constructed environments create powerful—and often autocatalytic—selection pressures on genes, and appear to have had a substantial impact on the patterns of genetic variation in the modern human genome" (Chudek & Henrich, 2011, p. 224).

As we learn more about the biology of inheritance, other ways in which culture and biology work together are becoming apparent. The recently discovered phenomenon of **transgenerational epigenetic inheritance** is an example. It is a passage of information from one generation to another that involves changes not in the genes, but in how genes are expressed to build proteins (Jablonka & Raz, 2009). I will discuss this further in the next chapter, as an aspect of prenatal development.

It should be clear, then, that we should not pit culture *against* biology, or suggest that if culture is important, biology is not. Much ink has been spilled in debates over the relative importance of nature and nurture, but in fact the two operate together as a team to such an extent that it is difficult to know where one ends and the other begins. This teamwork is the case in evolution, as we have seen in this chapter, and it is also the case in ontogenesis. For example, the picture we have today of the human brain, thanks to modern neuroscience, is again one of biology working with culture. What was described as the "most startling" result of the "decade of the brain" (the research program that ran from 1990 to 1999) was the discovery that new neurons continue to be created into old age. The human brain has turned out to be much more flexible and plastic than was previously thought, and this implies that a child's development involves a **biocultural co-construction** in which neurophysiological changes are crucial (Baltes et al., 2006). Throughout childhood, and into adolescence and beyond, complex neural networks are growing so as to link different regions of the cortex and connect them to subcortical structures. This process is not a consequence of genetically pre-programmed maturation, it occurs as an aspect of the child's activity in the environment. A flexible brain (in a body, of course) is transformed as it responds to the world around it, and as it transforms that world it is changed again. We will explore this complex interweaving of biology and culture in ontogenesis in more detail throughout this book, starting in Chapter 4 with what we know about the construction of the brain during prenatal development.

What we witness in human development is not an "interaction" between biology and culture in which the former involves genetic transmission and the latter involves social transmission, but changes in a living organism whose capabilities are emergent properties of its constant dealings with the environment, an environment which, importantly, has been greatly shaped by preceding generations. What we call "history" is the way people organize the conditions of the bio-cultural development of future generations. Biology and culture are tightly intertwined, and when we look back over the past 10,000 years, what is obvious is the increasing capacity of humans not simply to adapt to their environments but to transform them.

Nature and nurture, then, are not separate things that then come together. Organism and environment are completely interwoven, and they are both in constant change. The organism is a continually changing embodiment, and the environment too is constantly changing as a result both of human and animal activity and of natural forces. To understand ontogenesis we must consider the whole system of an organism, both physiology and psychology, acting in the complex field of an environment that has both human and non-human constituents. This is a new way of thinking about evolution, and also a new way of thinking about human development.

Viewing things this way involves **relational thinking**: "treating the organism not as a discrete, pre-specified entity but as a particular locus of growth and development within a continuous field of relationships. It is a field that unfolds in the life activities of organisms and that is enfolded in their specific morphologies, powers of movement and capacities of awareness and response" (Ingold, 2004, p. 219). Life itself is the creative potential not of an isolated organism but of a dynamic field of relationships. No animal can survive without a world in which to live: "In that sense, life is not so much in organisms as organisms in life" (Ingold, 2004, p. 219).

SUMMARY

WHAT IS EVOLUTION?

- Humans today are products of a process which began when life appeared on Earth around 4 billion years ago.
- Evolution is the process of change in all forms of life over generations. Central to this process is the inheritance, with variation, of characteristics of one generation by the next generation.
- Biological evolution involves not only genes but also the construction of niches.

EVOLUTION OF HUMAN BEINGS

- Humans and chimpanzees share a common ancestor that lived between 6 and 4 million years ago.
- Many species of hominin have been identified on the basis of their fossils.
- Even the earliest of these hominins, Australopithicus, used simple tools.
- Homo sapiens evolved around 200,000 years ago in Africa.
- Before they could expand beyond Africa, Homo sapiens experienced a dramatic drop in population, to no more than 10,000 individuals. All humans today are descended from these few individuals.
- After leaving Africa, Home sapiens quickly spread around the planet.

TRACING THE ORIGINS OF LANGUAGE

- There is disagreement about how long ago human language evolved.
- Neanderthals seem to have had the necessary prerequisites for oral language.
- Some research traces the origins of phonemic speech to southern Africa around 50,000 to 70,000 years ago.

EVOLUTION OF THE LIFE CYCLE

- The life cycle of hominins has evolved. Compared with primates, Homo sapiens have three additional development stages: childhood, adolescence, and the post-menopausal period for adult women.

(Continued)

(Continued)

- The human newborn has become increasingly premature, and the duration of childhood has increased.
- Childhood emerged by the time of Homo habilis.
- For Homo ergaster, childhood was even longer, with infancy ending around age 3 and the juvenile stage starting at six years and ending around age 14 years.
- The stage of adolescence appeared for the first time with Homo sapiens.

SOCIOCULTURAL EVOLUTION

- Unlike other hominid species, Homo sapiens have constructed complex technologies and complex social organizations.
- A human society is a constructed niche that enables humans to survive in larger groups with greater population concentration.
- Human sociocultural evolution involves the construction of societies with social institutions.
- The scale of human societies has increased: from the family group, to the local group, to the regional polity, to global society.

ONLINE RESOURCES

The Neanderthal survival game:

www.nature.com/news/neanderthals-bone-technique-redrafts-prehistory-1.15739

or www.youtube.com/watch?v=kwX7M9ydfRw#t=85

Human Origins at the Smithsonian's National Museum of Natural History:

http://humanorigins.si.edu/

University of California, Berkeley, Museum of Paleontology:

Geologic time scale www.ucmp.berkeley.edu/help/timeform.php

CHAPTER 4
PRENATAL DEVELOPMENT, BIRTH, AND THE NEWBORN
(CONCEPTION TO 6 WEEKS OF AGE)

LEARNING OBJECTIVES

In this chapter we will explore:

- The processes of conception and prenatal development, with an emphasis on the formation and growth of the human nervous system, including the brain, which is of course an organ of central importance.
- The moment of birth, a transition that is dramatic not only for the neonate but also for the mother and the other people involved.
- The possible evolutionary function of this dependence, and implications for the infant's further development.
- The capabilities of the newborn child.

FRAMING QUESTIONS

- If you (or your partner) were pregnant, what preparations would you make for your new arrival?
- Do your parents and other relatives have strong opinions about whether or not you should have a baby, and with whom?
- What do you think about arranged marriages?
- Where do you think a newborn baby should sleep?
- Should a father feed his newborn baby, or is this a job for the mother?

INTRODUCTION

Birth is the moment from which we begin to count the days, months, and years of a child's life. But birth itself is the culmination of a process which in one respect began nine months earlier, and in another respect— when we consider Homo sapiens as an evolved species—has roots that can be traced back billions of years.

1. PRENATAL DEVELOPMENT OF BODY AND BRAIN

There may be thousands of ways of imagining how kinships bring children into existence, but there is only, it is argued, *one* developmental physiology to explain how babies really grow in the womb. (Latour, 2005, p. 117)

Bruno Latour, in the quotation above, is rejecting the view that has been common in social scientific studies of other cultures: that each has its own way of imagining the world, and specifically the biological facts of "kinship" (the relationships among family members), but behind or beyond these ways is a single reality, grasped by Western science.

In this chapter I will summarize this scientific view of the facts of reproduction, the current scientific explanation of "how babies really grow in the womb." However, it will be worth spending at least a little time exploring other ways in which kinship and reproduction are understood.

The newborn baby is a product of millions of years of evolution and of nine months of **gestation**, the process in which a series of bio-chemical events, influenced by environmental factors, give rise to a new organism. We discussed evolution in Chapter 3; now we can turn to gestation.

Human beings, like all mammals, reproduce sexually. **Sexual reproduction** is a process of propagating new members of a species which are not genetically identical to their forebears: two individuals give rise to one new individual. In **asexual reproduction**, in contrast, a new organism carries genetic information identical to that of its parent. Sexual reproduction is not very efficient, but the big advantage it offers is that the new individual is not an exact copy of either parent. The genes of the two parents are shuffled together, in a process called **recombination**, so that the new individual starts life with a fresh deck. This greatly increases variability in the offspring, and variability in a population generally increases overall survival.

One could begin a description of human reproduction at any one of several points. Typically, descriptions start with fertilization, but it is equally appropriate to begin at the time when male and female **germ cells** (or **gametes**) form, for these will provide the cells that unite at the moment of fertilization. Starting here enables us to better understand the ways that the bodies of mother and father prepare for the possibility of a child.

Both male and female human embryos contain germs cells that are formed in the first weeks of embryogenesis and that, when they become adults, will be able to contribute to fertilization. In the male, each germ call is called a *spermatagonium*, while in the female it is called an *oogonium*. Each kind of germ cell contains 23 pairs of chromosomes, making a total of 46, the same as every adult human cell. The spermatozoa and oocytes they produce, however, each contain half this number.

In the case of a male, the growth and division of the germ cells occur in the testes. After puberty, the testes produce 200 to 300 million new spermatozoa each day, though each takes 74 days to mature. The spermatagonia divide, producing spermatozoa with half the genetic material of the original germ cells, selected at random. A spermatozoon can move, thanks to a tail formed of microtubules that rotate, causing a whipping motion. It is common to think of a spermatozoon as nothing more than a package of DNA, but in fact it also contains mitochondria to power the tail and other cellular components.

In the case of a female, the small germ cells (also called *egg cells*) grow and divide within the ovaries, to produce what are called *primary ooctyes*. These are large and complex cells; after all, they will need to regulate the many cellular and organic processes of ontogenesis. A typical body cell is 10 to 20 μm (micrometer: one millionth of a meter) in diameter; the oocyte is 100 μm, one thousand times larger in volume. A spermatozoon is much smaller than an oocyte: the spermatazoon's head is only 5 μm long and its tail 50 μm long. An oocyte's development takes more than 120 days, and then that development is put on hold: no further division takes place until and unless the oocyte encounters a sperm. At her birth, a girl's ovaries contain around a million oocytes. These slowly die, until at puberty about 400,000 remain, and only about 10 percent of these are released during a woman's life.

Until an oocyte is released from the ovary, and while its division is on hold, the mother's body performs many metabolic functions on its behalf. This arrangement may protect the oocyte's chromosomes from potential damage by the products of metabolism (such as free radicals), or it may be to postpone metabolic processes until they can make use of the DNA of *both* parents. The mother's body provides many cellular constituents, including proteins, RNA and ribosomes to transcribe genetic material, and mitochondria to create energy. The oocyte grows and stores this material away for future use.

Following puberty, hormones restart the oocyte's molecular processes and it finally undergoes **meiosis**, dividing into two cells, each with 23 chromosomes. These two cells do not separate, however: one forms a small container for the excess DNA (called the polar body). The remaining cell, called the *secondary oocyte*, starts to divide again, but this division will not continue unless fertilization occurs.

Each month one oocyte is released from the ovary (a process called *ovulation*), as part of the menstrual cycle. The oocyte begins to move down the fallopian tubes, but dies if not fertilized within a day of being released. Fertilization occurs if a spermatozoon encounters the oocyte and binds with its outer membrane. The membranes of the spermatozoon and the oocyte then fuse and become impermeable to other spermatozoa, and the spermatozoon loses its tail. The oocyte's second division now completes, and the chromosomes contributed by father and mother come together, so that the fertilized oocyte now has once again the full complement of 23 pairs of chromosomes. It is now called a **zygote**. The spermatozoon also contributes certain RNAs, proteins, and subcellular structures. The fused nuclear DNA now replicates, and this begins the zygote's first **mitotic** division.

In section 1.6 I will explore the way that fertilization is at one and the same time a biological and a cultural event. Every society in the world has customs and often laws that regulate who may engage in sexual reproduction and who may not. Fertilization is also the moment at which the fertilized egg begins to move along one of two fundamental bio-cultural trajectories—girl or boy—with profound consequences for subsequent ontogenesis.

At the same time, for this event to occur the two trajectories of female and male—mother and father—must converge. Already it will be clear that parents don't simply "transmit" something to their offspring: traits, or genes, or information. Their involvement amounts to much more than this. In the case of the mother it means first crafting 7 million oocytes, each of them a thousand times larger than a typical cell, filling them with an excess of organelles and cellular materials, then keeping them secure for more than a decade, before releasing them to the possibility that they will meet a passing spermatozoon. This is a fascinating combination of regulated cellular mechanics and happenstance!

In the remainder of this section I will describe the subsequent steps in the prenatal development of the zygote, and the two trajectories of this development along male or female pathways. I will also provide an overview of the structure of the human brain, discuss how the brain functions, and give a short description of prenatal brain development. I shall end the section with some remarks on the ways in which none of this is simply a matter of biology alone. Biology is no more fundamental than culture!

1.1 STEPS IN PRENATAL DEVELOPMENT

Prenatal development, embryogenesis, is a kind of assisted self-assembly, in which the complex structure of the human body is constructed within a women's uterus. The nine months of human gestation are often divided into three *trimesters* of three months each. However, neonatologists distinguish three broad steps in prenatal development. The **germinal period** begins at the moment of fertilization, when sperm and egg fuse, and lasts until the cell becomes attached to the uterine wall, about 10 days later. The **embryonic period** extends from implantation in the uterus until eight weeks after conception. The **fetal period** continues from the ninth gestational week until birth.

Within 24 hours after fertilization the zygote undergoes a series of cell divisions without growing in size, with the result that it becomes made up of many smaller daughter cells called *blastomeres*. These divisions are fueled by the stockpile of proteins and RNA molecules provided to the oocyte by the mother (Ogushi et al., 2008). By the time it contains four or eight cells, the zygote's genes and various biochemical pathways have become activated, so that new proteins are being formed (this is called the "maternal to zygotic transition"). The blastomeres are "totipotent": each one has the capacity to differentiate into any of the different types of cell in the body, something that will be crucial for the development of an organized whole organism.

The zygote moves further down the fallopian tube, and after four days of development it contains about 32 cells, which begin to reorganize into an inner cell mass (the *embryoblast*), which will develop into the embryo proper, and an outer cell mass (the *trophoblast*).

A cavity then forms within the zygote, absorbing fluid, and the embryoblast forms a compact mass on one side. The zygote, now called the *blastocyst*, reaches the uterus between six and nine days after ovulation and releases its surrounding membrane (a process called "hatching"). The blastocyst continues to float in the uterus until it reaches the uterine wall. At the point of contact specialized trophoblast cells burrow into the wall, in a process known as **implantation**. Implantation establishes an intimate biological connection between the mother and the embryo which will continue through the remainder of the pregnancy. This process is often described as an "invasion" of the mother's body by the trophoblast, but a more apt metaphor is that there is a "placental construction" in which the mother's body recognizes and responds to the fetus and is actively involved in the formation of the maternal-placental interface (Kincaid and McKitrick, 2007, p. 186).

The uterus and blastocyst both contribute, then, to the formation of the *placenta*, a little-understood organ that connects the developing fetus to the uterine wall via the *umbilical cord*, and also the *amniotic sac*, a membrane that surrounds the embryo and protects it (Kaiser, 2014). The placenta is an extraordinary organ, the life support system for the fetus. It is formed in an interaction of fetal and maternal tissues in which the mother's body contributes by permitting cells from the embryo to penetrate the blood vessels of the uterus. The human embryo is much more intimately bound into the uterus than is the case in other mammals, and this can be interpreted as the result of a greater investment by the human mother (Pijnenborg et al., 2008). As the blastocyst becomes tightly attached it secretes progesterone, and in response the uterine lining becomes highly vascularized. This ensures a rich supply of nutrients, and it prevents the shedding of the lining that is part of the normal monthly cycle of menstruation.

The placenta performs key physiological tasks that the embryo's growing organs are not yet capable of. It provides oxygen and nutrition, and it disposes of waste, doing the work of the lungs, kidneys, and other organs, all courtesy of the mother. When it follows the baby into the world at birth (it is also called the "afterbirth"), it weighs about a pound (half a kilo). It truly is a special ecological niche, a transformation of the environment of the embryo, in which the mother's body is induced to provide resources that are essential for the unborn child's survival and growth.

It is common to say that the placenta connects the growing baby to the mother. In fact, the placenta is what makes it possible for a baby to form in the first place, and then to differentiate from the mother. The placenta performs the physiological functions necessary to enable the formation of a separate circulatory system, for example, so that at birth newborn and mother can separate physically without grave damage to either.

The placenta has been viewed for many centuries as both important and mysterious. The ancient Egyptians created sculptures showing the Pharaoh's servants carrying his placenta, which they considered his soul. Hebrew texts referred to the placenta as an "external soul" and a "bundle of life." The ancient Greeks knew that the placenta nourishes the fetus, but it was not until the end of the eighteenth century that it was discovered that the circulation of the blood in mother and fetus is separate (Longo & Reynolds, 2010).

About two weeks after implantation, *gastrulation* takes place. This is a time when the embryo starts to form layers of new cells which are no longer identical but start to take on the specialized functions of organs and tissues. Gastrulation begins with the appearance of a longitudinal axis of growth: a faint groove forms along the now oval-shaped embryo, defining what will be the left and right sides, the bilateral symmetry, of the newborn, as well as the vertical (*cranial/caudal*) axis and the front/back (*ventral/dorsal*) axis. Cells begin to migrate along and around this groove, forming three distinct layers: the mesoderm, the endoderm, and the ectoderm. The *mesoderm* will become the muscles, bones, circulatory system, and reproductive system of the fetus. The *endoderm* will grow into the digestive system and the respiratory system. The *ectoderm* is the basis for skin and for the neural system, including the brain. These three are the primary **stem cell** lines that will give rise to all the structures of the human body.

These different populations of cells begin to interact to produce precursors to tissues and organs. This process is guided by complex cascades of molecular signaling, which turn on and off the expression of specific genes. For example, as the neural stem cells migrate they receive signals which induce them to differentiate into precursors of the different regions of the brain. The major organ systems differentiate between week 4 and week 8, in the period known as *organogenesis*. Precursor structures known as the *somites* form the basis for the vertebral column, skeletal muscles, and skin.

During the course of the *fetal* period, from nine weeks to birth at nine months, all the body organs and systems continue to develop. We still know very little about the regulation of these processes, or how cells interact with each other and with the environment of the early embryo. However, it is becoming clear that morphogenesis is not simply a matter of following a genetic blueprint, for the organs are in dynamic interaction. For example, in the chick fetus the olfactory bulb (the sense organ for smell) induces, through chemical signals, growth of the cartilage and bone of the beak (Szabo-Rogers et al., 2009).

1.2 TRAJECTORIES OF SEX AND GENDER

Morphogenesis includes the formation of the primary sexual characteristics—those physical traits that we take as indications of the child's biological sex. These traits include formation of the *gonads* (ovaries or testes) and the *internal and external genitalia* (uterus, vagina, penis, scrotum). Among the 23 pairs of chromosomes carried by every person are two, known as the X and Y chromosomes, that play an important part in determining their sex. In general women have two X chromosomes, while men have one X and one Y. However, we shall see that things are not always so straightforward.

The specific combination of these X and Y chromosomes at the moment of fertilization determines the sex chromosomes that the embryo carries. The oocytes produced by the mother have one X chromosome, while the spermatozoa produced by the father have either one X or one Y. The fertilization of the egg by the sperm leads, generally, to the zygote having either XX or XY. Generally, a fertilized egg with XX sex chromosomes will develop a female body type, while one with XY sex chromosomes will develop a male body type. This might seem common sense, but in many other species, including reptiles, turtles, and fish, the sex of the offspring is determined not by the genes but by some characteristic of the environment, such as temperature. Some fish, for example, change their sex during their lifespan.

In the case of humans, the embryo remains apparently undifferentiated for some time while the internal organs are forming. Then, activation of genes on the sex chromosomes produces hormones that generally drive the body down either the female or the male pathway. If the Y chromosome is present, androgen production will be switched on from about week 8 of embryogenesis, leading to the formation of a male body type. The Y chromosome also carries genetic instructions that cause the gonads of the embryo to grow into testicles, while in the absence of these instructions the gonads become ovaries. The physiological differences between the sexes follow from this starting point. Until puberty, boys and girls differ physically in rather subtle ways, but with the complex biological and psychological changes of puberty their physical differences generally become very evident, with the formation of what are known as secondary sexual characteristics, as we shall see in Chapter 13.

However, this is not the whole story. For one thing, the embryo's development may follow a pathway that is intermediate between male and female. For example, the embryonic tissue that usually becomes either a penis or a clitoris may develop features of both, in what is known as **hermaphroditism**. A combination of male and female primary sexual characteristics may result. It is estimated that around 1.7 percent of children are born **intersexual**. In some cases this happens because the fertilized egg contains an extra X or Y chromosome: XXY or XYY. In other cases it is due to other biological differences. In the past, gender reassignment surgery was performed to "correct" what were viewed as biological errors. This led to great difficulties for such babies as they grew up, and some people who were subjected to such surgery during infancy have vehemently rejected the gender to which they were assigned (Fausto-Sterling, 2000, 2012).

Second, if it were entirely a matter of chance whether an egg is fertilized by a sperm cell that has an X chromosome or one that has a Y then the ratio of male to female children would be 1:1. However, in many species, possibly including humans, there is variation over time in the proportion of sons and daughters that are born, and this seems to be a consequence of the mother's condition (diet, health, and possibly social status) at the time of conception (Rosenfeld & Roberts, 2004). This divergence from an equal probability suggests that some kind of feedback exists between environmental conditions and the process of fertilization, so that sperm containing either an X or a Y are favored.

Third, during the history of Western societies people have changed in their thinking about sexual difference and its relationship to gender. Our understanding of the biological basis of "male" and "female" is not written in stone. For thousands of years it was taken as obvious that women and men have the same genitalia, with the small difference that women have them inside the body, while men have them outside (Laqueur, 1990). This "one-sex model" was widely adopted, a model in which men and women are seen not as two distinct biological types but as individuals distributed along a spectrum of possible body types with a single underlying sex. Until about two hundred years ago it was assumed that the basic form of the human body was male, and that women were a lesser version of that same form. Today's "two-sex model" may seem factual and objective, but it too is a culturally and historically situated way of interpreting physiological data.

Fourth, it might be tempting to draw a straight line that connects a child's sex with their gender identity—whether they consider themselves a boy or a girl—and their sexuality—their **sexual orientation** or their **sexual preference**. However, as we shall see in the following chapters, a person's sexual preference does not follow directly from their gender identity, and this in turn does not follow directly from their biological sex.

In short, the biology of the embryo and fetus does not fit naturally into one of two boxes. However, when the child is born, adults in many societies immediately assign a **gender categorization** on the basis of the observable primary sexual characteristics, as we shall see in section 2 of this chapter. Most legal systems insist that every child is officially recorded as either male or female at birth, though in several countries, including Australia, New Zealand, and Germany, the law has now been changed so that parents can leave the gender blank, in effect reporting that their newborn's gender is "indeterminate."

Whether the route that is followed turns out to be determined or flexible, we see in prenatal development the first distinction among trajectories in children's development. Following the path towards a male or a female body type—or an intersex body—will have significant social and psychological consequences for the rest of a child's life. Sex is an evolved characteristic that humans share not only with other primates but also with all other mammals; however, the societal regulation and organization of sexuality and gender, and in particular the categorization into distinct genders, have profound consequences for human cultures and for children's development.

In gender and sex, culture and biology are interwoven. The distinction between genders does not simply have biological roots and cultural fruits. Cultural categorizations of gender get read back into physiological interpretations of the biology of children, even before birth. It would be wise to follow the advice that "sex and gender are best conceptualized as points in a multidimensional space" (Fausto-Sterling, 1993). For example, even if we restrict ourselves for the moment to consider the biology of sex, it turns out that we need to consider not only the genetic level but also the cellular level, the hormonal level, and the anatomical level.

1.3 THE STRUCTURE OF THE HUMAN BRAIN

The adult human brain is made up of around 170 billion cells. The two main kinds of brain cell are *neurons* and *glial cells*, and there are equal numbers of each (Azevedo et al., 2009). The cells in each organ of the human body are specialized for the tasks they perform, and the **neurons** are specialized cells that are electrically excitable. They send and receive electrical and chemical signals and so are considered information-processing cells, though they seem to function more like an analog computer than a digital computer.

Neurons vary in size and shape, but each has the same basic components. The *cell body* contains the central nucleus, like any other cell. In a neuron, however, the cell body is surrounded by numerous arrays of fibers called **dendrites**, which extend a short distance and receive electrochemical input signals from other neurons.

A neuron also has a long fibrous extension called an **axon,** which transmits electric impulses along its length by means of the flow of charged molecules, called ions, across its surface membrane. An axon can grow long distances to connect with selected targets that are far from the body of the cell. At its end, an axon branches and terminates in multiple **synapses**, where the arrival of an electric impulse stimulates the release of neurotransmitters which flow across the small gap to the dendrite of another neuron. A synapse is a junction between two nerve cells, where the membrane of one neuron comes very close to the membrane of another cell. Axons, then, are the principal means of sending signals from the neuron, while dendrites are the major sites for receiving input from other neurons. Each neuron can connect to more than 1,000 other neurons, so that the adult brain may have more than 60 trillion such connections. Think of the map of airline hubs and flights in the back of an inflight magazine, then imagine that there are 86 billion airports, and at least 1,000 flights arriving and leaving from each one. It is estimated that 1 cubic millimeter of brain tissue contains more data than all the photos uploaded to Facebook.

Neurotransmitters are the chemicals that transmit a signal from one neuron to another. Some neurons synthesize and release *small-molecule neurotransmitters*—such as amines and peptides—and *hormones*—such as cortisol and epinephrine—that permeate entire brain regions and modulate the activity of all the neurons in those regions, a process known as neuromodulation. Other neurons release neurotransmitters that pass directly to another single neuron via a synaptic junction. It is now believed that a dendrite does not simply passively receive electrochemical information, it actively processes this information before passing it to the rest of the neuron (Branco & Häusser, 2010).

On the basis of simple visual appearance, brain tissue is divided into gray matter and white matter. **Gray matter** consists of neurons, their dendrites, glial cells, and blood vessels. Glial cells (from the Greek word for 'glue') form the brain's connective tissue. As we saw above, there are as many glial cells in the brain as there are neurons. Glial cells hold the neurons in position and provide nutrition, and they guide axons towards their targets when they are growing. They may also play a key role in regulating synaptic activity (Shaham, 2005). One important kind of glial cell produces a fatty substance called **myelin** that wraps around the axons of the neurons to insulate them so they transmit electrical impulses faster and more efficiently. **Myelination** increases by a factor of 100 the speed with which an axon transmits impulses: presumably this helps to synchronize and coordinate signals among brain regions. **White matter** consists of this white, fatty myelin wrapped around axons, and the bundles of such axons that form **fiber tracts** connecting different regions of the brain, constituting processing networks that send information back and forth. The brain of an adult contains around 176,000 km of myelinated axons (Paus, 2009).

The brain is only one of the components of the nervous system. The **central nervous system** (CNS) is composed of the brain and spinal column, while the **peripheral nervous system** is a network of nerves that extend from the CNS to the rest of the body. The spinal cord is involved in reflex reactions to sensory stimuli and also consists of ascending and descending nerve pathways which communicate information between the body and the brain.

The brain is made up of three main parts: the *forebrain*, the *midbrain*, and the *hindbrain*. The *forebrain* is composed of the **cerebral cortex** (upon the surface of which four distinct **lobes** are visible) and subcortical structures, including the **basal ganglia** and the **limbic system**: the *thalamus*, the *hypothalamus*, the *amygdala*, and *hippocampus*. The *midbrain* is below the cerebral cortex and above the hindbrain, near the center of the brain. The *hindbrain* consists of the *medulla*, *pons*, and *cerebellum*. Often the midbrain, pons, and medulla are referred to as the **brainstem**.

At the center of the brain are interconnected cavities, **ventricles**, filled with cerebral spinal fluid, which as the name suggests circulates through both the brain and the spinal cord. The walls of these cavities are the site of most neuron production during brain growth.

The hindbrain manages basic organic functions such as breathing, heartbeat, and blood pressure. It is sometimes called the "reptilian brain," because the entire brain of reptiles resembles the human hindbrain. In evolutionary terms it is the oldest part of the brain. The pons relays signals from the forebrain to the cerebellum, and handles functions such as sleep, respiration, swallowing, and facial expression. The medulla also manages autonomic, involuntary functions. The hindbrain contains pathways which move information from the spinal cord up into the brain and down in the opposite direction.

The **cerebellum**, located at the bottom of the brain, regulates and coordinates balance, movement, and posture. It does not initiate movement, but it contributes to the coordination, precision, and timing of various kinds of voluntary movement. It receives input from sensory systems via the spinal cord and from the motor cortices and integrates them to regulate motor activity.

The **limbic system** is a set of brain structures at the interior border of the cortex at the base of the forebrain, which includes the thalamus, hypothalamus, amygdala, and hippocampus. The *thalamus* is a relay station, receiving information from all the sensory organs and sending it on to the cortex. The *hypothalamus* controls the autonomic nervous system and is involved in emotion, thirst, hunger, and circadian rhythms. The *amygdala* is involved in memory and emotion. The *hippocampus* plays a role in consolidating long-term memories, and in spatial orientation. It is one of the first regions to be damaged in Alzheimer's disease. The limbic system is closely connected to the brain's "pleasure center," the *nucleus accumbens* (Olds & Milner, 1954). The limbic system is also linked to the **endocrine system**, a network of glands that secrete various types of hormone, such as adrenaline and dopamine, directly into the blood. The endocrine system is the body's chemical signaling system, operating alongside the electric signaling of the nervous system and regulating metabolism and growth, tissue function, and mood. Organs such as the liver, kidney, gonads, and heart are linked to the endocrine system.

The cerebral **cortex** with its associated underlying structures is the largest part of the human brain. Mammal brains follow a basic pattern that is also found in frogs and birds, but while in humans the basic pattern is the same the overlying cerebral cortex is much larger, as are the associated basal ganglia. The cortex is the outermost layer of the cerebrum: it is a 2–4 mm thick sheath of gray matter. The human cortex has an area of 2400 cm^2 (in comparison, a cat's cortex is only 100 cm^2) and to fit within the skull it has become folded, with ridges (gyri) and folds (sulci). The outermost part, the **neocortex**, is evolutionarily the most recent, a thin sheet made up of six layers each of which contains a mixture of different kinds of neurons (the outermost is called layer 1, the innermost is called layer 6).

The human cortex, despite its relatively large size, contains only around 19 percent of all brain neurons (that is still around 40 billion), around the same percentage as in rodents and other primates (Azevedo et al., 2009). These neurons are organized into a complex network of local circuits and long-range fiber pathways. This network provides the structure to support interactions among various specialized brain regions (Hagmann et al., 2008). The cortex handles voluntary functions, both movements and thoughts.

It is divided structurally into four regions or **lobes**: the occipital lobe, the parietal lobe, the temporal lobe, and the frontal lobe. In the adult brain these have become broadly specialized to handle different functions. For example, the **occipital lobe** receives input from the eyes and handles processing of visual information. The **parietal lobe** is associated with movement, orientation, and recognition of stimuli. The **temporal lobe** handles auditory input and speech production. The **frontal lobe** (also called the frontal cortex) manages reasoning, planning, and problem solving. Increasingly, however, research on brain functioning is discovering that different regions of the brain work together on most tasks, so that linkages among regions are crucial and play a role of increasing importance during ontogenesis, as we shall discuss in the next section. The **prefrontal cortex** is that portion of the cortex at the very front of the brain, behind the forehead and above the eyes. In humans, the prefrontal cortex comprises from a quarter to a third of the cortex.

To the naked eye the human brain is shaped like a walnut, with two hemispherical sides, each with a wrinkled surface. These two cortical **hemispheres** are mostly symmetrical, but there are slight differences in their functioning. It has been held for a long time that the left hemisphere handles verbal tasks while the right hemisphere handles spatial tasks. However, there is now evidence that the left hemisphere becomes specialized in routine activities, while the right hemisphere becomes specialized in detecting and responding (often emotionally) to unexpected stimuli in the environment (MacNeilage et al., 2009). This account of hemispheric specialization explains why verbal tasks become handled by the left hemisphere, because oral language has become routine in adults. It also implies that the difference in language ability between the hemispheres is not innate, but is due to differentiation over time. This implication is confirmed by studies with children, as we shall see in Chapter 6.

The two hemispheres are connected by the fibers of the **corpus callosum**. Studies of "split brain" patients, whose corpus callosum was cut to prevent epileptic seizures, throw an interesting light on the functions of the two hemispheres (Baynes & Gazzaniga, 2000).

The brain consists, then, of very complex neural circuitry, bathed by chemicals that regulate and modulate the circuits' operation. The basic architecture of the human brain, the regions of the brain, is formed by the time a child is born, and only in extreme and atypical environmental conditions does this basic structure change. However, the anatomical details of the structure of the brain, together with its functioning, depend greatly on environmental input, and the links between the various parts of the structure become formed on the basis of experience and learning.

1.4 THE WAY THE BRAIN WORKS

The cortex of the adult brain can be divided anatomically into different regions or lobes, and it can also be divided into areas that perform different functions. The two divisions often do not clearly coincide. We have all seen phrenological heads and "homuncular maps" of the cortex, and every psychology undergraduate learns about the "language areas"—Broca's area and Wernicke's area. We may even hear about cells that respond to a single feature of a sensory input, or to a specific kind of object—the famous (and undiscovered) "grandmother cell," a specific nerve cell that recognizes the unique combination of features that define your grandmother (Gross, 2002). As we saw in Chapter 2, there has been a popular notion that the human brain is a collection of distinct and innate **modules**, each specialized to perform a specific function, and each operating largely independent of the rest (Chomsky, 1984; Pinker, 1998).

Evolutionary psychologists have argued that the brain is "a collection of dedicated minicomputers—a collection of modules" (p. 81). Indeed, the "first principle" of evolutionary psychology is "The brain is a physical system functioning as a computer," and evolutionary psychologists have declared that "Psychology is the branch of biology that studies (1) brains, (2) how brains process information, and (3) how the brain's information-processing programs generate behavior" (Cosmides & Tooby, 1997, p. 75). In this view, brain regions became specialized for solving specific problems in the environment of our ancestors, so that "our modern skulls house stone age minds" (1997, p. 99; cf. Tooby & Cosmides, 1992).

Evidence now suggests, however, that evolution has favored not specialized modules but an overall flexibility that permits environmental organization to influence the brain's function, and even its structure.

Today, researchers are beginning to understand how different brain regions grow and how their structural differentiation is linked to their functional operation. The evidence suggests that long-range neuronal networks play a crucial role in supporting the various psychological functions. We know that interconnected neurons that "fire" together will tend to become more strongly interconnected by synaptic connections, and this is presumably the basis for learning and memory. This property of neurons means that as information flows through the architecture of the brain, that architecture is altered.

It is now generally believed that brain tissue has **equipotentiality**: every area of the cortex has the same potential to carry out every possible function. This suggests that the function that a particular region comes to serve depends greatly on the kind of input it receives. For example, if a region of the cortex receives input from the eyes it will adapt to specialize in visual data. The immature cortex has been called "protocortex": it has the same layered structure throughout and it includes cell types which have the potential to respond to any of the sensory modalities. Usually the connections are wired in a specific way during prenatal development, but experimental interventions and circumstances such as blindness or injury can change the wiring diagram. In such cases, the cortex responds strongly to the sensory input from the environment that it actually receives, even when this is not what it typically receives. The brain grows as it learns, flexibly adapting to environmental input and accommodating to changes in this input. In addition, human brain development continues far longer than in other animals, presumably because of the benefit that comes from responding to this input for more time:

> Because human cortical development is much more prolonged and extensive than what purely physical limits predict, we think this suggests that the human brain's evolution has maximized its capacity to interact and be shaped by environmental structure through progressively building the circuits' underlying thinking. (Quartz & Sejnowski, 1997)

The fact that the information entering an area of the cortex plays an important role in the maintenance and further differentiation of that area, and may change its function and neuroanatomy, shows again that drawing a line between "nature" and "nurture" is not helpful.

What has been described as the "most startling" result of the "decade of the brain" (the 1990s) was the discovery that new neurons continue to be created into old age. The human brain has turned out to be much more flexible and plastic than we thought, and (as I mentioned in Chapter 1) we can think of the adult brain as the result of a "biocultural co-construction" (Baltes et al., 2006). During childhood and adolescence, complex neural networks form, linking different regions of the cortex and connecting them to subcortical structures, not as a consequence of genetically pre-programmed maturation but in response to what is happening in the environment, and what the growing individual is doing in that environment.

1.4.1 IS THE BRAIN A DIGITAL COMPUTER?

There is a heated debate in neuroscience today about the way the brain works. The classic theories of cognition assumed that the brain is an "information processing system" operating like a digital computer (e.g., Fodor, 1985; Newell & Simon, 1972; Pylyshyn, 1984; Tulving, 1983). As I have pointed out, some evolutionary psychologists have made the same claim. The programs of a digital computer operate on formal data structures that represent some state of the world. For example, the cells in a spreadsheet may contain information about prices and sales for some inventory of products. Similarly, the address book on your cell phone contains lists of the phone numbers, email addresses, and street addresses of people you know. In general, a digital computer's representations consist of formal lists that specify the characteristics of real-world objects outside the computer. In a sense, these data form a very simple *model* of some aspect of the real world. The spreadsheet "models" sales and inventory. The address book "models" your friends and acquaintances.

As we saw in Chapter 2, from the cognitive developmental perspective the brain functions in a similar manner, operating on **formal data structures** that represent features of the environment. A child's knowledge of the world is assumed to have this kind of organization. For example, if a young infant can recognize her grandmother, this is assumed to be because she has a mental representation, a model, of that person's features: red dress, slippers, makes blintzes, yells a lot (Gross, 2002).

These representations are assumed to be **amodal**, that is to say, they have been stripped of all information about the *sensory modality* through which the information was received—whether it was by vision, hearing, or touch. These representations are "formal" in the sense that they have form but no concrete content. Representational theories of knowledge and cognition assume a separation between brain and environment, with the body serving simply as the source of data input and a medium of data output, while the brain contains all the data ("knowledge") and handles all the processing ("cognition") (Myachykov et al., 2013).

This view of the brain as a computer has become part of our common-sense folk psychology. It is common to hear people talk of their brain forming and storing images of objects in the world, or memories of past events, or plans for the future. Recently, however, psychologists and neuroscientists have begun to suggest that the brain operates as part of a dynamic system, that it doesn't *represent* the external environment but is in a constant and dynamic *interaction with* that environment (Gallese & Lakoff, 2005; Van Gelder, 1995). Brain function, from this perspective, is an aspect of the whole organism's involvement in constant interaction with the environment which it inhabits. The brain is only a component—though a very important one—within this dynamic system. The rest of the body is equally important. The environment is also a component. At least at its most fundamental level of operation the brain does not need to create data structures that represent the world, because it is in continual contact with the world. When I walk across the room my brain doesn't need to form a representation of the floor, it simply needs to monitor and respond to the support the floor provides to my body, the upward pressure on my feet, the visual flow that my eyes detect, and so on. According to this view, knowledge is grounded in this interaction, as the brain and body work in and with the world to act and to detect flows of information (Lakoff & Johnson, 1999). We shall see in the next chapter that this view of how the brain works is closely related to an influential distinction between two distinct modes of reasoning and decision making, known as "dual systems theory." It is a view that also relates to a distinction I will draw in Chapter 5 between *representation* of the world and *residence* in the world. Neuroscientists and neuropsychologists are describing the neural contribution to residence. We will also see this **dynamic fields approach** applied to specific aspects of infant development in Chapters 5 and 6.

1.4.2 BRAIN AND BODY

The brain is of course literally embodied, and it would be a mistake to think of brain and body as two separate entities that somehow interact. When psychologists have thought of the brain as like a digital computer, they have envisioned it as enclosed in the skull and sending and receiving information to and from the external environment, both the world and the body. But the body is a bio-mechanical system with many organs, of which the brain is only one, and the body is also a material entity constantly involved with its environment, taking in air and food, eliminating waste products. The body is a highly integrated set of multiple subsystems that work together to sustain life, over both long and short time-scales. A major function of the brain is to coordinate these different bodily subsystems, largely through monitoring and managing our interaction with the environment. Our environment, too, involves continuous but structured change. We live in a world in which gravity pulls us, in which day and night follow one another in regular cycles, as do the seasons of the year. In addition, previous generations of humans have organized and arranged this world to suit their social purposes and activities, so that we find ourselves in organized and predictable spaces such as bedroom and dining room, field and barn, church and synagogue, and we find that our time is organized in terms of hours of work, rest, and sleep. Our bodies adapt to these adapted circumstances.

Human psychology is an aspect of this embodied engagement, and in the view of a growing number of psychologists this makes it completely different from the operation of a digital computer. Thought and reasoning are consequences of the brain working in partnership with the rest of the body and with environmental structures, in ways that we shall explore in the chapters that follow. Cognition, emotions, social interactions, and physiology are not independent processes, or even processes in "interaction," they are interrelated aspects of this embodied involvement. Bodily processes such as respiration, digestion, and locomotion are not separate from, or irrelevant to, what the brain does. The brain is not just about cognition, nor just about consciousness—it is at the core of all these aspects of the process of human life (Clark, 1998; Varela et al., 1992).

In the chapters that follow I will be tracing out some of the developmental implications of this emphasis on **embodied cognition**. For example, in Chapter 6 I will be suggesting that emotion in infancy is a psychological function that involves *two* people: infant and adult. In Chapter 7 I will suggest that *material* representations play a key role in human psychological functioning, while mental representations are actually sensory "simulations" that maintain the modalities of the experiences that they are based on. The result is an account of psychological development as a series of transformations in the way a child lives in the world.

This view of cognition and other psychological functions as embodied is related to **connectionist** theories, which view brain function as based on the formation of interconnected neural networks. At a basic level the units in these networks are neurons, and the connections are synapses. At higher levels, the units are regions of neurons and the connections are nerve fibers. These linkages transmit activation within each network, and from one network to another, including feedback (known as **reentry**). Such networks acquire information not as stored representations but as modifications of their connections: in this sense knowledge is distributed across a neural network. I turn now to one important account of brain function along these lines.

1.4.3 THE PERCEPTION–ACTION CYCLE

Anatomically, the brain is complex and confusing, but we can make some relatively straightforward statements about its overall organization, and these contribute to our growing understanding of how the brain works. First, sensory input is received at the back of the brain, while motor output is initiated at the front. Second, towards the base of the brain psychological functions are unconscious, automatic and reflexive, with the most basic role being played by the autonomic nervous system. As we move upwards in the brain towards the cortex and neocortex, processes become more conscious, deliberate, and reflective.

Let us explore these two aspects of brain organization in a little more detail. Most sensory input passes from the sensory organs—the eyes and ears, for example—first to the thalamus. Each sense has its own "nucleus" (a cluster of neurons) within the thalamus—for example, the lateral geniculate nucleus (LGN) receives visual input, the medial geniculate nucleus (MGN) auditory input. The thalamus connects into the lower cortex, from which there are returning connections. Other outward connections pass to regions involved in motor control, such as the basal ganglia and the cerebellum. All the sensory and motor systems make use of both input and output fibers, with information passing both ways.

This neurological linkage between the sensory systems at the back of the brain and the motor systems at the front forms the basis for a **perception–action cycle** (see Figure 4.1). The associative sensory areas at the rear of the brain are connected to the associative motor and planning areas at the front, and between front and back there is a continual flow of neural activity. The cycle is completed through the environment, in the sense that motor actions, oriented towards the attainment of goals, lead to changes in the environment. These changes are detected by the eyes, ears, and other sense organs, and this provides feedback to the posterior perceptual areas. These signals too are then passed again to the frontal areas, where they are evaluated and assist in the planning and executing of new sequences of action.

This perception–action cycle also has a vertical dimension, which corresponds to the second aspect of overall brain organization that I described above. The cycle operates on a series of levels arranged in a hierarchy. The lower levels of the cycle involve automatic and unconscious sensori-motor processes. The higher levels are responsible for complex, more conscious and deliberate, goal-directed actions. At the very top of the hierarchy are the prefrontal cortex and the polymodal sensory association cortex, which handle the highest level psychological functions, those that are most deliberate and thoughtful (Fuster, 2006).

Neuroscientists propose that during ontogenesis successively higher and higher levels of this hierarchy come into play. The neural substrate that supports psychological functioning at one level is supplemented as the neural structures on the next level of the hierarchy begin to function. The lower, earlier levels do not stop working, but they are subordinated to the higher-level neural structures, which pursue more complex and longer-term goals. This arrangement leads to the integration of the more automatic actions into developing systems of deliberate instrumental, linguistic, or logical thinking. At the highest level, the frontal and prefrontal cortices come to play the important role of monitoring and guiding the entire hierarchy, keeping track of goals, and activating relevant memories and knowledge. As we shall see in Chapter 9, the prefrontal cortex is not fully developed until adolescence or even early adulthood, so evidently the formation of this hierarchical perception–action cycle takes a considerable number of years.

As we shall see, this account of the relationship between lower and higher levels in the neurological perception–action cycle, which is based on cutting-edge contemporary neuroscience research, fits very well with Vygotsky's account of the relationship between the lower and higher psychological functions, which I introduced in Chapter 2.

In short, the picture we have today of the human brain, after several decades of intensive research, is of nature working hand in hand with nurture. The brain-and-body is in a process of continuous exchange of information with the environment, and of continuous transformation of the environment. The brain's perception–action cycle is flexibly transformed in response to changes in the world. Human psychological functioning is embodied and embedded (Barsalou, 2008).

One example of this flexibility is the cerebral consequences of learning to read, write, and calculate. (I will return to this in Chapter 8.) Writing and arithmetic are such recent cultural innovations that sufficient time has not passed for human neurology to have evolved and adapted. Instead, what happens is that learning to read and write, or to calculate, modifies the functioning of the human brain. These skills apparently invade evolutionarily established brain regions that have functional capabilities that can be exploited, and they transform these regions, putting them to new uses. Researchers have remarked on a surprising degree of "cerebral invariance of cultural maps" (Dehaene & Cohen, 2007)—the fact that in different societies with different writing systems the same regions of the brain support these activities. However, this invariance is surprising only to those who think that culture produces only differences.

Evidently the human brain has evolved to be continually adaptive to its circumstances, so that new patterns of behavior can be learned at any age. Societal change—technological innovation, institutional transformation, and so on—is both the product of this flexibility and adaptability and a provocative stimulus for further adaption and learning. The "cultural ratchet"—the accumulation of inventions and artifacts that we discussed in Chapter 3—depends on a social group being large enough that innovations can be passed around, but it also depends on the cerebral plasticity of the people who make up the group, so that when they encounter an innovation they can learn how to employ it.

Modern research is confirming the insights of neuropsychologist Alexander Luria, who proposed that the psychological functions are "complex functional systems" which "cannot be localized in narrow zones of the cortex or in isolated cell groups, but must be organized in systems of concertedly working zones, each of which performs its role in the complex functional system, and which may be located in completely different and often far distant areas of the brain" (Luria, 1973, p. 31, emphasis removed).

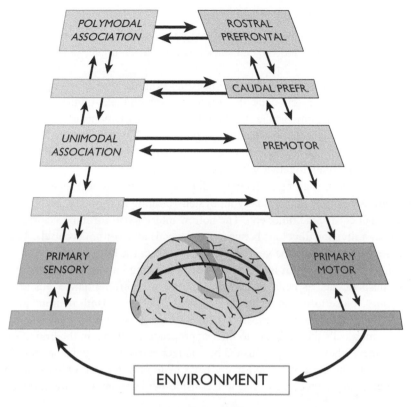

Figure 4.1 The cortical components of the perception–action cycle

Source: Fuster (2006)

Luria also insisted that these complex functional systems include, as important components, "extracortical" artifacts such as writing. When we talk about writing invading the brain, then, this is not to suggest that writing becomes an entirely "intracortical" process. On the contrary, what we are seeing are changes in the brain that allow the person to make use of script as a material artifact, reading and writing text.

In short, there is a growing consensus that the brain is not a computer that forms formal representations, models, or theories about an external world. The brain is a component of a system in which a hierarchical arrangement of perception–action cycles actively seeks sensory input, interprets familiar signs in this input, and responds with patterns of bodily action, many of which involve the use of material artifacts. The human brain is embodied; human beings are embedded in environments that have been constructed and reworked over many generations. As we shall see, uniquely human abilities, such as abstraction, imagination, and collaboration, do not transcend or escape from this embodied and situated basis—they build upon it in ways that depend crucially on cultural innovations such as material symbolic representations.

1.5 PRENATAL BRAIN DEVELOPMENT

We can now return to our account of prenatal development, picking up at the start of the embryonic period, when gastrulation occurs and the cell lines begin to differentiate, in order to explore how the brain is constructed.

We have seen that it is the ectoderm that produces the skin, the perceptual organs, and the nervous system. After gastrulation, those stem cells of the ectoderm which make up the neural cell line form the **neural plate**, around the same time as the first blood vessels and elements of the urogenital system are forming, along with the lining of the viscera and the body wall. The neural plate folds to form a hollow tube, the **neural tube**, which initially resembles a straw. It will change dramatically in size and shape to form the ventricules of the brain together with its major structures.

This tube now differentiates along its length, radius, and circumference. Its length becomes divided into the major subdivisions of the central nervous system, bulging to form the forebrain and midbrain at one end, and the spinal cord at the other end. The hollow interior will form the ventricles.

Around the tube, a division develops between top (dorsal) and bottom (ventral). The dorsal surface will form the sensory cortex, while the ventral surface will form the motor cortex.

Along the radial dimension, from inside to outside, a layering pattern starts to form. At the bulges, further morphogenesis occurs, as cells proliferate, migrate, and differentiate. Cells are born primarily in *proliferative zones*, close to the inner surface of the neural tube. Both neurons and glial cells are produced by cell division in these zones, from progenitor cells known as *neuroblasts* and *glioblasts* respectively. The young cells then migrate to their appropriate locations in the brain. Some cells move by passive displacement (they are simply pushed by younger cells); this is what happens in the thalamus, the dentate gyrus of the hippocampus, and many parts of the brain stem. Other cells move by active migration (described below), which gives rise to the inside-out laminar structure of the cortex and some subcortical areas.

By the end of the embryonic period, nine weeks after conception (when the fetus is still only about 3 cm in length), the basic structures of the brain and central nervous system are in place, and the central nervous system and peripheral nervous system have become distinct. At this time both cortical and subcortical structures grow and elaborate rapidly, and major fiber pathways become established. Between now and around 4.5 months gestation, in the fetal period, the majority of the brain's neurons are produced and move to their positions in the neocortex. Much of the brain development during the fetal period consists of these processes of neuron production, migration, and differentiation.

In short, human brain development is both orderly and patterned over time, and plastic and open to modification. Throughout the prenatal development of the brain and nervous system, biological and environmental processes operate together. The brain's increasingly elaborate structures and functions reflect the contributions of both at every point in its development. At birth, then, the neonatal brain has its key structures established, from the spinal cord to the cortex, and an initial patterning has been established within each of these structures. But the newborn's brain is flexible and resilient, and its patterning is changeable and not fully specified. In order that the complex organization of the adult brain be achieved, various kinds of environmental input will be necessary. The newborn is an "experience expectant" organism (Greenough et al., 1987). If typical adult patterns of neocortical organization are to emerge, input from the sensory systems will be necessary.

By birth, most of the cells of the human brain have been created (though not all, as used to be thought). However, the newborn's brain weighs only 25 percent of what it will weigh as an adult. Much of this added weight will come from the production of glial cells, so that by 2 years of age the brain will be about 80 percent of its adult size. In addition, after birth the neurons will make many new connections. Most of these connections are made early in life, but we now know that new synaptic linkages, as well as myelination of axons, continue until at least 40 years of age and probably older (Naumova et al., 2013). This growth in linkages and networks also adds to the brain's weight.

1.6 CULTURAL ORGANIZATION OF PRENATAL DEVELOPMENT

In the account of prenatal development of body and brain that I have provided, I have emphasized the interaction between the growing fetus and the environment of the womb. However, the role of culture extends way beyond what I have so far described.

First, every society has norms, and often explicit rules and laws, about who may engage in reproduction and who may not. These often include the prohibition of incest, which Freud considered to be the basis of civilization. It has also been suggested that avoiding sexual relations with someone with whom one has grown up is an evolutionary adaptation that is not unique for humans (Westermarck, 2003[1921]). Anthropologist Claude Lévi-Strauss suggested that the prohibition of incest required that each man must obtain a wife from outside his own clan, so that the exchange and circulation of women became the basis for social organization (Lévi-Strauss, 1971[1949]). The incest taboo is not in fact universal, and although many cultures view partnering between family relatives as inappropriate there is much variation. For example, in some cultures relations among types of cousin are accepted or even preferred, while in others they are prohibited. Marriage between brother and sister (although usually half-siblings) seems to have occurred among the ruling classes in ancient cultures in Inca, Egypt, China, and Hawaii, and among commoners in ancient Rome (Bixler, 1982; Strong, 2005). It is important to bear in mind, though, that social groups define these kinship relationships in different ways. Among the Matsigenka in the Amazon, for example, a man cannot marry the daughter of his uncle because she counts as his sister, but he can marry the daughter of his aunt because she does not (Johnson, 2003).

In addition, many societies have, or have had, laws prohibiting marriage between members of different "races," or "castes." In the USA such laws were not fully lifted until 1967.

Cultures define not only who should and should not engage in sexual activity but also *when* this activity can occur. For example, despite their different environments and practices, both the Copper Inuit in the Central Canadian Arctic and the Abelam of Papua New Guinea show seasonal variation in the number of conceptions and births. In the case of the Inuit this is due to social and economic responses to extreme environmental change. For the Abelam, whose agriculture centers around giant yams, it is a consequence of the belief that strong emotions, such as those provoked by the sexual act, should be avoided during the growing season because these would disturb the yams (Condon & Scaglion, 1982; Scaglion & Condon, 1979).

In some cases the cultural norms regulating marriage and reproduction are shocking to people who live in societies where adolescence is taken for granted and parenthood is delayed until the 20s or even later. According to the non-profit organization Too Young to Wed:

Marriage is a celebrated institution signifying a union between two adults and the beginning of their future together. Unfortunately, millions of girls still suffer from a vastly different marriage experience every year. Worldwide, many brides are still children, not even teenagers. So young are some girls that they hold their toys during the wedding ceremony. Usually these girls become mothers in their early teens, while they are still children themselves. The practice, though sheathed in tradition, can result in profound negative consequences for the girls, their families and their entire communities. (http://tooyoungtowed.org/#/explore)

We shall see in Chapter 14, however, that in many societies the teenage years are considered the start of adulthood, not a time of adolescence.

In other words, although the details vary, societal restrictions and norms play an important role in determining whose germ cells can combine to form a child. In considering fertilization and prenatal development, we should not think that biology comes before culture, or operates independent of culture. Conception is at one and the same time a biological event and a cultural event.

The sensitivity of the prenatal brain to environmental influence defines another role that culture plays during prenatal development. In many cultures there are powerful norms about what an expectant mother should eat and drink. In some, foods we would consider healthy during pregnancy are banned, including various kinds of meat, eggs, fish, and milk. A common belief is that eating an animal will lead to taking on its characteristics, and this is often extended to pregnancy. For example, the Sirionó of Bolivia believe that the characteristics of animals whose meat is eaten during pregnancy will be transferred to the unborn child (Holmberg, 1969). Similarly, the Doowaayo in the Cameroons say that a woman who eats warthog during pregnancy will have a child who resembles that animal. The Mbo and Bakweri say that if a pregnant woman eats monkey, her child will never stop jumping. They also prohibit eggs, saying that the baby of a women who eats this food would be bald and have a soft head all its life. Some cultures—the Desana and the Waiwai in the Amazon, for example—prohibit all meat during pregnancy and even once the child is born (Harper, 1975). The Bamum have a taboo against eating sugar cane, saying that it causes a baby to grow excessively (Leypey & Fomine, 2009). On the other hand, eating soil, clay, or sand (known as geophagy) is practiced by pregnant women in many parts of the world, and may provide necessary minerals (Allport, 2010). Such dietary customs and restrictions change the balance of protein and other nutrients that are important to prenatal growth, and this may have an impact on a child's weight and maturity at birth and their subsequent physiological and psychological development (Kaplan, 1972). Women who eat what researchers judge to be a better diet do have healthier babies (Jeans et al., 1955). Providing nutritional supplements for infants who are small in size due to maternal malnutrition can facilitate earlier walking, increased motor development, and more mature social-cognitive and emotional regulatory behaviors (Pollitt et al., 2000). On the other hand, early walking, for example, is not always viewed as healthy (see Chapter 6).

In addition, the decline in breastfeeding in many parts of the world, especially when people move to the city, has negative consequences for children's physiological and psychological development (Gussler & Briesemeister, 1980; Quinn et al., 2001). Amongst other benefits, breastfeeding nourishes the microbes that colonize the intestinal tract of the newborn, with beneficial consequences for health and well-being (Hinde & Lewis, 2015).

There is, in addition, evidence that women who live in stressful environments during pregnancy have more irritable babies, who when they are older have more attention difficulties and behavior problems (Mulder et al., 2002). Research comparing Navajo, Malay, Chinese, and Tamil mothers and infants found that maternal blood pressure during pregnancy was related to newborn irritability (a dimension of neonatal behavior measured by the Brazelton exam, which I shall describe later in this chapter). For example, Navajo women who lived in the city rather than in a Navajo community had higher blood pressure and more irritable infants. Living in fast-paced urban areas dominated by Anglos, often with little family support, led to stress and high blood pressure, which in turn influenced the characteristics of the newborn (Chisholm, 2009[1983]).

Temperamental differences can be found between Caucasian and Navajo infants very early, even at birth. For example, Navajo neonates are generally quieter and less irritable. The Navajo people value cooperation and reserve, quietness and nonintrusiveness, and respect for the dignity of each person. A pregnant woman in a Navajo community lives in a quiet and reserved way, has lower blood pressure during pregnancy, and her newborn is calmer and less irritable. It has been suggested that this is "facultative adaptation *in utero*" (Chisholm, 2009[1983], p. 244), presumably a form of the epigenetic inheritance that we discussed earlier. If this is the case, then the Navajo newborn has already begun to adapt to community norms and practices, with a temperament that will be sustained by the way she is subsequently parented and educated.

Last but not least, unborn children are able to hear the voice of their mother, transmitted through her body, and probably other environmental sounds as well. As we shall see, there is evidence that the unborn child becomes sensitive to the specific language that is spoken by and to the mother (Kisilevsky et al., 2009) and to vocal expressions of emotion (Mastropieri & Turkewitz, 1999), but that is a topic for later in this chapter.

The account of reproduction that I have given in this chapter is very culturally circumscribed. It has as its core an account of kinship: the emergence of the relationship that defines "parent" and "child." Anthropologists have paid a great deal of attention to kinship, and have often divided the social relationships in a society into two kinds: those of "descent" and those of "marriage." However, these are Western notions—the Western so-called "genealogical model of kinship"—that view family relationships as a combination of inherited biological attributes and derived social and cultural relationships. In this model, a "child" is defined primarily by a biological link to her "parents" and vice versa. Biology is viewed as fundamental, and family relationships are viewed as built from biological constituents. Kinship is based on a combination of biological reproduction (father, mother, child, sister, uncle …) and marriage law (husband, wife, brother-in-law, mother-in-law …). People related by marriage are distinguished from those related by biology, and biologically linked persons (parents and children, siblings) are prohibited from entering into social bonds of marriage or procreation with one another. The social bonds of marriage must be forged outside the biological bonds of the family.

However, in some cultures biological relations of birth are discounted as unimportant for kinship, and sometimes totally ignored. For example, the Kamea of New Guinea acknowledge no connection between children and those who conceived them (Bamford and Leach, 2009).

Similarly, in the Trobriand islands, studied by Bronislaw Malinowski in the 1920s, it is the spirit of a dead ancestor which impregnates a woman, while she is bathing in the sea. The Trobrianders consider intercourse as merely opening a path for the spirit, called "baloma," to enter the womb.

In such cultures, kinship is understood not a result of biology so much as a relationship among people who, as Marshall Sahlins puts it, "are members of one another, who participate intrinsically in each other's existence." Social relationships and participation can trump biology. As Sahlins says, "To the extent [people] lead common lives, they partake of each other's sufferings and joys, sharing one another's experiences even as they take responsibility for and feel the effects of each other's acts" (Sahlins, 2011, p. 14). The specific kind of kinship upon which the scientific account of fertilization and prenatal development rests is only one among many. That is not to say that we may one day find that spirits play a role, but it is to suggest that the priority we tend to place on biology leads to a one-sided view of the process of conception and prenatal development.

1.7 EPIGENETIC PROGRAMMING

It is becoming increasingly clear that the prenatal environment of the womb can prepare or "program" the developing child for their future life. This "epigenetic programming" occurs when there are inherited changes not in the genes themselves but in the ways genes are expressed to build proteins, changes which occur in utero and are then passed down to subsequent generations (Hochberg et al., 2010). Detailed records in Sweden enabled researchers to compare the health of several generations and to link this to environmental events (Pembrey et al., 2005). They found that men who were exposed as children to a famine in the nineteenth century had grandsons who were less likely to die of heart disease, but more likely to die of diabetes when food was plentiful. On the other hand, those men who were grandsons of men who lived when food was plentiful had increased rates for diabetes.

The opposite effect was found for women: women who were exposed to famine before birth (while their eggs were being formed) had granddaughters who died younger. These findings provide evidence that the environment can influence at least some of a person's biological characteristics, and that these altered characteristics can then be inherited by their children, or even their grandchildren.

These biological changes involve modifications not of the sequence of amino acids in the genes, but of various molecules on an "epigenetic level," that is to say "above" the genes. Methyls attach to the strands of DNA and influence their transcription to construct proteins. Transcription factors are proteins that bind to DNA and control the rate of its transcription. Such molecules provide a cell with a kind of memory, which is passed on to the next generation when the cell reproduces (Meaney & Szyf, 2005).

Conditions in the womb which reflect the mother's well-being shape the epigenetics of the embryo. It has been suggested that maternal nutrition, body composition, and levels of stress provide cues to adapt the developing child to later environmental conditions, in what is called the "Predictive Adaptive Response" (Bateson et al., 2014). We shall see further examples of this plasticity and adaptation to a predicted future environment in later chapters, especially the "psychosocial acceleration theory" of Jay Belsky and James Chisholm, who propose that attachment experiences in early childhood influence the timing of puberty and the subsequent "reproductive strategy" of the adolescent. Such phenomena are further illustrations of the intricate linkage of the processes of evolution and ontogenesis.

2. BIRTH: THE FIRST DEVELOPMENTAL TRANSITION

Birth is a dramatic transition in which one biological entity becomes physically separated into two parts, which then have to become reintegrated in a new way. In being born, the fetus separates physically from the woman who has carried her for nine months. This separation is remarkable, even traumatic, and it has profound consequences for both mother and baby. Inside the womb, the fetus was ingesting amniotic fluid and receiving nutrients and oxygen through the umbilical cord. After birth she is breathing air and absorbing oxygen through her lungs, and she must receive milk from her mother's breast, or from a bottle. However, although the newborn is no longer physically inside her mother her biological dependence on other people has by no means ended. The newborn baby is an "exoparasite," feeding on liquid food which is produced by the mother's body, in a process that is neither purely biological nor purely natural, but has been shaped by the cultural history of her group: human breast milk has evolved, apparently influenced by changes in human lifestyle (Hinde & Lewis, 2015). The neonate is no longer bound to her intrauterine environment by the direct physical connection of the umbilical cord; nonetheless, after birth her essential biological needs—nutrition, warmth and protection—must still be provided by other human beings. Newborn and caregivers, especially the mother, must explore and discover new ways to deliver these needs, and there is a risk that they will be unable to achieve this new coordination. Certainly, the forms of this coordination vary widely from one culture to another.

There is in fact great variation across cultures in the birthing process, though at the same time we can see universal aspects to this transition. Some cultures treat birthing as a natural event that requires no special preparation. For example, among the !Kung people a woman is supposed to give birth entirely alone. (Exceptions are made for the first birth, however.) Fear is thought to make childbirth more difficult, so the woman should remain calm. When she feels labor pains she should go out into the bush without telling anyone, deliver the baby, and cut the cord. Only when other members of the community hear the newborn's cries do they go to assist mother and baby (Konner & Shostak, 1987). A !Kung woman living in the Kalahari desert in the early twentieth century recorded that she accompanied her mother as she walked out of the village, sat with her back against a tree, and give birth to a baby boy. The woman recalled thinking, "Is that the way it's done? You just sit like that and that's where the baby comes out? Am I also like that?" (Shostak, 1981). Conversely, in other cultures childbirth is treated as an illness. Even when that is not the case, it is still generally viewed as a condition that requires medical intervention. The people who assist a women with childbirth vary with time and place: sometimes they are family members, sometimes experts. For example, among the Zinacantecos, a Mayan culture in southeastern Mexico, it is customary towards the end of the second stage of labor for the woman to kneel with the support of a midwife or her own mother, while her husband pulls on a cinch around her waist to place downward pressure on her uterus.

2.1 THE HISTORY OF CHILDBIRTH

There have also been historical changes in the practices of childbirth, as well as beliefs and attitudes. Today in the West, childbirth is treated as a medical event, usually located in a hospital, attended by doctors and nurses, described using medical terminology (*full term*, *premature*), and so as a matter of obstetrics or at least midwifery rather than as an event within the family. This medicalization began in the eighteenth century. Previously, childbirth had "belonged to women" rather than to doctors, and women managed childbirth in a coherent and systematic way (Wilson, 1990, p. 69). It was the husband's duty to call the midwife and other women to assist at the birth, perhaps half a dozen, often including the pregnant woman's mother, but he was excluded from the delivery. Midwives' techniques varied greatly, as did the woman's position—lying on her back or her side, sitting in a friend's lap, or kneeling on a cushion. The women who assisted were known as "gossips," a corruption of "god-sib" or "god-sibling," and the term came to mean what women did together.

The birth was an occasion for celebration, and once the newborn was delivered the cord was cut and the baby was swaddled and then shown to the mother. A lying-in ritual then began, to last perhaps a month. The mother was given this time to rest, often confined to bed for the first two weeks in a darkened room, then allowed to sit, then to stand and walk but confined to the house. In the first of these stages only women were allowed to visit the new mother, then later her male relatives. A nurse was hired to carry out household chores, though sometimes the husband did some of these. During the second stage of lying-in a "women's feast" often took place. Sexual intercourse between husband and wife was prohibited until the end of lying-in, during which time the couple slept separately. The end of lying-in was marked by "churching," a ritual of thanksgiving and purification which the new mother attended, veiled, with her female companions.

Organized in such a way, birth was a rite of passage, a ritual that defined a process of nature as being also a cultural event. This kind of childbirth had the stages that characterize rites of passage: stages of separation, transition, and reincorporation. It has been interpreted as reflecting a shared perception of female inferiority and impurity, but it has also been argued that the ritual persisted because it was in women's interests, and should be seen as a form of resistance to male patriarchy (Davis, 2008).

When we consider historical changes in the organization of childbirth we can see that, like prenatal development, although it might seem a solely biological process it is culturally organized and filled with cultural significance. Even when birth is medicalized, culture is still at work in the form of the application of technology to the process of childbirth.

In fact, technological assistance and intervention in childbirth is very old. The ancient Romans developed the technique of performing a Caesarean section to save a baby when a mother died during delivery, although the idea that Julius Caesar's name came from an ancestor born in this way is probably not true. The second emperor of India, Bindusara, born in the third century BC, is said to have been the first child born by this surgery, after his mother consumed poison and died in childbirth.

2.2. BECOMING A CAREGIVER

The family generally, and parenting specifically, are today in a greater state of flux, question, and redefinition than perhaps ever before. We are witnessing the emergence of striking permutations on the theme of parenting: blended families, lesbian and gay parents, teen versus fifties first-time moms and dads. One cannot but be awed on the biological front by technology that now renders postmenopausal women capable of childbearing and with the possibility of designing babies. Similarly, on the sociological front, single parenthood is a modern-day fact of life, adult–child dependency is on the rise, and parents are ever less certain of their roles, even in the face of rising environmental and institutional demands that they take increasing responsibility for their offspring (Bornstein, 2002, p. ix).

Conception and prenatal development not only lead to the creation of a child, they also lead to the creation of parents. Of course, "Put succinctly, parents create people" (Bornstein, 2002, p. ix). But the act of conception creates both a baby-to-be and parents-to-be.

What we call **parenting** is the way those directly responsible for the infant attend to her needs. The term comes from a Latin word meaning "bringing forth." Developmental researchers believe that parenting—what parents do—is of central importance to the kind of person a child grows up to become, and to how that growing up is brought forth.

In many respects, parenting actually begins before conception. The Misak, in Colombia, make offerings to the spirits when they ask them whether the time is propitious for starting a child. If the answer is in the affirmative, conception is timed so that the baby is born at the most desirable time of year, because the season of birth will determine that child's temperament. Parents in the USA are more likely to consult their bank accounts than the spirits to see if they can afford to have a baby, but in both cases the cultural practices of arranging a child's life begin before the biological processes of conception.

Parents influence their progeny in many ways: by protecting them, caring for them, teaching them, and arranging for their education. Children, of course, also influence their parents. We will explore many of these mutual influences in the following chapters. As the quotation that opens this section points out, parents come in many shapes and sizes. Is there anything general we can say about caring for the newborn baby?

Some anthropologists have suggested that there are universal goals for childrearing, but even if this were the case it does not mean that parenting is the same the world over. Parents differ in their age, temperament, preparation, and motivation. In addition, the people who care for a child may or may not be the biological parents. They may have adopted the child, or be a step-parent, or a hired nurse or nanny, or a professional who works in a childcare institution. The birth mother may not be the biological mother, if artificial insemination took place. Even when the caregiver is the biological parent she (or he) may be part of a couple, a single parent (divorced, widowed, or never married), and may have the assistance of parents, relatives, friends, and various kinds of childcare experts and professionals. When two caregivers are a couple they may or may not be working, may or may not be the same gender, and they may be of the same age or very different ages. There may be marital stress and even abuse. Caregivers may care for a single child or for a large family; the children may be of the same or mixed genders; there may also be stepchildren; there may be children with special needs. In short, parents come in many different shapes and sizes.

I will postpone until Chapter 5 a discussion of recent research that has identified distinct styles of parenting during infancy—styles which are associated with overall goals for development that are specific to different categories of culture.

3. INFANT DEPENDENCE: WHAT THE NEWBORN CANNOT DO

Birth leaves the newborn naked and exposed, gulping her first breaths of air, lacking a direct source of nutrients. The newborn has a variety of skills, as we will see, but at the same time, paradoxically, a newborn human can do far fewer things for herself than the newborn of other species. A puppy will be moving around and searching for food within a few hours. A newborn lizard, hatched from an egg, will probably never meet its parents and is completely independent from birth. The human neonate, in contrast, depends on other people for almost all her needs.

This dependence of the human infant is surely no accident. There is every reason to think that it has evolved, and presumably has survival value. We saw in Chapter 3 that infancy has become longer during hominin evolution. There is a close link between the relative immaturity of the human newborn, who will require years of nurturing before approaching anything close to self-sufficiency, and the fact that human beings inhabit a culturally mediated environment. The newborn's complete biological helplessness means that all her activity must follow a pathway through other people. All the newborn's behavior—feeding, changing, even turning over—is woven into this sociability, for it is possible only through other people's cooperation. The consequence is that the newborn's earliest contact with the world is completely socially mediated. For many months all movement through space, for example, takes places in the arms of adults, or being pushed in a stroller. The transition of birth places the human newborn in a situation where she is still effectively merged and intertwined with others, and within which her sense of herself has yet to be differentiated from other people. She has no choice except to participate in the ways of her culture, and in doing so she will learn them well.

One reason for the human infant's relative helplessness is that her brain will grow to a size that could not be achieved within the uterus. The adult human has a brain, and so a head, that is large relative to her body size. The newborn baby's head is already large compared with other mammals, though it will grow a lot. The female pelvic opening is simply not big enough to allow a baby with a larger head to pass through. This places limits on the brain construction that can take place before birth, and this presumably results in fewer abilities that are operating when the neonate enters the world.

The story doesn't end there, however. Why is the human brain so large? The newborn's large brain reflects the fact that she must learn a great deal in her lifetime. Her helplessness reflects her plasticity and adaptability. Birthing that is relatively early in terms of brain growth has the consequence that further growth and neurological development take place when the baby is outside the womb, in a complex, stimulating environment. This permits the interaction between biologically programmed brain development and environmental stimulation which we considered earlier in this chapter, an opportunity which would be much reduced if the child stayed longer in her mother's womb or if her brain were more fully developed at birth.

However, this evolved strategy of dependency is certainly risky. If parents or other people do not meet the newborn's needs, the result is death. The human infant's survival is literally completely in the hands of other people. The benefits that follow from the newborn's dependency must be considerable indeed to make this risk worth taking.

To survive, the newborn must act in a qualitatively different way than was the case before birth. Now, her actions have significant effects on the world around her. She makes urgent vocal demands on the people caring for her. The way these people interpret the behavior of their new charge depends greatly on their own experiences, and their hopes and expectations for her. This is shown in reactions to learning the baby's gender (this research took place before tests provided this information during pregnancy).

We saw earlier in this chapter that from the moment of conception the child has been committed to one of the two fundamental developmental trajectories: being a boy or a girl. Parents' comments such as this one, made by a father—"It can't play rugby. Everyone said it was going to be a boy" (Macfarlane, 1977, p. 109)—reflect cultural interpretations of these biological characteristics, which are immediately projected into the child's future. The developmental trajectory of boy or girl is transformed from an aspect of biology into a way of living. This projection has been called **prolepsis**, namely representing something as existing before it actually does (Cole, 1995). Of course such interpretations can change— today women do indeed play rugby—and so the parents' projections may not become reality. But they define a trajectory for the child that is based on her parents' past, is expressed in the present moment, and anticipates a likely future. As caregivers act on the basis of their own projections about the possibilities for their child, they establish the material conditions for her development. For example, researchers have found that adults treat the same infant quite differently when dressed in pink or blue clothing! They will bounce a baby wearing blue and comment on his manliness, while they treat *the same baby* wearing pink in a gentle way and talk about her beauty and sweetness! Gender stereotyping begins even before birth (Rubin et al., 1974).

Another example is the traditional Mayan interpretation of signs in or on a newborn child. A future shaman will be born with worms or flies clutched in the fist, a future midwife is born with the amniotic membrane draped over the head, while a baby that will threaten future siblings is born with a double whorl on the top of the head (Paul & Paul, 1975). The Maya also believe that the date of the child's birth in their calendar defines her destiny, though what is made of this is up to her (Rogoff, 2011).

Parents weave their newborns not only into the future of their family and community, but also into its past:

> On the Alaskan North Slope, the Iñupiat will name children and sometimes adults after dead persons, thus making them members of their namesakes' families. Over a lifetime … an Iñupiat may acquire four or five such names and families, although those who bestow the names were not necessarily related before, and in any case they are never the birth parents. Begetters, begone: natal bonds have virtually no determining force in Iñupiat kinship. Kinship statuses are not set by the begetters of persons but by their namers. Indeed, it is the child who chooses the characteristics of birth, including where he or she will be born and of what sex. (Sahlins, 2011, p. 3)

The way in which adult humans anticipate the trajectory of their infant's development and begin to put it into practice is very different from care of infants in our primate cousins. Only humans can populate the environment of their newborns with plans, projects, and expectations for the future that they immediately begin to implement in the present, in their choice of clothing and toys, by putting the child's name on school waiting lists, or by starting a college fund in their bank account. The parents' capacities to anticipate a future and plan in order to bring it about—in short, their *higher psychological functions*—are already having an impact on their newborn's development.

In preparing for their infant's future in these ways, parents are also contributing to the continuity of their culture—and also, at times, to its discontinuities. When a parent says that they want their child to have opportunities they never had, this expresses an intention that things will be different for the next generation. In acts such as these, parents create the future that their children will live in and will in turn hand down to subsequent generations.

As we shall see, however, children do not passively accept the plans their parents have for them, or the values their parents might wish them to share. The dynamic character of the relationship between caregiver and child, in which there will be times when the child needs to assert her independence and difference as part of the process of growing up, assures that there is not a smooth transition from one generation to the next, or a simple socialization of the newcomer by oldtimers. An adolescent girl, for example, might by horrified by her parents' sense of what is an appropriate occupation for a woman!

In addition, cultural innovations—new forms of communication, new media for representation, new energy technologies—propagate through society and have unanticipated impacts that are different for child and adults and can make parents' plans obsolete. Because the infant's brain is still growing, a new technology can become part of her psychological functioning much more smoothly and deeply than is the case for an adult. Young children today are using smartphones at an age when they are still pruning synaptic connections. Technology and brain interact, and the consequence is that no parent can fully anticipate the adult their child will become. (More on this later.)

As we shall see in the next chapter, an extreme form of this projection occurs when parents treat their newborns and infants as though they are not true persons. There are cultures in which the infant is not viewed as a person at all until she is walking and talking (Lancy, 2013). Often this seems to be a consequence of the fact that parents cannot with any certainty anticipate a future for their newborn due to the high rate of neonatal and infant morality.

It is an undeniable fact that the human newborn is fragile and vulnerable. In general, infancy is a very risky stage of the life cycle. Worldwide, around 4 million infants die during the first month of life, and neonatal deaths account for 36 percent of deaths among children less than 5 years of age (Black et al., 2003). Infant mortality (defined as the ratio of infant deaths to live births) varies considerably around the world, but today it is much lower than in even the recent past. The current average worldwide rate is around 45 deaths for 1000 births; in 1950 it was 152. It has been estimated that through much of human history the rate was around 200 deaths per thousand. Infant mortality began to decline in Western Europe in the late nineteenth century; in some countries (such as Singapore, Iceland, and Japan) it is now as low as 2.3. In the USA it is estimated that the infant mortality rate in the 1850s was 216.8 per 1000 for whites and 340.0 for African Americans; today it is around 7 per 1000. The improvement is largely due to the control of infectious diseases through basic health care. Breast-feeding also makes a significant difference: the risk of neonatal death is higher when infants are bottle fed, or when they are given milk-based fluids or solids in addition to breast milk (Edmond et al., 2006).

Around the world today, neonatal mortality rates are highest where resources are most scarce. Levels in economically developed countries are around 3 to 4 per 1000, in middle-income countries they are around 20 per 1000, and in poor areas such as sub-Saharan Africa they are around 30 per 1000. Parents in societies with high infant mortality rates, such as the Gusii, of Nyansongo in Kenya, may not consciously feel anxious about the immediate well-being of their infants, but their practices of childcare are designed to monitor the infant's physical status and respond quickly to signs of distress (LeVine & LeVine, 1988). The Kogi, in Colombia, consider their infants to enter the "human" phase only once they begin crawling (see the Case Study below). It is likely that this attitude is partly a response to the high level of infant mortality in the community due to the difficult circumstances in which these indigenous people have been forced to live, high in the Sierra Madre mountain range. Lower atmospheric pressure and oxygen level at higher altitudes increase infant mortality; for this reason pregnant women of cultures in the high Andes and Tibetan mountains often descend to lower altitudes to give birth.

Technology has played a role in the reduction in the rate of infant morality, though basic sanitation and health care have probably been the major factor. In a society with low infant mortality, such as Sweden, parents may still express anxiety about the physical well-being of their unborn or newborn infant, but nonetheless their childcare practices assume that the infant has a good chance of physical survival and so they can focus their energies on developing emotional connections with their child (Welles-Nystrom, 2006).

4. NEONATAL CAPABILITIES: WHAT THE NEWBORN CAN DO

The result of the physical separation of fetus from mother in childbirth is that the newborn enters an extrauterine environment that is filled with sights, sounds, tastes, and smells. As a fetus she had been somewhat sedated, by placental chemicals and the low oxygen tension in her blood. This resting state usually changes at delivery: the neonate now becomes fully awake for the first time, though she often sleeps shortly afterwards (Lagercrantz & Changeux, 2010). Research suggests that the newborn child perceives not distinct sensations but each situation as a whole. The infant's first responses are not to isolated stimuli but to an "intricate, complex, emotionally colored whole" such as the caregiver's face. At this stage we have to assume that no distinction is known or experienced between self and things, nor between social and physical objects, nor between drive, affect, and sensation (Lagercrantz & Changeux, 2009).

4.1 NEONATAL ASSESSMENT

Children born in hospital are often evaluated on the basis of observations of five vital signs, and given what is known as an Apgar score (Apgar, 1966). This evaluation is valuable to clinicians, but laboratory studies can tell us much more about what neonates can and cannot do. An examination known as the Brazelton Neonatal Behavioral Assessment (BNBA), designed by pediatrician Berry Brazelton, provides more detailed information about neonatal capabilities (Als et al. 1977; Brazelton & Nugent, 1995). The BNBA was designed to document the contributions that the neonate makes to the parent–child system, and the active contributions that the neonate makes to her own development. It was based on the assumption that the newborn is not a passive recipient of stimuli from the environment, but actively seeks and responds to sensory input. A neonate can respond to stimuli by changing her **behavioral state**, from sleep to alertness or vice versa. Some newborns have a lower threshold for stimuli and are hypersensitive, others respond in a disorganized way. These individual differences present challenges to caregivers, and can lead to the risk of neglect or abuse. The BNBA was designed to observe the neonate's behavior as she defends herself against intrusive and negative stimuli, and as she controls her motor and autonomic responses so as to attend to social and nonsocial stimuli. It is used in areas such as obstetrical medication, the prediction of neurological deficits, with low birth weight infants, and the exploration of cross-cultural differences.

4.2 THE NEWBORN'S SENSORY ABILITIES

Researchers have explored the sensory abilities of young infants in the laboratory by presenting various kinds of stimuli and observing the response. One common technique is to present a stimulus repeatedly until the infant stops paying attention—a phenomenon called **habituation**. Then the stimulus is changed in some small way; if the infant shows renewed interest (**dishabituation**) we can infer that she perceived the change. Sometimes the infant's attention is simply observed, but brain waves can also be measured.

Newborns have all their sensory systems functioning, though at different levels of development. Hearing is one of these sensory systems. In the uterus, outside sounds are reduced in intensity by about half but the mother's voice is conducted to the fetus through her body. Newborn infants show a preference for the sounds of the language they have been hearing in utero. In addition, a newborn can distinguish between her mother's voice and the voice of a stranger. Responses to auditory stimuli include turning the eyes and head in the direction of the sound in 30 percent of cases. For example, in a study using the habituation technique it was found that 2-month-old infants are sensitive to the small differences in the timing of speech sounds (Eimas, 1985). In Chapter 5 I will describe the basic sound units of language, the phonemes. Adults who have learned a specific language lose the ability to perceive differences in speech sounds that are not relevant to that language's phonemes. For example, differences in the timing of "voicing," the vibration of the vocal cords, are important in distinguishing phonemes. Studies in various countries suggest that infants everywhere are born with the same sensitivity to several categories of voicing, whether or not these distinctions are used in their community's language. This does not mean that newborns can perceive the phonemes of that language—in fact we know from other studies that it is not until around 6 or 8 months of age that infants develop the kind of categorical perception of phonemes that adults have. What it means is that newborns have perceptual abilities that are tuned to the acoustic differences that define phonemes in the various languages of the world, which prepares them very well to learn the phonemes of the specific language they hear around them. Once again, we see that evolution has prepared the human infant to be able to learn the specific practices of her cultural group.

Another important sensory system is vision. As we learned earlier in this chapter there are four pathways from the eyes into the brain. Visual **orienting**—turning the eyes and head in the direction of a stimulus—seems to develop as these brain regions mature and as experience influences how they function. I have described how at birth inputs from the two eyes project onto common neurons in layer 4 of the visual cortex. During the next six months, axons originating from the eyes are pruned so that stereo-acuity improves. During this first six months there is also a slow shift from subcortical processing of visual input to cortical processing, though even in the newborn cortical activity is not completely absent. Information from the eye already enters the deeper levels of the primary visual cortex, although the input is weak and disorganized.

Many studies have shown that newborns can discriminate visual patterns with relatively fine detail, and that they show a preference for high contrast and for movement. Newborns see most clearly when the object of their gaze is about a foot away, and they have difficulty focusing on objects further away. The newborn is capable of tracking, and preferential orienting. Even in the first hour after birth she will **track** a moving object: locking onto it with her eyes and following it as it moves, with her eyes, and then with eyes and head when she is a few days older. Infants' vision also seems intrinsically tuned towards people (Haith & Campos, 1977). The features of the human face seem to be particularly salient.

A classic study showed that newborns just two days old can perceive different patterns, and that they prefer a schematic face over a pattern of concentric circles. Much research since then has explored infants' responses to faces. Some researchers have suggested that the newborn has an innate ability to process the visual appearance of the human face, while others argue that this ability must be learned. Either way, a very young infant is able to recognize faces, orient towards them, and identify those that are familiar. It seems most likely that the newborn is born prepared to respond to the world in a way that ensures that faces are salient, especially when there is social feedback—an adult giving praise for her attention. As a result, neural tissue rapidly becomes dedicated to this kind of stimulus. The newborn also seems predisposed to track a face more than other objects. Neonates can distinguish among happy, sad, and surprised expressions posed by a live model, and their facial movements in the brow, eyes, and mouth regions show evidence for imitation of the expressions they see (Field & Walden, 1982).

Mutual gaze—eye contact between the infant and another person—occurs early in life. Newborns fixate longer on a face that is looking directly at them than on a face looking to one side. Infants as young as 1.5 months react when an adult they are interacting with holds their face still with a neutral expression while still maintaining eye contact: this is called the **still-face procedure** (Bertin & Strian, 2006). Joint attention—looking in the direction in which another person is looking—begins around three or four months, though at first only when the other person has made eye contact with the infant. It seems likely that eye contact facilitates subsequent processing of information about a face. In adults, the superior temporal sulcus (STS) responds in a highly selective manner to the perception of eye movements in another person. In infants, this same area also responds to non-eye motion, suggesting that at first it is not specialized and becomes so only with experience. In the next chapter I will explore these face-to-face interactions in more detail.

The visual system comes under increasing voluntary control. During the first week of life increasing time is spent awake, and responses to both visual and auditory stimuli improve, as assessed in the Brazelton exam. The 1-month-old may show "sticky fixation," unable to shift her attention away from one focal stimulus; this seems to be because her cortex is now involved in such a way as to inhibit automatic eye movements. She can now stop her eyes from moving reflexively, but she cannot yet direct them deliberately.

Psychologists now agree that perception is an active process. The eyes and ears don't passively receive information, they actively seek it out:

> our eyes actually "feel" the environment in a manner quite analogous to the ways that one's hands "feel for" a handkerchief in our pocket or reach into a shopping cart and pick up objects without looking, so that we have to "come to" identify the object. One does not pick up a bottle in the same way that one picks up a banana; any such action is a form of orientation, a process involving complex back-and-forth interactions of the person and the object. (Cole & Wertsch, 2011, p. 9)

The newborn is beginning to learn how to explore the world with her senses, a skill that will continue to develop over many years. By 6 months—though we are stepping here into the territory of the next chapter—there is evidence that not only the cortex but also specifically the prefrontal cortex is starting to control visual attention, though only at 12 months do we find brain waves that show cortical planning of saccades—the rapid movements of the eyes between fixation points.

Turning finally to the senses of taste and smell, evidence shows that both these senses are functioning at birth, and the newborn's responses seem to be influenced by the tastes and smells she has been exposed to prenatally. For example, she shows a preference for the smell of her mother's body and clothes, of her milk, and of amniotic fluid. In newborns, different brain responses are found to smells that adults judge to be pleasant and unpleasant, and newborns show a preference for sweet liquids and aromas over sour or bitter ones, responding with facial expressions that seem to display liking or disgust.

4.3 COORDINATION BETWEEN NEWBORN AND CAREGIVER

Here we are moving into aspects of the newborn's behavior that are rapidly influenced by her interactions with caregivers. The newborn's abilities include the important capacity to display her behavioral states to other people. Crying—a combination of sounds, movements, and facial grimaces—is one way an infant signals both her vigor and her need to receive care (Soltis, 2004). Crying is contagious among newborns—if one cries, others will tend to follow, though the newborn can distinguish her own cry from those of other babies. Studies using fMRI have begun to explore the neurological basis of caregivers' responses to cries and other signals. It appears that such displays by the infant activate regions in the adult basal forebrain, circuits which regulate specific nurturing and caregiving responses, and also activate the general circuits for emotions, motivation, attention, and empathy—all of which play a central role in effective parenting (Swain et al., 2007). The ways that caregivers respond to their newborn can critically shape the child's current and future behavior. We will explore the caregiver–infant relationship in more detail in the following chapter.

If the newborn is to learn the ways of her society and culture, she and her caregivers must rapidly coordinate their participation in these ways. The adults must come to know their new child, and adjust to her temperament and needs. The newborn must learn how to get those needs met through the intermediary of other people, since her own repertoire of behavior is so limited. How should we conceptualize these mutual adjustments?

For example, families all over the world have to coordinate the sleep patterns of adults and infant. But the results of their efforts to do this are quite different. In American urban families, infants a few weeks old quickly move towards the adult day/night cycle, averaging about 8.5 hours of sleep between the hours of 7 p.m. and 7 a.m. by the end of the second week. Between four and eight months their longest sleep episode increases to 8 hours from about 4 hours a night.

For Kipsigis infants in rural Kenya, on the other hand, the course of getting on a schedule is very different. At night these infants sleep with their mothers and are permitted to nurse on demand. During the day they are strapped to their mothers' backs, accompanying them as they take care of the household, work in the fields, and socialize. Infants do a lot of napping while their mothers go about their work. At 1 month old, the longest period of sleep reported for babies in a Kipsigis sample was three hours, and their longest sleep episode increased little during the first eight months of postnatal life (Super & Harkness, 1982).

Sleep is ubiquitous and it is often assumed to be biological in character and universal in form. Yet in fact sleep takes diverse forms in different cultures. Sleep is a highly organized and supported activity, "embedded in behaviorally, socially, and culturally constituted environments enabling safe sleep" (Worthman & Melby, 2002, p. 71). Sleeping arrangements reflect the tacit moral norms of a community (Shweder & Jensen, 1985), so that when and with whom infants sleep is one of the earliest ways in which they begin to participate in the customary practices of their family and community (Welles-Nystrom, 2005).

The sleep ecology provided to an infant appears to have consequences for the regulation of state and the management of attention. The Balinese, for example, acquire at a young age the odd ability to fall asleep if they are afraid! This suggests that the regulatory processes governing the transition between sleep and wakefulness can become differently organized in different cultural circumstances. The typical Western practice of infants sleeping alone may deprive them of the stimulation that facilitates the development of regulatory systems.

It is not only simple cultures that practice co-sleeping, but also technologically advanced cultures such as that of Japan. Japanese parents believe the infant needs to be drawn into relationships with other people. American parents, in contrast, believe that the infant must become independent (Jenni & O'Connor, 2005).

Feeding the infant is another area where coordination is crucial. In the 1940s, Mead and Macgregor (1951) set out to test Gesell's ideas (see Chapter 1) about the relation between maturation and learning, through cross-cultural research. All biologically normal infants are born with a reflex to suck that can be triggered by many different stimuli. Mead and Macgregor argued that the way that cultures interweave learning and maturation would be visible in the management of the change from reflex sucking to nursing, and in the long-term consequences of this change. Some cultures, they reported, take advantage of the sucking reflex by putting the newborn to the mother's breast immediately to stimulate the flow of milk, although the infant remains hungry. Other cultures provide a wet nurse until the mother has milk. Others will give the baby a bottle, and so on. In an immediate sense, all of these routes to nursing are equally adequate. However, they have different long-term implications. For example, babies who are bottle fed until the mother's milk is available may learn to nurse in ways that subsequently interfere with breast-feeding, with consequences for both the infants' nutrition and the quality of their social experiences during nursing. Recent research has shown that mothers who breast feed their infants also engage in more touching and gazing at the child than do bottle feeders (Lavelli & Poli, 1998), so the choice of feeding method influences the character of mother–infant interactions.

I will return again to sleeping and feeding arrangements in the next chapter, where we will trace the linkages between their organization during infancy and the environmental setting of the community.

CONCLUSION

In this chapter I have traced the developing human organism from its origins in the fusion of sperm and egg to its exit from the environment of the womb. The prenatal processes that create a fetus are subtle and complex, and we are still a long way from understanding all the mechanisms involved.

Fetal growth is both genetically programmed and at the same time a response to the environment of the womb, as well as to the behavior and choices made by the mother, and the support and services available to her during pregnancy. The newborn has already started to adapt to community values and practices (Chisholm, 1980).

Prenatal development is also sanctioned by cultural norms and laws that dictate who is permitted to have sexual relations, and who is prohibited. These regulations have changed historically, but often only with significant controversy and social conflict. Reproduction is generally viewed as central to kinship, and the link between parent and child generally is considered to be the primary social relationship, though whether this link is understood as biological, or as cultural, or as both, varies across cultures.

In this chapter I have focused on the prenatal formation of the human brain. We still know remarkably little about how the brain works. I have contrasted the view that the brain is like a digital computer, operating on formal representations, with the view that the embodied brain and the environment form a system, and function as parts of a unity. I will explore the implications of these two views in more detail in the pages to come.

Birth is a transition that is both biological and cultural. It is a normal event—half a million babies are born on planet Earth every day—but it is also a crisis, a traumatic event for the people involved. It requires significant adaptation on the part of the adults (and often older children) whose responsibility it will be to care for the baby. As the mother's body prepares itself for the abrupt event of **parturition** so too does the family make preparations for this new arrival. Birth requires rapid and significant adaptation on the baby's part too. The newborn is abruptly separated physically from her mother but she is still biologically dependent: she must obtain oxygen and food from new sources, and this not only requires a significant physiological and behavioral adjustment, it also requires that other people will be disposed to offer their care.

Indeed, it is a striking fact about human development that the human newborn is so completely dependent on other people for the most basic necessities of life. I have suggested that this dependence is an important *condition* for later development. We shall see in the chapters that follow how dependence provides the basis for the **intersubjectivity** that permits advancement of the child's development. At each stage the child is able to build on what she has already achieved.

It is not enough simply to be dependent, however. The human newborn has to be able to learn from the intimate interactions with other people that her dependency requires. The neonate enters the world already acutely attuned to the people around her, and this provides important learning opportunities. In time, the infant will learn how to actively and deliberately solicit adult caretaking. But even before she is capable of such deliberate behavior, adults can and do take care of her. To be effective caregivers, the adults who are in charge of a newborn human baby must allow themselves to become dependent on their child, in the sense that they must allow the baby's demands to dictate their actions. A process of mutual negotiation and adjustment has begun, one that will continue throughout life because it is crucial to the child's psychological development.

Birth transforms the child's relationship with her surroundings. A whole new environment has opened up and new experiences have begun, for an organism that is still undergoing rapid and profound biological changes in brain and body. The newborn baby will rapidly learn the ways of this new world, in what Vygotsky called the "Great-We."

SUMMARY

PRENATAL DEVELOPMENT OF BODY AND BRAIN

- Fertilization is when spermatazoon meets oocyte. It is both a biological event and a cultural event.
- The nine months of prenatal development are a process of guided self-assembly.
- The brain is a component in the perception–action cycle.

BIRTH: THE FIRST DEVELOPMENTAL TRANSITION

- Birth is a physical differentiation of mother and baby.
- Birth too is both a biological event and a cultural event.

INFANT DEPENDENCE: WHAT THE NEWBORN CANNOT DO

- The human baby has evolved to be extraordinarily dependent on other people for her survival.
- Caregivers weave the newborn into both the future of their community and its past.
- When infant mortality is high, caregivers will avoid forming an emotional bond with their newborn.

NEONATAL CAPABILITIES: WHAT THE NEWBORN CAN DO

- The human newborn is tuned and responsive to the people around her.
- Newborn and caregivers need to coordinate basic activities such as feeding and sleeping.

ONLINE RESOURCES

- Video about neurons:

  www.youtube.com/watch?v=xysT9JD7i0w&feature=relmfu

- Video about the nervous system:

  www.youtube.com/watch?v=tqvJZ1STLos&feature=relmfu

- Brain anatomy: a 3-D tour:

  www.pbs.org/wnet/brain/3d/index.html

(Continued)

(Continued)

- Alice Proujansky's photos of childbirth in various cultures: http://aliceproujansky.com/a/galleries/delivery-2/

- The process of gender inheritance is animated here: www.kscience.co.uk/animations/gender.htm?

CHAPTER 5

INFANCY

(6 WEEKS–12 MONTHS)
A PRACTICAL UNDERSTANDING OF THE WORLD

[I]t was the lengthening of infancy which ages ago gradually converted our forefathers from brute creatures into human creatures. It is babyhood that has made man what he is. The simple unaided operation of natural selection could never have resulted in the origination of the human race … In order to bring about that wonderful event, the Creation of Man, natural selection had to call in the aid of other agencies, and the chief of these agencies was the gradual lengthening of babyhood. (Fiske, 1909[1871], p. 1)

LEARNING OBJECTIVES

In this chapter we will look at the first stage of human development, infancy. We will consider:

- Piaget's account of how the infant develops a practical understanding of the world through active exploration.
- The world of infancy, based primarily on investigations of the way infants respond not to objects but to other people.
- The concerns of caretakers of the human infant.

In studying these aspects of infancy you will come to understand the particular way the human infant lives in the world, and how caregivers must respond to her needs.

FRAMING QUESTIONS

- In what sense might this statement be true? "It is babyhood that has made man what he is." Think about possible evidence in favor of this view, and against it.
- Do you consider that caring for an infant is something that comes naturally to parents and other caregivers? In your opinion, is the biological mother of an infant the best caregiver? If so, why?
- If you had just become a parent, what material preparations would you be making?

INTRODUCTION

The human newborn leaves the womb and enters an environment that has been shaped and worked over by previous generations of her community, as we saw in Chapter 3. She has inherited the genetic information needed to grow a skilled, agile, relatively graceful body with a big brain and a large cortex. She has also inherited the artifacts created by her predecessors in her community, which are being used in such a manner as to meet her present and future needs. However, she herself has yet to acquire the ability to employ these artifacts appropriately. We saw in the previous chapter that the human newborn leaves the womb completely dependent on other people, and at the same time sensitively attuned to them: to their faces and voices, for example. She is relatively immature compared with the young of other species, and she will take a comparatively long time to grow to adulthood.

Infancy—from a Latin word meaning one who does not speak—is widely, though not universally, considered a distinct stage of development that extends from birth until approximately 1 year of age. In some cultures, and in some psychological theories of development (such as Piaget's), infancy is considered to extend to 2.5 years of age, but I will be describing a transition that occurs towards the end of the first year of life, when the infant begins to walk and talk, as the end of this first developmental stage.

The proposal that the immaturity and duration of infancy are related to the qualitative difference between humans and other animals has been around for a long time. For example, the American philosopher John Fiske (1842–1901), whom Charles Darwin called a lucid expositor and thinker about evolution, made precisely this proposal in 1871. Human evolution has arranged human infancy, said Fiske, so that the child is "born with the germs of many complex capacities which were reserved to be unfolded and enhanced or checked and stifled by the incidents of personal experience in each individual." He went on to explain, "It is not that our inherited tendencies and aptitudes are not still the main thing. It is only that we have at last acquired great power to modify them by training, so that progress may go on with ever-increasing sureness and rapidity."

If Fiske was right, we would expect to see during infancy, during the first year of life, important changes as the newborn's capacities start to be "unfolded and enhanced, or checked and stifled." We ought to find important learning taking place during infancy.

And indeed we do. It has been recognized for some time that infancy is a time for learning about the immediate environment in a direct, practical manner. How, though, should we conceptualize the practical understanding which the infant acquires? In this chapter I shall examine several different conceptualizations.

My conclusion will be that the kind of understanding that an infant acquires is practical, intuitive, emotional, and social all at once. This is an age, and a developmental stage, at which there is as yet no clear differentiation between the social and the intellectual, between the cognitive and the emotional, between physical movement and intelligent action. The infant is interacting with the world around her in terms of a simple kind of interpretation, understanding the world in terms of its contingencies.

1. THE INFANT'S PRACTICAL UNDERSTANDING

For a long time, psychologists have recognized that an infant rapidly acquires a practical understanding of her surroundings. One of the key figures in the study of infancy was Jean Piaget, who we met in Chapter 2. Piaget proposed that infancy is the stage of **sensory-motor intelligence**. In this section I will review Piaget's account of the first four substages of sensory-motor intelligence, and then discuss what is known as the **A-not-B error**. I will compare Piaget's account with two other competing views of how an infant understands the world: theory theory and dynamic field theory.

1.1 THE EARLY SUBSTAGES OF SENSORIMOTOR INTELLIGENCE

Piaget's developmental theory provides an important perspective on the abilities of the human infant. Piaget viewed the first two and a half years of the child's life as the period of sensorimotor intelligence, because the process of adaptation during this period involves coordinating sensory perceptions with motor actions in increasingly complex ways (we discussed Piaget's concept of psychological **adaptation**, and its two component processes, **assimilation** and **accommodation**, in Chapter 2). Piaget argued that infants do not experience the world the way adults do: they have to construct an understanding of the reality that adults take for granted. Piaget's two great books on infancy—*The Origins of Intelligence* (1936) and *The Child's Construction of Reality* (1937)—describe how the infant, and then the toddler, constructs successively more complex practical **schemas**, which amount to a practical understanding of space, time, causality, and objects. "Schema" is Piaget's term for an enduring psychological structure: in the sensorimotor period the schemas are patterns of practical activity. Schemas provide the "forms" or "categories" that the influential philosopher Immanuel Kant argued are innate and universal and imposed by each person on the raw data of experience. Piaget believed that the forms of space, time, causality, and object are not innate, and that it takes an infant two or three years to construct them.

Piaget described *six substages* to the sensorimotor period. In *The Origins of Intelligence* he described the schemas that characterize each substage. The first schemas are simple *reflexes*, though Piaget insisted that even reflexes are active responses by the newborn, not just passive reactions to external stimulation. Reflexes become *circular reactions*, and these then become more complex, organized, and differentiated. A **circular reaction** occurs when the infant repeatedly tries out an action with some particular object, learns how to control its action in that context, and then works to generalize it to other contexts. You will see that it is a similar idea to the perception–action cycle we discussed in Chapter 4. Piaget distinguished among **primary circular reactions**, **secondary circular reactions**, and **tertiary circular reactions**.

In *The Child's Construction of Reality* Piaget described the substages again but this time in terms of the different ways the infant experiences the world. For example, it is not until substage 6 that the child understands that objects exist in their own right, independent of her perception of them and her action on them. This **object permanence** has become a focus of much subsequent research.

In the earlier substages, space, time and object are not yet differentiated. Well-known phenomena such as the "A-not-B error" (see below) illustrate how around 8 to 12 months of age objects have their special places for the infant, and are understood as linked to the actions that have been carried out on them.

In sum, Piaget proposed that our human understanding of space and time, of objects, and of causality, is not innate, that it has to be constructed over the course of our development. In his account, the human baby is doing something quite amazing in the first two years of life: constructing a practical understanding of the basic aspects of what humans take to be reality. She constructs this understanding through her practical activity, by exploring the environment with her body. This is "the construction of reality in the child," to which the title of Piaget's book refers. Confusingly, most textbooks focus on only a single aspect of sensorimotor intelligence, that of object permanence. This is certainly important, but to understand it correctly we need to place it in the overall picture that Piaget painted of the sensorimotor period.

Piaget's sensorimotor period corresponds to what I am calling in this book both *infancy* and *toddlerhood*. In this section I will focus on the four substages that occur during the first year of life. In Chapter 5 I will describe the last two substages, which occur during the toddler stage.

1.1.1 SUBSTAGES 1 TO 4 OF SENSORIMOTOR INTELLIGENCE

Piaget's account of sensorimotor development was based on his observations of his own children: Laurent, Lucienne, and Jacqueline. I have illustrated each substage with one of his observations. (Piaget's convention for representing the child's age is "year; month (day)," for example, "0;8(20)" is zero years, eight months and 20 days of age.)

Substage 1: Reflex Schemas (Birth to 1 month). From birth to around 4 or 5 weeks of age the infant is learning to control and combine the reflexes with which she was born. The sucking reflex, for example, is an innate reflex response to stimulation of the lips or cheek that functions to obtain food, but it will also be applied by accident to non-nutritive objects such as the infant's thumb. The *assimilation* of this reflex is seen in the fact that for an infant in this substage everything is a "suckable": the familiar sucking reflex is applied to every new object. These early reflexes do not permit much *accommodation*, but they produce stimulation that leads to further development. In this substage the infant does not search for objects that have been removed from sight. Apparently, out of sight is out of mind: the infant shows no expectation that objects will continue to exist when they are no longer visible.

Observation 1.– From birth sucking-like movements may be observed: impulsive movement and protrusion of the lips accompanied by displacements of the tongue, while the arms engage in unruly and more or less rhythmical gestures and the head moves laterally, etc.

As soon as the hands rub the lips the sucking reflex is released. The child sucks his fingers for a moment but of course does not know either how to keep them in his mouth or pursue them with his lips. Lucienne and Laurent, a quarter of an hour and a half hour after birth, respectively, had already sucked their hand like this: Lucienne, whose hand had been immobilized due to its position, sucked her fingers for more than ten minutes. (Piaget, 1952a[1936], p. 25)

Substage 2: The first acquired adaptations and the primary circular reactions (1 to 4 months). Starting around 4 weeks of age the infant begins to apply her simple reflexes and action patterns to new objects in a systematic way. Whereas in substage 1 the infant might accidentally suck on her thumb, now she will actively bring the thumb to her mouth in order to suck it. Piaget interpreted this as a repeating of pleasurable actions. He called such action patterns **primary circular reactions**; they are *circular* in the sense that the infant repeats them; they are *primary* in the sense that they don't extend into the world beyond the infant's own body.

Observation 11.– Laurent at 0;0(30) stays awake without crying, gazing ahead with wide open eyes. He makes sucking-like movements almost continually, opening and closing his mouth in slow rhythm, his tongue constantly moving. At certain moments his tongue, instead of remaining inside his lips, licks the lower lip; the sucking recommences with renewed ardor.

Two interpretations are possible. Either at such times there is searching for food and then the protrusion of the tongue is merely a reflex inherent in the mechanism of sucking and swallowing, or else this marks the beginning of circular reaction. It seems, for the time being, that both are present. Sometimes protrusion of the tongue is accompanied by disordered movements of the arms and leads to impatience and anger. In such a case there is obviously a seeking to suck, and disappointment. Sometimes, on the other hand, protrusion of the tongue is accompanied by slow, rhythmical movements of the arms and an expression of contentment. In this case the tongue comes into play through circular reaction. (Piaget, 1952a[1936], p. 50)

These simple circular reactions are subsequently *differentiated* and *integrated*. The infant will learn to suck in different ways on different objects, and to combine action patterns in various ways. The schemas become more complex, and the infant's understanding of the world develops. Piaget insisted that an infant is active, seeking stimulation, and actively solving the problems that confront her in her environment.

Substage 3: Secondary circular reactions and procedures to make interesting sights last (4 to 8 months). Between 4 and 8 months of age the infant shows growing interest in the environment around her. Now she repeats interesting and pleasurable actions not only on her own body, but also on things out in the environment. Piaget called these action patterns **secondary circular reactions**. For example, if we place a brightly colored rattle in the hand of a 7-month-old infant she will grasp it, move it, perhaps look startled at the noise it makes, and begin to wave it more systematically, while watching it intently. Piaget believed that this behavior was evidence for the infant's growing understanding that objects are distinct from her body.

Observation 94.– At 0;3(5) Lucienne shakes her bassinet by moving her legs violently (bending and unbending them, etc.), which makes the cloth dolls swing from the hood. Lucienne looks at them, smiling, and recommences at once. These movements are simply the concomitants of joy. When she experiences great pleasure Lucienne externalizes it in a total reaction including leg movements. As she often smiles at her knick-knacks she caused them to swing. But does she keep this up through consciously coordinated circular reaction or is it pleasure constantly springing up again that explains her behavior?

That evening, when Lucienne is quiet, I gently swing her dolls. The morning's reaction starts up again, but both interpretations remain possible.

The next day, at 0;3(6) I present the dolls: Lucienne immediately moves, shakes her legs, but this time without smiling. Her interest is intense and sustained and there also seems to be an intentional circular reaction. (Piaget, 1952a[1936], pp. 157–158)

Substage 4: Coordination of secondary circular reactions and their application to new situations (8 to 12 months). Starting around 8 months of age the infant begins to coordinate these secondary circular reactions; that is, to put them together into more complex action sequences. For example, the infant may reach out and drop an object in a cup, then pick up the cup. She may reach out to pick up a cover, then snatch an object that has been uncovered. In these **coordinated secondary circular reactions** we see behavior that is organized and directed towards a goal. Schemas have become coordinated so that the first schema serves as a means and the second schema defines the goal. Piaget considered this stage to show the earliest form of intentional action and problem-solving ability. At this age, moreover, the infant begins responding to objects and people when they are out of sight. After she has seen an object being hidden, she will lift the cover to retrieve it.

Observation 121.– […] At 0;8(20) Jacqueline tries to grasp a cigarette case which I present to her. I then slide it between the crossed strings which attach her dolls to the hood. She tries to reach it directly. Not succeeding, she immediately looks for the strings which are not in her hands and of which she only saw the part in which the cigarette case is entangled. She looks in front of her, grasps the strings, pulls and shakes them, etc. The cigarette case then falls and she grasps it.

Second experiment: same reactions, but without first trying to grasp the object directly. (Piaget, 1952a[1936], p. 215)

Piaget believed that these early and simple sensory-motor schemas contain what he called a "practical logic": an organization analogous to what in mathematics is called a "group." A group is a system of elements and operations with four fundamental properties. The first property is that the group is **closed**—an operation on any element in the group yields another element, but one which is still a member of the group. Second, a group shows **associativity**—if P, Q and R are operations, the order of the operations is not important: $(P \times Q) \times R$ is equivalent to $P \times (Q \times R)$; that is, "the end result is independent of the route taken" (Piaget, 1970, p. 20). Third, there is an **identity** operation, which leaves an element unchanged, identical to itself—an operation I such that $P \times I = P$. Finally, the group shows **reversibility**—for every operation P there is an operation P' that reverses it, such that $P \times P' = I$.

To put this in simpler terms, the infant discovers in her everyday actions that she can (1) act on things without changing them, (2) follow various routes to the same goal, (3) not act, and (4) return to her starting point.

These are fundamental properties for any logical system, and Piaget insisted that they exist in the infant's actions. He proposed that at first these practical groups exist only from an observer's viewpoint, but with the passage of time the infant comes to recognize them herself, and this provides the basis for her logical thinking when she is older. We can see here Piaget's interest in how the infant—who I think he would have called a biological organism—becomes an adult who is logical—able to understand and follow the laws of logical reasoning. For Piaget, adult logic is inherent in the child's physical activity in the world. As she develops, she becomes consciously aware of this logical potential.

Infancy 0–12 months	**Sensory-motor stage**	*Substage 1:*
Toddler 1–2.5 years	Sensory-motor stage	*Reflex Schemas (Birth to 1 month)* *Substage 2:*
Early childhood 2.5–6 years	Preoperational stage	*Primary circular reactions (1 to 4 months)* *Substage 3:*
Middle childhood 6–12 years	Concrete operational stage	*Secondary circular reactions (4 to 8 months)* *Substage 4:*
Adolescence 12–	Formal operational stage	*Coordination of secondary circular reactions (8 to 12 months)*

Figure 5.1   The first four substages of sensory-motor intelligence, according to Piaget

1.1.2 THE A-NOT-B ERROR

The character of an infant's understanding of the physical objects in her environment was assessed by Piaget in a number of ways. One task that has attracted a great deal of attention involved simply hiding an object the infant was interested in and observing her response.

A newborn, in substage 1, will not respond at all when an object in her line of sight is hidden. In substage 2, when an object is hidden the infant will orient (turn her eyes and head) to the place where it was last seen. In substage 3, the infant will reach for a partially hidden object but will stop if the object disappears completely (see Table 5.1).

However, around the end of infancy, in Piaget's substage 4, at 8 to 12 months of age (the substage of Coordinated Secondary Circular Reactions), the infant shows a surprising response. She will search for an object that has been completely hidden, which suggests that she understands that objects continue to exist when they are not directly visible. However, the infant at this age makes an interesting "error" which suggests that she does *not* yet understand objects the way adults do. At this substage, when the infant searches for a completely hidden object she looks in the *original* location of the object even when it has been moved to another location in full view. This is called the **A-not-B error**.

Sensorimotor Substage	Response to Hidden Object
Substage 1 Reflex Schemas Involuntary rooting, sucking, grasping, looking	Infant does not search for objects that have been removed from sight.
Substage 2 Primary Circular Reactions Repetition of pleasurable actions, on or near the body	Infant orients to the place where an object was last seen.
Substage 3 Secondary Circular Reactions Repetition of actions that produce interesting change in the environment; dawning awareness of the effects of one's own acts	Infant orients to the place where an object was last seen. Search for objects that are partially hidden.
Substage 4 Coordinated Secondary Circular Reactions Combining schemas as means to achieve a desired end; earliest form of problem solving	Infant will search for a completely hidden object; keeps searching in the original location of the object even if it is moved to another location in full view of the infant—but makes the A-not-B error
Substage 5 Tertiary Circular Reactions Deliberate variation of problem-solving activity; experimentation to discover consequences	Infant will search for an object after seeing it moved, but not if it is moved while out of sight
Substage 6 Inventions Through Sudden Comprehension Invention of new means of problem solving through insight and imagery	Infant will search systematically for a hidden object, apparently certain that it exists somewhere. Shows the ability to follow invisible displacements of an object

Figure 5.2   Piaget's six substages of sensorimotor intelligence, and the typical responses to a hidden object

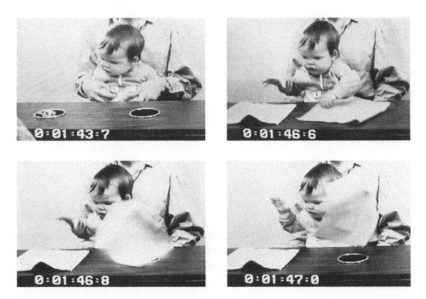

Figure 5.3 The A-not-B error

In a typical administration of what has become a very popular Piagetian task, an infant is seated at a table on which two small cloths have been placed, one of them at the location we will call A, the other at location B. An object—usually a small toy—is placed at location A, and when the infant's attention is focused on it, it is covered with the cloth. The infant in substage 4 usually has no difficulty reaching out to grasp and remove the cloth, and then retrieve the object. The researcher hides the object again two or three more times. Then the object is moved to location B, and hidden there.

This time, what usually happens is that the infant reaches out and picks up not cloth B, as one would expect, but cloth A. This "A-not-B" behavior is an "error" from an adult's point of view, but Piaget argued that the behavior must make sense for the infant.

Of course, we could say that the infant "lacks object permanence," but what does this phrase really mean? Many textbooks leave out Piaget's own explanation of the infant's behavior when she makes the A-not-B error. Here is what Piaget wrote:

> The object is still not to the child as it is to us: a substantial body, individualized and displaced in space without depending on the action context in which it is inserted … Hence there would not be one chain, one doll, one watch, one ball, etc., individualized, permanent, and independent of the child's activity, that is, of the special positions in which that activity takes place or has taken place, but there would still exist only images such as 'ball-under-the armchair,' 'doll-attached-to-the hammock,' 'watch-under-a-cushion,' 'papa-at-his-window' etc. … Whereas we think of the ball as able to occupy an infinitude of different positions, which enables us to abstract it from all of them at once, the child endows it with only a few special positions without being able, consequently, to consider it as entirely independent of them. (Piaget, 1954[1937], p. 62)

Piaget's explanation, then, was that the original location where the object was hidden, location A, has become that object's "special position." Furthermore, to the infant, lifting cloth A is an action that has brought back the object successfully in the past, so it is sensible to perform this action again, even though the object was hidden in a new location. For the infant in substage 4, object-action-place are not yet differentiated, as they will be by the end of the sensorimotor period. She does not yet understand that every object is an individual entity, independent of other objects, and permanent even when it is acted upon or moved. The infant's practical understanding of objects, and also of space, time, and causality, is by no means complete.

1.2 COGNITIVE DEVELOPMENTAL RESEARCH WITH INFANTS AND THEORY THEORY

The phenomenon of the A-not-B error has become something of a testing ground for competing theoretical frameworks. Piaget's constructivism, cognitive developmental psychology, and cultural developmental psychology each have a different view of what is going on during infancy, and consequently they have different interpretations of the A-not-B error.

Cognitive developmental researchers have suggested, for example, that the young infant *does* in fact know that the object continues to exist in location B but cannot *display* her knowledge. Researchers have invented new tasks that can be used with infants who are too young to reach out and pick up a cover. In a typical **visual preference task** the infant is seated in front of a display in which an object moves behind a screen and the direction in which she looks is monitored and recorded. In such a task the infant does not have to reach for the hidden object, she merely has to look in the direction where she expects it to be, and the researchers assume she will look longer when she sees something unexpected. Researchers find that even young infants are surprised when a hidden object does not reappear again (Baillargeon, 2004).

Researchers using this task hypothesize that young infants learn about the role of factors such as height and transparency separately for each kind of event that is shown to them (events such as covering, containment, or occlusion). For example, infants younger than about 7 months are not surprised when a tall object seems to be hidden inside a short container.

Other cognitive developmental researchers have varied other details of the task to see how the infant responds. For example, if the infant is allowed to respond immediately when the object is hidden she may correctly search in location B. If her response is delayed, however, she will shift back to location A (Diamond, 1985). This suggests that her *understanding* of what has occurred is quite sophisticated, but her *memory* of what has occurred is not very good.

Cognitive developmental researchers have concluded that "from an early age infants interpret physical events in accord with general principles of *continuity* (objects exist continuously in time and space) and *solidity* (for two objects to each exist continuously, the two cannot exist at the same time in the same space)" (Baillargeon, 2004, pp. 393–395). Some of these researchers believe that these general principles may in fact be innate. This is very different from Piaget's view that it takes two years for the infant to construct an understanding of spatial continuity and physical solidity.

It certainly seems that young infants quickly develop expectations about the ways physical objects will and will not behave. By five months of age, infants expect that an occluded object will reappear, and that objects will not occupy the same location in space. It takes more time, though, for them to understand more complex transformations and displacements.

However, what is the nature of these "expectations"? Here is where perspectives diverge. Piaget proposed that infants and toddlers cannot form **mental representations** until they are 20 or perhaps 30 months old. In his view, as we have seen, sensorimotor understanding is a practical, embodied way of knowing the world, *knowing-how* rather than *knowing-that*. Sensorimotor intelligence is non-representational: indeed, for Piaget the infant's inadequate understanding of the permanence of objects is in part due to her lack of an ability to create mental representations of the objects she sees around her. As we will discuss in Chapter 7, Piaget argued that the ability to create mental representations emerges only at the end of the sensorimotor period, at around 2.5 years of age. Only at that point can the toddler construct what Piaget called an "object concept," with which she can represent objects even when she no longer sees them. In Piaget's view, as we shall see, such early concepts may be very simple but they provide the child with a new way of understanding the world that he considered to be a dramatic advance upon sensorimotor understanding.

However, Piaget's claim that mental representation is not possible until 2.5 years of age runs counter to the central presumption of the cognitive developmental theoretical framework, which, as we saw in Chapters 3 and 4, is that the brain is like a computer. Infancy researchers who work within the cognitive developmental framework assume, then, that even the youngest infants already have mental representations—"concepts"—of the world around them. Some argue that these concepts are innate. As the information included in these representations becomes richer, the infant's expectations change. The figure below shows one attempt to model the infant's understanding of physical objects as a process of building cognitive representations.

In fact, some infancy researchers claim that the youngest infants are forming "theories" about the world. This view has been called **theory theory** (Gopnik, 2012; Gopnik & Wellman, 1992). These psychologists have a theory that the infant knows the world by forming theories about it. They explicitly propose that evolution has equipped the human baby with the ability to create and manipulate rules and representations with a structure and a function just like scientific theories, and just like computer programs. They propose that a child's cognition develops in the way that theories develop

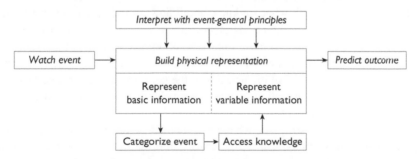

Figure 5.4 One proposal for the kind of mental representation that an infant may construct

Source: Baillargeon (2004)

in science: the infant tests and revises her theory about the properties of objects by making predictions of what will and will not happen.

For example, when an infant shows that she expects an object to reappear after it is hidden, this is because she has constructed an enduring theory of that object. A typical conclusion is that "young infants' understanding of occlusion events is strikingly similar to that of adults" (Baillargeon, 1993, p. 266).

To a cultural psychologist, however, it appears that these researchers are ignoring an important distinction between two kinds of knowledge. Cognitive developmental researchers assume that the only possible kind of knowledge is representational. Any evidence of an infant understanding something about the world is interpreted by these researchers as evidence for representational knowledge, in the form of "concepts," "models," or "theories." Cultural psychology, on the other hand, follows Piaget in interpreting the knowledge that is formed in infancy as practical, embodied know-how. Cultural psychology differs from Piaget, however, in two important respects. First, it sees this knowledge as being thoroughly social in character. Second, it considers this kind of knowledge to remain important throughout life, whereas Piaget thought that sensorimotor intelligence was replaced by intellectual and representational ways of knowing. I will expand on the first of these points in the next major section of this chapter. First, however, I want to introduce exciting new research on infancy which explores the notion that the understanding of physical objects does not require mental representations.

1.3 DYNAMIC FIELD THEORY

A line of research that has explored in some detail the kind of knowing involved in the A-not-B error is **dynamic field theory** (DFT). Linda Smith, Ester Thelen, and their colleagues have argued that Piaget was correct to see embodied knowledge as central to infancy, but that he was wrong to think it is replaced by a different kind of understanding at 3 years of age (Smith et al., 1999; Thelen et al., 2001).

Where the cognitive developmental psychologists have tried to explain the A-not-B error in terms of the infant's mental representations and theories, Smith and Thelen have instead explored the possibility of explaining the A-not-B error in terms of the way interconnected neurons handle the continuous flow of information that arrives from the senses. This information, they propose, is reorganized within the brain and then sent to the muscles to initiate action.

Dynamic field theory starts with what we know about how an individual neuron operates and then builds mathematical models of how thousands of interconnected neurons—**neural networks**—would behave. DFT proposes that rather than forming some kind of representation, or theory, or model, a neural network maintains an overall pattern of activation that changes dynamically as new information arrives. The information is distributed across all the neurons in the network, and the properties of the network, operating as a field, lead to the generation of intelligent behavior, in the form of complex, real-time, dynamic responses to the environment.

For DFT, cognition is what takes place when an embodied organism acts within a structured environment. Any organism will actively search for sensory information, its motor activity will be tuned to features of the environment, and its activity will flow seamlessly forward in space and time. Brain, behavior, and environment operate together, and we misunderstand the development of cognition if we

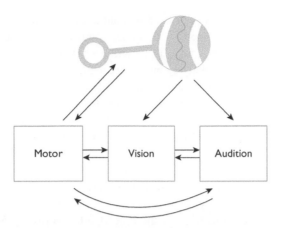

Figure 5.5 The auditory, visual, and motor systems are all activated by shaking a rattle

take the infant—either literally or theoretically—out of her environment. Thelen and Smith argue not only that cognition has sensory-motor origins, as Piaget recognized, but also that cognition continues to have a sensorimotor basis throughout development, a non-representational basis upon which more complex kinds of knowing can be built. As you can see, this is consistent with the new view of brain function that I introduced in Chapter 4.

The research conducted by Smith and her colleagues provides a compelling explanation of the A-not-B error (and of other infant behaviors) in terms of this dynamic flow of information in neuronal fields. I described earlier the secondary circular reaction that occurs when we place a brightly colored rattle in the hand of an infant between 6 and 10 months of age. She will grasp it, wave it, listen to the noise, and then move it more systematically, watching intently. The infant's auditory, visual, and motor systems are all operating and they are functionally interconnected, due to the fact that the rattle moves and shakes and is a bright color. The inputs to the different sensory systems are different, but they are correlated with one another and their mutual dependencies enable patterns to be detected across the sensory modalities.

DFT proposes that when the infant reaches out in the hidden object task, her action is instigated by an integration of visual input in the present and the motor memory of reaching in the past. When she searches in location A, not B, this is because she is responding to the current situation in a continuous, dynamically evolving manner, that depends both on her looking in the present and her memory of what happened (Erlhagen & Schöner, 2002). When the object is first hidden at A, activation rises in the corresponding point in the neural field and continues for a while. As the object is being hidden at B for the first time, there is renewed activation at A due to memory for prior reaches. When the object is hidden, activation rises at B but this fades away and the traces of previous motor actions—reaching for A—dominate the field. This increases the activation at A, leading to reaching for A, and the A-not-B error.

In other words, the A-not-B error occurs because the infant's memory of the desired object is embodied in the processes that plan spatially directed action. It is not a question of forgetting where the object was hidden: Piaget was right, the object has become bound to a specific location in space. The more immediate memory of the B event competes—within neurophysiological fields in the infant's brain—with the memory of the previous event, and of prior actions at A, and the latter wins out. Evidence for this is that the error can be made more likely by increasing the salience of A (making it a bright color, for example), and made less likely by increasing the salience of B.

DFT suggests that it is not necessary to postulate that the infant has some kind of internal representation of the objects and events, a "know-that" that amounts to a theory. The A-not-B error arises from the sophisticated practical understanding of the world that the preverbal infant is acquiring. Each neurological field is coupled to the world through the infant's body, so that the infant's spatial orientation and posture play an important role in how she understands and responds to events. For instance, if we make the infant stand up between the events at A and the event at B the error disappears, because the memory for A, and the preliminary plan to reach to A, are reset by the change in posture. The infant's body and the objects and locations of the task together form a practical field within which certain actions become inviting, and in which it makes no sense to distinguish between what the infant perceives and what she "knows." This is strong evidence that the infant's understanding is embodied rather than representational.

There are similarities between DFT and the concept of the perception–action cycle that I introduced in Chapter 4. DFT is an account of the infant's behavior and knowledge of the world in terms of the lower levels of the perception-action hierarchy. It also fits well with what is known as "dual systems theory."

1.4 DUAL SYSTEMS THEORY

Over the past decade or so, psychologists have become very interested in **dual systems theory**, perhaps because a Nobel Prize was won for the first investigations (Tversky & Kahneman, 1974). There appear to be two distinct modes in adult reasoning and decision making: these have been called **System 1** and **System 2** (De Neys, 2006; Evans, 2008; Lieberman, 2000). System 1 is rapid, intuitive and unconscious: this mode of reasoning involves quick judgments about a situation when there is no time for a careful examination of the facts. System 1 operates automatically and quickly, with no sense of voluntary control.

System 2 includes a lot of different functions, but they all share the characteristic that they require focused attention. This mode of thinking is deliberate, effortful, thoughtful, rational, and relatively slow: it is what we usually think of when we think about thinking. When we carry out System 2 processes we have the subjective experience of agency, choice, and concentration. That is to say, we need to focus on what we wish to accomplish, we have a sense of making an effort, and we know we have various options among which we will deliberately select.

These two systems have also been named to emphasize their central characteristics: System 1 has been called System X because is "refleXive," while System 2 has been called System C because it is "Conscious." An adult tends to think about themselves in terms of the deliberate, conscious system: "When we think of ourselves, we identify with System 2, the conscious, reasoning self that has beliefs, makes choices, and decides what to think about and what to do" (Kahneman, 2011). Indeed, until recently psychology as a whole has tended to focus on, and to value, System 2 (Bargh & Chartrand, 1999). But each of the two systems serves an important function, and it is necessary that we pay attention to both. Each system has both its strengths and its limitations, and it seems that the relationship between the two systems changes during development. We will be exploring this in the chapters that follow.

A lot of research has focused on the "errors" of System 1. For example, when people make intuitive judgments about their chances of winning the lottery they overemphasize their possible losses, and underestimate likely gains. People tend to misjudge probabilities, and especially combinations of possibilities. For example, when a young person is described as a young female and people are asked a series of questions about her possible occupation they are more likely to affirm that she is "a bank teller and a feminist" than that she is "a bank teller." But logically the second statement *has* to be more probable, because there are necessarily more bank tellers than there are feminist bank tellers (Kahneman, 2011).

But are these errors? Perhaps practical logic is not the same as formal logic. Presumably the intuitive system wouldn't exist if it were leading people to frequently make significant mistakes. Perhaps people intuitively assume that the statement that someone is "a bank teller" would include the information that she is "a feminist" because who would leave out something so noteworthy! Another line of research has focused on the *strengths* of intuitive thinking. It turns out, not surprisingly, that experts in a specific activity have become intuitive and automatic in their skills: for example, firefighters become able to make quick, intuitive judgments about danger in a burning building (Klein & Jarosz, 2011). This kind of expertise appears to be in large part a matter of educating System 1. And this means that System 1 is not simply full of biases and errors, it also becomes full of expertise and wisdom.

Neuroscientists have begun to explore the neurological basis for these two systems. Their findings suggest that System 1 involves the lateral temporal cortex, the basal ganglia, and the amygdala. They propose that System 1 is made up of connectionist networks in which information is stored in a widely distributed manner, in synaptic connections and fiber linkages. This system employs parallel functioning: it is performing many simultaneous operations at the same time, finding patterns in sensory input, and assimilating data into valleys of coherence (to talk in systems terms).

Central among these operations is the basic, ongoing perception of the world in which we live. One might say that the fundamental contribution of System 1 is to construct our taken-for-granted world. Each of us experiences a world external to us that we assume without question to be real, with enduring objects that are physical, but also have emotional and meaningful characteristics. On reflection, though, we can see that this experience is a product of our active engagement in the environment, and the brain's active processing of energy flowing into the senses. The processes of this perception are largely unconscious: our conscious awareness is of the *results* of our unconscious perceptual processes.

System 2, in contrast, handles deliberate controlled psychological functions, and contributes to our *reflective* awareness: our sense of our own agency in the world. System 2 appears to be instantiated in the anterior cingulate, the hippocampus, and the prefrontal cortex.

System 1 is operating smoothly most of the time, but when System 1 encounters some problem or hitch, then we turn to System 2. A problem activates the anterior cingulate, which in turn activates the prefrontal cortex. As we have seen, System 2 involves deliberate and conscious reasoning, and as a consequence it can use symbolic logic to solve problems in a way that System 1 cannot, and System 2 uses this ability to influence or override System 1. It seems that the hippocampus records the occasions in which System 2 was activated, possibly to facilitate problem solving the next time a similar situation is encountered.

System 1	System 2
Unconscious (you know only its products)	Conscious (you also know its operation)
Output is experienced as reality	Output is experienced as self-generated
Fast, automatic	Slow, deliberate
Parallel (many at once)	Serial (one at a time)
Learns slowly	Learns quickly
Intuitive, analogical	Formal, propositional
Phylogenetically older	Phylogenetically newer
Ontogenetically younger	Ontogenetically older

Figure 5.6   System 1 and System 2

Source: Lieberman (2002)

Although most research on System 1 and System 2, both behavioral and neurophysiological, has been conducted with adults, it seems highly likely that in the newborn all brain processes are unconscious and automatic, involving only System 1. I have said that System 1 handles the unconscious processing of sensory input so as to give rise to our experience of a stable world, in which people and objects are solid and enduring, continuing to exist even when out of sight. The sensorimotor period can be viewed as the time when System 1 is learning how to do this work, so that as a result the way the infant experiences the world is continually changing. In this case, the dynamic fields that developmental researchers have been exploring are aspects of System 1.

Only with time, experience and adult help will conscious, controlled psychological functions begin to emerge. In the chapters that follow I will be describing the development of various kinds of self-regulation and self-control: these presumably show the increasing operation of System 2. Interaction with other people will turn out to be crucial for the operation of System 2 (Ardilla, 2008). In fact, during infancy it is the caregivers who provide System 2 for their child. Infant and caregivers together form the dual systems, as we shall see in section 5.

In later chapters we shall see how System 2 both builds upon the basis of System 1 and acts back on System 1 to transform it. The relationship between the two is a dynamic one: System 2 would not be possible without the existence of System 1; on the other hand, System 1 is changed once System 2 emerges. Indeed, if we take seriously the model of the perception–action cycle, there are multiple levels of functioning, not merely two.

We can see in infancy, then, a practical understanding of the world that grows in power and effectiveness. During the first year, the infant becomes capable of simple physical manipulation of physical objects, elementary toys, and apparatus. Using one object to influence another is a fundamental but crucial form of practical intelligence, the basis for tool use (Lockman, 2000), and importantly it is a type

Piaget	Cognitive Developmental Psychology	Dynamic Field Theory	Dual Systems Theory	Cultural Psychology
A practical sensory-motor understanding of the physical world.	Concepts, perhaps theories, about the world.	Neural networks with dynamic activation generate intelligent behavior of an embodied and embedded organism	System I operating to experience of a stable world. The caregiver provides System 2.	An understanding of social spaces and times that is practical, intuitive, emotional, and social.

Figure 5.7 How different theoretical frameworks view the type of understanding constructed during the first year of life

of intelligence that is prior to and independent of language. We shall consider in the next chapter the emergence of speech in the first year.

Piaget viewed sensorimotor intelligence as the result of the infant's interaction with her physical surroundings and adaptation to those surroundings. The infant's sensorimotor intelligence, then, is her practical understanding of the world around her. It is also her way of *evaluating* things and events in that world. As I pointed out in Chapter 2, Piaget ignored the cultural character of the environment and the infant's social relations with other people. However, the infant's practical intelligence involves not only actions on objects but also interactions with people. A separation between interaction with objects and interaction with people would be artificial and inappropriate at this stage: the infant encounters objects *through* the people who care for her. In the following section, then, we turn to the ways an infant interacts with the adults who are assisting and managing her life, and how this helps us understand the world of infancy.

2. THE WORLD OF INFANCY: THE "GREAT-WE"

Piaget emphasized that infancy is a time for exploring the environment, but he focused primarily on the physical characteristics of this environment. In fact, however, the space and time in which every infant lives are social, so that the circular reactions she engages in have social goals and social consequences, and the objects she interacts with are cultural artifacts. For example, the space in which an infant lives is first of all *home*, whether it be a thatched hut, a terraced house, or a palace, and a home is known not simply by moving within it but by living in it. In addition, home has been organized and arranged, divided and structured, by the adults who live there. It has a character: familiar smells, sights, and sounds. It is inhabited, by people who are "familiar" in the sense of both being known and being family. It has a temporal rhythm, ordered by the hours of the working day, the days of the week, and the seasons of the year. The infant soon becomes familiar with dinner time and bed time. Before very long she will experience the event known as a birthday. Objects too are culturally defined: they are artifacts used in particular ways, at specific times and places. Contact with these objects is generally through other people and, equally, contact with other people is often achieved through objects. Piaget did not pay attention to this social character of the infant's world and of her sensorimotor actions in this world.

For example, Piaget recorded this observation of his daughter when she was in sensorimotor substage 4:

> at 0;10 (3) Jacqueline takes my hand, places it against a singing doll which she is unable to activate herself, and exerts pressure on my index finger to make me do what is necessary. This last observation reveals to what extent, to Jacqueline, my hand has become an independent source of action by contact. (Piaget 1954[1937], p. 260)

Piaget's interpretation was that during this substage the infant begins to attribute causal powers to another person's body. In his view, since she still does not understand that persons have permanent existence, Jacqueline views their actions as depending on her own presence and influence. In short, for the infant at this stage, persons don't differ intrinsically from objects.

2.1 THE INFANT'S SOCIAL SENSITIVITY

Was Piaget correct? In the late 1960s, researchers using the new technology of portable film cameras noted that 1-month-old infants responded differently to persons and to objects. Infants only a few weeks old engaged in direct face-to-face interactions with their caregivers, interactions in which there was a notable synchrony and coordination of the partners' vocal, oral, and gestural displays (Trevarthen, 1974; 2004). Films of interaction between mothers and newborns, for example, showed an intricately coordinated, rhythmic patterning between the two, each responding to the other's actions. Here are some written observations from the time:

> the mother and infant were collaborating in a pattern of more or less alternating, non-overlapping vocalisation, the mother speaking brief sentences and the infant responding with coos and murmurs, together producing a brief joint performance similar to conversation, which I called 'protoconversation.' (Bateson, 1969, cited in Trevarthen, 1998, p. 23)

This coordination between adult and infant was called **primary intersubjectivity** (Trevarthen, 1979; Trevarthen & Aitkin, 2001). **Intersubjectivity** is a term used in philosophy, psychology, sociology, and anthropology to emphasize a fundamental relatedness among people, often taken to be unconscious and emotional. It is usually used in contrast to solipsistic individual experience, to emphasize our inherently social being. It refers to phenomena such as language and social practices which cannot be reduced to subjective experience but are also not objective in the sense that they would continue even if no people existed.

This **protoconversation** generally includes specific behaviors by the infant, including mutual gaze, smiles of recognition, and vocalizing declamations. During the first six months of infancy, these proto-conversational abilities seem to outpace the child's manipulation of objects, suggesting that interaction with people can be a richer and more fundamental source of learning than interaction with physical objects. It occurred to the researchers that the newborn's innate abilities "are adapted to learning through communication with a known person" (Trevarthen, 2004, p. 37). The infant is evidently born equipped and motivated for organized emotional interchanges with other people (Trevarthen, 1998, 2005). One implication is that research needs to focus not only on what an infant can do alone, but also on what she can do with appropriate human support.

When caregivers—at least in the cultures that psychologists have usually studied; that is, their own— are face to face with their infants aged 2 to 3 months they will spontaneously interact in a rhythmic way, creating a joint pattern of activity and mutual orientation. The adult treats the infant's sounds and gestures as intentional and conversational. Presumably at this young age this is not in fact the case, but this experience offers the basis for them to become so. These rhythmic interactions serve to capture the infant's attention and so they provide an occasion for learning. Adults spontaneously become interpreters of the infant's gestures and vocalizations, responding to them "as if" they are linguistic acts. As we shall see, this establishes the conditions for *actions* to become *gestures* and then *symbols* (Lock, 1978).

Certainly, caregivers interpret the appearance of **social smiling** at around 2 months of age as a sign that their infant recognizes them. They respond to this change in various ways, including increasingly the complexity of their speech to the infant, at least in Western middle-class families (Henning et al., 2005).

These interactions are a form of communication prior to language, employing on the infant's part both sounds and gestures but without the phonemic character of oral language. There is evidently "an innate emotive foundation for language and the learning of culture, and for the making of emotionally-regulated, and emotional health-regulating, social bonds" (Trevarthen, 1998, p. 23). We shall see in Chapter 8 that this kind of patterned interaction supports, in particular, the toddler's learning of names for objects.

After 3 months of age, these protoconversations develop into participation in simple interactive and strongly rhythmic songs and nursery rhymes, and ritual play routines such as peek-a-boo. These "person–person games" involve highly predictable repetition. At first it might seem that the adult is responsible for scaffolding these interactions, but closer observation discloses that the infant can often take the initiative and become the leader.

By six months of age, infants can recognize familiar behaviors, and can distinguish between animate action and the movement of inanimate things. Around this time, games between infants and adults begin to include the use of objects. For example, Barbara Rogoff watched how several adults played with her infant son and daughter with a jack-in-the-box. In the early months, the adults tried to focus the infant's attention by working the toy and, as the bunny popped out, by saying things like "My, what happened?" By the end of the first year, in contrast, the interaction centered on how to use the toy: the adults guided the infant's hand in turning the handle and putting the rabbit back in the box. During the second year, the adults helped from a distance, using gestures and verbal prompts, such as making a turning motion with the hand (Rogoff et al., 1984). These different ways of acting together on an object enable the infant to understand, through active participation, the customary ways in which artifacts are handled. She gains a practical understanding of the objects in her world, guided by adults in ways that are adjusted to her ability and comprehension.

The discovery of these characteristics in early infant–adult interaction made psychologists and other social scientists who study young children aware that infants should be considered active agents in their social relationships. This discovery also made it seem very likely that both individual and cross-cultural differences in the ways that infants are treated and cared for can have major long-term implications for their development. A careful examination began of the ways that adults care for infants in other cultures.

This led to the awareness that there are cultures that do not foster this kind of face-to-face interaction, which has become called the "distal style" (see section 4.3 below). The distal style has been assumed to be necessary for healthy development. As we shall see, however, in many cultures a different kind of interaction, the "proximal style," is the norm.

Towards the end of this chapter I will describe the dramatic changes that take place in the infant's social sensitivity at around 12 months of age, as the threshold of independent locomotion is reached: in particular, the appearance of what is called "secondary intersubjectivity."

But for the moment let us return to Piaget. It turns out that even the A-not-B task has a social character. If you watch the YouTube video of the A-not-B error you may notice that the adult researcher responds to the infant's vocalizations and gestures as though these are bids at communication. The researcher is talking throughout the task, treating what the infant does as contributions to their interaction. For example, she asks that the object be returned to her, and while the infant is too young to place it into the researcher's hand she does seem to drop the object in a collaborative way. Researchers have noted that an experimenter is often in the position of a teacher "inasmuch as the infant's achievement also depended on the experimenter's attention to the infant's behavioral/emotional state and on optimal arrangements of learning tasks" (Papousek & Papousek, 2002, p. 184).

Indeed, 10-month-old infants commit the A-not-B error much less often when the object is hidden without the experimenter giving the usual communicative cues, such as eye contact, talking to the infant, using her name, and pointing or looking back and forth between the hiding location and the infant (Topál et al., 2008). This social dimension of laboratory research with infants has generally been ignored, presumably because we simply take for granted these patterns of adult interaction with very young children.

2.2 THE GREAT-WE OF INFANCY

The infant's dependency has the consequence that her ability to get things done in the world depends on other people's cooperation. From the outset the infant finds herself in a world that is throughly social, and the newborn has an innate "general relational capacity" (Selby & Bradley, 2003). The newborn's innate abilities, which I described in Chapter 4, are adaptations that predispose her to learn through interaction and communication with members of her family.

Although the infant may not appear very socially skilled she actually has a specific and unique kind of sociability, and we can in truth say that this provides the basis for all her future development. Dependent on other people and exquisitely tuned to them, the infant interacts with them in an embodied way and in doing so begins to learn her family's ways of doing things. As a result, during the first year of life the infant becomes increasingly skilled at communicating to other people what she wants from them. In a later section we shall see how this provides the basis for her active participation in the community of oral language.

However, the infant is already participating in the culture of her community, exploring the way her environment has been organized, and interacting with her caregivers. Here involvement also takes the form of people interacting with her using everyday artifacts. At first, all behavior—feeding, changing, moving—is possible only with other people's cooperation, so that the infant's contact with the world is largely **socially mediated**.

It is hard to judge the degree of self-consciousness of another person, but the evidence suggests that this early communality with others takes place before the infant becomes conscious of her own existence as a differentiated and separated "I." The infant is merged and intertwined in a shared situation, which Vygotsky called the **Great-We**. The term refers to a form of consciousness prior to the differentiation between a "you" and an "I." The Great-We of infancy provides the basis for a later differentiation in which an "I"—a first, simple sense of self-awareness—will start to form.

Infancy, Vygotsky wrote, is a time of a psychological life without a center: "He lives, but he is not conscious of his life himself" (Vygotsky, 1932–1934/1998, p. 233). Vygotsky referred to research (by Henri Wallon, a French philosopher and psychologist) on the child's understanding of the body: the infant doesn't at first distinguish her own body from objects in the world, then she becomes aware of objects before becoming aware of her body, and she first understands her own hands and feet as though they are foreign objects, learning to coordinate their movements before recognizing that they are parts of her own body.

Vygotsky also argued that for an infant the adult is at the center of every situation, and as adults come and go this "arms and disarms the activity of the child" (p. 231). The infant's contact with objects occurs within a context with other people. Sara Fajans, a colleague of the famous Gestalt psychologist Kurt Lewin, found that an infant loses interest in an object that is out of reach unless an adult moves close to that object. Then the infant becomes interested again, and with the object rather than with the adult (Fajans & Lewin, 1933). It seems that for the infant the perceived object changes its properties depending on the kind of structure it is part of, a structure that includes other people.

We can see the Great-We when infants act in ways that Piaget dismissed as "magical actions," such as reaching for an object when it is clearly out of reach. Vygotsky suggested that the infant is in fact trying to obtain an adult's help: "the infant's solipsistic behavior is actually social behavior characteristic of the infant's 'Great-We' consciousness" (Vygotsky, 1932–1934/1998, p. 241). This proposal bears upon the point I just made about laboratory research with infants. Such research is usually carried out with adults present—the researcher, and often the mother or father—and yet attention is not paid to the possibility that the infant is trying to influence these people. However, trying to influence others must be natural to an infant; it is the only way she can get anything done. Research is needed to explore the possibility that when an infant reaches towards location A instead of B, she is trying to elicit the help of other people to get back the hidden object.

2.3 UNDERSTANDING OTHER PEOPLE: THE CONTINGENT STANCE

How should we interpret the infant's growing capabilities in social interactions? What kind of understanding is she demonstrating of other people's actions, and of the social world? This question has become the focus of great interest, the center of attention in a number of laboratories of infant research. Does the infant come to recognize that people have mental states such as motives and desires? Is it even possible that the infant has begun to form a "theory of mind"?

In 1989 philosopher Daniel Dennett published an influential book titled *The Intentional Stance*. Dennett defined the **intentional stance** as a strategy of predicting and explaining the behavior of an entity—living or nonliving—by attributing to that entity beliefs, desires, and other "intentional" states.

A stance, as he defined it, is a cognitive-perceptual filter or bias that influences how the person interprets events. A stance is a specific way of interpreting the world.

However, the intentional stance is only one possible way to interpret the "complex system" that is a person. There is growing evidence that each stage of development involves a different stance. The stage of infancy involves what I will call the **contingent stance**.

The most likely explanation for the emergence of primary intersubjectivity is that the infant is paying attention to, and responding to, the "causal texture" of the world. **Contingency** is a fundamental property of this texture. Two events are "contingent" when from the occurrence of one the occurrence of the other is possible, but cannot be predicted with complete certainty. Evidence suggests that an infant uses contingency information to determine very rapidly whether something, or somebody, is responsive to her. Indeed, "All humans are capable of detecting rhythmic impulses and qualities of other persons' behaviors that are contingent upon and related emotionally to their own expressions" (Trevarthen & Aiken, 2001, p. 31).

Infants are sensitive to the contingencies between their own behavior and events in the environment; that is, to the degree of causal relatedness between stimuli and responses. For example, when her leg movements produce a movement in a hanging mobile, a young infant will pay attention and move her leg more vigorously. Perhaps the most important innate ability of the human infant is "The capacity to accurately interpret stimulation as contingent or not" (Gergely & Watson, 1999, p. 101).

Detecting contingencies is important for coming to understand how physical objects operate. But it is central to coming to understand social interactions. From this perspective, what is most important in the face-to-face interactions of protoconversation is their contingencies: the way that one event in the exchange depends on the occurrence of another. Detailed microanalysis of these early interactions has indeed found that the adult unconsciously responds in a way that is contingent on the infant's actions, adjusting to her behavioral state and displays of emotion (Papousek & Papousek, 2002). When this contingency is disrupted, the infant quickly reacts. For example, when an infant interacts with her mother's live image on a video monitor all is well, but when a recording of the mother is played instead, the infant becomes upset because the contingencies are now missing (Murray & Trevarthen, 1985).

Similarly, the **still-face experiment**, where the person interacting with the infant holds their face still for a while, shows how sensitive the young infant is to the contingency pattern of face-to-face interaction, and how she will actively search to reestablish this pattern when it is disrupted. The infant quickly becomes distressed and even depressed in this situation (Papousek, 2007).

It is likely that by paying attention to contingencies, infants become able to understand other people's behavior in terms of their **dispositions**—their characteristic inclinations or tendencies (Watson, 2005a). For example, a mother may tend to be friendly on some days, and inclined to be impatient on other days. Impatience and friendliness are dispositions, in both the psychological sense and the statistical sense: a disposition is a tendency to respond with certain contingencies to specific events. The ability to grasp dispositions by detecting contingencies is an example of how a person's behavior can be understood without having to infer mental beliefs and desires, or even wishes and goals.

The following example illustrates how an infant can come to interpret her mother's behavior as a sign of her dispositions. Notice that the mother is also interpreting her infant's signs:

Imagine an infant who enjoys extended interaction with his mom. Sometimes when she tucks him in and he smiles at her, she turns out the light and leaves. Sometimes, however, she tucks him in and if he smiles, she picks him up again and interacts with him for a while longer. Alternatively, if he pouts when she tucks him in, sometimes she leaves but other times she picks him up and interacts a little longer. As a determinist [Watson uses the term "determinist stance" rather than "contingent stance"], our infant rejects the notion that his mother is behaving randomly. The fact that she might be caused to stay (or likewise caused to leave) by a smile or a pout presents no special problem, since lawfulness allows alternative causes for a specific kind of effect. However, the fact that his smile (and likewise his pout) appears to sometimes cause her leaving and sometimes cause her staying in an otherwise equivalent situation calls for remedy of the infant's formulation of the lawful efficacy of his behavior. He needs to posit a disposition of state in his mother in order to maintain his commitment to determinism. With additional experience on his part, we might imagine ... that he will eventually uncover cues to her state variation that he has been logically forced to assume. If he is successful, then he will cope well with the fact that, in this example, his mother sometimes has rewarding days at work and sometimes has days that have depleted her reserves of nurturance. On rewarding days she views his smile as a sign he is content (so she leaves) but his pout as a sign that he needs additional comforting (so she picks him up). On her difficult days, she views his smile as a sunny reprieve (so she picks him up) but his pout as a sign that he is asking for unnecessary support that she is not prepared to give at this time. (Watson, 2005b)

Detecting contingencies is important not only for making sense of other people's behavior, it may also enable the infant to become aware of her *own* dispositional states—that is, her own emotions. Caregivers often respond to and reflect their infant's displays of emotion, in ways that are contingent on those displays. This provides an opportunity for the infant to develop a dawning awareness of her own emotions and to start to control them (Gergely & Watson, 1999).

Emotions in infancy are, as I will describe in the next chapter, instinctive and involuntary responses to environmental events. Caregivers spend a lot of time monitoring, interpreting, and evaluating their infant's displays of emotion, and responding in a contingent manner. The caregivers' responses to an upset infant can help calm her, and at the same time can provide an opportunity for the infant to learn that her display of emotion will lead to regulation of that emotion, via the route of another person. This process of **social-biofeedback** builds on the infant's natural capacity to detect contingencies and respond to them, and on the adult's tendency to respond to the infant's emotions in specific ways. Together, the two participants constitute a system: "The currently dominant biosocial view of emotional development holds that mother and infant form an affective communication system from the beginning of life ... in which the mother plays a vital interactive role in modulating the infant's affective states" (Gergely & Watson, 1999, p. 112). In short, the infant's ability to detect contingencies provides the basis for the subtle interactions with caregivers that involve her in her family and culture from the very start.

We shall see in the following section that researchers have begun to identify culture-specific patterns of contingency between mothers and infants, and are exploring their developmental consequences.

3. CARING FOR THE INFANT

3.1 IS PARENTING INTUITIVE?

Taking care of the infant is a necessity in every part of the world, and one might think that the relatively simple and persisting demands made by infants would lead to a universal pattern of caretaking. Researchers have debated the question of whether there is a biologically based prototypical form of infant care: in particular, whether it is the biological mother who should have primary responsibility for an infant. This has been the position of some psychiatrists (e.g., Bowlby, 1980; Spitz, 1965), as well as pediatricians (Klauss & Kennell, 1976), and ethologists (Blurton-Jones, 1972).

For example, parenting has often been described in terms of **maternal sensitivity**: "sensitive responsiveness to infant signals and communications" (Ainsworth et al., 1978, p. 152). Sensitivity is defined as a mother's ability to perceive the infant's signals accurately and to respond to them promptly and appropriately. But what is an accurate perception? What is an appropriate response? Caregiving is not only a matter of responding to signals, it is also a matter of interpreting these signals, and caregivers' interpretations depend on their own values and expectations and on the norms of their culture. As we shall see below, systematic differences in maternal responsiveness exist in different cultural settings.

Furthermore, caregiving involves more than paying attention to the physical needs of an infant, it is also a matter of engaging her in the social interactions which we have seen provide opportunities for learning and development.

Researchers continue to debate the extent to which parenting practices are universal and innate, and the extent to which they vary from one culture to another. On the one hand, as we saw in the previous section, mothers and fathers in many different cultures tend to behave in a gentle, playful way with their newborn. On the assumption that this behavior is unconscious and doesn't need to be learned it has been called **intuitive parenting** (Papousek, 2007).

However, we have to be careful before assuming that such "intuitive parenting" is universal, or innate. Caregivers may respond unthinkingly to the smiles and frowns of their infant, but these unconscious reactions may be quite different from one culture to another. It has been suggested that all parents share the tasks of caring for their infant, socializing her, and transmitting culture to her (Bornstein, 2002). Nonetheless, before we accept this proposal we would need to spell out what is meant by "socialization" and "transmission." Socialization seems the wrong term if it means that the infant needs to *become* social for, as we have seen, the newborn already has an innate sociality, and adults adapt the practices of their culture to include her. Transmission doesn't seem the correct term either, as we saw in Chapter 3—certainly, there is much about any culture that caregivers do not deliberately transmit to their child, in large part because they take it for granted and don't notice it. Learning the ways of a culture is an active process on the part of the child, not merely a matter of transmission.

3.2 PARENTING, CULTURE, AND ECOLOGY

Moreover, caregiving depends on much more than the characteristics and capacities of the infant. Anthropologists have since the mid-twentieth century explored the relationship between parenting and culture, and a brief summary of the history of this research will set the stage for our examination of caregiving in the different stages of children's development, both in this chapter and those that follow (Harkness & Super, 2002).

Early on there was a strong interest in how the customs, practices, or belief systems of a culture lead parents to structure the experiences of their children in such a way as to create a specific type of personality, typical for the community. Ethnographers turned to psychology, in particular to Freud, in efforts to see if, for example, Oedipal conflicts exist in matrilineal societies. In one analysis, the Ifaluk practices of bathing infants each day in cold water and weaning them abruptly were seen as creating a sense that the world is threatening, explaining the persisting belief in malevolent ghosts in Ifaluk society. In another example, political differences between the Gusii and Nuer, pastoral communities in Africa, seemed related to differences in father–son relationships.

An interest rapidly grew in exploring how parenting was shaped by the local ecological circumstances of the community. One such investigation was carried out by Barry et al. (1959) in a comparison of 104 cultures. Their conclusion was that child rearing tends to be an adaptation to the "subsistence economy" of the community: the way the local environment is exploited for food. Hunting and gathering societies, which are not able to accumulate a surplus of food, tend to foster initiative, self-reliance, and independence in their children. In contrast, pastoral and agricultural societies, which are able to generate and store a surplus of food, tend to encourage obedience and responsibility. In general, this correlation between the "economy" and parenting is due to the ways parents involve children in various kinds of work, but it begins in the way parents handle and relate to their infants. The distinction between self-reliance and achievement on the one hand, and obedience and responsibility on the other, has continued to be important for research in this area, as we shall see below.

Anthropologists John and Beatrice Whiting organized the *Six Cultures Study of Socialization*, a large comparative study of child rearing and child development conducted in the 1960s. They proposed a general model of the relevant causal relationships (see Figure 5.8 below). In this model, childrearing depends upon the "domestic organization" of the family, which in turn rests upon the basic "maintenance systems" of a society, which in turn are determined by its local ecology. The maintenance systems include the basic economy and elementary aspects of social structure. The crops that can be grown, and the success of fishing, hunting, or herding animals, will depend on the soil, the rainfall, and linkages to other communities, with whom goods can be exchanged along with innovative ideas. These aspects of how the community derives a living from the local ecology influence the ways that dwellings are constructed and arranged spatially, and the way the household is organized: the size of the family, relations among the generations, the sexual division of labor, and so on. The practices of child rearing—who takes care of the infant, tasks assigned to older children, discipline—then depend upon this domestic organization. The Whitings hypothesized that the learned aspects of adult personality would be the products of these childrearing practices, and personality would be expressed in aspects of the culture: religion and magic, ritual and recreation, even rates of crime and suicide (LeVine, 2010; Whiting, 1963).

The Six Cultures Study tested this model with a detailed investigation of societies at the high end of the "food accumulation" dimension. The fieldwork included naturalistic observations of children between 3 and 11 years of age. The focus was on identifying the cultural pressures for parents to encourage either nurturant-responsible behavior in their children, or dependent-dominant behavior. The effect

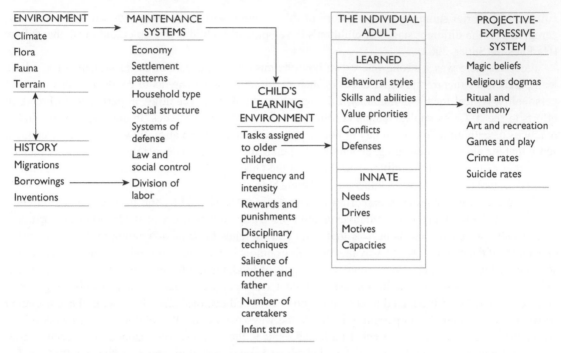

Figure 5.8 Whiting's model for psychocultural research

Source: Whiting (1977)

of parenting was assumed to take place in daily routines that were dictated by environmental factors. The main finding was that the "complexity" of the culture was an important factor. Simpler societies require cooperation, while complex societies, with a hierarchical structure and multiple roles, require competitiveness. In simpler societies, household tasks are carried out by women with their children helping. In more complex societies, children are not involved in adult work. Both the quantity and character of children's tasks were important in encouraging a nurturant-responsible attitude. In this model, culture was viewed as a "provider of settings," while parents were viewed as "organizers of settings" in which children develop. In particular, parents "assign" children to settings in which they then interact with different kinds of people.

The finding of a general association between economic subsistence and child-rearing practices and goals has been corroborated in many small-scale, non-Western, traditional societies.

3.3 ETHNOGRAPHIES OF INFANCY

In the 1960s researchers started to fill a gap in the Six Cultures Study: they conducted ethnographic studies of infancy and infant care, mostly in sub-Saharan Africa but also in Japan, and among the Navajo of New Mexico (many were reprinted in LeVine & New, 2008). Infants do have simple needs, but this means that great variation is possible in how those needs are met. Anthropologists have now documented a wide variation in the arrangements made for infants in different cultures. They have paid particular attention to hunter-gatherer societies, assuming, rightly or wrongly, that this lifestyle resembles that of early Homo sapiens, since, as we saw in Chapter 2, agriculture was invented only 15,000 years ago. Let us consider some examples of such cultures.

A study of infant care among the !Kung bush people in Botswana found that mothers are indulgent with their infants, and place few restrictions on them (Hewlett et al.,1998). They care for the infants in a dense social context, in constant contact with relatives and friends. At night the infant sleeps beside the mother. The !Kung believe that lying down while awake is bad for the infant and so when not sitting the infant is held in a sling on the mother's hip, which provides access to the breast. The infant is fed whenever she cries, or when she is in the sling she feeds whenever she wishes. Weaning is gradual and may continue until the child is 4 or 5 if a sibling isn't born. At the end of the first year the infant begins to spend more of her time with a multi-age group of children.

!Kung infants and children are ahead of American children in tests of motor skills. In contrast, children of the Ache, in eastern Paraguay, are behind in these tests: infant Ache start walking around a year later than average. This is because the Ache live and forage in the subtropical forests. They move camp frequently, and rarely clear ground or build structures. The women focus their attention on childcare, generally doing very little work while they are carrying an infant, and children younger than three years of age stay very close to their mother: they are within a meter of her almost all the time, and in physical contact more than 80 percent of the time. Mothers are reluctant to let their infants or toddlers explore. The young children themselves only leave their mother's lap tentatively and for brief periods. Infants are almost never punished, and obtain what they want by whining and crying. When they are older they are usually obedient and helpful. However, the lack of opportunities to move around and explore the environment leads to delays in the achievement of milestones in motor development during infancy, such as sitting up, crawling, and walking. That this is not due to intrinsic biological differences is shown by the fact that older children quickly make up for these delays. They spend much of their time climbing high trees, and chopping branches and lianas with machetes. They become much more physically skilled than children the same age in the USA.

The Efe are hunters and gatherers in the forests of the Democratic Republic of Congo (formerly Zaire). They live in small groups of one or more extended families and forage with bow and arrow, or work as laborers in nearby farm communities. The Efe employ a system of multiple caretaking (Tronick et al., 1992). They live in camps of from 6 to 50 people and are semi-nomadic, moving every four to six weeks. They value cooperation, sharing and identification, and there is continuous social contact and interaction among community members. Infants spend a lot of time away from their mothers, passed among many individuals and suckled by other women. Their access to plenty of milk and continual physical contact meets the infant's need for nutrition and warmth, in an environment where the temperature is between 22 and 17 degrees Celsius. Toddlers are free to wander around the camp to watch adults at their work, making tools or cooking, and they are allowed to enter, uninvited, into most of the huts. From the age of 3 young children go with their parents to gather food, collect firewood, and work in the gardens. There are very few activities where adults focus exclusively on their children; instead the children participate alongside adults in whatever they are doing. We will explore the opportunities this provides for learning and development in Chapters 6 and 7.

Among the Aka, hunter-gatherers in central Africa, fathers provide more direct care for their infant than in any other human group that has been investigated. A study here included behavior observations of infants aged 3 to 4 months and 9 to 10 months and their caregivers. The data showed that an Aka father will be close to his infant or holding her on average more than 50 percent of every 24-hour period. In this community father and mother have virtually interchangeable roles. This pattern is in part a consequence of the fact that adults spend about 80 percent of their time hunting and gathering. Men and women collaborate to hunt hogs, duikers (small deer), and monkeys with woven nets, with the men driving the animals and the women killing them once they are caught. The fact that the women are involved in this activity means that infants are carried on the hunt, in a sling on their mother's hip, which gives the fathers an opportunity to contribute to their care. It also means that older children (or grandmothers) do not take care of infants, as occurs in many other hunter-gatherer societies, because they are not able to carry the infants on the long trips that hunting requires (Hewlett et al., 1998).

Aka husband and wife cooperate extensively and spend much time together, not only when hunting but also when in camp. Presumably this enables the infant to form emotional attachments to both of them, and this may be another reason why caregiving by the father is so prevalent. A father's care varies with the setting: he will spend more time with his young children when he is in their camp than when he is involved in economic activity in the fields or hunting. The Aka are patrilineal and patrilocal, meaning they live with the father's family or nearby. They value sharing, cooperation, non-violence, and independence. They live in camps of around 25 to 35 people, and they move to a new location every three or four months. Infant mortality is high: a female Aka will have an average of 6.3 live births, but 20 percent of infants will die before they are a year old. Although the degree of the father's involvement does not seem to relate to child mortality, an Aka infant who is born without a known father usually dies within six months.

This new anthropology of infant development, with its detailed observations of infant behavior and interactions in a cultural context, confirmed not only that infants were already participating in the practices of their communities, but also that striking variations existed in infant care among hunter-gatherer communities.

Notwithstanding the variations among such societies, agricultural societies are different again. One agricultural community that has been studied is that of the Zinacantecos. These people live in settled households, which presumably can be made safer than the jungle or forest. In such circumstances, a mother tends to delegate the care of an infant to her older children, and she spends more of her own time involved in working rather than in childcare. This may seem surprising, but the arrangement provides stimulation to the infant and may promote her development.

In addition, the researchers who studied the Aka made similar observations with the Ngandu, an agricultural community who live in the same tropical forest. Despite the infant mortality rates being similar to those of the Aka, Ngandu infants were both more stimulated by their caregivers and more often left alone. They were carried on the back rather than in slings, they were dressed more completely, and small chairs, beds and mats were made for them. The difference between the Aka and Ngandu confirms that local ecology alone does not determine parenting, rather what plays a role is the style of subsistence—foraging versus agriculture.

From about 7000 BC until around two hundred years ago, the majority of children lived in agrarian societies, centered around agriculture. Today, although many children still live in such communities, many more live in urban and industrialized settings: in cities. Fundamental differences can be seen in how these two ways of living arrange childhood. In an agricultural society, children provide labor for their parents and offer them security in old age, consequently it makes sense for parents to have many children. In an urban, industrialized society, family ties are less strong and parents expect to contribute to their children's growth and education without receiving much in return, because children are expected to become autonomous, moving away from home to follow their own line of work and form their own family. The child-bearing years are relatively short, and old age is usually a time of few contacts with offspring. These differences in the relationship between parent and child become evident as early as infancy, as we shall see.

In short, different environments present different challenges to the health and well-being of infant and child, and caregivers will focus on meeting those challenges. Where infant mortality is high, caregivers will focus on health and survival. Where economic competition is fierce, caregivers will want their children to learn how to work and gain an income (LeVine & White, 1987).

These ethnographies draw attention to the wide variation in circumstances of infancy. We have already mentioned the variation in infant mortality across the globe. Those cultures in which infant mortality is high tend to be those in which mothers must work long and hard to obtain the basic necessities of life. In the West we tend to think of the first year of life as a time when infants and parents, especially mothers, should have close and intimate contact. But in impoverished communities such contact may be impossible, and it may be undesirable in the sense that parents may be reluctant to form close emotional bonds with their infant when the chances are high that their child will die.

3.4 SPECIFIC PRACTICES OF INFANT CARE

As we saw in the previous chapter, an example of a caregiving practice that varies widely across cultures is the decision over something as seemingly simple as where, and with whom, the baby sleeps (Shweder et al., 1995). The question of which family members share sleeping space always evokes strong feelings about what is right or wrong, but there is considerable variation across cultures. In North America the infant is usually not expected to sleep in the parents' bed, at least in white middle-class families. Outside the USA, however, this attitude is often viewed as cruel. In Japan, infants usually sleep with their parents, and co-sleeping continues until early adolescence. Not to sleep in this way is seen as very strange (Caudill & Plath, 1966). Research in a Hindu town in India found that sleeping was arranged so that young children were protected at night by sleeping with someone older. In addition, unmarried girls should not sleep alone so their chastity can be protected, and arrangements for older brothers and sisters prevent incest. If to do this requires that a husband and wife must sleep apart, this is not considered a problem (Shweder et al.,1995).

Similarly, in a Mayan community in Guatamala, infants slept with their mother until a new sibling arrived; then they moved into someone else's bed. Throughout childhood, both boys and girls generally slept with other family members (Morelli et al., 1992).

The issue of who sleeps alongside whom is resolved by making social arrangements of space and time which the infant inevitably participates in, and which become routine and customary. The social circumstances of a family are experienced as a natural necessity by the infant, who without knowing it has entered the specific social position that her family occupies in the community.

3.5 PROXIMAL AND DISTAL STYLES

In another move to make sense of the cultural variation of caregiving, researchers have identified distinct styles of caregiving with infants: the distal style and the proximal style (Keller et al., 2004).

Heidi Keller and her colleagues compared a sample of middle-class families living in Athens, Greece, with a sample of families in the rural Nso community in the Cameroon. The first of these is considered a culture of *independence*, in which autonomy and separateness are valued. The second is considered a culture of *interdependence*, in which hierarchy, obedience, and respect are valued. As we have seen, traditional agricultural societies tend to have these values of interdependence.

Families were visited in their home when their infants were 3 months of age, and again between 18 and 20 months. A free-play situation was videotaped, and analysis of the interaction between mother and infant disclosed two distinct styles.

The Greek mothers tended to emphasize face-to-face interaction with mutual eye contact, and the displaying of objects to the infant. The researchers called this the **distal parenting style**, because the mothers kept their infant at a distance, and they hypothesized that this style established a framework of mutuality between mother and infant, within which the infant had a relatively high degree of control over the interaction, and that it started the infant along a developmental trajectory towards independence and autonomy. (This is the style we saw early in face-to-face protoconversation.)

The Nso mothers, in contrast, emphasized body contact and physical stimulation. The researchers called this the **proximal parenting style**, and they hypothesized that this style promoted interdependence, unity and fusion rather than separateness, and established synchrony between mother and infant, rather than reciprocity.

In Chapter 7 I will describe the relationship between these styles of interaction in infancy and measures of later development, including the toddler's self-recognition at 20 months of age. Here, I want to describe two further developments of this line of research.

First, Relindis Yovsi extended the study of parenting style into the practice of breastfeeding (Yovsi & Keller, 2003). She visited two ethnic groups in Cameroon: the sedentary Nso farmers we have already met and nomadic Fulani pastorals. These two groups live in the same region, they suffer similar degrees of poor health in a dangerous environment and the same high rate of infant mortality, but they have different economic systems, and correspondingly different values and goals for their children's development.

Among the Nso, who live in a subsistence-based farming ecology, the infant is cared for not only by her parents and relatives but also by neighbors, since childcare is considered a responsibility of the whole community. As we have seen, the Nso value interdependence. They encourage in their children obedience and respect for authority, a responsibility to others, and a commitment to social harmony. Breastfeeding of infants is highly encouraged, because it brings mother and child together and also because the community values strong healthy children.

Among the Fulani, in contrast, children are cared for only by their immediate family, including older siblings. After birth the grandmother takes the infant away so her mother can rest. Since the Fulani believe that colostrum is bad for the infant, she is fed only water until the mother's breast milk is available. After that, the infant is breast fed for about two years, due to the belief that a child not fully breastfed will mismanage the herd and tend to depend on other people for a living.

Among the Fulani, eye contact between children and parents is forbidden, because it is believed that intimacy should not be part of their relationship. Hugging and holding are considered erotic and sexual, and are forbidden between parent and child. It is said that if a mother shows interest in her child the evil eye will curse or kill the child. The Fulani, who have to protect, manage, and accumulate their cattle, value competence, a respect for elders, commitment, and self-reliance.

When their infants were around 4 months of age Yovsi visited each family in the two communities and observed a routine breastfeeding session. Infant and mother behaviors were coded. Nso and Fulani mothers differed significantly in their modes of interaction during breastfeeding. The Nso engaged more in tight body contact, tactile stimulation, and were more involved. Infant and mother often smiled at one another. The Nso mothers were concerned and responsive to cues from their infant, with the consequence that the infant was kept in an alert state. The Fulani were more distant and less affectionate with their infants during breastfeeding. They engaged in very little eye contact, generally looking away from the infant, and were unlikely to respond to cues such as vocalizations or movements.

This identification of differences in style of mother–infant interaction is important, but so too is the implication that in *every* culture the infant is encouraged through everyday practices of caregiving to become the kind of person that is valued in her culture. This investigation shows us that breastfeeding not only meets the nutritional needs of the infant, it is also an adaptive process in which parental goals are embodied in the practical activity in which mother and infant interact. The infant is learning to participate in the practices of her community in such a way that her development begins to follow a specific trajectory.

The second extension of the research on proximal and distal parenting styles is the proposal by Joscha Kärtner that these two styles begin to establish distinct developmental trajectories because they involve culture-specific patterns of contingency. Kärtner (2015) applied the social-biofeedback model (Gergely & Watson, 1996) that we discussed earlier in this chapter to review similarities and differences in maternal contingent responsiveness toward infants, in research with 159 3-month-olds across six different sociocultural contexts. His conclusion was that systematic and predictable differences in contingency patterns did exist across these cultures. There is strong evidence that visual contingencies are significantly higher in cultures that value autonomy and independence (such as Berlin and Los Angeles), whereas in cultures that value relation and interdependence, such as the Nso families, the contingencies occur in the proximal modality.

For example, in a comparison between middle-class German and Nso mothers, the pattern of mothers' contingent responsiveness to their infant was identical at 4 and 6 weeks after the birth, but differences started to emerge around week 8. By week 12, the Nso mothers were showing significantly higher levels of proximal contingent responses to their infant. The German mothers, in contrast, showed a steady increase in visual contingencies during the second and third months, and a steady decrease in proximally contingent responses during this time. That is, they shifted from a proximal to a visual (distal) style.

As a result, infants in the two cultures were already very different at the time of the "two-month transition," when, as we saw earlier, face-to-face social interactions between infant and adult increase greatly. This increase did indeed take place for the German infants. However, the pattern of the two-month transition was very different for the Nso infants. Like the German babies they showed a sharp increase in awake alertness between the ages of 6 and 8 weeks, but their mothers offered them little opportunity

	Distal Style	Proximal Style
Characteristics	Face-to-face interaction; stimulation with objects	Body contact and physical stimulation
Caregivers' values	Independence and autonomy	Interdependence, compliance and obedience
Developmental outcomes during infancy	Social smiling from 2 months	Absence of social smiling
Cultures	Urban families in Athens, Berlin, Los Angeles	Nso and others

Figure 5.9   The distal and proximal caregiving styles

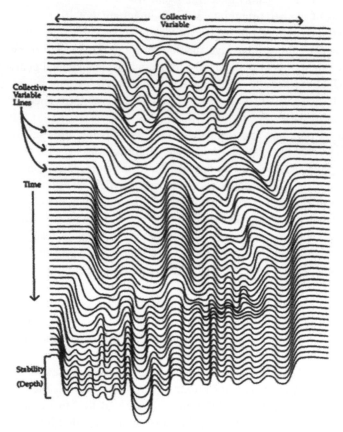

Figure 5.10   Development depicted as an epigenetic landscape

Source: Thelen (1995)

Copyright © 1995 by the American Psychological Association

for face-to-face interaction, and their interest in their mothers' faces (i.e., their gazing behavior) did not increase with age. In fact, the amount of mutual gaze remained low from 1 month of age to 3 months of age.

Evidently, the face-to-face interactions of primary intersubjectivity and social smiling are not universal characteristics of infant development, but are characteristics of specific cultures with specific caregiving styles and particular goals for development. For the Nso the ideal infant is emotionally neutral, and calmness is considered desirable. Smiling and laughing are considered signs of overexcitement and a disruption of emotional equilibrium (Kärtner et al., 2013). Nso mothers spontaneously interact with their infants in ways that foster precisely these desired characteristics, though they would be judged "insensitive" by Western standards.

This divergence of possible trajectories during development has been described in terms of an **epigenetic landscape** (Waddington, 1940). In the figure each horizontal line is a slice in time, and the curves represent the probability that the

Figure 5.11   Nso mother encouraging motor development

Source: Keller (2003)

system will adopt a specific behavioral configuration, represented as a valley. Development can be visualized as a movement towards increasing possibilities, represented by the larger number of valleys as time moves downward. But along the way choices must be made—one valley will be followed rather than another, and some possibilities are lost because there is no turning back. Shallow valleys are easier to move out of, deeper valleys are harder. The term for a process of development that can follow any one of many trajectories is **equifinality**: many ends are possible.

Figure 5.12   Nso, practice in walking

Source: Keller (2003)

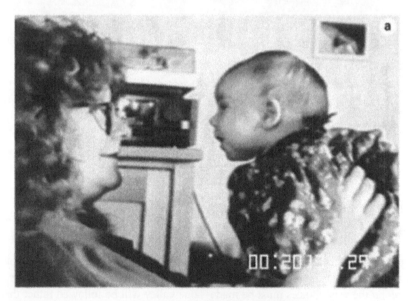

Figure 5.13   German mother engaging her infant in face-to-face interaction

Source: Keller (2003)

3.6 CAREGIVING AS NICHE CONSTRUCTION

One final way that caregiving and parenting have been conceptualized is in terms of the construction of a "developmental niche" or "ontogenetic niche." This approach has obvious connections with the proposal in Chapter 3 that evolution involves organisms that actively construct for themselves and their offspring an environmental niche. Human caregiving can be considered as a "culturally constructed interface between the larger environment and the development of children" (Super & Harkness, 2002, p. 271). The emphasis here is not so much on why parenting varies from culture to culture, but on how parenting works. Caregivers not only choose settings and establish routine activities within these settings, they also actively construct the settings in which they interact with their children.

Adult organisms of many species make material arrangements for their offspring, specialized niches that foster their development, survival, and in time their reproduction, and humans are no exception. In ecology these specialized arrangements are known as "ontogenetic niches" (Werner & Gilliam, 1984). These niches are enormously diverse—even with young infants they range from pouches in which they are carried (Tronick et al., 1994), to the cribs in which they sleep, the nurseries in which they are sheltered, and many more. These are adaptive modifications of the environment, to which not only parents contribute but also other kinds of caregiver, and they reflect historically shaped customs and practices of care and rearing. They also result from parents' beliefs about development and their aspirations for their children.

One influential proposal has been that the human **developmental niche** comprises three subsystems. First is the physical and social setting. Second are the historically formed customs and practices of childcare and child rearing. Third is the psychology of the caretakers, in particular their **ethnotheories** about childcare: these are, by definition, shared with other members of the community (Harkness & Super, 1994; Super & Harkness, 1986).

Charles Super and Sara Harkness suggest that the operation of these subsystems has several important consequences for the child's development. One of these is **redundancy**, the repetition of influences from several parts of the niche in a way that is mutually reinforcing. A second is **thematic elaboration**, the repetition and accumulation of significant symbols and interpretive frameworks. A third is **chaining**, in which no single element of the niche is sufficient to produce a particular outcome but the linking of disparate elements creates qualitatively new phenomena (Super & Harkness, 2002).

The notion of the ontogenetic niche contributes to what Harkness and Super (2002) have described as the central challenge to our understanding of caregiving in a cultural context—"reconceptualizing culture in relation to development," namely recognizing that culture is a dynamic system not a static entity. This calls, in their view, for the "developmental study of culture," an exploration of how culture "is created across the lifespans of individuals in families and communities" (2002, p. 276). How the developing child becomes capable of contributing to this continuous recreation of culture is a significant aspect of the account in this book.

In conclusion, faced with their newborn, adults have to adapt to their new role as parents. The dependence of the newborn baby has obvious implications for her caregivers, who have to provide for their new arrival. They have to arrange every aspect of their baby's daily activity, from feeding and sleeping to changing diapers and clothing. But parents will have to balance their own growth and development with their investment in their new charge. They will also have to balance the needs of the child with the requirements of work and the other daily demands of their family and community.

At the same time, of course, infants change their parents. As Marc Bornstein has pointed out, "By their very coming into existence, infants forever alter the sleeping, eating, and working habits of their parents; they change who parents are and how parents define themselves" (Bornstein, 2002, p. 3). It seems most accurate to say that infants and caregivers are necessarily involved in each other's activity, and because the parents are already skilled in the ways of the culture the infant starts to engage with cultural artifacts, learning the ways of her community and starting to understand the social world in which she lives.

Parents also take for granted a certain balance of relatedness and autonomy. As a consequence, they start to adopt a style of caregiving which unconsciously fosters a specific pathway in their baby's development (Kagitcibasi in Chapter 10). Since infancy is that stage of maximal dependency, the infant is generally woven especially tightly into the caregivers' daily activity, especially that of the mother.

Whatever arrangement a culture makes for an infant's care, her dependence means that she has no other option but to be deeply involved with caregivers. In addition, her sensibilities and sensitivities, including the dramatic ongoing growth and development of the brain which we have discussed, mean that she will be importantly influenced by these involvements.

I have emphasized that the human infant lives in a social world, within which her actions are mediated by other people. I have called this social situation of infancy the "Great-We." Parenting is a matter of how adults make arrangements in order to meet an infant's needs, since she cannot satisfy these needs by herself. The practices of parenting vary from one culture to another, as do the beliefs and expectations about their infants' development that parents express when psychologists interview them. This suggests that even if parenting has some kind of biological basis, so that "intuitive parenting" is spontaneous, parenting is also a product of culture. Indeed, we should surely expect this.

Parents are adults who have grown up in a particular culture and learned to be skilled in its practices. It is inevitable that their skills and attitudes play a role in the way they respond to an infant. This means, however, that parenting is not just a matter of taking care, it is also a **pedagogic interaction**. The social moment in development is of central importance.

Adaptive needs	Population-level patterns	Cultural goals of child care
Subsistence: Provision of food	Economic systems: foraging, agrarian, industrial	Economic competence
Reproduction: Somatic continuity	Marriage and kinship systems, demographic regimes, norms of infant care	Childbearing and survival, acquisition of gender roles
Communication: Sharing of information	Languages and other symbol systems	Communicative competence
Social regulation: Maintenance of order	Social hierarchies, conventions of face-to-face relations	Self-control, situationally appropriate behavior

Figure 5.14 Framework for the comparative analysis of child care

Source: LeVine et al. (1996)

CONCLUSION

The newborn enters the stage of infancy completely dependent on other people, and sensitively attuned to those people. Infancy is a year of important learning, as the infant builds a practical understanding of the world around her. This is a cultural world, with social spaces, times, and artifacts; the infant lives in an "ontogenetic niche" that has been constructed by her caregivers to meet her needs (and theirs) in a manner that reflects their projections of her future. Of course, the infant understands this niche in a very simple way. She is sensitive primarily to the contingencies of events—the conditional relationships between what she does and what other people and objects do. Adult responses to her emotions, for example, provide an opportunity to grasp contingencies. This is a very basic level of understanding: the infant does not yet even recognize that something that has been partly hidden is still a whole object. Yet this simple, practical understanding paves the way for what is to follow.

The infant's practical understanding can be viewed in a variety of ways. It can be understood in terms of the *schemas of sensorimotor intelligence*. An emphasis can be placed on *primary intersubjectivity* (and later on *secondary intersubjectivity*). It can also be considered the operation of the unconscious and intuitive *System 1*. And it can be viewed as a *grasp of contingencies*.

In other words, infancy is a stage when the perception–action cycle (see Chapter 4, section 1.4.3) is functioning on its most fundamental levels. For an infant, to see something is to act towards it, though her action generally requires the assistance of another person. Perception, action, emotion, sociality are all aspects of an infant's way of being in the world; they have not yet become distinct. We lose sight of this important fact when we study, or write about, infancy in terms of distinct domains of physical, social, emotional, and cognitive development.

Caregivers the world over probably share many goals and concerns for their infants. Yet the diverse circumstances in which they live prompt them to employ different caregiving styles. Some aspects of caregiving may be intuitive and innate, but many aspects have to be learned: from relatives, from experts, or through trial and error. Caregivers play an especially crucial role at this stage in a child's development. They do for the infant what she cannot do for herself, and this is a matter not only of her biology—feeding and cleaning her—but also of her psychology.

SUMMARY

THE INFANT'S PRACTICAL UNDERSTANDING

Infancy is a stage of what Piaget called "sensorimotor" intelligence. He proposed that the infant is actively constructing a practical understanding of the world: of space, time, causality, and objects. Researchers working with different theoretical frameworks have different views about what this practical understanding consists of.

(Continued)

(Continued)

THE WORLD OF INFANCY: THE "GREAT-WE"

The extreme dependence of the human infant means that all her action in the world must be mediated by other people. The infant lives in a Great-We, in which she has not yet differentiated psychologically from her caregivers. The infant is able to detect contingencies in her interactions with other people—technically speaking, the conditional probabilities between stimulus events and responses, and in more simple terms, the degree to which events happen together. When adults respond contingently to an infant, they provide bio-social feedback.

CARING FOR THE INFANT

Ethnographic studies of caregiving in different cultures have found great variety in how the simple, basic needs of infants are met. Two particular caregiving styles have been identified: the distal style, which encourages independence and autonomy, and the proximal style, which encourages interdependence and obedience.

FURTHER READING

LeVine, R. A., & New, R. S. (2008). *Anthropology and Child Development: A Cross-cultural Reader*. Malden, MA: Blackwell.

Learn more about Dynamic Field Theory:

www.uiowa.edu/delta-center/research/dft/index.html

Shonkoff, J. P., & Phillips, D. (2000). *From Neurons to Neighborhoods: The Science of Early Childhood Development*. Washington, DC: National Academies Press.

'Shaping the Developing Brain: Prenatal through Early Childhood': Fifth Annual Aspen Brain Forum, November 11–13, 2014, The New York Academy of Sciences:

www.nyas.org/Events/Detail.aspx?cid=4757ae98-7fa3-4f07-a77d-d8693dd50a42

ONLINE RESOURCES

See the A-not-B error on YouTube:

www.youtube.com/watch?v=lhHkJ3InQOE

CHAPTER 6

INFANCY

(6 WEEKS–12 MONTHS)
TOWARDS BIOLOGICAL DIFFERENTIATION

LEARNING OBJECTIVES

In this chapter we continue our examination of the first stage of human development, infancy. We will consider:

- The emotions of infancy, and how at this age emotion is distributed between infant and adult.

- The dramatic and highly important biological and physiological changes during the first year of life.

- The transition that occurs towards the end of the first year, when the abilities to move independently and to speak recognizable words are aspects of an important change: a biological separation from significant others that involves new strengths as well as new anxieties.

In studying these aspects of infancy you will come to understand how the world of the infant slowly changes, leading to an important developmental transition around 12 months of age.

FRAMING QUESTIONS

- What is an emotion? Can you define emotion? Can you list the constituents of an emotion such as anger?

- During the first year of life, the infant's brain doubles in its weight. What changes inside the brain do you think might be going on?

- Consider how your life would be different if you were unable to walk or talk.

INTRODUCTION

In Chapter 4 I emphasized the helpless and dependency of the human newborn when compared with the young of other species. It takes the human infant a year to reach the level of motor development of a newborn great ape. This helplessness pays off in the channeling of resources to the brain growth and development that we explored in the first section of this chapter. The cost, however, is that the newborn baby cannot survive without help from other people. This dependency must convey some advantage to the newborn, or it would not have been selected through evolution. As I suggested in Chapter 4, the advantage appears to be that the human infant is malleable and receptive, open to learning the specific practices of her family and community. Human development appears to involve **canalization**: the newborn is adaptable and open to many possible outcomes, and with time her behavior and personality become relatively rigid and options become more closed.

The direction that development takes is not hard-wired from the start, but nor is it completely open all the time to the influence of environment. Initial experiences give direction to subsequent development. For example, during the first two years of life a child can easily learn whatever language her family happens to speak. Later in life, learning a second language is much harder, and a second-language learner is never able to unlearn the phonemic distinctions of their first language (see later in this chapter). However, we now know that even people in their 60s who learn a new language will generate new neurons, so the options are never completely closed.

In infancy, we have started to understand some of the trajectories that development can follow. Whether it is the distal style or the proximal style of parenting, or whether adults don't treat the infant as a true human being for some time, the influence of adults is occurring at a time when fundamental brain growth and organization are taking place. The world over, boy and girl babies are treated differently, and these two fundamental trajectories of prenatal development are extended and usually move further apart from each other.

This canalization of human development has evident advantages. It has a biological basis, with regulatory genes opening and closing windows of opportunity and so establishing the general timing and sequencing of developmental processes, but it allows the infant to adapt to her specific cultural niche, of which language is one important element, and to begin to adopt the ways of her family and community. In this sense, human biology establishes an openness to culture (and relies on this openness). And we have seen that with "[i]n infancy, the key developmental task is the acquisition of a social matrix (i.e., formation of relationships through social interaction)" (Keller & Kärtner, 2013, p. 80).

1. PRECURSOR EMOTIONS AND THEIR REGULATION

The sensorimotor understanding that becomes increasingly complex during infancy is not just a way of knowing the environment, it is also a way of evaluating what is going on. The infant's actions and interactions are accompanied by strong emotions. Indeed, emotionality is at the core of the kind of organism that is an infant, and her emotions are strongly salient to the people who care for her. The infant shows her exquisite responsiveness to the presence of people primarily in bodily and facial expressions which adults interpret as displays of emotion. Emotion is a key element in the social interactions and relations of infancy, and emotional displays are the main way people become aware of an infant's needs.

We have already encountered emotion in this chapter. Piaget noted the emotion that accompanied the infant's discoveries about the world: he observed his infants' seriousness when accommodating, and their happiness and excitement during playful assimilation.

We have also seen that communication for the infant, while she lacks the capacity to speak, is primarily a matter of emotion, of negative or positive reactions to the presence of adults (Tronick, 1989).

And we saw in the previous section that parents in different cultures have different senses of what are appropriate emotions and emotionality, and interact with their infants accordingly.

But what is emotion? There is much disagreement among psychologists about the answer to this seemingly straightforward question. Each emotion has a bodily component, for example sweaty palms or a heightened level of arousal. But an emotion also has a feeling tone, and an evaluative aspect: each emotion can be said to involve an evaluation of the environment in terms of the person's goals. Emotion has a behavioral element too: each emotion involves a movement or an impulse to act, one that generally functions to either maintain or change the person's relationship with their environment.

In general, we can say that an emotion is, at least initially, a fast, intuitive appraisal of the environment's relevance to some goal or need, and ultimately its relevance to the person's survival. An emotion is a functional, behavioral, and experiential change in a person's relation to their environment, including other people. Each emotion involves an involuntary and unconscious evaluation of the situation and an action response of some kind. Emotion, in short, is an aspect of System 1. In an adult, this response is generally followed, or restrained, by deliberate evaluation and reappraisal, but of course this is not yet possible for an infant. Emotions are also flexible, contextually bound, and goal directed (Campos et al., 1994). They are rapidly noticed and responded to by other people: although it might seem that an emotion is fundamentally a personal experience, increasingly emotion is being viewed as inherently interactional and interpersonal.

Emotion in childhood has been of interest at least since Charles Darwin published his *The Expression of the Emotions in Man and Animals* in 1872 (Darwin, 2002[1872]). Darwin focused on the way emotions are displayed in facial expression, gesture, and bodily movement. Paul Ekman (on whose work the TV show *Lie to Me* is based) has identified muscle movements involved in the expression of each emotion (Ekman, 1980). But facial movements are not merely external "expressions" of inner states, they are social displays with a communicative function. Taken as a sign, an emotional display indicates the feelings of the sender and leads the receiver to feel an impulse to act in response.

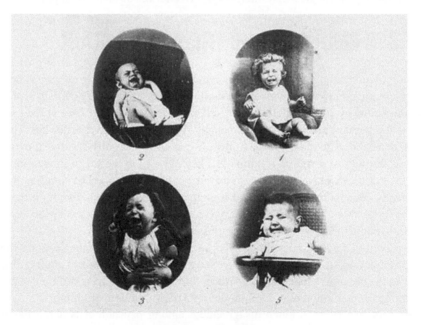

Figure 6.1 Darwin's photos of his son's expressions of emotion

Some developmental researchers have argued that facial expressions of emotion are innate and universal (Ekman, 1994), and that very young infants show **precursor emotions**, including distress, disgust, fright (startle), interest, and pleasure (Izard, 1992). These "prototypical emotions" are considered innate responses to physical stimuli that are significant to the infant's survival. The expressive and bodily components of these precursor emotions are reflexive, automatic, unconscious, unfocused, and uncoordinated.

However, more recent research has not supported the claim that specific facial expressions correspond to distinct emotions. Linda Camras has proposed that emotions start to differentiate during infancy, and that a young infant experiences a diffuse excitement which in time differentiates to become delight or distress, and then in turn fear, anger, elation, or affection. She has suggested that facial expressions of emotion follow a similar path: an expression will at first display a general intense excitement and later become specific to a discrete emotion. At the same time, the infant's facial expressions may come to resemble adult expressions. In addition, adults help organize their infant's emotions by expressing emotion themselves, by appraising the infant, and by sanctioning whatever has made the infant emotional (Camras & Shutter, 2010).

A fundamental distinction that may be universal is that between "positive" emotions—such as happiness and relief—and "negative" ones—such as anger, fear, or shame. However, what undoubtedly varies across cultures is the relationship between emotion and context: anger towards a parent may be seen as appropriate in some cultures, but highly inappropriate in others.

Certainly, early emotions begin to take on a culturally defined form as caregivers interpret them as appeals for action. Parents identify very young infants' facial expressions in terms of familiar emotion words, such as anger, sadness, happiness, and fear. Mothers generally say that their infants have expressed interest and joy by 1 month of age, and many believe they have also seen surprise, fear, and sadness by this time (Sroufe, 1997). Since what an infant experiences during the first few months of life are more likely to be nonspecific feelings than discrete and specific emotions such as anger or sadness, parents have to work to figure out what their infant wants. Parents interpret their infant's displays of emotion on the basis of cultural categories for emotion, and their culturally derived sense of which emotions are appropriate for a given situation (Hochschild, 1979). They respond to the infant accordingly, and work to manage her arousal and behavior and meet her needs.

The study of emotions is yet another area where an emphasis on either biology or culture is being replaced by a recognition of a complex synthesis: emotions have been called **bio-cultural processes** (Engelen et al., 2009). There is general agreement that aspects of human emotion reflect our ancestral past, have a physiological basis, and are shared with other animal species. Nonetheless, emotions change as caregivers interpret them and respond in the way they consider appropriate.

We still know comparatively little about the brain regions implicated in emotion. There is growing agreement that the brain basis of emotion lies in circuits or networks of structures rather than localized brain centers, and involves the orchestration of many different brain regions (Dalgleish, 2004; Izard, 1993; LeDoux, 2012). Figure 6.2 illustrates two pathways in the activation of fear.

We are starting to learn about cultural differences in the display and perception of emotion (Scherer et al., 2011). To the extent that people living in different cultures face similar survival problems, it might seem that emotions would have a common character. However, the same problem may be understood and handled differently in different cultures, and this implies that emotions vary cross-culturally. Cultural groups vary in their conceptualization of emotion, and in their norms and customs for the display and regulation of emotion. In an infant's emotions, then, we see not only her earliest evaluations of her circumstances, and her efforts to act on them, but also her parents'—and hence her culture's—interpretations.

Moreover, it seems likely that what happens in emotional development during infancy (and beyond) is the education of System 1. The infant responds intuitively to the here and now, the ebb and flow of sensory experience. An infant's emotions show her earliest spontaneous evaluations of her circumstances as she acts on them.

We might play with Piaget's terminology and call this a period of **sensory-emotional** intelligence. Emotional displays are important in infancy precisely because the infant needs to call upon the actions of others to accomplish her goals. Emotion displays are taken by adults to be salient signs, though of course they are not deliberate signals by the infant, at least at first.

As a child grows physically and develops psychologically there are changes in the neurobiology of emotion, changes in the emotions she will display and experience, changes in the objects and goals of her emotions, and changes too in the kinds of emotions she can recognize and understand in other people. We are only just starting to understand how these developments take place.

Displays of emotion play an important part in helping parents feel connected to their new baby. Smiling is an especially rewarding emotional expression. Between 1 and 2.5 months, infants will smile at almost any stimulation. Social smiling, smiling at another person, appears at around 2.5 to 3 months of age (though not in every culture, as we have seen). At this point parents often report a new sense of reciprocity in their relationship with their baby. In Navajo culture, the occasion of a baby's first smile calls for a ceremony (Leighton & Kluckholm, 1969[1947]). Until the end of infancy, however, an infant will

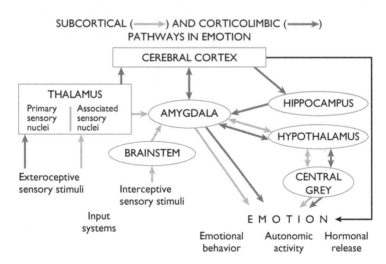

Figure 6.2 Neural substrates of emotion: subcortical and corticolimbic pathways in emotion activation

Source: Izard (1993)

Copyright © 1993 by the American Psychological Association

smile at virtually anyone who engages their attention. Later, smiling will become selective to specific people. As we have seen, however, in cultures such as the Nso, parents act in ways that do not encourage social smiling.

Crying is another powerful display of emotion. The tears that are part of crying are a uniquely human phenomenon. Much expert advice to parents has centered around the issue of how to respond to crying, and how to reduce its frequency and intensity. The old advice to "let them cry it out," based on the assumption that to respond to a crying infant rewards the behavior and reinforces it, has been rejected by researchers who find that crying is reduced, not increased, when parents are responsive to cries rather than ignoring them (Bell & Ainsworth, 1972).

At the same time, infants provide us with evidence that their understanding of other people's emotions is rapidly growing. We saw in Chapter 4 that neonates can distinguish some facial expressions of emotion. At 3.5 months, infants respond more to emotions on the faces of people they know than to strangers' facial expressions, suggesting that they are guided in their recognition of emotions by the familiarity of their parents, before generalizing to others (Walker-Andrews et al., 2011). After 4 months of age infants will look at facial expressions posed by a variety of people of both sexes and recognize when they are the same, responding in a categorical manner (Nelson, 1987). Late in the first year, an infant will check with her mother before responding to a person's facial expression, showing that she is seeking the adult's help in interpreting its significance.

Emotional displays from other people can both produce emotion in the infant and regulate those emotions. For example, newborns together in a nursery show **emotional contagion**, where the crying of one induces crying in others. In addition, we have already seen how in primary intersubjectivity the emotions of infant and adult are mutually interdependent. And at around 9 months of age the infant begins to show emotional responses to an adult's facial, vocal, and gestural signals about an event that is an object of joint reference.

It seems likely that emotional displays are highly salient in infancy precisely because the infant needs to call upon the actions of others to accomplish her goals. These goals may be simple—perhaps no more than staying comfortably warm, secure, and fed—but other people need to provide them. While the infant lacks the capacity to speak, communication is largely a matter of emotion, of negative or positive displays in the presence of adults.

Emotions develop: we do not expect to see an adult displaying the same emotions as a 3-year-old. An important aspect of the development of emotion is their regulation. We can think of emotions themselves as serving to regulate behavior and interaction: an emotion sets in motion a coping action, in the form of an impulse to act—for example fear is an impulse to flight, anger is an impulse to attack—and in this sense an emotion regulates a person's behavior. At the same time, we all recognize that emotional reactions cannot be given free rein, so that emotions themselves must be regulated (for example going for a run can reduce strong anger) (Röttger-Rössler & Markowitsch, 2009).

Two complementary processes are at work here: emotions regulate actions, and actions regulate emotion. This complementarity can establish a feedback loop, where strong emotion leads to action which can lead to reduced emotion.

Recognizing this feedback loop may be key to understanding how emotions develop, because the actions that regulate one person's emotions may be performed by another person. In infancy, this is in fact almost always the case. When an adult encounters a problem in practical activity that arouses emotion, they stop and think. When an infant encounters a problem, she cries! This emotional response is an appeal to another person—the infant turns to her caregivers to solve her problem. Adults must perform the actions that the infant's emotion calls for, and in doing so they regulate that emotion. For example, when an infant cries her parents must try to interpret what she needs, and try various ways to satisfy or calm her.

Charles Darwin observed that emotional expressions come under voluntary control during infancy, and suggested that this was in part due to the response of adults:

> every true or inherited movement of expression seems to have had some natural and independent origin. But when once acquired, such movements may be voluntarily and consciously employed as a means of communication. Even infants, if carefully attended to, find out at a very early age that their screaming brings relief, and they soon voluntarily practice it. (Darwin, 2002[1872], p. 351)

More recently, Manfred Holodynski has suggested that interaction with caregivers provides **natural biofeedback training** (Holodynski, 2013). Caregivers interpret the infant's displays of emotion as signs of desires and needs, and act on behalf of the infant to try to satisfy her. This response offers the infant the opportunity to detect the contingencies among her own emotion displays, the causes of her emotions, and the caregivers' responses. In addition, caregivers mirror the infant's emotions in a symbolized manner, with conventionalized facial displays, words for emotions, and so on. As a consequence, the infant begins to acquire an implicit use of cultural symbols.

The dynamics of emotion between infant and caregiver provide an example of **co-regulation,** "a form of coordinated action between participants that involves a continuous mutual adjustment of actions and intentions" (Fogel & Garvey, 2007, p. 251).

The interaction enables the infant to take increasing control over her own psychological processes. Over time there will be a shift from **interpersonal regulation** to **intrapersonal regulation** of emotion. At first, as I have said, the regulation of emotion is accomplished largely by the caregiver. With time, the child will become able to control her own emotions. Intrapersonal regulation will never completely replace interpersonal regulation, but it becomes increasingly important—though presumably there is variation across cultures in the balance between interpersonal and intrapersonal regulation.

As I mentioned earlier, it has been suggested that this **social-biofeedback**—when an adult selectively responds to and reflects an infant's displays of emotion—is necessary for the infant to become aware of her own emotions as distinct and discrete, and as having regular patterns (Gergely & Watson, 1996, 1999). When a caregiver responds contingently to an infant's display of emotion this provides feedback through which that infant can become sensitized to the cultural categorization of her own emotion-states. This helps her to recognize her own emotions, to regulate them, and contributes to the building of a communicative code of emotion expressions.

In conclusion, we have seen how an infant engages in simple but emotionally powerful interchanges with her caregivers. In these exchanges, cultural learning takes place. The infant starts to learn the appropriate use of cultural artifacts. She begins to recognize that vocalizations can serve to designate objects. And, centrally, her precursor emotions begin to differentiate and the shift from interpersonal regulation to intrapersonal regulation begins.

Emotion is a fundamental aspect of our residence in the world. We can say that an infant's emotions are rapid intuitive evaluations that correspond to what has been called System 1. In this stage of development, System 2 functions—a conscious and deliberate response on the basis of the emotional evaluation—are provided not by the infant but by the caregiver. In this sense, during infancy (and for some time to come) the components of each emotion—physiological changes, evaluation, feeling, behavior—are distributed *between* child and adult.

I will trace subsequent development of the regulation of emotion in subsequent chapters. However, what we have described here is enough to enable us to see again the interpenetration of culture and biology. The case of emotional development clearly illustrates Vygotsky's General Genetic Law, which I described in Chapter 2: an interpersonal process provides the basis for an intrapersonal process. We have to say of the infant that "the rational and cultural forms that constitute its inner nature are wholly external to it, embodied in its parents" (Vygotsky, 1997a, p. 143). The infant's potential is considerable, and she will in time become fluent in both language and logic; for the moment, however, this potential lies not solely in her genes, not merely in her brain, but also in her caregivers and the other people around her.

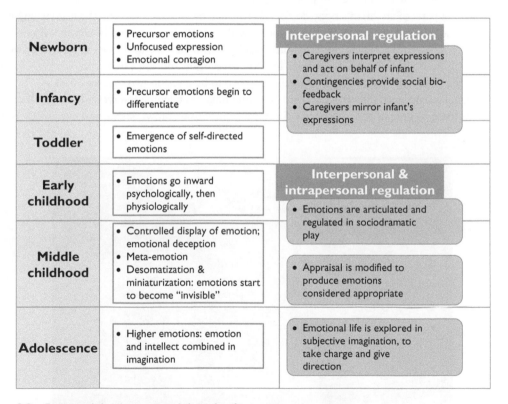

Figure 6.3   Emotional development and the role of interpersonal regulation

Source: Author, based on Holodynski (2009)

2. BIOLOGICAL DEVELOPMENTS DURING THE FIRST YEAR

2.1 PHYSICAL GROWTH AND MOTOR MILESTONES

Physical growth is continuous and rapid during the first 12 months of life, as the infant becomes larger and stronger. In the United States a newborn baby weighs on average 7 pounds and is about 20 inches in length. At the end of the first year the weight of a typical infant increases to about 22 pounds and her length to 30 inches. That is, during the first year the infant has tripled in weight, and her length has increased by 50 percent.

These figures, however, represent circumstances where an infant receives plentiful nutrition. Growth is affected both by the food that is available and by her parents' beliefs about what is appropriate for their baby. In many parts of the world food is scarce and infant growth is slower. Size and shape are also influenced by the infant's genes and so there is much individual variation. Gender differences also exist: boy infants tend on average to be taller and heavier than girls. Girl infants, however, tend to mature faster in such areas as the growth of bones and the organ systems.

The different parts of an infant's body do not all grow at the same rate. At birth the head is one-quarter the length of the whole body, while at 2 years old it will be just one-fifth, and in adulthood one-eighth. This illustrates a pattern known as **cephalocaudal** growth, in which the head and upper body grow first and the rest of the body follows. The change in body proportions during infancy makes it increasingly easier to lift the head and control its movements, and then to balance on two legs and walk.

Bones become harder as minerals are deposited, and muscles become longer and thicker. Increase in muscle mass leads to greater ability to move the body, to turn over, crawl, stand, and eventually to walk.

Figure 6.4　The infant has a lot of growing to do

For normal development to occur, however, experience, stimulation, and activity are essential. Infants in orphanages who spent most of their first year lying in cribs could not sit up at 21 months, and only 15 percent of them could walk at age 3. In cultures where parents discourage independent locomotion for reasons of safety, walking is delayed.

These are biological changes in the infant, but they are are at the same time social and cultural changes. Childrearing practices influence the infant's rate of growth, and are in turn influenced by her physical characteristics. An infant in a family living at subsistence levels is likely to grow more slowly, and will develop learning deficits if her malnutrition is severe, with implications for how her parents must care for her and for her role in the family. An infant who has adequate nutrition will grow rapidly, and her parents must adapt when she begins to move independently. Biologically and behaviorally, infancy is a time of rapid changes which are monitored anxiously by parents, who must respond to these and will attempt to influence them.

As her body changes the infant is learning how to control it: physical growth puts more resources at her disposal. What are often simply viewed as "motor milestones"—reaching and grasping an object, stacking one block on top of another, crawling and then walking—are actually psychological milestones, because the body is the infant's way of knowing the world and acting on the basis of what she knows.

Milestones such as sitting and crawling are some of the most obvious achievements during the first year of life, and the development of motor skills was the first focus in the scientific study of infants. Gesell and others (see Chapter 2) interpreted growth in motor ability as an indication of brain maturation.

Birth to 3 months	Lifts head Supports weight on elbows Makes reflexive stepping movements when held upright Sits with support 3 to 6 months
3 to 6 months	Kicks feet when lying Plays with toes Turns from back to side Sits with support Starts to crawl
6 to 9 months	Rolls from back to stomach Crawls with both hands and feet Pulls to standing position Sits up Stands with support
9 to 12 months	Walks with support Sits without falling Stands alone Attempts to crawl up stairs Grasps object with thumb and forefinger

Figure 6.5   Milestones of motor development during infancy

Subsequently, however, as developmental psychology shifted its attention to cognition and the mind, interest in movement and the body was lost. Only in recent years have researchers returned to the topic, as they began to understand that brain, body, and environment work together in a dynamic system.

The traditional studies of infancy described a linear sequence of achievements which were assumed to reflect preprogrammed neurological growth. However, bodily movements require the coordination of body segments, joints, multiple muscles, nerve cells, and brain cells—a coordination in which maturation certainly plays a role but so too do the mass and weight of the limbs, the configuration of the joints, the strength of the muscles, together with characteristics of the environment within which an infant is acting. Movements are the result not only of the brain, but also of the mechanical and biological characteristics of the body, the physics of the environment, and the particular task that is at hand. New motor abilities are the result of changes in any or all of these, as the infant discovers new potentials within her body as it rapidly changes and grows (Thelen, 1995).

For example, the stepping reflex that is present at birth usually disappears at around 2 months of age. This change was at first interpreted as a sign of brain maturation, but this is also the age when an infant usually gains subcutaneous fat, so that her limbs become heavier. If the infant is floated in a tub of water the reflex reappears, evidence that its disappearance was related to the biomechanics of the legs and body rather than to neurological changes (Thelen & Fisher, 1982).

The implication of such findings is that motor development does not follow a fixed timetable but is sensitive to the context, and that motor behavior is an emergent property of a combination of factors. The body is embedded in the world, and what a body can do at any given age depends on what the world enables it to do. For example, putting an infant in a walker, or a jolly jumper, opens up new possibilities for the motor system as a whole.

As we shall see in more detail in Chapter 7, changes in motor abilities are linked to changes in perception and to learning. Within a few weeks the infant will bring objects to her mouth to explore them. When she is able to sit up (something that will depend on the availability of cushions, baby seats, and so on) she can manipulate objects in a focused way, and this provides a new opportunity to learn about their qualities. Once she can crawl, she can explore the space of her home and search for things that are interesting to examine. Once she can walk, space becomes explorable in a completely new way.

2.2 BRAIN GROWTH AND DEVELOPMENT

The infant grows rapidly in brain as well as body. The brain doubles in weight by age 1, to reach more than half its adult weight. Dramatic transformations have taken place in the way we think about postnatal brain growth. It was long believed that the formation of new brain cells stopped before birth and that children and adults could only lose neurons. However, neuroscience research has found that neurogenesis occurs after birth in humans (Seki, 2011), as well as in other mammal species and non-mammalian vertebrates (reptiles and fish). In an infant brain thousands of young neurons are born and migrate every day, though only a fraction survive and differentiate.

Here too ontogeny has often been reduced to phylogeny, by which I mean that researchers have often assumed that evolution has selected our genes and that brain development simply follows genetic instructions. This is no more the case after birth than it was prenatally: brain development during the first year is an active process in which the biological structure is built differently in each individual, through complex and variable interactions between organism and environment.

Since the neonate has a brain that is only one quarter its adult size obviously much brain growth must take place after birth. The high rate of growth that occurred in the human fetus continues for a full year after birth, compared with only a month for chimps and macaques. Even after that, substantial brain development continues for a considerable time. Brain size increases four-fold by age 6, and by that age the brain is 90 percent of its adult size. Structural changes in grey and white matter continue into adolescence. It is not clear when this degree of postnatal brain growth evolved, but it has been estimated that an adult brain size of 850 ml would have been sufficiently large to require high rates of brain growth after birth—due to the limits of the pelvic opening—and this probably occurred before Neanderthals, and possibly with Homo erectus.

It would be incorrect, however, to assume that the small relative size of the newborn brain is unique; in fact it is about average among mammals. The brain of a kitten is only 10 percent of the weight of an adult cat's brain. However, the human newborn brain has much more cortical surface whose function is open-ended rather then being hard-wired. The so-called "association regions" are larger, while the dedicated sensory and motor regions are relatively smaller. Furthermore, it takes an unusually long time for the cellular circuits in many regions of the human brain to form. Some brain circuits that are close to sensory input, such as the visual system, are in place by 6 months of age, but those in the language areas, for example, do not begin to complete their development until 6 or 8 years of age (Quartz & Sejnowski, 1997). These areas of the human brain are responding to environmental influence for much longer than is the case in other species. In addition, cortical areas which are further away from the sensory regions can wait for the development of lower areas. This not only provides increased flexibility, it also means that recovery from damage is much better. A human infant who suffers brain damage will usually show little sign of it later in life, compared with adults who suffer similar damage, or the young of other animal species. The brain, like the body, heals more easily in youth, and the young human brain is the most resilient.

The brain grows and develops on many different and interacting levels during infancy, from its gross anatomy to its subcellular biochemistry. Neurobiologists have come to see brain development as "a complex series of dynamic and adaptive processes operating within a highly constrained, genetically organized but constantly changing context" (Stiles & Jernigan, 2010, p. 327). New neural structures and functions continually emerge and differentiate, and the structures of the human brain develop at different rates. For example, as I mentioned in Chapter 4, at birth the cortex seems to have regions that are only minimally prepared for specific kinds of sensory input. The consistent structure-function relations that are found in the adult brain are the result of multiple intrinsic and extrinsic constraints, rather than being hard-wired. The way that brain regions influence each others' development, through feedback and top-down interactions, has been called **embrainment** (Westermann et al., 2007).

What, then, are the principal ways in which the brain grows during infancy? We now know that the postnatal development of the human brain involves several interrelated dynamic processes which play out in a context that is both biological and cultural, both genetically organized and culturally arranged (Stiles & Jernigan, 2010). The general pattern of brain growth appears to be in two directions. One is the **progressive differentiation** of brain structures and their neural elements, as patterns of input cause these structures to become dedicated to specific tasks. The other, at the same time, is the organization of

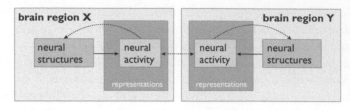

Figure 6.6 Embrainment: two functional brain regions develop interactively

Source: Westermann et al. (2007)

these structures into **integrated functional systems** that coordinate and unify the complex hierarchical and dynamic networks which I introduced in Chapter 4.

The increase in volume of the brain during infancy is due to several different processes: (1) the creation of new neurons; (2) the creation of glial cells; (3) a dramatic increase in the number of synaptic connections between cells followed by a pruning of these connections; (4) an extension in the length of axons; (5) a large increase in the number of dendrites; (6) the formation of fiber bundles between brain regions and the myelination of these bundles. I will consider each of these processes in turn.

First, more nerve cells are created. The adult brain—and presumably the infant brain too—contain neural stem cells. Labeling of DNA has shown that new neurons are generated from progenitor cells in the dentate gyrus of adult humans, and that the human hippocampus retains its ability to generate neurons all through life (Eriksson et al., 1998). The subventricular zone, which lies along the walls of the lateral ventricles, continues to be a source of new neurons into adulthood, and these cells migrate to other parts of the brain (Alvarez-Buylla & García-Verdugo, 2002). It is difficult to conduct studies of neurogenesis in human infants, but if it occurs in adults it presumably occurs in children too. At the same time, existing neurons grow in size and they continue to migrate, actively following the fibers of glial cells.

Second, the glial cells themselves also continue to proliferate and migrate during infancy, and apparently do so throughout childhood and into adult life. Their main role seems to be that of myelination of axons. The glial cells differentiate and migrate into the cortex, striatum, and hippocampus. When they reach their destination, each extends itself to form the insulating membrane that wraps around the axons of nearby cells, until it is tightly wrapped in multiple layers. These cells also synthesize chemicals that maintain the integrity of the axon and help the neuron survive, and some of them seem to form excitatory and inhibitory connections with neurons and hence may influence their signaling. The glial cells, then, play an important role in the functional development of neural circuits.

Third, and probably most significantly, the synaptic connections among neurons are first produced in great number and then are subsequently eliminated, in processes known as **exuberant production** and **synaptic pruning**.

The first of these processes, exuberant production, is a dramatic increase in the synaptic connections among neurons. We saw in the previous chapter that massive neurogenesis occurs in the period roughly 6 to 24 weeks after conception. The exuberant phase of **synaptogenesis**, a build-up of synaptic connections among the neurons, then begins. At birth, the synaptic connections among neurons are relatively sparse, perhaps only 10 percent of the number an adult has. During infancy this rich network of neural connections begins to grow. Studies of human brain material show a rapid increase in synapse density until around 20 months (Huttenlocher, 1979).

Somewhat counterintuitively, however, this mass of interconnections makes an inefficient brain, and so those connections begin to be slowly and selectively eliminated, in the process known as synaptic pruning. This pruning is driven by the child's interactions with the world, and it continues throughout life, until a more streamlined connectivity is achieved. Pruning helps establish networks of white matter connections within and among areas of the brain. The retention or elimination of synaptic connections seems to involve competition for resources and reflects the presence or absence of incoming sensory stimulation, and it is an important source of plasticity and adaptivity in the young brain.

The processes of synaptic production and pruning occur at different times in different areas of the brain. In the visual cortex, for example, exuberant production peaks at 3 to 4 months of age, then pruning continues until preschool age. Much the same occurs in the primary auditory cortex. In the medial prefrontal cortex the production does not occur until 3 or 4 years of age, and pruning continues through adolescence.

By the time a child is 5, it is estimated that 90 percent of the neural connections she will have as an adult have been established. In general, younger brains have more connections among areas that are close together, while older brains have more connections among distant regions. In an adult, each neuron may have links to 5,000 other neurons or to receptors around the body (Fair et al., 2009).

On a microscopic level, individual neurons can form and retract connections very rapidly, over periods of hours or even minutes. Especially early in life, transient connections form in many parts of the brain—something that is not observed in adults. As axons grow they appear to sample the space around them, and form or retract synaptic connections in a dynamic and systematic manner (Hua & Smith, 2004).

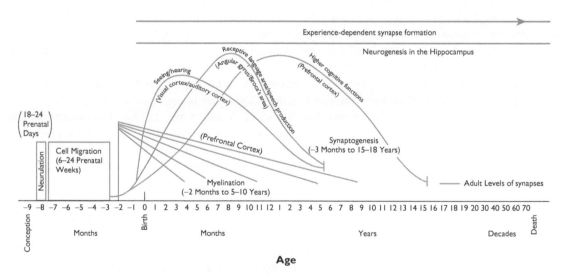

Figure 6.7 Processes of prenatal and postnatal brain growth

Source: Thompson and Nelson (2001)

Fourth, our study of the neural pathways of the visual system has suggested another mechanism of brain development, namely the growth of axons (Hubel & Wiesel, 1972). The axons extend, branch out, and form increasingly complex connections with other cells. This growth depends heavily on the amount of activity in the system in which the axon is located, and so is influenced by environmental circumstances.

A fifth mechanism of growth in the infant brain is the extension of dendrites. For example, the dendrites of a cell in the frontal cortex grow over ten times in length between birth and 6 months, and they continue growing into adulthood, reaching over 30 times the length they had at birth. The majority of this growth occurs after age 2, but it begins in infancy. Growth of dendrites appears to be an adjustment to the demands placed on the brain, and enables the formation of regions of correlated activity.

Recent research has found that different cell types follow distinct developmental timetables, even when they are close together. Cells in layers of the visual cortex, for example, receive different kinds of information from the retina and this seems to be what induces their growth. In addition, a number of animal studies have experimentally manipulated environmental conditions and found systematic effects on synaptic number and density, along with suggestions that these effects are reversible.

Sixth, during infancy there is also the formation of fiber bundles among brain regions. At birth the most developed regions of the brain are subcortical areas which handle fundamental functions such as respiration and the beating of the heart. Regulation and control of these subcortical regions by higher cortical centers arise later, as the corpus striatum matures and then the cortex. In the newborn, only the primary areas of the cortex are myelinated, those that are connected to peripheral organs. Over the first six months of life these primary areas become connected to the intermediate and terminal areas. As a consequence of these brain changes, instinctual reactions are differentiated and then integrated into more complex forms of sensory-motor activity (Simmons & Barsalou, 2003).

In the past, researchers assumed that information from each of the senses—sight, hearing, smell, and touch—enters the brain separately and must then be combined, in what is called **binding**. However, it seems that information from the various senses is bound together in multiple sites along the processing stream, so that there is no single localized area in the brain where perceptual binding is carried out. Infants have multimodal perception from the outset.

As the way that a brain region responds to information comes to depend on its connections with other regions and their patterns of activity, different regions of the infant brain begin to interact in organized patterns, in a process known as **interactive specialization**. A region may at first have loosely defined functions, so it will be activated in many contexts and tasks. With development, as this region becomes linked to other regions, its functions may become more defined and its activity more restricted and specific. For example, a region that responds to a variety of visual objects may come to respond, with time and experience, only to upright human faces.

All of this implies that the brain responds to environmental stimulation not merely with selective elimination, but with active construction. Synapses *are* eliminated, but at the same time other connections of various kinds are constructed. Once again, we see a dynamic interaction between sensory information from the environment and the biological mechanisms of neural growth, so that neural circuits are built and modified in a directed manner. This implies that no rigid distinction can be drawn between learning and maturation: experience guides the biological processes through which the brain matures. With all these ongoing changes in neurological structure and function, the architecture of the infant brain becomes adapted to the organization of her particular ecological niche.

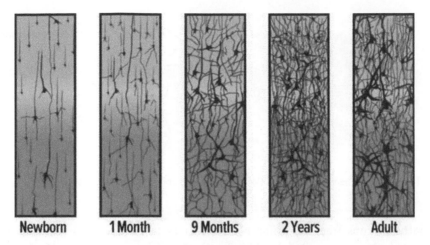

Figure 6.8   Changes in synaptic density over time

Finally, there is currently a debate over the degree to which the *prefrontal cortex* (PFC) is already functioning during infancy. The prefrontal cortex is generally associated with self-control and with the higher psychological functions, such as deliberate reasoning and planning. Since infants are not yet capable of these higher functions we have assumed that the PFC is largely inactive at this stage.

However, research with infants using new neuroimaging techniques (functional near-infrared spectroscopy: fNIRS) has found activity in two portions of the PFC (the medial and lateral portions) that control emotional and cognitive responses, respectively (Grossmann, 2013).

In adults, the medial aspect of the PFC (mPFC) is known to be more involved in control of emotion, while the lateral aspect (lPFC) is involved in control of cognition. Of the two, the lPFC is thought to have evolved much later. It has been said that the mPFC provides "hot" executive function, while the lPFC provides "cool" executive function. After all, both calm problem-solving situations and highly emotional emergencies can call for self-control.

However, we don't know to what degree the PFC in an infant is coordinated into functional networks, as it is in an adult. Consequently, while the PFC may be active, it may not yet play a role in controlling other regions of the brain. Evidence for **cortical hubs** in the PFC—regions that are heavily connected with other parts of the cortex—has been found first at around 12 months of age, and it seems that these hubs become more complex during subsequent development. There is also evidence that the PFC is involved when a new task is first learned, but that subsequently more posterior regions take over, so the activity seen in the infant PFC may reflect the high degree of learning that is taking place at this age.

2.3 DORSAL AND VENTRAL STREAMS: WHAT AND WHERE

Let me offer one example of how research is throwing light on the way an infant's growing understanding of spatiality and of objects is related to what is happening in her brain. We now know that visual sensory input about objects is divided in the brain into two relatively separate streams of information.

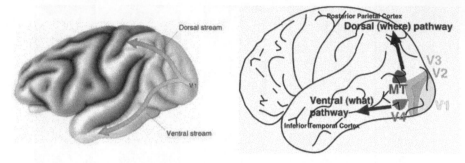

Figure 6.9 The dorsal (*Where?*) and ventral (*What?*) pathways for visual information

A **ventral pathway** runs from the primary visual cortex to the temporal lobe and accomplishes recognition of objects, so it is called the ***What?* pathway**. A **dorsal pathway** runs from the primary visual cortex to the parietal lobe, and organizes sensory-motor responses to perceived objects, so it is called the ***Where?* pathway**.

The dorsal stream handles those properties of visual input that are relevant to acting in the world. Action requires understanding of space, and in the dorsal pathway there are multiple systems for spatial processing. Some neurons in this pathway update the body-centered sense of visual space. Others mark where the person is looking. Others track moving stimuli, and many of these continue to respond when the stimulus disappears. Still others attend to changes in relative size and motion as a stimulus moves towards the person. Flow in the optical field is detected, along with the size, shape, and orientation of figures in the field. These aspects of spatiality seem to be attended to in parallel, in a manner that is neither solely sensory nor solely motor, but truly sensory-motor. The neurons in this stream are identifying *where* a stimulus is located.

The cells in the ventral pathway, in contrast, respond to increasingly complex clusters of features. Some cells detect the internal features of a stimulus, wherever on the retina it occurs: they respond to consistent features irrespective of position. Some of these cells respond only to features in a specific orientation, others equally no matter what the orientation is. The neurons in this stream are recognizing or identifying *what* the stimulus is.

At the moment we know only a little about when and how the dorsal and ventral pathways develop. Studies of infants show that the two pathways consume glucose equally at rest, meaning that they are both using energy at the same rate, but this tells us little about how they are functioning when active. Some researchers have suggested that the dorsal pathway develops first in infancy, but it is equally possible that the two pathways differentiate from each other during the course of postnatal development. Either way, this research would seem to have identified two of the brain's central pathways involved in sensory-motor intelligence, pathways which are involved in an infant's growing understanding of what things are and how they are arranged in space. Both the Where? and What? pathways are presumably central to System 1.

Does this neurophysiology help us understand the A-not-B error? The discrepancy between looking and reaching in these tasks may reflect a lack of integration between the dorsal and ventral pathways.

If a 4-month-old infant is watching something and a barrier is placed between her and the object, there is evidence that she is unable to hold on to both the information processed in the dorsal stream and the information in the ventral stream. What seems to determine the kind of information that is maintained is the degree to which the object invites action. In addition, it is not until 8 months of age that infants begin to show the high frequency "gamma" EEG waves that occur in adults when spatially separate features are "bound" together into the perception of a single object, something that is accomplished in the ventral pathway (Mareschal & Johnson, 2003).

3. THE TRANSITION AT 1 YEAR: BIOLOGICAL DIFFERENTIATION

As the infant grows in physical strength and coordination she becomes increasingly able to perform at least some of the practical activities of her everyday life more independent of the adults upon whom she has been completely dependent. She is also working hard to communicate her increasingly complex needs and desires to these adults, who are of course using language to communicate. In particular, two highly important achievements towards the end of the first year of life are starting to walk and to talk. (Some infants, of course, start to learn sign language, rather than spoken language.) These achievements lead to a dramatic developmental transition. When the infant becomes able to stand on her own two feet and move without adult help, and when she becomes able to produce sequences of sounds that adults recognize as words in their language, she comes to live in the world in a new way, and experience that world in a new way. In a real sense she becomes a different kind of human being.

During the first year, as the infant gains energy, moves with more skill, and becomes more dextrous, the extent of her influence grows and her ways of using the path through an adult to get what she wants become more varied. The infant becomes increasingly proficient in the primary sociability that we have seen characterizes this stage, deliberately influencing others to obtain what she wants. Her physical growth extends her interactions with adults within the Great-We. However, at the same time a contradiction develops "there is a heightened basic contradiction between the increased complexity and variety of social relations of the child and the impossibility of verbal communication" (Vygotsky, 1998[1932–1934], p. 232). There is tension between, on the one hand, the complexity of the infant's involvement with other people, as her energy and mobility increase and her interests expand, and on the other hand, the limitations inherent in trying to communicate without words. While she is unable to move independently, there is much that she can achieve only when others cooperate. With a limited capacity for verbal communication, she can communicate only by means of "surrogates": gestures, such as pointing and vocal calls. This tension motivates transformation.

3.1 STARTING TO WALK

When infants start to walk they resemble Charlie Chaplin, taking small steps with their legs wide apart and toes pointing out. We call this "toddling." At first, toddlers are literally falling into each step. But improvements are rapid over the next three to six months, due to increased strength and better control of posture. By 4 or 5 years of age young children are walking like adults, pushing upward with the supporting leg.

For an infant, walking is an invention that is made possible by a combination of physical growth and neural growth. Physical growth provides greater muscle mass and strength, together with a lowering of the centre of gravity. Neural growth improves motor responses to perceptual information (Adolph et al., 2003). Frontal lobe EEG activity surges around the age that infants start to walk. Practice provides useful feedback and improves the infant's speed of movement and her adaptation to different surfaces, and walking while supported by an adult also helps. These factors interrelate: practice probably promotes brain development, and it builds muscle strength; neural development allows more and more skillful practice. Statistical separation of these factors suggests that practice is the most important (Adolph et al., 2003).

Infant locomotion is becoming viewed by researchers as the product of a dynamical neuromuscular system (Forrester et al., 1993). Walking emerges from the simultaneous cooperation of many elements, influenced by the environment and the tasks of balance and coordination. Put simply, there are many ways to move one's legs, and the infant has to organize sustained, coordinated movement patterns, under challenging conditions. In the process, older behaviors are decomposed and reorganize into new ways of moving. For example, once an infant has enough strength in her arms and legs to be able to hold her torso off the ground she starts to explore various ways of moving those arms and legs, such as moving only one limb at a time, or moving both limbs on one side of the body at the same time, and then the opposite limbs.

The various kinds of movement that we have all seen in infants—such as crawling on their belly, using their hands and knees, cruising (walking while holding on to furniture) sideways, cruising forward, and of course walking (Vereijken & Adolph, 1999)—are achieved in a general sequence, though the order may vary, and some may be skipped altogether. As we shall see shortly, their timing varies greatly. An infant may revert to a previous stage, or achieve two, such as starting to crawl and cruise, at the same time. Most infants find that simultaneously moving diagonally opposite limbs, such as the right arm and left leg, is most efficient and stable. This outcome is not preprogrammed, it is the natural outcome of trying to achieve the most dynamically efficient solution. The particular task an infant faces often dictates the method of movement she will use.

However, all infants eventually settle on walking as a stable solution to the problem of how to locomote. Practice builds motor skills, and what an infant learns from one kind of locomotion can transfer to another, even though the patterns of movement are quite different. Successful experience with one way of moving may increase their motivation to try something new. What might seem simply the product of biological maturation is actually a result of active interaction with the environment.

Once they are walking, toddlers will do so for an average of six hours per day, with between 500 and 1,500 steps per hour (that's the length of 29 football fields every day!). Walking development proceeds from a process of adjustment one step at a time to an ability to control the overall path of movement (Adolph et al., 2003).

Becoming able to walk provides a good example of the way the body is at the center of development. The central nervous system can play only a limited role in motor control. The brain initiates muscle actions, but the force exerted in a bodily movement is a matter of gravity, inertia, and the mechanical properties of the joints, none of which are controlled by the CNS.

Walking also depends on culture. We saw earlier in this chapter that Ache infants are delayed in their motor development because they are discouraged from exploring. Similarly, anthropological

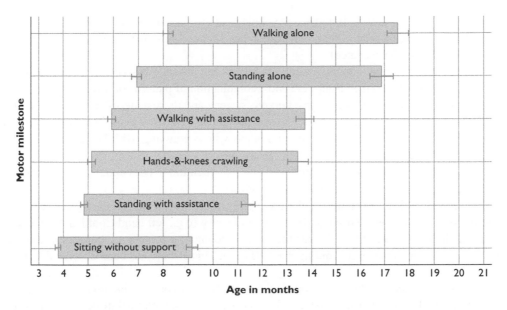

Figure 6.10 World Health Organization motor development milestones for standing and walking

fieldwork in Java in the 1950s found that at that time infants were not allowed to move about alone until their muscles were strong enough to support their weight. Instead, they were carried in a shawl or bounced on the parent's lap. This treatment reflected a concern the Javanese had with bodily equilibrium and spatial orientation (Geertz, 1959). The result was that Javanese infants entirely missed the crawling stage.

The data in Figure 6.10 show an interesting pattern. They were collected by the World Health Organization from over 800 children aged 4 to 24 months in Ghana, India, Norway, Oman, and the USA. A common sequence was found for five of the six motor milestones for over 90 percent of the children, but as the figure shows there was an increasing divergence in the age at which these milestones were reached. There is a range of 5 months in the age at which infants sit without support, but a range of 10 months in the age at which they walk unaided. This growing variation suggests the increasing influence of the cultural environment in the motor capabilities of the developing child, so that children in different cultures become increasingly different in what they can do and when. An infant may start to walk alone as young as 8 months, or as late as 17 months. This translates into a considerable variation in the age at which infancy ends and the stage of toddlerhood begins.

3.1.1 THE PSYCHOLOGICAL CONSEQUENCES OF LOCOMOTION

We now know that independent movement leads to dramatic psychological changes. Crawling and then walking will lead to changes in an infant's perception, her spatial cognition, and her social and emotional behavior. Locomotion initiates a psychological reorganization that is both context-specific and broad-based (Campos et al., 2000). The outcomes share a common origin, but they may not be closely linked (in time, for instance).

Locomotion transforms an infant's perception of depth and distance. Moving in space produces a patterned flow of information in the visual field and a combination of patterns of information in the visual, vestibular, and somatosensory aspects of the nervous system, and these patterns enable an infant to build up expectations about what will come next. These expectations will be violated by the change in depth at a drop-off, and this is why a walking infant, but not one who is crawling, will display anxiety when she encounters a vertical drop and will avoid trying to cross it.

The infant who is moving independently must also pay attention to cues about distance, and distance perception becomes more accurate as walking develops.

Moving around leads to encounters with new aspects of the spatial environment, and this appears to motivate the shift from an **egocentric** understanding of space (e.g., left hand/right hand) to an **allocentric** understanding (e.g., near the wall/near the door). Locomoting infants are better at finding hidden objects, and they are also better at avoiding the A–B error. This change has been described as follows:

> Based on observations of infants performing the A-not-B task in our lab, locomotor infants appear not only more attentive and less distractible than prelocomotor infants but they appear also to actively search for communicative signals from the experimenter. It is as if they work harder to understand the 'game,' as it were, and try to glean such an understanding from the experimenter. (Campos et al., 2000, p. 194)

Not only does this observation provide some support for the suggestion made in the previous chapter that we should see the A-not-B task as a social situation, it also supports the idea that once an infant is moving independently she needs to communicate in a more active manner.

Researchers have suggested that the new ability to walk shows us how "development involves organizing (orchestrating) many component processes into more and more complex levels" (Campos et al., 2000, p. 211). For example, fear of heights seems to emerge as a result of several different processes: changes in the flow of visual information, the mismatch between this visual input and vestibular information, and the sense of postural instability that a change in the surface induces. Locomotion can be said to operate as the orchestrator of these processes, and in this sense changes in multiple domains have a single agent of control, one which is dramatically changing the relation an infant has with her environment.

Indeed, walking has been called the "psychological birth" of the infant (Mahler et al., 1975) because it breaks the symbiotic relation between infant and caregiver and leads to both willfulness and autonomy. Certainly, independent locomotion introduces new challenges for parents, who must encourage exploration while discouraging conduct that risks danger or damage, to either the infant or her surroundings. I will call this, however, a biological differentiation rather than a psychological differentiation. Locomotion reorganizes the family system. The infant now "gets into everything."

The ability to move independently has implications, then, for the infant's relationship with her caregivers, and for her communication with them. Once an infant begins to crawl and walk, her location—and consequently her safety and security—are no longer under the complete control of her caregivers. The toddler's new differentiation means that new safeguards have to be arranged. Caregivers can no longer directly prevent mishaps, no matter how carefully they arrange the environment. The moving infant encounters objects and situations that will alarm her parents and require their intervention.

Indeed, this transition is often the start of a "testing of wills." A tug of war begins between caregivers' demands for compliance and their infant's willfulness. Caregivers report that temper tantrums start at this age, along with more displays of delight and happiness. They also begin to expect that their child will comply with their wishes and commands, because they now consider the toddler to be more responsible for her actions. They use verbal prohibitions more often than in the past, and they also more often express anger verbally—many mothers say that they became angry with their infant for the first time when she started to walk. But there is also more affection, and more frequent hugging.

Not surprisingly, newly mobile infants keep a watchful eye on their caregivers to obtain feedback about what they are doing—this is called **social referencing** (Tamis-LeMonda & Adolph, 2005). Indeed, when an infant starts to crawl and walk she receives dramatically increased "social signaling," especially "distal" communication: parents will use verbal warnings to try to influence from a distance what the infant is doing (Tamis-LeMonda et al., 2007). A mobile toddler understands better when her parents are trying to draw her attention to something, and she also understands better the spatial landmarks through which she is navigating. When a parent points, a prelocomotor infant will looks at the finger. But an infant who is crawling or walking becomes able to follow the referential gesture toward its target. She will orient first to her parent, and then to the target of their verbal or gestural message (Campos et al., 2000).

In short, then, the infant's new ability to move without the help of other people involves a collection of interconnected changes in how she perceives the world and the people in it, in how she understands space, in her characteristic emotions, and in her relations and communication with other people. For her caregivers it involves new responsibilities and concerns, but also a new appreciation of their child as an active agent. The end of the first year is a time at which "a single acquisition, in this case the onset of locomotion, sets in motion a family of experiences and processes that in turn mobilize both broad-based and context-specific psychological reorganizations" (Campos et al., 2000, p. 150).

3.2 STARTING TO TALK

The second important milestone that defines the transition between infancy and toddlerhood is the child's first use of the powerful resources of the language of their community. Caregivers usually say that their child has started to talk when she speaks her first recognizable word, and this generally occurs somewhere between 10 and 15 months of age. However, for some time before this the infant will have been learning to recognize and even to understand aspects of the speech she hears around her, and to produce the basic sounds of her language. Nonetheless, the first words are an important milestone.

What is language? Linguists have offered a variety of definitions, each focused on a different aspect of language. Obviously there are many different languages in the world, and not all of them involve speech—the sign languages used by people who are deaf are just as complex and subtle as any spoken language—but it is spoken language that I will focus on here. Spoken language can be viewed, in very simple terms, as a system in which sequences of sounds, acoustic wave patterns, *count* as words, which in turn *stand for* classes or categories of objects and events in the world. Language is both a system of action and a system of meaning, and words and grammatical structure are tools for producing meaning—"propositional content"—in order to carry out an action. Language involves both doing and saying. In the first words of an infant, however, only the first of these is present. As we shall see, the infant speaks to act and not to represent.

3.2.1 THE LEVELS OF LANGUAGE

It is helpful to think of a language as organized on four distinct levels: those of its **sounds**, its **words**, its **sentences**, and its **utterances**. In a sense, language at each of these levels is a code that the child has to crack. At each level there are conventions which must be discovered. Children's discoveries show a common pattern, so that even though we cannot yet fully *explain* how they learn language, we can *describe* the ways they do so.

The Level of Sounds. All spoken languages are made up of a fixed and finite set of sound units, called **phonemes**. English, for example, has 40, while Spanish has 24. (We saw in Chapter 3 that mapping the number of phonemes in each of the world's languages has enabled us to identify the likely place and time for the evolutionary origin of language.) The study of the sounds of language is called **phonetics**. Phonemes are the *vowels* and *consonants* of a language. When we speak, we force air from our lungs up through the larynx, over the vocal folds, and into our mouth and nasal cavities, where it leaves between the lips and through the nostrils. The sound is shaped by movements of the tongue, lips, and glottis. Vowels are made with an open flow of air, varying in the shape of the mouth and where the tongue is placed. For example, in the "e" of "beat" our tongue is raised towards the roof of our mouth. The consonants may be *stops*, where the flow of air is completely halted for a fraction of a second ("t" as a "tree"), or *fricatives*, where the flow is restricted but not stopped ("v" in "thrive"). A phoneme may be *voiced*—accompanied by vibrations in the vocal folds—or *unvoiced*—without such vibration. These characteristics are the **distinctive features** of each phoneme: features such as voicing, plosion, and place of articulation. Each phoneme consists of a unique combination of these features.

The level of sounds also includes **intonation**, the pattern of changes in pitch when words are spoken, which has one foot in the linguistic camp and the other foot in **paralinguistics**, those non-verbal aspects of communication that include facial expression and gesture. Pitch and tempo display the biology of emotionality—we speak more rapidly and with more pitch variation when we are angry—but also cultural dimensions such as politeness. In some cultures it is polite to speak slowly, while in others what is polite is speaking rapidly.

Even a newborn is able to distinguish between the sound of speech and non-language sounds, and shows a preference for the former, and within a few days she can distinguish the sound of her family's particular language from other languages, probably because she was hearing speech in the womb. By 6 months of age she is able to recognize the phonemes of her particular language, and this means, seemingly paradoxically, that she no longer notices the differences among sounds that fall within the same phoneme. She has learned not to pay attention to differences in sound that do not make a difference in the language she is learning. (This learned ability—or inability—is one reason why it is much more difficult to learn a second language as an adult; adults can no longer hear the important sound differences in a new set of phonemes.) By 6 months of age, even though she cannot yet speak its phonemes, the infant has adopted the intonation patterns of her language so that even untrained listeners can tell the difference between the sounds made by infants raised in families speaking French and those raised in families speaking Arabic or Cantonese (Locke, 1983; Vihman, 1992).

By 7 months the infant is babbling, vocalizing combinations of vowel and consonant sounds (even if she is exposed to two languages; see Oller et al., 1997), and around 9 months she begins to narrow her babbling to the specific phonemes of her language. By the end of the first year she is using the stress, intonation, and phonemes of her native language. At first, the infant will utter sequences of phonemes that are not recognizable words, vocalizations that are called **jargoning**. But with time she will combine phonemes in such a way that her parents will hear a word, and a milestone will have been reached.

In short, in dealing with the level of the sounds of any spoken language, an infant has to learn first to recognize the phonemes of her community's language and then to produce them, in sequences that are often complex. As she combines phoneme sequences she will invent **simplifying phonological strategies**, such as treating all the stop consonants (where the flow of air is completely stopped for a fraction of a second) in a word as the same, for example saying the word *pancakes* not as "pankakz" but as "panpaps."

Of course, before the infant produces vocalizations that her caregivers recognize as words, she is able to communicate using **vocal gestures**. Some infants imitate the sounds they hear around them, others do not, but all use vocal gestures in a functional way, consistently and systematically, as a form of action that has an impact on other people. For example, an infant might say *nananana* to mean something like "I want that thing now" (Halliday, 1975). This is an example of the **instrumental function** of language: using speech to get things done. In the next chapter I will describe these language **functions** in more detail.

The Words of Language. Just as each language is made up of a specific set of phonemes, so each language contains its own words, so that words in French differ from those in Italian. Each word is made up of a sequence of phonemes. While there is some debate over the degree to which phonemes carry meaning, there is no doubt that words convey meaning. "Dog," for example, in English conventionally means a four-legged, domesticated, carnivorous animal with a long snout and a barking voice. People speak and understand words without a thought, but the issue of how to study and analyze word meaning has been a matter of considerable debate. The study of meaning is called **semantics**. Let's briefly explore some of the semantic characteristics of words, issues that the young child has to master.

First, a word such as "dog" can *refer* to a particular animal, but it can also be said to have the *sense* of *dog* in general. What is the relation between these two aspects of word meaning: **reference** and **sense**? And where can the sense of a word be found? Is it a **concept**? Is it in the speaker's mind? Or is it in some timeless, universal realm, as some philosophers have proposed? A child has to figure out not only what object, or categories of object, each word refers to, but also the sense that the word conveys when it is used.

For when words are used in utterances they have **interpersonal meaning.** When "dog" is said in a specific situation, it will be interpreted in a way that depends on that context. In a picnic, saying "dog" could be taken to mean a request for another hotdog, or it could be taken to mean a warning that someone's pet has stolen the hamburgers. This shows the important role of **context** in word meaning.

Second, the basic unit of meaning in language is actually not the word, it is the **morpheme**. A morpheme may be a whole word or part of a word, such as a prefix or suffix. Words such as "in" and "on" are morphemes. The plural suffix "-s" is a morpheme, as is the past tense suffix "-ed." Some languages use many suffixes and prefixes to combine meanings, while others do this by stringing words together in a sequence.

The Sentences of Language. Words may be spoken individually, but usually they are combined into sentences. Sentences are sequences of words that follow the rules which define the **grammar** or **syntax** of a language. Utterances of two words or more can be said to have a grammatical "structure." A child has to learn which combinations of words are grammatically acceptable, and she has to discover the syntactic rules that underly a sentence. I will postpone until Chapter 9 a detailed discussion of this third level of language, since children generally do not speak in more than single words before they are toddlers.

The Utterances of Language. The fourth level of language concerns the uses of language—the way people speak words in sentences in specific circumstances to achieve particular goals in interaction with the people around them. The study of this level of language is called **pragmatics**. This level turns out to be of primary importance in the first stages of learning to speak a language: the infant learns to speak in the course of trying to have an effect on the people around her. The elements of language at this level are known as **speech acts** (Austin, 1975; Searle, 1969).

3.2.2 LEARNING HOW TO MEAN

There are many different accounts of children's language acquisition. Some focus on specific details, others aim for the big picture. Some emphasize the role of syntax (e.g., Pinker, 2000), while others highlight the role of pragmatics (e.g., Tomasello, 2003). I will focus on an account that is not the newest but remains one of the most significant, that of linguist Michael Halliday.

Halliday carried out a very interesting case study in which he shifted the focus from grammatical structure to the functions of language, an example of a "usage-based approach" to language acquisition (Ellis et al., 2016; Halliday, 1975). At the time, Noam Chomsky's analysis of syntactic structures (Chomsky, 1965) had been adopted as the basis for empirical studies of children's speech and their language acquisition. As we shall see in Chapter 8, because these studies were interested in syntax the researchers focused on utterances with two or more morphemes and did not look at single-word utterances (Brown, 1973; Brown & Fraser, 1964). One implication of Halliday's focus on the functions of language was that single-word utterances were no longer considered irrelevant. From a functional perspective, there is language as soon as an infant produces meaningful expressions, even when these have no grammatical structure.

Halliday studied the way his son Nigel learned to speak, starting at 9 months of age. Nigel's earliest language, which Halliday called "Phase I," consisted of only two levels, sounds and meanings, with neither words nor syntactic structures. Phase II, which appeared when Nigel was around 17 months of age, was a transition in which he added a third level which Halliday called **lexicogrammar**, and in which he also mastered the speech conventions of dialog. (In contrast to Chomsky, who argued that syntax is an autonomous part of language, Halliday considers syntax and the lexicon—that is, grammar and vocabulary—to be intimately connected. Lexicogrammar is his term for the combination of the two.)

Phase III of Nigel's language skills, at around 30 months, was what Halliday considered his entry into the adult language system. Over the course of these phases, the functional organization of Nigel's language system evolved and transformed in significant ways. I will discuss Phase II in Chapter 8, and Phase III in Chapter 9.

During Phase I, Halliday identified the following basic functions in Nigel's language:

Instrumental: "I want"
Regulatory: "Do as I tell you"
Interactional: "Me and you"
Personal: "Here I come"
Heuristic: "Tell me why"
Imaginative: "Let's pretend"

The Functions of Language at Phase I (with permission, from Halliday, 1975)

Phase 1 Language (9–12 months). In this first phase an utterance can perform only a single function. At 10.5 months, Nigel's utterances were not yet recognizable words from the adult language, though his family could understand these and respond. He was using the first four of the functions in the table above: Nigel was vocalizing to obtain material needs (the *instrumental* function), to influence the behavior of other people (the *regulatory* function), to make contact (*interactional*) and to express himself (*personal*). Just before he moved to Phase II he began to vocalize to pretend (*imaginative*) and to ask the names of things (*heuristic*).

In Chapter 8 I will continue the account of Nigel's growing skill with language. The most important point to emphasize here, however, is that in Phase I of his language, Nigel was using speech to interact with other people but not to share or seek information. Speech at this age neither represents nor informs. This confirms what other researchers have observed: language is used first as a pragmatic resource rather than a semantic resource. As I mentioned above, pragmatics turns out to be more fundamental than syntax in the acquisition of language. Of course, the fact that language is not yet used by the infant to communicate information does not mean that it cannot be used to do other things. This may seem contradictory; obviously, for an adult the infant's vocalizations do precisely that: they convey information. However, the infant's vocalizations do not *encode* information. They convey information to the adult because of what the *adult* brings to their interaction, not because of what the infant brings. The infant simply tries to have an effect.

3.2.3 THE FIRST WORDS: HOLOPHRASTIC UTTERANCES

When the first recognizable words are produced, they are fitted into the kind of simple linguistic system that Nigel illustrated at Phase I. The infant's first words are different from adult speech both in their

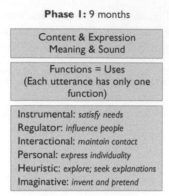

Figure 6.11 Phase I language

sounds and their meanings. When an infant starts to speak her language is **holophrastic**: what for an adult would be a whole phrase is boiled down into a single word. The meaning of these first words is always complex, and a single word functions as though it were a whole phrase or a sentence. A word is often first used in a specific initial situation, then applied in other settings where the meaning is evidently derived from separate parts of the original situation. An infant's first utterances can often be understood only by the adults with whom she has a history of interaction, and even then only in concrete settings. Communication between the infant and adults is quite different from communication among adults: adults can use words to *replace* a situation, to talk about things and events that are not present, but an infant's words cannot serve this function, they can only pick out a single aspect of a situation. This means that adults must continue to adapt to the child. As Vygotsky put it, "before a child begins to speak in our language, he compels us to speak in his language" (Vygotsky, 1998[1932–1934], p. 249). We will explore these holophrastic utterances further in Chapter 8.

As I have said, an infant uses her first words to **indicate** (or designate), but not yet to represent; she uses neither the grammar nor the abstract concepts of adult speech. These utterances are preliminary forms of speech acts, and for this reason they have been called **proto-imperatives** and **proto-declaratives** (Bates et al., 1979); they are **performatives** that accomplish personal and interpersonal functions. Each single-word utterance is in many respects still a vocal gesture.

What we have at this point, then, is a **protolanguage**: a form of speech that as yet does not have any syntax, any grammatical organization, but does have what we can call a protopragmatics, so that an infant is able to speak in order to direct other people's attention to objects, without saying anything specific about those objects.

In truth, the basic unit of language that an infant starts with is not the word, but the utterance: the act of speaking. She understands the utterances of the members of her family on the basis of the shared background of joint attention, the Great-We, and by building on her understanding of non-linguistic actions, including gestures. It seems most likely that the infant learns the words of her family's language as she tries to understand utterances, and as she hears words repeated across utterances in situations with similarities. So-called "mapping" theories of language acquisition propose that an infant builds a "map" of links between words and objects (e.g., Smith & Yu, 2008). However, this cannot be the whole story, because the goal of understanding a person's utterance is not to identify its referent, the object referred to, it is to understand the speaker's intention and their motive in speaking (Tomasello, 2003). For this goal, a map of words and objects would not be sufficient. Clearly, the infant's growing comprehension of language builds upon her understanding of other people, as well as contributing to it.

Compared with the adult language, then, an infant's first speech is different in its phonetics, semantics, pragmatics, and syntactics. But it serves as a bridge that the child can cross, to make the transition from the vocal but non-verbal communication of infancy to the verbal communication of the toddler. These early words play an essential transitional role. They show the infant's dawning recognition that her needs are not obvious to other people so they must be communicated, and that one central way to do this is using language. And although the infant is speaking only in one-word phrases, adults talk to her in syntactically complex sentences with a large vocabulary, adjusted to her level of comprehension.

BOX 6.1 THE QUESTIONS THAT MUST BE ANSWERED ON EACH LEVEL OF LANGUAGE

I.   THE LEVEL OF SOUND

What are the basic units of sound?

Phonemes:

In English there are 40: /p/ /b/ /r/

How to recognize them?

Categorical perception: /pa/ & /ba/

How to produce them?

Distinctive features: voicing, plosion, place

How to combine them?

Simplifying phonological strategies

2.   THE LEVEL OF MEANING

What are the basic units of meaning?

Smaller than the word: morphemes

"cat/s" prefixes, suffixes (plural, tense, inflections)

(Continued)

(Continued)

English has 100,000, making 500,000 words

Grammatical morphemes ...

Where are the word boundaries?

"Why are you weary?"

How do words refer to things?

The problem of reference ...

How do words relate to other words?

Semantic relations ...

3.   THE LEVEL OF SENTENCES

How to string words together?

Sequences of words

How to speak grammatically?

Grammatical categories: noun, verb, adjective

4.   THE LEVEL OF USES

How to do things with words?

Pragmatics

What are the basic units of communication?

Speech acts

How to be polite?

Conversational implicature

3.3 BIOLOGICAL DIFFERENTIATION AND ATTACHMENT

Walking and talking contribute to, and feed back into, a substantial transformation in the relationship between infant and caregivers. Often this change is described as the formation of an **attachment relationship**, but it is more accurate to view it as a change in the way the infant relates to the people with whom she is already involved in the Great-We. What is undeniable is that around the time an infant begins to walk and talk she starts to respond in a new way to the important people in her life. She starts to show strong emotional responses to separation from and reunion with these people. This "attachment" demonstrates again how biology and culture are interwoven.

I mentioned earlier that walking has been called the "psychological birth" of the infant, as she discovers the new possibilities of exploring the world without adult assistance. I have mentioned that caregivers describe their infant displaying new delight and happiness, but also as starting to have temper tantrums. We will see that it is not until around 2.5 years of age that the toddler becomes **self-conscious**, conscious of herself as an object in the eyes of other people. However, at the end of infancy she becomes aware of herself as a source of agency in the world, a phenomenon I am calling **self-awareness**.

Attachment might be said to reflect the infant's dawning recognition of her own dependence on other people, precisely because of her new independence. It is as though as she discovers the new things she can do by herself, she recognizes for the first time her own dependence and vulnerability. During the first year, the infant has become increasingly skilled at enjoying the company of other people and influencing them to obtain what she wants. When she starts to walk and talk this seems to provide her with a new sense, an awareness, of her own agency. Until this point she has needed others to fetch and carry for her; now she can begin to do so herself. The fact that the attachment "bond" now appears is evidence, somewhat paradoxically, for this differentiation, what Vygotsky called a "biological separation." Although the infant can now do things for herself she still is greatly dependent on her caregivers, and she seems to recognize this for the first time, and this is evident in new anxieties and fears.

3.3.1 BOWLBY'S THEORY OF ATTACHMENT

There are competing theories of how and why there is a new emotional quality to the relationship with caregivers around the transition from infant to toddler (Cassidy & Shaver, 2008), but much research takes as its starting point the work of John Bowlby.

Bowlby (1969, 1982) was trained in the United Kingdom as a child psychiatrist, and he worked during the Second World War with children who had lost their mothers or been separated from their families. He arranged for the observation of hospitalized or institutionalized children, and identified three phases in their response to this separation from parents: first protest, which included throwing tantrums and trying to escape; second despair and depression, and finally detachment, a state of indifference to other people.

Bowlby drew on work from ethology (such as Lorenz's work on "imprinting" in young goslings), cybernetics (the study of control systems), and psychoanalysis (which emphasized the enduring importance of early relations), to propose that the emotional connection between child and mother is based not on satisfaction of the infant's needs, such as hunger, but on instinctual responses which, in the human infant, take the form of a behavioral system that involves control through feedback.

Specifically, Bowlby proposed that an infant shows "a number of species-characteristic behavior systems, relatively independent of each other at first, which emerge at different times, become organized toward the mother as the chief object, and serve to bind child to mother and mother to child" (Ainsworth, 1969, p. 27).

He argued that we should interpret an infant's behavior in terms of the environment in which our species evolved, the "environment of evolutionary adaptedness." In his view, behaviors that might seem irrational today were once crucial to survival, and became part of the human biological repertoire through natural selection. These behaviors work together as a system which has the general function of maintaining a child in a defined relationship with her environment. Viewed from this perspective, attachment behaviors are products of a system that maintains proximity between the child and her caregivers, and its evolutionary function is protection of the child from danger. Young infants signal this need for proximity indiscriminately to anyone around them, but with time these behaviors become focused on the primary caregivers, who then serve as a safe haven from which the toddler can explore, but to which she can return when there is danger. The attachment system maintains a dynamic balance between security and comfort, on the one hand, and exploration and learning, on the other.

Later, Bowlby (1969) proposed that we can view the behaviors of the toddling infant and her caregiver as a simple cybernetic arrangement: a feedback loop that functions rather like a thermostat. A thermostat is a simple system: it maintains a constant temperature in a room by varying a source of heat or cooling. If the temperature starts to rise, the input of heat is reduced. If the temperature starts to fall, the heat is increased. In an analogous manner, the attachment system maintains a constant level of security in the toddler, by varying the distance (or proximity) to the attachment figure. If all is safe, the toddler moves away from the secure base to explore. If some threat of danger appears, she will move back towards the base to reestablish her sense of security.

Attachment has been defined as "an affectional tie that one person or animal forms between himself and another specific one—a tie that binds them together in space and endures over time" (Ainsworth & Bell, 1970, p. 50). Once the infant can walk she is able to explore the environment independent of her caregivers. This gives her new opportunities to learn but it also introduces new risks. The emotions of the "attachment system" assure that she has the security to be able to explore and learn, but also that she will return to the safety and protection of her caregiver when necessary. There is a "dynamic equilibrium" between seeking proximity and exploration. However, as Ainsworth noted, "[e]ven though the baby, once mobile, strongly tends to seek proximity, he is still not very competent to do so, and he tends to explore without much discrimination or judgment about dangers; therefore the responsibility still remains largely with the mother" (Ainsworth, 1969, p. 34). With time the balance shifts, and the child spends much longer exploring, with the approval of her attachment figure.

At first, psychologists interpreted Bowlby's observations as indicating that an infant needs to be with her biological mother (Vicedo, 2011). We now know that infants and toddlers can also form attachments to their father, and to other caregivers. They can form multiple attachments to several different caregivers. The fact of attachment does not mean that daycare for infants and toddlers is a bad idea; on the contrary, good daycare provides great opportunities for them to develop their capabilities in the process of meeting new adults and other children.

Research with animals has also contributed to our understanding of attachment. Harry Harlow conducted research with rhesus monkeys (Harlow, 1958; Harlow & Harlow, 1965; Meyer et al., 1975). One important finding was that infant primates also show attachment behavior, which supports the notion that attachment evolved before the separation between humans and other primates. In addition, the attachment that infant primates form is made on the basis not of receiving food but contact and physical comfort. Sigmund Freud had argued that the mother is the most important figure to an infant because she provides milk. Behaviorist researchers argued that the infant learns to value her mother through **drive-reduction**: being fed satisfies and reduces the infant's impulsive "drive" to seek nourishment, and this is rewarding to the infant. Harlow and his colleagues found instead that soothing contact was

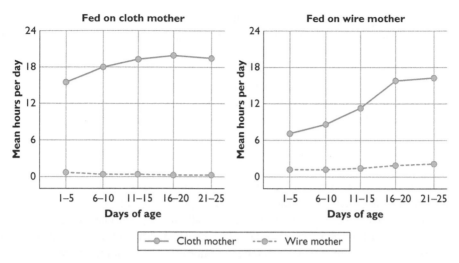

Figure 6.12 Time spent on cloth and wire mother surrogates

Source: Harlow (1958)

the basis for the formation of attachment. Infant rhesus monkeys were raised with surrogate mothers, either covered in cloth or made from wire. Even if the wire surrogate provided food, the infant monkeys preferred to spend time with the cloth-covered surrogate. Harlow wrote that "We believe that contact comfort has long served the animal kingdom as a motivating agent for affectional responses" and that this is the basis for "the development of love in the neonate and infant" (Harlow, 1958).

3.3.2 AINSWORTH'S RESEARCH

Bowlby's attachment theory was soon developed through studies by his colleague Mary Ainsworth, who conducted interviews and naturalistic observations of mothers and babies in Uganda and then a more detailed study in the United States (Ainsworth, 1967; Ainsworth et al., 1978). Ainsworth was struck by the fact that children in these two cultural groups exhibited similar patterns of behavior. These patterns included distress during brief, everyday separations from the mother, fear of strangers, and use of the mother as what Ainsworth called a **secure base** from which to explore. However, the Ugandan children seemed to express these behavior patterns more readily and more intensely than the American children.

Ainsworth also noted differences in maternal sensitivity which seemed to be associated with distinct patterns of attachment: **sensitive** mothers had **securely attached** toddlers who cried little and happily explored when their mother was present; less sensitive mothers had **insecurely attached** toddlers who cried frequently, even when their mothers held them, and who explored little. Infants who were not yet attached showed no differences in their behavior with their mother and with other people.

Ainsworth developed a laboratory procedure called the **Strange Situation** for studying attachment and exploratory behavior in 1-year-olds. This procedure is a 20-minute sequence of eight episodes. First, mother and infant are brought into a laboratory playroom, where they are later joined by an unfamiliar person. While the stranger plays with the infant the mother leaves, and then returns a little later. The stranger leaves, and then the mother too, so that the infant is alone. The stranger returns first, and then a little later the mother.

Ainsworth found that the majority of infants, as expected, sought interaction, proximity, or contact with their mother on reunion with her. However, surprisingly, a few of the infants were angry when their mother returned. These infants cried and evidently wanted contact, but when they were picked up they showed ambivalence, kicking or swiping at their mother. Another group of infants seemed to avoid or ignore the mother when she returned, even though they looked for her when she was gone (Ainsworth et al., 1974). On the basis of these findings Ainsworth distinguished three patterns of response to separation from the parent and subsequent reunion: Type A—**avoidant** (also called anxious-avoidant); Type B—**securely attached**; and Type C—**resistant** (also called anxious-resistant, or ambivalent). Subsequent work has identified an additional pattern, Type D—**disorganized** (Hesse & Main, 2000; Main & Solomon, 1990). Table 6.1 summarizes these patterns. A great deal of research has explored these different patterns of attachment behavior, and we shall return to this topic in the next chapter, where I will explore the phenomenon of attachment in more detail, including research that explores the antecedents and consequences of these distinct patterns of attachment behavior.

A. **Avoidant:** Little distress at departure, or response at return. Treats the stranger like the caregiver.
B. **Secure:** Uses the caregiver as a secure base. Protests departure and seeks proximity.
C. **Resistant:** Seeks proximity before separation. Anger and ambivalence on return.
D. **Disorganized:** Freezes or rocks on return. Contradictory behaviors such as approaching but with the back turned.

Four patterns of attachment

	Seeking Proximity	Maintaining Contact	Avoiding Proximity	Resisting Contact
A: Avoidant	Low	Low	High	Low
B: Secure	High	High (if distressed)	Low	Low
C: Resistant	High	High (often before separation)	Low	High
D: Disorganized	Inconsistent	Inconsistent	Inconsistent	Inconsistent

Figure 6.13   Behavior in the Strange Situation in each attachment pattern

3.3.3 AVOIDING ATTACHMENT

We will see in the next chapter that many psychologists maintain that infants and toddlers everywhere need to be parented—and in particular mothered—in a way that establishes a strong "attachment relationship": an emotional bond. However, ethnographers have noted in many cultures the casual way in which a mother may attend to the needs of her infant, carrying her on the back while engaged in routine tasks, putting her to the breast without engaging in interaction, and in general not paying very much attention.

In such cultures the practical concern that parents must confront is to "avoid forming a premature attachment" (Lancy, 2013). Several issues seem to play a part in this. High rates of infant illness and mortality mean that it is sensible to wait and see whether the infant survives. The multiple responsibilities that confront a new mother mean that her attention cannot be focused entirely on her infant. Practices of fostering and alloparenting mean that an infant is often cared for by people other than the mother, whose emotional involvement is correspondingly reduced. Unwanted births, due to a lack of contraception and other factors, also reduce affection for the infant. Finally, the view that a child's central role is to contribute labor to the family reduces the formation of an emotional relationship with an infant, who cannot yet work, and so is not yet a true member of the family.

The consequence of these issues is that in many parts of the world an infant is not considered a full person, not yet ripe, until she is able to talk or walk—in fact, there seems to be very little consensus about the age at which personhood emerges. Some cultures view the young infant as not yet connected, others see her as still in another world: pure and innocent, or channeling evil forces, or a trickster who does not intend to become human (Lancy, 2008). On the other hand, there are a few cultures, such as the Beng people in West Africa, where infants receive *lots* of attention because they are believed to be reincarnated ancestors who must be discouraged from returning to the afterlife (Gottlieb, 2015)!

3.4 SECONDARY INTERSUBJECTIVITY

Between 9 and 12 months of age, as an infant reaches the threshold of independent locomotion, another dramatic change takes place with the appearance of what has been called **secondary intersubjectivity**. Several new phenomena appear.

First, the infant's interest in objects and her interest in people become integrated: she begins to engage in cooperative games and tasks in which she and an adult share joint attention to objects of interest. This has been described as "the systematic combining of purposes directed to objects with those that invoked interest and interaction from a companion" (Trevarthen, 1998, p. 31). The infant's interactions are no longer dyadic, person to person, they are **triadic interactions**, in which the infant is able to interact with both another person and an object.

Second, the infant can now follow another person's gaze, and also their pointing gestures. She herself begins to point to things in order to draw people's attention to something that interests her (Tomasello et al., 2007).

Third, the infant starts to use other people's emotional responses towards ambiguous situations to guide her own actions, in what is called **social referencing**. The infant will turn to check how her caregiver is reacting to an unexpected event, such as the appearance of an unfamiliar person, before responding.

Sometimes these new phenomena have been interpreted as indicating that the infant now understands other people's visual perspective, and even their intentions. However, as we shall see in the next chapter, this is an unlikely explanation of what is going on (Carpendale & Lewis, 2004). It makes more sense to see the infant's new behaviors as emerging within the interactions of the Great-We.

First, it is important that we not overestimate what the infant is now capable of in understanding other people. At first, she will simply follow the turn of someone's head (Corkum & Moore, 1998). When she first starts to point she does so without checking whether anyone notices. Second, these new phenomena have an emotional core. For example, it seems that an infant will looks to her mother not to share a focus of attention but because she is stressed and seeking support (Baldwin & Moses, 1996). When she encounters a new object she will pay close attention to the emotions that adults display (Moses et al., 2001). I mentioned earlier that Vygotsky argued that to an infant the adult is center of every situation, and as adults come and go this "arms and disarms" her activity. As the infant becomes a toddler, able to move independently, her dependence on others is reduced only minimally, and it makes great sense for her sense of security to continue to depend greatly on the presence of her caregivers.

Certainly, however, around the end of the first year there is evidence for an important change in the way other people's actions are understood by infants. They begin to recognize that these actions are directed towards goals, and that there is intention *in* these actions. This is not to say, though, that they understand the intentions *behind* such action. For instance, by about 10 months of age an infant will respond differently when someone handing them a toy accidentally drops it, compared with how they would respond if the toy is withdrawn in a teasing manner (Behne et al., 2005). She will imitate a person's actions on objects and collaborate in actions. In the next chapter I will describe this transition from the *contingent stance* of infancy to the *teleological stance* of toddlerhood.

These developments in expressive bodily communication, and the subtlety of the timing and detail of these infant–adult interactions, seem to have a clear continuity with, and presumably pave the way for, the linguistic communication that emerges at the end of infancy.

CONCLUSION

The first year of life is a time when action is not separated from perception or emotion. Practical, embodied understanding is the infant's mode of psychological functioning. This practical understanding can be studied and described in a variety of different ways. In Chapters 5 and 6 we have explored four of these. The first is in terms of the increasingly complex schemas that Piaget described as underlying infants' sensorimotor understanding of the world. The second is in terms of brain function, where we can see the lower levels of the perception–action cycle, and the ways that System 1—the unconscious and intuitive system—is slowly modified. The third is in terms of the practical interpersonal interactions of this stage. The fourth is in terms of emotionality.

These approaches complement each other. For example, we have seen that emotion, a process of appraisal-and-action, is not possessed in its entirety by an infant but is a characteristic of the infant–adult system. The caregiver and infant *together* comprise a complete combination of System 1 and System 2. Emotion is centrally important at this stage. It is the primary way that young infants communicate, without conscious intention, with adults. It is the evaluative aspect of sensorimotor intelligence, of the perception–action cycle. And attachment at the end of infancy is not a new bond so much as the infant becoming aware for the first time of her dependence on others, and so of the potential threat when a caregiver leaves.

Towards the end of the first year (with wide individual and cultural variation), an infant begins to move independently and speak her first recognizable words. New doors are opened, and new steps are taken, literally and figuratively. The infant's biological dependence is lessened, as she can move by herself and obtain things that catch her fancy. Her psychological dependence, however, does not end. If anything, it increases, in that caregivers now have to be vigilant to protect the infant—now a toddler—when she gets into situations that she cannot handle. At the same time, speech enables the infant to influence people in new ways, through verbal communication—the first appearance of a new kind of understanding, in which sounds count as acts. Both child and adults have to adapt to these changes. A new stage begins, and a new chapter of the child's development.

SUMMARY

PRECURSOR EMOTIONS AND THEIR REGULATION

- The regulation of emotions is a key aspect of an infant's development. An infant depends on her caregivers to help her regulate her emotions. Caregivers provide natural biofeedback training. The dynamic of emotion between infant and caregiver is an example of co-regulation: the caregivers provide control that the infant herself lacks. This illustrates Vygotsky's General Genetic Law.

BIOLOGICAL DEVELOPMENTS DURING INFANCY

- During the first 12 months there is rapid, continuous physical growth. An infant in the USA on average triples her weight. Growth is cephalocaudal, with the head and upper body growing first. The brain doubles in weight during the first year. New neurons and glial cells are created, synaptic connections grow and then are pruned, axons and dendrites grow, and fiber bundles connect brain regions.

THE TRANSITION AT 1 YEAR: BIOLOGICAL DIFFERENTIATION

- The transition at 1 year has three main constituents: the first steps, the first words, and the first assertions of independence.

- Independent movement leads to dramatic psychological changes in perceptions, cognition, and social and emotional behavior. Walking changes the infant's relationship with caregivers, who must intervene when the infant gets into trouble or puts herself in danger.

(Continued)

(Continued)

- The infant starts to produce her first recognizable words at around 12 months. This simple "Phase I" language involves only two levels: sounds and meanings. Speech by the infant is not yet representational or informative. Each utterance is produced as a tool rather than as a sign.

- In this transition at 1 year old, the attachment relationship starts to form: the infant shows strong emotional reactions when she is separated from and reunited with caregivers. John Bowlby proposed attachment is a bond between child and mother that evolved to ensure that the child seeks security. In research using the Strange Situation, Mary Ainsworth discovered three patterns of attachment behavior, apparently associated with differences in maternal sensitivity. Type A is avoidant; Type B is securely attached; Type C is resistant. Subsequently a Type D, disorganized, was also distinguished.

CHAPTER 7

TODDLERHOOD

(1 YEAR–30 MONTHS)
A WORLD OF IRRESISTIBLE INVITATIONS

LEARNING OBJECTIVES

In this chapter we explore the second stage of human development, between 12 months and 30 months of age. We will consider:

- The world of the toddler, in which independent locomotion has opened up new invitations which she is at first unable to resist.
- The character of caregiving at this stage, which will bring us back to the attachment that began to appear at the end of infancy, as we saw in Chapter 6.
- The way a toddler understands other people.
- The substantial biological changes that take place during this stage, in body and brain.

FRAMING QUESTIONS

- Imagine you have a 1-year-old. She is starting to walk, and she gets into everything! Would you punish her for this?
- Do you consider that the mother is the most important caregiver for a baby?
- At what age would you expect a child to experience the emotions of pride and shame? Why?

INTRODUCTION

As we saw in the previous chapter, what appears to initiate the transition to a new developmental stage is the ability to move independently on two feet. We saw that an infant may become able to walk unaided as early as 8 months of age, or as late as 17 months. That is to say, the transition between infancy and toddlerhood occurs at different ages in different circumstances. Equally, the achievements that mark the end of toddlerhood and the transition into early childhood show much variation. However, let us say that this stage spans roughly the period from around 12 months of age to around 2.5 years (30 months).

Whether it begins earlier or later, toddlerhood is a stage in which key developments take place, and in many societies it is also a stage that is increasingly scrutinized by professionals (Edwards & Liu, 2002).

Once an infant becomes capable of independent movement—to "toddle" is to walk with short, unsteady steps—the world changes: now it includes accessible and inaccessible places, things, and people to which the toddler responds with enthusiasm. In addition, once the infant can use not only sounds and gestures but also recognizable words of her family's language new possibilities open up here too. As we saw at the end of the last chapter, once an infant begins to walk and talk her relationship with her surroundings and with other people is transformed.

Toddlerhood is a stage of mastering the simple skills of daily life, such as feeding and dressing, and in doing so coming to understand the customary uses of everyday artifacts—their functions, and the norms for using them. As the toddler participates in a widening range of activities with other people she shows a growing ability to understand the aims in other people's actions, and she also starts to understand the tacit social norms and customs that her family lives by and to hold other people accountable to these (Edwards & Liu, 2002). She observes how things are done in her family, and she understands this as how things *ought* to be done.

1. THE WORLD OF TODDLERHOOD: IRRESISTIBLE INVITATIONS

One fact about toddlers that rapidly becomes clear to every caregiver is that they get into everything. A toddler cannot resist the invitations offered her by the world: once she sees or hears something interesting she has to explore it. The sensorimotor linkages of an infant continue in a toddler and become increasingly elaborate. However, for a toddler the world is very different from what it was for an infant, and she interacts with it in a radically different way. For toddlers—moving on two legs, with the hands free to touch and grab—the world is a kind of forcefield in which they are constantly on the move: a stairway must be climbed; a door must be opened; a ball must be rolled. For toddlers, interesting things impel action.

1.1 AFFORDANCES

I have emphasized that every child is actively involved in the world. Piaget insisted that infants actively explore and adapt. Dynamic field theorists emphasize that the human senses are not passive receptors, but active exploratory systems. As a child acts in the world, her senses encounter streams of structured and constantly changing energy. As she moves, some sensory information remains invariant while other information changes. Space is defined to the senses by these visual, auditory, and tactile gradients of textured information. For example, as a toddler moves across a surface, information streams past the periphery of her vision while information from what is in front stays relatively still and constant.

These streams of information define possible ways of acting for the child. The term **affordance** was coined by psychologist James Gibson, who defined it as the "action possibility" between an organism and its environment (Gibson, 1966). Affordances exist as a *relationship* between an organism and its environment. If you are scrambling up a steep grassy slope, a tree branch could afford a useful handhold and rocks could afford a steady support. The infant discovers the physical affordances in her environment: she learns which things she can grasp and which she can hit, how things will respond when she acts on them.

Using an **affordance** is a process of interpretation. A feature in the environment is understood as permitting, as affording the possibility of, a specific kind of grip, or grasp, or action. We shall see that as a child develops new kinds of affordance emerge: as her physical and psychological capacities grow and change, she will discover and make use of new possibilities for action in the world around her. One can say that the toddler is a dynamic *part* of each situation, her actions adapting to the structure of affordances. Her body is engaged in the world through the perception–action cycles that her brain supports and regulates. She explores her environment with her increasingly sophisticated practical understanding and responds to the information that flows from it into her eyes, ears, and hands. This is skilled and intelligent activity, though of course it lacks the planning, reflection, and forethought that she will have when she is older.

Like the infant, the toddler does not yet understand the world as a place of stable, independent objects. However, we would expect that now the toddler has started to move more freely through her environment her understanding of it will dramatically change. And indeed, research using the **visual cliff experiment** shows that it is only when an infant starts to crawl that she develops a fear of heights. Surprisingly, when she starts to walk she has to learn once again that high places are risky: her different methods of locomotion seem to teach her different things. Experienced 12-month-old crawlers will avoid a steep drop-off, but novice walkers at the same age will step over the edge. At 18 months, however, when these walkers have gained more experience, they will refuse to walk over risky drop-offs and look for another way to descend. Findings like these suggest that when a toddler starts to move she learns how to identify and respond to the affordances relevant to a specific action, first crawling, and then walking (Kretch & Adolph, 2012).

The **gestalt psychologist** Kurt Lewin showed, in a famous demonstration that he captured on film, both the strengths and limitations of toddlers' practical intelligence. The toddler in Lewin's film had great difficulty sitting down on a rock, because when she turned around to sit she could no longer see the seat. She solved this problem by looking between her legs to keep the rock in sight as she lowered herself onto it. The rock offers the new possibility of sitting down: one can only sit down if one can stand up! But because the rock is not yet a permanent, independent object, the offer disappears when it is no longer in sight.

The behavior shown in Lewin's film is an extension of the fusion of perception, affect, and action that was characteristic of infancy. This is why Piaget considered sensorimotor intelligence to continue beyond the stage of infancy into the stage of the toddler (as I have noted, he saw only a single stage here, the sensorimotor stage). Vygotsky suggested that each situation the toddler encounters has an emotional valence for her, attracting her or repelling her, arousing the motivation to touch or avoid, to pick up or put down, to approach or run away. Blue things seem cold, and yellow things seem hot. Piaget emphasized that a toddler is able to explore the environment in ways that an infant is not, and this makes important new developments possible. He saw the second year as a time during which two final substages of sensorimotor intelligence are achieved. Our examination of these substages will lead to a discussion of whether or not the toddler is becoming capable of mental representation and mental action, as Piaget believed.

Figure 7.1   A still from one of Kurt Lewin's films of toddlers trying to sit

Source: With permission from The Virtual Laboratory, Max Planck Institute for the History of Science, Berlin

1.2 SENSORIMOTOR SUBSTAGES 5 AND 6

Substage 5: Tertiary circular reactions, and the discovery of new means through active experimentation (12 to 18 months). The fifth substage of sensory-motor intelligence is marked by increased flexibility and creativity. The toddler becomes engrossed in the many things she can make happen, and starts to systematically vary and combine actions to produce results that interest her. She invents new ways to achieve her goals. Piaget considered the toddler now to be experimenting like a scientist, albeit in a practical manner. For example, the toddler may try dropping a ball from different heights to see how high it will bounce each time. Piaget called these explorations **tertiary circular reactions**. Here is an example:

> *Observation 141.–* […] At 0;10(11) Laurent is lying on his back but nevertheless resumes his experiments of the day before. He grasps in succession a celluloid swan, a box, etc., stretches out his arm and lets them fall. He distinctly varies the positions of the fall. Sometimes he stretches out his arm vertically, sometimes he holds it obliquely, in front of or behind his eyes, etc. When the object falls in a new position (for example on his pillow), he lets it fall two or three times more on the same place, as though to study the spatial relation: then he modifies the situation. At a certain moment the swan falls near his mouth: now, he does not suck it (even though this object habitually serves this purpose), but drops it three times more while merely making the gesture of opening his mouth. (Piaget, 1954[1937], p. 269)

Substage 6: Inventions Through Sudden Comprehension (18 to 30 months). The sixth and final substage of sensory-motor intelligence is marked by an understanding of practical relationships that takes the toddler beyond trial-and-error. She shows evidence of premeditation, originality, and novelty, and Piaget observed what he took to be inventions achieved through sudden comprehension.

In addition, the toddler now has the ability to follow an object through invisible displacements: if an object is hidden and then moved while it is out of sight, the toddler will search persistently for it. She finally shows what Piaget called **object permanence**—understanding that an object continues to exist even when it is not visible.

How are these striking new achievements of substage 6 possible? Certainly, the fact that the toddler now searches systematically for hidden objects suggests that her understanding of the world has changed by the time she reaches 30 months of age. The world of invitations has become a world of stable objects. Piaget considered this, and other new developments, to be evidence that the toddler has become capable of forming **mental representations**.

In Piaget's view, the capacity for mental representation is also behind **deferred imitation**, where the toddler copies what she saw someone do hours or days earlier. It is also evident in the **make-believe** or **pretend play** that toddlers begin to engage in. In Piaget's account, mental representation makes possible a new way of solving problems, in mental action rather than physical action. In this way toddlers, in Piaget's view, prepare for the transition to the **preoperational intelligence** of early childhood.

Here is an example of an invention through sudden comprehension:

Observation 181.– [...] Jacqueline, at 1;8(9) arrives at a closed door – with a blade of grass in each hand. She stretches out her right hand toward the knob but sees that she cannot turn it without letting go of the grass. She puts the grass on the floor, opens the door, picks up the grass again and enters. But when she wants to leave the room things become complicated. She puts the grass on the floor and grasps the doorknob. But then she perceives that in pulling the door toward her she will simultaneously chase away the grass which she placed between the door and the threshold. She therefore picks it up in order to put it outside the door's zone of movement. (Piaget, 1952a[1936], p. 339)

Piaget's account was as follows: "This ensemble of operations, which in no way comprises remarkable invention, is nevertheless very characteristic of the intelligent acts founded upon representation or the awareness of relationships" (Piaget, 1954[1936], p. 339). Certainly we can see here indications of insight, of a problem-solving ability that is more advanced than trial-and-error. But is this evidence of mental representation? It seems that Jacqueline was able to anticipate what would happen when she opened the door to leave the room, but it is not at all obvious that this imagination requires mental representation.

Piaget also observed the toddler for the first time recognizing and understanding simple symbols: he called this the **semiotic function**. Certainly, during the second half of toddlerhood we can see a growing understanding of *material* representations, such as models, pictures, and signs. But does this ability really depend on a new ability to form *mental* representations? I will return to this question in Chapter 8.

Infancy 0–12 months	Sensory-motor stage	**Substage 5:**
Toddler 1–2.5 years	**Sensory-motor stage**	*Practical experimentation (12 to 18 months)*
Early childhood 2.5–6 years	Preoperational stage	**Substage 6:**
Middle childhood 6–12 years	Concrete operational stage	*Object permanence. Deferred imitation.*
Adolescence 12–	Formal operational stage	*Use of symbols (18 to 30 months)*

Figure 7.2   Characteristics of the final sensory-motor substages, according to Piaget

2. CARING FOR THE TODDLER

As the toddler starts to move independently, her relationship with caregivers is transformed. As we saw in the previous chapter this is especially true of walking, though research suggests that crawling can also be important. Now a toddler no longer needs the help of another person in order to seek out and obtain an interesting object, whether this is a toy or an item of food. However, this doesn't mean that caregivers can step out of the picture. If anything, they need to be even more attentive. If the toddler cannot say "no!" to herself because she is caught up with the irresistible invitations of the things around her, her parents need to say it for her. I was recently with the parents of a 2-and-a-half-year-old who was intent on trying to climb down the steep concrete stairs at the entrance to the house. She seemed drawn to the stairs like metal to a magnet and her parents needed to step in to hold her back, or block her access, or tell her to stop. Caregivers need to monitor what a toddler does, and intervene frequently in her impulsive actions. A toddler still needs adults to protect her from dangers in the immediate environment, to keep an eye on her, to pick her up and comfort her when she falls, to prepare food for her, and to put her to bed. We can say, though, that there is now a triangular relation among caregiver–toddler–world, rather than the dyadic caregiver–child relation of infancy.

Caregivers will respond in different ways to this change in their baby. Some will see her new-found independence as something to celebrate. Others will focus on the increased potential for mischief and havoc and will find themselves challenged by their toddler (Biringen et al., 1995).

Indeed, emotions continue to play a major role in caregiver–toddler interaction, in several respects. A toddler's response to affordances is deeply emotional, and this includes her response to adults. Assertions of independence may not be universal, but when they do occur they are impressive: a toddler can show a strong willful opposition. For example, a toddler who is told she cannot have what she wants, or one whose demands are simply misunderstood, may yell and scream, stomp, or throw herself on the floor. Prohibitions seem to be intolerable at this age. While an older child will contentedly allow herself to be led by the hand, the toddler who is starting to walk will insist on exploring by herself and resist adult guidance. This is the age when caregivers will resort to calling "goodbye!" to try to get their toddler to follow them. In doing so, they are making use of the emotional connection that, as we have seen, is generally called "attachment."

We saw at the end of Chapter 6 that the transition around 12 months is, at least in the USA and similar cultures, marked by a new emotional quality in the relationship with caregivers, as though the infant becomes aware for the first time of her dependence on others for care and comfort, and consequently feels threatened when they are not around. A toddler who is left alone will cry because her very existence seems at stake. In this section I will explore this phenomenon of **attachment** in more detail, and then turn to studies of the ways different communities care for toddlers and organize their learning.

Freud wrote of the **anal stage**, at 2–3 years of age, as a time when the toddler views the world as a hostile place and battles with parents over issues such as bowel control. Erik Erikson also viewed aggression and a struggle for autonomy as part of the toddler's emerging personality, though he emphasized that some cultures are much more relaxed than others over toilet training. He recommended that parents should allow their toddlers to make choices and support their assertions of independence.

Certainly, the standard picture of the transition into toddlerhood is that it involves demands and assertions of independence—the temper tantrums mentioned in the last chapter. However, careful research has shown that in some communities toddlerhood is quite different. In Zintatecan Mayan communities, for example, it is often a time when the mother is attending to a new baby and her toddler is displaced. Rather than independence being something the toddler has to struggle for, it is thrust upon her. Zulu toddlers are also weaned abruptly; at first they respond with withdrawal and aggression, then they bounce back and act more independently (Albino & Thompson, 1956). In such societies, the toddler starts to spend time with a group of other children of various ages, rather than being with her parents most of the time. The emphasis on independence as something the toddler must struggle for may have been overstated, and it certainly seems to be culturally specific.

If we return to the categorization of cultures into those that value independence and those that value interdependence, it seems likely that during the toddler stage this distinction will become more clearly visible. In addition, when independence is expected of the toddler this can either take the form of a toddler striving for autonomy, or the caregiver (usually the mother) pushing for separation.

There is certainly evidence that caregivers in different parts of the world have quite different expectations of their toddlers. In the USA, caregivers generally say they value assertiveness, while Italian parents expect sensitivity and graciousness, for example. Toddlers in the USA are often expected to follow the same rules as older children. In other communities, however, toddlers are given a special status: they are allowed to do and have what they want because it is assumed that they do not yet understand how to cooperate (Mosier & Rogoff, 2003). In addition, in many cultures toddlers are encouraged to participate in household activities, even when many of us would consider them risky and dangerous. Among the Efe, toddlers use machetes. Likewise the Aka teach toddlers to throw small spears and use pointed digging sticks. By age 3 or 4, Aka children can cook themselves a meal on an open fire (cf. Grove & Lancy, 2016).

It has to be said, however, that once again cultural variation makes it very difficult to draw general conclusions. In some cultures, toddlers and even young children are discouraged from participating in adult activities, for fear they will mess them up. They are considered to "lack sense" before they are around 6 years of age (Lancy, 2011; see also Broch, 1990).

2.1 THE TODDLER'S ATTACHMENT TO CAREGIVERS

We saw in Chapter 6 that John Bowlby observed a pattern in toddlers' responses to separation from caregivers that he took to be innate, evolved, and universal. He suggested that an "attachment system" has evolved between child and mother to facilitate both proximity and exploration. Harry Harlow's studies with rhesus monkeys showed, moreover, that the bond is not unique to mothers, because a "secure base" can be provided by anyone who provides comfort. Mary Ainsworth's research in Uganda and in Baltimore provided cross-cultural evidence in support of Bowlby's ideas, and also developed a methodology—the Strange Situation—with which to study them.

The central proposal was that a toddler needs a secure base from which to explore, and to return to when there is danger. We can view this as a solution to the challenges that arise once independent locomotion becomes possible. We saw at the end of the last chapter that at around 12 months the toddler will start to check back with caregivers when she encounters anything strange or threatening. This *social referencing* along with attachment behaviors show that caregivers are still the center of the child's world. Emotion remains a psychological process distributed across child and caregiver, because the toddler cannot yet regulate her emotions. At this age emotion still cuts to the core of the toddler's existence, as well it ought: it is the most basic level of our will to survive.

However, Ainsworth's research led to continuing controversy by finding not a single, universal pattern of attachment behavior, but three distinct patterns. As we saw, these patterns have been named avoidant (Type A), secure (Type B), and resistant (Type C). The debate since then has centered around how to interpret these patterns. If the attachment system is innate and universal, why do we find these differences?

Bowlby's own view was that variation from the pattern of favorable development should be considered a "disturbance" of the child's psychology, and is due primarily to a mother's responses to toddler behavior:

> The association which constantly impresses itself upon me is that between form and degree of disturbance and the extent to which the mother has permitted clinging and following, and all the behaviour associated with them, or has refused them. In my experience a mother's acceptance of clinging and following is consistent with favourable development even in the absence of breast feeding, whilst rejection of clinging and following is apt to lead to emotional disturbance even in the presence of breast feeding. Furthermore, it is my impression that fully as many psychological disturbances, including the most severe, can date from the second year of life when clinging and following are at their peak as from the early months when they are rudimentary. (Bowlby, 1958, p. 70)

However, there are problems with these notions of favorable and disturbed development.

2.1.1 WHAT LEADS TO ATTACHMENT PATTERNS?

Researchers have certainly been very interested in investigating the styles of caregiving that *lead* to these different patterns of attachment behavior, and also to explore the *consequences* of each pattern, in both the short and long term (cf. Cassidy & Shaver, 2008). There is evidence that the three principal attachment patterns found in the Strange Situation reflect the early caregiving history, and also that they can predict key aspects of a child's subsequent social development. Interestingly, attachment pattern has not been found consistently related either to the sex of the child or to birth order. As we review this research we shall see that it has led to a heated debate over whether the various attachment patterns should be judged to be "healthy" or "unhealthy."

Let us first explore what leads to these different attachment patterns. Ainsworth suggested that the different patterns of response were due to differences in mothers' "sensitivity." When Ainsworth analyzed the data she had collected in the homes of the toddlers in Baltimore, she concluded that the mothers of Type B toddlers were generally sensitive in their responses to their child, while the mothers of Type A infants were rejecting, and the mothers of Type C toddlers were inconsistently responsive. It was usually the toddler's reaction to being reunited rather than their reaction to separation that correlated best with the mother's sensitivity. This finding has been replicated (de Wolff & van IJzendoorn, 1997), but what might be the explanation? How does a mother's sensitivity influence the way the attachment system operates? As we saw in Chapter 5, responding to an infant's signs requires interpreting these signs. So what counts as a "sensitive" interpretation?

One problem is that sensitivity is often *defined* as encouraging autonomy in the child. Ainsworth wrote that a sensitive mother will "respect the baby as a separate, autonomous person" (Ainsworth, 1976, p. 4) and avoid imposing her will on her infant. Here, what is judged to be sensitive depends on assumptions about appropriate developmental goals—goals which we have seen are not universal. In cultures where interdependence and connection are valued and encouraged, rather than autonomy, the relationship between infant and caregivers is often evaluated as "insecure attachment," and the caregivers are seen as "insensitive." It seems more appropriate to conclude, however, that what counts as sensitive caregiving varies from one culture to another (Rothbaum et al., 2000).

One hypothesis about the way caregiving styles lead to different attachment patterns is that each toddler adapts flexibly to the specific caregiving environment in which she finds herself, so as to maximize the biological protection she can receive. For example, when a caregiver responds inconsistently to a toddler's signs the child is likely to adapt by increasing her bids for attention, and this is evident as extreme dependence, which is identified as the resistant attachment pattern, Type C (Main, 2000).This strategy can maintain proximity, but it also preoccupies the infant and reduces her exploration and learning: the strategy is adaptive biologically, but maladaptive psychologically.

In general, evolution tends to favor a *variety* of behavioral responses in an organism, each of them often an adaptation to a specific environment. If we apply this idea to attachment, it would seem that we have to abandon the idea that Type B attachment is healthy while the other patterns are unhealthy. We would need to consider Type A as healthy in one environment, and Type C in another.

In addition, the proposal that maternal sensitivity leads to specific attachment patterns tends to treat the caregiver–child relationship as a one-way street, in which the toddler is adapting to the adult, but not vice versa. Other studies have found that patterns of *co-regulated* interaction predict attachment patterns, implying that both partners play a role in forming the attachment (Evans & Porter, 2009; Fogel & Garvey, 2007). For example, it has been suggested that the behavior categorized as insecure/ambivalent may be satisfying to a caregiver who is threatened by the toddler's emerging autonomy, so that the toddler's insecure behavior will encourage the caregiver's inconsistency, which will lead to further insecure behavior in a cycle of mutual adaptation (Cassidy & Berlin, 1994).

An important question is whether insecure attachment results from parents sharing with other people the task of caring for their toddler. Many parents have to make arrangements for their toddler while they go to work. Since the caregiver–child bond is strong at this age, it might seem that daycare or similar arrangements could have negative consequences for the toddler. The issue has been controversial. Initial research findings suggested that toddlers who received more than 20 hours a week of care outside the home were more likely to show insecure attachment patterns (Belsky et al., 1996), and this alarming finding led to a US government study. That study found, however, that toddlers who spent more time in childcare were slightly less likely to have a secure attachment, but that by far the greater effects were attributable to "insensitive mothering" and family socioeconomic status (NICHD, 2003a, 2003b).

Cross-cultural research has important relevance here. We saw in Chapter 5 that there are cultures in which infants and toddlers are cared for by many people, both adults and children, not just by parents. For example, grandparents can be a very important resource for childcare. The relative isolation of parents with young children that we tend to take for granted in the industrialized West is by no means universal; toddlers seem entirely able to form secure relationships with multiple caregivers. Attachment researchers have often taken as natural and universal the nuclear family with two parents, and assumed that it is the mother who is centrally responsible for childcare. However, this assumption does not hold up cross-culturally or historically (Ambert, 1994).

2.1.2 WHAT ARE THE CONSEQUENCES OF ATTACHMENT PATTERNS?

When he first formulated attachment theory, Bowlby proposed that the attachment system ensures the continued protection and nurturing of the toddler once she is able to move independently. At the same time, it also ensures that she spends time with her close relatives and learns their ways of living.

The general consequence of attachment for the toddler, then, is twofold: it provides needed protection and at the same time opportunities for learning. In the phenomenon of attachment we see again the interweaving of biology and culture. Some kind of bond with caregivers would seem to be necessary and universal, a consequence of primate evolution that will be found in all human cultures. It would be overstating the case to say that "cultural learning begins with the attachment relationship" (Grossmann & Grossmann, 2005, p. 208), because we have seen that cultural learning begins even before birth. However, it is certainly true that attachment facilitates learning the ways of one's culture, and that "It seems as if nature wanted to make sure that infants begin their lifelong education by first learning about the values of their own people" (2005, p. 207). If attachment is a biological bond it certainly works nicely with culture—it ensures that the toddler relates primarily with kin at the age when she is developing important social and cognitive abilities, especially language.

Investigation of the consequences of patterns of attachment behavior should throw light on the question of whether some forms of attachment are healthier than others. Infants assessed as securely attached at 12 months have been found to form better relationships at 3.5 years than insecure infants, and to be more socially skilled, have more friendships, and be more self-confident at 10 and at 13 years of age (Sroufe et al., 1999). Longitudinal studies have found continuity in attachment pattern into adulthood.

In one such study, 72 percent of children assessed as infants and then as adults 20 years later received the same attachment classification both times (Waters et al., 2000; Waters, Merrick et al., 2000). One explanation of this continuity has been that the child forms an **internal working model** of their relationship with caregivers and that this model endures over time and is applied whenever intimate relationships are formed; only under unusual conditions is the model modified or replaced.

Indeed, those people who had different attachment patterns as adults from those when they were children have been found to have experienced some kind of negative life event, such as the death of a parent, parental divorce, a life-threatening illness, or physical or sexual abuse by a family member.

Researchers have even found that early attachment patterns predict romantic relationships in adolescence and young adulthood. I will return to this topic in Chapters 13 and 14. However, there is not complete agreement about the degree to which attachment patterns persist. One study, conducted by Michael Lewis, found that the attachment pattern at 1 year had *no* relationship to relationships as a young adult of 18 years, or to assessments of metal health at that age (Lewis, 1999).

Lewis concluded that this illustrates an intrinsic difficulty in developmental research: life is full of dramatic events and unpredictably changing circumstances, but most of our developmental theories, including attachment theory, assume that children's development is "organismic"—that it is a slow process of gradual change towards a specific outcome (Lewis, 1998). Lewis argues instead for a "contextualist" model of development, which recognizes the complexity of the developmental process, the multiple determinants of behavior, the role of accidents and chance encounters, and in addition the fact that a child becomes capable of conscious, deliberate choice. "Adaptation" does not always mean gradual change, because the environment changes too, often in dramatic and unpredictable ways. An economic crisis, the illness of a parent, the birth of a sibling: all of these can have an impact on a child's development, but none of them can be predicted. Consequently, any strong correlation between early attachment and later relationships would be expected only in those increasingly rare cases in which the environment has been stable.

- After the global sociality of the first year …
- The toddler forms her first *specific* social relationships.
- This attachment shows culture and biology working together.
- It assures that a toddler learns the ways of her own people.
- The toddler relates primarily with kin, at an age when important social and cognitive abilities are developing

The value of attachment

2.1.3 CULTURE AND ATTACHMENT

An obvious question is whether not only caregiving styles but also cultural styles might influence patterns of attachment. For at least two decades there has been sharp disagreement among developmental scientists concerning the data about attachment in different cultures. Research initially suggested that the proportion of toddlers showing each of the three attachment patterns varied considerably across cultures. Now, however, the picture has become considerably more complicated.

For example, several decades ago children living in some Israeli kibbutzim (collective farms) were raised communally from an early age. Although these children saw their parents every day, the adults who took care of them for much of the time were usually not family members. When placed in the Strange Situation at age 11 to 14 months with either a parent or a caregiver, many of these toddlers became very upset. Half were classified as anxious/resistant, and only 37 percent appeared to be securely attached (Sagi et al., 1995). The researchers suspected that the high rate of insecure attachment was due to the fact that the communal caregivers could not respond promptly to the individual children in their care, since their schedule did not allow them to provide individualized attention. To test this hypothesis the researchers compared the attachment behaviors of toddlers in these traditional kibbutzim, where they slept in a communal dormitory at night, with those of toddlers in kibbutzim where they returned to sleep in their parents' homes at night (Sagi et al., 1994). Once again, the researchers found a low frequency of secure attachments among the toddlers who slept in communal dormitories, whereas the toddlers who slept at home displayed a significantly higher level of secure attachment, supporting the idea that differences in the degree of sensitive caregiving accounted for the differences in attachment quality.

Some have argued, however, that these different proportions of attachment patterns are actually cultural differences in what counts as attachment, and that the very notion of human relatedness which is part of the categorization of attachment is culturally specific (Rothbaum et al., 2000). For example, a low percentage of securely attached babies has been observed among northern (but not southern) German children. Researchers in one study found that 49 percent of the 1-year-olds tested were anxious-avoidant and only 33 percent were securely attached (Grossmann et al., 1985). Having made extensive observations of home life in northern Germany the researchers were able to reject the possibility that a large proportion of the parents were insensitive or indifferent to their children. Rather, it seemed that these parents were following a cultural norm that called for the maintenance of a relatively large interpersonal distance from their children, and that they believed that babies should be weaned from parental bodily contact as soon as they became mobile. (This seems consistent with the finding of a *distal style* of parenting in Germany, discussed in Chapter 5.) The researchers suggested that among northern German mothers, "the ideal is an independent, non-clinging infant who does not make demands on the parents but rather unquestioningly obeys their commands" (1985, p. 253).

For example, these mothers aimed to satisfy their infants' needs without disrupting the family routine, and they avoided "spoiling" their child with too much attention. The toddler slept in her own room, and the mother left the toddler alone there for some time when she woke in the morning. Toddlers were left alone at home when the mother went shopping. Any anxiety the toddler might feel was viewed as not having serious consequences. Such patterns of interaction would presumably lead toddlers to become more tolerant of separations from their mother, and this may be what the Strange Situation measured.

In the USA today, in contrast, leaving a toddler unattended is illegal in many states. However, it is important to recall that in the 1920s and for several decades afterwards the standard advice to parents in the USA was very similar to that practiced in northern Germany in the 1970s. It was only after World War II that a more emotionally responsive and child-centered style of parenting became advocated. The goal of parenting shifted away from physical health towards mental health, though it was still taken for granted that there was a single pathway to this goal.

Other researchers have argued that toddlers show secure attachment in the same way everywhere but that *insecure* attachment takes different forms in different cultures (van IJzendoorn et al., 2006). For example, Japanese researchers found a large proportion of anxious-resistant toddlers among traditional Japanese families, and no anxious-avoidant infants at all (Miyake et al., 1985; Nakagawa et al., 1989). They explained this pattern by pointing out that traditional Japanese mothers rarely leave their children in the care of another person and encourage interdependence. Consequently, the experience of being left alone with a stranger in the Strange Situation is particularly unusual and upsetting to these toddlers. This interpretation is supported by a study of non-traditional Japanese families, in which the mothers were working and consequently had to leave their toddlers with other people. Among these toddlers, unlike those in the more traditional families, the frequency of the various patterns of attachment was very similar to what has been found in the United States (Durrett et al., 1984).

Confusing the picture is the fact that a number of studies have found no cultural differences in the frequencies of the different attachment patterns. An important review of research in many cultures concluded that although the proportion of toddlers showing each pattern of attachment behaviors may vary in a few cases, the overall frequency distribution is highly consistent with Ainsworth's initial findings and with Bowlby's theory (van IJzendoorn & Sagi, 1999, p. 731): a distribution with 21 percent Type A, 65 percent Type B, and 14 percent Type C. The authors of this review concluded that there is more variation *within* countries than *between* countries.

Finally, when researchers tried to replicate the Japanese research but with older children, using a procedure to assess attachment between 6-year-old children and their parent (Main & Cassidy, 1988) together with an interview to assess adult attachment (Main et al., 2002), they found a distribution of A, B, and C patterns that was very similar to these worldwide norms. Strikingly, however, they also found that 47 percent of the Japanese children were in category D or were unclassifiable (Behrens et al., 2007).

If "sensitive" parenting (especially mothering) has the same form in all cultures and for all times then there has apparently been "widespread neglect, indifference, maltreatment, sexual abuse and abandonment of infants and children over the ages, particularly during the 18th and early 19th centuries" (Grossmann, 2000, p. 86). Can it really have been the case that for much of human history there have been "epochal derailments" of the attachment system (Grossmann et al., 2006)? This would seem very odd if attachment indeed has universal survival value. It may be more logical, if equally disturbing, to conclude that what seems to us in hindsight to have been maltreatment of children had functional value in the society of the time.

Moreover, as I have pointed out, Ainsworth's definition of caregiver "sensitivity" took for granted that the goal of parenting is encouraging the child's autonomy and self-reliance (Rothbaum et al., 2000). Ainsworth wrote that "it is a good thing for a baby to gain some feeling of efficacy. She [the sensitive caregiver] nearly always gives the baby what he indicates he wants" (Ainsworth, 1976, pp. 3–4). As has become clear, however, autonomy is not a universal goal: caregivers in many cultures encourage interdependence. This raises important questions. For example, in families in such cultures, how is the attachment system mobilized in the service of interdependence? Should caregivers in such families be judged insensitive? For example, mothers of children classified as ambivalent have been described as "insensitive to the child's cues and developmental needs for autonomy" (George & Solomon, 1996, p. 201) and as likely to "endorse the advantages of closeness, emphasizing descriptions of the positive aspects of the relationship" (George & Solomon, 2008, p. 845). As we have seen, however, this seems appropriate caregiving for a culture in which closeness is considered more important than autonomy.

Attachment researchers have proposed the "competence hypothesis": that "secure attachment is related to higher competence in dealing with developmental, social, and cultural challenges." However, it is important to recognize that competence has to be defined "in accordance to each specific cultural group" (Grossmann et al., 2006, p. 83). For example, in the USA maternal sensitivity is correlated with toddlers' tendency to explore in challenging situations, while in Japan maternal sensitivity is correlated with toddlers' cooperativeness. In one culture, competence is considered to be exploration, while in the other to be competent is to cooperate. It may well the case that securely attached children are the ones most likely to "grow up to value their parents' values" (2006, p. 83), values which differ across cultures. However, this then raises further questions, such as the role of attachment in societies where innovation and value change play a significant role, so that simply adopting the values of one's parents is neither desirable nor effective.

In sum, some researchers have found different proportions of attachment patterns around the world, while others have not. Differences that do exist may reflect the possibility that caregiving is less appropriate and sensitive in some cultures. Alternatively, the observed differences may be due to inconsistencies in the way the Strange Situation is implemented, or because the Strange Situation itself is culture-bound and is in some settings an inappropriate measure of attachment. Equally, however, it may be the case that what counts as "healthy attachment" varies from one culture to another, and that caregivers' agenda for their children's development is different. It has been suggested that "attachment research may legitimately be seen as imposing on the study of normal personality differences a form of moral evaluation framed in terms of mental health and psychopathology and claiming the authority of biomedical science for what are basically moral judgments" (LeVine & Norman, 2001, p. 97).

There is now increasing insistence that "attachment theory as it stands does not adequately reflect cultural variation in relationship development" (Keller, 2013, p. 179). Such critics argue that attachment theory presumes a Western middle-class emphasis on independence and autonomy as essential for healthy human development, and has defined parental sensitivity and optimal parent–child interaction on the basis of that presumption. As we saw in Chapter 5, however, the distinction between proximal and distal styles of interaction calls this presumption into question. The consequence is that "what is normative in one cultural environment is regarded as a pathological condition in another" (2013, p. 182).There is a pressing need to reconceptualize attachment theory to take account of the ways cultures define different pathways for children's development so that they become adults in different ways.

2.1.4 PSYCHOSOCIAL ACCELERATION: PLASTICITY AND PROGRAMMING

Much of our thinking about the ways toddlers respond to aspects of their environment, such as specific kinds of caregiving, is cast in terms of "healthy and unhealthy," or even "normal and abnormal." When we judge some caregivers as "insensitive" and some toddlers, as a consequence, as "insecurely" attached, it is difficult to ignore the evaluative character of these labels.

Of course, it is perhaps inevitable to ask what is best for children and what is bad? It might, however, be more helpful to consider whether differences among toddler and caregivers might amount to alternative developmental strategies, different means to a common end. One such approach to the developmental consequences of caring for toddlers is "psychosocial acceleration theory."

Psychosocial acceleration theory predicts that the character of the environment in early childhood influences the timing of puberty in adolescence, along with other aspects of the "reproductive strategy" adopted in adolescence and adulthood (Belsky, 2012; Belsky et al., 1991; Chisholm, 1993). In effect, a toddler's environment encourages her, tacitly and unconsciously, to begin to adapt to a *future* environment. A child's early experience shapes the lifecourse of her development.

The observation that led to this theory was that young women from families in which the father was absent when they were children act as though their own relationships with men will not last, and that these men will not invest in their children. These young women do so by acting promiscuously: becoming sexually active at a younger age, moving from partner to partner, and having more children, on average, than young women from families in which the father was present.

This would be conventionally judged "bad behavior," but Belsky and others saw it instead as a specific "reproductive strategy," attuned by expectations established early in life. Early experiences "program" the developing child and prepare her for her future environment. This programming include physiological components: puberty occurs earlier in girls who experience absent or problematic fathering (Belsky, 2012). Indeed, key aspects of their development seem to be accelerated. The consequence is a shift in the balance between the effort put into locating and courting a mate and the effort put into parenting, including gestation and childbirth as well as postnatal care. The age of puberty in boys, however, appears to be unchanged.

Lacking a father is not the only factor that accelerates development and alters its direction. Parental conflict and economic hardship play a similar role. Inconsistent parenting seems to lead to a mistrustful view of the world, and an opportunistic orientation to other people. Chisholm proposed that it is an underlying and unconscious appraisal of the risk of dying that shapes the young person's capacity for intimacy and parenting, and prompts the reproductive strategy of having more offspring, earlier, and investing in them less. When survival is difficult there is benefit in having more children, and having them earlier, but when conditions are good, the benefit comes from investing time and energy in a few offspring so as to increase their own likelihood of reproducing.

In addition, it has been suggested that a young child will commit to a particular developmental pathway earlier if her environment is stable. When the environment is changeable, the future is harder to predict and so the optimal strategy is less clear.

The character of her attachment relationship with caregivers, then, can be considered as providing the toddler and young child with a source of information about the degree of danger in the wider world. Different patterns of attachment are not simply healthy or unhealthy, they reflect adaptations by a plastic organism to local conditions (caregiving in the family) and to the environmental circumstances that those conditions indicate. Attachment patterns are different strategies that all serve a common goal of survival and reproduction.

It remains to be seen whether the prenatal epigenetic programing we discussed in Chapter 4 also plays a role in the adoption of a reproductive strategy. There is some evidence that peer relations in middle childhood play such a role, having an influence on adrenarche (see Chapter 11, section 1).

2.2 CAREGIVING AS GUIDED PARTICIPATION

Attachment theory emphasizes a key aspect of caregiving—providing the toddler with a secure base. However, there are other aspects, one of which is to guide a toddler's participation in the practical activities of her culture.

In addition, attachment research puts a great deal of weight on a single technique for the assessment and measurement of caregiving: namely, the Strange Situation. A different approach to the study of caring for toddlers has been to focus on the details of caregiver–child interaction in natural settings. Here the assumption is that in all cultures there a process of **guided participation** between adults and children. Guided participation is defined as the structuring of children's participation in activities and a bridging between their understanding and that of their caregivers (Rogoff, 1990). Adults do not simply respond, sensitively or otherwise, to their toddler's signals, they make arrangements for her to participate in cultural practices, and they also make adjustments as she gains skill and knowledge. Caregivers provide support and guidance to the toddler's psychological development. The notion of guided participation is intended to emphasize that development is a process in which children are already participants, either central or peripheral, in ongoing activity. They participate in cultural activities *as* they learn to manage them, to "appropriate" them.

In one way or another, children in every culture are involved in the practices of their elders. However, there are some important cultural differences in the form of guided participation.

Barbara Rogoff and her colleagues studied toddlers in four cultures: a Mayan Indian town in Guatemala; a middle-class urban group in the United States; a tribal village in India; and a middle-class urban neighborhood in Turkey. In each case, one or more members of the research team spent time in the community. Fourteen families were recruited in each, and interviews and observations were conducted at the children's homes. Everyday activities were observed, and each family was also given a collection of novel and interesting objects and the caregivers were invited to encourage the toddler to play with them. Differences were found across cultures in the goals of development, in the means of communication, and in adults' and toddlers' responsibility for learning (Rogoff, 1990; Rogoff et al., 1993).

In general, in the middle-class communities (the USA and Turkey) the adults played and talked with their toddlers and emphasized the verbal instruction and structuring of each child's involvement and motivation. In the rural communities (Guatemala and India), on the other hand, the emphasis was on non-verbal communication, sensitive assistance, and skilled sharing of attention. Those toddlers were embedded in group activity for much of the time, and they learned through what Rogoff called "keen observation" rather than through instruction in lessons organized by adults. Here we see once again the distal and proximal styles of caregiving.

Rogoff argues that developmental research has often paid attention *either* to the individual *or* to the environment, as though these are separate or independent. Even when both have been considered, they have still been regarded as distinct units or elements. She recommends an approach in which the environment and person are taken to be mutually defined and interdependent. Her approach involves analysis on three inseparable, mutually constituting planes—personal, interpersonal, and community. On each of these, Rogoff argues, we can distinguish distinct developmental processes. On the **plane of community activity** the key developmental process is **apprenticeship** (see Chapter 12). On the **interpersonal plane** the process is **guided participation**. On the **personal plane** the process is **participatory appropriation**. Children participate in the activities of their community by engaging with other children and with adults in routine and tacit collaboration, as well as explicit collaboration, and so become increasingly skilled (Rogoff, 2008).

Research might focus on the interpersonal plane, in which processes of interaction occur, and on the interpersonal arrangements between children and their caregivers, such as observation and participation, or explicit verbal instruction (as did Rogoff's own research that I have described here). However, the background to these interactions is the community plane, in which processes occur such as the historical role and changing practices of schooling, age segregation, families, and work. In addition, important consequences occur on the individual plane, in which learning occurs through processes of appropriation. Rogoff's central argument is that "children's cognitive development is inseparable from their social milieu in that what children learn is a cultural curriculum: from their earliest days, they build on the skills and perspectives of their society with the aid of other people" (Rogoff, 1990, p. 190).

The differences that Rogoff and her colleagues identified—differences, you will recall, in the goals of development, in the means of communication, and in who had responsibility for learning—have their *origins* in the community plane, are *evident* in the interpersonal plane, and have *consequences* in the personal plane. An example of a study that examined all three planes is research on the Girl Scouts, also conducted by Rogoff and her colleagues, which I will describe in Chapter 12.

In attachment theory, the caregiver is a secure base that the toddler can return to after exploring the world in order to learn. The notion of guided participation, in contrast, emphasizes the way that adults explore the world *with* toddlers, and in doing so guide their learning.

Leading by the hand is a metaphor for guided participation, and at the same time it is a good example. A toddler can walk, but she still lacks the ability to plan her own preambulation. She responds spontaneously to the environment's invitations. Consequently, we will often see a caregiver leading a toddler by the hand, guiding her in the direction that the adult chooses. However, that direction is not always entirely the adult's decision—the united hands provide communication in both directions, and the toddler will make her desires known by pulling the adult in the direction that *she* wants to go. Together, they form a system that has its own logic.

Is there a way of reconciling these two perspectives on the caregiver–toddler relationship: attachment theory and guided participation? Recall that Bowlby proposed that attachment behavior is part of a "system" in which feedback maintains the toddler's security while permitting her to explore and learn. What if the learning comes not necessarily from exploring, but from participating?

Bowlby himself suggested that during the early years, while a toddler is slowly acquiring the capacity for self-regulation, the mother functions as her toddler's ego and super-ego. He argued:

> It is not surprising that during infancy and early childhood these functions are either not operating at all or are doing so most imperfectly. During this phase of life, the child is therefore dependent on his mother performing them for him. She orients him in space and time, provides his environment, permits the satisfaction of some impulses, restricts others. She is his ego and his super-ego. Gradually he learns these arts himself, and as he does, the skilled parent transfers

the roles to him. This is a slow, subtle and continuous process, beginning when he first learns to walk and feed himself, and not ending completely until maturity is reached … Ego and super-ego development are thus inextricably bound up with the child's primary human relationships. (Bowlby, 1951, p. 403)

In Sigmund Freud's theory of the psyche, the superego is the part that passes judgments on actions; it embodies the conscience and ideals (Freud, 1920, 1923). Freud himself suggested that it is based on what caregivers do early on in a child's life: "the installation of the super-ego can be described as a successful instance of identification with the parental agency," and with further development "the super-ego also takes on the influence of those who have stepped into the place of parents—educators, teachers, people chosen as ideal models" (Freud, 1933, pp. 95–96).

Bowlby phrased his point in psychoanalytic terms, as though the toddler provides the "id" and the adult provides the "ego" and "super-ego." In more modern terms, we could say that the child has System 1 capabilities while the adult provides System 2 abilities to plan and evaluate. The toddler has separated both physically and biologically from her mother, but has not yet separated psychologically. She still needs an adult to guide her as she seeks what she wants and needs.

Moreover, as a student of Bowlby's early writing has pointed out, "This sounds more Vygotskian than Freudian" (Bretherton, 1992). She adds, "However, in emphasizing infant initiative and sensitive maternal responding, Bowlby's (1951) earlier theorizing on the mother as the child's ego and superego was regrettably lost."

It seems entirely possible that when we study guided participation we are seeing this external super-ego in operation, in practical activities that the caregiver and infant participate in together. Indeed, the reaction of a toddler to separation may indicate her attitude to this external super-ego. She may experience anxiety at the potential loss of guidance when a parent leaves. Or she may experience relief at the freedom from guilt that the external super-ego had been imposing. After all, Erik Erikson described toddlerhood as the stage in which there is a basic conflict between autonomy on the one hand and shame and doubt on the other hand.

2.3 WEANING

Weaning [among the Ache] is an extremely unpleasant experience for mothers (and apparently for their children), with children screaming, hitting, and throwing tantrums for several weeks. The parent–offspring conflict of interest over interbirth interval and lactational investment … is an obvious and important life history event. During this time a woman will often apply some bitter plant substance to her nipples in order to discourage her child from trying to sneak a suckle when she is resting or sleeping. (Hill & Hurtado, 1996, p. 221)

Because human children remain dependent on their caregivers for such a long time, meeting their nutritional needs is a continuing concern. Among the issues that confront the caregivers of a toddler is whether to breastfeed, how to combine breast milk with other kinds of food, and when to withdraw the breast. Breast milk provides nutrition and antibodies to the growing child, but providing it places demands on the time and energy of the mother. When and how to wean is a decision based on the needs of the toddler and the needs of the mother, who is often pregnant again and if so will soon have to care for a new baby. It is a practical concern that all caregivers must confront. In addition, weaning usually leads to the toddler finding herself in new social circumstances, often being cared for by alloparents.

Weaning is the replacement of breastfeeding with other sources of food. It can be defined as the time when breast milk is no longer offered, or as the time when other kinds of food are first introduced. Weaning involves changes in behavior and relationships, as well as the loss of an important source of nutrition. It is a time when the needs of the mother may clash with those of her toddler. Many psychologists (including both Freudians and evolutionary psychologists) have suggested that a toddler will resist and challenge the removal of the breast, seeking to maximize the resources that are provided to her by caregivers. However, a temper tantrum also has its costs to a toddler, and compromise rather than confrontation may be the best strategy. In addition, it is presumably advantageous to a child to be weaned at some point. The character of weaning and its consequences are likely to vary with timing and context.

Weaning generally occurs while the child is a toddler, but the precise age varies considerably from culture to culture, and indeed from family to family. In addition, weaning may be abrupt or it may be a gradual process. For mothers who persevere with breastfeeding (that is, who do not stop breastfeeding in the first few weeks or months after birth), the age of weaning varies from 18 months to 2, 3, or even 5 years. The average age across cultures is around 2.5 years. As I have mentioned, there is also variation within a culture. Some mothers never breastfeed, opting for bottle milk instead. Others breastfeed for a few months and then switch to the bottle. Single mothers tend to wean their children earlier than do women with a partner, at least in industrial societies (Quinlan & Quinlan, 2008).

Historically, the duration of nursing and the timing of weaning would have been linked to the maintenance of the size of a population and rates of infant mortality, as well as to maternal health and nutrition. Breast milk provides nourishment and immunological benefits to the growing child. But nursing also places demands on the mother's body, and it delays the reappearance of fertility and reduces the likelihood of a subsequent pregnancy (this may be regarded as a benefit or as a problem by caregivers). When another pregnancy does occur, the mother's resources of time and energy are likely to be redirected to the new baby, and the toddler will be abruptly weaned.

Attempts have been made to estimate a "natural" age for weaning, on the basis of biological comparisons between humans and other animals, in terms of, for example, when the permanent teeth erupt, weight at birth, how rapidly body weight increases, and the length of gestation. Estimates made in this way range widely, from 25 months to 7 years of age (Dettwyler, 2004). It seems, though, that compared with other animals, humans wean their offspring early. Apes, for example, continue to breastfeed until their infant is around 6 years of age.

Compared with other primates, humans also seem to have an unusually flexible strategy for feeding their young. For example, human mothers often continue to nurse when their infant has begun to eat, a strategy that may have been adaptive as humans evolved but that creates the potential today for a mismatch between optimal and actual feeding practices (Sellen, 2007).

The World Health Organization recommends exclusive breastfeeding for the first six months of life and complementary breastfeeding (that is to say, breast milk completed with other food) up to 2 years of age or beyond. The American Academy of Pediatrics recommends the same period of exclusive breastfeeding, and that it should continue for at least 12 months after solid foods are introduced. Some researchers are concerned that in local ecological contexts where mothers are stressed, six months of exclusive breastfeeding may be insufficient to meet an infant's nutritional needs. At the same time, there is evidence for benefits from breastfeeding beyond 12 months of age, though this often doesn't happen.

To supplement or replace breast milk, infants and toddlers require specially prepared food. In agricultural societies, the supplement is often grain (rice, wheat, or maize) that has been mashed into a pap or gruel, sometimes mixed with animal milk. Urban caregivers have access to commercial baby food, which is made for children aged 4 months to 2 years. Medical professionals recommend that baby food not be introduced before 6 months of age, but food companies market "practice" food for 4- to 6-month-olds.

In eighteenth- and nineteenth-century Europe a solution employed by many mothers was to hire a "wet nurse"—an employed lactating woman, who had often lost her own child. This practice enabled the wealthy to enhance their fertility and increase the likelihood of their infants surviving. Strategies such as this show that whatever instinctual component there might be to childcare in humans, it clearly also depends on the cultural setting and the individual circumstances in which a woman finds herself (Hrdy, 1999).

For example, among the Sebei in Africa, toddlers are generally weaned only when they choose to stop nursing at the breast. The exception to this is when the mother becomes pregnant again, for continuing to nurse is considered harmful to a pregnant woman, and in such a case the toddler is often weaned abruptly by putting pepper or tobacco juice on the breasts, or by pinching her when she tries to suckle (Goldschmidt, 1975).

In many cultures, though probably less now than in the past, the first non-milk food offered to an infant has been premasticated—chewed first by the caregiver. One-third of those ethnographic studies that have collected data on infant feeding report premastication. Although the practice is discouraged by medical professionals, 63 percent of Chinese university students today report receiving premasticated food as an infant, including grain and rice, meat and dried meat, nuts, vegetables, dumplings, and eggs (Pelto et al., 2010).

After weaning has occurred, the toddler will still need assistance from other people while eating for several more years. Weaning is by no means the end of biological dependence. However, once the mother is not the only source of nutrition, alloparents can be recruited—such as pre-teen females, grandmothers, aunts, and female friends. For example, the Case Study below illustrates how among the !Kung weaning is a gradual process which can continue until a child is 4 or 5 years of age, unless a new baby comes along, in which case the toddler comes under the care of people other than her mother. Many anthropologists have observed toddlers who are weaned early and separated from the mother to be cared for by a grandmother or siblings. Some have interpreted this as rejection of the toddler, but others see it as the child's entry into the wider family system (Weisner & Gallimore, 1977, p. 176). As we shall see in the next chapter, young children are often given caregiving responsibilities for younger siblings. Sarah Hrdy has suggested that growing up with a number of caregivers helps children become able to understand the needs and desires of other people, and so more skilled at figuring out who will help them and who might hurt them (Hrdy, 2009).

As we saw earlier, the !Kung people live in the Kalahari of Southern Africa, and survive by hunting and gathering. Their population remains relatively constant, in large part because the average spacing between births is four years, which is unusually long. The result is that the population grows by only 0.5 percent a year. This low fertility occurs despite not using contraceptives or abstaining from sexual intercourse. Average age of menarche is 16.5 years, and first birth occurs on average at 19.5 years. Infant mortality is between 10 and 20 percent in the first year: death is usually from infection. Each !Kung woman has on average 4.7 live births, of whom about half survive into adulthood (Konner & Shostak, 1987).

The !Kung are very active, and consume relatively few calories, and both of these are factors known to reduce fertility. Children under 4 are carried by their mother while she works. Equally importantly, however, !Kung mothers breastfeed their children very frequently, and until the child is relatively old. Each child is fed perhaps four times each waking hour, and several times during the night. This high frequency continues until the child is around 4 years of age, or until the woman becomes pregnant again, in which case weaning occurs.

Blood tests show that nursing !Kung women have lower levels of the hormones estradiol and progesterone, and that those who feed most frequently have the lowest levels. They also have strikingly high levels of prolactin, an important protein that controls milk production and suppresses the ovulatory cycle.

Overall, then, the traditional practice of frequent breastfeeding has physiological consequences (which may be increased by physical activity and restricted nutrition) which lead to longer spacing between pregnancies. This has been interpreted as a "biocultural adaptation," since it slows population growth, which is necessary for a community living with scarce resources. The combination of frequent nursing and late weaning seems adaptive in at least three respects. First, it ensures a stable source of nutrition for the infant in the face of high infant mortality and illness. Second, widely spaced births lead to more infants surviving. Third, breastfeeding increases infant and toddler resistance to microorganisms (Konner & Shostak, 1987).

This interpretation is supported by historical changes that have taken place in !Kung culture. Since the 1970s the !Kung began to adopt a more pastoral lifestyle, and they became more sedentary. They started to feed their toddlers cow's milk, and as a result pregnancies and births became more closely spaced. Weaning occurred earlier, and births became more frequent, leading to an increase in population. The dynamics of reproduction had shifted in response to the change in lifestyle.

Figure 7.3 shows a model of the relationship between birth spacing, population growth, the frequency of nursing, and the timing of weaning, along with other biological and cultural influences.

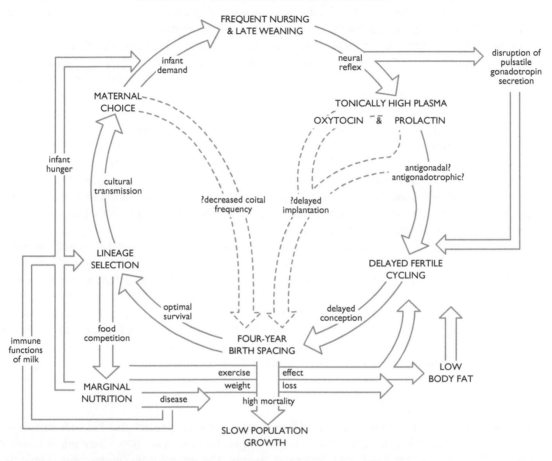

A MODEL OF !KUNG NURSING AND FERTILITY

Figure 7.3 Nursing, weaning, birth spacing in the !Kung

Source: Konner & Shostak (1987)

3. UNDERSTANDING OTHER PEOPLE: INTENTIONS IN ACTION, AND FAMILY CUSTOMS

The research on how adults care for their toddlers raises questions regarding to what extent and in what manner a toddler is able to understand the actions and intentions of other people. In what way does she understand what her adult caregivers are doing? This question has been a focus of research in several child development laboratories. I will focus on the work of György Gergely at the *Institute for Psychological Research* in Budapest with colleagues such as Gergely Csibra, and research by Michael

Tomasello, co-director of the *Max Planck Institute for Evolutionary Anthropology* in Leipzig, and his colleagues. They have demonstrated that toddlers show a growing ability to understand other people's intentions and actions, and in addition the customary ways in which artifacts are used.

In Chapter 5 I described the interactions between infant and adults that begin shortly after birth. We saw that by around 6 weeks of age, at least when caregivers have a distal style, infants show great pleasure in face-to-face interaction with people, a phenomenon known as primary intersubjectivity (Trevarthen, 1979). At first this kind of interaction does not require deliberate or specialized communicative acts on the part of the infant (Trevarthen, 2005), though increasingly she does come to *initiate* these interactions. These preverbal interactions are best described as the operation of a single dyadic system rather than as two individuals transmitting coded information. This preverbal communication system operates through co-regulation, apparently because the infant is able to adopt a *contingent stance*, in which she is able to detect contingencies in interaction, and understand other people in terms of their dispositional characteristics. On this basis she has the experience of causal control over events in her interactions with other people, something which she finds exciting and pleasurable. The infant's later verbal communication builds on the basis of this preverbal interaction.

Between 12 and 18 months of age there are impressive developments in toddlers' ability to understand other people's actions and emotions, and also to understand the customs and norms of her family. These developments provide the basis for both moral conduct and immoral behavior! Some toddlers honor family customs in the breach—that is, by deliberately violating them. By the end of this stage, at around 3 years of age, a toddler acquires the capacity to apply these norms to herself, in what I call the **customary stance**. At the same time, she can adopt what is known as the **teleological stance**. She can now grasp the goal or aim that is visible *in* a person's action (its *telos*), though she can not yet understand the intention that someone might form *prior* to acting.

3.1 THE TELEOLOGICAL STANCE

To understand the character of this teleological stance, let us consider research that has been carried out by György Gergely and his colleagues. They designed an experiment to see how 12-month-olds would understand the actions of "rational" and "irrational" agents. The infants were shown three simple figures: a small circle and a large circle, with a rectangle between them. The figures then started to move: the large circle expanded and then contracted. The small circle then did the same. Then the small circle moved towards the large one; however, the rectangle blocked its movement. The small circle retreated, then it jumped over the rectangle. When the two circles finally met, each of them expanded and then contracted.

A second condition showed the same behavior except that this time the rectangle was located not between the circles but behind the small circle. It was no longer an obstacle; consequently jumping over it was no longer a "rational" action.

Two test events were also presented. In the first, the small circle simply moved directly towards the large circle. In the second, the small circle jumped while moving towards the large circle.

Twelve-month-olds watching either of these two conditions rapidly habituated, as we would expect. However, their reactions to the test events differed. Those who initially saw the circle jumping over the rectangle showed no surprise to the first test event, but they were surprised by the second, even though the first test showed a new action, one they had not seen before. The researchers' interpretation was that these toddlers had understood the small circle to be acting rationally by jumping over the rectangle, and so when they saw the circle jumping in the second test condition they were surprised because the act of jumping seemed unmotivated, since no rectangle was present. Those in the second group, who saw initially the circle jumping "irrationally," showed surprise at either of the test events.

This is certainly a rather artificial situation within which to try to study how toddlers understand real people. However, let us put those doubts aside for the moment, and look at the way the researchers interpreted their findings.

Gergely and his colleagues initially proposed that the 12-month-olds were able to take what they called an "intentional stance" (Gergely et al., 1995). The toddlers, in their view, were attributing an intention to agents who behaved in a manner that seemed to them goal-directed. The evidence for this proposal was that the toddlers formed expectations about the circles' behavior in a new situation (the test events). The researchers concluded that these 12-month-olds "can identify the agent's goal and interpret its actions in relation to it" (1995, p. 165). This was, in their view, evidence for:

> the appearance at the end of the first year of the ability to attribute causal intentional states to others ... it is during this developmental phase that the infant starts to adopt a mentalistic strategy to interpret and predict the behavior of other agents ... infants are indeed capable of taking the intentional stance (Dennett, 1987) in interpreting the goal-directed behavior of rational agents. (1995, p. 184).

However, Gergely and his colleagues came to see that they were failing to draw an important distinction. To understand that an action is goal-directed it is not necessary to infer or imagine a mental state such as a belief or a desire. Philosophers have drawn a distinction between **intention-in-action** and **prior intention** (Anscombe, 1957; Searle, 1980).

Many goal-directed actions are carried out without the agent forming any prior intention to do them. As philosopher John Searle explains:

> We need first to distinguish those intentions that are formed prior to actions and those that are not ... Suppose you ask me, 'When you suddenly hit that man, did you first form the intention to hit him?' My answer might be, 'No, I just hit him'. But even in such a case I hit him intentionally and my action was done with the intention of hitting him. I want to say about such a case that the intention was *in the action* but that there was no *prior intention*. (Searle, 1980, p. 52)

A "prior intention" is a commitment to act that is made in advance of acting. A prior intention is usually understood to involve an "intentional state" such as a belief or a desire, because it needs to include some kind of representation of its "conditions of satisfaction"—namely, what is aimed for. An "intention-in-action," on the other hand, is visible *in* the action. Searle points out that all intentional actions have intentions-in-action, but they do not all have prior intentions. As anthropologist Alessandro Duranti puts it:

Our body, through postures and conventional as well as non-conventional gestures, is a continuous source of information for others to get access to our conscious and unconscious attitudes or to the possible direction of our future actions. (Duranti, 2008, p. 492)

For example, we may see James at the window and interpret what he is doing as indicating that he is trying to open it. This would be to recognize his intention-in-action. We may go further, and infer that James intends to get some fresh air. This would be to attribute a prior intention. The toddler, however, is not yet capable of this.

Since there is an intention "in the action" of every intentional action, it seems plausible that a toddler begins to understand intentional action by recognizing intentions-in-action, far earlier than she can imagine or infer prior intentions.

For example, we know that a 14-month-old toddler will copy an adult's unusual action (such as turning on a lamp with her head) more often when that action seems freely chosen (the adult's hands are empty) than when it is forced by some constraint (her hands are full) (Gergely et al., 2002). Once again, the researchers who conducted this study presumed that in the first case, but not in the second, the toddler needs to infer that the adult has an "intentional state"—a desire—to turn on the lamp in an unusual way. However, it seems more likely that the toddler may recognize the *intention-in-action* of turning on the lamp, and the intention-in-action of carrying books, and recognize the connection between the two. The intention that is visible in the action is somewhat different in the two cases, and the toddler is able to see the difference, without needing to infer prior intentions.

Indeed, Gergely and his colleagues changed their minds about the capabilities of 12-month-old toddlers in their experiment with the three shapes (Gergely & Csibra, 2003). They came to draw a distinction between the intentional stance and a **teleological stance**, and proposed that the toddlers were in fact using not the former but the latter. The *teleological stance* is "a non-mentalistic interpretational system" in which a toddler "can come to represent the agent's action as intentional without actually attributing a mental representation of the future goal state to the agent's mind."

As Figure 7.4 illustrates, *teleological* understanding is understanding an action in terms of the telos towards which that action is directed, as well as the contextual affordances. In comparison, *intentional* understanding involves the attribution of intentions, beliefs, and desires. In other words, the researchers now suggested that the 12-month-olds were recognizing not intentional states, but intention-in-action.

In the experiment that we first described, then, the 12-months-olds did not attribute to the small circle a *desire* to get to the large circle and a *belief* about the impenetrability of the obstacle, they simply recognized that the small circle was *trying to get to* the large circle.

Contingent stance	When James moves his leg, the mobile jiggles	Contingency
Teleological stance	James is trying to open the window	Intention-in-action
Intentional stance	James intends to obtain fresh air	Prior intention

Figure 7.4   Illustration of the contingent, the teleological, and the intentional stances

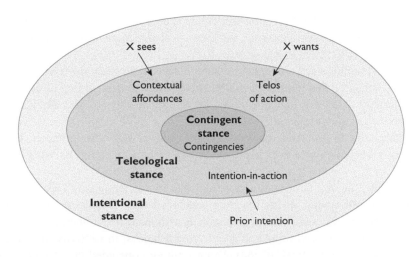

Figure 7.5   Constituents of the contingent stance, the teleological stance, and the intentional stance

Source: Modified from Gergely & Csibra (2003)

To repeat, then, Gergely now suggested that "According to our alternative proposal, one-year-olds can represent, explain and predict goal-directed actions by applying a non-mentalistic, reality-based action interpretational system, the 'teleological stance'" (Gergely & Csibra, 2003, p. 289).

This was a significant step forward in research on how infants and toddlers understand other people. Teleological understanding—recognizing intention-in-action—is a powerful form of understanding, even in adults. And as we shall see in Chapter 10, research suggests that 3-year-old children presented with what are called "false belief tasks" also understand the actions in these tasks teleologically, not in terms of beliefs and desires but in terms of contextual affordances and the telos that is visible in action (Perner & Roessler, 2012).

It is important for us to recognize, though, that teleological interpretation will lead to *mis*understanding of an action when that action is based on pretense, or, importantly, if the person who is acting holds false beliefs. For example, if I believe that there is chocolate in the fridge but you know that there is not, you will not correctly recognize my intention-in-action when you see me searching in the back of the fridge. To correctly understand what I am trying to do, you will first need to recognize that I am mistaken about the location of the chocolate. To deal with such cases a child will have to learn to employ other ways of understanding, and we shall see that this is precisely what happens in subsequent stages.

Research with non-human primates highlights what is unique to humans. Recognizing what other people can is an important aspect of understanding what they are doing. By 3 years of age, toddlers start to recognize that what they can see may not be visible to another person, and that the other person can see an object that they cannot see. This has been called **level 1 perspective taking** (Flavell et al., 1981). We will consider visual perspective-taking in detail in Chapter 10. However, this achievement is not unique to humans. For example, socially subordinate chimpanzees attend not just to the presence of a dominant chimp but also to what they infer that chimp is able to see (Tomasello & Carpenter, 2007). They are capable of level 1 perspective taking, and they can also recognize deliberate actions (Call et al., 2004; Hare et al., 2000, 2001, cited in Rakoczy, 2010).

This suggests that humans share with other primates the ability to grasp the intentions that are visible in another animals' behavior. But there is no doubt that toddlers' understanding of other people rapidly outpaces that of primates, and that human children develop other ways of understanding that are more sophisticated than the teleological stance.

There is another notable difference between human children and other primates. Children, unlike apes, can apparently become aware not simply of the *outcome* of an action but also the *means* of the action.

Rather surprisingly, the ability of apes and monkeys to imitate actions is very limited (Tomasello, 1996). The authors of one review of the literature concluded that "Despite the strong anecdotal evidence for imitation of gestural and postural behaviors in chimpanzees, imitation of a novel tool-using behavior has never been witnessed in unambiguous circumstances, in captivity or in natural environments" (Visalberghi & Fragaszy, 1994, p. 264). Another author concluded that, "after nearly 100 years of research, there is still no unequivocal evidence of motor imitation in any primate species and even if there were, it would not imply the possession of mental state concepts" (Heyes, 1998, p. 103). There is now some evidence, however, that chimpanzees can imitate when they have had explicit training to do so, or prior experience interacting with humans (Heyes, 2001).

This limitation is apparently due to the fact that chimps are able to focus only on the *outcome* of another's action, while human children can also focus on the *means*: "For example, if a demonstrator opens a nut in a clever way, chimpanzees learn that the nut opens, while humans learn in addition the clever strategy used" (Rakoczy & Tomasello, 2007, p. 121). (This may explain why chimps do not recognize helpful pointing: they focus on the object pointed at, and ignore the act of pointing.)

In short, humans have much greater ability than apes to imitate the way in which a tool, or other artifact, is used by another person to achieve an outcome. This ability has important consequences. Since human children can focus on the means, and not just the outcome, they can copy the means, and not just seek the outcome. This makes it possible for toddlers to learn the customary uses of cultural artifacts, their conventional "functions"—what "we do" with scissors, for example. I will return to this important point in section 3.3.

3.2 SHARED INTENTIONALITY

Unlike other animal species, human beings use language, make mathematical calculations, create social institutions, build skyscrapers, use maps, marry one another, form governments, play symphonies, use money, and on and on. For some years now we have been trying to figure out what enables humans, but not our nearest primate relatives, to do these things …. The big Vygotskian idea is that what makes human cognition different is not more individual brainpower, but rather the ability of humans to learn through other persons and their artifacts, and to collaborate with others in collective activities. (Tomasello & Carpenter, 2007, p. 121)

At the same time as toddlers acquire the ability to recognize the intentions in other people's actions, they are "sharing" intentions with other people. This is the proposal that comes from Michael Tomasello's laboratory.

Tomasello and his colleagues argue that humans are crucially different from other animals in our ability to collaborate, and that this ability is based on sharing goals and intentions (Behne et al., 2008; Tomasello et al., 2005). During the toddler stage, Tomasello suggests, two lines of development converge and interact. The first is the line of understanding that others are goal-directed agents. The second line is a "motivation to share psychological states with others" (Tomasello et al., 2005, p. 675).

The first of these lines is the one I described in the previous subsection, but Tomasello believes that it develops more rapidly than I have suggested. Tomasello proposes that by 14 months of age toddlers "begin to understand full-fledged intentional action," by which he means understanding how an agent can form plans based on rational decisions about goals in specific situations. In other words, Tomasello believes that 14-month-olds can adopt the intentional stance.

He argues that this ability to understand other people's goals and decisions is what enables toddlers "not only to predict what others will do, but also to learn from them how to do things conventionally in their culture" (2005, p. 680). Humans engage in forms of "cultural learning" that are absent in primates.

The second line, of shared intentionality and the sharing of emotions, experiences, and activities, emerges, in Tomasello's interpretation, when "the goals and intentions of each interactant … include as content something of the goals and intentions of the other" (2005, p. 680). The result is a double-sided understanding on the basis of which, in Tomasello's view, habitual social practices provide the groundwork for societal institutions.

However, this account is open to the criticism that it fails to appreciate that toddlers participate in already existing social practices and institutions. Routinely, a toddler finds herself participating in collective activities without needing to form prior intentions to do so. Guided participation ensures this, as we have seen. As far as a toddler is concerned, collaborative activities are not the *results* of shared intentions, they occur as a context *within* which intentions can be shared. The evidence suggests that toddlers are not yet capable of forming a deliberate goal for themselves, let alone forming a goal for themselves and another person together.

Tomasello presumes that a toddler *starts* with the ability to form mental representations of her own goals and of "goals with respect to the other's goals" (2005, p. 680); all of this is "in the head," as Tomasello puts it. However, it seems more likely that the ontogenetic sequence is in fact the other way around: that the ability to participate in everyday collective activities, things that people do together, highly supported by family and kin, helps a toddler become able to form her own goals.

Is the teleological stance sufficient ability for toddlers to be able to collaborate in joint activity? It seems to be. Take for example the activity of walking together (Gilbert, 1990). An adult takes the toddler's hand and walks towards the door. The toddler is able to read the signs and grasp the intention-in-action—to leave the room. She evaluates this, and responds positively (going along with a happy smile) or negatively (holding back with a frown). In the first case there is a shared intention-in-action, but no mental representation by the toddler of a specific goal, either for herself or for the adult. This is a "triadic interaction"—toddler and adult are oriented towards the door. One can also imagine a toddler initiating such a joint activity, by grasping an adult's hand and pulling towards the door. In Tomasello's terms this would be "coordination of roles," but a simpler interpretation would be that it is a coordination of intentions-in-action.

To put it another way, what is unique to the human child is not what she brings to collective activities, but what she takes from them. The toddler is apparently motivated to be helpful, and in this sense "collaboration" is indeed apparently uniquely human. Collaboration in this sense, however, does not require grasping the other person's mental representations of goals; it can be based on recognition of intention-in-action. A chimpanzee that sees another reaching for food is likely to grab it for itself. A toddler who sees the same thing is likely to pass the food to the other person. The difference here is not primarily cognitive, it is motivational. In fact, there is no reason why the ability to form a mental representation of another person's goals should lead to helpfulness. (Indeed, we know that some children grow up to be malevolent rather than benevolent, while understanding other people's goals very well.)

3.3 THE CUSTOMARY STANCE

Caregivers in many different cultures recognize that by the time they turn 3 years of age toddlers become aware of the customary norms for permitted and prohibited behavior. The Utku Eskimo, who live on Hudson Bay, call this *ithuma*, or reason, while for the Fijians it is *vakayalo*, a sense of what is proper (Kagan, 2005).

A popular topic for research with toddlers has been **compliance**: the extent to which they comply with customary norms, and with the requests and prohibitions made by their caregivers. The interest has mainly been to help reduce the clashes between adult and child, but the studies also provide interesting information about toddlers' growing understanding of practical norms, and the rules used to enforce them. We know, for example, that during the second year caregivers' praise and disapproval become increasingly salient to the toddler, and she will start to work to gain praise and avoid disapproval.

As we have seen, before 2 years of age toddler behavior is to a large degree under the control of other people. However, once a toddler becomes more skilled in directing her own behavior, compliance is by no means automatic. Studies in North America and Europe find a peak of non-compliance around 2 years of age: the age of the "terrible twos." After that, compliance with adult requests and commands increases; indeed, many toddlers enjoy following adults' instructions, especially in play settings. However, boy toddlers remain somewhat less compliant than girls. Caregivers begin to use persuasion and negotiation to guide their toddler's behavior—and the toddler starts to do the same in return!

Toddlers certainly hear more and more simple commands and rules: "Don't touch that!" "That's not for playing!" As we have seen, in some communities a toddler will be given simple tasks and responsibilities, in which norms can be learned (Edwards & Whiting 1993; Weisner, 1989). In many cases, caregiver pressure for appropriate behavior increases towards the end of toddlerhood, when the child becomes more interested in participating in adult activities, and when looking after her becomes more complicated for caregivers.

What we witness here is the way that toddlers the world over are exposed to the customary activities of their family and culture: everyday practical activities that embody unspoken norms. A toddler is learning not only what she can and cannot do—her physical possibilities and limitations—she is also learning what she *may* and *may not* do—the customs that define her community. She is learning what is socially appropriate and effective, as well as what is feasible and efficacious. Norms may become verbalized in explicit rules and commands, but many norms are simply implicit in what people do and what they don't do. Whether it is through participation, observation, or instruction, a toddler shows a growing comprehension of this basic level of the normative character of her social world.

Of course, a toddler cannot show compliance to a norm or standard before she understands what it is. Towards the end of this stage toddlers begin to make simple evaluations of "good" and "bad" to events, actions and people, and to themselves. Psychologists interested in morality have in the past argued that for a child who is so young these words can mean no more than parental praise and punishment, but research shows that towards the end of the toddler stage an understanding of social agreements emerges. A 3-year-old whose father promised to set up a toy train set but was unable to do so may complain, "You made a deal!"

In one experiment, 2- and 3-year-olds were taught simple games with objects. These toddlers were shown an action and told, "this counts as *daxing*." They were given the opportunity to imitate how the researcher played the game, and then watched while a puppet performed a different action with the same objects. In the control condition, this action was performed outside the context of the game, so that it was not inappropriate. Both the toddlers (aged 2) and the young children (aged 3) showed more normative responses in the first condition, though the 3-year-olds did so on a more explicit level. They protested vehemently when the puppet broke the agreement, and they offered to teach the puppet what was correct. The toddlers in the control condition had no such reactions (Rakoczy et al., 2008). Evidently the 3-year-olds not only recognized the social agreements that were established in this simple game, they also respected these and actively enforced them on others. However, even the 2-year-olds showed a basic understanding of the normative character of the game.

Other laboratory studies have shown that when a toddler is cooperating with an adult in an activity, if the adult partner suddenly stops participating, 18-month-olds and 2-year-olds, and to some degree even 14-month-olds, will actively try to re-engage their partner.

Similarly, 14-month-olds and 18-month-olds will spontaneously help an adult who they see struggling to open a door, or who has accidentally dropped something (but not if they see the adult deliberately throwing it down).

Two-year-olds will comfort and try to help someone in physical or emotional pain, because they have bumped their knee or their toy has been broken. They will also be more likely to help someone who has helped them in the past.

In addition, from 2 years of age toddlers are paying attention to the gender character of tasks around the home. If Daddy irons shirts, the ironing board will be male equipment.

Judy Dunn studied toddlers' growing understanding of norms and rules about possession, rudeness, and wild behavior through naturalistic observations in the home of second-born children in England, during the year between a toddler's first and second birthdays. She noted how during that time adult standards become increasingly evident to the toddler, and are "a source of curiosity, distress, delight, and shared humor" (Dunn, 1990, p. 91). Dunn paid particular attention to conflict in the family, to discussions between parents and toddlers about rules and feelings, and to pretend play with siblings. She reported:

At the 14-month visits none of the mothers explicitly referred to social rules in talking to the child, other than using the words 'naughty' or 'good.' From 16 months onward, however, each mother made reference explicitly to social rules and to transgression of such rules. Such references were usually made in 'conversational' form. Rather than simply stating the rule, the comments were usually in question form, as if the mothers expected and made 'space' for an answer. It was striking that as early as 16 months, four of the children took part in these 'conversations' about rules with appropriate responses, either shaking head, nodding, or answering verbally. (Dunn & Munn, 1985, p. 486)

Here is an example:

Family N, child 16 months. Child throws biscuit [cookie] on the floor.

Mother: What's that? Biscuit on the floor? Where biscuits aren't supposed to be. Isn't it?

[Child looks at mother and nods.]

Mother: Yes. Now, what's all this? [points to toothbrush and toothpaste on kitchen table]. Who brought that downstairs?

[Child looks at mother and smiles.]

Mother: Yes, you did. Where does this live?

Child: Bath. (Dunn & Munn, 1985, p. 492)

In fact, to say that biscuits aren't supposed to be on the floor, or that the toothbrush lives upstairs, is not a rule, it is a norm. It is an explicit statement of what is customary: what we do, and do not do. A rule tells you what to do, and often defines the sanctions. It has imperative form. A rule is an explicit regulation or principle that governs conduct within a particular activity. "Don't drop cookies on the floor!" would be a rule. Researchers need to draw a clearer line between norms and explicit rules.

Dunn found in addition that teasing between siblings increased during the year, showing toddlers' "pragmatic understanding of how to provoke and annoy the sibling" (1985, p. 94). Increasingly, this teasing was verbal in form. Toddlers also increasingly referred to social norms in occasions of conflict. They took care to avoid detection when doing something that was prohibited, and began to use words such as "naughty" and "bad" to refer to themselves and others who had transgressed. They were increasingly interested in behavior that was permitted or prohibited, though this didn't necessarily mean they followed the norms. Sometimes they took sides with an older sibling who had misbehaved. One mother told the researchers, "Collusion and conspiracy have begun." In those families where the mother frequently talked about norms, and about her children's feelings, the toddler showed more complex behavior at 24 months, such as acts of conciliation, justifying prohibitions, and verbal teasing.

These toddlers showed both increasing empathy and an increasing ability to tease and provoke. They were learning how to be both moral and immoral! Both these kinds of conduct are based on an understanding of family norms and customs, as well as the emotions of family members. Emotions seem to play an important role in early moral understanding. Dunn suggested that "it may well be in part *because* of the emotional urgency and significance of [family] relationships that children begin to attend to, explore, and exploit moral understanding" (Dunn, 1990, p. 110).

There are other signs that toddlers are starting to recognize the customs of their family and community. With help from their caregivers, toddlers begin to apologize, to offer sympathy, and to try to help other people. Empathic responses to other people's pain emerge during the second year (Kagan, 1981), and when a caregiver explains and shows concern, their toddler now shows more empathy (Zahn-Waxler et al., 1979). Altruistic behavior (giving up something to another person, rather than simply sharing with them) is more difficult and develops later (Svetlova et al., 2010).

As we shall see in the next chapter, around 30 months toddlers start to display emotions such as shame, guilt, reparation, empathy, and pride. These are called **secondary emotions**. A toddler will show pride in something she has done, and will seek recognition and approval by calling attention to it. She will begin to actively seek the help of adults in order to reach goals and standards (Kagan, 2005).

It is evident that toddlers have available to them two interrelated ways of understanding the people with whom they live. The first of these is the teleological stance: they can see the intention-in-action of what these people do. The second is to recognize the customary activities of family members. Adults model normative activities with artifacts, and they also provide a toddler with evaluations, both tacit and explicit, of the way that she participates in such activities. For a toddler, then, patterns of conduct, joint activities, in the family become typical, and then become taken as obligatory. That is, the toddler recognizes what the people in her family *typically* do, and she begins to view this as the *necessary* way of doing things.

Although one way to understand someone's actions is in terms of their beliefs, goals, and desires, there is a second way: their action can be understood in terms of the social situation, with its norms, obligations, rights, and responsibilities. This second kind of understanding has largely been neglected by researchers, but they have started to notice its importance. It has been called the "normative stance" (by Rakoczy and Schmidt, 2013; cf. Clément et al., 2011):

> Children not only interpret social activities as instances of individual intentional actions ("I see what she intends") ... Rather, they view and acquire many social activities as actions that are governed by conventional, communally shared social norms ("This is how one does it"). (Rakoczy & Schmidt, 2013, p. 17)

I will call the kind of normative stance that toddlers adopt the **customary stance**, because they are acquiring the ability to focus on the customary means that people use to accomplish goals using material artifacts. As the figure below illustrates, the customary stance builds upon the contingent stance of infancy, and it will provide the basis for the "conventional stance" of early childhood.

Morality has often been treated by psychologists as a separate and distinct "domain" of development, but we have seen in this chapter that this is not the case. The way we understand a person's actions is closely linked to our evaluation of those actions and vice versa (Chandler et al., 2000; Wainryb, 2004). What we see someone do is inevitably compared with what we consider they *ought* to do.

During the toddler stage, developments in understanding both people's actions and the customs and norms of the family provide the basis for moral conduct, and also for misbehavior. We have seen that during this stage a toddler comes to adopt the teleological stance and grasp intention-in-action. She is not yet capable of the intentional stance and inferring prior intentions. She is a long way from being able to adopt the mentalistic stance and attribute beliefs and desires to other people (or to herself).

Of course, the toddler's understanding of social norms is still very simple. Tomasello and Amrisha Vaish, in a review of the literature on the evolution and the ontogenesis of morality, suggest that "before about 3 years of age [children] may not really understand social norms as such. Instead, they may be responding only to adult imperatives and not to the force of any agreements among members of their group … They only later come to understand how these norms and rules essentially work as agreements among peers of equal status in a community" (Tomasello & Vaish, 2013, p. 240).

However, the term "norm" has an interesting ambiguity. It can mean what is usual, typical—what is normal. It can also mean a standard, what is expected, what should be complied with. This gives us a clue to what happens with toddlers: patterns of conduct in the family become typical, and then are taken as obligatory. That is, the toddler first recognizes what the people in her family typically do, and then begins to view that behavior as necessary. The "daxing" research, for example, used explicit agreements (and not "rules," as the researchers claimed), but toddlers are also exposed to many implicit norms.

Tomasello and Vaish are correct to conclude, "Thus, even very young children are social, collaborative, and cooperative beings who view their collaborative and cooperative efforts as inherently joint. Such jointness makes children interdependent; they need the other to achieve their (social) goals, and they know that the other needs them" (2013, p. 241). Toddlers' prosociality and cooperation grow from the Great-We of infancy. And, as we shall see in the next chapter, at the end of this stage a toddler shows awareness of her dependence on other people, as she at the same time starts to assert her independence.

The understanding of normativity will continue to advance. In early childhood, children will begin to understand that these norms in action are agreements among specific people, and that they have a situational character—that people act accordingly in distinct, specific, repeatable situations. For example,

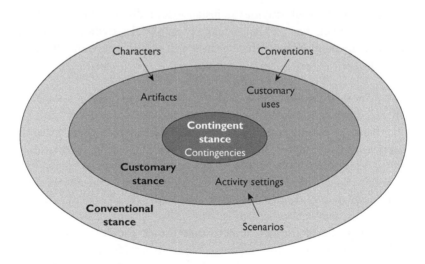

Figure 7.6   The contingent stance, the customary stance, and the conventional stance

dinner time has its own normative character, bed time has another. "Playing a game," as we shall see, requires defining a situation, with norms that apply for the moment, and it is in early childhood that we will see the skillful creation of situations (see Chapter 10). A toddler is not there yet.

In middle childhood, children will recognize that these norms have an institutional character: that people's actions reflect the roles they play in societal institutions (see Chapter 11).

4. BIOLOGICAL CHANGE DURING TODDLERHOOD

During the toddler years, body and brain continue to change rapidly. At 30 months, a girl will be on average between 34.5 and 36.5 inches in height and 27 to 31 pounds in weight, while a boy will between 35 and 37 inches in height and 28 to 32 pounds in weight. This represents more than half their adult height, and as a toddler's trunk and limbs grow longer and their stomach becomes tighter their appearance is less chubby and infantile. Muscles become stronger, and bones harden. At first standing and walking unsteadily, a toddler rapidly learns to run, to climb stairs and ladders, and to peddle a bicycle. Fine motor skills also improve rapidly. Toilet training usually begins during these years, and all the baby teeth will have erupted by 30 months.

Important changes are taking place in a toddler's brain. Competitive elimination of synapses continues, as does growth of dendrites and axons. Myelination, which started in the base of the brain after birth, has by the end of infancy begun to occur in the frontal, parietal, and occipital lobes of the cortex. During the toddler years, white matter increases in volume and becomes more myelinated, though less rapidly than during infancy. The left hemisphere develops more rapidly than the right hemisphere, and in particular the left frontal cortex develops rapidly. However, the remodeling of gray matter and white matter is by no means complete; it continues until the adult years (Lenroot & Giedd, 2006; Matsuzawa et al., 2001).

CONCLUSION

When an infant becomes a toddler she becomes able to respond in a new way to the irresistible invitations of the world around her, responding without hesitation or thought to things she can seek and grasp. Affordances are the action-possibilities that things offer: a toddler, now walking, is surrounded by new affordances to which she is impelled to respond. What a toddler sees, she has to pursue. In these affordances she does not yet identify stable, permanent objects. Perception is her primary psychological function, although it is still interwoven with action, affect, and memory.

Much research has focused on the operation of an "attachment system" during the toddler years. However, in many cultures caregiving is shared by a variety of people—biological parents but also other relatives and sibs—so it would be a mistake to see the mother–child bond as universal. Certainly, however, a toddler seems to recognize, at least at an emotional level, her dependence on caregivers. She needs their guidance as she begins to explore the world and particulate in cultural practices, and in this sense caregivers act as an "external ego" for the child at this age, monitoring and when necessary curtailing her impulses to act.

There are certainly important differences in guided participation in different cultures. In some cultures adults teach explicit lessons, while in others a toddler learns through participation. In addition, in some cultures a toddler seems to need to make assertions of independence and autonomy, while in others she is often displaced by the arrival of a new infant. In some cultures but not others, the caregiving style fosters self-consciousness.

At some point during this stage the majority of children will be weaned. The removal of the mother's milk may happen earlier, especially if a new baby is born, or later. It may be a slow process or an abrupt one. It amounts to a change in the relationship between toddler and mother than can be significant for both. The mother becomes able to give more time to her work or other siblings. The toddler eats new kinds of food and often spends more time with other people.

In the next chapter we will continue to explore toddler psychology, looking at how their use and understanding of language improves, the impact of this on their relationship to the world, and the important transition at around 30 months.

Teleological stance	Intention-in-action	Its telos	Given contextual affordances
Customary stance	Artifacts	Their customary uses	In practical activity

Figure 7.7   The two ways of understanding other people in toddlerhood

	Moral	**Conventional**
Toddler 12m–36m	• No distinction between the moral and the conventional. • *Teleological stance*: intention-in-action. • *Customary stance*: use of artifacts in activity settings. • Second-person normativity, based on customary practices in personal relationships. • Prosociality: collaboration & cooperation. • Equitable sharing. • Distinguish between "mean" and "helpful" others. • Secondary emotions (pride & shame).	

Figure 7.8   Morality in toddlerhood

SUMMARY

THE WORLD OF TODDLERHOOD

- Toddlerhood begins with the infant starting to move independently, as early as 8 months and as late as 17 months. She is unable to resist the invitations of the world around her: "the affordances"—the action possibilities between organism and environment. These illustrate how she is embodied and embedded in the environment.

CARING FOR THE TODDLER

- Caregivers in different cultures have very different expectations of their toddlers. For example, US parents value assertiveness, while Italian parents expect sensitivity.

- The phenomenon of attachment has been the focus of a great deal of research. However, the definition of "sensitive" caregiving assumes that the goal is to encourage autonomy in the child. However, many cultures value interdependence and obedience. This suggests that what counts as sensitive varies from one culture to another, and some researchers have suggested that the concept of attachment does not adequately reflect the cultural variation in caregiver–child relationships.

UNDERSTANDING OTHER PEOPLE

- The toddler moves from the contingent stance to the teleological stance: she is able to understand intention-in-action—the goal or telos that is visible in a person's action. However, the toddler is not able to recognize prior intention—the intention someone forms before acting. By age 3, toddlers also recognize the customary norms for permitted and prohibited behavior in their family. Morality might be said to emerge at the end of the toddlerhood stage: 3-year-olds evaluate their own actions and those of other people, and show self-conscious emotions such as pride and shame.

BIOLOGICAL CHANGES DURING TODDLERHOOD

- During the stage between 12 months and 30 months of age, boys and girls grow in height and weight, but their growth is much slower than during the first year. During the second year, they typically become able to go up and down stairs, kick a ball, and perhaps run.

ONLINE RESOURCES

Learn more about the MacArthur-Bates Communication Development Inventory: www.sci.sdsu.edu/cdi/cdiwelcome.htm

- Interview with Barbara Rogoff about guided participation

  www.youtube.com/watch?v=bDJBSsiTuks

- Developing destinies www.youtube.com/watch?v=pxu_yrFUKrl

Sensorimotor substages:

  www.youtube.com/watch?v=U7YZIVOc5zE

CHAPTER 8

TODDLERHOOD

(1 YEAR–30 MONTHS)
TOWARDS PSYCHOLOGICAL DIFFERENTIATION

INTRODUCTION

During the second and third years toddlers make great strides in several areas. In terms of their oral language abilities, their speech moves beyond the simple "protolanguage" of sounds and meanings, and becomes the systematic use of utterances to accomplish two general "macrofunctions," the *pragmatic* and the *mathetic*. They start to combine words, with utterances of two words and then more. Their vocabulary grows rapidly, and they become able to participate in turn-taking dialog and to use language to learn about the world.

Caregivers have now become attachment figures: a toddler has become aware of her dependence on others, and she will cry when she is left alone because her very existence seems at stake. A caregiver provides a secure base. We will see that several different patterns in toddler attachment behaviors have been identified, and there is an ongoing debate about what leads to these different patterns, and what their consequences might be for later development. Some psychologists argue that cultures have different definitions of what counts as a secure, healthy attachment between a toddler and caregivers; others argue that caregivers are more sensitive in some cultures than in others; and still others propose that the attachment relationship is defined by biology and evolution and works in the same way in every culture.

As part of this, a form of self-consciousness begins to emerge in which the toddler starts to understand that she too is held accountable to these norms, along with a dawning understanding of the distinction between males and females (though it is far too early to speak of "gender identity"). The toddler's regulation of her own emotions improves, and her impulses become more controlled.

The *theoretical issue* in this chapter will be whether or not toddlers need to form mental representations in order to understand material representations.

1. THE TODDLER'S TALK

The second year of life is a time of rapidly growing ability with spoken language. Increasingly, the communication between caregivers and toddler is by means of the "mother tongue." A toddler becomes more skilled in both the comprehension and the production of speech, and this enables successful communication over greater distances.

It might seem that learning language is simply a matter of imitation. After all, the words and syntax of English have accumulated over cultural-historical time, and now they seem fixed. We can find them in a dictionary, and in books on grammar. In this sense, certainly, a toddler inherits the language of her culture. However, learning a language is a constructive and creative activity. Language is acquired within the family context, and in the everyday practices of family life: a toddler learns words in and through social activity—she strings words together into simple sentences with the help of other people, and she discovers how words can influence people by trying them out on her relatives. There is plenty of evidence that learning to use a language is not simple copying, but active construction. A toddler has to creatively reconstruct for herself the organization of the language she finds herself in.

1.1 PHASE II OF LEARNING HOW TO MEAN

We saw in the previous chapter that around 12 months of age a toddler starts to make sounds in such a way that adults will recognize words of their language. For some time afterwards speech takes the form of single-word utterances, which we have seen are called "holophrastic." Speech at the start of toddlerhood is and is not adult speech. It differs from adult speech in its sounds, its meaning, and its word sequences, and this means that a toddler can only communicate effectively in specific situations with people who know her.

Adults understand, of course, that toddlers mean more than they say. But how much of this "more" does the toddler actually know? Psycholinguistic researchers in the 1980s and 1990s put a lot of effort into writing **grammars** of toddler speech, in which they attributed a great deal of

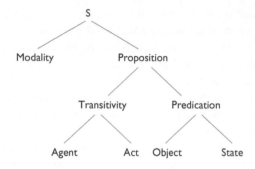

Figure 8.1   A syntactic reconstruction of a sentence

structure "implicit" in utterances of two words, or even one. These researchers argued that while most of the elements in the grammatical structure of an utterance were optional, or eliminated, the structure itself still had psychological validity.

For example, one proposal was that when an infant produces a one-word utterance several semantic notions are involved: notions such as the *agent*, the *act* they perform, the *object* acted on, and the *state* the act leads to. The utterance, from this point of view, expresses the relation of *predication* (that the object is in a specific state), and the relation of *transitivity* (the kind of change that occurs), and it combines these relations into a *proposition*, to which is attached a *modality* (the action *may* happen; or *will* happen; or *has* happened) (Ingram, 1971). For example, the holophrastic utterance "ball!" could be analyzed as an expression of the structure "Daddy kicked the ball into the bushes." Such utterances were then described with diagrams like the one in Figure 8.1, where *S* stands for the *sentence structure* attributed to the infant.

The proposal was that although only one constituent of this structure is actually expressed as a word, the other constituents may be communicated by gesture, or facial expression, or expression of emotion.

This kind of approach attributed a great deal of abstract knowledge to the toddler who is only starting to use language. It seems more parsimonious to say that the meaning of a toddler's words is to be found in the Great-We, not in what she knows as an individual. Adults assist the toddler by attributing linguistic skills to her that she does not yet have, and this may be precisely how she acquires these skills. These structural descriptions are actually reconstructions of *adults' interpretations* of toddler's speech, and they draw upon and incorporate all the knowledge that adults have about language, not simply what the toddler knows.

Let us return to the case of Michael Halliday's son Nigel, which I began to describe in Chapter 5. Recall that Nigel's Phase I language, which emerged at 9 months of age, consisted of the two levels of sound and meaning, and employed several basic functions (*instrumental, regulatory, interactional*, and *personal*, and later the *heuristic* and *imaginative*). These basic functions of Nigel's language were transformed when he entered Phase II at around 17 months, at the same time as his vocabulary started to grow rapidly. Many of the words that he now started to use still fitted into the existing functions. For example, "syrup" was used to mean *I want my syrup* (*instrumental* function).

But Nigel now became able to combine several functions in a single utterance, saying, for example "cake" to mean both *Look, there's a cake—and I want some!* (the *instrumental* function plus the *regulatory* function).

Other new words did not fit into the basic functions, but nor were they used to convey information. It seemed that Nigel adopted words such as "dog" and "bus" as he began to employ language to learn about his environment: these words were used in utterances to make known occasions in which he observed something interesting or recalled something previously seen (a blend of the *personal* and the *heuristic* functions). As Halliday put it, "the child develops a linguistic semiotic for the interpretation and structuring of the environment in terms of his own experience … Hence the new words function mainly as a means of categorizing observed phenomena" (Halliday, 1965, p. 251). (This fits well with our discussion later in this chapter of the way language changes a toddler's world.)

In these simple utterances that combine functions, we can start to see two new **macrofunctions** emerging in Nigel's speech: Halliday called them the **pragmatic** (combining the *instrumental* and *regulatory*) and the **mathetic** (combining the *personal* and *heuristic*). In utterances with a *pragmatic* function a toddler is acting on and in the environment, and expresses her attitudes towards it. In utterances with a *mathetic* function, on the other hand, a toddler is separating herself from the environment to start to talk about it, interpreting what is around her. Speaking now includes *learning* (the word *mathetic* refers to learning, or the science of learning). With *pragmatic* utterances a toddler seeks to influence people in a variety of ways. With *mathetic* utterances she seeks to learn about the world. *"Was 'at?"* ("What is that?") is a typical example of an utterance with a mathetic function.

In summary:

- The **pragmatic** macrofunction is talking as action (*doing*).
- The **mathetic** macrofunction is talking as learning (*understanding*).

Halliday proposed that when Nigel's utterances came to have these mathetic and pragmatic functions this was an indication that his relationship with the world was changing. I will explore the significance of this changed relationship later in the chapter.

In short, Nigel's spoken language began in infancy as a "protolanguage" in which single-word utterances—holophrases—served a number of simple and distinct functions. This Phase 1 was a pre-syntactic form of speech, with a protosemantics that enabled Nigel to direct other people's attention to objects without yet saying anything about them. Around 17 months, when words were combined into two-word utterances, his language formed a speech system (Phase II) in which there were two general macrofunctions, the *pragmatic* and the *mathetic*.

Adult language, of course, is able to *combine* the *doing* and *understanding* in every utterance: these two are components of *every* utterance. The first is concerned with the speaker's involvement in the speech situation, while the second component is concerned with the speaker's interpretation of the world. This is what is so powerful about grammatical structure: it is the combining of words so as to enable meanings that have derived from these two different functions to be encoded together.

The three phases of language acquisition (Halliday, 1975):

- Phase I: single-word utterances, each of which has a single function.
- Phase II: combining words enables combining of functions. Generalized **macrofunctions** emerge from these combinations: *pragmatic* (instrumental and regulatory) and *mathetic* (personal and heuristic). The latter enables the child to use language to learn about the world. Grammar is the combining of words to have *either* function. Dialog is the adopting of linguistic roles.
- Phase III: structure emerges, enabling every utterance to combine *both* ideational and interpersonal **metafunctions**.

Learning Words. It is obvious that a toddler does not learn the names of objects all by herself—she relies on other people to help her learn words. Indeed the social dimension of learning new words is central: it is the social practice that we call "naming"!

> In showing a child something, when I use a word to name it, the first requirement that must be met for this word to take shape in the child's consciousness is the existence of a certain relationship between the child himself and the thing I have named. The content of this relationship will be the first thing to appear in the meaning of the given word for the child. (Leontiev, 2005, p. 24)

Researchers have tried to discover more about what happens when adults name things for toddlers, through detailed study of videos in which both parents and 18-month-old toddlers wore motion-tracking sensors on their head and hands (Pereira et al., 2008).

It turned out that the toddlers learned more words during interactions in which there were occasions when either the caregiver was still when the toddler was acting, or the caregiver was acting when the

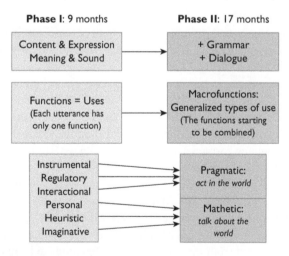

Figure 8.2 The transition from Phase I to Phase II of language acquisition

toddler was still—that is, either the adult waited until the toddler's attention was directed to one thing and then named that thing of interest, or the adult named an object while the toddler was watching it. Interactions with these characteristics seemed to create the greatest opportunity for a toddler to learn a new word. And it was, not surprisingly, largely the caregiver who was responsible for the organization of their interaction.

It also seems that when a toddler hears a new word she will treat it as a name only when it is used in the social act of naming. A toddler will ignore a new word if she hears it over a loudspeaker, or while the speaker is behind a curtain, or when the speaker is watching TV. But if the speaker says a word while looking at an object, the toddler will start to use that word as the name for that object. Or, if there is no object present when an adult uses a word, the toddler will look around for one, or look inquiringly at the speaker (DeLoache, 2004).

The process or activity of naming seems to pass through several steps. Words seem to start as "proper names" for people—"*Mummy*"—but the toddler also treats objects as though each has its own name. Words then begin to become "common names" (names of classes), first through the naming of concrete experiences (where for example the toddler says "Bus!" and her caregiver responds "No, that's a taxi"). This helps toddlers learn the conventional boundaries among classes of object. Classes are generally considered by linguists and psychologists of language to form a hierarchy, a "taxonomy" of classes— fruit is a food; a berry is a kind of fruit; a raspberry is a kind of berry. However, toddlers seem to organize the words they use in terms of how these occur together in concrete situations, rather than in a hierarchy.

To look ahead, by around 4 or 5 years of age young children can grasp words that refer to abstract entities, such as "fair." The entry into grammar (syntax), in early childhood, provides the key for learning new vocabulary for logical and grammatical relations. Later, grammatical abstractness will provide the key for entering into written language (Halliday, 1993).

However, toddlers are not yet consciously aware of the words they use to name objects. Although toddlers speak, they do so without being conscious of *how* they speak, or of the *process* of speaking: "the word itself is a transparent glass through which he looks at what is hidden behind this glass, but does not see the glass itself" (Vygotsky, 1998[1933], p. 279). While a toddler is now conscious of objects and activities as distinct from her, at first she treats these words as *parts* of the objects that they name. Just as a shirt has a label attached, each object has its name attached.

Language Without Speech. It is important to recognize that our learning language does not require speaking. Humans have a biological predisposition for language—every baby is born with the ability to learn to communicate with language—but this predisposition operates at a very general level, and in no way depends on specific brain regions dealing with hearing or vocalization. Language can use other modalities such as gesture.

First, hearing children between 13 and 18 months of age can learn non-verbal "labels" for objects just as easily as verbal labels. They will accept as a label not only a novel word, but also a whistle or some other type of non-verbal human sound, or a gesture, or a pictogram. Starting around 20 months, however, a child living with caregivers who talk starts to show a preference for the verbal modality, and this grows increasingly stronger with time (DeLoach, 2004).

Second, children who are born deaf show a normal pattern of early language acquisition, whether they are (1) monolingual in sign language, (2) bilingual in oral and sign language, or (3) bilingual in two different sign languages. Deaf children with deaf parents show the same pattern of development as hearing children raised to sign by deaf parents (Pettito, 2005). However, children born deaf to hearing parents who do not believe that it is useful for their children to sign—insisting instead that they learn to interact through oral language—are a different story (Goldin-Meadow, 2007; Goldin-Meadow et al., 1994). Such children live in an environment that is rich in culturally mediated social interaction, but they lack a conventional representational system to communicate. They cannot use verbal language, and they are prevented from using sign language. Under such circumstances, deaf toddlers spontaneously begin to employ **home sign**—a kind of communication with gesture which shows several of the properties that are found in the early stages of spoken language. For example, around their second birthday they begin to combine signs into sequences, at about the same time that hearing toddlers create multiword utterances. Moreover, home sign takes very similar forms in very different cultural/linguistic environments: Chinese and American deaf children show the same patterns of early gesture combinations.

This spontaneous gestural language emerges without difficulty from biology and early prelinguistic interaction (Goldin-Meadow & Mylander, 1998). However, the language development of deaf toddlers who do not have access to a developed sign language comes to a halt at this point. Unless they are able to participate as members of a community of signers their signing will not develop more complex linguistic features.

However, when a deaf child's signing community is large enough, or when their home sign language can be passed down from one generation to the next, their use of signing will become complex and sophisticated. For example, children who had each invented home sign were enrolled in a new school for the deaf in Nicaragua. Instruction was in Spanish and proved to be not very successful. Outside the classroom, however, the children pooled their different home signs to create their own language, which new arrivals made richer and more complex. After 25 years it had become as grammatically structured as any natural language (Senghas et al., 2004).

Such phenomena demonstrate that the biological predisposition for language which every child has operates at a very general level, for it is independent of modality (hearing or vision). One of its components seems to be a sensitivity to rhythmical and distributed patterning (Petitto, 2005). However, whatever form language takes, it will only develop when it is used in social interaction with people with whom the infant and then toddler has a close relationship. The interpersonal is the gateway through which language is entered (Halliday, 1993).

1.2 COMBINING WORDS

Most children begin the year between their second and third birthdays with a sizable vocabulary of words, at least 50 words by most counts. Many have even begun to combine words to form their first phrases and simple sentences. But the age of 2 marks the beginning of a year of great linguistic effort. By the end of this year, most children will have acquired much of what they need to know for forming sentences and making conversation. (Bloom, 1991, p. 1)

At around 19 months of age, Nigel began to combine words to produce two-word utterances, forming a linguistic structure. He moved from combining an utterance with a gesture (for example, "star" + shaking his head in negation = *I can't see the star*) to stringing two words together (for example, "bubble no-more"). Some of these two-word utterances combined the *instrumental* and *regulatory* functions ("butter on"), others were *mathetic* ("mummy book").

At this point (which Halliday named Phase II) Nigel also became able to participate in true dialog. *Dialog* requires adopting and assigning the conventions of communication, such as a speaker, questioner, respondent, persuader, and so on. At around 18 months Nigel was able to respond to *Wh-* questions, commands, and statements, and to initiate dialog by saying "*What's that?*" For example, told to "Take the toothpaste to Daddy and go and get your bib" he replied "*Daddy... noddy... train,*" that is "*Daddy (give) noddy (toothpaste, and get bib with) train (on it).*"

This was Nigel's first step towards a new function that is defined by language itself—the *informative* function. Language can not only be used to refer to an object, or to communicate one's attitude, it can also be used to seek and convey information. When a toddler starts to understand this function, they can learn directly from language, by asking for and providing information, by arguing and exchanging points of view. Dialog also opened the way to grammatical components such as "mood" (declarative, interrogative, etc.). Phase II of language, then, has *three* levels: sound, meaning, and grammar, and it includes dialog in the form of adopting and assigning linguistic roles.

In Halliday's terminology the macrofunctions (*pragmatic* and *mathetic*) had been transformed into **metafunctions** (*ideational* and *interpersonal*) (Halliday, 1993).

During the second year, then, there are dramatic advances in toddler vocabulary, in the grammatical structure of their utterances, and in their ability to participate in dialog. We have seen that as their vocabulary grows with the addition of new words, several new language functions are mastered. Toddlers begin to speak in order to make observations, report past events, and predict future ones. Asked "*Did you tell Daddy what you had for tea?*" Nigel, aged 1year 6 months, responded with an excited "*ayi ... ayi!*" (egg, egg!). The transition to two-word utterances has been called "perhaps, the single most disputed issue in the study of language development" (Bloom, 1998). Typically, a toddler will begin to combine words when she is between 18 and 24 months of age.

The first two-word utterances show a number of specific characteristics. First, they are simpler than adult speech in systematic ways. For instance, function words are generally not used. Inflections, such as -s, -ing, -ed, are not used, which shows again that the toddler is not simply imitating what she hears. Conjunctions (*and*), articles (*the, a*), and prepositions (*with*) are omitted too. This may be because using them would require extra effort, which the toddler is not yet capable of. Or it may be because the toddler does not yet understand them.

Once toddlers start to speak with syntactical constructions, their vocabulary grows rapidly. In languages with suffices, the distinction between a syntactical combination and a single word may be hard to draw, suggesting that lexical development and grammatical development are intertwined: consider *Dámelo!* in Spanish—is it a syntactic construction or a single word (Tomasello, 2003, p. 93)?

Around 30 months old a toddler's utterances will become yet more complex as she adds additional words and also affixes other **grammatical morphemes**.

One of the first ways that researchers tried to characterize two-word utterances was to say that they were **telegraphic speech**. These utterances omit words such as articles, auxiliary verbs, inflections, prepositions, and the word *is*. Those words that are used tend to be nouns, verbs, and adjectives, and their order tends to resemble the order in what one presumes the equivalent adult sentence would be.

These characteristics make early utterances sound like telegrams—messages sent using the telegraph, for which the cost depended on the number of words. The implication was that adding these words was a cost to the toddler.

A second approach was to suggest that two-word utterances are the product of simple structural rules (Braine, 1963). The **pivot-open pattern** consists of a simple rule: one standard word plus a empty slot that can take many other words: such as "More ___." In this analysis, each pair of words follows a simple rule that selects from a small set of words—called "pivots"—that occur in many utterances and always in a fixed position (either as the first word, or the second). For example, "Allgone" is a first-position pivot: a toddler might say *allgone egg*, *allgone shoe*, but never *shoe allgone*. Or a pivot could be in the second-position: *shirt off*, *water off*, etc. The choice of the second word is more "open."

However, the evidence suggests that two-word utterances are not organized using abstract syntactic or semantic rules. If toddlers were using syntax we would see them not simply combining words, but combining them in a way that showed their awareness of syntactic categories such as *noun* and *verb*, and also in such a way that the word order made a difference to meaning. If, for example, when a toddler said "*Ball gone*" she evidently meant something different from "*Gone ball*," this would be evidence that she was using some kind of syntactic rule. In fact, the pivot-open pattern involves a fixed order of elements, so it is not a true syntax. In these respects, the toddler speaking two-word utterances is not yet using syntactic categories. It seems more accurate to say, as Halliday did, that her utterances are combining two or more functions of language in a concrete way.

The first psycholinguists who studied children's language made two crucial and related decisions, which in retrospect introduced unnecessary restrictions on their research. First, they equated language with syntax, largely due to the influence of the linguist Noam Chomsky (see Chapter 2), and assumed that language is an abstract structure. Chomsky had proposed that the grammar of any language is a system of formal rules that will generate an infinite number of well-formed sentences (Chomsky, 1957). Researchers viewed toddlers learning to speak as though they were linguists studying a new language, and assumed that they were acquiring a grammar of precisely the kind Chomsky had described. Roger Brown, of Harvard University—one of the first psychologists to systematically study children's language—presumed that speaking a language is a matter of following the syntactical rules for grammatical sentences, and that language acquisition is a matter of coming to know those rules. In his view, the task for a researcher studying children's language acquisition was to figure out the grammar underlying each stage of speech development. Brown set out to study the word order and word combinations in young children's speech (Brown, 1970).

In the introduction to his book *A First Language: The Early Stages*, published in 1973, Brown explained what the book was about: "It is about knowledge; knowledge concerning grammar and the meanings coded by grammar" (Brown, 1973, p. 58). In an earlier book, Brown had summarized the elements that Chomsky had suggested make up a **transformational grammar**:

A generative grammar is a system of rules that derives an infinite number of well-formed sentences and assigns them correct structural descriptions. The most demanding form in which to pose the question of the child's knowledge of structure at any time is to ask for a generative grammar that represents his knowledge. (Brown, 1970, p. 103)

A grammar is (1) a system of rules (formal re-writing rules) that (2) derives (generates)] (3) an infinite set of sentences (thus it is creative and open-ended) that are (4) well formed (grammatical, according to the intuitions of a native speaker), and it (5) assigns to each sentence a correct structural description (a phrase structure) through its (6) phase structural component (operating on hierarchical "tree" structures, not just the surface sequence of words). A complete grammar also contains a (7) lexical level (that replaces grammatical symbols with words), (8) the latter two comprising the grammar's "base structure." In addition it contains a (9) transformational component (that permutes phrase-structure elements to generate related forms such as imperative, interrogative, etc.), and a (10) phonological component (operating on the morphophonemic level to replace lexical items with appropriate sounds).

The conclusion of Brown's research was that "order of development, conceived in the right abstract terms is invariant across both children and languages and is primarily determined by the relative semantic and grammatical complexity of constructions" (Brown, 1973, p. 59).

This focus on grammar led to the second decision that in retrospect may have been a mistake. Because they had decided to study word order and word combinations, Brown and his colleagues focused their attention on the period during which toddlers produce utterances containing more than one word. Single-word utterances simply involve no syntax, so there was no benefit to be gained from studying them. Yet, as we have seen, toddlers are learning very important things during the period of time in which they speak in single-word utterances.

Brown quickly discovered, however, that syntax was not enough to explain how children learn to talk, it was also necessary to pay attention to the semantics of their speech—the meaning—and not only the grammar. However, his approach here was to assume that meaning is carried (coded) entirely in the grammar, and hence he did not look at the context in which the child was speaking. Consequently, what Brown meant by the term "semantic" was the semantics of propositions or assertions (cf. Brown, 1973, p. 29). He was studying *sentences*, not *utterances*, in the sense I defined in the previous chapter.

However, researchers now recognize that the meaning of an utterance depends on the context, on the identity of the speaker and the hearer, and on the circumstances of production. Meaning depends, also, on the surrounding linguistic context, on presuppositions, and on other tacit knowledge that is not part of the sentence (or even part of the utterance). Children naturally learn to attend to and use these elements when they comprehend and produce spoken language.

Consequently, semantics is not only a matter of the propositional content of a sentence. In addition to "truth-conditional" theories of meaning there are also "use-conditional" theories of meaning. These theories give:

> logical priority to utterance-meaning over sentence-meaning … All boundaries between formal and contextual aspects of language are seen as artificial and ill conceived; the system as a whole is completely contextual and does not possess autonomous components. If it is agreed that the task of pragmatics is the study of language use in context, and if all language is inherently contextualized, then pragmatics is the most general discipline encompassing all aspects of language. (Ninio & Snow, 1999, p. 349–350)

It is now generally accepted that in order to understand the acquisition of language we need to look at how language is used and not at its abstract structure. This, after all, is what children do—they pay attention to how adults are using language to get things done. Learning a language is not simply a matter of learning rules (Pinker, 2000), it is a matter of understanding what people are trying to do when they speak: that is to say, the pragmatics of speech. Halliday's approach is an example of an analysis that focuses on the pragmatics of children's speech, not merely on its syntactics. Today, pragmatics has moved to the center of explanations of children's language acquisition.

This makes sense—after all, a toddler's comprehension and production of speech are guided by communicative intentions (namely, her own and those of the people she interacts with in concrete situations). It is the *use* of verbal utterances to understand what people are doing and intending to do, and to communicate one's intentions to others, not the acquisition of formal patterns, that is central to learning language. A toddler learns new words in order to learn about her environment, not in order to learn language.

For example, 2-year-olds can correctly follow instructions such as "*Make the rabbit push the duck*," showing that they comprehend word order, but only with specific verbs. These **verb island constructions** show that early two-word combinations are built around concrete patterns of word sequence that the toddler has identified (Tomasello, 2011).

More abstract constructions start emerging between the ages of 2 and 3, though still not as abstract rules but as patterns conventionally used for specific communicative functions, which the toddler can identify in adults' utterances: "*Spot got hit*"; "*He gave it to Mommy*"; "*Daddy cut the grass.*"

All this is evidence that when a toddler learns language this is not because she has some kind of innate language-specific capability, what Chomsky called a "Language Acquisition Device." She learns language using general cognitive and social skills. She is able to detect patterns in the speech that she hears, based on details of sound that can be quite subtle. And, as we have seen, she is able to understand people's actions and intentions, and this is extremely useful for understanding their words.

The fact that languages are to a great degree conventional means that they can be learned only by paying attention to what other speakers are saying. The toddler learns new words as she tries to comprehend other people's utterances. Her understanding of speech builds upon the preverbal interaction and communication of infancy—protoconversations—and also upon the joint attention and joint reference of secondary intersubjectivity. It builds upon the shared background of the Great-We. And it builds upon the toddler's growing understanding of people's intentions-in-action and customary uses of artifacts.

Another attempt to rethink explanations of language acquisition is found in the approach known as "emergentism," which views language acquisition as a dynamic process—one that is located not in the individual but in a system, a matter of "simple learning mechanisms, operating in and across the human systems for perception, motor-action, and cognition as they are exposed to language data as part of a communicatively-rich human social environment by an organism eager to exploit the functionality of language" (Ellis, 1998, p. 657; cf. Ke & Holland, 2006; MacWhinney, 2006).

Certainly, as her speech becomes more complex the toddler has to become capable of identifying patterns at a higher level of abstraction. For example, even though the following two utterances have no words in common, and they contain different numbers of words, they encode the same **semantic roles** (see above): *agent*, *action*, and *patient* (Tomasello, 2003).

"*I kicked the ball*"

"*Daddy threw his keys*"

As she hears words repeated across utterances, in situations with similarities, the toddler becomes famil-iar with the semantic roles they convey. This is not just a matter of forming associations between words and objects, as "mapping" theories assume, because, as we have seen, to understand a word is not simply a matter of knowing its reference but of being able to use it with intention and motive.

An illustration of the centrality of social interaction to language learning can be seen in that fact that before the toddler is able to string words together into two-word utterances by herself, she does so with the help of other people. Toddlers produce **vertical constructions** before they produce **hori-zontal constructions**. A vertical construction is a sequence of single-word utterances that are related. For example, a little girl aged 1 year 7 months picked up her mother's shoe and said "*mama. mama. mama. mam. sh. shi. shish. shuk. shush*" (Scollon, 1976). In doing so she expressed a semantic relation that was not possible with each word by itself. However, each word had the intonation pattern of a separate utterance.

Adults respond to these hesitating efforts with contributions of their own—suggesting what the next word might be, and correcting poor pronunciation. With time, and with this help from caregivers, vertical constructions become horizontal: the toddler starts to speak two words with the intonation contour of a single utterance. Vertical construction still continues, however, actively helping the toddler to build more complex constructions.

In this regard, the toddler's language is a product of adult psychology as much as infant biology: learning a language and being a member of a community go hand in hand. The members of the toddler's family are competent speakers who use the adult form of the language, and the toddler's growing ability to talk is woven into this web of social relations and interactions. Parents provide a "dynamically adjusted frame in which infants' communicative capacities may unfold" (Papousek, 2007, p. 259). After all, "the primary concern of caregivers is to ensure that their children are able to display and understand behaviors appropriate to social situations. A major means by which this is accomplished is through language" (Ochs and Schieffelin, 1984, p. 276). Once again we see that a capability, in this case that of linguistic complexity, is achieved socially, with other people, before it becomes an individual skill.

The evidence that I have reviewed supports the conclusion that toddlers' comprehension and pro-duction of speech are guided by communicative intentions: their own, and those of the people they are interacting with in concrete situations. The *use* of verbal utterances, first to influence other people and then in addition to communicate information to them, is central to learning language, and the acquisition of formal patterns is at best secondary. The basic unit of language acquisition is not the isolated word or the morpheme but the *utterance*. As Tomasello put it, "An utterance is a linguistic act in which one per-son expresses towards another, within a single intonation contour, a relatively coherent communicative intention in a communicative context" (Tomasello, 2001, p. 63). Increasingly complex linguistic struc-tures follow on from and build upon concrete language usage. Adults are able to talk in abstract terms about abstract entities, but "children's language is structured by much weaker and more local linguistic abstractions" (Tomasello, 2003, p. 324). The abstract structures of adult language are not yet present in toddler speech. In short, there is little empirical evidence for the existence of a universal grammar, or a Language Acquisition Device, as Chomsky proposed. Grammatical structures emerge, in ways we have started to explore in this chapter, in part as a *consequence* of using language in speech, rather than being a necessary *prerequisite* to language use.

2. HOW LANGUAGE CHANGES THE WORLD OF THE TODDLER

As a toddler's use of language becomes more extensive and sophisticated her relationship with the world begins to change, and she starts to perceive the things around her as objects in specific cultural categories—as *types* of thing.

It has long been recognized that every language embodies the categories of the culture of the people who speak it. The **Sapir–Whorf hypothesis** is the proposal that language shapes perception and even thinking; it is based on the work of the anthropological linguists Edward Sapir (1884–1939) and Benjamin Whorf (1897–1941). For some time this proposal was out of favor, but recent research has brought to light evidence that supports it (Reines & Prinz, 2009; Regier & Kay, 2009).

We now know, from research with both toddlers and adults, that our experience with language encourages our perceptual systems to become tuned to particular features in the environment. This perceptual tuning can then influence the formation of early categories and concepts. Learning to talk changes the way a toddler sees.

2.1 CULTURAL CATEGORIES AND GENERALIZATION

Languages encode perceptual features and dimensions in many different ways, even in domains that one might think are simply a given, such as color, space, and time. For example, English speakers tend to talk about the future as "in front" of them. But the indigenous community of the Aymara in South America talk about the past as "in front" and the future as "behind"—after all, we can "see" what happened in the past, while future events are "out of sight," as though behind our back. There is one community in which people always gesture in whichever direction is downhill when they speak of the past, and uphill when they speak about the future (Boroditsky, 2011). Communicative practices such as these guide toddlers' understanding of the world.

A growing number of studies indicate that during the second year of life significant changes take place in a toddler's visual recognition of objects, as she learns to use language (Lupyan et al., 2007; Smith, 2003; Son et al., 2008; Waxman & Booth, 2001). The language she is learning serves to channel the direction of the toddler's attention (Stapel & Semin, 2007).

Toddlers seem to spontaneously categorize objects on a "thematic" basis: that is, they put together things that work together, rather than things that resemble each other. In one study, 2- and 3-year-old children were asked to select "another one that is the same as this." The children paired a dog with food (a bone) as often as they paired a dog with another dog. However, when a name was provided to apply to one of the objects, the children chose another object that looked similar (Markman, 1991). They apparently treated the words as labels for objects that are similar in appearance—that is, as defining categories of objects. Apparently names for objects seem to be the words that are most salient to toddlers, perhaps because they are relatively common, even though every language has other kinds of words, such as verbs and prepositions, and terms such as "up" and "down." Furthermore, the words that are learned first are names for "basic level" categories, a notion we shall explore further in Chapter 7.

Subsequent studies have shown that once a toddler has learned the name for something she generalizes it to name other things that are similar in appearance. For example, the name for an object that has eyes or legs will be generalized to other animate things, while the name for a solid artifact will be generalized to things of the same shape, and the name for something non-solid will be applied to things made of similar material. In the past it was proposed that this behavior was explained by "innate modules" that are able to distinguish animate from inanimate, substances from objects, and so on. The evidence now indicates that these distinctions are learned, and that language is a central source of the learning. The toddler seems to recognize that words co-occur with particular features of objects, and her attention shifts to those features. This enables her to draw distinctions between *types* of objects, and the effect increases as her vocabulary grows. In addition, use of the same word across different situations invites her to notice similarities among the things talked about, so that new categories can be learnt. This has been called **structure-mapping**.

It seems, then, that the cues provided by language guide a toddler's attention to features of things in the environment, and this enables her to draw distinctions not just among things but also among *types* of thing. Strong evidence that this recognition of types of things on the basis of the words that name them is a cultural phenomenon, not an innate ability, comes from the fact that the features a toddler pays attention to will depend on the language she is learning. For example, the Japanese language marks the distinction between animates and inanimates more clearly than English does. But English distinguishes more coherently than Japanese between objects and substances, using the distinction between count nouns and mass nouns, and especially so in the kinds of nouns that toddlers typically learn. In English one cannot say "a sugar" or "three sugars." Sugar is not counted. As one might predict, a toddler speaking English learns the solid/non-solid distinction earlier than a toddler speaking Japanese, and she learns the animate/inanimate distinction later.

A second example is provided by the way English and Spanish differ in their treatment of the count-mass distinction. A piece of wood can be viewed as an object (a block) or a substance (wood). In English the word *block* is always a count noun that refers to an object. At the same time, the word *wood* is always a mass noun that refers to the material. An English speaker can say "a block" or "some wood," but not "some block" or "a wood." However, in Spanish a wooden block can be called "*un bloque*" (*a block*) or "*algo de madera*" (*some wood*), but it can also be called "*una de madera*" (*a wood*). In Spanish many nouns can function in this way, as either count terms or mass terms. The linguistic distinction is made not with the noun but elsewhere, in the syntax.

So what impact does this linguistic difference have on toddlers who are learning one of these two languages? It turns out that Spanish-speaking toddlers learn to make the distinction between an object (countable) and a substance (mass) faster than do English-speaking toddlers (Colunga et al., 2009).

In short, the language a toddler is learning provides her with categories and distinctions that have proved useful for her community in the past, and have become enshrined in the words people use. These distinctions influence a toddler's perception. Put a button in the palm of someone's hand, and ask them to slowly close that hand. When does the button stop being *on* the hand and become *in* the hand? The perceived situation changes gradually, continuously, but the linguistic categorization is discontinuous, abrupt and binary. Here too, the categorical distinction differs across languages. Spanish uses *en* for both *in* and *on*. Dutch uses *op* for objects placed on a horizontal surface, or securely attached to a non-horizontal support (such as a magnet on a fridge door), but *can* for an object attached to a non-horizontal surface by a restricted point (such as a picture hanging on the wall).

Or consider this. In English the prefix *un-* makes a "covert" semantic distinction: it is applied only to verbs with a covering, enclosing, or surface-attaching meaning. So we say *uncover, uncoil, undress, unfasten, unlock, unroll, untangle, untie,* and *unwind,* but not *unbreak, undry, unhang, unheat, unlift, unmelt, unopen, unpress,* or *unspill.* How do children learn this odd kind of category? We don't really know, but once they have learned it, their perception of the world has subtly changed.

The words a toddler is starting to use contain these cultural distinctions and categories, and they highlight some features and background others. Just as the phonemic categories of a language use and highlight specific phonetic features (in English the difference between a nasal stop [n] and nasal fricative [m] is important, but the difference between a glottal stop and glottal fricative is not), in a similar way the semantic categories of a language highlight specific features of the world.

2.2 PAYING ATTENTION TO SHAPE

Among the features that are highlighted by language, one of the most important is shape. A central way in which language transforms a toddler's perception is by drawing her attention to the shapes of things. We can see her growing ability to understand and employ shape-based categories in her actions when a collection of objects of various shapes and sizes—blocks, dolls, utensils, etc.—is put in front of her. At 12 months a toddler is more likely to touch a toy she just picked up than other toys that have the same shape. At 18 months, she will put two or three objects of the same shape together in front of her. At 24 months she will divide objects into two distinct categories, working on one category at a time. At 30 months she will simultaneously coordinate work on two major categories and create subcategories in which the objects are grouped not only by shape but also by color. Increasingly, the toddler touches an object not because it simply stands out, but because it has a similar shape to the last object she handled (Sugarman, 2011).

Why do toddlers start to pay attention to the shapes of objects? It turns out that words draw their attention to the shape. Shapes play an important role in the cultural categorization of objects. What makes something a cup is of course its use, but this is largely a matter of its shape rather than its color, size or material. The word "cup" will tend to be applied to objects with the same shape, even when they are different in color and size, or made of different material. And indeed, toddlers tend to learn the names of things that are similar in shape: this is known as **shape bias** (Samuelson et al., 2011).

This toddler attention to shape then feeds back to increase their learning of new vocabulary: longitudinal studies of individual toddlers have found that when they start to show shape bias there is

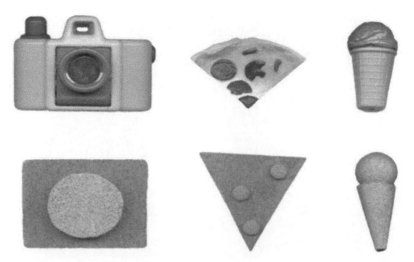

Figure 8.3   3-D objects and their caricatures. Toddlers recognized the detailed objects, no matter the size of their object-name vocabulary, but only those toddlers with a larger vocabulary were able to recognize the shape caricatures

Source: Smith & Jones (2011)

an acceleration in their vocabulary for object names. The more words a toddler aged 18 to 24 months knows, the better able she is to recognize "shape caricatures," such as those in Figure 8.3 (Smith & Jones, 2011). In this experiment, toddlers recognized the detailed objects in the top row no matter the size of their object-name vocabulary, but only those toddlers with a larger vocabulary were able to recognize the shape caricatures in the bottom row. This suggests that learning the names for objects changes the way a toddler perceives their shape, possibly by encouraging her to pay attention to the whole object rather than just its parts. It seems that a toddler first identifies objects on the basis of their detailed, specific components—for example, she identifies anything with a smile as a face. Naming helps her start to recognize the *overall* shape of an object, and categorize it accordingly. Then, at around 24 months of age, toddlers start to talk explicitly about similarity, using terms such as "same as" and "is like."

This language-focused attention to shape may explain the "fast mapping" I mentioned earlier—the fact that a toddler starts to learn new words surprisingly quickly so that her vocabulary grows very rapidly. Once she has learned to pay attention to shape and recognize similarities so as to categorize objects, this may enable her to quickly learn the names for new categories. She is not simply "mapping" words to objects, she is starting to pay attention to shape as a basis for naming.

Another way in which language influences toddlers' perception of the world is through providing one or more **frames of reference**. In order to move around, they need a practical understanding of the arrangement of objects in the space around them. Psychologists have sometimes assumed that this is provided by a frame of reference that is innate, built into human neurocognition. Others, like Piaget, have argued that the frame is constructed by a toddler as she navigates through the world. However, we

Figure 8.4 Frames of reference

now know that reference frames vary cross-culturally—for example, people in Western cultures tend to use a Relative reference frame, while people in other cultures often use an Absolute or an Intrinsic frame of reference. For example, look at the fork and spoon in Figure 8.4. We could say that the spoon is to the left of the fork: this would be using a Relative (or egocentric) reference frame. We could say that the spoon is to the east of the fork: this would be using an Absolute reference frame, based on fixed bearings. Or we could say that the spoon is near the handle of the fork: this would be using an Intrinsic, or object-centered, reference frame.

A culture's frame of reference is encoded in its language, and this presumably is how a toddler gains access to it (Majid et al., 2004). We know now that toddlers easily and quickly acquire any one of these reference frames (and sometimes more than one):

- Relative (or egocentric) reference frame: the spoon is to the right of the fork.
- Absolute (using fixed bearings): the spoon is to the west of the fork.
- Intrinsic (or object-centered): the spoon is near the handle of the fork.

What might be the neurological basis for these linguistically induced changes in the toddler's perception? We saw in Chapter 5 how researchers have used Dynamic Field Theory (DFT) to develop Piaget's idea about sensorimotor intelligence, and to explain the A-not-B error in terms of neurophysiological fields. These fields embody memory and they initiate action, and they are coupled to physical objects and events in the world through the orientation and posture of the body (Smith, 2005). We saw that properties of these fields enable them bind together actions, objects, and locations, just as Piaget proposed.

There is evidence that similar dynamic neurological processes are involved in early language acquisition. As a toddler learns her first words she can be said to be binding names to things. What makes this binding possible? It seems that location in space is crucially important. When an object is regularly placed in a specific spatial location, a toddler more quickly and easily learns its name (Samuelson et al., 2011).

How is the toddler using the stable location of an object to help her bind a word to that object? We have seen that DFT proposes that neurological fields can function as dynamic maps, and that two fields can be coupled together, so that activation in one field drives activation in the other. Let us suppose that one field is a map of objects in (body-centered) space, just as was the case in the hidden object task. This field initiates actions in space such as turning, looking, reaching, and pointing. Let us also suppose that we place an object at a specific point in space, and name that object several times. This would enable the toddler to form a second field: a map of words in space. This field is also a sensorimotor field: it is a mapping between a word and the location that is attended to when the toddler hears that word.

On the basis of these two fields a third field can be created. This third field is an object-word map, an association field that links the name to the thing. This third map does not involve any information about space. Spatial location enabled the toddler to *form* this connection between a word and a thing, but the connection is no longer bound to space—it has broken free from the here-and-now.

In other words, with help from her environment (people placing objects in particular locations and naming them) the toddler's sensorimotor system, which is bound in space and time to the real world, could enable her to construct a link that transcends her concrete circumstances. Names of objects can float free from space.

This shape bias appears around 18 months, at the time when a toddler has about 50 object names in her productive vocabulary. At first, she will attend to shape also when she learns a new adjective, which is of course usually the incorrect thing to do, but by 5 years of age she has learned that adjectives usually name something other than shape. Figure 8.5 summarizes data from several studies to show the changes

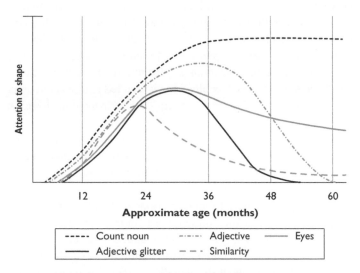

Figure 8.5 How the shape bias changes with age, for different kinds of word

Source: Jones & Smith (1993)

with age in the extent to which toddlers and young children pay attention to shape when they learn and apply various kinds of new word: new count nouns; new count nouns for objects with eyes; new adjectives; and new adjectives when a property other than shape is made salient. When learning a new noun, the child's attention to shape continues undiminished. With the other types of new word, attention to shape rises during toddlerhood and then decreases with age (Jones & Smith, 1993).

In short, the categories that a toddler or a young child creates when she learns new words involve the perceptual characteristics of the things being named, in systematic ways. She is looking for observable patterns in the world. This suggests that the concepts are based on what the young child perceives rather than on theories about core properties, or essences. Even children as young as 2.5 years do know that objects have non-obvious properties, such as insides—however, it seems that they do not use only these core properties as they develop concepts to define categories.

2.3 WORDS AND SELF-CONTROL

As a toddler becomes able to recognize the way her language—and hence her culture—categorizes the environment in which she lives, the immediate connection with the world with which she entered this stage starts to rupture. Whereas at 12 months the toddler was responding impulsively to the invitations offered by affordances, by age 2 language has provided her with the opportunity to pause and consider before she acts. How does this happen?

An illustration of this power of language comes from an experiment not with toddlers but with two adult female chimpanzees, Sheba and Sarah. The experimenter placed two treats in front of them, and the arrangement was that when Sheba pointed to a treat it was given to Sarah and Sheba got the one left over. This was repeated many times so the chimps could learn the arrangement. Sheba wanted the larger treat, but no matter how many opportunities she had to make a choice she repeatedly pointed to the larger treat, which then went to Sarah, so that Sheba always ended up with the smaller (Boysen et al., 1999).

What we see here is the irresistible invitation offered by the larger treat. Sheba could not resist being drawn to it, even when she had had every opportunity to learn the negative consequences of doing so. The researchers proposd that the chimps' behavior got "captured" by their practical routines (System 1), which were quick and efficient in their usual ecology but which led to unwanted outcomes in this unusual experimental situation. Reaching for a bigger piece of fruit works in a chimpanzee's natural environment, but it doesn't work in the laboratory.

If, however, the treats were placed in containers with material representations (numbers) on the top, Sheba quickly learned to point without hesitation to the container with the *fewer* treats. This treat went to Sarah, and Sheba was now getting more treats, which of course was what she had wanted all along (Boysen et al., 1996).

What had changed? Adding the material representations had altered the way the chimps interacted with their situation. They offered Sheba something other than the treats to focus on and attend, and this freed her from her own impulsive actions, enabling her to gain control of what she was doing. Focusing on the representation—on what by custom *indicates* the treat rather than the treat itself—enabled her to escape the treat's invitation and achieve what she actually wanted. The representation helped to decouple the intelligent agent from the immediate tugs of the encountered scene; it loosened "the bond between agent and world, and between perception and action," and it seemed to do this by "providing a new target for selective attention and a new fulcrum for the control of action" (Clark, 2006, p. 4).

A toddler is in a situation similar to that of these chimpanzees. She lives in an environment that is full of invitations that she cannot resist, at least at first. But her environment is also rich in layers of material representation. Spoken language is one of these, but there are many others. Her caregivers may be reading picture books with her. She may have toys that are tiny people, vehicles, and animals. She may be watching television with her family. She is an embodied agent embedded in a world that is material and symbolic at the same time. As she begins to recognize and understand how to use these material representations, they provide cognitive resources that loosen the bond between her and the world. Words, in particular, provide something concrete that she can focus on, and offer her a fulcrum to be better able to control her own actions. The chimpanzees could make only simple use of these resources, but for the toddler they open up vast new potentials. Focusing on the words and other signs that *stand for* objects, she no longer responds simply to the objects' natural features, she responds to these as members of customary cultural categories. And in doing this she develops a certain distance from them.

3. UNDERSTANDING MATERIAL REPRESENTATIONS

Language is both a way to influence people and a way to *talk about* the world by creating representational content. The first of these uses is grasped first by the toddler, but she soon begins to recognize the representational possibilities of speech and make use of this potential to express herself.

Toddlers begin to *create* material representations, in several ways. They start to draw and paint in simple ways, and they begin to engage in "pretend" play, in which they have one object stand for another.

This new ability has been called the "semiotic function." How does it become possible? We will consider Piaget's explanation, and this will lead us to consider two very different theories of semiosis.

3.1 LANGUAGE AS MATERIAL REPRESENTATION

> When humans engage in symbolic processes, they are engaging in cultural practices for seeing as. (Hutchins, 2008, p. 2014)

Developmental psycholinguists have often assumed that when a toddler begins to speak the language of her community this shows that she now carries around in her head an internal model of the language system: a set of syntactic rules, a grammar, although much simpler than the grammar that an adult knows. Cultural psychologists point out, in contrast, that language is part of the ecological niche of human beings. The toddler, like the infant, is surrounded by language, and this means that learning to speak "does not require the organism to possess an internal model of the grammar of a language ... any more than the building of a nest requires a prior internal model of the nest. The grammar of the language is *in the language*, just as the structure of the nest is in the nest" (Sinha, 2006, p. 113, original emphasis). Language is a material system of representation.

The sociologist Emile Durkheim insisted on the importance of "social facts," which he characterized as "manners of acting, thinking, and feeling external to the individual, which are invested with a coercive power by virtue of which they exercise control over him" (Durkheim, 1895). A language is a "social fact"; it lies outside of, and independent of, individual cognition, as a constituent of the biocultural niche that is specific to human beings. Language exists in the *talk* that each of us witnesses, and participates in, every day. In many communities it exists also in the *texts* that a child will probably become able to read. Central to Vygotsky's account of children's development is the proposal that individual human cognition is possible only because language is a shared social resource, available to the child as her capabilities grow.

Psychologists have tended to think of speech as an "expression" of thoughts and experiences in the mind. But in the next chapter we will explore the proposal that speech *is* the young child's first thinking. We are starting to see that language is "a vehicle of social life and social interaction that enables and constitutes the uniqueness of the human mind" (Sinha, 2009, p. 3). The toddler doesn't need to carry language in her head, she needs to learn how to participate in this vehicle.

The toddler has started to participate in customary ways of talking, just as much as she is involved in customary ways of wearing clothes, consuming food, going to bed, and so on. These social activities are regulated by tacit norms, which quickly become taken-for-granted ways of acting, and indeed ways of living, ways of being. Talking occurs upon this background of joint activity. Talking is, from one point of view, simply another kind of social action. It is a way of doing things together.

I have suggested that the "we" of shared intentionality does not come from some kind of sharing of mental states, or from one person's mental representations of another person's mental states, but arises in joint practical activity—the activities that people do together without needing to plan in advance. Going for a stroll, eating a meal, bath time, singing a song: these are joint practical activities, regulated by customs and unspoken norms. Toddlers' involvement in these activities occurs on the practical level that we have explored in Chapters 5 and 6: it is embodied, emotional, intuitive. A central aspect to speech is its pragmatic power, as a way to influence other people. This is how toddlers first encounter and deploy language.

However, there is a second, and equally important, aspect to speech: its capacity to *represent*. As we have seen, a toddler begins to discover this "mathetic" function of oral language—the fact that people talk to share information. Her understanding of the character of this information grows by leaps and bounds.

A toddler's first words do not yet have a representational character. At the start of this stage words simply point to things, and even to categories of things, but they do not yet *stand for* those things. It as though each word were a proper name. If I can correctly name someone "John," this doesn't mean that the word "represents" the person, or that I have the concept of "John." The word simply names the person, as though it were a label. A toddler initially treats all words as labels for objects (and for events). It is true that she often names objects that have characteristics in common, especially shape, and in this sense words not only label, they also generalize. However, for a toddler words do not yet stand for objects.

Toddlers now start to discover that words can be used to share information with other people. The social activity of naming is a matter of establishing what *counts as* a member of a class of objects. This animal "counts as" a dog (since we name it "dog"). And that animal too, though in color and size it is quite different. Learning the names of objects helps a toddler pay attention to those objects' shapes, because shape is often the basis for cultural categories: people tend to give the same name to objects with the same or similar shapes. Attending to shape enables her to perceive things as *kinds* of objects, as though she were saying to herself, *there goes banana again!* You can see that this ability could contribute to object permanency—the ability to understand that an object continues to exist even when it is out of sight.

This ability to perceive things as *kinds* of objects, as members of categories, also contributes to a kind of *double vision* that is necessary for understanding other kinds of material representations. A toddler starts to see generalized objects, not particular things. Her perception *classifies* what she sees. She becomes able to see something and at the same time see that it *counts as* a specific *type* of thing. This **seeing-as** is an important new ability.

To use language to its full extent, then, requires understanding that one thing *counts as* another. For example, the sequence of sounds *doggy* counts as the word "doggy" (technically, it counts as a *token* of a particular *type*), as a coin counts as 50 cents. Using language also requires an understanding that one thing *stands for* another. The coin does not *stand for* the value of 50 cents, it simply *is* 50 cents. The word "doggy," however, not only *counts as* a specific recognizable word in English (but not in Spanish, for example), it also *stands for* a four-legged animal. Language *represents* objects, events, actions, and situations that are outside of language. We saw in the case of Nigel that it took some time for him to grasp that a sequence of sounds not only *counts as* a word but also *stands for* something.

At first a toddler cannot yet talk about objects that are not actually present, she can talk only about what she sees. This suggests that for toddlers the connections among words are primarily situational and concrete, and so if we are to talk about the meaning of a word for toddlers this is also situational, so that the same word will at one time label one thing, at another it will label another. We could say that at first each thing has various names, depending on the situation. For example, a toddler will name a colored object depending on the colors of other objects, or the background: color names are relative, not absolute. In part this is because her speech is affective and volitional; she talks to make judgments and exclamations about things, not to describe them neutrally.

Toddlers begin to use language, then, to talk about the world they live in, although of course they have not yet grasped its full representational potential.

3.2 CREATING MATERIAL REPRESENTATIONS: STARTING TO DRAW

One way in which a toddler shows her growing understanding of material representations is that she begins to *create* representations herself. She starts to scribble and draw.

As we saw in Chapter 3, *Homo sapiens* is apparently unique in possessing the ability to create and comprehend drawings, paintings, and sculpture. No other animal species alive today has this ability. It is still unclear whether Neanderthals possessed it, but it seems unlikely than any of our other *hominin* ancestors did. Consequently, it is extremely important and interesting to understand when this ability appears in human ontogenesis, and certainly it takes significant steps during toddlerhood. Toddlers show a growing understanding that pictures, models, and toys serve as representations of other things.

These material representations—artifacts that are indices, signs, and symbols—are crucially important to modern life, and we can find them everywhere. We are surrounded by books and pictures, films and videos, signs and models, diagrams and maps, graphs and drawings, photos and plans, calendars and clocks. In fact, virtually anything can be used to represent something else: someone describing a holiday in Paris to friends around the dinner table can use a salt-shaker to represent the Eiffel Tower; the designer of a new enclosure at the zoo can demonstrate their work to colleagues by using a pen to represent an elephant.

It is sometimes said that to understand a sign is to identify the intention of the person who produced it (Deloach, 1998). However, this seems to introduce a circularity, because the intention is never directly visible; one has to infer the intention on the basis of interpreting the sign. It seems more likely that a sign is established by the norms that operate in the particular circumstances in which it is encountered. For example, in a formula, the sign "X" signifies an unknown variable. On a treasure map, an "X" identifies the location of buried gold.

Why do humans have so many representations? In part it is because they provide us with information about what is not directly present. Pictures can inform us about the North Pole, or the Moon, or the bottom of the ocean. Photos can inform us about people we have never seen. Diagrams can show us a hidden, internal structure. Maps provide a bird's eye view. Most of our knowledge today comes not from a firsthand, direct contact with things but from reading signs. Language, both spoken and written, is of course an important and central type of material representation, but humans have invented many others, and children come to understand and use them.

Between 1 and 3 years of age, toddlers begin to produce material representations— not only speech but also drawings. However, before we examine research on children's creation and understanding of drawings and paintings, let us reflect a little on the characteristics of pictorial representation. A picture has to be "read" in order to be understood as a sign of its object. Its "resemblance" to what is pictured is governed by many conventions: even the most "realistic" of pictures is actually highly conventional. And, as we shall see, the drawings made by toddlers are extremely conventional representations.

Oddly, many psychologists have assumed that pictures, models, and real objects are perceived in the same way by infants and toddlers. Developmental researchers often study children's responses to pictures (or models) as though they are the real thing, and they assume that this substitution makes no difference. For example, research exploring whether infants are able to identify the category of "animate" objects has presented not dogs and cats, but plastic toy dogs and cats! One shouldn't have to point out that nothing made of plastic is animate! The assumption that toddlers treat models as real is dubious, and it is one whose validity has never been systematically tested (Ittelson, 1996, p. 177). It would be wise to expect that at some point for children, "The processes involved in the visual perception of the world and in the visual perception of pictures differ in important ways. Generalizations from one to the other must be undertaken with caution" (1996, p. 181).

Given paper and crayon or pencil, toddlers will spontaneously draw. When they first do so, they show what has been called "the canonical bias." Typically, toddlers and young children do not accurately draw what can literally be seen from their viewpoint. For example, asked to draw a cup, they will typically include the handle even when they cannot see it. Asked to draw two objects, one of which occludes the other, they will typically draw both objects fully. In other words, they will draw "canonical" objects— typical examples of the *kind* of object—rather than the details of the *particular* object in front of them.

Piaget called this phenomenon "intellectual realism": he proposed that children draw not what they see, but what they know (Piaget & Inhelder, 1966/2008). It seems likely, however, that they will draw what they are conscious of seeing. That is to say, when they look at a cup they will unconsciously interpret the visible part of that cup as a sign for the whole, and they will be conscious of the whole cup, including its handle even if that handle isn't visible. Learning to draw only the visible aspect instead of the whole object is a complex matter, and requires becoming conscious of the automatic inferences of visual perception (which we discussed in Chapter 4).

Equally, learning to see the drawing of a cup as a cup is a complex matter. An infant may see that a picture of a cat resembles the animal, and she may even group the image and the animal together, but she will not grasp that one *represents* the other, but not vice versa.

We know this because a 9-month-old will try to pick up an object she sees in a realistic photograph or on a TV screen. Infants respond to pictures merely as interesting kinds of object: "though infants can perceive a difference between real and depicted objects, they do not understand the significance of that difference, so they investigate" (Delouch, 2004, p. 68). In contrast, 24-month-old toddlers were taught the word "whisk" by pairing a picture of the object with the sound of the word. Then they were offered either the object, or the picture of the object, and asked which one was the "whisk." They chose the object: evidently they assumed that the word named the object, not its picture, even though they had learned the word with the picture (Preissler & Carey, 2004).

A 2-year-old knows, then, the picture *is not* the object. Does she understand that in a special sense the picture *is* the object? In fact, a 2-year-old toddler will have difficulty using a picture to find an object hidden in the room. At 2.5 years of age, she has figured this out and can use a picture in order to find an object.

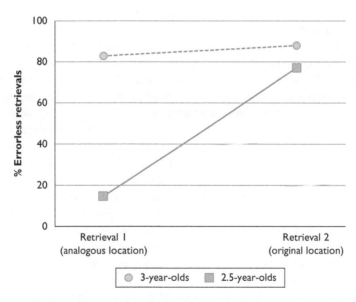

Figure 8.6 Performance of 2.5- and 3-year-old children in the model task

Source: DeLoach (2011)

But she still has difficulty if given not a picture but a scale *model* of the room. A model is more complex than a picture, even though that model has three dimensions, just like the room. At 3 years of age, a toddler understands that a model too is a representation of the room, and she can use what has been shown her in the model to find an object hidden in the real room (see Figure 8.6). Evidently, between 2 and 3 years of age a toddler comes to understand the basic operation of pictures and models as material representations: that they are designed both to *resemble* and to *stand for* something other than themselves.

3.3 CREATING MATERIAL REPRESENTATIONS: TODDLERS' PLAY

A second kind of creation of signs by toddlers is seen in the activity we call "play." During the second year a toddler starts to engage in creative activities in which one action or object stands for another. **Pretend play** has been called behavior in an "as if" mode. This behavior may be an action carried out without the usual materials, such as "pouring tea" from an empty pot. Or it may be one object substituting for another, such as "pouring tea" when there is sand instead of water in the pot, or using a banana as a telephone, or a block as a train.

We all know that children play, but what precisely is play? This question is more difficult to answer than one might think. Even infants play, in the sense that they explore with pleasure the physical properties of the objects in their environment, and they also enjoy rhythmic interactions with adults. If by play we mean pretense, however, this starts during the second or third year of life.

Pretend play has been viewed by psychiatrists and clinical psychologists as a window into the inner feelings of toddlers and young children, but more recently interest has focused on its linkages to social and cognitive development. Attempts to relate the ways young children play to events in their real life have not been very successful, though it seems that when their circumstances are pleasant, young children play with rich imagination.

A toddler will start making pretend actions, such as pretending to feed herself, as early as 12 months. Toddlers in poor villages in Guatemala show similar patterns of pretend play as middle-class American children (Fenson et al. 1976; Kagan et al., 1978), as do Italian children (Bates et al., 1977). At this point, however, most of a toddler's play is still sensorimotor activity that explores the physical properties of objects, but focusing now on their conventional functions.

For example, a toddler will pretend by using objects in a socially appropriate manner—"drinking" from an empty cup or saucer, for example. This kind of play generally increases from the start of toddlerhood and then decreases. Between 15 months and 20 months there is a shift towards directing these pretend actions towards a toy or a doll. A doll isn't a real person, of course, but it resembles a real person—it stands for a real person. It might seem that when a young toddler feeds her doll this is pretend play. But it may not yet be deliberate play: the toddler may simply be responding to the affordances of her doll. It this case it is "play-for-others" but not yet "play-for-self"; adults see her actions as play and respond accordingly, but the toddler is not yet *making one thing stand for another*.

Still more advanced is manipulating the doll as though it were the agent. In early childhood we will see more elaborate role play with dolls.

At around 18 to 24 months, toddlers will begin to make one object stand for another. At first, a toddler finds this easiest to do with objects that are realistic and highly prototypical: in other words, objects that strongly exemplify a category (Jeffree & McConkey, 1976). Progressively, however, pretend play becomes possible when resemblance is absent. Toddlers from 14 to 19 months will occasionally use a block to stand for a person: by 24 months 75 percent of them will be doing this. At 24 months, 94 percent will be using a cup to pretend to feed a realistic toy, and 70 percent will also be using a cup to pretend to feed a block. But only 33 percent at this age will be using one block to pretend to feed another block, play which requires a double substitution. (These figures are from a study by Fein, 1981.)

The playful substitution of one object for another usually occurs when they have a similar shape: a toddler uses a bucket as a hat, for instance. In addition, this kind of substitution play is also related to the toddler's vocabulary for objects, and to the ability to recognize caricatures. It has been found that toddlers who can recognize the caricatures I described earlier are more likely to engage in play that substitutes one object for another. Toddlers with a smaller vocabulary engage less in this kind of play. This suggests that pretend play is based on the role that language plays in enabling a toddler to recognize that things are similar in shape (Smith & Pereira, 2010).

Naming enables a toddler to see that one thing is *like* another. Her next step is to make one thing *stand for* another. In pretend play she is *creating* a material representation, not merely understanding one that someone else has created. When we study early childhood in Chapter 9 we will see just how vital a developmental step this is. Furthermore, much of pretend play is accompanied by speech, and even accomplished using speech. The toddler announces, "This is my dolly!" One researcher gave the example of his daughter climbing into an upturned box and saying "Bathtub!" (Scollon, 1976).

It has often been assumed that when pretend play begins it is an individual activity, and much research has studied toddlers' solitary play. However, there is convincing evidence that their pretend play has social roots. For one thing, when adults provide a toddler with realistic toys they are supporting her pretend play. Dolls, trucks, blocks, and so on, represent the categories of the culture, and "toy" is itself a cultural category (Sutton-Smith, 1986). For example, toys are often gender-marked, first by adults and then by children—dolls are for girls; trucks for boys.

Research indicates that pretend play lasts longer, and it is more sophisticated, when a toddler plays with her mother than when she plays alone. Similarly, her play is even more complex when she plays with an older sibling.

Moreover, when toddlers start to engage in pretend play they often imitate other people and they practice joint games of pretending (Rakoczy et al., 2005). When a toddler plays with caregivers her pretense goes on for longer and is more diverse and complex than when she plays alone (Youngblade & Dunn, 1995). During the second year of life the duration, level, and diversity of symbolic play increase when toddlers are with a caregiver. Caregivers respond to and participate in the play of their toddler, providing verbal commentaries, and when an adult provides a model for the toddler to imitate, symbolic play becomes more complex. Reciprocal forms of interaction, with active turn taking or simultaneous involvement in a shared activity, lead to more complex symbolic play (Fiese, 1990). Toddlers who have an older sibling also engage in more pretend play, and usually it is the older child who initiates it (Dunn, 1990). These observations suggest that play with others is important for pretense to develop.

Research also shows that a toddler's imagination is often not captured merely by an object but by a story which gives meaning to that object and defines specific actions on it. At first, the story is often provided by adults, although soon toddlers start to create their own narratives for play: "When adults play roles and dramatise a chain of events, they open a door to a play world which the children can enter" (Lindqvist, 2001).

3.4 ORIGINS OF THE SEMIOTIC FUNCTION

Piaget called this new capacity to understand and create material representations the "semiotic function" (sometimes this was translated as the "symbolic function"). Central to Piaget's account of this important development was the proposal that at the end of the sensorimotor stage the toddler starts not only to understand and create material representations but also to form *mental* representations. To understand his account, we need to explore briefly semiotics and semiosis.

Semiotics is the study and theory of **semiosis**. "Semiosis" is the process of interpreting and responding to some aspect of the environment as a **sign**. A "sign" in turn, by its dictionary definition, is "an object, quality, or event whose presence or occurrence indicates the probable presence or occurrence of something else". We recognize the process of semiosis when we say that an artifact "signifies something"—for example, that a round piece of metal signifies a quantity of money. However, responding to something as a sign can be both simpler than this and more complex.

A simple example is the way a dark cloud can be taken as a sign of rain. This semiotic process works because there is a causal connection between rain and dark clouds. However, in many semiotic processes the connection is not causal, it is one of resemblance. A photograph of a dog resembles that animal. In other signs the connection is one of convention. The red, green, and amber lights of a traffic light are conventional signs. However, despite the differences, in each case we have one thing—an object, quality, or event; the color of a cloud; an image; the color of a light—that can be responded to as indicating something else—an impending storm, a loved pet, a command to stop.

3.4.1 DE SAUSSURE AND PIAGET

Many semiotic theories draw upon a model proposed by the linguist **Ferdinand de Saussure** (1857–1913). As illustrated in the following figure, Saussure suggested that a sign has two aspects, its *signifier* and its *signified* (in French, *signifiant* and *signifié*) (Saussure, 1915).

Saussure was concerned mainly with the signs of language, that is to say with words. One might think that as a sign, word has two components: a sound and an object to which it refers. However, Saussure's analysis was more complex than this.

In the case of a spoken word the signifier is what Saussure called its "sound-image": this is a mental image of the way the word sounds. The signified is also something mental: Saussure called it the "concept." In the case of the example on the right, the (French) word "*arbor*" is a sign that is composed of a signifier that is an image of a string of sounds, and a signified that is the concept of a tree. The concept would presumably be something like "a woody perennial plant, with a single tall stem or trunk and lateral branches." This model emphasizes the *conventional* or *arbitrary* relation between the two components of a sign: the same concept can be attached to many different sound-images: "*arbor*" in French, "tree" in English, and "*arbol*" in Spanish.

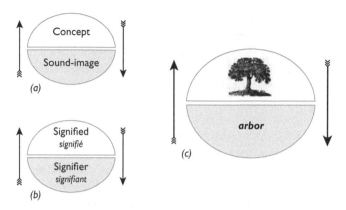

Figure 8.7   The structure of a sign, according to de Saussure

However, Saussure's model of semiosis raises several questions. For one thing, it seems to have no place for the actual tree that the word "tree" might be used to refer to. The object *tree* can be referred to using the word "tree," and understood in terms of the concept [tree], but it is separate from the word/concept pair. In addition, the status of the "concept" is unclear. Is a concept in the mind? Or in the language? There seems, once again, to be a dualism built into this account of semiosis.

At the time that Piaget wrote *Play, Dreams, and Imitation in Childhood*, Saussure's analysis of signs was widely accepted (and in addition, both Piaget and Saussure were Swiss). One might expect, then, that Piaget would try to explain the semiotic function by tracing the developmental roots of its two components, the signifier or "sound-image," and the signified or "concept." And this is precisely what he did!

Unlike cognitive developmental psychologists, Piaget maintained that infants are not born with the capacity to form mental representations of the world around them. Sensorimotor schemas are, Piaget insisted, not mental representations, they are patterns of action. He proposed that the capacity to form mental representations is a consequence of developments during the sensorimotor stage, and starts to appear only in the sixth and final substage. The lack of object permanence in younger infants and toddlers, according to Piaget, is due to their lack of the ability to form a mental representation of the object, a representation that persists even when the actual object is no longer visible.

Piaget's book *Play, Dreams and Imitation in Childhood* is about the form of intelligence found between the sensorimotor intelligence of infancy and later "operational" intelligence. First translated into English in 1951, this book was originally published in French in 1945.

Piaget argued that the capacity for representation is constructed. It is constructed from one kind of component provided by play, and another provided by imitation. Piaget saw the balance between assimilation and accommodation swinging in the direction of the former when the child **plays**, and in the direction of the latter when the child **imitates**. As Piaget puts it, play is a primacy of assimilation; imitation is a primacy of accommodation. When the child plays they are applying their existing schemas to the world around them: pretending that a pencil is a laser gun, for example. Their egocentrism is maxed out. When the child imitates they are modifying their action patterns to copy a model they find in the world.

This is why play and imitation are highlighted in the title of this book. (Dreams are there because Piaget takes time to consider theories of unconscious symbolism in Freud and others.)

Piaget's story of sensorimotor intelligence ends with the child achieving, in substage 6, a new kind of play and a new kind of imitation. The play in which one object stands for another, which we have been considering, Piaget called **symbolic play**. Imitation of a model that is no longer in front of the child he called **deferred imitation**. In this kind of imitation, Piaget claimed, accommodation has become "interiorized." Imitation is now based on "mental images." Both, according to Piaget, have an important role in the appearance of the semiotic function.

Piaget argued that the semiotic function becomes possible when two contributions come together, one from imitation, the other from play: "Representation begins when there is simultaneous differentiation and co-ordination between 'signifiers' and 'signified'" (p. 3). Put briefly, imitation—through accommodation—provides "**signifiers**," in the form of "**mental images**" that are actual or mental imitations of something in the world that is now absent, but continues to serve as a model. On the other hand, play—through assimilation—provides "**meanings**": the "**signified**."

Signifier and signified have to separate at the sensorimotor level, Piaget proposed, so that they can be coordinated or combined, and this combination makes it possible for the toddler to "to be capable of going beyond the immediate present" (p. 3) using, now, *mental* assimilation and accommodation.

For Piaget, then, the semiotic function involves the two components of "signifier" and "signified," and for the toddler at the end of the sensory-motor stage these are "mental image" and "meaning" respectively. With these two the toddler can construct "individual symbols." Later these will be combined with "collective signs" (chiefly language), but for now the toddler can only engage in "egocentric representative activity." This is sufficient, however, to get mental representation started. Representation, Piaget says, "begins and gradually develops at the beginning of the second year" (p. 165).

It is true that in the earlier sensorimotor substages there were already "signifiers" in the form of "indices" by means of which an infant recognizes an object or situation. But since these indices were *aspects of* the object or situation, there was no differentiation between signifier and signified.

The image, on the other hand, is a signifier that is *differentiated* from what it signifies. When images are constructed, a genuine mental representation is possible. However, an image still *resembles* the object that it stands for. This means that the image is not yet a truly "arbitrary" signifier. In addition, the image is individual in origin, not social. In both these respects, the image differs from the signs that are found in language, in Piaget's view. The role of language, for Piaget, was a secondary one: "the acquisition of language is itself subordinated to the working of a [semiotic] function."

In the third section of the book, Piaget traces the way that mental representation is put to use by the toddler, in a new kind of *mental action* that is now possible. He describes in some detail the transition at the end of the sensorimotor stage, and the entry into "intuitive thought," thinking that is intermediate between image and concept, a kind of thinking that represents something by imagining it (and so by moving from general to particular), not by deducing it (by moving from particular to general).

In short, in Piaget's explanation of the semiotic function, sensorimotor schemas (in toddlerhood) lead, first of all, to individual symbols which will later (during the preoperational stage in early childhood) be combined with the collective signs of language, so as to give rise to the true concepts of concrete operational thinking (in middle childhood).

Some psychologists today follow Piaget in arguing not only that the semiotic function depends on mental representations, but also that a **dual representation** is required to understand a picture or a model: that a toddler must form a mental representation of the picture or model as an object, and then also form a mental representation of what it stands for (DeLoache, 2004):

> Representational insight – and successful symbol use – requires dual representation. To use a symbolic artifact as a source of information, children must mentally represent both the concrete entity itself and, at the same time, its abstract relation to its referent. (DeLoache, 2011, p. 321)

3.4.2 PEIRCE AND VYGOTSKY

A different semiotic theory was proposed by the logician and philosopher **Charles Sanders Peirce** (1839–1914). Peirce suggested that semiosis involves not two components but *three*: the *sign*, the *object* it is taken as, and the *interpretant*, the *taking* of the sign as the object. He defined a sign as "something which stands to somebody for something in some respect or capacity" (Peirce, in Buchler, 1955, p. 99).

Consider the object in Figure 8.8. Seeing this artifact you might, especially if you are English like me, grab it and use it to prepare a pot of tea. The name the English give to this artifact is, of course, "teapot." All this is obvious; my point is that seeing and grasping this artifact *as* a "teapot" is a process of interpretation, a process of semiosis. Seeing an object as a teapot is a simple kind of semiosis: one responds to the artifact as an instance, an example, of a teapot: as an implement that is customarily used to prepare tea. One responds to it *as* a teapot, by using it to prepare tea!

In Peirce's terms, the teapot is a shaped piece of ceramic whose various characteristics (the *sign*) allow it to be taken as a familiar kitchen item (the *object,* which we name "teapot"), for example by the action of preparing a hot beverage (*interpretant*).

As users of signs, we are often more aware of the object that we take the sign to be than we are of the sign itself. Our awareness is of *teapot*, not of the curved ceramic surface. As witnesses to other people's use of signs, we generally infer their interpretation on the basis of their actions. When we

Figure 8.8   An artifact. What is it?

see someone preparing tea, we infer that they too interpret the artifact as a teapot (and not as a prized heirloom, for example). That is, their *interpretants* become for us signs to be interpreted. Signs chain together in this way.

One important advantage of Peirce's semiotics over Saussure's is that all three components—sign, object, and interpretant—are material. The *sign* is an object, quality, or event. The *object* is what the sign is taken to be: for example, a dark cloud is taken as coming rain. Both the cloud and the rain are material. And the *interpretant* is the response: running for cover, or looking for an umbrella.

This "taking one thing as another" is a process of interpretation, a process of semiosis. Philosopher Ludwig Wittgenstein emphasized the importance of "seeing as" (Schroeder, 2009). As cognitive psychologist Edwin Hutchins says, "When humans engage in symbolic processes, they are engaging in cultural practices for seeing as" (Hutchins, 2008, p. 2014). Peirce's semiotics, and the semiosis of "seeing as," offer an alternative way of thinking about the origins of the semiotic function in toddlers.

In the next chapter we will consider Vygotsky's hypotheses regarding the motives for pretend play and its developmental consequences. Here I want to focus specifically on his account of how object substitution play contributes to the development of the semiotic function: the ability to see one thing as a representation of another.

Consider how we respond to the question "What is that?"

We can respond with a name: "That is an elephant."

Or we can respond with a definition: "That is a heavy plant-eating mammal with a prehensile trunk, long curved ivory tusks, and large ears, native to Africa and southern Asia."

"What is that?" is a question toddlers start to ask. We saw in section 4 that '*Was 'at?*' is a *mathetic* utterance with which a toddler seeks to learn about the world. What is it she seeks to learn? Simply the name of an animal? Perhaps at first. But rapidly she will want to learn what the animal *is*. Of course the definition would be beyond her comprehension, but in asking her question she is starting to enter the way a language is used to define the reality of entities in the world.

In Vygotsky's view, early pretend play, object-substitution play, is where a distinction begins to develop between how something appears and what it is. As he put it, "in play a new relationship is created between the semantic and the visible—that is, between situations in thought and real situations" (Vygotsky, 1934). In short, object-substitution play doesn't *depend on* the semiotic function, the capacity to see one thing as another. Rather, it *sets the conditions* for the semiotic function.

Let's suppose (to borrow one of Vygotsky's examples) that a toddler uses a stick as a horse, riding it around. She selects the stick because it has the right characteristics: it can be placed between the legs, held with one hand, and ridden like a horse. The stick, the substitute object, resembles a horse only in a vague way, but it permits (affords) a similar action.

Importantly, she now applies the word "horse" to the stick. In a sense, then, the word "horse" has been separated from the object it initially named, the animal. When "horse" is applied to a new object, the stick, it becomes clear that words do more than refer and label, they also "mean" something. In separating the word "horse" from the object *horse*, the the toddler discovers that a word carries a semantic content—a "meaning"—that can be transferred from one object to another. As Vygotsky puts it, the pivot "steals" the name of the object it replaces, and in doing so "frees" the meaning of the word. The stick, he says, is "the necessary material pivot to keep the meaning from evaporating." Once the meaning of a word is freed, it can be applied freely to *any* object. A carrot could be called a "horse"! Vygotsky called this a process of "emancipation," and one can see why (Vygotsky, 1966). (Note that the term "pivot" should not be confused with the proposal that a toddler's two-word speech has a "pivot-open" grammar.)

Several things have changed here. A meaning has become evident "in" the word. The word has ceased to seem a part, an aspect, of the object it names, so that it—or rather its *meaning*—can be applied to other objects. Equally, a distinction appears between an object and its meaning; between, for example, the animal we call "horse" and what it means to be a horse.

As a consequence, the toddler's perception is transformed. Instead of seeing a horse, she starts to see an animal *as* a horse. Vygotsky said that perception now becomes "interpreted." However, we know that perception is always a process of interpretation (now we can see that it is a process of semiosis)— what happens to the toddler is that a *new kind* of interpretation begins, in which one thing is seen as something else.

Language helps make the world become more stable and objective for the toddler. She begins to understand the world as something separate from her. She starts to grasp the fact that words have both sound and meaning. As yet, though, "[I]n play a child unconsciously and spontaneously makes use of the fact that he can separate meaning from an object without knowing he is doing it" (Vygotsky, 1966[1933], p. 13).

The young child also now begins to recognize that one object can *stand for* another object, functioning as a picture, a model, or a symbol. All of this means that she now has all the necessary psychological requirements to start to distinguish between the way things *appear* and the way they *are*. This object *seems* to be a horse, but it is *really* a stick. This distinction will be a crucial accomplishment of early childhood.

The similarities between Vygotsky's account of semiosis and that of Charles Peirce have been noted (Hildebrand-Nilshon and Seeger, 2006; Ma, 2014; Perinat & Sadurní, 1999). Like Peirce, Vygotsky focused on semiosis as an aspect of the child's interaction with the world, not as an internal mental process. He emphasized a transformation in the toddler's perception of the world, her consciousness of the world, that is a consequence of her growing sophistication with language. Language makes it possible to ask "What is that?" and the answers to this question open up for the toddler an entirely new way of living in the world: "seeing as" and living "as if."

It seems entirely possible, then, that the emerging ability to understand material representations does not rest on a capacity to form mental representations.

Rather, what the toddler acquires is the ability to see that one thing can *stand for* another: the ability to see one thing *as* another. This *seeing as* requires a kind of creative perception, a capacity for imagination, that far outstretches anything that any other primate is capable of. However, the ability to understand material representations is not a mysterious mental process that emerges suddenly and dramatically at the end of the sensorimotor phase, at around 30 months of age, as Piaget seems to have believed. It is an ability that the toddler steadily acquires since she turned 1 year old, based on prior accomplishments.

This ability to "see as"—to see an animal as an example of the general category of *dog*, to see marks on paper as a picture of a dog—is probably the most important development of toddlerhood. It is certainly crucial for her understanding and use of material representations. In Chapter 7 we will see that this ability remains central in early childhood, the next developmental stage.

4. SELF AND SYMBOL: THE TRANSITION AT 3 YEARS

The steady changes that I have been describing over the months of toddlerhood build towards a dramatic transition that occurs at around 2.5 or 3 years of age. We have seen that toddlerhood began with a new kind of *self-awareness*, a sense of self as an active agency in the world, able to bring about interesting effects without the direct mediation of other people. This stage now ends with what we can call *self-consciousness*: the toddler shows a new understanding of herself. She recognizes that she is visible in the eyes of other people. We see this change in the toddler's self-recognition, in her growing understanding of norms and standards, and in the so-called secondary emotions.

4.1 RECOGNIZING A MIRROR IMAGE

A common task that researchers use to determine a child's degree of self-awareness is to present a mirror and observer her reaction to her own reflection. Often they will surreptitiously apply a red spot to her nose, and observe her response when she sees this in her mirror image (this is called the **rouge test**). Of course, mirrors are artifacts that are not available in every culture, and not every infant or toddler will have the opportunity to see her reflection. The results of this task, consequently, must be interpreted as contingent on cultural practices. In a study with children in a rural village in Kenya, who presumably had little or no experience with mirrors, only 2 percent of the youngest passed the mirror mark test. Instead, even children as old as 7 years "stood transfixed, staring frozen and inhibited at their image" (Rochat & Zahavi, 2011, p. 212).

In societies where mirrors are common, however, a developmental sequence of self-recognition has been observed. A small study of five infants found the following pattern, through the ages associated with each stage varied (Dixon, 1957). In the "Mother" stage, at around 4 months, the infants did not respond to their own reflections, but smiled and vocalized at their mother's image. In the "Playmate" stage the infants responded as though their reflection was another infant. In the next stage, at about 7 months, the infants repeated simple actions, such as opening their mouth, while watching their reflection. In stage 4, at 12 months, the infants recognized their own image and distinguished it from those of others, as well as responding correctly when asked "Where are you?" (And at the end of this stage, at about 18 months of age, the infants also started to respond to their own names.)

A toddler's reaction is different, however. Most toddlers will start to touch the red dot at around 20 months, and when asked "Who's that?" will answer "Me." Then, generally, the experience starts to become increasingly troubling, and they start to show wariness. Interestingly, autistic children will remove the spot from their own nose when they see it in the mirror, but will not show any coyness or embarrassment (Hobson, 2002). For normal toddlers, the anxiety wears off again in time. Next comes the toddler's recognition of her own physical characteristics, and then verbal self-description (both neutral and evaluative).

The ability to recognize one's own physical features is not present in other animal species. Of course, animals encounter their reflections very rarely in the wild. Studies of wild-born chimpanzees in captivity given a mirror for the first time found that they first discovered how to move their image in the mirror without showing any signs of recognizing that they were seeing themselves. Within a few days they had learned to use the mirror to see parts of their bodies that were usually invisible to them, but still seemed unaware that the image "was" them. They seemed to have grasped a sensorimotor connection between image and body part, but without identifying with their image. Monkeys, too, can use a mirror to find food that is otherwise not visible, but they do not respond to their own image with recognition (Gallup, 1970).

The cognitivist interpretation of the mirror self-recognition test is that the toddler who evidently recognizes herself now possesses a "concept of self" (Gallup, 1970, p. 87), or "an internal model of self" (Keenan et al., 2003, p. 11), or "an idea of me or self-representation" (Lewis, 1995, p. 281). There is even speculation now about the existence of a possible "self-network" in the brain (Keenan et al., 2000). However, once again the material artifact has been forgotten. A mirror is an artifact that offers something unique: it permits someone to see herself as others see her, to become a spectator of herself (Rochat & Zahavi, 2011). Adults can recognize themselves in a mirror because they have seen their image before, perhaps on a daily basis. But until she is first offered a mirror, the toddler has never seen herself. She has no idea what she looks like, or perhaps even that she is visible to other people. The toddler presumably discovers that the image in the mirror is herself by moving in front of it and discovering that the reflection's movements are completely coordinated with her own. To make this discovery is to realize for the first time how she appears. Visible for the first time to herself, she realizes that she is visible to other people, and how she looks to them. The mirror offers the toddler a perspective or viewpoint on herself analogous to the perspective others adopt towards her. The existential philosopher Maurice Merleau-Ponty wrote:

> At the same time that the image makes possible the knowledge of oneself, it makes possible a sort of alienation. I am no longer what I felt myself, immediately, to be; I am that image of myself that is offered by the mirror … In this sense I am torn from myself, and the image in the mirror prepares me for another still more serious alienation, which will be the alienation by others. For others have only an exterior image of me, which is analogous to the one seen in the mirror. Consequently others will tear me away from my immediate inwardness much more surely than will the mirror. (Merleau-Ponty, 1964, p. 136).

The toddler discovers a new aspect of her own existence, discovers that she is visible to other people, and discovers that they are both observing her and evaluating her.

In the last chapter I introduced the distinction between two caregiving styles, the **distal style** and the **proximal style**, which are apparently related to different sociocultural orientations (Keller et al., 2004):

- The **distal style** tends to emphasize face-to-face interaction with mutual eye contact, and the displaying of objects to the infant. This style is thought to establish a framework of mutuality within which the infant has a degree of control over the interaction, and to start the infant along a developmental trajectory towards independent self-construal.

- The **proximal style** tends to emphasize body contact and physical stimulation. This style is thought to promote unity and fusion rather than separateness, and synchrony rather than reciprocity.

These parenting styles during infancy (at 3 months of age) have been found to be associated with differences at 18–20 months in self-recognition (using the rouge test) and also self-regulation (using a compliance task: inhibiting a forbidden act and performing a requested behavior).

You will recall that these researchers compared parent–infant interactions in Cameroonian Nso (a culture of *interdependence*, valuing hierarchy, obedience, and respect) and Greek middle-class families (a culture of *independence*, valuing autonomy and separateness). They also studied Costa Rican middle-class families; a culture of what has been called *autonomous relatedness*, emphasizing both autonomy and relatedness.

The Greek toddlers, whose mothers used the distal style, showed the greatest self-recognition (68.2 percent) but the lowest compliance (47.7 percent of them did not comply with either requests or prohibitions). The Cameroonian Nso toddlers, whose mothers used the proximal style, showed very low self-recognition (3.8 percent), but the greatest levels of self-regulation (71.9 percent complied). The Costa Rican toddlers, whose mothers combined both styles, were between the other two groups in both their self-recognition (50 percent) and their self-regulation (41.7 percent complied).

When the researchers looked in more detail at the various aspects of parenting style they found that the parental practice that best predicted the toddlers' self-recognition was presenting objects to stimulate the infant, in particular the degree of mutual eye contact. They concluded that "the more mutual eye contact the children experience the more likely it is that they recognize themselves at 18 to 20 months" (Keller et al., 2004, p. 1753). This kind of interaction with parents apparently strengthened "the sense of autonomy and the experience of being a distinct and separate person" (2004, p. 1755).

Turning to self-regulation, it was the toddlers who had experienced a proximal parenting style who demonstrated most self-regulation at 18–20 months of age. Body contact turned out to be the central predictor for this relation. The researchers interpreted the toddlers' compliance with requests and prohibitions as an indication of obedience and interdependence.

This research supports the proposal that there are distinct cultural trajectories to development during infancy and toddlerhood. Here, these styles appear to be linked to the new sense of self that appears to emerge around 30 months to 3 years of age. Toddlers in families in which parents use the distal style and who foster independence will become self-conscious at a younger age. They are also less compliant, suggesting that they are beginning to assert their independence in the family.

Joscha Kärtner (2015) has argued that the distal caregiving style draws the toddler's attention to "subjective mental states," because of the character of the contingent biosocial feedback that it provides. If this were the case, it would contradict what I have suggested earlier in this chapter about a toddler's ability to understand intention-in-action but not prior intentions or intentional states. However, Kartner assumes that "Mirror self-recognition reflects a representation of the self as an autonomous intentional agent that is based on subjective self-awareness" (2015, p. 1304). It seems more reasonable, however, to suppose that the reverse is the case: that subjective self-awareness is based upon mirror self-recognition, amongst other things. The toddler is *discovering* herself: she is not yet conscious of her intentions, let alone does she consider herself an "autonomous intentional agent." We see just the beginnings of autonomy in the way some of these toddlers studied by Keller and her colleagues were showing a lack of compliance. They were discovering their own agency in clashes with parental authority.

4.2 SELF-REFERENTIAL LANGUAGE

The second indication of the discovery of a new self-consciousness at the end of toddlerhood is that toddlers begin to use self-referential terms, such as their name or the personal pronoun ("I"). Between 18 and 24 months a toddler begins to produce utterances that will include an explicit reference to herself as the agent of the action she is talking about: "Tommy finished," or "Uh-oh. I fix." The first single-word utterances, as we have seen, are generally used to refer to some object or action. But once toddlers start to combine words they can, as we have also seen, combine language macrofunctions and begin to talk about their own agency.

This raises the interesting question of whether language, which we have seen is transforming toddlers' understanding of the world, is also transforming their understanding of themselves. We saw earlier in this chapter that Halliday suggested the new linguistic macrofunctions that emerge in the second year—the pragmatic and mathetic—involve a separation of self from the environment (the "non self"). Halliday proposed that in utterances with a pragmatic function a toddler is interacting with the environment, to act on it and express her attitudes towards it. In utterances with a mathetic function, on the other hand, he suggested that the toddler is separating herself from the environment, with the result that she starts to interpret that environment in a new way, as we have seen, and that she also starts to become conscious of her self.

A toddler starts to use the mathetic function when she grasps the need to communicate an experience to someone, and this leads to recognizing that different people have different experiences. Piaget believed that toddlers and young children assume that everyone sees the world as they do: he called this **egocentrism**. He also argued that this shows that a toddler is not yet socialized—though it seems more accurate to say that she is still only slowly differentiating from other people. In the next chapter I will explore the notion of egocentrism in more detail.

4.3 SECONDARY EMOTIONS

The third indication of a new self-consciousness is that the toddler now shows new kinds of emotion. In Chapter 5 I described how the first displays of emotion are responded to by parents, and how this establishes the conditions for the infant to begin to regulate her own emotions. At 12 months of age we still saw the primary emotions, such as joy, fear, anger, surprise, sadness, disgust. These emotions have a simple, direct relation to the events that elicit them.

A **primary emotion** can be defined as "a complex, organized response disposition to engage in certain classes of biologically adaptive behaviors. It is characterized by a distinctive state of physiological arousal, a distinctive feeling, or affective, state, a distinctive state of receptivity to stimulation, and a distinctive pattern of expressive reactions" (Epstein, 1984).

Darwin noted the lack of self-consciousness in young toddlers:

Children at a very early age do not blush; nor do they show those other signs of self-consciousness which generally accompany blushing; and it is one of their chief charms that they think nothing about what others think of them. At this early age they will stare at a stranger with a fixed gaze and unblinking eyes, as on an inanimate object, in a manner which we elders cannot imitate. (Darwin, 2002[1872], p. 346)

Between 18 and 24 months, however, a toddler begins to show new emotions such as embarrassment, pride, shame, guilt, and envy (e.g., having a self-satisfied smile, hanging the head, covering the face, trying to hide). Each of these is what has been called a **secondary emotion**, "a culturally established syndrome, modeled after the primary emotions, that is not characterized by a biologically adaptive response disposition … [which] consists of a widely shared positive or negative reaction to a designated stimulus situation" (Epstein, 1984). To put it in simpler terms, the secondary emotions involve an evaluation of oneself in the eyes of other people, in terms of shared norms and expectations. They are responses to a realization of one's own success or wrongdoing in the eyes of others. These have been called **self-conscious** emotions (Lewis, 1995) and **self-directed** emotions (Holodynski, 2009).

These secondary emotions are products of both biology and culture. We have seen that all emotions are based on a physiologically based evaluation or appraisal, but the secondary emotions involve self-evaluation: the object of the emotion is no longer some thing or event in the world, but the toddler herself as an agent in that world. Secondary emotions are displays for other people, but they are also displays to the child herself. They are more flexible than the primary emotions in the kinds of event that produce them, and they are products of culture in the sense that they reflect the evaluations that adults have been making of the toddler. In addition, they contribute to the reproduction of culture in the sense that a child who feels guilt or shame at violating a social norm is likely to conform to that norm in the future.

The self-conscious emotions reflect a toddler's increasing ability to recognize, talk about, and think about herself in relation to other people (e.g., in terms of some social standard, rule, or desired goal). The perception of approval by significant others leads to pride, and a sense of worth. In contrast, the perception of their disapproval—perhaps together with disappointment and frustration at failing in a task—leads to shame (Campos et al., 1994). Indeed, a toddler first shows guilt and shame when she is literally in front of other people, and only somewhat later does she show these emotions when she is alone. Importantly, these new emotions appear around the same time as self-recognition in the mirror (Lewis et al., 1989).

These new emotions emerge as caregivers begin to expect their toddler to regulate her own actions and emotions and to conform to family and cultural norms with appropriate emotions (Holodynski, 2009). Secondary emotions reflect the continuing movement from interpersonal to intrapersonal regulation that I introduced in Chapter 5. Emotional expressions now begin to be directed not only towards other people but also towards the self. Secondary emotions direct the toddler's behavior in ways that are in agreement with family norms (Holodynski, 2009). The toddler is learning that her actions have consequences for other people. She is also starting to learn how to manage her emotions herself without always needing the support of her caregivers.

Since cultures differ in their expectations and norms, the emergence of secondary emotions is culturally directed and contextualized. For example, in a sample of Canadian families, 2-year-olds were shyer if their mother was punitive, and less shy if their mother was accepting and encouraging. In a Chinese sample, however, the opposite was the case: 2-year-olds were shyer when their mother was warm and accepting (Chen et al., 1998)! And although we often assume that aggression should be discouraged in children, a mother in a tough neighborhood may encourage her toddler to be hostile when attacked by another child (Miller & Sperry, 1987). Aggressiveness, however, is accepted only in appropriate contexts. There is a long-standing notion that some cultures emphasize guilt while others emphasize shame.

In their third year, toddlers discover that their actions can lead to praise or blame by their caregivers, and begin to try to obtain the first and avoid the second. They start to voluntarily suppress or postpone their impulses to act. How do they do this? We have seen that in large part this is due to a toddler's changing relationship with the world, as she becomes able to focus on material representations, and on the cultural types that define objects and events. This contributes to the acquisition of techniques a toddler can use for distracting and calming herself. She starts to become capable of reinterpreting her situation, and putting multiple motives in order of importance (Bischof-Köhler, 2012). Her ability to reflect on and regulate her own emotions is increasing. The consequence is a trend towards less intense emotions, and less frequent strong emotions.

The ways caregivers respond is important, as we have seen. Researchers have found that when the mother of a 2-year-old toddler makes many negative evaluations, especially of what the toddler does and the results of her actions, the child will show more shame when she is older. In contrast, when the

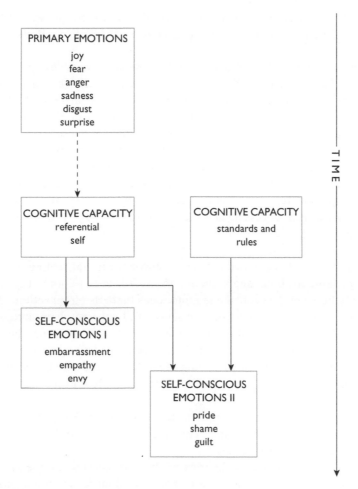

Figure 8.9 The development of self-conscious emotions

Source: Lewis et al. (1989)

mother makes mainly positive evaluations, and provides helpful feedback, her child will later show more persistence on tasks, a characteristic known as **mastery motivation**. And when a mother supports her young toddler's autonomy that toddler is less likely to avoid challenging activities at 3 years of age (Kelley et al., 2000).

4.4 PSYCHOLOGICAL DIFFERENTIATION: SELF-CONSCIOUSNESS

The secondary emotions are further evidence that during the stage of toddlerhood there is a movement from **self-awareness** to **self-consciousness**. A 12-month-old infant acts in the world and celebrates the consequences: this is self-awareness. A 30-month-old toddler understands that she is responsible for the consequences of her actions: this is self-consciousness.

This new kind self-consciousness has been described in a variety of ways. Michael Lewis has described the difference between **subjective self-awareness** and **objective self-awareness**:

> Human beings are complex, multilevel, self-regulating organisms capable of perceiving, emoting, thinking, remembering, and learning. We possess elaborate feedback loops that do not require our objective self-awareness in order to operate. For example, we regulate our bodily functions as well as our cognitive ones without focusing on the fact that we are doing so (indeed, most of the time we are unaware of this aspect of our being). All living creatures have similar processes. However, at some point ontogenetically, human beings gain a new capacity: awareness of their own operations. The capacity for objective self-awareness allows humans to process information and to decide on the best action (whether it be motor behavior, thought, or emotion). The objective self can reflect on and reject any solution generated by the subjective process. It allows us to stand back from our own processing and thereby increases the possibility of generating new solutions. (Lewis, 1997, p. 122)

A similar distinction has also been drawn between a **non-conceptual feeling** of one's own agency, and a **conceptual judgment about one's agency** (Synofzik et al., 2008). The infant's feeling of agency is presumably based on perceptual and motor cues that arise from action. On this level, self-agency would be experienced as "a rather diffuse sense of of coherent, harmonious ongoing flow of action processing" (2008, p. 228). On the other hand, the *judgment* of agency involves the application of beliefs and desires to this feeling. This judgment is an explicit interpretation of the feeling of agency, usually when there is some kind of feeling of *not* having the anticipated agency, or when the effects of actions are highly culturally mediated or ambiguous. It is influenced by both the context and current beliefs.

In adults, the feeling and the judgment contribute to the overall sense of agency. In toddlers presumably the feeling is present, and judgments are beginning to be made, so that the toddler is starting to evaluate the consequences of her own actions.

There are suggestions that the prefrontal cortex might be responsible for the self-attribution that is involved in a sense of agency, because this is based not only on modal sensory inputs and intersensory correlations but also on the contingency of these with motor intentions, and the latter are largely formed and stored in the prefrontal cortex (Synofzik et al., 2008, p. 233).

Psychologists have also distinguished between an infant's **emotional core self** and a toddler's **interpersonal self**. The interactions between infant and adults built emotionally colored expectations on a level that was not accessible to consciousness, but which contributed to a fundamental sense of self: its "emotional core" (Emde et al., 1991). The sense a toddler comes to have of her own worth and possibilities will depend, in addition, on her social context and on the dynamics of her relations with caregivers. This is an "interpersonal self," based on her involvement in a social world within the Great-We (Neisser, 1991). This sense of self has its roots in the infant's biological needs and the toddler's motivations, as well as in the patterns of response of her caregivers. It is not a "self-concept," but something that is still more tacit and basic. It is an aspect of the toddler's residence in the world, not yet something that she represents to herself or to others.

Findings such as those I have described suggest that the caregiving relationship—whether we conceive of it as attachment or as guided participation—gives a toddler a sense of her own worth, or the lack of it. As we have seen, in his earlier writing Bowlby proposed that the caregiver becomes the ego and the superego for their infant and toddler.

If a toddler gains her first sense of her own value in her relationship with caregivers, this would explain why attachment has such a strong influence on her subsequent behavior and relationships. The clinical psychologist Erik Erikson (1950) suggested that in the first year of life we acquire our fundamental sense of trust or mistrust in the world. In the second year, the balance is between autonomy or shame and doubt. A toddler who is criticized, overly controlled, or not given the opportunity to assert herself will acquire a sense of shame or doubt in her own abilities, and may become overly dependent upon others, lacking self-esteem. Attachment does not simply ensure that the toddler learns from kin, it also establishes the basis for the kind of person that toddler will become.

This self-consciousness is also apparent in the negativity and stubbornness that can appear around 3 years, when a toddler refuses to do what parents ask or even demand. "You're not the boss of me!" is the slogan with which some toddlers initiate a revolution and become a young child. As we have seem, however, in some communities it is the parents who initiate this revolution, when the toddler is displaced by the arrival of a new infant.

Caregivers with different styles will respond to such changes in different ways, as we have seen in the last two chapters and shall see again in the following chapter. Up until this point, the very existence of the infant and toddler would have been impossible outside the emotional ties to the family. But now, relationships with other people change. The toddler has been content to be led by the hand. But now she insists on walking independently. An "I" has emerged, albeit still within the Great-We.

To repeat, then, we saw that in the transition at 12 months an infant came to recognize her own agency, distinct from that of the people around her, as she began to walk and talk. We said that she was *self-aware*. Now, in the transition at the end of toddlerhood at 3 years of age, she starts to recognize that she is the *subject* of her actions, and this means that she is visible in the eyes of other people. She is now self-conscious.The emergence of self-consciousness at the end of toddlerhood at 3 years of age amounts to a **psychological differentiation** between the child and her caregivers.

Whether she struggled to assert her autonomy or found herself displaced by the arrival of a new infant, a new separation has taken place for the toddler. The "I" that emerges, however, still exists within the Great-We rather than being completely separated from it. In the next developmental stage the young child will still depend greatly on her caregivers.

As I have mentioned, many developmental psychologists have assumed that the infant is born an aso-cial creature who must be **socialized**, through adult instruction, or feedback, or discipline. As we have seen, it makes much more sense to say that the infant is born social, and only with time becomes *differentiated* from other people. At birth the newborn is separated physically but not yet biologically. The toddler who starts to walk is separated biologically, but not yet psychologically. Now, at the end of the toddler stage, she starts to separate psychologically: to have consciousness of herself as a separate psychological entity.

A toddler begins with very little sense of herself as a separate being, distinct from other people. She is starting to contrast herself with the artifacts she encounters, but still within a social situation in which she is merged with other people. Vygotsky proposed that the first distinction that is made in the toddler's consciousness is between "I" and "object," not between "I" and "other person." We can see this in the extent to which the toddler continues to assume that other people will know her wishes immediately. Although the toddler becomes frustrated when adults cannot correctly interpret her one-word utterances, in general she is able to continue assuming that others will give her what she wants, in large part because they are continually working to interpret what she is doing in order to figure this out. Initially the tod-dler still "does not separate what is in his consciousness from what is in the consciousness of the adult" (Vygotsky, 1998[1932–1934], p. 266). Now this is changing.

Finally, in the previous sections of this chapter I have suggested that there are two new accomplish-ments that mark the end of the stage of toddlerhood, around 3 years of age. One is the emergence of self-consciousness. The other is the capacity to understand material representations.

An obvious question arises here: is there a connection between these two? Some psychologists have suggested that there is–that to comprehend and create representations leads to a self-conscious subject, so that in the development from a pre-representational to a representational relationship with the world the "subject" is formed (Kristeva, 1992; Lacan, 1956). Their argument is that the recognition of the rela-tionship between a representation and the object that is represented not only "frees" the object, but at the same time, the subject is "freed" as well, "in the form of a greater self-consciousness, a new distance and separation from the object, a sense of standing over against it and no longer being englobed by what is depicted" (Taylor, 1989, p. 202). The proposal here is that to represent the world is to objectify it, con-sequently to become more detached from it, and to begin to draw the boundary between self and world that is so characteristic of modern, Western psychology.

The dawning distinction between the way things appear and they way they are, which we explored in section 6, and the growing sense of self as distinct from both the world and from other people, seem to be interrelated. They make up the transition, the revolutionary change in a toddler's relationship with the world, that leads to the next developmental stage—early childhood. The young child discovers that she has the power to *impose* representations, in the form of words, on the world. She can tell objects, and people, what they are!

CONCLUSION

During the period from around 1 year to around 3 years of age, dramatic and importance changes occur. At the start of this stage, a toddler responds without hesitation to the invitations of the world around her.

Her spoken language begins as a "protolanguage" in which single-word utterances, holophrases, serve a variety of distinct, simple functions. Around 18 months, when words are combined, this transforms into a speech system in which there are two general functions, the *pragmatic* and the *mathetic*. With pragmatic utterances the toddler seeks to influence people in a variety of ways. With mathetic utterances she seeks to learn about the world. "Was 'at?" is a typical example. By the end of this stage the toddler is beginning to be able to combine these two functions in her utterances, using true syntax.

As her language improves the toddler engages with adults in the social practice of naming. Naming draws her attention to the shapes of objects, and also provides access to the ways her culture categorizes artifacts and objects. Names also provide access to material representations: a drawing of a dog generally has the same name as the animal that it represents. Piaget accepted Saussure's account of signs as signifier/signified pairs, in which both signifier and signified are mental entities.

Language specifies the categories into which a culture divides the world, and as she talks the toddler's attention is directed to specific categories of object, and to specific characteristics of those objects, especially their shape. As this happens, her immediate and impulsive way of being in the world starts to change. That world becomes more stable and objective, defined by culturally defined categories of artifact, which the toddler now starts to recognize are used in customary ways.

Language also aids the toddler's recognition that one object can *stand for* another. She begins to comprehend pictures, models, and signs—that is, she starts to understand material representations. We see one thing standing for another in her first attempts at drawing, and in her pretend play, when she substitutes one object for another—for example, calling a stick a horse and starting to ride it. When she pretends that the stick is a horse, although she knows that it is not "really," she is controlling what the stick appears to be within her play activity. Drawing and pretense will become centrally important in early childhood.

At first, words do not *represent* objects. The toddler treats words as though they are labels for objects (as a shirt might have a label). However, as she applies the word "horse," for example, not to the original object but to a stick that she is pretending is a horse, the word starts to detach from what it names, and its meaning starts to become evident to the toddler. Words start to have *sense* as well as *reference*. In using words to pretend that one thing is another toddlers are taking their first steps in making use of the representational links between words and the world that every language provides.

There are certainly important differences in guided participation in different cultures. In some cultures adults teach explicit lessons, while in others a toddler learns through participation or observation. In addition, in some cultures a toddler seems to need to make assertions of independence and autonomy, while in others she is often displaced by the arrival of a new infant. In some cultures but not others, the caregiving style fosters self-consciousness.

At the end of this stage, at around 3 years of age, the toddler starts to differentiate between herself as object and herself as agent. In the previous transition, at 12 months, as she began to walk and talk, the infant came to recognize her own agency, distinct from that of the people around her. She became self-*aware*. In the transition at the end of toddlerhood she starts to recognize that she is the *subject* of her actions, visible in the eyes of other people. As a consequence she starts to show self-conscious emotions such as pride and shame. Now she is self-*conscious*. She **differentiates psychologically** from other people.

The toddler still assumes, however, that her wishes and desires are visible to other people, and that they will do her bidding. In a sense this is in fact the case, because adults can see her intentions in her actions. And when these are not clear, adults do indeed work hard to figure out what the toddler wants, in this way contributing to her stance towards other people.

During this period of time between 1 and 2.5 years of age, then, however, both objects and people become increasingly stable and permanent, though their affective quality remains central. Language contradicts a toddler's immersion in concrete situations, and this contradiction grows increasingly intense: "Speech instantly starts to shatter sensory-motor unity and to break up the situational connectedness of the child" (Vygotsky, 1998[1932–1934], p. 269). Language—through social practices of naming— enables toddlers to make sense of what they perceive.

During toddlerhood the world of affordances is transformed into a more stable and objective reality. Language slowly but steadily undoes the connection between a toddler and her world. The sensorimotor unity of infant and toddler is broken and "Suddenly, the child becomes entirely different … and a new age-level begins" (Vygotsky, 1998[1932–1934/1998] p. 268).

The toddler's growing language ability slowly creates a stable world of objects, *types* of entity. As the world stabilizes it becomes something distinct from the toddler herself. What were at first irresistible affordances now become invitations which the toddler can decide whether or not to accept. With the transition at age 3, a toddler develops a new sense of self, as separate from the objects around her, and from other people, and able to use words to *represent* those objects. She has started to use and understand material icons (pictures), not just indices.

We see this in pretend play, in which toddlers use one thing to stand for another. Young children begin to differentiate between the way things appear and what they are—the cultural categories they fall into—as examples of classes. We have seen how learning names helped the toddler make this distinction. On this basis a young child can create a "closed field" in which objects and people are deliberately turned into something else, by renaming them. Objects are consciously and deliberately named and generalized—"This is a horse!"—without losing track of what they really are.

We have also seen that words at first are fused with objects. For a toddler the word is a name which is part of an object, one of its features. Now, in pretend play, the toddler starts to remove a word from its object—remove "horse" from the animal, for example—but only by moving it to another object. The word "horse" is removed from the animal by being applied to the stick. The stick "becomes" a horse.

In doing this a toddler is taking the first steps towards understanding the conventional, arbitrary link between word and thing. They are beginning to imagine one thing as another—the stick as a horse—and in this regard they are starting to think. Now their ideas decide what something is, rather than what something is determining their ideas (as with preschoolers).

The crisis at age 3 seems to involve the toddler applying this capacity for generalization to herself, and differentiating between self as object and self as agent. The toddler came to recognize herself as a source of agency distinct from that of the people around her. In the transition at the end of toddlerhood, however, she starts to recognize herself as an object in the eyes of other people, and this is why she shows secondary emotions such as pride and shame.

SUMMARY

THE TODDLER'S TALK

- The toddler makes rapid advances in spoken language. Her vocabulary grows, and she begins to combine words.

- Language acquisition is not simple imitation: it is an active process of construction.

- As the toddler combines words, her Phase II language consists of two macrofunctions: the pragmatic and the mathetic.

- The toddler's pragmatic utterances enable her to act on and in the environment, and influence people. The toddler's mathetic utterances enable her to talk about her environment, interpret it, and so learn through talk. A typical example is *"Was 'at?"* The toddler can now participate in dialog.

- At first, the toddler treats words as proper names (like the name of a person). Then they become names of categories of objects.

HOW LANGUAGE CHANGES THE WORLD OF THE TODDLER

- Every language embodies the categories of the culture of the people who speak it.

- Experience with language draws the toddler's attention to specific features of objects, in particular their shape. Toddlers show shape bias: they learn the names of things that are similar in shape.

- This perceptual tuning influences the formation of early categories and concepts. The toddler starts to recognize categories of objects with similar shapes, and names them with the the same word.

- The experiment with chimpanzees Sheba and Sarah shows how material representations can provide a fulcrum for the control of action, and loosen the bond between agent and world.

UNDERSTANDING MATERIAL REPRESENTATIONS

- Language is a "social fact," part of the ecological niche in which a toddler lives. She doesn't need to carry language in her head; she needs to learn how to participate in this vehicle of social life and social interaction.

- Understanding material representations requires a kind of double vision: a drawing both *is* and *isn't* what it represents.

- Toddlers tend to draw what they know, not what they see: Piaget called this intellectual realism. Or perhaps they draw what they are conscious of seeing.

- Pretend play in which one object substitutes for another, is also the creation of a material representation. One object *stands for* another.

(Continued)

(Continued)

SELF AND SYMBOL: THE TRANSITION AT 3 YEARS

- At the end of this stage, a toddler shows indications of a new self-consciousness. These indications are self-recognition, an understanding of norms and sanctions, and secondary emotions. In all of this, she recognizes that she is visible in the eyes of other people.

- When they have had experience with mirrors, toddlers respond to the rouge test from around the middle of their second year by touching the red dot on their nose that they can see in the mirror.

- However, cultural differences in caregiving style are important here. Toddlers of Nso mothers, who used the proximal style, showed very low self-recognition on the rouge task. Toddlers of Greek mothers, who used the distal style, showed high self-recognition. Mutual eye-contact seems to encourage a sense of autonomy, and the experience of being a separate person.

CHAPTER 9

EARLY CHILDHOOD

(3–6 YEARS)
HOW THINGS APPEAR AND HOW THEY ARE

Understanding physics is child's play compared to understanding child's play. (Albert Einstein)

LEARNING OBJECTIVES

In this chapter we will consider:

- The new kind of play that characterizes early childhood: sociodramatic play.
- New skills with oral language.
- The question of how a young child understands the world around her.

FRAMING QUESTIONS

- When you go to the theatre to see a play, or you watch a television drama, which of your psychological functions are you using?
- List as many different things as you can that you do by speaking.
- How old were you when you first saw a cow?
- Name some of the things that exist in your society that a member of a hunter-gatherer society in Africa would not understand. Can you imagine things that exist in their society that you would not understand?

INTRODUCTION

The psychological differentiation and the new self-consciousness that mark the end of toddlerhood introduce a new way of relating to the world, and this defines the stage of early childhood. From 3 years to around 6 years of age a child is often called a preschooler, though this term takes for granted what is not always the case, that in the future she will be attending the institution of school. Instead, I will use the less culture-specific term "young child."

Let's look back, briefly, to put this stage in context. We have seen that the infant was immersed in the lives of the people around her. Then, the toddler was immersed in her immediate interaction with the physical environment and with other people, but in the period from 1 year to 3 years of age she became

Freud	Phallic stage: Oedipal conflict
Erikson	Initiative v guilt
Piaget	Preoperational intelligence: mental actions, based in perception
Vygotsky	Age of play: with other children

Figure 9.1   Key theorists' views of early childhood

increasingly able to turn down its irresistible invitations, or at least to consider whether or not to accept them. She began to understand the cultural categories of the things around her, the *kinds* of things that they were, and their normative functions as artifacts. She began to understand, with the help of language, that one thing could stand for another. Now, as a young child, she continues to *create* material representations, and to explore the relationship between appearance and "reality."

1. SOCIODRAMATIC PLAY

> We have to conclude, therefore, that civilization is, in its earliest phases, played. It does not come from play like a babe detaching itself from the womb: it arises in and as play, and never leaves it. (Huizinga, 1955[1933], p. 173)

In general, Vygotsky stated that child development is a process in which "a human being as a specific biotype is transformed into a human being as a sociotype, an animal organism becomes a human personality" (Vygotsky, 1993, p. 160). He also added that "the social mastery of this natural process is called education" (1993, p. 160), and that "Play is the natural means of a child's self-education, an exercise oriented towards the future" (1993, p. 161). We shall see in the next chapter how societies arrange schools to master this process; here we will focus on the young child's "self-education" in play.

In early childhood, the pretense that began in toddlerhood is expanded into **sociodramatic play**: pretend play in which several children play at being some other kind of person. This is often referred to as "role playing," but I will reserve the term "role" for the particular way of behaving that is defined by a social institution. Young children do not yet understand institutions or roles. What we see in their play at this stage, I believe, is the fact that they are beginning to recognize the categories of person that are distinguished in their culture and some of their typical actions, governed by conventions.

What we have in sociodramatic play, then, are not truly "roles," because a role is defined by a social institution, but **characters**, types of person—like characters in a theatrical play or a story. (A "character" was originally a stamping tool used to create tokens or types.) Characters do not have rights and responsibilities, they have characteristic patterns of behavior (see Corsaro, 1979).

Let's consider an example of sociodramatic pretend play. Two young children, one 5 years old and the other 4, are walking across the playground of their preschool kindergarten towards the climbing structure. They have just left their classroom for "playtime," as the adults call it, and they are deciding what to do.

Josh:	That's a shark. And I'm gonna be Laser Bat, that's a bat. Which has a, has a (…) for a laser. *[They break into a run towards the climbing structure.]*
Brendan:	(…) cause it has a propeller in it
Josh:	Why don't I laser that out? Ugh, psshhh. I lasered, I lasered the propeller out, Brendan.
Brendan:	(Bad) jet engine. (Shot) jet engine.
Josh:	Use your jet engines off your … your jet engines are hooked onto your arm and you go like this … pshhh *[thrusting out his arms]*… and they'll shoot … but I have a little laser hooked into my pack *[Josh jumps down off the climbing structure and walks to the other end. Brendan soon follows]*
Josh:	I don't like the look of this place. Laser Shark?
Brendan:	Yes?
Josh:	My name's Laser Bat. My name's Laser Bat. Um, I don't like the look of this place. Looks like a … the Mediterranean to me.
Brendan:	I'll blow it up. *[Brendan lasers more of the area]*
Josh:	No *[Josh pushes Brendan's arms down]*. Quit that. Sheez. *[They begin to walk behind the structure]*
Brendan:	Whoa! *[Brendan falls]* You know what (…) … (I don't) like those little things that grow along the ground.
Josh:	Jump the pits, that's where they live. *[Josh jumps]* Jump that. They live in there (…) jump. *[Josh runs back to the back of the structure, then more laser noises]* Come on, let's get outta here.

We can make several observations about the activity of these young children. First, it has the "as-if" character that defines pretend play. The boys act as if they have laser weapons and jet engines, the playground is seen as if it were the Mediterranean, the holes in the sand as if they were pits in which something dangerous lives. To "pretend" originally meant to make a claim, as is evident in the use of the word "pretender" to mean someone who makes a claim to the throne. The boys make claims not only about what they are doing and seeing (claims which they both accept, though an observer might doubt their veracity) but also about *who they are*.

Second, this "as-if" character is applied to the participants themselves. The boys talk as if they were "Laser Beasts." Each is a different beast: Josh is Laser Bat, Brendan is Laser Shark. A little later, Josh explains to another boy what this means: Laser Beasts, he says, "are beasts with lasers!" They are constructing a drama in which each of them has an assigned character.

Third, the boys' play extends across the whole playground: they race from one side to the other, up the climbing frame and down again. It is very active play with lots of running and jumping. Josh directs most of the activity. He is the older boy, and he establishes something of a hierarchical organization, with himself as leader and Brendan and other children as followers. This kind of peer structure emerges in early childhood.

Fourth, other boys are drawn into this play. One little boy in particular is designated the "Monster," and he is delighted as Josh and Brendan run away from him as if in terror. Indeed, one of the central elements of this drama turns out to be running away from monsters. Josh calls out at one point, "The monster: Where is it, and what is it?" The pretense is shared, and constructed together.

Fifth, it is striking that this play does not involve any girls. At one point Josh and Brendan run over to a sand tray where three girls are playing, and those three immediately leave. The Laser Beasts don't invite any girls to join in their play. This **gender self-segregation** is very typical of early childhood play. Often it is said to contribute to the development of "gender identity," a topic which we shall consider later in this chapter. However, just as I have said that young children do not understand institutional roles, so too I think that "identity" is the wrong word here. Male and female, boy and girl, are two types of person in many cultures, and young children are beginning to understand the conventional behavior of each of these types. We know that for preschool-age children, the constancy of gender—the fact that a person remains male or female their whole life, except in rare circumstances—is not obvious or easy for young children to understand. For example, they think that a boy who wears a dress becomes a girl. Once again, underlying reality has not been distinguished from appearance. However, their grasp of gender becomes better once they understand that the genitalia are the defining attribute for male and female (Bem, 1989). Playing mainly with peers of the same gender seems to be part of the process of understanding it. (More on this later.)

Starting around 3 years of age young children are able to create imaginary situations, within which they interact together in ways that are conventional for the characters they pretend to be. During the stage of early childhood the time spent in sociodramatic play steadily increases, at least among the urban children who have been studied most often. Taking on the characters of parent and child and playing family is common, especially among younger children, but with time the characters become more varied and often come to involve imaginary participants. Around age 4, some children (estimates range from 12 percent to 65 percent) create imaginary friends and playmates. Young children also get better at tying together the activities of the different characters in an imaginary situation.

For better or worse, young children's behavior in sociodramatic play often follows gender stereotypes, and this is further evidence that they are adopting the conventional actions of typical characters. Around 20 months of age boy and girl toddlers start to differ in the toys they select to play with, and they play with those toys in different ways. Parents often praise play that they consider to be gender-appropriate, and fathers respond negatively if their sons play with girls' toys, though gender is probably more salient and clearer to the adults than it is to the toddlers. Sociodramatic play during early childhood also shows gender differences in the characters that young children create, with boys somewhat more likely to create fantasy situations and girls more likely to create domestic situations. Boys' play is considered by some researchers to be more dependent on the material objects around them. Again, we can see here that young children are using their play to work out their dawning understanding of gender categorization.

Messages in pretend play are paradoxical: they don't mean what they seem to mean, taken literally. **Metacommunication** is often required to set up the appropriate context within which to understand what is said. Metacommunication is communication about communication, indicating how a message should be interpreted. An example is when Josh says, "I'm gonna be Laser Bat, that's a bat." Such a message establishes a **constitutive speech act**: it defines one of the characters in the game. Later, in middle childhood, both constitutive and **regulative rules** will define the players and what they have to do ("You're pitcher, and you throw the ball under these conditions … "), but in early childhood what happens is talk about who the characters are ("Will you be the monster?") or what they do ("Let's take turns"). Young children are also more likely to make proposals about their own actions than make suggestions for the actions of their playmates, as did Noah.

Observation of young children in preschool finds infrequent solitary play, while interactive pretend play increases during the period from 3 to 6 years. Object-substitution play continues during early childhood, and it becomes more complex. By 4 years of age, it becomes what is called "ideational"—the object doesn't have to be physically present. Sociodramatic play increases until around age 5 or 6, and then it apparently begins to disappear. In middle childhood, games with rules outnumber occasions of sociodramatic play. Some psychologists have argued that this is because the child becomes more adapted to reality, but in the next chapter I will suggest a different explanation.

Here is an example of girls playing:

Andrea and Kathryn are sitting on the tire swing—a car tire suspended by three chains from a metal frame.

Cici:	[*Cici runs up to the tire swing*] Can I ride?
Kathryn:	Sure. Andrea, could you slow down?
Andrea:	OK.
Kathryn:	Yikes. [*taking one hand off the tire*]
Cici:	Listen. [*She climbs onto the tire*] Whose turn is it gonna be next?
Kathryn:	My turn.
Cici:	OK, and after yours, it's gonna be mine.
Andrea:	Right. [*She starts to turn the tire, stretching down to push with her feet against the sand underneath them*] (And then it's gonna be Gigi's) turn
Kathryn:	… the teacher's turn and then it's gonna be the teacher's turn after Cici.
Cici:	Right. And then Andrea's turn, and then your turn, then my turn and then the teacher's turn again, right?
Kathryn:	Right. Like a pattern of people pushing.
Andrea:	It's gonna be a pattern, a pattern going on and on.
Kathryn and Cici:	A pattern.
Kathryn:	… with people.
Cici:	No, a pattern is with colors.
Kathryn:	It can also be with pushing … people … different people pushing again and again …
Cici:	Yeah.
Kathryn:	Like different colored … or it could be different colored coats or jackets.
Cici:	Or it could be the same color, but different shapes. Right?
Kathryn:	Right.

The girls' play is distinct from the boys' in several ways. First, it uses only a specific, localized part of the playground. However, it is still play that is very active and physical, as the girls take turns to make the tire spin while they are seated upon it, legs flying outwards.

Second, it is very clear who is included, whereas in Laser Beasts other boys came and went. Girls' play in early childhood tends to define participants more clearly.

Third, the girls' primary concern appears to be with organizing the taking of turns, in a way which will be fair. For the participants to have fun the tire they are sitting in must spin, and in order to spin it must be pushed. The issue they are facing is how to arrange the pushing. Kathryn's proposal seems to be for an egalitarian organization, in which everyone takes a turn at pushing. That is, we don't see here the hierarchy that characterizes the boys' play.

Fourth, this is neither pretend play nor sociodramatic play as these are usually defined. These girls do not assign characters, nor does the tire stand for something else, such as a spaceship. However, in the girls' talk we can see them creating a representation to describe what they are doing together: when they talk of their turns being "like a pattern of people pushing," they are using a simile to represent what they are doing. This illustrates that their understanding of what they are doing has an "as-if" character, even though they have not invented a fantasy situation.

In fact, the girls' play illustrates what is perhaps the central feature of young children's capabilities: they are able to initiate and sustain a social situation of face-to-face interaction. They do so by drawing on the resources of the social conventions that they have come to recognize in daily life, in TV, and the movies, together with the conventions that they can establish and negotiate on the spot. "Let's take turns" is such a convention.

Of course girls in general, and these girls in particular, certainly do engage in sociodramatic play. One can find them playing Princess Pony, and house, and so on. There is one other way in which their play resembles that of the boys: it does not involve participants of the opposite gender. (Boys are actively excluded: a little later, when Andrea has gone to ask a teacher to push them, a boy runs over and tries to climb onto the tire, but both Kathryn and Cici tell him "No!") Like the boys, the girls, too, appear to be working out something about gender categories in their activity with peers. This is evidently an important aspect of development in early childhood.

Sociodramatic play builds upon the pretend play of toddlerhood. It involves transferring the properties of one thing to another and the creation of imaginary situations. It shows the young child's new relationship to the world: distinguishing between how an object or person *appears* and how it *is*. The toddler started by doing what the things around her told her to do, but ended up able to tell things what they were. In early childhood the boot changes foot once again: the young child not only tells things what they are, she also tells *people* what they are, including herself! This is clearly no longer play-for-others but true play-for-the-child—a process of deliberate and conscious dramatization in which action occurs within an imaginary situation that children themselves have created. Language evidently continues to have a central function in such play: the young child uses the power of language to define what things and people are. The "as if" quality of the young child's relation to the world is most evident in sociodramatic play, but it permeates all aspects of the young child's life.

People often think of play as freedom from constraints. Play seems rather frivolous, a diversion from the demands of real life. It may come as a surprise, then, that Vygotsky described it as an activity in which young children impose constraints on themselves. When playing, the young child actually does two things: she creates a **situation**, and she establishes the **conventions** that she—and others—have to follow. The conventions define the situation, and the situation is a transformation of the world. The situation is the context within which objects and people are "as if" something else. Later in this chapter I will explore the proposal that sociodramatic play can help young children develop self-control through this self-imposition of constraints.

In the sociodramatic play of early childhood the imaginary situation is quite obvious, but the conventions are less evident: they are often implicit or simply improvised on the spot when needed. We shall see in Chapter 7 that the games of middle childhood involve rules that are explicit and obvious to everyone, though the imaginary character of the situation is more difficult to see. However, when we stop to think about it we can appreciate that even a game such as baseball, which is certainly taken very seriously by both players and fans, is imaginary in the sense that one plays the game "as if" a batter, or a pitcher, or a fielder.

1.1 WHY DO YOUNG CHILDREN PLAY?

There are many theories about why young children engage in sociodramatic play, and here it is interesting to compare Piaget's view with that of Vygotsky.

For Piaget, as we have seen, play—both pretend play and sociodramatic play—is an activity in which assimilation predominates over accommodation. He observed that play tends to occur after the young child has accommodated to a new experience, and thus saw it as an attempt to make sense of that experience. However, he also considered play to be at root a **failure of adaptation to reality**, something that the young child must grow out of in order to become able to reason logically and think scientifically.

Vygotsky, in contrast, viewed play as an opportunity for the development of the imagination, not something opposed to reality but in a dialectical relationship with the real world. He argued that imagination is of central importance for reasoning in adults, and so play has a central and necessary role in the development of cognition. For Vygotsky, play is the **central line of development** in early childhood. It may be an attempt to make sense of the past, but it is also anticipation of a possible future. The young child who plays doctor may be trying to make sense of a trip to the doctor, and she may also be exploring being a doctor as a possible future occupation.

Vygotsky proposes, then, that far from growing out of play as they get older, as Piaget proposed, children grow deeper into play. Play is imagination, and imagination is central to the way humans live in the world. It has been said that "the capacity to imagine other worlds ... is the very foundation of the sociality of modern human society" (Bloch, 2008, p. 2055).

We tend to think of imagination as disconnected from reality, a matter of solitary daydreams about things we know not to be true or real. But imagination can deal with things we know to be true, things that are very real. For Vygotsky, play—and imagination in general—are not an escape from reality. Play's dialectical relation to the world consists of the way it enhances the young child's perception and understanding of reality by transforming it. Although when they play young children suspend what we adults take to be everyday reality, they still make use of the knowledge they have gained about that reality and its causal and psychological powers. They play to explore the possibilities of these powers. Play is imagination in action: whereas an adolescent imagines in daydreams, or in her diary, the young child imagines in her activity.

Vygotsky argued that play emerges from a young child's desire to participate more fully in the society of adults, and it is her first attempt to take on adult roles. The young child lives with a tension between her desire for immediate gratification and her growing ability to formulate desires which *cannot* be satisfied at once—especially the desire to do what adults do, a desire which in most cases is impossible. But what is impossible in reality can be acted out in play.

We saw in Chapter 7 that the toddler begins to understand the norms of conduct that are considered appropriate in her family. Vygotsky suggested that in early childhood there is a gap between knowing the norms and conventions, on the one hand, and a genuine desire to follow them, on the other. A young child wants to be "good" in the eyes of her parents, but she also wants to be autonomous. This gap leads to a tension or conflict in the young child's personality, and play fills that gap.

Play does so by resolving, at least for a few minutes, the contradiction between desire on the one hand, and norms and conventions on the other. In play a young child explores the contradictions between social norms and personal motivations. Play is pretend and in this sense unreal, but the young child experiences real emotions when she plays, and consequently learns to articulate and regulate those emotions, and this leads to new and more complex emotions.

Both Piaget and Vygotsky, then, saw an element of wish fulfillment in pretend play. But while Piaget saw play as a failure to adapt to reality, Vygotsky viewed it as important preparation for the future. Play is a resolution in fantasy of conflict and anxiety; in play, the young child has control that she lacks in real life and, as we shall see later in this chapter, early childhood is a time of stressful change in young children's relations with caregivers, especially for boys. There is lots of motivation for young children to play.

Many developmental researchers since Vygotsky have argued that play is crucial for children's healthy development. They propose that sociodramatic play in early childhood provides opportunities to develop new competences and skills, several of which we will explore further in this chapter:

First, sociodramatic play, with its distinction between that is *pretense* and what is *real*, apparently helps a young child master the distinction between *appearance* and *reality*—the ways things appear, and how they really are.

Second, play provides an opportunity for the young child to increase their ability for self-control.

Third, it contributes to a more sophisticated understanding of other people's intentions and beliefs—to what has been called "mentalizing"—as well as to their understanding of "social affordances" (see below, section 3).

Fourth, play gives assists the young child in their acquisition of language, in their grasp of material symbols, and in their growing ability to construct material symbols. This in turn contributes to her ability to know the world by conceptualizing it. It extends the separation between object and word that we discussed in Chapter 6.

Fifth, it provides an opportunity to create and explore social situations, and experiment with the conventions that these situations demand in the young child's family and culture.

Sixth, this opportunity to explore social situations contributes to her understanding that each culture defines *types* of person. One of these central definitions in every culture is that of types of gender.

However, the existing research evidence does not support strong causal claims about the unique importance of pretend play for development (Lillard et al., 2013). It is possible that pretend play is simply one of many routes to positive developments. It is also possible that other factors drive development, and pretend play is a result of these.

1.2 PLAY ACROSS CULTURES

> Play is an integral part of everyday childhood activities in most cultural communities around the world … though some have argued that parent-child play is a product of modernization in Western societies and is relatively absent in many communities. (Roopnarine & Krishnakumar, 2006, p. 19).

This emphasis on the importance of sociodramatic play in early childhood would be beside the board if in fact such play only occurred in Western culture. Certainly, that is where most of the research has been conducted, typically with children in preschool settings.

However, caregivers' beliefs about the importance of play vary across cultures, and the frequency and character of play vary too. In technologically advanced societies, play is usually considered central for cognitive and social developments. Play is valued and encouraged, and parents join in. In other cultures, however, play is not valued in this way. In such cultures, caregivers more likely to emphasize early academic activities for their young children than encourage play.

In addition, because young children's play is located in family and social contexts which vary widely from one part of the world to another, the ways children play, where, when, and with whom, also vary. It has been suggested that the functions of play are culture specific. As we look at play we have to appreciate its location within specific trajectories of development, rather than making universalistic claims about its form and function. However:

> cross-cultural generalizations about children's play continue to be hampered by issues of conceptualization, operationalization, measurement, and theoretical propositions that tend to ignore the cultural properties of childrearing and childhood experiences. (Roopnarine, 2010, p. 20)

So what do we know about cultural differences in play? In agricultural and hunter-gatherer societies children take on work tasks early, because their labor is important to the community, and it is possible that because of this play is less important as a way to learn. At the least, play may be seen as less important by adults in such communities. In industrialized societies in which schooling is customary, caregivers may value their young children's academic success, and expect or pressure them to study rather than play. In such circumstances play may not seem relevant to the goals considered important. On the other hand, caregivers who have been more academically successful themselves are more likely to value the benefits of play.

In societies where interdependence is valued, such as Indonesia, Thailand, and India, young children are indulged, though obedience is expected, and play is viewed as largely incidental and unimportant— work-related activities are valued more. Again however, better-educated caregivers are more likely to value play. The Yucatek Maya, for example, view play as largely unimportant, and considered it simply as a sign that children are healthy.

When adults believe that play has educational value, or that it is is a valuable part of being a young child, they are not surprisingly more likely to provide opportunities for play (such as play times and play spaces), and also more likely to play with their young children (the proto-conversations we considered in Chapter 5 might be considered an early form of this). When adults participate in young children's play they are likely to arrange activities so that play includes opportunities to learn. Young children engage more in pretense play when caregivers engage them in such play. On the other hand, in traditional societies, both agricultural and hunter-gatherer, when young children engage in pretend play it is usually older siblings and other children who arrange the circumstances.

Children's play (without adults) has been richly described in many cultures. The themes of play often reflect local cultural practices. For example, !Kung children play at tending to animals. Baka children play at hunting, as well as playing house and dancing and singing. But Baka have also been observed playing at driving and flying toy airplanes made from papaya stems (Kamei, 2005). In many societies the objects that children play with are constructed by the kids themselves, rather than factory-made toys.

There is little direct evidence that playing at adult activities helps young children master adult skills, though this seems quite likely. When children have an opportunity to observe adults working, they are more likely to include work-related themes in their play.

If young children make use of pretend play to make sense of their experiences and to explore and express their anxieties and frustrations, this may explain the observation that in some cultures there is very little fantasy play. The Yucatec Maya, for example, allow their young children significant control over their own daily lives and make few demands of them (Gaskins & Miller, 2009). Adults and older children do not play with young children, nor do they supervise their play much, and in fact they prefer that young children spend their time doing household tasks. Young Maya children play with siblings or relatives who live nearby, the older of whom may have been assigned as caregivers. This means that children of a range of ages interact together regularly, so that when they play it must be in a way that incorporates a family hierarchy and respect. In circumstances such as these play certainly occurs, but it is often not pretend play.

When pretend play is observed among the children in such circumstances is usually about familiar scenes such as the household. For example, one group of three Maya girl cousins aged 6 to 10 played at making tortillas: going to town in a truck to shop, grinding corn into tortilla *masa*, preparing for a dance, sweeping, and washing dishes. There was little variation or elaboration in their play over time. Mayan children, it appears, do not pretend to be something other than people—at being animals, for example. Nor do they play at being babies or younger than they really are, nor do they create imaginary objects or people in their play (Gaskins & Goncu, 1992). The peak age for symbolic play in this culture is not early childhood but age 6 to 8, perhaps because what occurs in this play is not the creation of an imaginary world but the mastery of adult activities.

Piaget's theory doesn't have much to say about cultural differences such as these. Nor does it predict whether these differences in how young children play are of any importance for their development. Vygotsky's theory doesn't speak directly to cultural differences in play either, but one can imagine that there might be differences between cultures where the emphasis is mainly on reproducing traditional practices, and cultures where innovation is valued and encouraged. Young Maya children have little opportunity to meet new playmates, and they are expected to conform to the guidance of their older siblings. In societies in which schooling has become taken for granted, special places are created—preschools and nurseries—that are designed not only to prepare young children for their entry into school, but also to acknowledge that their interests and abilities differ from those of school-age children.

In such societies, play is often considered centrally important to young children (though today there is heated debate over whether the focus of preschools should also be academic). The Maya, in contrast, see play as something that is natural but has little function, to be tolerated rather than encouraged. This may mean that play in their culture no longer has all the developmental functions that Vygotsky attributed to it. A young child learns to play in ways that are acceptable and relevant to the people around her, both adults and other children. Among the Maya, where young children's play is structured by older children, sociodramatic play seems culturally organized to function as an arena for practice and escape (Gaskins & Goncu, 1992).

The way that play emerges in specific sociocultural contexts, and is a social activity before it becomes individual, was evident in a study in the homes of nine affluent, middle-class families in the USA.

In such families, both the physical ecology and the social ecology support play. That is, young children are provided with large quantities of specialized objects to play with, and time and space are arranged so that other children and adults are available as play partners, as is shown by the following excerpt from researchers' field observations:

> It is late morning. Three-year-old Molly and her five-year-old sister Rachael are lying side by side on their bedroom floor (ostensibly 'picking up'). Molly asks repeatedly to play with Rachael's Tropical Skipper doll, but Rachael refuses. Eventually, the distraught Molly bites Rachael, who authoritatively reminds her of the prohibition on biting and then threatens to 'tell.' Molly explains, 'I'm a doggy who bites.' Rachael begins to scold the doggie and then realizes, 'Baby doggies don't like Tropical Skipper!' Apparently satisfied that the issue is revolved, she turns away and begins to sing, 'The sound of music!' (Haight & Miller, 1993, p. 10)

This episode shows various characteristics of how young children are raised in affluent circumstances: the freedom from tasks and responsibilities (these children should be tidying their room but they don't bother), the personal ownership of toys by young children, the threat to call down adult authority, the use of pretense to justify misbehavior and avoid sanctions. It also shows the status of the elder child, the refusal to share, the competitiveness between the two sisters, and the understanding of rules by both young children, as well as the recourse to the physical act of biting when verbal persuasion fails. Molly reads back from her own biting an "as-if" identity—if she bites, she must be a doggie.

The researchers emphasized that play has not only cognitive consequences but also cultural ones. In working-class families the physical and social economy supports different kinds of activity. For example, anthropologist Shirley Brice Heath (1983) observed that in the white working-class community of Roadville, young children had little experience of fictional or fantasy stories at home. Adults in their family asked them to recount events they had experienced, but frowned upon invention. When these young children attended nursery school they encountered for the first time many materials—books, DVDs, stories—that didn't follow real-world constraints. Even so, they would tell make-believe stories only when an explicit frame was provided, either by the children themselves or by teachers. This frame seemed to release them from the need to stick to the facts and tell the truth. When they returned home they continued to frame their play in this way so as to suspend reality. Even then, they often paradoxically insisted that real-life behavior be enacted. For example, they would play house only if they could use real water or flour.

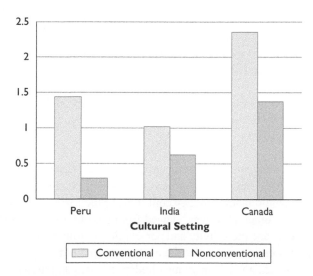

Figure 9.2   Mean number of object-substitution acts per minute across cultural setting and type of toy (conventional or nonconventional)

Source: Callaghan et al. (2011)

For example, a comparison of object-substitution play among 3-year-olds in three different settings— middle-class rural Canada, traditional rural Peru, and India—found much more object-substitution play in the young Canadian children. The researchers attributed this to the fact that while all the Canadian mothers reported engaging in pretend play with their child, less that half the Peruvian mothers and less than one quarter of the Indian mothers reported doing so (Callaghan et al., 2011). The young Canadian children were also more likely to recognize when the experimenter adopted a pretend attitude, and to respond with pretense of their own.

In short, the small amount of research that has been conducted on the question of cultural variation in sociodramatic play in early childhood suggests that it is neither inevitable nor universal either in its structure or in its functions.

1.3 THE COLONIZATION OF YOUNG CHILDREN'S CREATIVITY

The encouragement and cultural organization of play in Western societies go beyond the family and preschool, and extend into the media and the marketplace. Young children creatively imagine some of the characters that they play, but clearly they draw others from the world they see and hear around them. Play in early childhood incorporates elements and themes that are made available by the culture.

Increasingly, the marketing of fantasy to young children is a pervasive feature of everyday life. Television programs and movies are designed to appeal to young children, and also to turn them into consumers of the media and commercial products. When I saw young children playing at being Laser Beasts I was impressed by their creativity and imagination. Only years later did I discover a website selling a line of small toys—animals with weapons—that a Japanese company had been marketing around the time I was observing the children.

A review of the *Toy Story* series of children's movies by the *New York Times*' film reviewer E. O. Scott captures perfectly what is going on here. He wrote:

> Perhaps no series of movies has so brilliantly grasped the emotional logic that binds the innate creativity of children at play to the machinery of mass entertainment. Each one feeds, and colonizes, the other. (Scott, 2010)

Viewed from one side, this colonization of young children's creativity is precisely the process of child development, where culture provides the conditions within which young children can grow psychologically. In addition, as young children develop they contribute to the formation and transformation of their culture, so that each feeds the other. However, viewed from the other side, it is disturbing to recognize the power the media have to shape the activity and personality of young children. This is "colonization" in the sense of entering and coming to control a place—the young child's imagination—where one really has no right to be. The mass media work on young children's needs and motives, in order to create new desires. Who, exactly, benefits when young boys play at being Laser Beasts?

1.4 THE PRESCHOOL AS A DEVELOPMENTAL NICHE

We have talked about young children's play without saying much so far about where that play takes place. In many industrialized societies, play during early childhood occurs in specific, specialized settings, arranged for its occurrence. Young children play at home, for sure, but they are also expected and encouraged to play in a kindergarten or preschool. The word *kindergarten* is German, and means "children's garden." The first kindergartens were designed to be sheltered and protected places where young children could grow and develop in multiple ways, without the narrow focus on academics that is found in formal schooling. The kindergarten is a constructed environment for young children in which sociodramatic play is encouraged.

The organization of a kindergarten or preschool is significantly different from that of the home: it is a novel social institution with new demands to which young children have to adapt. Unfamiliar adults who are not parents or family members are **teachers**, figures of authority who participate in a status hierarchy that a young child will not yet completely understand. There will be many other young children, mostly strangers to one another. They will find themselves in a building whose structure is unlike that of any family house or apartment. Its division into classrooms, the presence of an outside play area, and the array of materials, tools, and objects that are available will be completely new. At the same time there will be new rules and regulations, implemented by the teachers and enforced with various sanctions. The young child has, without knowing it, become a "student" for the first time in her life, and she must discover what this role entails. The familiar routine of the family has been left behind, at least for a few hours each day, and a new order must be discovered.

Discovered, but also made. In preschool, young children start to form, perhaps for the very first time, relationships with **peers**—children of the same age who are not members of their family. Young children in a nursery school will begin to develop reputations among their peers, as they interact together to produce a **peer culture**.

Investigation has found diverse norms, customs, and rules among preschool teachers in different cultures. Local assumptions about the abilities of young children and how they should be treated vary greatly. For example, a study conducted in 1985 with teachers in Japan, China, Hawaii, and the USA found that teachers had markedly different views about what was proper in a preschool classroom. The researchers showed recordings of classroom interactions to teachers and other audiences in each of these countries, to evoke their interpretations and identify the "informal cultural logic" of preschool education (Tobin et al., 1989).

For example, in the Japanese preschool, Hiroki was misbehaving: he waved his penis at the visiting researchers! He started fights with the other children and interrupted their play. American teachers watching this on video disapproved not only of Hiroki's conduct, but also of how his teachers handled the situation. They couldn't understand why he had not been sent to "time out" as punishment. And they were astonished that the Japanese classroom had 30 young children and only a single teacher.

The Japanese teachers' view, however, was that a large class gave young children the valuable experience of being able to relate to lots of peers. Their ideal class size was 15 students or more, while the American preschool teachers said a preschool class should ideally have only four to eight young children. To the Japanese teachers such a small class seemed empty and sad. One said, "I wonder how you teach a child to become a member of a group in a class that small" (Tobin et al., 1989, p. 38).

The American teachers wondered whether Hiroki misbehaved because he was smart, and consequently became bored. The Japanese teachers disagreed, saying that for them being smart was equal to being well-behaved. Hiroki, in their opinion, had become overly dependent because he did not live with his mother. He hadn't learned how to get along with others and be sensitive to them. He needed to learn how to relate to other children, so isolating him would be the worse thing to do.

The Japanese teachers also disagreed with teachers in the USA about how to handle conflict, saying that a teacher should try not to intervene when there were conflicts among the young children, in order to give them the opportunity to learn how to manage such situations themselves. They also maintained that a child's success in the long term had more to do with effort and character, which they felt could be taught in school, than with innate ability,

The researchers returned 20 years later, to explore whether there had been significant historical changes. Teachers and other adults in Hawaii, Japan, and China were shown the original recordings, and they also viewed new recordings made in preschool classrooms in each country (Tobin et al., 2009).

Two decades on, the Chinese preschool had changed dramatically. A concern in 1985 with spoiling the young child had been replaced by an emphasis on promoting independence and creativity, for these were now considered "characteristics needed to succeed in entrepreneurial capitalism" (Tobin et al., 2009, p. 226). At the same time, there was growing concern about the need to ensure that young Chinese children did not lack social and moral values.

In Japan, after more than a decade of economic difficulties, the teachers told the researchers that preschools should conserve traditional values, perspectives, and skills. The Japanese teachers spoke critically of modernization. In the USA the researchers found a growing emphasis on academic readiness, accountability, and scientifically based teaching. Preschool curricula that emphasized play were now being rejected, even though teachers maintained that play was very valuable for young children, and there was pressure on both preschool teachers and preschool programs to obtain credentials.

Nonetheless, the researchers suggested that in each country the implicit cultural logic had not changed, largely because it was not explicitly noticed. Class size in Japanese preschools remained larger than in the USA, in part because of the implicit cultural value that young children needed to be socialized to relate to others and their group. In China an implicit emphasis on mastery and performance was unaltered. In the United States, freedom of choice and individual self-expression were still taken for granted. We can see here how culture influences children development due to unexamined norms about "how things work." These invisible influences surely have major consequences in the long-term formation of a young child's personality.

Early childhood is generally viewed as a time when young children begin to leave the family for periods of time and spend time with peers, other children of the same age, in institutional settings such as daycare and preschool. However, this discontinuity between family and other sites of child–child interaction (daycare, preschool, school) has been introduced in developed countries. It does not exist for the Yucatec Maya, for example. Consequently, many of the characteristics and features of the social interactions and relations of young children that have been taken for granted by researchers turn out to be highly culture specific. The centrality of friendship, the assumption that a young child interacts primarily with others of the same age … all of these certainly characterize some cultures, but not all.

Friendship in the USA is defined as a voluntary association, an exclusive relationship between equals that involves reciprocity. However, if friendships are crucial for healthy development, the Maya are in trouble! Children there grow up in a familial network of siblings, cousins, and young aunts and uncles, and it is simply not possible to leave this network to spend time with a friend from another family. Phenomena such as social isolation and rejection, which have been greatly studied in the peer interactions of young children in the USA, would be very strange events in Maya society. In addition, the Maya do not arrange children into groups of the same age the way that childcare centers do as young as 2 or 3 years of age. Conversely, the opportunity to take care of younger children begins early for Maya children, while it is a practice that is virtually absent in the USA, or indeed illegal (Gaskins, 2006):

> Children are also allowed to make serious decisions about their lives, particularly when these decisions do not have serious consequences. Three-year-olds decide if they want to go to preschool or not (often having to argue with their parents in either case). One five-year-old, whose parents divorced and left the village to earn money, was allowed to decide with which grandparent he wanted to live, essentially being allowed to determine his own child custody. When asked why children are allowed to make these decisions, people shrug their shoulders and point out that the children will go where they want anyway on a daily basis, so why try to make them do something against their wishes? (Gaskins, 2006, p. 294)

1.5 PEER CULTURE IN EARLY CHILDHOOD

Johan Huizinga, the author of a book titled *Homo Ludens*—man the player—(1955[1938]), defined play in these words:

a free activity standing quite consciously outside 'ordinary' life as being 'not serious' but at the same time absorbing the player intensely and utterly. It is an activity connected with no material interest, and no profit can be gained by it. It proceeds within its own proper boundaries of time and space according to fixed rules and in an orderly manner. It promotes the formation of social groupings that tend to surround themselves with secrecy and to stress the difference from the common world by disguise or other means.

Huizinga proposed that play does not occur *within* culture, because culture *is* play. If he was correct, then the ability of young children to create sociodramatic play is evidence of their growing ability to participate actively in the reproduction of the culture in which they live.

As a child gets older, her relationships and interactions with peers outside the family will become increasingly important. I have emphasized that development is a collective process, not an individual one. Childhood is not simply a time of preparation for adulthood, it is a form of life in its own right in which children are active producers of **peer cultures** which are handed down from one **cohort** of children to the next. We can see this as new students arrive in a childcare center or preschool.

At first, of course, young children are participants in the social practices of their family, but in interactions with peers outside the family they create a series of peer cultures within which they acquire knowledge and skills.

Peer culture is a social reality that is produced by children themselves. In the preschool, peer culture exists for the moments of its production—unlike adult culture it leaves few lasting traces. But over time, as a consequence of interactions with peers, young children move from being treated as equivalents by their teachers to viewing themselves as equal members of a small community. This group membership shows up in various ways, including shared rituals and activities, and sometimes a collective insubordination to adult authority, both of which provide young children with a sense of having some control over their daily lives. We can see here very clearly that young children do not simply live within the culture created by adults, they are active agents in the creation of culture.

As yet, there have been no longitudinal studies of children's transition through peer cultures at preschool, school, and then in adolescent peer groups. However, it is clear that these peer cultures are autonomous and creative social systems in which young children do not simply imitate adults or copy from the adult world (Corsaro & Eder, 1990; Corsaro & Nelson, 2003).

Most studies of peer cultures in early childhood have been conducted in the preschool or the playground, though there has been some research in the neighborhood and the family. Toddlers are often introduced to same-age playmates at the home, under their parents' supervision. But it is in early childhood that the opportunity for interactions with peers increases greatly.

Young children often use these peer interactions as a chance to challenge adult authority and gain some control over it. They may challenge or mock their adult caretakers and find subtle ways to violate their regulations, such as smuggling forbidden personal items into a preschool. Young children put a lot of time and effort into establishing social contacts, and joining an existing social group is a complex matter, perhaps because those groups are still fragile and easily disrupted. Young children must learn appropriate "access strategies" to make a successful entry into a group. They begin to use the word "friend" at this age, and although studies have found few enduring relationships among young children, they do cultivate specific relations with their playmates (Gottman, 1983).

Routines and rituals are common in early childhood play. Approach-avoidance games—such as the Laser Beasts running from the Monster—which have been identified in several cross-cultural studies, incorporate real fears into activities the young children can control, so they can share the tension, excitement and relief. Playing together, young children learn and practice discourse strategies and refine their communicative competence.

Sociologist William Corsaro undertook participant observation on the preschool playground, where he became known as "Big Bill." His detailed study of young children's talk during sociodramatic play found differences in speech style that showed how they understood the characters they adopted in their play (Corsaro, 1979). The young children seemed to grasp *status*—that social positions are embodied with honor, prestige, and power. The young children whose character had higher status, "the boss," (e.g., mother, teacher, doctor), spoke more and used more imperatives, and more of these towards the young children with lower status (e.g., baby). The young children assuming lower-status characters produced more informative statements, and they regularly displayed deference, by obeying their playmates' imperatives or asking their permission. These young children apparently understood status as the power to direct others' actions: the baby never told the mother what to do, for instance. However, they used relatively simple sociolinguistic devices to manage status in play.

Moreover, these children showed a limited understanding of the duties and expectations associated with what Corsaro considered the social *roles*, and they were confused about the character of social institutions such as the family and the workplace. For example, two young children playing at husband and wife did perform duties that were typical of sex-role distinctions. The "husband" introduced the activity of moving furniture, for example, while the "wife" accepted the responsibility for cleaning. But the children showed a limited understanding of the range of duties associated with certain social positions, and these duties were often embodied in short "scripts" in their play (big sisters do whatever they want, husbands help wives with the more physical chores, etc.). They also showed some confusion about the coordination of roles: for example, whether it was possible for a wife to have two husbands.

These confusions show that young children are only starting to understand the "institutional facts" that define social "roles" in any society. Their pretend play was the enactment not of institutional roles, but of the conventional actions of familiar characters.

1.6 WHEN YOUNG CHILDREN WORK

Educator Maria Montessori said that "Play is the work of the child," and developmental researchers often assume that the best way for young children to learn is through playing, both with peers and alone.

However, there are many societies in the world in which early childhood is the time for assuming responsibilities for work inside and outside the household. These provide an interesting contrast with how young children are cared for in the West, raise important and interesting questions about the developmental consequences of different parental expectations and circumstances, and throw light on the character and importance of play.

Cultures differ greatly in the degree to which young children are allowed into the world of adults. Western caregivers tend to create a specialized space for young children in which they are supervised by adults—parents, or teachers, or both. But in many cultures, young children are members of an extended family network, among which they move freely with little direct supervision, or are supervised mainly by older children. These differences in the niche that is created for young children may also be the basis for differences in kinds of play around the world.

1.6.1 CASE STUDY: THE KWARA'AE

The Kwara'ae people are one of the many hunter-gatherer tribes who live in the islands in the Pacific known collectively as Oceana. Their first contact with Europeans was in the fifteenth century, but their way of life changed little before their islands became parts of empires at the end of the nineteenth century. They used only stone tools until very recently. Karen Watson-Gegeo and her husband have spent many years with these people, in rural villages on the island of Malaita, in the Solomon Islands off the north-east coast of Australia.

The Kwara'ae assign their children adult responsibilities and tasks at a young age. Young children participate at home and in gardens from 3 years of age. At this age girls are given their first machete and start to take care of younger siblings. They carry firewood and build cooking fires, prepare vegetables, and keep the house and garden clean and tidy. By age 7 or 8 they may have the younger children in their sole care for several hours each day, and they will also often have their own garden, growing produce that they will prepare for the family or sell at the market. By 11 years of age, the end of middle childhood, a Kwara'ae girl has the ability to manage a household and its gardens by herself.

Boys are considered to be rather less capable than girls, but they too are given chores by 3 or 4 years of age. At age 5 the boys may also have their own garden, and will build their own small houses.

Figure 9.3 Children from the Solomon Islands

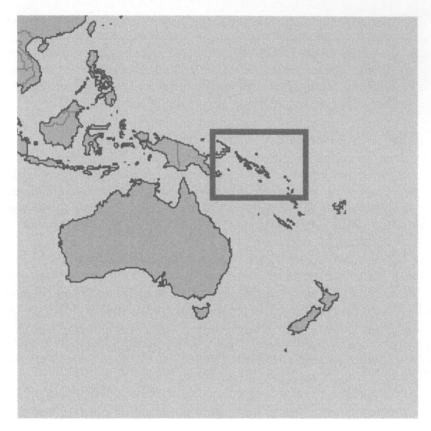

Figure 9.4 The Solomon Islands

The Kwara'ae do not have a word for fantasy. The word *Sokesoke* signifies "false" or "not real." Children are punished if they exaggerate or tell stories. This is due in part to the fact that young children carry oral messages and deliver gifts, and are expected to report back to their parents, so they need to be truthful. Children are also often witnesses in court cases, because adults view their testimony as reliable since children do not deliberately or maliciously lie, though they may be mistaken or misled. From infancy, children are raised to tell the truth. If a young child does lie, her parents may be called into court and fined.

Young Kwara'ae children have little time for imaginative play. Adults don't encourage or demonstrate the framing of alternative realities. In short, they encourage their children to accept and adopt the specific reality of the community. They also mark the distinction between "acting adult" and "pretending to be an adult." Children as young as 3 display two distinct modes. In "child mode," they run about, are shy, giggly, or moody, and engage in pretend play in which they often imitate adults.

When they are involved in work, however, they display an "adult mode," in which they are calm and rational, and speak and carry their bodies as adults do. Watson-Gegeo provides the following illustration:

Namokalitau [the father] is cleaning the family kitchen while baby-sitting with his three-year-old daughter Faluta (who is in child mode) and Faluta's infant sister. Faluta's conversational utterances exhibit the substitution of l for r typical of her and her age-mates' habitual speech. Seeing the family machete caked with mud, Namokalitau scolds Faluta, saying that she and her siblings are always borrowing his knife and not properly caring for it. Instantly Faluta shifts into adult mode. She boldly scolds him back in the manner of an adult woman, saying that the knife is not his knife, it belongs to her mother who purchased it with money she made selling potatoes in the market. In her retort, Faluta correctly pronounces and rolls all her r's. Embarrassed, her father changes the subject. Faluta returns to child mode, again pronouncing all her r's as l's. Faluta's retort is more than a mere counter reprimand to her father. She is using a cultural insult that implies that her father, being poor, is not a good provider such that her mother had to buy an essential work tool herself with her own money. (Watson-Gegeo, 2001, p. 144)

Adult mode is generally based on what a child has heard or seen adults do, as well as routine interchanges with adults in which they are directly taught the appropriate presentation of self in various social situations. The young children themselves initiate these kinds of interchange with the toddlers they are in charge of. One can sometimes hear a child "revoicing" familiar adults when she is using adult mode.

When in adult mode, a child is more likely to be efficient and quick. Watson-Gegeo suggests that this mode has a self-regulative function, a function that other researchers have often attributed to dramatic play. It seems, then, that adult mode is make-believe, "a form of sociodramatic play that accomplishes real work" (2001, p. 146). Adult mode is *both* work and play, and both children and adults recognize its double character. The young child's performance has to be *accepted* as "real" to be successful, and it sometimes fails, to adult laughter, or adults have to help repair it. Young children using "adult mode" show that they already have a great deal of understanding of the adult world. They also sustain and monitor this mode when there are no adults around.

This is also a society in which adults often turn their work into play, to compensate for its difficulties. This brings out the important point that adult work is also an "as-if" activity. Work, too, is a performance of various kinds.

However, young Kwara'ae children do engage in sociodramatic play when they are apart from adults, in the realm of the child mode. Such play often imitates the work that young children do; now they are *playing* at doing real work. Young children are somewhat embarrassed if an adult comes across them while they are playing in this mode.

For the Kwara'ae the world of young children and the world of adults intersect in work, rather than in play or in school.

2. TALKING AS BOTH DOING AND UNDERSTANDING

Much of the new psychological phenomena that emerge in early childhood appear to be related to the role that oral language is coming to play in the life of the young child.

In previous chapters we followed Michael Halliday's son Nigel as he passed through Phase I and Phase II of language acquisition. Phase I began around 9 months of age with Nigel's first holophrastic utterances, each serving a distinct function. His language had a simple structure with two levels: expression/content (*or* sound/meaning). Phase II began around 16 months, when Nigel began to put words together, became able to carry on a simple dialog, and when each of his utterances served one or the other of two macrofunctions: the *pragmatic* and the *mathetic*.

Let us pick up the story from there. Around the end of the toddler stage, when Nigel was 30 months old, he began to be able to *combine* these two macrofunctions in his utterances, using true syntax. First, the restriction that a specific utterance could serve only one macrofunction disappeared, and Nigel became able to use any two-word utterance with either function. Then, he began to construct utterances which contained *both* mathetic and pragmatic components. At this point the young child, in Halliday's words, "makes the crucial discovery that, with language, he can both observe and interact with the environment at the same time" (Halliday, 1975, p. 262). In Halliday's terminology the macrofunctions (*pragmatic* and *mathetic*) have become transformed into **metafunctions** that can occur together in any utterance. These two metafunctions are named the *ideational* and the *interpersonal* (Halliday, 1993). Halliday has also called these the "observer" and "intruder" metafunctions respectively.

As Halliday put it, "Grammar makes it possible to mean more than one thing at a time" (Halliday, 1975, p. 254):

> Perhaps the most important single principle that is involved in the move from protolanguage into mother tongue is the metafunctional principle: that meaning is at once both doing and understanding. The transition begins with an opposition between utterance as action (doing) and utterance as reflection (understanding). (Halliday, 1993, p. 101)

The language we speak as adults is easily able to do these two things at once: to talk about the world, and to accomplish some kind of (social) action in the world. That is, adult speech combines the two metafunctions, the *ideational* (which one can also call representational, referential, cognitive, and denotational) and the *interpersonal* (which one can also call expressive-conative, oretic, evocative, and connotational). The ideational function is representing the speaker's interpretation of the world, while the interpersonal is a matter of the speaker's involvement in the speech situation.

Nigel's language now had three levels, in place of two. Previously, his utterances combined sound and meaning. Now they were composed of sound, grammar, and meaning.

Once grammar and dialog are within her abilities, a young child has achieved the transition to the adult language system, though of course many of the details of adult language must still be worked out. Halliday called this Phase III. This new, more complex semiotic system provides young children with a variety of strategies. The system can be expanded in various ways.

First, they can refine the meanings they have built up in the system by introducing more delicate distinctions. For example, they can add "it may be" between "it is" and "it isn't," or elaborate a verb such as "go" into "walk/jump/run/climb" and so on.

Second, young children can extend meaning into new areas of experience or forms of interpersonal relationship (semantic domains) that were not previously available. New vocabulary can be added on "vertically" in this way; for example, the move into logical-semantic relations of "when" and "if" and "because."

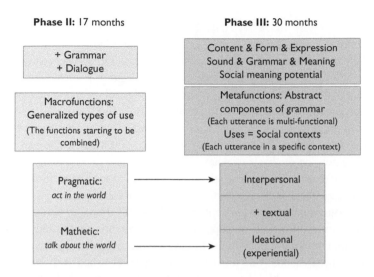

Figure 9.5   From Phase II to Phase III of language acquisition

The third strategy is a powerful combination of these first two; it is the strategy of deconstructing and recombining—for example, demanding "iced coffee" when the alternatives offered are "hot coffee" and "iced tea."

In learning how to mean, Halliday suggests, the interpersonal metafunction leads the experiential metafunction: "There are numerous smaller steps that have to be taken; and it seems to be the case that, most typically, each critical step in learning language is taken first of all in the interpersonal metafunction—even if its eventual semiotic contexts are going to be primarily experiential." In this sense, there is "a generalized *interpersonal gateway*, whereby new meanings are first construed in interpersonal contexts and only later transferred to ideational ones, experiential and/or logical" (Halliday, 1993, p. 103). Discovering how to use speech to manage social interaction provides a gateway to discovering how speech can convey experience and reasoning.

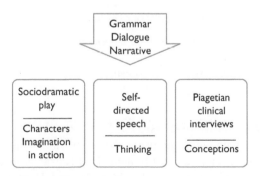

Figure 9.6   The psychological consequences of Phase III of language acquisition

3. THE WORLD OF EARLY CHILDHOOD: BREAKING FROM THE VISUAL

While infants and toddlers gain a great deal of practical knowledge of the world around them, and begin to learn how to handle both things and people in ways that are considered appropriate, by the time a toddler reaches 3 years of age she is clearly acquiring a different kind of knowledge—the kind she can talk about, and can be told about. So how does this verbal knowledge relate to practical understanding? What does the young child now know about the world, what form does her knowledge take, and how does she use what she knows in order to reason and act? These are questions that researchers have tried to answer.

First, let's define some terms. We can say that **inference** is the automatic and unconscious understanding of something new on the basis of what was already known. **Thinking** can then be defined as an advanced form of inference, in which a person deliberately coordinates their inferences to serve a purpose, such as to make a decision, plan an action, and so on. **Reasoning** can be defined as an advanced form of thinking that consciously follows accepted standards of rationality (Moshman, 1998).

In these terms, infants and toddlers are capable only of *inference*, but young children will begin to *think*, although of course thinking will continue to develop throughout adolescence and into adulthood. As we shall see in the next chapter, this thinking is first accomplished with speech. Thinking can be more or less successful, and as a child develops she will evaluate her own thinking, applying standards of rationality so that her thinking becomes reasoning. What develops *after* early childhood is knowledge about when logical inferences are justified, together with metacognitive awareness, and deliberate control of inference. The young child, in contrast, is only starting to become aware of her own thoughts:

> Very young children routinely make instantaneous deductions without even realizing they have done so. But that's precisely the problem. Lacking awareness of inference, they cannot explicitly evaluate arguments. Even as children gain some degree of awareness of and control over their inferences, they initially remain oblivious to the logical form of those inferences. (Moshman, 2004, p. 228)

What do young children know about the world, and how do they think about the world? In this section we will try to answer these questions.

Inference	Automatically and unconsciously anticipating the new from what is known
Thinking	Deliberately making inferences for a specific purpose
Reasoning	Applying self-imposed standards of evaluation to one's thinking

Figure 9.7 Definitions of inference, thinking, and reasoning.

Source: Based on Moshman (1998)

3.1 THE YOUNG CHILD'S THINKING ABOUT THE WORLD

Young children's new facility with language means that early childhood is an age at which psychologists can start to conduct simple interviews with them. This is exactly what Piaget did in some of his earliest studies (*The Child's Conception of the World*, 1926, and *The Child's Conception of Physical*

Causality, 1927). He conducted what he called **clinical interviews**, in which he asked preschoolers and school-aged children to explain aspects of the world around them. In Piaget's view, early childhood is the age for an important transition, from the practical intelligence of the sensorimotor stage to a new kind of intelligence. Piaget believed that this new intelligence is based no longer on physical actions, but on mental actions, performed on mental representations. In the last chapter I raised questions about this way of describing the transition, but certainly there is a qualitative change in the way young children approach the world, compared with infants and toddlers. Later in this chapter I will explore Vygotsky's suggestion that this difference is due to young children's increasing grasp of oral language.

Despite his emphasis on the importance of this new form of intelligence in early childhood, Piaget found what he considered to be a number of limitations and deficits in the thinking of the young children who he interviewed. For example, he reported that until about 6 years of age a young child may say that people think with the mouth, and may identify thoughts with the voice:

With SCHMI (5½ y): What do people think with?—*The mouth.*

With BARB (5½ y): You know what it means to think?—*When you can't remember something, you think.*—What do you think with?—*The ears.*—If you were to stop them up, could you think?—*Yes ... no ...*

Piaget was dismissive of this childish belief that, as he put it, "there is nothing subjective in the act of thinking" (Piaget, 1960[1929], p. 38). However, we shall see later in this chapter that there is a strong element of truth in the children's view!

Piaget also questioned children about natural things, and found that they often viewed inanimate things as alive, and natural things as man-made.

With BARB (6 y): Tell me some things that are alive. – *Butterflies, elephants, people, the sun.* – The moon? – *Yes, also.* – Are stones alive? – *No.* – Why not? – *I don't know?* – Why? – *Because they aren't alive.* – Are motors alive? – *No.* – Why not? – *I don't know.* – What does it mean to be alive? – *To be able to move all alone ... Are stones alive? – No. –* Not when they roll? – *Yes, when they roll they're alive. When they're still, they're not alive.*

Piaget's interpretation was that a young child first views any type of activity as indicating life. Next, she views movement as the criterion of being alive. Then, she views anything that moves spontaneously as alive. Finally, her conception of life becomes restricted to animals and plants.

In answers like these Piaget believed that he could see characteristics that anthropologists of his time claimed also to have found in the thinking of "primitive" peoples. He called these characteristics *realism, animism, artificialism,* and *syncretism.*

Realism is the belief that thoughts and dreams are material. In addition, names are believed to be parts of objects, and so they cannot be changed.

Animism is the belief that all things possess life and consciousness. Piaget argued that animism gives young children a sense of unity with the world. It leads them to have what Piaget considered magical beliefs—that the natural world was created for them, and that since it is alive they are able to control it.

Artificialism is the belief that natural phenomena, including living things, were created by and for human beings; for example, that the sun was created by a man with a match.

Finally, **syncretism** is thinking that is based entirely on what can be seen and experienced firsthand. A young child, in Piaget's view, is incapable of inferring beyond she can observe, and cannot make deductions and generalizations. As a consequence, events are linked together when in reality they are not related, for example:

> Why does a stone sink, and wood float?—*Because the stone is heavy. The wood is light.*—Why doesn't the sun fall down?—*Because it's warm, it sticks.*

Piaget proposed that young children fail to make the **ontological** distinctions that in his view every rational person has to accept. In his view, they lack an understanding of the **dualisms** of the mental and the material, the internal and external, the biological and nonbiological, and of objects and representations. However, as we shall see in Section 3.4, he was here adopting a specific, Western cosmology.

Later on, Piaget began to use a variety of empirical tasks to further explore the thinking of young children. His **conservation tasks** are a famous example. In a liquid conservation task, for instance, Piaget presented a young child with two containers of equal size and shape. He poured the same quantity of liquid into each container. Next he poured the liquid from one container into a third container that was either taller and thinner, or shorter and wider, than the others. He asked the young child whether the amount of liquid was still the same.

On the basis of tasks such as this, Piaget described the young child's thinking as **preoperational** and **precausal**—as lacking the capacity to think in a logical manner, and in particular lacking the ability to explain causal relationships. In Piaget's view the young child specifically lacks the ability to **distinguish appearance from reality**.

We have seen that "object permanence" is achieved by the end of toddlerhood, and I have argued that objects become stable by this time. However, objects are evidently not so stable that conservation tasks are solved by young children. Consequently, we have to be careful not to make too strong a claim about toddlers. It seems that by the end of toddlerhood objects (and people) have become permanent, experienced as enduring in time and recognized as "the same" when they reappear. A toddler has some sense of an object's identity over transformation (at least in simple transformations of appearance and disappearance). But it is only during early childhood that an object starts to have a *hidden* identity, one that endures even when transformations alter that object's appearance.

Infancy 0–12 months	Sensory-motor stage	*Mental representations that are static.*
Toddler 1–2.5 years	Sensory-motor stage	
Early childhood 2.5–6 years	Preoperational stage	*Failure to conserve.*
Middle childhood 6–12 years	Concrete operational stage	*Egocentric speech.*
Adolescence 12–	Formal operational stage	*Egocentric thinking, concrete and irreversible.*

Figure 9.8 The key characteristics of Preoperational Intelligence, according to Piaget

In all cultures, people draw a distinction between the way things *appear* and the way they *really are*. The notion that there is a real world "underlying" and "explaining" the apparent one is common to modern science, to "folk philosophy," to religion, and to myth. This notion also implies that how things appear may be relative to the person who observes them, and so it has implications for one's understanding of self. For these reasons it is important to understand when young children begin to make this distinction. Unfortunately, much of the research has been flawed, failing to recognize that the distinction varies culturally and historically, and assuming that how we in the West today draw the distinction between appearance and reality ought to be what all children learn, no matter where they live.

Piaget argued that young children are concrete in their thinking: they can make inferences only about what is real and what is in front of them. However, even very young children can think about counter-factual premises—statements about what is not actually real—when these are presented in the form of a fantasy, such as a fairytale (Hawkins et al., 1984).

3.2 CAPTURED BY APPEARANCES

> Play is a reality in which children tend to believe when by themselves, exactly as the real is a play which children tend to play with adults and all those who believe likewise. (Piaget, 1924, p. 93)

It is in early childhood that young children begin to draw the distinction between how things appear and how they really are. At the start of this stage, at around 3 years of age, they have a tendency to focus exclusively on the most striking aspects of an object (that is, its surface appearance). They see a stick placed in water as really bent. They become frightened when someone puts on a mask. They believe that a cat with a dog mask actually turns into a dog. During early childhood, the world of stable, generalized, and meaningful objects becomes progressively differentiated into what is visible, and what is real but invisible.

Both Piaget and Vygotsky recognized this change, but they interpreted it in different ways.

Let us return to Piaget's **conservation** task. You know that when a liquid is poured from one container to another that has a different shape, the quantity of the liquid remains unchanged. The quantity is a physical property that is "conserved." You know that if a lump of Play-Doh is squashed flat, the amount of material has not changed. You know that when two rows of coins with an equal number in each are lined up and then one row is spread out, they still have the same number.

Young children, however, will disagree with you in each case. They will say that the quantity of liquid has changed, that the amount of Play-Doh has changed, and that the number of coins is different. When a single cracker is broken in two, a young child will be content that they now have the same as another child who has two crackers! She shows a **failure to conserve**.

What is going on here? We will consider first Piaget's explanation and then some alternatives.

3.2.1 PREOPERATIONAL INTELLIGENCE

As you will know, Piaget believed that at the culmination of sensorimotor intelligence, aged around 3 years, a toddler becomes capable of forming mental representations of the world around her. In his view this frees her from being able only to solve problems about the here and now. Now she can represent past events, and anticipate future ones. Her new ability to act not only on real objects, but also on mental representations of those objects, makes possible the earliest form of thinking, which Piaget called **preoperational thinking**.

He viewed the capacity for preoperational thinking as a major step forward from the sensorimotor intelligence of the first three years. However, what he emphasized were the limitations in the young child's thinking.

The young child's thinking is confused and slow, and it is concrete, still tied to her practical action. In addition, in Piaget's view it is **egocentric**: the young child is unable to understand the point of view of another person, or even recognize that they have a point of view different from her own. Piaget added that she lacks any sense of the need to justify her thinking, and she also lacks the ability to think about her own thoughts.

All these limitations in the young child's thinking abilities, according to Piaget, stem from the underlying fact that her mental representations are not very sophisticated. She can represent in her mind, Piaget argued, the **states** of physical things, but not the **transitions** between states. For example, she can represent the height of the liquid in a container, but not the transition of pouring that liquid into a second container. Her thinking is **static**. In addition, when she forms a mental representation of a physical state, she is unable to grasp all of it. Instead, she has a tendency to focus on one aspect and ignore the others. Here, her thinking shows what Piaget called **centration**. Finally, because she cannot represent the transitions among states her thinking lacks **reversibility**: she cannot reason about the consequences of reversing a transition.

In Piaget's view, the young child fails to solve conservation tasks because of these limitations. Her thinking lacks the flexibility that it will have later. Although she is now capable of **mental actions**, those actions are not yet **operations** in the technical sense in which Piaget used this term. We will discuss mental operations in Chapter 12; here it is enough to know that they are mental actions that have systematic logical properties. This explains the naming of this stage: in Piaget's view intelligence in early childhood is **pre-operational**—that is to say, it is not yet operational.

It is helpful to reflect on the question of how it is that you, as an adult, know that a squished piece of Play-Doh still contains the same amount of material. You know that nothing is added or taken away, so it is the same piece of Play-Doh. It may be longer, but it's also thinner. You saw it being squished, and squishing it doesn't change the amount. You could roll it back into a ball, and it would look the same as the way it started. You conclude that although the Play-Doh *looks* different it is *really* the same.

In Piagetian terms, your adult reasoning shows the following characteristics: **identity constancy**—it remains the '*same*' Play-Doh; **decentration**—*both* the width and the length change; **reversibility**—the transformation could be *reversed*; and you distinguish **appearance** from **reality**—it may *look* different, but it's "*really*" the same. A young child's thinking *does not yet* have these characteristics.

This helps us understand that it is only when the transformation can be *seen* (and when it can be remembered) that a person can reason in a way that is not based only on the way that things appear. A young child is strongly influenced by the perceptual properties of the conservation task: by the way the liquids look. She does not yet understand that appearances may be deceptive. Piaget proposed that she is unable to represent the transition, which means that she cannot remember it, so she cannot think about its consequences.

3.2.2 THE ALLURE OF THE VISUAL

Rather surprisingly, however, even young children can think correctly about the transformation that occurs in a conservation task if the liquids are *hidden* from their view! This suggests that Piaget was wrong to think that the limitation in young children's cognition is a result of not being able to represent the transition. It seems, instead, that young children are *misled* by seeing the movement of the liquid from one container to another.

Let's repeat the conservation of liquid task, but this time with the three containers hidden behind a screen. Only the top of each container is visible. The researcher pours the contents of one of the narrow containers into a wider container of the same height, as before, but now the transformation is not visible (Bruner, 1964). The young child is asked, still without seeing the containers, whether or not they have the same amount of liquid.

The number of correct judgments given by young children increases dramatically in this way of conducting the task, compared with results in the regular form of the task. Among 4-year-olds the increase is from 0 percent to 50 percent, it is from 20 percent to 90 percent among the 5-year-olds, and from 50 percent to 100 percent in the 6-year-olds. Most of the children will justify their answer by saying "It's the same water," or, "You only poured it."

Then the screen is removed. All the 4-year-olds change their mind! It seems that "The perceptual display overwhelms them and they decide that the wider beaker has less water" (Bruner, 1964, p. 7). In contrast, almost all the 5-year-olds stick with the decision they have given, and often justify this by talking about the difference between appearance and reality. All of the 6- and 7-year-olds also stick to the answers they have given. A few minutes later another test is done with no screen: a post-test. The 4-year-olds show no influence as a result of what has gone before: they all fail the task. But the 5-year-olds improve from 20 percent to 70 percent, and with the 6- and 7-year-olds performance improves from 50 percent to 90 percent (see Figure 9.9).

In this modified task the screen prevents the young children from seeing the visual appearance of the liquid in the containers. In this situation, even some of the youngest children are able to think correctly about the task. This suggests that the difficulty they have with the regular conservation task is not due to the limited character of their thinking so much as the power of the visual. Young children are "captured"—one might say "captivated"—by what they see. Even though they observe the transformation, which should enable them to solve the task, the way the liquid looks in the containers *interferes* with their thinking. The problem is not how they mentally represent the states and transformations, it is the *appearance* of the material that is transformed.

Certainly the liquid *looks* different in the two containers. Even adults are influenced by the visual appearance of things when they don't have the information necessary to reason that things are not as they appear. For example, they are likely to pour more liquid into a short, wide glass than into a tall, narrow glass. An experiment with college students and with bartenders found that the students poured 30 percent more liquid into the short glasses, and the bartenders, who presumably have much more experience with this task, still poured 20 percent more into the short glass. The quantity of liquid simply *looks* less when it is in a short glass.

Adults, though, when they have seen the transition or been told about it, can reason that the amount of liquid *must* be the same. Young children, in contrast, are overly impressed by the way the liquids look. This implies that when children become able to solve the regular conservation task (where everything is visible) it must be because they have acquired an ability to "break away from" what they see. What could make this possible? One possibility is that here too language plays a role: "if a child is to succeed in the conservation task, he must have some internalized verbal formula that shields him from the overpowering appearance of the visual displays" (Bruner, 1964, p. 7). Putting into words what is seen may enable a young child to reason:

> Once language becomes a medium for the translation of experience, there is a progressive release from immediacy. For language, as we have commented, has the new and powerful features of remoteness and arbitrariness. (Bruner, 1964, p. 14)

We have already seen that language is a cultural tool. This tool makes many things possible: one of them is going beyond the immediate situation. Talking "invokes" things and events that occurred in the past, or that may occur in the future. We can also talk about what exists but is not visible.

Remember the research with Sheba and Sarah in an earlier chapter? We saw that material representations helped these chimpanzees overcome the irresistible impulse to action that was created by the sight of the treats. In the case of the conservation task, we again have an irresistible tendency to draw conclusions about what has taken place created by the sight of the liquids. In young children we seem to witness something similar to the change that took place for the chimpanzees. As they begin to use words

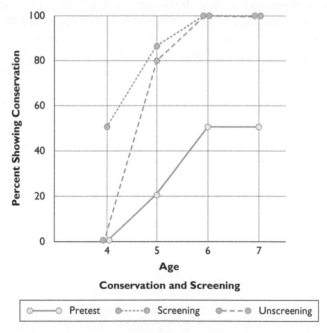

Figure 9.9 Conservation responses before screening (pretest), during screening, and after the screen is removed (unscreening)

Source: Bruner (1964)

as a material representation of what they see, they start to see in a new way. In the last chapter we talked about the way language provides toddlers with cultural categories in terms of which to see objects. We saw that language helps a toddler make a distinction between herself and the world. Now, in early childhood there is a growing ability to talk about things in non-perceptual ways.

At the start of early childhood, then, young children continue to be swayed by the visual appearance of objects and events. However, during this stage they are increasingly able to draw a distinction between the ways things appear and they way they really are. One factor in this ability is language: young children are able to talk about the situation, and the way they talk influences their thinking.

Young children can talk about the conservation task in a way that continues to focus on the way it looks—talking about the height, the width, or the "bigness" of the liquid. They can also talk about the action of pouring the water. In contrast, words such as "volume" and "proportion" can "stand for" something that is not directly visible, but which the young child can learn to identify. Recall the distinction between "inference," "thinking," and "reasoning" that we introduced earlier in this section. A young child's first *inference* might be that the liquid has changed, but she now starts to *think* about what has happened, and she is able to conclude that actually the liquid remains the same.

As the distinction is drawn between appearance and reality, the former becomes shifting and transient, and what is now taken to be stable, enduring, and objective is a realm that cannot be perceived directly. When a young child masters this distinction, this contradiction and paradox, she will solve Piagetian conservation tasks.

3.3 THINKING ABOUT THE NATURAL WORLD

Presumably it is the young child's involvement in the world that makes it possible for her to attend to regularities in that world and start to understand them, and also to understand what the people she knows tell her about the world. At this point in our account you will not be surprised to learn that this involvement varies from one culture to another.

Piaget claimed that young children demonstrate animism, realism, artificialism, and syncretism—that they are "primitive" in their thinking.

Animism, in particular, is an apparent tendency to confuse living and non-living things. Margaret Mead set out to test Piaget's claim about animism through anthropological fieldwork. Her question was the following: "Was this type of child-thought which confused cause and effect, imputed personality or spirit to inanimate objects and insisted upon an anthropomorphic interpretation of the universe, characteristic of all children of a certain age, or only of children who had been subjected to a particular set of environmental conditions?" (Mead, 1932, p. 174).

Mead's answer to her question was a resounding "no!" She found that among the Manus people on the Admiralty Islands north of New Guinea, adults would attribute spirit powers to the operation of wind chimes, whereas young children explained the movement of the wind chimes as due to the wind! It was the *adults* who appealed to forms of explanation that many Western social scientists would call "animistic," "primitive," or "childish," while their children did not. Mead concluded that she found "no evidence for spontaneous animistic thought in the uncontrolled sayings or games of these Manus children during five months of continuous observation" (1932, p. 180). The difference between young children and adults seemed to be due to the fact that the children did not yet participate in adult rituals, so they did not yet understand spirit relations. In addition, Manus children were taught at a very early age the properties of fire and water, how to estimate distance, to allow for illusion when objects are seen under water, and to judge when a canoe can pass under an obstacle or through shallow water. Mistakes brought immediate and severe punishment. This meant that the child's attention became focused on cause-and-effect relationships, with no time or place for fanciful speculation.

Mead concluded that "The Manus child is less spontaneously animistic and less traditionally animistic than is the Manus adult" (1932, p. 186), and she suggested that animism is not inevitable, that it arises from the particular language and traditions that young children hear and see adults using.

Mead's investigations show that Piaget's claims about the thinking of young children ought to be examined in a cultural context. However, researchers working with young children from contexts similar to that of Piaget's Swiss participants have also cast doubt on his analysis.

For example, researchers have found that 4- and 5-year-old children in the West can distinguish between psychological causes and biological causes. This has suggested that when they say that living things have a vital energy ("vitalism") they are not confusing people and animals, they are simply applying their greater knowledge of people in order to think by analogy—to make "educated guesses"—about plants and animals (Inagaki and Hatano, 1993, 2006). Young children growing up in post-industrial societies have very little direct experience of plants and animals—how old were you when you first saw a cow?—and so they can really only think about them by analogy to people. A young child who lives in the city but does have some direct experience of living creatures—for example, from taking care of a goldfish—will think more adequately. She will still draw analogies, but to the familiar animal rather than to humans (Inagaki, 1990).

In addition, we now recognize that it is unfair to compare the thinking of a young child against the standard of how scientists reason, no matter what culture that child lives in. Researchers have increasingly come to recognize that scientific reasoning is not the only endpoint to children's conceptual development. For some time it seemed that in every human society studied, adults tended to think about plants and animals in terms of a **hierarchical taxonomy**, organized around species with a common essence (e.g., oak or robin, rather than tree or bird), and that they think about the features of these species in the same way (Atran et al., 2005). This way of thinking differs significantly from scientific biological reasoning, which considers humans to be animals and deals with interrelated genera, rather than species with distinct essences. In other words, the majority of adults don't reason like scientists.

Furthermore, research has now uncovered distinct ways of reasoning about biology among adults in different cultures. Adults in industrialized societies tend to see biological creatures as a hierarchical taxonomy, as the earlier research found. However, in contrast, the Yukatek Maya, for example, are primarily concerned with ecological relationships and reason in a **systemic** way (Atran et al., 2005). Their **ecological thinking** puts two biological entities together not because that have similar characteristics, but because they are related in the ecology in which they both live.

In industrial societies, even adults lack both a scientific knowledge of animals and plants and direct practical experience with these living things, because unlike their ancestors who farmed, and unlike other people who hunt, they no longer have daily contact with animals and plants. Their children's reasoning is likely to be limited as a consequence. Children in the USA show an **anthropocentric bias**: they base their thinking about animals on what they know about humans, probably because of their lack of familiarity with animals and plants, other than family pets and cuts of meat in the supermarket. Who knew that chickens have feathers?! In cultures where young children and adults have regular contact with plants and animals, even young children quickly become capable of complex ecological reasoning (Atran et al., 2001).

For example, young Yukatek Maya children, aged 4 to 5, were compared with Maya adults on a task in which they had to reason about a shared property. They were shown a picture of a wolf and told "Now there is this stuff called *andro* that is found inside some kinds of things. One kind of thing that has *andro* inside is a wolf. Now I will show you other things and you tell me if you think they have *andro* inside like wolves do." They were then shown a second object, such as a raccoon, an eagle, or a rock. The researchers were interested in discovering which of these were viewed as similar to the wolf. The question was then asked again, this time not about a wolf but about a human, a bee, a goldenrod plant, or water. Again, the researchers wanted to see if the child or adult would reason that *andro* would also be found in something in the same category: human, animal, bird, plant, inanimate.

The Maya adults' reasoning showed that they assumed greater similarity between humans and other living kinds than between humans and non-living kinds, following the pattern predicted by standard biological taxonomies. But when it was a bee that contained *andro* they often reasoned that its properties would be shared not only with other invertebrates, but also with trees and humans. This pattern was interpreted by the researchers as indicating ecological reasoning. The inference appeared to be that bees build their nests in trees and humans eat their honey, so that one might reasonably expect a property of bees to transfer to those things they interact with. Indeed, the participants often explicitly used ecological justifications in their responses.

Most importantly, the young Maya children's responses were very similar to those of the Maya adults. Whatever first object contained *andro*, the children assumed less similarity when the second object was a tree than when it was a mammal. And, like the adults, the children showed no indication of anthropomorphism: inferences from humans did not differ from inferences from animals or trees, and the Mayan children did not appear to favor humans as a basis of inference. They did not interpret the biological world anthropocentrically.

This is evidence, then, that knowledge and thinking about biology do not show inevitable limitations in early childhood, but depend on the particular experience that a young child (or adult) has gained from living in specific circumstances. It supports the conclusion that the anthropocentric bias observed in urban American children comes from their lack of everyday contact with plants and animals. Over the past two hundred years, children who live in urban environments and go to school have had less and less contact with the natural world, and know less and less about it (Medin et al., 2007). We are often told today that we ought to reason ecologically, and in fact young children whose culture brings them into close, everyday, practical contact with plants and animals are capable of sophisticated ecological thinking. The "less advanced" thinking of young children in urban, technologically dependent settings seems to reflect their lack of experience, and in this sense is illustrates a "devolution" of knowledge over time (Atran et al., 2004; Wolff & Medin, 2001; but cf. Ergazaki & Andriotou, 2008).

Moreover, studies such as those I have described raise important methodological questions. Frequently, the form of investigation is still that used by Piaget—questioning by an adult interviewer. In this approach, language is treated as though it were a transparent medium of communication in which a word has the same meaning for adult and child. For example, in one study young children were asked to name drawings of animals. When the name was "correct" they were told so, when the name was "incorrect" the researcher provided the "correct label," and then asked questions ("Can Xs think?") that required only a yes/no answer (Coley, 1995). This approach offers the young child little opportunity to articulate their own understanding of the name, and it actually discards useful information about their understanding that is contained in their "incorrect" names. We need to be open to the possibility the meaning of a word for a young child is quite different from its meaning for an adult.

3.4 CULTURE AND COSMOLOGY

There is, however, a deeper problem with this line of research about the character of thinking in early childhood. Ever since Piaget sat down with young children to ask them about the world, research on children's conceptions has taken for granted that people may think about and conceptualize the world in different ways, but there is a single underlying reality.

For example, Piaget, as we have seen, assumed that the distinction between mind and body is a real and unavoidable one, along with the distinction between subject and object, and consequently the internal nature of thought. For Piaget, the young children's answers to his questions began by being "primitive" but ended up being "correct."

It seems common sense that we all live in the same world, though we understand it in different ways. However, in cultural anthropology today there is a heated debate about this apparently obvious issue. In the so-called **ontological turn**, some anthropologists are proposing that different cultures have not merely different ways of conceptualizing a single world, they inhabit different worlds. The task of ethnographic fieldwork has long been considered that of grasping the "worldview" of a people, the way they perceive and conceptualize the reality around them—their **cosmovision**. The "ontological turn" is the proposal that people in a different culture don't simply have different perceptions and conceptions of the world, they actually live in a different world, and that ethnography must aim to grasp its ontology—that is, not its cosmovision but its **cosmology** (Kohn, 2015; Pedersen, 2012; Viveiros de Castro, 2012).

Let me try to make this apparently bizarre claim seem obvious! The British live in a country in which there is a queen, a prime minister, and a Conservative Party. In the USA, people live in a world of senators, freeways, dollars, and hedge-fund managers. The Matsigenka in the Amazon live in a world of spirits, co-wives, cotton-spinning, and manioc beer. These three ontologies are quite different.

In Chapter 3 I explained John Searle's analysis of **institutional facts**. Searle argues that these are "the glue" that enables "the construction of social reality" (Searle, 2005, p. 1). Despite the name, an institutional fact is not an item of information; it is an aspect of the reality in which people live. Institutional facts add up to an ontology, created not by what individuals believe but by public practices in which everyone participates.

Institutional facts define rights and responsibilities, and so possibilities for action. Among the Matsigenka, as I mentioned in Chapter 3, the daughter of a man's uncle counts as his sister, so he cannot marry her (Johnson, 2003).

It might be objected that institutional facts make up the culture of a society, but that the natural world remains, well, natural! Surely nature is the same everywhere? A lion is a lion, a rock is a rock. However, anthropologists of the ontological turn point out that the very distinction between "cultural" and "natural" has very different forms in different communities, and that the way Western scientists view this distinction is very contradictory. We tend to assume that humans are cultural while animals are natural. On the other hand, we acknowledge that humans are animals too! And we claim that culture is part of human nature! We tend to assume that the distinction between nature and culture is natural. But doesn't it make more sense to see it as cultural? It is, in fact, very difficult to define culture and nature in a way that is not circular.

We have seen that Piaget detected "animism" in young children's conceptions. As he noted, the thinking of indigenous peoples has also been called "animistic." In some cultures, people maintain that "the world is full of persons, only some of whom are human, and that life is always lived in relationship with others" (Harvey, 2006, p. xi). Even a stone is understood as containing energy and life. Anthropologists are now suggesting that animism is not a "primitive" conception, it is an ontology which postulates that relations between humans and non-humans are social, and that the space between nature and culture is social. Animists recognize a wide range of "persons" and do not take humans as the primary exemplars of personhood. In Amerindian societies, in the Amazon region, it is taken for granted that animals see themselves as people, and see humans as animals. Animism is an ontologically distinct way of engaging the world and making sense of it.

To be human is to be able to take a reflexive relationship to oneself. This means that salmon see themselves as human, because this is the relation a subject takes to itself. Peccaries cannot see themselves as peccaries, because this is how *humans* see them.

Animism is not a narcissistic projection of humanity onto nature, but a consequence of the fact that the Amerindian world comprises a multiplicity of subject-positions. In this cosmology:

> all beings see ('represent') the world in the same way—what changes is the world that they see. Animals impose the same categories and values on reality as humans do: their worlds, like ours, revolve around hunting and fishing, cooking and fermented drinks, cross-cousins and war, initiation rituals, shamans, chiefs, spirits … But the things *that* they see are different: what to us is blood, is maize beer to the jaguar. (Viveiros de Castro, 2012, p. 107)

In the Amerindian cosmology, "there are no autonomous, natural facts, for what we see as 'nature' is seen by other species as 'culture,' i.e., as institutional facts—what we see as blood, a natural substance, is seen by jaguars as manioc beer, an artefact; our mud is the hammock of the tapirs and so on" (2012, p. 111).

Once again, we seem to have assumed that what we in the West take to be reality is the only possible way to understand the world. We take for granted the distinctions among physical, biological, and psychological phenomena, assuming that this is simply how the world works. The research on young children's conceptions of the world has been concerned with the question of whether their knowledge fits into these distinct "domains," such as animate and inanimate, biological and psychological, which have been called **natural kinds**: "Natural kinds are categories of objects and substances that are found in nature (e.g. tiger, water, cactus)" (Gelman & Markman, 1987). What the ontological turn implies is that there are no such things. Scott Atran, deeply involved in this program of research, remarks in a footnote:

The conception of 'natural kind', which supposedly spans all sorts of lawful natural phenomena, may turn out not to be a psychologically real predicate of ordinary thinking (i.e. a 'natural kind' of cognitive science). It may simply be an epistemic notion peculiar to a growth stage in Western science and philosophy of science. (Atran, 1998, p. 569)

Philosopher of science Ian Hacking puts it more bluntly: "*there is no such thing as a natural kind*" (Hacking, 2007, original emphasis).

This analysis can be extended to the proposal that *within* a society there are multiple cosmologies. Surely the ontology of medicine is different from that of the law? That of the economy is different from that of politics? This the proposal made by Bruno Latour in *An Inquiry into Modes of Existence* (Latour, 2013).

It has been show that young children can already distinguish fictional worlds from real worlds. In fact, they can distinguish multiple fictional worlds. They recognize that Batman and Robin are fictional, not real. They grasp that Bob Squarepants is not real either. And they also appreciate that Batman and Robin don't know Bob Squarepants (Bunce & Harris, 2014).

Why, then, could it not be the case that young children are already starting to distinguish the multiple real worlds of their community and society?

Cognitive Psychology	Cultural Psychology
Each culture has a cosmovision: a specific way of knowing the world we all live in	Each culture has a cosmology: a specific world with particular entities
A child knows the world with concepts	A child knows the world on several levels, from sensory-motor to conceptual

Figure 9.10   The differences between cosmovision and cosmology

CONCLUSION

In early childhood we see a new form of activity, sociodramatic play, in which young children create an "imaginary" situation together, adopt recognized social characters, and metacommunicate about their conventional actions. The norms of play are implicit at this stage; later, in middle childhood, play will have clearly defined rules. The game of Laser Beasts illustrates these qualities.

Sociodramatic play is linked to several other developmental achievements of early childhood. It is an activity in which young children explore their new understanding of gender: we see this, for example, in their spontaneous self-segregation along gender lines. It is too early, however, to speak of "gender identity"— young children's understanding is limited to seeing the cultural categorization of people into (usually) two genders, plus the behaviors conventionally associated with each category, such as wearing specific clothes. As a consequence, the young child assumes that a change in clothes will be a change in gender.

Boys and girls not only generally play apart, they also play in different ways, and they tell different stories. Sociodramatic play is an exercise of the imagination in practical activity, and it is an opportunity to practice, understand, and anticipate adult situations and conventional actions.

However, the constraints that young children impose on one another in their sociodramatic play, whatever gender category they now place themselves in, lead to improvements in their self-control.

Sociodramatic play seems to emerge in all parts of the world. However, the degree to which adults involve themselves in young children's play varies greatly. The preschool setting that we may take for granted is one extreme: the preschool playground is a deliberately developmental niche deliberately constructed by adults in order to facilitate young children's play. In many cultures, adults largely ignore their children's play, neither discouraging it nor facilitating it. We have also seen that young children's sociodramatic play also reflects efforts by the media and marketing to shape their desires and influence their purchases.

A young child's understanding of the world takes important steps beyond the practical understanding of the infant and the toddler. Piaget's interviews with young children led him to describe their understanding as having the characteristics of realism, animism, artificialism, and syncretism. He concluded that a young child does not recognize fundamental distinctions, such as between mind and world. She fails conservation tasks, he argued, because her mental representations are static, and her thinking suffers from centration. In short, she cannot distinguish appearance from reality.

We have seen that there is a kernel of truth to Piaget's conclusions. It is true that young children are still captured by the visual qualities of situations such as the conversation task. The amount of liquid in two differently shaped containers does look different, even to adults, and a young child's reasoning is swayed by this. However, it seems likely that what enables her to break away from the visual is language, not a better kind of mental representation.

At the same time, Piaget assumed that the divisions that Western science finds in the world—the mental and material, the psychological, biological, and physical—are simply how the world is. Anthropologists are increasingly turning to the view that different cultures have different ontologies: they inhabit different worlds. The fact that young children are becoming able to understand the multiple realities of fiction suggests that they might also be starting to grasp the ontology of their own culture.

SUMMARY

SOCIODRAMATIC PLAY

- In early childhood, play often takes the form of sociodramatic play—pretend play in which several children play at being some other kind of person. Sociodramatic play has an "as-if" character, applied to the participants themselves, as characters in their drama. Play is not simply freedom from constraints. In fact, in play young children impose constraints on themselves. In their play, they engage in gender self-segregation. They are starting to recognize the conventions of gender.

(Continued)

(Continued)

- For Piaget, play was a failure to adapt to reality, an activity in which assimilation predominates. He saw play as something a child must grow out of. For Vygotsky, play is an opportunity to develop the imagination, and it is the central line of development in early childhood, an anticipation of a possible future. Play is imagination in action.

TALKING AS BOTH DOING AND UNDERSTANDING

- A young child is able to combine the interpersonal and the ideational metafunctions of language, so that her speech both accomplishes a social action and says something about the world.

- Her language now has three levels: sound, grammar, and meaning.

THE WORLD OF EARLY CHILDHOOD

- Piaget considered early childhood to be the stage of preoperational intelligence, in which mental actions are performed on simple mental representations. He emphasized the limitations in young children's thinking: limitations such as realism, animism, artificialism, and syncretism, and proposed that they fail to distinguish between appearance and reality, and also fail to understand the dualisms that he considered real.

- However, young children are beginning to learn the key ontological distinction of their culture's cosmology. They are captured, or captivated, by what they see. However, during early childhood they start to draw a distinction between the way things appear and how they really are. This distinction is made in every culture. However, it varies culturally and historically—each culture has a distinct cosmology.

RESOURCES

The "keen attention" of Mayan and Mexican-heritage children points to the importance of understanding the different strengths that children bring to their learning:

http://stemforall2016.videohall.com/presentations/693

Vivian Paley, reading from her book:

www.youtube.com/watch?v=LfCx6th9Y4o

"How Does Childhood Differ Between Traditional Societies and Modern Societies?" Lecture by Jarod Diamond:

www.youtube.com/watch?v=BvqOaWwLtjo

Parenting Across Cultures: The Different Ways We Raise Our Children

www.youtube.com/watch?v=BJic9NrYk0Y

Harvey, G. (2006). *Animism: Respecting the Living World*. New York: Columbia University Press.

CHAPTER 10

EARLY CHILDHOOD

(3–6 YEARS)

TOWARDS INNER AND OUTER

LEARNING OBJECTIVES

In this chapter we will explore the following aspects of early childhood:

- The way young children understand other people, now not only recognizing their intention-in-action but also inferring prior intentions, and so using what is called the intentional stance.
- The origins of verbal thinking in the young child's self-directed speech.
- The different styles of caregiving that have been identified in Western society, and the family models that define distinct developmental trajectories for young children.
- Ways in which the young child is becoming a *type* of person.
- The biological changes that occur during this stage.

FRAMING QUESTIONS

- You see someone sweeping water in the street. How many different explanations can you imagine for this person's actions? How many of these explanations make reference to the psychology of the person? What do the other explanations make reference to? How many of these explanations do you think a young child could understand?
- What are the differences between a man and a woman?
- At times, do you hear your own voice in your head?

INTRODUCTION

In the previous chapter we saw how a young child shows in sociodramatic play her ability to use language to make one thing count as another. We considered Piaget's conclusions about the way young children conceptualize and think about the world. Piaget conducted interviews, something that is possible now that young children are able to use language to talk about the world in interpersonal interaction.

We also saw that every child lives within a culture with a specific cosmovision: a specific way of living in the world that defines entities and domains. The very distinction between "cultural" and "natural" varies across cultures. The young child progressively becomes able to distinguish between how things "appear" and how they "really are," presumably grasping her culture's cosmovision in the process.

In this chapter we continue this exploration of early childhood. We consider first how young children understand other people, introducing two new interpretive stances—the intentional stance and the conventional stance.

We then consider how young children are cared for in different parts of the world. At this age, people outside the family frequently contribute to this care. Distinct parenting styles have been identified, and also four distinct kinds of family model, which define distinct developmental trajectories.

Next, we explore the origins of the verbal thinking that young children become capable of. As we shall see, Piaget considered self-directed speech to be egocentric, while Vygotsky considered self-directed speech to be the earliest form of thinking.

1. UNDERSTANDING OTHER PEOPLE: PRIOR INTENTIONS AND CONVENTIONAL SCENARIOS

Three-year-olds take the world they see to be the world as it is. They don't recognize that people have different visual perspectives—that a person standing in a different place has a different point of view. They don't understand that people know different things about the world—that someone can have, for example, a false belief. Indeed, they don't yet draw a distinction between the world and knowledge about the world.

During early childhood, however, young children's understanding of how other people perceive and know the world changes and advances in important ways. These changes are the focus of this section.

1.1 UNDERSTANDING PERSPECTIVE

Once again we will start with Piaget. His famous **three mountains task** explored the ability of young children to understand visual perspective. A young child is shown a model representing a scene with three miniature mountains, together with tiny trees, huts, and other objects. The child is allowed to examine the model from all sides. Then she sits in front of it and is asked to describe what she sees. A doll is then placed on the opposite side of the model, and the young child is asked what the doll can see. Piaget found that usually the young child will say that the doll sees exactly what she, the child, sees.

Piaget called this lack of ability to understand another person's visual perspective **egocentrism.** What he meant by this was not that the young child is selfish, but that she has a strong tendency to consider the world entirely in terms of her own point of view. She assumes that everyone sees the world in the way that she does. She simply assumes that the world *is* as she sees it. At first, Piaget proposed that in order to recognize that other people have different perspectives, the young child needs to be socialized. Later, he suggested that the young child makes no distinction between herself and the world she lives in, and that in order to recognize other perspectives she must become conscious of herself:

> In order to be objective, one must have become conscious of one's 'I.' Objective knowledge can only be conceived in relation to subjective [knowledge] ... originally the child puts the whole content of consciousness on the same plane and draws no distinction between 'I' and the external world. (Piaget, 1960[1929], p. 241)

Figure 10.1 Piaget's three mountains task

For Piaget, the young child's cognitive development was a matter of overcoming egocentrism by progressively **decentering**: recognizing the distinction between how the world appears from her own point of view and an objective, perspective-independent understanding—drawing a distinction between how the world *appears* and how it *is*.

This suggestion is similar in some ways to Vygotsky's proposal that the young child is only beginning to *differentiate psychologically* from other people and from the world around her. As she becomes aware of herself as a distinct person, she will come to understand that she has a perspective on the world which other people do not share. The young child starts to appreciate that reality appears in different ways to different people.

We saw in Chapter 7 that 3-year-olds can appreciate that another person may be able to see an object that they themselves cannot see: this has been called **level 1 perspective taking** (Flavell et al., 1981). In fact, however, the label is misleading insofar as there is no understanding of perspective. The same 3-year-olds do not recognize that an object which is visible to both themselves and another person will be seen *in different ways*. This ability is called **level 2 perspective taking**, and it seems to emerge at around 4 years of age (Aichhorn et al., 2006).

For example, a 3-year-old can tell a researcher where to place the figure of a naughty boy so that he will be out of sight to a toy policeman. She can tell whether not the policeman can see something that she can see. However, the same young child will be unable to correctly describe the appearance of an object as seen by someone seated on the opposite side of the table. She is capable of level 1 perspective taking but not level 2. She assumes that the *way* she sees something is how it appears to everyone.

1.2 UNDERSTANDING BELIEFS

In Piaget's view, egocentrism is also illustrated by the young child's failure to understand other people's mental states: their beliefs, desires, thoughts, and intentions.

Piaget asked young children about their own thinking and the thinking of other people. As we saw in the previous chapter, he concluded that young children fail to distinguish the physical from the psychical, attribute intentions to material things, and often propose that thoughts are material—he called this *realism*. The young child apparently fails to realize that people have private and personal mental states.

Many researchers have followed Piaget's lead, exploring young children's understanding of beliefs and desires, and they have aimed to document when this understanding emerges.

A very popular way of studying how children at different ages understand what other people believe and know is the **false belief task**. A young child is shown a toy character, Max, who hides something—a candy, for example—in one of two locations. Max then leaves, and while he is gone the candy is moved to the second location. Max returns, and the young child is asked where he will look for the candy, or to explain where Max will think the candy is.

Older children, aged 6 or 7, answer correctly in this task, just like adults. They say that Max will look in the wrong place because this is where he *believes* the candy is. However, younger children (aged 3 years) answer incorrectly. But they do not give random answers: they consistently say that Max will search in the second location, where the candy actually is (Wellman, 2011).

In another version of this task the child is shown a situation in which someone has false expectations about the contents of a container. For example, she may be shown that a tin with an image of candy on the lid is actually empty. The child is then asked what Max, who sees the closed container, will expect it to contain. Once again, younger children will typically say that Max will think that the container is empty. She has apparently confused her own knowledge with that of Max, rather than understanding that Max will have a belief that is false because his knowledge of the situation is different.

What is behind such errors? Does the young child fail to understand that Max's belief is no longer correct? Does she fail to distinguish between what she herself knows and what Max believes? Or does she not yet draw a distinction between what she knows about the world and how the world actually is? Does she in fact not recognize beliefs at all?

The validity of the false belief task has been questioned, though many researchers have concluded that the phenomenon is a real one: young children do not grasp that a person can believe something about the world that is not true (Wellman et al., 2001). This phenomenon is then generally taken as evidence that young children do not recognize that people have mental states such as beliefs. The young child, it is said, lacks a "theory of mind."

However, before we accept this conclusion we should take into account the finding that young children show similar difficulties with tasks that don't require an understanding of mental states (Bloom & German, 2000). For example, 3-year-olds have as much difficulty with a false photograph—one that doesn't accurately portray how things look—as with the false belief task, while 4-year-olds perform better. Younger children also have difficulty with stories about a false signpost—one that points to an object that has been moved—and about a false label—one that indicates incorrectly what is in a container. This suggests that what is difficult for young children is false representation in general (Leekam et al., 2008). What we may be seeing is that the young child cannot understand how one thing may "point to" another incorrectly. The young child simply assumes that a tin contains what its label indicates, that a sign points where it seems to, and that a person's action "points" towards their goal. Yes, this implies that young children do not yet understand people's actions in terms of mental states. But as we have seen, they *do* understand people's actions in terms of intention-in-action.

During early childhood, as the young child moves beyond this limited understanding, it appears that the teleological stance, the ability to grasp intention-in-action, is supplemented by a new ability, the **intentional stance**, as the young child acquires the ability to infer **prior intention**.

1.3 THE INTENTIONAL STANCE

In Chapter 6 I introduced "theory theory"—the theory that young children, and even infants, form theories about the world. One form of theory theory is the proposal that during early childhood young children start to form a **theory of mind**—a capacity "to construe people in terms of their mental states and traits" (Lillard & Skibbe, 2005; Wellman, 2011). The understanding of beliefs and desires is presumed to require a theory because they are assumed to be interior, subjective mental states which are invisible to observation.

Theory of mind is based on the representational model of mind as a computer that we saw has been central to the cognitivist theoretical framework (Chapters 2 and 4) (Byrnes, 1992). The theory-theory psychologists believe that in order to understand another person a young child has to form a theory about that person's mental states. This may be an unnecessarily complex assumption—after all, "It is important to remember that a theory is a reflective, rational construction, based on advanced language and aimed at the causal explanations of phenomena, which can be used as a tool for theorizing ... Before children develop language to a sufficient degree, explaining their responses as a result of their 'theories' can be misleading" (Subbotsky, 2014, p. 18).

It seems more likely that the young child builds on the ability that she acquired as a toddler to understand people's intention-in-action, and that her understanding is still largely emotional—intuitive, evaluative, and embodied—rather than theoretical.

Western adults take for granted a "mentalistic" way of describing and explaining what people do, in terms of subjective and interior beliefs and desires. But this way of thinking has a history—it began in Greece around the time of Homer (Olson, 1994)—and it is not shared by all cultures. Around the world, people speak about and presumably understand beliefs and desires in an enormous variety of ways (Lillard, 1998; Vinden, 1998). In terms of sheer number, English is at an extreme, possessing more than 5,000 words for mental states. By contrast, the Chewong people of Malaysia are reported to have only five words to cover the entire range of psychological processes, words translated as *know, remember, forget, miss, want,* and *want very much* (Howell, 1981). Anthropologists have also described a number of cultures in which people actively avoid talking about each other's psychological states (Paul, 1995). Researcher Angelina Lillard has concluded:

> The EA [EuropeanAmerica] mind concept may well be culture specific. Other cultures appear to give much more emphasis to souls and seem to have different ideas about the main functions of minds (by including, e.g., health and fertility). Some cultures identify mind with heart more

so than with brain, and others do not make the mind–body split. Finally, many cultures do not discuss minds. Cultures that do not discuss mental states either do not overtly explain actions or overtly explain actions as emanating from something besides minds. (Lillard, 1998, p. 14)

For example, the Ifaluk, who live on a coral atoll of four islands in the Pacific Ocean, have only 100 words for emotions, and of these only a core group of 10 to 15 are used regularly. The Ifaluk understand emotions in terms of the events or situations in which they occur, and rarely if ever in terms of feelings, or physiology: "To utter an emotion word on Ifaluk is not primarily to evoke an image of an image of internal churnings or of particular ways of hotly thinking; rather, it is to evoke an image of a particular kind of of event, a particular relationship between a person and the world" (Lutz, 1987, p. 294).

Cross-cultural research has explored whether or not theory of mind is a universal developmental phenomenon, and has provided confusing findings (Lillard & Skibbe, 2005; Liu et al., 2008). In one of the first studies in non-Western cultures, young Baka children in rural Cameroon seemed to have the ability to make inferences about people's false beliefs (Avis & Harris, 1991). All the 5-year-old Baka children answered correctly in the false-belief task, and some of the younger children, aged 3.5 years, did so too. Other studies have found, however, that performance on the false belief task is poor in cultures where people are less likely to talk of mental states. For example, even 8-year-old Quechua children in Peru had difficulty solving the task (Vinden, 1998, 2002). However, a study of young children from a variety of small-scale, low-technology groups in Cameroon and New Guinea found that they were able to understand how beliefs affect behavior, though they had difficulty predicting an emotion based on a false belief (Vinden, 1999).

As I said, findings such as these are hard to interpret. Poor performance on the false belief tasks could be because people lack the vocabulary to talk about beliefs, or because they understand beliefs in a different way than we do. To avoid the impact of vocabulary on the task, studies have been conducted in which it was not necessary to use difficult-to-translate words such as *belief* and *emotion*. In one such study, a toy was hidden under one of three bowls with two adults present. Then one adult left and the other indicated to the young child to put the toy under a different bowl, then asked her to point to the bowl the first adult would pick up when they returned (Callaghan et al., 2005). This version of a false belief task uses language only at a simple level, since the child responds by simply pointing, and the task does not use words for belief or desire. The children were asked simple questions about behavior, not about beliefs or thoughts.

A large number of children between 2.5 to 6 years of age were tested in this way in Canada, Samoa, India, Peru, and Thailand. A common pattern was found: performance improved with age, with 50 percent of young children of 4.5 to 5 years of age performing correctly, and all children of 5.5 to 6 years of age responding correctly. This finding has been interpreted as showing that young children's understanding of false beliefs develops in a single way that is independent of culture or the language that is spoken.

However, in a task in which young children were asked to *explain* the bad behavior of a story character, there were cultural, regional, and class differences in whether the explanation was given in terms of mental states (or traits) or in terms of external circumstances (Lillard et al., 2001). Children in all the groups gave both mental and situational explanations, but the frequency and patterns of these explanations varied. The researchers attributed the results to the language practices in the different communities.

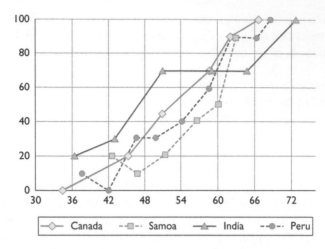

Figure 10.2 Percentage of children passing the false-belief test as a function of age, plotted separately for Canada, Samoa, India, and Peru

Source: Callaghan et al. (2005)

They suggested that parents in poorer and rural communities are more likely to explain actions to their children in terms of situations, while parents in wealthier and urban communities are more likely to explain actions in terms of mental states.

Overall, it seems that when carefully simplified versions of the false belief task are presented to young children in widely different cultures they perform roughly the same, but cultural variations appear when language is made part of the task—when the children have to explain their answers, for example.

This suggests that there may be a universal basic way of understanding other people's behavior, but that when young children come to adopt their culture's way of talking and thinking about what people know and want, differences start to appear (cf. Stone et al., 2012). One might hypothesize that the basic understanding uses System 1, the implicit teleological understanding we have discussed, while verbal explanations require System 2.

An illustration of the different ways that young children around the world come to understand beliefs and desires comes from the culture of Java, a large island that forms part of Indonesia. Young Javanese children are taught to be acutely aware of other people's moods and desires, and are required to learn extreme self-control and renunciation. They are first told that they can trust their mother and family completely but that the rest of the world is composed of strangers and evil spirits who will do them harm, especially if they do wrong (Geertz, 1959). They must show *wedi*, the word for fear. As young children, they are told that strangers will disapprove of them if they do wrong, so that they feel *isin*, shame. Then as they grow older their parents start to respond differently, ignoring them if they cry, and punishing them if they don't do what they are told. *Wedi* now includes showing respect for parents.

It would be a mistake to think that young children's understanding of other people is an individual accomplishment. Adults help children to make sense of what other people know and want. Indeed, several investigations have showed that a young child's family is important for an understanding of other people. For example, Judy Dunn and her colleagues (Dunn et al., 1991) observed young children interacting with their mothers at 33 months of age, and then gave the children various tasks at 40 months (3 years 4 months). They found that in a false-belief task a third of the children were able to offer explanations in terms of belief, and that the ability to do this was related to conversations between child and mother about feelings and about causality at the earlier time, and to the child's talk about feelings at the earlier time: "For example, during the observations mothers frequently attempted to sort out disagreements between siblings by explaining how the other child's (often mistaken) beliefs governed his or her actions: 'He thought you had finished yours'; 'She didn't know I had promised it to you'; 'He thought it was his turn'" (Dunn et al., 1991, p. 1363).

As such research might lead us to predict, young children perform better on false-belief tasks when they have more siblings (Perner et al., 1994), older siblings (Ruffman et al., 1998), or have mothers who encourage them to reflect on their feelings (Ruffman et al., 1999) and who talk about mental states (Ruffman et al., 2002) and emotions (Taumoepeau & Ruffman, 2008).

It has been proposed that caregivers' talk facilitates a young child's understanding of mental states because their "emerging implicit understanding about mental life is made explicit" (Taumoepeau & Ruffman, 2006, p. 478). Moreover, a general caregiving style (warmth/sensitivity) is not associated with young children's performance on theory of mind tasks (although it is associated with their cooperative behavior), suggesting that what improves the young children's understanding is a specific type of talk rather than a general style (Ruffman et al., 2006).

When one stops to think about it, it is rather odd that in the false belief task the young child is usually asked about the beliefs of a doll or puppet! Dolls and puppets don't actually have beliefs, though psychologists seem to forget this. Dolls and puppets don't act in realistic ways, either. In such a task, what the young child is actually being asked to do is enter into a game of *pretense* with the researcher, a game in which beliefs are *attributed* to a toy, a material representation of a person. The false belief task, in its most common form, takes for granted a young child's ability to understand pretense.

We have seen that sociodramatic play in early childhood builds on the object-substitution pretense play in toddlerhood, which itself rests on the fact that some objects resemble other objects—something that toddlers learn to pay attention to as they learn the words of their language. When young children engage in pretend play together this is an activity in which they deliberately make claims about objects that are not true, and in that sense they create false beliefs which they can apparently understand. Seth doesn't really believe that he is a Laser Bat, but he is able to pretend that he is. What is the difference, exactly?

There is evidence to suggest that young children understand the distinction between what is pretend and what is real before they understand the distinction between appearance and reality (Flavell et al., 1987). For example, young children become able to engage in pretend play before they are able to successfully solve false-belief tasks (Lillard, 1993). This suggests that it may be in play that young children learn to master the distinction between true and false beliefs. It also suggests that the capacity to understand other people is based on a capacity for imagination.

It might seem obvious that when young children can solve the false-belief task, at around age 5, this is because they have begun to reason about beliefs and desires (Wellman, 2014).

However, there is evidence that these children still are not reasoning about beliefs, they are inferring an intention based on a specific situation. The primary evidence for this comes from the surprising finding that at the point when young children begin to pass standard false-belief tasks, they begin to fail "true-belief" tasks!

What I mean by this is that at the age (around 5 years) when young children will correctly say that Max will not look in the cupboard to which the candy was moved when he was not present, they will *not* say that he will look in the correct cupboard when the candy has been moved and then moved back to its original location! They answer randomly, and the percentage of children responding correctly drops to 50 percent.

This strange phenomenon was initially discovered by accident. It has subsequently been explored more carefully. For example, in one true-belief task Max watched his mother place candy in the red cupboard. During his absence, his sister took the candy out and considered moving it to the green cupboard, but then changed her mind and returned it to its original location. As Figure 10.3 shows, young children at the base of the U-shaped curve said that they did not know where Max would look when he returned. They said things like, "He didn't see his sister do it," or "He never knew where his sister put it" (Fabricius et al., 2010).

As Hedger and Fabricius point out, these findings suggest that young children acquire "an intermediate level of understanding" that is between the "reality reasoning" where what is seen is taken as real, and the "belief reasoning" characteristic of children in middle childhood. It seems that when young children start to solve false-belief tasks, they do not in fact yet understand false beliefs! The researchers conclude that children "do not acquire an understanding of beliefs, and hence a representational theory of mind, until after 6 years of age, or 2 years later than most developmental psychologists have concluded" (Hedger and Fabricius, 2011, p. 429).

What is this intermediate level? Fabricius proposes that these young children are paying attention to what a person does and does not see, and assume that the person's action will be based on this "perceptual access" (Fabricius et al., 2010, p. 1404). In this "perception–action reasoning" young children have discovered that seeing leads to knowing, which is an important milestone. They do not yet understand, however, that a person can form beliefs that do not correspond with what that person sees. In a false-belief task they infer that when Max hasn't seen where the candy has been moved he will be "wrong," and so they cannot predict where he will look. They infer ignorance, not a false belief.

These young children are, then, paying attention not only to what a person *does* see, but also to what the person *did* see. The fact that these young children are able to solve false-belief tasks shows that, in contrast to how they responded at age 3 (assuming that someone who wants candy will go where the candy in fact is), they now understand that someone can form an intention (to obtain candy) but then perform an action that will not in fact lead to that goal, because since the intention was formed (on the basis of specific knowledge and desires) the conditions have changed.

The young child has come to understand that an intention can be formed some time in advance of an action being performed. She has become able to attend to two conditions: the initial situation, in which Max formed his intention to get the candy, and the subsequent situation, in which Max's intention-in-action sometimes doesn't get him what he wants.

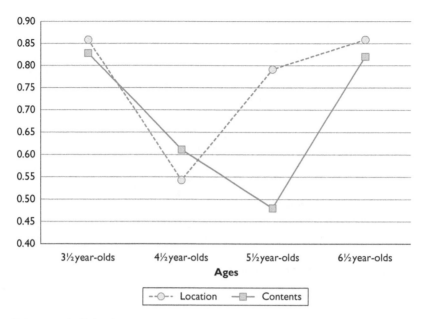

Figure 10.3 Failing true-belief tasks

Source: Hedger and Fabricius (2011)

Moreover, the U-shaped curve pattern of results in true-belief tasks shows that what is attributed to Max is not an intention based on a belief, in the adult sense. To an adult (at least a Western adult) a belief is a mental representation that is maintained over time, even when reality changes. In the true-belief task, the situation is changed and then "un-changed" while Max is absent. If he formed a belief it would still be true. When he returns, he should perform the correct action! But the young children say they do not know where he will look.

I suggest that the kind of intention these young children are attributing to Max is a *prior intention*. We saw in Chapter 7 that while an intention-in-action is visible *in* an action, a prior intention is a commitment to act that is made in advance of acting. In the example we used in that chapter, when we see James trying to open the window we might attribute to him a prior intention to get some fresh air. An adult could in addition infer that James also has beliefs and desires: for example, the belief that the air outside is cooler than the air inside, and the desire that this colder air enter the room so that he will be more comfortable.

A prior intention is formed on the basis of knowledge about a situation. When James forms a prior intention to let fresh air into the room this is based on his knowledge that the window is closed and the room is hot. If, however, the situation changes without his knowledge, his prior intention may no longer be relevant.

Of course, an adult can go further, and consider whether James's intentions might still be appropriate to the changed situation (as indeed they are in the true-belief task). This would require comparing

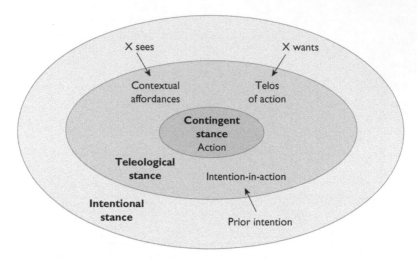

Figure 10.4 The intentional stance of early childhood

James's knowledge of the original situation (his beliefs) with the facts of the new situation. Evidently young children at the bottom of the U-shaped curve are unable to do this. They attribute intentions made in advance—prior intentions—but not yet enduring beliefs. Because the situation has changed, they conclude that his prior intention is no longer relevant, so they can't predict how he will act. They evidently cannot compare Max's beliefs with the current situation, because if they could, they would find that they correspond.

In short, these young children, at around 4½ years of age, have moved beyond the teleological stance, in which they understood actions in terms of intention-in-action, to understand **prior intention**, in what we can call the **intentional stance**. They infer a prior intention based on what the person sees in a specific situation, and what that person wants. If the situation changes, whether or not the person knows this, the young child assumes that the prior intention no longer holds.

1.4 THE CONVENTIONAL STANCE

Inferring someone's intentions—intention-in-action or prior intention—is not the only way to understand their actions. As we saw in Chapter 7, toddlers are able to understand actions also in terms of the customary norms of everyday activity. There is growing evidence that in early childhood young children become able to understand the conventions that apply to specific characters in recurrent scenarios.

For example, when one person says to another, "Hello, nice to see you!" it would be odd to try to explain this action in terms of their beliefs and desires. They are simply performing the conventional action in a familiar scenario. When someone asks you to stick out your tongue, it may be because that is what a doctor does with a patient, whether they like it or not. When someone hands over a candy, it may be because they have promised to do so. Personal desires, beliefs, and intentions are not the most important factors here. We again we see the importance of a "normative stance." As Henry Wellman and Joan Miller have noted:

> Particularly problematic, we believe, is that the traditional belief-desire framework portrays everyday psychology as an enterprise where behavior is conceptualized in freely chosen terms, with little attention given to the extent to which behavior is situated in a social-psychological context and may be undertaken in response to social rules, obligations, duties, and responsibilities that must inevitably also be at play. Equally, persons tend to be conceptualized exclusively as individual, autonomous agents, with little attention given to the extent to which they are social agents, whose psychological identity is socially based. Instead, beliefs and desires – and so the core of everyday psychology – are seen as exclusively self-directed, private states of unique individuals, satisfied by getting what one wants. (Welman & Miller, 2008, p. 107)

The authors argue that "a deontic focus is also required for an adequate characterization of everyday naive psychology and its development" (2008, p. 108). Even in the individualistic USA, nearly a quarter of the explanations that people give for everyday behavior refer to aspects of the social context (Miller, 1984). In other cultures, social role is much more important (Chinese, Japanese, Indian, etc.).

Is a psychological core necessary to understand obligation and permission? Some would argue that "deontic knowledge is (conceptually, for adults) inherently mentalistic" (Wellman & Miller, 2008, p. 109). I would disagree.

In obligation, some action is required. In permission, some action is allowed. In both cases, it is the normative character of social action that provides the basis.

Tomasello and colleagues have conducted a series of studies of how young children understand and respond to normativity—to norms of various kinds.

Recall the "daxing" study we described in Chapter 7. The 3-year olds in that study enthusiastically enforced the agreements that had been established in a simple game. Tomasello and Vaish (2013) propose that this illustrates the first of two steps in the ontogenesis of morality: an initial second-personal morality, evident in toddlers. This is followed, in their view, by a more norm-based morality in early childhood. The first of these steps illustrates nicely the continued role of the Great-We for toddlers. The evidence suggests that the second step, in early childhood, is a stage in which the norms that are understood are social conventions, agreements made among members of a group. For this reason, I am calling this the **conventional stance**. Tomasello and Vaish suggest that these two steps "take infants into a full-fledged human morality," but we shall see in the following chapters that additional steps are necessary.

In addition, in early childhood a distinction becomes drawn between transgression of these social conventions and moral transgressions. Young children understand and enforce agreements that are binding on the members of a group. On the other hand, they view harming anyone, not just a group member, as a different kind of transgression. They apply agreements to group members, and to themselves. Indeed, 3-year-olds will enforce agreements *only* on those children who actually entered into the agreement. And they only see an agreement as binding if there was complete consensus. If as few as 10 percent disagreed, the norm would not be considered established for anyone (Schmidt et al., 2016).

Young children enforce these agreements using generic normative language, rather than stating a personal preference: saying, "You can't do that!" They will actively intervene, including on behalf of a third party who is also a group member, when a agreement is violated. When someone outside the group is harmed, in contrast, they will respond on behalf of that person, and appeal to adults to sanction the wrongdoer. And 3- to 4-year-old young children are less likely to help someone who they have witnessed causing or intending to cause harm to another individual.

Between 3 and 5 years of age young children also show an increasing concern with equitable sharing, especially in contexts where they have obtained a reward from collaborating with peers.

The proposal that during early childhood there is a recognition of social conventions receives support from a study conducted by Larry Nucci and Eliott Turiel, which involved observations and interviews on the playground of 10 preschools, with attention given to actions that were responded to as violations, either by the teachers or the young children themselves (Nucci & Turiel, 1978).

Interviewed about events both they and the researchers had witnessed, the young children distinguished between moral transgressions and transgressions of conventions in a way that agreed with adult judges. Examples of social conventional transgressions included activities in a place or at a time designated for something else, diverging from the group in group activities, eating a snack while standing rather than sitting, and so on.

Events classified as moral, by both the children and the researchers, involved people's justice, welfare, or rights. Moral transgressions involved physical or psychological harm, such as intentional hitting, taking someone's possession, and failing to share with others.

Interestingly, while the young children recognized transgressions of social conventions, it was mainly adults who *responded* to such transgressions. Ninety-two percent of these events had an adult as the sole respondent, while 3 percent had a child as the sole respondent, and 5 percent had both adults and children as respondents. It seems that the young children recognized the school's conventions but treated them as matters for adult authority.

Adults responded to moral transgressions by explaining what had been wrong, and by talking about people's feelings, while they responded to transgressions of social conventions by focusing on features of social organization, such as commands, rules, sanctions, and disorder. The young children responded to moral transgressions generally as victims, with emotional reactions, expressions of injury or loss, physical responses, commands, and by involving the adults:

Communications between the children involved in moral events generally included statements about the injury or loss experienced by the victims of the transgressions. Physical reactions and responses expressing emotional reactions to the transgressions were also prevalent in the moral events. Moral transgressions also produced commands from the children to refrain from behaving in a given way. In sum, the children's responses revolved around the intrinsic consequences of the actions. (Nucci & Turiel, 1978, p. 406)

Nucci and Turiel concluded that social conventions and morality are understood as two distinct domains by children as young as 4 years of age.

However, it has to be noted that the adult judges who classified transgressions as either moral or social conventional were of the same Northern California culture as the children. What was viewed as a convention there might be considered as a moral matter in another cultural setting. In Chapter 12 we will look at research with older children exploring the issue of cultural variation in morality.

Vygotsky also saw early childhood as a stage of growing understanding of social conventions. For example, he described two sisters, aged 5 and 7, playing together. One suggested to the other, "Let's play sisters." It might seem odd that two sisters would play at being sisters, since this would be playing at being what they already are—imagining what is already in fact true. But Vygotsky argued that playing in this way provided the young girls with an opportunity to explore the conventions and obligations of sisterhood in general, as opposed to the responsibilities of their particular relationship. To understand why they would do this it is important to recognize that in everyday life a young child would never need to think of herself as being her sister's sister. She knows her sister not as "sister" but as a particular person within her family. Even when her parents say "Share with your sister" she has little reason to reflect on the character of the relationship of brother and sister as these have been defined in her specific culture.

However, such awareness grows during early childhood. The play of these two girls explored the rights and responsibilities of the kinship type of "sister." The girls' play was about *trying* to be sisters, about being *ideal* sisters. They explored what sisters conventionally do, something that goes unexamined in everyday life, so as to bring it to conscious awareness. The "conventions" of sociodramatic play enact, explore, and clarify the specific concerns of real life. Play, then, is an opportunity to become conscious of the conventions and responsibilities of kinship of a specific culture.

Paying attention to social conventions provides a way for a young child to understand and explain people's actions without needing to form theories about beliefs and desires (Rakoczy & Schmidt, 2013), and to build upon the understanding of customary behavior that they acquired as toddlers.

There is also evidence that young children begin to understand, and arrange, agreements and bargains. For example, in one experiment British and Nepalese young children aged between 3 and 7 were told stories in which two protagonists agreed to an exchange of mutual benefit. For example:

> This is a story about Susan and Simon. Look—Susan has a green brick to play with and Simon has a gray brick to play with. They say that they'll do a swap. Susan says that she'll let Simon play with her brick if Simon let's her play with his. And Simon says that he'll let Susan play with his brick if Susan let's him play with hers. (Harris et al., 2001, p. 756)

They were then shown pictures that illustrated four possible outcomes: (1) both children still holding their original item; (2) the girl in possession of both items; (3) the boy in possession of both items; (4) each child holding the other's original item. The young children were able to accurately identify (1) when either protagonist had reneged on the agreement (been "naughty") and (2) when both protagonists had kept the agreement. Apparently they could understand the obligations that are established by making an agreement, and they recognized how people who have entered into an agreement are bound by its terms.

The fact is that agreements—promises, "making a deal"—become salient during the stage of early childhood. It makes sense that this coincides with understanding prior intentions, for a prior intention can be considered an agreement that one makes with oneself. And it is during early childhood—as we shall see in the next section—that young children begin to formulate plans in advance; that is, to make agreements with themselves.

These researchers—María Núñez and Paul Harris—also explored the linkages between young children's understanding of other people and their understanding of "deontic concepts" (Núñez & Harris, 1998). (Deontic means concerning duty and obligation.) They pointed out that if someone apparently transgresses a convention (or a moral prescription, for that matter) it is generally important to assess their intentions, for "a deliberate failure to meet an obligation is blameworthy whereas an accidental failure is not" (1998, p. 157). Piaget had proposed that young children ignore intentions and judge a violation only in terms of its consequences: for example, judging it worse to break ten plates accidentally than one plate deliberately.

However, in an experiment with a similar methodology to their research on agreements, Núñez and Harris found that young children aged 3 and 4 from Cali, Colombia, and Oxford, England, responded similarly when they heard stories about "conditional permission" rules made by a parent, followed by pictures of four possible outcomes. For example:

This is a story about Sally. One day Sally wants to play outside. Her Mum says that if she plays outside she must keep her hat on.

Here's Sally playing outdoors. Look! She's taken her hat off!

Or: Here's Sally playing outdoors. The wind has blown her hat off!

The young children typically chose the deliberate transgression as the one that was naughty, showing that they had paid attention both to the social conventional permission and Sally's intentions. As the researchers concluded, "the interpretation of an agent's action cannot draw exclusively on psychological concepts; it has to be informed by an appreciation of naive physics on the one hand and deontic obligation on the other" (1998, p. 168).

Indeed, there is evidence that young children pay *more* attention to deontic matters than to psychological ones. In one experiment, stories were told in which the subject was described with a novel category label (e.g., "a Lissian") or with an individual proper name (e.g., "Lisa"). Preschool-age children were more attentive to the normative properties of the social categories, while it was younger school-age children who were more attentive to the psychological properties of individuals (Kalish, 2012).

In short, it seems that young children's understanding of other people's actions is based on a practical grasp of agreements among members of a group, and that "in order to develop the capacity to have beliefs about others' mental states, one must first have a grasp of these basic embodied practices.

Moreover, embodied intersubjectivity continues to be our principal mode of social interaction even in adulthood" (Spaulding, 2014, p. 198).

It has been proposed that activity settings are scenarios provide children with **deontic affordances** that indicate to a young child not only "what I *can* do," but also "what I *should* do." They are "observable, *shared*, *public* opportunities for perception and action … Unlike mental states, generally characterized as internal, hidden, and unobservable properties of minds, deontic affordances are entirely out there, in the open, to be perceived" (Kaufmann & Clément, 2014, p. 8).

These deontic affordances "enable social perceivers to *fore*-see what will or should happen next" and "are the perceptual basis of the deontic inferences" people make all the time in their social relationships.

Another proposal is that the stories young children love provide them with lessons in how to understand how *types* of persons act, and why. Daniel Hutto (2011) suggests that children acquire the ability to make sense of what it is to act for a reason by engaging in narrative practices:

> Stories like 'Little Red Riding Hood' and 'Goldilocks and the Three Bears' are paradigmatic folk-psychological narratives. The narratives provide exemplars of how agents act according to reasons in order to attain some goal. The child and her caretaker jointly attend to the narrative, and through guided interaction with a caretaker, the child becomes acquainted with forms and norms of acting for reasons. (Spaulding, 2014, p. 199)

In a similar line of reasoning, anthropologist Laurence Hirschfeld argues that what he calls "Theory of Society" is more important than "theory of mind," because it is a "generally more 'accurate' strategy for predicting and interpreting the actions of others." Hirschfeld argues that theory of mind:

> despite the attention it has received and the importance attributed to it, is ultimately of sharply limited utility in interpreting and predicting the behavior of others in both the contemporary world and the sociocultural environments in which mentalizing evolved. (Hirschfeld, 2013, p. 101)

Hirschfeld goes on to propose that "humans are in fact quite poor at appraising what others and indeed what we ourselves are thinking and feeling," but we "excel at interpreting and predicting behavior in terms of unseen social and cultural (nonmental) qualities (ranging from 'fixed' qualities such as gender and race, to 'variable' ones such as age, rank, or occupation, and to 'episodic' or transient ones such as coalition partner or teammate)" (2011, p. 101).

Overall, it seems entirely possible that deontic matters (such as customary practices, characters, and conventional scenarios) play the central role in young children's understanding of other people, while attention to intentions, beliefs, and desires may play a smaller part (Kalish & Shiverick, 2004). Certainly, developmental researchers are paying growing attention to the ways that "behavior is situated in a social-psychological context and may be undertaken in response to social rules, obligations, duties, and responsibilities that must inevitably also be at play" (Wellman & Miller, 2008, p. 103).

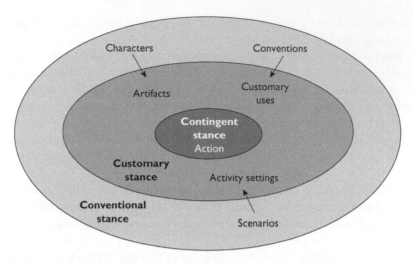

Figure 10.5   The conventional stance of early childhood

	Moral	**Conventional**
Early childhood 3y–5y	• *Intentional stance*: understand prior intentions. • Understand morality as harming anyone, not just a group member. • Respond to harm on behalf of third party • Use normative language, with generic terms ("You can't do that"). • Appeal to adults to sanction wrongdoer. • Apply moral norms to themselves.	• *Conventional stance*: understand & enforce conventions as agreements binding on members of a group (characters in scenarios). • Apply conventions only to group members. • Apply these conventions to themselves. • Actively intervene, including on behalf of third party, when a convention is violated. • Use normative language, with generic terms ("You can't do that").

Figure 10.6   Understanding of morality and of social conventions in early childhood

2. CARING FOR THE YOUNG CHILD

> The notion of parents, especially of mothers, as the necessary source of children's current and later personal stability does not hold cross-culturally nor, for that matter, historically. Much more research is needed in this domain. (Ambert, 1994, p. 531)

This section is titled "Caring for the young child" rather than "Parenting the young child" because early childhood is often a time when people outside the immediate family contribute markedly to childcare, as do older children within the family. Anthropologist Margaret Mead called infants "lap children," toddlers "knee children," and 4- and 5-year-olds "yard children," because although the latter are not allowed to wander too far away, they can leave the immediate vicinity of their primary caregivers.

Mead's comparison of different societies also helps us question some of our basic assumptions about young children: for example, that they have fixed names, live with their parents, and are clearly of a distinct generation. Mead wrote about childhood in the islands of Samoa in the South Seas:

> Samoan children's names change often, at the whim of any relative. As soon as they are old enough, they are allowed to choose new ones for themselves upon any occasion. And similarly they choose their own homes, living now with a grandmother, now with an uncle. Families are not made up of father and mother and children, but of some fifteen or twenty relatives among whom there is no oldest child, because a young aunt or cousin will be nearly of an age, among whom the same child is never 'youngest' for long. And in these great households the mothers take little care of their children after the babies learn to crawl. The nurses are not young girls but toddling five-year-olds, who trundle about on their hips babies that are too heavy to be lifted into their arms. (Mead, 2008, p. 23)

A young child in Samoa will be asked to contribute to the care of her younger siblings, and she is considered old enough to change her own name and even to pick who she lives with! Such a young child will have no toys to play with, not even a doll. She will be expected to sweep and tidy up the house. This doesn't mean that life is dull, however:

> Yet they have their games, playing at ball with square light balls made of pandanus [the fruit of a local tree], stringing necklaces of flowers, playing round games to merry songs of their own improvising in the dusk. (Mead, 2008, p. 23)

Young children in Samoa play together, just as young children do in the USA. But the way in which they are taken care of is very different.

The goals for caregivers and the tasks facing them change as a child reaches the early childhood stage. In many cultures the primary goal during the first year is simply an infant's survival, and during toddlerhood it is ensuring safety. As the term "caregiver" suggests, adults everywhere try to promote the survival and success of offspring, but we have seen that the way they do this is adapted to their specific socioeconomic and demographic conditions (LeVine, 1988). In places with high rates of infant mortality caregivers tend to keep their infants close to them, respond rapidly when they cry, and nurse them frequently. They also tend not to engage the infant in vocal play or elicit smiles from them. Caregivers in agrarian and in urban-industrial societies will behave differently, and local cultural traditions will result in further differentiation. And when local circumstances threaten these goals, caregivers will modify their strategies.

The strategies that caregivers use to achieve their goals for young children, as distinct from their infants or toddlers, need to change. Caregivers can now use more indirect tactics to influence a young child's behavior, such as reasoning with her and appealing to her understanding of norms, rules, and expectations. After the transition at age 3 the young child has now differentiated psychologically from adults, developing self-consciousness in part by opposing them, at least in societies that value independence. She is gaining the ability to control her own actions and impulses, she asserts herself more often, and she begins to plan activities, make up games, and initiate activities with others. At this age, caregivers in many cultures begin to expect the young child to contribute to the organization and order of the household, and to behave appropriately in a range of situations (LeVine et al., 2008, p. 57).

Erik Erikson considered the central conflict of this stage to be between initiative and guilt. Young children are acting increasingly assertively, especially with peers. Caregivers, however, may interpret this as aggression, and if they respond with criticism or attempt to control their child, the young child, in Erikson's view, would develop enduring guilt and a sense of "being a nuisance."

As we shall see, however, researchers have identified distinct goals that are considered appropriate by caregivers in different cultures. Some caregivers will try to encourage their young child's autonomy. Others will encourage obedience and interdependence. Others will allow the young child to do what she wishes, letting her development take its own course. Many parents in the USA—though by no means all—emphasize independence and autonomy, and psychologists trained in the West have often focused on this characteristic. As we have seen, however, this is not a universal trajectory of development.

2.1 STYLES OF CAREGIVING

A very influential research project on the character of caregiving during early childhood was conducted by Diana Baumrind, who studied families of young children in Northern California.

Baumrind was interested in exploring differences in the ways caregivers respond to a young child and try to influence her behavior, and in exploring the psychological consequences of these differences. She observed parents interacting with their young children and focused on the ways in which parent and young child made bids for control. The following is an example of an interaction in which a young child makes a demand of the parent who fails to comply, although the young child uses increasingly greater power:

> JOHN: "Can I go out?"
> MOTHER: "Yes. Oh no, I guess you can't. I didn't realize how late it was."
> JOHN: "Please, Mother. (*Crying, beseeching, being terribly cute.*) I never get to go down the street."
> MOTHER: "No dear."

On the basis of observations such as these, Baumrind identified three distinct styles of parental control: permissive, authoritarian, and authoritative.

The **permissive** parent is accepting and positive, and does not punish the child's actions or desires. Such parents make few demands of their young child. They explain family rules and involve the young child in decisions. The young child has few responsibilities around the house, and is not expected to be orderly or especially well-behaved. The permissive parent is a resource for the child, rather than an ideal to be emulated, and does not believe that it is necessary to shape or change the young child's behavior and attitude. The child is permitted to act as she pleases whenever possible, and the permissive parent avoids trying to control, or to impose explicit rules and standards. Instead this kind of parent tries to use reason, and sometimes manipulation, but not overt power.

The **authoritarian** parent, in contrast, applies a fixed standard of conduct to the young child. Such parents see obedience as a virtue, and they are in favor of punishment and force when their child seems disobedient or willful. When the young child does something that the parent views as inappropriate, the authoritarian parent will put her in her place, restricting the child's autonomy and imposing tasks as punishment. The parent believes that young children should not talk back, and that a parent's decision is final and should be accepted. Such a parent makes strong demands on their young child, using force and punishment when necessary to impose these demands, and will withdraw affection and intrude psychologically when the young child misbehaves.

Finally, the **authoritative** parent tries to direct the young child by using reason, and by encouraging discussion about what is right and wrong. Such a parent explains the reasons behind decisions, and asks the child for her point of view when there is disagreement. The parent values both disciplined conformity and autonomous self-will, and so although the parent exerts firm control they do not unduly restrict the child. The parent recognizes that the young child has her own perspective, as well as individual interests and characteristics. The authoritative parent validates the young child in the present but also sets standards for her future behavior, using both reason and rules to achieve these objectives. This parent does not base decisions on consensus or on the child's wishes, but instead provides reasons for the demands that are made of the young child, and is generally consistent in enforcing these demands and explaining them.

Baumrind argued that what is optimal for the young child's development is a style of parenting that steers between the extremes of a hierarchical authoritarianism that focuses on obedience, on the one hand, and a permissive attitude that lets the young child get away with anything, on the other hand. The *authoritative* style of parenting provides this synthesis of the two extremes. Her prediction was that "authoritative control can achieve responsible conformity with group standards without loss of individual autonomy or self-assertiveness" (Baumrind, 1966, p. 905). Subsequent studies have largely borne out her prediction.

Baumrind herself explored the relationship between the style of parents' caregiving and the characteristics of their young children. She identified three groups of young children (average age 47 months) enrolled in a nursery school. Observations showed that some young children were assertive, self-reliant, and self-controlled. The second group were children observed to be unhappy and disaffiliated. The third group were young children observed to be dependent on others, with poor control over their impulses. Home visits were then conducted, including observations of parent–child interactions and interviews with the parents. Young children in the first group were found to have parents who were demanding but communicative and loving. Parents of the second group were relatively controlling and detached; and parents of the third group were non-controlling, non-demanding, and relatively warm. In other words, the first group of young children tended to have parents with the authoritative style, while those in the second group tended to have authoritarian parents, and those in the third group tended to have permissive parents.

In her longitudinal research program the *Family Socialization and Developmental Competence Project*, Baumrind went on to explore the linkages between patterns of parenting and outcomes at school age and adolescence (see later chapters).

One of the strengths of Baumrind's research is that she did not view caregiving simply as socialization, as having as its goal only the young child's conformity to social norms. Baumrind recognized that the young child is still acquiring the ability to control her own actions, and so parents must act as the superego of their young child, acting in a sense as her conscience (we saw that Bowlby also made this suggestion). Baumrind's view was that optimal childrearing leads both to moral character—the capacity to *will* the good—and moral competence—the capacity to *do* the good. She insisted that children are born neither wicked nor good: they have both moral feelings and destructive impulses, and their character is formed in their interactions with caregiving adults, interactions in which the adults have more power to control what is going on than do the children. In these interactions, the internal structure of the young child's conscience is formed, and ideally she develops accountability, persistence, and self-discipline. Good caregiving will involve helping, solidarity, compassion, and generosity.

Viewed this way, parenting is about *emancipating* a young child, encouraging her consciousness and her ability to exercise responsibility. Responsibility, here, is not simply a matter of conforming to rules about what is right and wrong, but freely choosing to do what is considered to be right, and for the right reasons. It would be a mistake, then, to view authoritative parenting as some psychologists have done, as no more than "an instrumental competence characterized by the balancing of societal and individual needs and responsibilities" (Darling & Steinberg, 1993). Caregivers have to protect their children. But they also have to protect their culture—both *for* their children, and at times *from* their children.

Baumrind was indeed focused on the kind of caregiving control that seemed most likely to foster independence and autonomy. She argued that:

> the infant is enslaved by virtue of his ignorance, his dependence upon others for sustenance, and his lack of self-control. The experience of infantile omnipotence, if such he has, is based on ignorance and illusion. His is the freedom to be irresponsible, a freedom reserved for the very young child and the incompetent. (Baumrind, 1966, p. 903)

The young child is certainly less dependent than the infant or toddler, but she still needs the guidance of a caregiver to help decide what to do. In Baumrind's interpretation, this means that the caregiver is an authority in the sense of being "a person whose expertness befits him [or her] to designate a behavioral alternative for another whether the alternatives are perceived by both" (Baumrind, 1966, p. 887). Her view was that if a young child is to become able to act responsibly and autonomously, neither the **assertion of power** nor the **withdrawal of love** is an appropriate style of parenting. The withdrawal of love had been described as a powerful aspect of parenting in Russia (Bronfenbrenner, 1970). Baumrind argued that the young child needs to learn how to dissent, to disagree, in an appropriate way, because it is only by exercising her will that she will become capable of "responsible (i.e., chosen) action" (Baumrind, 1966, p. 904).

Similarities exist between Baumrind's views and Erikson's description of the conflict of early childhood: between initiative and guilt. Erikson proposed that if given the opportunity, a young child will develop a sense of initiative, and feel secure in her ability to lead others and make decisions. Conversely, if this tendency is squelched, either through adult criticism or control, the young child will develop a sense of guilt. She may come to feel that she is a nuisance to other people and will consequently remain a follower rather than a leader, lacking in self-initiative.

As Baumrind pointed out, it is important to remember that there have been the historical changes in the practices American (USA) parents have used to influence their children, based on views of children which have changed over time.

Permissive Parent	Characteristics of Young Child
+ Attempts to behave in a nonpunitive, acceptant, and affirmative manner. + Makes few demands for household responsibility. + Presents herself to the child as a resource for him to use. + She allows the child to regulate his own activities as much as possible. + Attempts to use reason and manipulation, but not overt power.	Dependent on others, poor control over their impulses

Figure 10.7 Permissive parenting style

Authoritarian Parent	Characteristics of Young Child
+ Attempts to shape and control the child in accordance with a set standard of conduct. + Values obedience and favors forceful punishment. + Believes in keeping the child in his place, restricting his autonomy, and assigning household responsibilities. + Believes that the child should accept her word for what is right.	Unhappy and disaffiliated

Figure 10.8 Authoritarian parenting style

Authoritative Parent	Characteristics of Young Child
+ Attempts to direct the child's activities in a rational, issue-oriented manner. + Encourages discussion, shares reasoning behind her policies, and solicits the child's objections when he refuses to conform. + Values autonomous self-will and disciplined conformity. + Enforces her own perspective, but recognizes the child's individual interests and special ways. + Uses reason, power, and reinforcement to achieve her objectives.	Assertive, self-reliant, and self-controlled

Figure 10.9 Authoritative parenting style

It has been suggested that the three parenting styles that Baumrind identified can usefully be arranged on two dimensions, *responsiveness* and *demandingness* (Maccoby & Martin, 1983). Responsiveness refers to efforts to foster a young child's individuality, self-regulation, and self-assertion, by being supportive and attuned. Demandingness refers to efforts to supervise, discipline, and confront a disobedient child (Baumrind, 1991).

In this analysis, authoritative parents are high on both dimensions, while authoritarian parents are high in demandingness but low in responsiveness. This dimensional approach distinguishes two types of parenting where Baumrind's identified only one. In place of the permissive style we can now distinguish between **indulgent** parents, who are high in responsiveness but low in demandingness, and **neglecting** parents, who are low in both responsiveness and demandingness.

By Baumrind's definition, Bofi parents in Central Africa are authoritarian: they value obedience and respect and exercise considerable control over their children. However, their children are not withdrawn and aggressive, as the research findings based on Western samples suggest. Instead, they show initiative and empathy (Fouts & Lamb, 2005).

2.2 EMANCIPATION OR COMPLIANCE AS A GOAL OF CHILDCARE?

A central issue that faces developmental science is how to grasp the multiplicity and diversity of human cultures. As I explained in Chapter 1, researchers have looked for ways to grasp and conceptualize this diversity. A well-known and popular approach has been to distinguish between "individualistic" and "collectivist" cultures, and there is surely validity to the criticism that psychology has often unquestioningly adopted a Western-centric focus on individual agency and autonomy. Individualism tends to be unquestioningly considered the norm, and it is exported around the world as the only healthy model of human development. Individualism tends to be treated as natural, even biologically based, even though many theories of human evolution have stressed the importance of cooperation.

Such a view, however, tends to confuse *autonomy* (being separate from other people) with *agency* (acting effectively). Being an independent individual is not the only way to have agency. Presumably *both* connection with other people and agency are necessary in human life, and necessary in children's development, and every culture must find a way to combine these two considerations. In addition, a sense of agency might arise not only from "individuation"—becoming an independent individual—but also from being related and connected to other people. Cigdem Kağitcibaşi has proposed that we consider the degree of connection amongst people (interpersonal distance) and the capacity to act effectively (agency) as two orthogonal dimensions (Kağitcibaşi, 2005). If we then treat each dimension as dichotomous this would define **four kinds** of childcare context, each of which involves a distinct **developmental trajectory**.

Kağitcibaşi has pointed out that there is a global tendency towards urbanization—families from traditional settings are moving into urban settings. This change in setting motivates a transformation in family dynamics: traditional patterns of interdependence among the generations of the family are no longer adaptive. It becomes less important that family members provide each other with economic assistance, though psychological interdependence continues to be valued. Autonomy is now considered important in the children, in part because it is an asset in the new social context. Children need to become autonomous to be successful in the big city. However, this autonomy is fostered and encouraged through close connections in the family. In the new urban setting, parents tend to remain controlling rather than permissive (though not in a way that should be considered authoritarian).

The result is a new kind of self: an *autonomous-related self*, a person who is capable of autonomous agency but maintains strong family connections. This has been described as "a dialectical synthesis" of the two more familiar kinds of family organization, and as something that psychologists should acknowledge and find ways to facilitate:

There is a need for professionals to be more culturally sensitive and to develop a more encompassing understanding of healthy self-other relationships, involving control, autonomy, and connectedness, rather than separation. (Kağitcibaşi, 2005, p. 416)

I described in Chapter 3 some of the ways of categorizing different cultures. One well-known approach has been to distinguish cultures that foster independence from those that foster interdependence.

A more recent approach, however, is to treat independence and interdependence as two independent *dimensions*, both of which are important in every culture. Turkish psychologist Cigdem Kağitcibaşi has suggested we should distinguish four different kinds of sociocultural context, each of which fosters a "family model" with specific practices of childcare and with distinct goals for how children will develop independence and interdependence.

1. **Interdependent Family Model**. This family model emphasizes interdependence and obedience. It corresponds to the proximal caregiving style that we witness among the Nso. For families in traditional rural farming societies, but also for poorer families in urban settings, interdependence among the generations is crucial. Children are a valuable resource for their parents, and they will need to contribute to the family's economic and social activities. Family size tends to be large, and siblings support and care for one other. As parents get older they become increasingly dependent on their children, so interconnection continues to be emphasized. Interdependence is encouraged rather than independence, and autonomy in a child can be seen as a threat, so that parenting tends to emphasize obedience. Obedience is in fact adaptive when children will take on simple agricultural or manual labor as they grow up. This interdependent family model has been found in large parts of Asia, in traditional cultures, as well as among ethnic migrants in Western societies. It is also found in poorer groups in the West, such as lower-income African Americans

2. **Independent Family Model**. This family model emphasizes autonomy and independence. It corresponds to the distal style of caregiving, found in many Western nuclear families, which tend to value independence and self-sufficiency. Greater economic resources and higher levels of education mean that older adults are unlikely to become dependent on their children, and may even view such dependence as unacceptable. Children represent a cost to the family rather than a resource, so family size is smaller and each child receives focused attention from their parents. The child's autonomy is not viewed as a threat to the family; instead it is valued and encouraged. The goal of parenting tends to be the child's separation from the family, to establish their own independent nuclear family.

It is often assumed that there is a general historical movement from the interdependent family to the independent family, as economic development and urbanization increase. However, while this may occur in some circumstances, there is evidence that in many circumstances a third model is emerging, the *autonomous relatedness* family model. A global tendency for traditional families with patterns of generational interdependence to move to urban settings has created the conditions for a transformation in family dynamics. In many parts of the world—such as Japan, Taiwan, and Singapore—urbanization and economic development have taken place without a shift towards individualism.

3. **Autonomous Relatedness Family Model**. This family model emphasizes both autonomy and interdependence or connection. It is typical of a family that has moved from the countryside to the city. With the increasing affluence that often comes from participating in a wage economy, intergenerational economic and material support within the family may no longer be necessary. However, members of the family will continue to value their connection and emotional interdependence, so that psychological interdependence continues to be valued in their children. At the same time, there is space for children to develop autonomy, because this is no longer considered to be a threat to family survival. On the contrary, autonomy, as a characteristic of the children, has value to the family because both school and workplace require individual decision making. Parents continue to exert control, but children understand this as a sign of involvement and support, rather than as authoritarian manipulation. Both relatedness and autonomy are encouraged, rather than obedience. In addition, the overall goal of parenting is not that the child's will ultimately separate from the family.

In addition, Kağitcibaşi has proposed that in their new setting, mutual economic assistance among family members becomes less important but psychological interdependence remains valued. Autonomy is encouraged in young children, in part because it is an asset in the new social context, but it emerges on the basis of a continued emotional connection within the family. Parenting tends to be controlling rather than permissive, though not in a way that can be considered authoritarian.

One difficulty with such a conceptualization of developmental trajectories, however, is that it seems to suggest that parents and families define the same pathway for their boy and girl children. However, we first introduced the term "trajectory" in our discussion of the formation of two (or more) sexes in

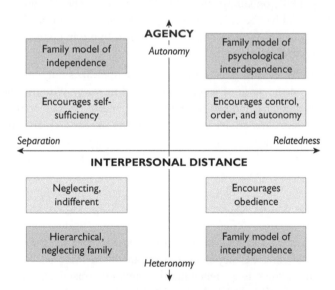

Figure 10.10   Dimensions of agency and interpersonal distance, and the four family models that they define

Source: Kağitcibaşi, 2005

prenatal development, and the subsequent assignment of one of two (or more) genders to the infant. Talk of family models risks ignoring the fact that caregivers often have quite different, if complementary, goals for boys and girls as they grow to adulthood. In many societies, parents expect their boys to become more independent, and their girls more interdependent.

We would expect, then, that parents would interact differently with children of different genders. In addition, birth order often implies a trajectory. In some cultures, for example, the youngest daughter is expected to remain at home and take care of her parents as they age. Older daughters, in contrast, are encouraged to marry and form their own households.

One of the puzzles with the research on caregiving styles and family model is the lack of any finding so far of differences in how caregivers treat their boy and girl babies. As we shall see in section 3, there is every reason to think that caregivers treat young boys and girls differently, precisely on these goals of independence and interdependence.

The concept of trajectory needs to be used carefully. We want to avoid the traditional conception of culture as static, homogeneous, and bounded. In fact, cultures are dynamic, contested, and assembled, and this implies that the assumption that there is a single developmental trajectory common to all children in all families in a common setting must be questioned.

Rather than treating the dimensions of interpersonal distance and agency as dichotomous, it may make more sense to see each of them as a continuum. This would mean that, conceptually, there are not simply four possible types of families, but rather four spaces within which each family could be positioned. However, if we were to go to the extreme and presume that each family, and perhaps each child within that family, has a unique developmental trajectory, generalization would become very difficult.

In the next chapter I will describe some of the developmental consequences of these different styles of caregiving, as well as Kağitcibaşi's proposal that these developmental trajectories lead to the formation of different kinds of self.

2.3 PARENTING RESEARCH TODAY

Comparative research, that is to say studies of parenting in other animal species, especially in non-human primates, has demonstrated that there is a wide variation in caregiving practices across species, as well as large individual differences within species. It has also shown us the importance of considering the *interaction* between parent and child at different ages, and the effect of the situation on this interaction (Hoffman et al., 1982).

Researchers studying human caregiving have, as a consequence, moved towards a more "interactional" model, in which caregiving is seen not as a one-way influence of adult on the young child but a process of mutual adaption. There is general agreement that the influence between child and caregiver flows both ways, that the family is not an isolated unit but part of a larger network, and that young children's behavior is a consequence of genetically based temperamental factors as well as their parenting. There is also recognition that caregiving changes with the age and developmental stage of the child, and that fathers are just as influential parental figures as mothers (Lamb & Lewis, 2011). It remains to be seen what impact this reconceptualization has on attachment theory, on categorizations of caregiving style, and on the theory of family models.

3. THE ORIGINS OF VERBAL THINKING

We saw in Chapter 9 that the young child's skills with oral language develop considerably during early childhood, and the ways that speech is *used* change considerably. Using the ideational and interpersonal metafunctions, the young child is both doing and interpreting. She starts to use speech to organize and direct her own actions. In this sense, as we shall see, speech is the first form of *verbal thinking*.

In Piaget's view, the egocentrism of early childhood is illustrated not only by the lack of visual perspective taking in situations such as the three mountains task, but also by the character of young children's talk, which he called **egocentric speech**. In this section we will compare and contrast the views of Piaget and Vygotsky, and see that they offered very different interpretations of young children's speech and its role in psychological development.

3.1 SELF-DIRECTED SPEECH

It is a common observation that young children are constantly chattering, talking about what they are doing. They don't even need to have an audience; they will chatter on even if no one else is around. This **self-directed speech** seems to be a very important aspect of development in early childhood.

Piaget noticed this kind of speech during his earliest research with young children, and it became a central part of his first theories about development. As I mentioned in the previous chapter, he called this chattering **egocentric speech**, and he proposed that it illustrated the way a young child's thinking is not yet socialized and is centered on the self, and even at times verging on the autistic (not in the clinical sense, but in the sense that a very young child, Piaget argued, is completely in her own world). Piaget proposed that the young child's egocentric *thinking* is evident in her egocentric *speech*. Preschoolers tend to engage in **collective monologues** in which although there appears to be a conversation among them, each young child is in fact talking about their own interests. Consequently, according to Piaget, when a preschooler speaks it is not really in order to to communicate.

In his earliest books, Piaget proposed that if she is to become able to think logically the young child needs to be socialized. It is only in contact with other people and discussion, he argued, that she is forced to recognize the subjective character of her own thoughts, and modify her thinking to fit with adult logic.

As we have seen, Piaget believed that in early childhood young children must learn to recognize three distinctions: the distinction between objects and signs, the distinction between what is internal to her mind (mental states) and what is external (the material world), and the distinction between thought and matter. For Piaget, accepting these dualisms is part of adapting to reality and a step towards thinking logically and scientifically.

The baby: a biological individual ⟶	the force of socialization ⟶	The social adult
inner, autistic thinking and fantasy	egocentric thinking	logical thinking
absence of speech	egocentric speech	social speech

Figure 10.11   Piaget's early view of the socialization of children's thinking

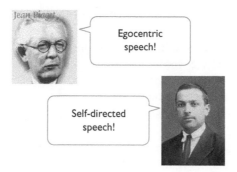

Figure 10.12 A difference of opinion about young children's speech

Vygotsky, in contrast, argued that Piaget had missed the point about the seemingly egocentric speech of young children, and had explained it backwards. It is not the case, Vygotsky suggested, that a young child is not yet social. On the contrary, her chattering to herself shows that she is not yet individual.

Vygotsky argued that the kind of talking that young children engage in when they are alone is not egocentric speech, it is **self-directed speech**. As we have seen, he insisted that children are social from birth and do not need to be socialized. He argued in addition that what this phenomenon shows us is the important role that oral language plays in the development of thinking. Early childhood, he proposed, is the stage in which thinking becomes verbal, and speech becomes intellectual.

Vygotsky carried out a series of studies in which young children were engaged in practical activities such as free drawing or painting. The researchers introduced some simple obstacles to the young children's activity: for example, they arranged that the child did not have to hand the colored pencil, or the paper, that she needed. As Vygotsky put it, "we experimentally caused disturbances and difficulties in the free flow of the child's activity."

The researchers found that when the young child found herself faced with such difficulties, she talked to herself! The greater the difficulty, the greater the amount of self-directed speech. There was every indication that this speech was an attempt to make sense of the situation in words and find a solution to the problem. The obstacle had produced a goal for the young child's activity. It was not simply that the young child was motivated to overcome an obstacle in order to achieve a pre-existing goal; the goal had not even existed until the obstacle was encountered. Once the obstacle defined a goal, the young child's psychological functions were exercised and improved in her efforts to achieve that goal.

Furthermore, this self-directed speech changed as the young child became older. Initially it occurred during points when she was changing direction in her practical activity, or when the activity was completed. With time, however, the self-directed speech shifted towards the start of the activity, and increasingly it took on the function of planning and directing her actions.

The same happened when problems arose independent of the researchers. For example, one boy aged 5½ years was drawing a streetcar (a kind of bus that runs on rails). He pressed heavily on his pencil to draw a circle for one of the wheels and the point broke. The child muttered to himself, "It's broken." Then he put the pencil to one side and picked up a brush and paints, and proceeded to paint a wrecked railroad car, being repaired after an accident. He continued to make comments to himself about the change in the subject of his drawing.

In this case the young child seems to have followed his own words, hearing them as though they were instructions. When he spoke the words "It's broken" this was a comment, a description, of what had just happened to his pencil. When he *heard* his own words, however, they functioned as a direction, an instruction or suggestion, about what to draw next.

Self-directed speech, then, occurs when a young child is trying to solve a problem. At first the child talks to herself after a problem occurs, to try to decide what to do next. Over time, she begins to speak to herself before beginning an activity, to form a plan in advance. In short, self-directed speech is a form of thinking; it is "thinking out loud." Vygotsky's interpretation was that the young child's talking to herself, her self-directed speech, is the first appearance of true verbal thinking, over and above the practical intelligence of sensorimotor understanding.

Of course, every adult talks to themself on occasion. We tend to think that to do so is a little crazy, but in fact this is not the case. The Japanese Industrial Safety and Health Association found that speaking out loud to oneself is a powerful technique for preventing errors. They studied workers on the trains in Japan, and found that vocalizations and gestures directed to oneself heightened the workers' mental focus at key points on the job where accidents were likely to occur. Workers asked to complete a simple task made 2.38 errors per 100 actions when no special steps were taken to prevent errors. When told to add just calling or just pointing, their error rate dropped significantly. But the greatest reduction in error—to just 0.38 mistakes per 100 actions—was achieved when workers used both steps together. The combination of pointing and calling reduced mistakes by almost 85 percent (see Table 7.1).

The technique of pointing and calling is now required on Japanese trains. Let's say the worker's task is to make sure a valve is open. The worker has to look directly at the valve and confirm that it is open, and then call out in a clear voice, "Valve open!" Then, still looking at the valve, the worker draws back their right hand, points to the valve in an exaggerated way and calls out, "OK!" This technique is called *shisa kanko*, which in English means "pointing and calling."

	Neither Pointing nor Calling	Calling Alone, or Pointing Alone	Both Together
Error rate:	2.38 per 100	1.50 per 100	0.38 per 100

Figure 10.13 Findings from the Japan Industrial Safety and Health Association research on self-directed vocalizing and gesturing.

3.2 WHAT IS THINKING?

At this point in the chapter we have encountered two quite different views about the nature of thinking in the young child. Piaget's view was that thought is mental action, carried out using mental representations, which are not yet very sophisticated in the young child. Vygotsky countered that in early childhood thought is self-directed speech, spoken out loud.

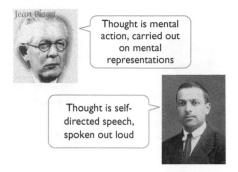

Figure 10.14   A difference of opinion about young children's thinking

Why does the young child fail to solve conservation problems? Piaget's position is that a young child's mental actions do not yet have the necessary logical properties, because her mental representations are static and centered on a few aspects of the situation. Vygotsky's position is that the young child is captured by the power of visual appearances, but that language has begun to reorganize her perception.

Figure 10.15   A difference of opinion about why young children fail conservation tasks

Piaget believed that thought is first personal and individual, then it is expressed in language, and only then does the young child begin to learn to communicate with other people. Vygotsky, on the other hand, maintained that thought is first social, and gradually becomes individual.

This should remind you of Vygotsky's *General Law of Cultural Development*, which I introduced in Chapter 2. This law proposes that every psychological function is first interpersonal, and second personal.

There is indeed a developmental sequence during early childhood. First, we see the young child using speech socially, in her interactions with other people. She directs speech to them; they direct speech

Figure 10.16 A difference of opinion about the origins of verbal thinking

to her. Of course, a lot of what parents say to young children takes the form of *directives*: instructions about what the child ought to do. Second, we see the young child using self-directed speech, talking to herself when she is engaged in a task. Finally, there is **covert speech**, where all we hear is a few muttered snatches of speech, or we hear nothing at all. Figure 10.17 shows the pattern of changes with age.

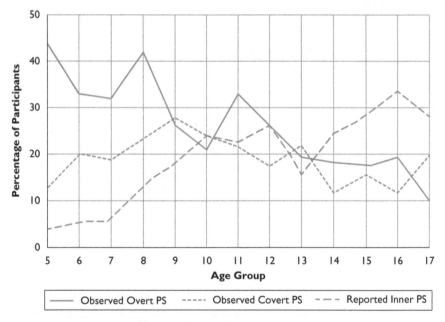

Figure 10.17 Age-related trends in children's use of overt, partially covert, and covert private speech

Source: Winsler & Naglieri (2003)

3.3 INTERNALIZATION OR NEW FUNCTIONAL ORGANS?

Many psychologists say that the movement from speech out loud to "silent" speech is explained by **internalization**. "Internalization" is one of the most popular terms used when people talk about Vygotsky.

But what does it mean? That something in the world goes inside the mind? It is true that "internalization" is a word that Vygotsky used, but he did not simply mean that speech is initially in the world and then subsequently speech is in the mind.

Vygotsky himself drew a distinction between two different kinds of "inner." He did indeed suggest that speech "goes inward," but he added that *first* it goes inward *psychologically*, and *then* it goes inward *physiologically*.

What does this mean? The first step here is directly in line with the General Genetic Law. To say that speech goes inward psychologically is to say that speech first appears as social, then as psychological; first as a form of cooperation among people, and then as a means of individual behavior. This is exactly what we observe: first social speech, then self-directed speech. This is speech going inward *psychologically*.

General Genetic Law	Self-Directed Speech
First, social, interpsychical	First, social speech: directed towards others (and from others)
Second, individual, intrapsychical	Second, self-directed speech: telling oneself what to do

Figure 10.18   The changes in self-directed speech follow Vygotsky's General Genetic Law of Cultural Development

However, we can also observe a second step. Self-directed speech moves from being overt—spoken "out loud"—to become covert—inaudible to other people. This is what Vygotsky refers to as speech going inward *physiologically*.

In neither of these steps does Vygotsky talk about speech going "into the mind." What he emphasized was not some kind of transfer from "outside" the mind to "inside" the mind, but the fact that the "social moment" comes first, that psychological functions are first social. Self-directed speech develops *from* social speech, and *this* is already, for Vygotsky, a matter of "internalization."

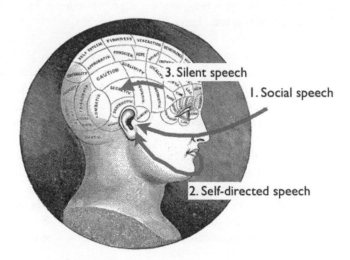

Figure 10.19   The three forms of speech to self that define the two steps of "internalization" of speech

But what does it mean to say that self-directed speech goes inward "physiologically"? To understand this we need to explore the neurophysiology of speech. The principal brain region involved in speech *production* is **Broca's area**. The principal brain region involved in speech *recognition* is **Wernicke's area**. (There are other areas involved too, but I'll ignore those subtleties for now.) In adults, these two areas are connected by a bundle of nerve fibers, called the *arcuate fasciculus*. Lesion studies show that this fiber pathway is involved in language. It is much larger in adult humans than in chimps or monkeys, who of course lack speech. Most importantly, MRI studies of children have found an increase in the white matter density of the *arcuate fasciculus* with age, from 4 to 17 years, but only in the left hemisphere, which is the speech-dominant hemisphere (Paus et al., 1999).

When a person speaks out loud, they hear the sound of their own voice. Broca's area is involved with the production of their speech. The sound emerges from the mouth, enters the ear of the person speaking, and is passed to Wernicke's area. But what if there were a way of connecting these areas directly within the brain? The *arcuate fasciculus* is exactly such a direct connection. And once this connection has been established, it should be possible for Broca's area to produce speech that is not actually spoken out loud, but which travels within the brain to be "heard" by Wernicke's area.

If this account is correct, it explains why many of us have the experience of hearing ourselves speaking, without being able to say very clearly where this voice is located. We get around this difficulty by saying that the voice is "in the mind" but, as we have seen, this is the **folk psychology** of Western culture, not a scientific explanation.

This is what Vygotsky meant when he said that the move from *overt* self-directed speech to *covert* self-directed speech was one of *going inwards physiologically*. As his friend and colleague Alexander Luria wrote:

> Social history ties the knots that produce new correlations between certain zones of the cerebral cortex, and if the use of language and its phonetic codes gives rise to new functional relationships between the temporal (auditory) and kinesthetic (motor-sensory) areas of the cortex, then this is the product of historical development relying on 'extracerebral connections' and forming new 'functional organs' in the cerebral cortex. (Luria, 2002, pp. 21–22)

What we are seeing here is the development of **verbal thinking** in early childhood. The young child has the experience every day of people telling her what to do. She will also tell them what to do, or at least she will try! With time, the young child will begin to tell *herself* what to do. And with the passage of more time, this self-directed speech will become inaudible to other people, due to the direct connection that has been established in her brain. The young child now talks to herself privately: and this is one major form of thinking.

Thinking at the stage of early childhood still occurs *in* action, or when there is a breakdown in practical activity. The young child is still not able to think about hypothetical or imaginary situations: though she is able to create these in action in her sociodramatic and pretend play. In this sense her thinking has not broken completely with the sensorimotor intelligence of the previous stages. But her thinking now takes a verbal form: the young child can think by talking to herself. We can say that two lines of development have come together. The practical speech of the toddler—words spoken in order to have

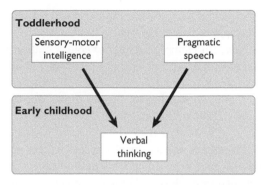

Figure 10.20   The combining of practical intelligence with practical speech provides the basis for verbal thinking in the form of covert speech

an influence on other people—has combined with the practical sensorimotor intelligence of the toddler to form self-directed speech that is used to solve practical problems. This self-directed speech is the first form of verbal thinking, and it then goes inward physiologically to give rise to the experience we all have of speaking "in the mind."

4. BECOMING A TYPE OF PERSON

We saw that the toddler came to understand that there are different types of objects and events. In early childhood, the young child starts to understand that there are also different types of person in her society as well, and that she is one of these types—or more. For example, every cultural cosmology has kinship types: brother, sister, father, mother. The young child has specific relationships with the particular people in her home; she has been calling them "mommy" and "daddy," but now she starts to understand that these are cultural "characters." In addition, an important distinction between type of person in many cultures is "male" and "female," and early childhood is that stage in which young children begin to form their understanding of **gender types**. However, true gender identity is a later achievement.

These aspects of cosmology operate in different ways. Someone can be both a father and a brother. Someone can begin as a sister and then become a mother. But in many cultures (although this is changing) gender is an exclusive and unchanging binary distinction: a person cannot be both male and female, and cannot change from one category to the other, except in exceptional circumstances.

4.1 GENDER AND RELATIONS WITH PARENTS

It is in early childhood that young children come to recognize that they are one gender or the other and begin to understand the consequences. Of course, their parents have known this from the moment they were born, or even before. But a newborn baby had no understanding of her gender. It is when she turns

3 or 4 years of age that the young child herself comes to recognize the cultural typology of gender that has been applied to her, and she applies this to herself.

But understanding one's gender isn't simply a matter of cold cognition. Gender is a profound aspect of one's identity, and its formation entails drastic changes in a young child's relations with parents and with peers.

One account of the ways that understanding of gender grows out of changes in the relationship between parent and child in early childhood comes from psychoanalytic theory, and was proposed by Sigmund Freud.

Freud believed that early experience has a crucial impact on later personality and mental health. Early childhood is the period of what Freud called the **Phallic Stage**—from 3 to 6 years—a stage in which physical pleasure is obtained through stimulation of the genitals. In Freud's view this is also the stage during which a young child discovers their gender, in part by noticing that they do or do not have a penis. Freud suggested that during this stage the young child begins to direct their affection towards the parent of the opposite gender, and begins to strongly resent the parent of the same gender.

Freud's theory of **infantile sexuality** has always been controversial. He proposed that infants and young children can derive sexual satisfaction from any part of the body, and that adult heterosexuality is not inevitable but is the consequence of society channeling this **polymorphous perversity**: the human ability to obtain gratification from behaviors that are outside what is normative.

Freud argued that around age 3 young children start to become aware of their own bodies and those of other people, and become curious about undressing and exploring the genitals. This is how they learn the physical differences between "male" and "female" and the gender differences between "boy" and "girl."

He also argued that in early childhood a young boy's attachment to his mother becomes sexualized, and he starts to view his father as a rival who can destroy or castrate him. To cope with this **castration anxiety** and defend against the threat (though it is fantasized rather than real), the young boy must deny and repress his connection with his mother and instead engage in a process of **identification** with the father who he both admires and fears. It is in the process of this conflict, Freud argued, that the boy forms a **superego**, an internal version of the controlling father.

Freud named this dynamic in little boys' development the **Oedipus complex**, referring to an ancient Greek tragic play in which a king named Oedipus kills his father and marries his mother. Little girls experience something similar, which Freud's follower Carl Jung named the **Electra complex**, after a play in which a woman named Electra plots with her brother against their mother and stepfather in revenge for the murder of their father.

Freud suggested that when a young girl realizes that she does not have a penis, she feels that she cannot sexually possess her mother. Instead, she directs her desire towards her father. Her **penis envy** is the basis for her heterosexual femininity in which bearing a child replaces the absent penis.

The suggestion that early childhood is a time of psychosexual drama and conflict remains controversial. One reason for the controversy is that Freud himself apparently believed that the outcome of the psychosexual conflicts of early childhood was positive for boys, and negative for girls. He argued that because a young boy has to separate from his mother he becomes more rational and less emotional, better prepared for the challenges of life. The young girl, in contrast, becomes an adult woman who remains emotional, and who lacks the detachment and capacity for reason that are needed to handle the challenges of life. It is not hard to see why many people have viewed Freud as having sexist opinions.

However, Freud's suggestion that the young boy and young girl have divergent experiences during early childhood has been developed in interesting ways.

A somewhat different account of the consequences of the changing relationships between parents and the young child has been given by the feminist sociologist and psychoanalyst Nancy Chodorow.

Chodorow argued that neither biological sex differences not deliberate socialization are adequate explanations for the differences between adult masculine and feminine personality and gender roles, which she suggests are almost universal (Chodorow, 1999[1978]). Biology does not determine gender identity, but neither are male and female behavior conventions simply taught to children. Even for young children these gender differences become tenaciously maintained and filled with emotion, and Chodorow argues that this is because **gender personality** becomes deeply central to young children's sense of who they are.

The universality of gender differences is, Chodorow proposes, a result of the fact that it is women who are responsible for the care of infants and young children in almost every society, as well as for the care of older girls and young women. This means that the relationship between mother and child, and especially between mother and daughter, is centrally important. It also means that boy and girl children have different positions and experiences in the social environment of the family and community.

The result is that feminine personality is defined in relation to and connection with other people. Women are less **individuated** than men. Masculine personality is defined in terms of separation and independence. For a boy, being male is tied in complex ways to his initial dependence on, and then his subsequent differentiation from, his mother (Chodorow, 2001). One consequence, Chodorow suggests, is that women fear and generally try to avoid separation, while men fear and generally try to avoid intimacy.

These characteristics operate not at the level of conscious roles, but at a level of unconscious desires and anxieties. They are the result not of things that parents do deliberately, but of social relationships that are emotional, unintentional, and tacit.

As we have seen, infants and toddlers are dependent on other people for all their basic needs. Often it is the mother who meets these needs, though sometimes she has assistance from the father and other family and community members. Only slowly does the child begin to differentiate from the mother: biological differentiation at 1 year, psychological differentiation at 3 years. A strong attachment relationship bonds the toddler and the primary caregiver who, again, often is the mother.

The fact that it is the mother who lactates is presumably the basis for the convention that she often has primary responsibility for the child, but clearly this biological fact does not dictate that fathers cannot participate, cleaning and comforting the baby, for example. Indeed, we have seen that there are cultures where this is exactly what happens. But in many cases both boy and girl infants and toddlers will form their strongest emotional attachment with their female caregiver. Some psychologists call this attachment relationship the child's **primary identification**.

Chodorow argues that primary identification is a two-way street: it is based not only on the toddler's needs and desires but also on the feelings of the mother towards her baby. A mother will often identify more strongly with a daughter, while with a son she will adopt a more ambivalent relationship, pushing him to be aggressive and independent. She points out that, for example, mothers among the Brahmins in South India are more lenient and affectionate with daughters than with sons, and they say this is due to their sympathy for the fact that a daughter will have to leave her family when she marries, and live in her husband's household. In general, mothers help their sons differentiate from them more than they do with their daughters, though in ways that, in Chodorow's view, may be damaging for children of both genders.

All this begins before the child has established any understanding of gender. When, in early childhood, young children begin to understand the cultural system of gender types and conventions, boys recognize that they are "male" and girls that they are "female," and they also learn that these categories are mutually exclusive and unchanging (Kohlberg, 1966). Toddlers, in contrast, think that a person who is wearing a skirt is female, and that if this person puts on pants they will be male.

In addition to this knowledge, however, what is also required is an emotional and personal **secondary identification** with someone of the same gender, usually personified by the caregiver of that gender. Chodorow argued that after about age 3 there is a dramatic reorganization of young children's relations with their parents. The father becomes a more important figure, for both girls and boys. The young boy identifies with his father, even though in many cultures the father works outside the family and is not very accessible to his children. As a result, the young boy identifies with the *position* that his father seems to adopt, more than with the *person*. Rather than forming a close personal relationship with the parent who he now realizes is the same gender as himself, he has to try to understand a depersonalized role of "masculinity." He does this, in part, by rejecting and opposing everything feminine that he sees around him. Being *male* must be the opposite of being *female*.

The young girl is in a different situation. The parent she now identifies with is the same one with whom she formed an attachment relationship, and on whom she has been dependent, namely her mother. She does not have to break this connection, or reject her primary identification, in order to form her secondary identification. In addition, femininity and female roles are evident to her in the daily life of her family. Consequently, her sense of her gender is grounded in the real emotional relationship she has with her mother.

The discontinuity that must come in the girl's life will occur later on, in adolescence, when she has to transfer her primary emotional connection—and her sexual attraction, according to Freud—from her mother and other females to her father and other males, in order to attain culturally sanctioned heterosexuality.

In short, the young boy's development in early childhood generally involves a discontinuity in his emotional connections within the family, while development of the young girl does not require such a discontinuity. The young boy has to **differentiate** himself from the parent with whom he formed his first attachment, his mother. The young girl is not required to differentiate, and so is able to maintain her **affiliation** with her mother. When, in middle childhood, children begin to prepare for adult work, either through apprenticeship or by attending school, these differences will play out in their motivations, as well as in the expectations of the adults who teach them.

It is important to recognize that this **asymmetry** between the requirement imposed on young boys and girls by their cultural circumstances—differentiation for the young boy, affiliation for the young girl—follows on from the fact that the primary caregiving role is often assigned to women. As we have noted, there is no biological necessity to this. If fathers were the primary caregivers it would be the young girl who would need to restructure her emotional attachments in early childhood, breaking the connection with her father in order to form an identification with her mother. It is the particular cultural arrangements for childcare and parenting that establish the unconscious, emotional basis for the young

	Girl	Boy
Infancy	Attached to mother	Attached to mother
Early childhood	Seeks to identify with mother	Seeks to identify with father
	No differentiation required	Must differentiate from mother

Figure 10.21   The typical relations for a boy and girl in infancy and early childhood

child's sense of what it means and requires to be a boy or a girl. The fact that many cultures adopt similar arrangements means that male and female personality, and masculine and feminine characteristics, are similar in many parts of the world

4.2 CULTURAL CONSTITUTION OF GENDER

It may be difficult to accept that male and female are culturally constituted types, because it seems obvious that the two genders have a biological basis. Most of us take for granted that gender is a dichotomous category, with two mutually exclusive possibilities. We assume that this is because people fall into two biological types, based on their reproductive organs and their DNA. However, none of this is necessarily the case.

We saw in Chapter 4 that the biology of sex is complex, with components on the genetic level, the cellular level, the hormonal level, and the anatomical level. We saw also that some babies are born intersexual, with both male and female reproductive organs. Some parents today are raising their children in a gender-neutral manner.

If sex is complex, so too is gender. Many indigenous cultures in the Americas—over 130 tribes—have long recognized a third gender category, who they call "Two Spirit people" (Roscoe, 1992). Such people wear clothing and perform tasks associated with both men and women, but they have distinct social roles in the community. They are believed to contain both a masculine and a feminine spirit, and they are often healers, foretellers of the future, or singers of the traditional songs. In many indigenous communities, a child's gender assignment is based not on their biology but on their preferred activities. Two-spirit people with male bodies would go to war and attend the sweat lodge with men, but they would also cook and perform domestic tasks. Female-bodied two-spirit people would usually marry only females.

If the obligations and conventions for "man" and "woman" are culturally constituted, as is the number of genders, then this means that here too what young children have to recognize is not a natural category. First, they have to learn the conventional distinctions between (or among) the genders. Then they have to learn conventional behavior by men and women. Then in many societies they will learn the institutional roles of a gendered division of labor. Only then will they have constructed their own "gender identity."

To say that gender is culturally constituted is not to say that it is simply a matter of "categories." The constitution of gender is a profound practical process, as we have seen in this section. Changing young children's understanding of gender, or changing gender identity in later childhood, may be desirable, but it would require difficult transformations in the practices of childcare and in the division of labor in the household.

5. BIOLOGICAL CHANGES IN EARLY CHILDHOOD

5.1 PHYSICAL GROWTH

Physical growth was rapid during infancy and toddlerhood, but it slows somewhat during early childhood. After the third birthday, the rate of growth in height is about 2½ to 3 inches per year, and growth in weight is about 5 pounds per year. Individual differences in height and weight become more pronounced, as do cultural differences due to diet and genetics. Among the Efe, who we met earlier, the average 5-year-old is smaller than 97 percent of children the same age in the USA (Perry & Domini, 2009). Boys continue to be somewhat taller and larger than girls. Nonetheless, compared to other mammal species the young child's body size is small relative to what will be her adult size, and her resting metabolic rate is higher than in all other mammals.

Young children become slimmer than they were as toddlers, as their percentage of body fat decreases. Body proportions become more like those of an adult, and the internal organs become more enclosed by the longer, wider torso. Balance and posture improve as a result of the altered proportions, and the young child's way of walking is more more like that of an adult, with her hands at her sides rather than spread wide for balance. Fine motor skills can be carried out with greater ease: young children become more agile in controlling their eating utensils, whether these are knives and forks or chopsticks. They can generally now unbutton a coat, though probably not button it up. They have improved control of pencils and crayons, and can now pour liquid into a container relatively successfully.

The young child continues to have immature dentition, one indication of her dependence on other people for care and feeding. It is only at the end of the stage of early childhood that the 20 deciduous teeth—"baby teeth"—start to be replaced by permanent teeth.

5.2 BRAIN GROWTH

The young child has a brain that is still relatively large for her body size, and which continues to be fast-growing. During early childhood the brain grows from 80 percent of its adult weight at age 3 to 90 percent at age 6. Between the ages of 2 and 5 years there is a dramatic increase in neuronal growth in the dorsolateral prefrontal cortex (DL-PFC) (Diamond, 2000).

Cognitive functions seem to become both more localized and more interconnected. For example, brain lesions limited to a single hemisphere have little long-term effect on language development when they occur before age 5 or 6.

Growth of the prefrontal cortex is associated with increased executive function—in simpler terms, self-control. Between the ages of 2 and 5 years there is a dramatic increase in neuronal growth in the dorsolateral prefrontal cortex (Diamond, 2000). Research has documented individual differences in executive function by the third year of life (Carlson et al., 2004).

In early childhood the left cerebral hemisphere is the more active, though this imbalance is reduced as activity in the right hemisphere increases through to the end of middle childhood. This change probably reflects the growth in oral language ability, since language is usually located in left-hemisphere structures. The right hemisphere generally handles spatial abilities, which continue to be acquired after early childhood.

No other mammalian species shows all these characteristics, or has a comparable developmental period (Locke & Bogin, 2006). As we saw in Chapter 3, the developmental stage of (early) childhood appeared in human evolution for the first time in Homo habilis, inserted between infant and juvenile. Presumably its evolutionary value was that once a mother no longer needed to nurse her young child she could give birth to another infant while other people would provide food and care for the youngster. Reproductive output was increased, with no additional risk to the mother or her children.

CONCLUSION

A great deal of attention has been paid to young children's understanding of other people. Do they form a "theory of mind"—a mental theory about the mental states, the beliefs and intentions of other people? Do they arrive at a belief-desire psychology? We have seen that it is more likely that the young child builds on her ability as a toddler to understand intention-in-action, and that her understanding continues to be primarily practical—emotional, intuitive, evaluative, and embodied—rather than theoretical. She begins to draw inferences about "prior intention," as something that will carry over from one situation to another. She does not yet grasp that people can have beliefs and desires that endure over time and can be compared with the facts of a situation.

During early childhood, speech directed to self provides the first form of verbal thinking. The young child talks to herself to direct her own activity—to understand problems and figure out solutions. This kind of speech increasingly goes underground: it is "internalized," first psychologically and then physiologically, as connections are formed in the brain between the regions responsible for speech production and those responsible for speech reception and comprehension. As a result, the young child begins to hear her own voice "inside her head."

Caregivers have new goals and expectations for the young child. They expect more self-control, and start to reason with her. We have discussed four different parenting styles in Western society, with corresponding characteristics in young children. In addition, we have seen that four distinct family models were identified in an analysis with a much broader cross-cultural scope. Early childhood is often a stage in which young children are taken care of by people outside the family—teachers and childcare workers—or in some cultures have responsibility themselves for taking care of younger siblings.

During early childhood the young child comes to recognize the cultural cosmology of kinship. Around her are *types* of person: parent, teacher, sister, brother, male, and female. In early childhood, young children start to figure out what it means to be male or female: they recognize the conventions associated with gender.

The various psychological developments that are achieved during early childhood are woven together in interesting ways. Sociodramatic play provides an opportunity to learn about social conventions, to exercise imagination, to practice self-control, to start to follow the conventions of one's gender, and to anticipate what it will be like to be an adult. In this regard, this new kind of play is the central line of development during this stage.

There are important changes in the *ontology* of the young child's world, not just in her conceptions. She comes to distinguish between the way things *appear*, and the way they *are*. She starts to solve conservation tasks, grasping that the liquid may look different after it is poured, but is really the same. She starts to solve false-belief tasks, grasping that prior intentions are formed in one situation, and carried into another. She recognizes social conventions and agreements, which once made will bind current activity. And she recognizes that her culture defines distinct, enduring types of person.

As we shall see in the next chapter, the young child increasingly applies this distinction between appearance and reality to herself. The former becomes shifting and transient, and what is now taken to be stable, enduring, and objective is a realm that cannot be perceived directly. The classic Piagetian conservation tasks are "failed" until the young child masters this distinction, this contradiction, and paradox. It now becomes clear to the young child that she can apply the same distinction to herself: she too is not simply what she appears to be.

She comes to understand that she really is a girl, no matter what clothes she puts on in the morning. She, too, has an appearance and a reality. How she knows herself is different from how she is known by others. They may see her goals in her actions, but they cannot perceive her beliefs and desires. This is a new psychological differentiation, between "inside" and "outside." A new world opens up for the child: the "inner" world of her personal and private thoughts and feelings. In the next stage, middle childhood, with the aid of various adult guides she will begin to explore this inner world.

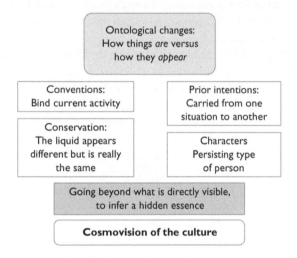

Figure 10.22   Ontological changes during early childhood

Intentional stance	What the person sees (+ contextual affordances)	What the person wants (+ telos)	Prior intention (+ intention-in-action)
Conventional stance	The characters (+ artifacts)	The convention for action (+ customary uses)	The scenario (+ activity setting)

Figure 10.23   The two ways of understanding other people in early childhood

SUMMARY

UNDERSTANDING OTHER PEOPLE

- Three-year-olds take the world as they experience it to be the world as it is. They don't recognize that people literally have different perspectives: that a person standing in a different place has a different point of view. They don't understand that people know different things about the world: that someone can have, for example, a false belief.

- Young children do, however, understand other people's prior intentions. They are capable of the intentional stance. At first, young children may infer prior intentions on the basis of what they observe that someone can see. This is called "perception–action" reasoning. As a result, they pass false-belief tasks, but fail true-belief tasks.

- Young children can also recognize the "social affordances" (or deontic affordances) of agreements and conventions. They can adopt the "conventional stance."

CARING FOR THE YOUNG CHILD

- Frequently people outside the family will contribute to the care of a young child. In some cultures, young children will be contributing to the care of their younger brothers and sisters, and will participate in household chores. She may even be allowed to pick who she lives with, and to change her own name.

- Baumrind distinguished three parenting styles: permissive, authoritarian, and authoritative. However, she assumed that independence and autonomy are the goals of good parenting.

- Cross-cultural comparison has distinguished four kinds of family model: independence, interdependence, psychological interdependence, and hierarchical-neglecting. These models define four distinct developmental trajectories: the autonomous-separate self, the heteronomous-related self, the autonomous-related self, and the heteronomous-separate self.

THE ORIGINS OF VERBAL THINKING

- Piaget considered self-directed speech to be egocentric. In contrast, Vygotsky considered self-directed speech to be the earliest form of thinking. The movement from self-directed speech out loud to covert speech—speech to oneself "in the mind"—involves two steps of internalization. Speech first "goes inward" psychologically: what was social becomes individual. Second, speech "goes inward" physiologically, as new functional organs form in the cortex.

(Continued)

(Continued)

BECOMING A TYPE OF PERSON

- The young child starts to recognize types of person: "characters," including gender types. The young boy has to differentiate from his mother, while the young girl does not. This difference creates a different basis for adult gender identity. The types of gender, however, depend upon both biology and culture.

BIOLOGICAL CHANGES IN EARLY CHILDHOOD

- Physical growth slows in early childhood, and physical proportions become more like those of an adult. Cognitive functions become more localized in the brain, and more interconnected. Extensive neuronal growth occurs in the prefrontal cortex.

- No other species of mammal shows a developmental stage equivalent to early childhood in humans.

RESOURCES

McGill University Brain Website:

http://thebrain.mcgill.ca/flash/i/i_10/i_10_cr/i_10_cr_lan/i_10_cr_lan.html

Bronfenbrenner, U. (1970). *Two Worlds of Childhood: U.S. and U.S.S.R.* New York: Russell Sage Foundation.

CHAPTER 11

MIDDLE CHILDHOOD

(6–12 YEARS)

UNDERSTANDING INSTITUTIONAL REALITY

[W]hat is most important has not yet happened to the child, namely, consciousness of his own processes of thinking … often he does not control them. They flow with him just as actions flowed previously, that is, in a purely reactive way. Only gradually, only with the passage of years does the child learn to control the course of his thoughts and just as he earlier controlled the course of his actions, he begins to regulate and select them. Piaget correctly notes that regulating thought processes is a voluntary act, an act of selection, to the same extent as a moral action. (Vygotsky, 1997a, p. 250)

LEARNING OBJECTIVES

In this chapter we shall explore:

- The 5-to-7 transition, describing its biological and psychological aspects.
- Some of the forms that education takes in cultures where the child does not go to school.
- The proposal that there is a feedback loop between the way adults arrange the circumstances for children in middle childhood, and the kinds of adult those children become.
- How other people are understood in middle childhood: research on moral judgments, the mentalistic stance, and the institutional stance.

FRAMING QUESTIONS

- Which skills that you use daily did you learn outside school? List as many as you can. Now list the skills you use daily that you learned at school. Which list is longer?
- At what age do you think you would have been capable of taking care of yourself if your parents had left on a month-long vacation?
- Most likely you are studying within a social institution. What are its most obvious roles and rules?
- Are there games that you learned from other children when you were a student at school?

INTRODUCTION

In many Latin American cities there are children living on the street—estimates range up to 80,000—and thousands more are *trabajadores jovenes*, who earn a living on the streets instead of attending school and return home at night.

Lewis Aptekar explored the daily life of these children in Cali, Colombia (Aptekar, 1988, 1990). With a team of students from the Universidad del Valle, Aptekar established contact with street children in a store-front program, then his team divided up to talk to the children in four different areas of the city. All were boys, mostly between 7 and 16 years of age, with 43 percent younger than 12 years of age. He also conducted tests of intelligence, and emotional and neurological functioning. Around one quarter of the children had problems in one or more of these areas, but the majority were of normal ability. It seemed that the children who were surviving on the streets were the stronger ones, and also that their membership of a peer group provided friendship and support.

There were indications, too, that street life had sharpened their problem-solving skills. These children were able to undertake and complete a variety of self-managed, non-supervised activities, they had extensive knowledge of their environments, and they showed high social awareness. In fact, compared with brothers and sisters who had stayed at home, the street children were in better physical condition.

Aptekar identified two styles among the preadolescent street children. One was the *gamine* (urchin), who had left their families and chosen to live on the street, where they survived through a combination of cunning and wit, and maintained their independence. They made money in inventive ways such as singing on public buses, or selling recycled popsicle sticks. They obtained food by strategies such as stealing from the plates of people dining in local restaurants. Adolescence brought challenges to such children: they became no longer satisfied with being mischievous, and many choose to become full-blown delinquents.

The second group, the *chupagruesos*, had genuinely been abandoned or thrown out by their families, and they survived by serving more powerful older children. They were less intelligent that the *gamines*, with poorer scores on the emotional and neurological measures.

Two kinds of peer group were evident too. The first were groups from 5 to 25 children in size, run by an adolescent boy. They collaborated to get money, but rarely stayed together after work. The power of the *jefe* was maintained mainly by his ability to sell the items the group obtained. The *chupagruesos* fit well in such groups.

The second kind of group was formed by two or three preadolescent children, successful in begging for food because of their youthful appearance. These groups operated with less hierarchy and more intimacy and emotional connection, more like family or friends. Group members ate and played together. The *gamines* moved in and out of this kind of group.

Most of these street children came from families of indigenous or Afro-Colombian origins who had moved to the city. These were families with extremely limited financial resources. Most of them were **matrifocal**, reflecting their African traditions: that is, the mother was the authority in the family. Often she had chosen to live without a male companion.

The *gamines*, in particular, had been raised to become independent early, and only a few had left home because of rejection or abandonment. For most of them, life on the street was part of a specific developmental trajectory, for which they had been deliberately prepared. Most of them remained in contact with at least one parent, usually the mother, and they sometimes returned to their mother's home for short periods. They had entered street live gradually, returning home frequently until they felt comfortable with life on the streets. But in general these boys were expected to leave home before they reached puberty, and they were given plenty of opportunities to do so. Their mothers considered it important that they explore the city without supervision to learn survival skills.

Figure 11.1   Street children in Bogotá warming themselves at a fire fueled by posters torn off the wall

Daughters, on the other hand, generally stayed close to their mother, sometimes leaving if they had a child of their own but then usually soon returning. These girls were in general taught to become independent of men. Both boys and girls assumed that they would not necessarily have a long-term relationship with one partner, and that marriage would not be an important part of their lives. They accepted that the family unit was defined by a mother and her children, without a male figure.

Middle childhood for these boys was short; adolescence came early, before puberty, and it ended early too.

In these street children of Cali we can see many of the characteristics of middle childhood, despite their extreme and distressing circumstances. Middle childhood is a stage of development in which the child is thrust outward in three ways. She moves out of the family into the peer group, she enters the world of work and of games that require more complex physical and psychological skills, and she makes a tentative entrance into the world of adult logic, symbolism, and conceptualization (Havighurst, 1972). Most developmental researchers consider middle childhood to start between 5 and 7 years of age, and to end around 11 years of age. Changes in the child around 6 years of age—the **5-to-7 transition**—are recognized by adults in most cultures, and their response is generally to introduce new responsibilities. In some cases, adults will send the child to a new institutional setting in which she will begin to learn the expertise needed for the work she will perform as an adult. In other cases, the child starts to work alongside adults, collaborating with them in activities in which they guide her more or less explicitly (Lancy & Grove, 2011).

In those cultures where the child enters a new institutional setting this is often, and increasingly, the school. There are many cultures, however, in which schooling is not the norm. Children may be taught by adults in an apprenticeship. Or they may learn through participating in work tasks with adults or with older children, and learn by observation, practice, and example. Middle childhood is a stage in which children in different parts of the world diverge even more markedly than before in their developmental trajectories. It is also a time when boys and girls are often involved in very different kinds of activity, as they move closer towards the gender differentiated roles of adult life.

Most of what developmental researchers know about middle childhood comes from studying children who attend school, and often studying them in the schools that they attend! It will become clear in this and the following chapter, however, that this limited focus has constrained our knowledge of children's development in several respects.

In this chapter we shall first explore various aspects of the transition that takes place between 5 and 7 years of age, and next consider the kinds of learning and teaching that occur in settings outside school. Then we consider the manner in which the child now understands the actions of other people. In the next chapter we will focus on the institution of school, consider the psychological consequences of attending school and the kind of reasoning that children become capable of at this stage. Finally we will explore what children do when they are outside school and work.

1. THE TRANSITION AT 5 TO 7 YEARS

The 5-to-7 transition brings the child into a stage that is called middle childhood, but could equally well be named the juvenile stage. As we saw in Chapter 3, juveniles have physiological characteristics and sufficient psychological ability that they could probably survive if their caregivers were no longer available, but they are not yet capable of sexual reproduction—that is, not yet biologically able to have children themselves.

1.1 CHANGES IN BODY AND BRAIN

The 5-to-7 transition involves psychological, cultural, and physical changes. In terms of the latter, there are important developments in the body and brain.

During the time between 5 and 7 years of age children experience a growth spurt that is matched only by the growth that took place during the first months of life, and by the accelerated growth that will be an aspect of puberty. An average 4-year-old in the USA is about 39 inches tall and weighs about 36 pounds. By the end of this stage, when they are 10 years old, they will be 5 feet and 90 pounds on average, and much of this growth takes place in the 24 months centered around age 6. During middle childhood height increases steadily, as the bones grow. Historical data show that children have grown increasingly taller, heavier, and faster over the past two hundred years.

By the end of the 5-to-7 transition, boys are on average stronger and larger than girls, with more muscle mass, and they show greater capacity than girls in activities that require force and strength. Girls excel in activities requiring manual dexterity, or fine foot movements, or balance. These differences reflect biological maturation, but they probably also stem from differences in what are considered appropriate activities for boys and girls. What happens, for example, in cultures where boys weave? As a consequence of these bodily changes children now have the requisite motor skills and physical capacities to engage in many adult activities, such as carrying materials, setting a trap, and working around the house.

It is during the 5-to-7 transition that the 20 deciduous teeth—the "baby teeth"—start to be replaced by permanent teeth. The age at which this begins is influenced by genetic factors: for example, it happens in girls before boys. But nutrition also plays a role, as do other environmental factors; young children in the USA get their first permanent teeth at around age 6½, while in other countries it is earlier. In addition, young children who live with smokers have more tooth decay (Shenkin et al., 2004), as do those who drink sugary beverages. The last of the 32 permanent teeth, the "wisdom teeth," grow in between 18 to 25 years of age.

This dental change makes a difference in the foods children are able to eat: they no longer need specially prepared meals. Many cultures have rituals around this loss of deciduous teeth, often associated with mice or other rodents which have sharp teeth that never fall out. In England and the USA the "tooth fairy" replaces a tooth hidden under a pillow with a coin. In France and Belgium the "Little Mouse" plays the same role. In Greece, Turkey, Vietnam, and other countries the lost tooth is thrown onto the roof of the house, or under the floor. In India, the tooth may be buried so that a new one will grow.

Although puberty will not occur until the end of middle childhood, important biological processes of sexual maturation do occur early in this stage. At around 6 to 8 years of age the adrenal cortex secretes increased levels of androgens, in a process known as **adrenarche** (Parker, 1991). Hair grows under the arms and in the pubic region, and the bones grow more rapidly. This is probably a consequence of changes in the adrenal cortex. However, it is only when the hypothalamic-pituitary-gonadal system matures that puberty will begin, marking the start of adolescence in some cultures, and the start of adulthood in others (see Chapter 13).

After the 5-to-7 transition the rate of physical growth declines and, surprisingly, during the rest of the years of middle childhood physical growth is at its slowest rate since infancy. This slowing may provide time and energy for brain growth (and learning). It may mean that there is less competition for food between adults and children than would be the case if children continued to grow, and it may be that the relatively small body of the human juvenile is less threatening to adults.

By the start of middle childhood the brain is 90 percent of its adult size, and its gross anatomy is now largely formed. Brain function, on the other hand, may differ from functioning in adulthood, though we don't have much evidence because brain processes are difficult to study in children. It is known that brain hormones influence the way large populations of neurons operate, so the rise in adrenal androgens around 7 or 8 years of age is likely to influence brain functioning. In animal species these hormones are associated with increased aggression and dominance in males, but we have no evidence yet of a similar association in humans, and probably the influence is bidirectional, with behavior also stimulating hormone production.

During middle childhood the brain grows little, but it undergoes steady reorganization. MRI studies show that gray matter volume is considerably *larger* in school-age children than in adults (Johnson & De Haan, 2011). The general pattern is of cortical thinning, as synapses continue to be pruned. Gray matter declines after age 7, with timing that varies by region. This loss of gray matter occurs first in the sensory-motor cortex during early childhood, and then progresses in the secondary cortex, then the multimodal cortex, then supramodal areas of the cortex, and finally in the parietal and frontal lobes around puberty and into adolescence. In other words, it appears that phylogenetically older areas of the cortex are pruned earlier than the more recently evolved, higher-order association cortex. This pattern of differential development across regions seems not to occur in primates, though it may not have been observed because it takes place more quickly.

At the same time, cerebral white matter increases in volume during childhood, and this increase continues into early adulthood.

From around 6 years of age onward the **prefrontal cortex** is developing, especially the part that covers the lateral and anterior convexity of the frontal lobe. New and higher layers are added to the perception–action cycle that I described in Chapter 4. These layers take the form of cortical networks that handle actions and goals in increasingly complex and sophisticated ways. The prefrontal cortex builds on the operation of lower cortical networks. It receives three kinds of information: input from the brainstem and limbic system about biological drives, attention, and reward; input from the posterior association cortex about memories and values; and input from the sensory organs, monitoring the outcomes of actions. The higher-order logical reasoning that we shall see becomes possible in middle childhood presumably requires the integration of all this information.

There is evidence (from patients with cortical lesions) that skilled tasks are handled by the prefrontal cortex until they become routine. Then they are passed to lower structures of the perception–action cycle, such as the basal ganglia: "The perception–action cycle continues to operate, but mainly at subcortical levels" (Fuster, 2005, p. 79).

In addition, at this stage the two hemispheres seem to be coming to specialize in different tasks, although there is debate about this. The traditional account is that the right hemisphere is involved in spatial cognition, while the left hemisphere is involved in linguistic and perhaps musical and logical cognition, though the two hemispheres collaborate. There is evidence that the right hemisphere becomes committed to visuospatial processing around age 10, which should lead to an ability to perform visuospatial tasks more accurately and efficiently. However, there is also evidence that the left hemisphere handles cognitive strategies that have become routinized, while the right hemisphere is involved in exploring novel situations to which existing skills and strategies are not useful. As a task becomes routinized it may be moved from the right to the left hemisphere. If this is the case, the traditional language/nonlanguage dichotomy may simply be a special case of this functional differentiation, since language has become routinized by the time its location is usually studied.

Furthermore, the frontal lobes in particular appear to be specialized hemispherically. The left frontal lobe seems to be involved in deliberate and context-independent activities that are based on known information, while the right frontal lobe seems to be involved in deliberate, context-dependent activities that are guided by the environment (Goldberg et al., 1994; Podell et al., 2001).

The psychological manifestation in this specialization has not yet been explored. However, as we shall see in this chapter, from around 6 years onward the child becomes increasingly less dependent on what is directly perceived, and her actions and thoughts become more governed by curiosity, knowledge, and innovation. In other words, her behavior becomes less reactive, and more autonomous and spontaneous. These behavioral changes match what we know about the increased function of the prefrontal cortex, as well as the increasing importance of language (Fuster, 2002).

1.2 DIFFERENTIATION OF OUTER AND INNER

We think of our thoughts, ideas, or feelings as being "within" us, while the objects in the world which these mental states bear on are "without" ... But as strong as this partitioning of the world appears to us, as solid as this location may seem, and anchored in the very nature of the human agent, it is in large part a feature of our world, the world of modern, Western people.

The localization is not a universal one, which human beings recognize as a matter of course, as they do for instance that their heads are above their torsos. Rather it is a function of a historically limited mode of self interpretation, one which has become dominant in the modern West and which may indeed spread thence to other parts of the globe, but which had a beginning in time and space and may have an end. (Taylor, 1989, p. 111)

We saw in the last chapter that at the start of early childhood the young child was the same inwardly as she was outwardly. When she played, she was completely absorbed in her play; her actions flowed seamlessly and unconsciously from her desires and wishes. During the course of early childhood this changed: the young child came to draw a distinction between the ways things appear and the way they are. She now applies this distinction to herself. The child starts to understand that she, too, has both an appearance and a reality. On the one hand there is how others see her, and on the other there is how she knows herself to be.

In particular, by the end of early childhood the child had become conscious of thoughts and feelings that are private, evident only to herself. In Chapter 10 we saw how speech became self-directed (psychologically inner) and then inaudible to other people (physiologically inner). Self-directed speech became, it seemed, "inside" the child, in a private personal space that in many cultures is called "the mind" (though we have seen that each culture has its own **ethnopsychology**). Now the child has thoughts in the form of a voice that she can hear "in her mind" and which other people cannot overhear.

The new world that opens up for the child at the start of middle childhood is this new private and personal "inner space" in which thinking and feeling occur, differentiated from the "outer" realm of actions, objects, and people. The child's psychological functioning now has both an internal and an external aspect, and it becomes apparent to her that each person has direct, first-person access to their own inner world. We shall see in section 3 of this chapter how this is evident in her understanding of other people.

As a result, the transition into middle childhood involves the introduction of a "wedge" between the child's experience and her actions. Because her verbal thinking is now "in her mind" it can become differentiated from her actions: she can *first* think what to do, *then* act on her thinking. She is now able to deliberate before acting, and she can formulate her own plans and follow them. She is better able to deliberately maintain her attention and focus on complex problems. As a result, the child sometimes now seems rather artificial and affected; she has lost the directness, spontaneity, and naïveté she had in early childhood. She can now deliberately adopt a pose, and her parents may see her conduct at times as contrived and showing off, or as alternating between clowning and deliberate moodiness. On the positive side, she can manage and regulate her emotions in more sophisticated ways (see section 3.4).

1.3 NEW EXPECTATIONS

Adults certainly notice these changes. Middle childhood has long been recognized as an age at which adults prepare children for their adult responsibilities. The Jesuit motto "Give me a child until he is seven and I will give you the man," attributed to Ignatius Loyola, implies that what happens before middle childhood is crucially important in forming a person's character, and also that by age 7 this process has in important ways been completed. In medieval times people viewed this as the age when childhood ended.

One historian has claimed that "Once he had passed the age of five or seven the child was immediately absorbed into the world of adults" (Aries, 1962, p. 329). For example, since 1769 English common law has held that a child older than 7 years is capable of knowing right from wrong and can be tried in a court of law.

However, in many parts of the world today the 7-year-old child is no longer absorbed into the world of adults. And in those cultures where she is so absorbed, it is not exactly as an equal. It would be more accurate to say that the change that has occurred is that the child is now seen as able to make a contribution to the family and community through participation in adult work activities, albeit with a status that is not yet adult. In many societies this is the age at which children are sent to institutions of instruction, often to become educated in the local techniques of inscription (reading and writing). In other societies they are sent to work alongside adults.

I have said that middle childhood extends from 6 years to 11 years, but when we look at this statement in historical and cultural context we find that it must be qualified. On the one hand there are cultures today in which young children, especially girls, begin to be assigned household tasks at 4 years of age or even younger. On the other hand, as recently as two hundred years ago a new developmental stage was generally recognized to start at around 7 or 8 years of age, but this stage was considered to continue past puberty until adult status was finally reached in the 20s. As we shall see in Chapter 13, adolescence is a relatively recent phenomenon. (More accurately, adolescence has apparently emerged and disappeared over the course of recent human history—the past 2000 years or so—for specific social groups.)

For example, in preindustrial society in Europe and the United States people recognized a long, slow transition from childhood into adulthood: from around 8 years of age until around 25. Youth was a period of relative independence, but one during which one did not yet have either adult status or adult responsibilities. Within this period not much distinction was made on the basis of age. Families were large, adults were surrounded by children, and so consequently they probably didn't pay them much attention (Gillis, 1974).

For both the working class and the aristocrats a surplus of children was necessary, because of the high rate of infant mortality. For example, in one village in France at the end of the seventeenth century 18 percent of infants died in the first month after birth, 35 percent died in the first year, and 53 percent of children had died before they reached age 20. For a couple to merely replace themselves with two children who reached maturity they had to engage in considerably more child bearing and child raising than today. They needed at least four children to have a 60 percent chance of a male heir surviving his father. Moreover, children were an important investment, offering security for the family property, and support in old age.

In short, these conditions defined a developmental stage of "youth" that began around 8 years of age and continued until perhaps 25 years of age. This stage was supported by both formal and informal institutions. Among the formal institutions was the practice of sending young people to be servants in other households. Many children left home aged around 7 or 8 to become household servants, and then when they were 13 or 14 sometimes became formal apprentices. Even the rich sent their own children away, while taking in others as servants. These children remained semi-independent until they were old enough to obtain other kinds of work, or until they inherited from their parents and married. Another institution was apprenticeship, which began as young as 8 or 9 and continued to 12 or even 24.

However, the pattern I have just described was by no means universal; it varied with the local conditions. For example, the Puritans who emigrated from England to the USA found themselves with plenty of land to farm and a favorable climate. Their family organization was patriarchal, they were able to have large families, and they kept their children at home to work on the farm instead of sending them away to become servants (Mintz, 2004, p. 12). This meant that many of these children could afford to marry at a younger age—women at around age 20 compared with 25 in England. These women went on to have an average of eight children in their own families. In conditions such as these, the stage of youth was somewhat shorter.

In many societies today, the most striking change in the organization of children's lives around age 7 is that they begin to attend the institution known as school. Indeed, children in the stage of middle childhood are commonly referred to as "school-aged children." However, school is not the only social institution in which children learn, as we shall see in the following section of this chapter.

It was in the early nineteenth century that the assumption appeared, at least among middle-class Westerners, that childhood—from around age 6 up to age 13 or 14—should be a time for schooling rather than work. These years became a time for deliberately shaping the future adult: character was no longer considered something inherited from ancestors, it became viewed as the result of active formation by parents and teachers (Mintz, 2004). Children were viewed as innocent and pure, as blank slates, and parents, especially mothers, were told they were responsible for protecting and nurturing them. School became the second institution, alongside the family, where this formation would take place.

The early nineteenth century was also a time when programs to reduce family size through various forms of birth control were dramatically effective: the average number of births per family in England dropped from seven or ten at the start of the century to five in 1850, and to an average of only three children per family in 1900. In middle-class families, children became a form of social capital rather than a source of labor, and parents began to see that they should invest in their child, through appropriate parenting and providing a quality education. The state began to regulate how children lived, both at school and at home. Rigid school curricula were designed, to impose order and foster self-discipline.

At this same time working-class families, in contrast, became even more dependent on the earning power of their children. Children's labor, in the factory or in the fields, was crucial for the survival of the family. For a working-class child it was either impossible to attend school, or to do so required a major sacrifice by the rest of the family.

Differences in access to schooling for children from different socioeconomic classes continue today in many of the parts of the world that have adopted formal schooling, as do differences in grades and rates of graduation for children with working- and middle-class family backgrounds. We shall consider schooling and its consequences in detail in the next chapter.

A developmental transition, such as the 5-to-7 shift, is not a biologically preprogrammed event, a result only of maturation. Even though there are maturational constituents, each transition is actively anticipated and orchestrated by adults. The community defines the setting and manner of a developmental transition, responding to what the child can and cannot do, and to what they must in the future be able to do. This is another example of *prolepsis*, the anticipation of an event before it actually happens—we saw in Chapter 4 how parents react to the discovery of their newborn's gender by anticipating her future life possibilities and starting to organize the material conditions to realize them. Transitions bring both new hopes and new dangers. The equilibrium of the family, and even the community, is disrupted, and for this reason transitions are often marked with rituals and celebrations. The 5-to-7 transition is no exception.

For example, adults will frequently arrange special activities at the end of the final year of preschool, when the transition to elementary school is about the occur. An ethnographic study in a **Reggio Emelia preschool** in Italy found that towards the end of the third year the young children were asked for the first time to do work individually, "and no copying!" (Corsaro & Molinari, 2000). The teachers defined this activity as "homework in class," thereby explaining something new in terms that were already familiar. They arranged a field trip to the elementary school. The young children began to talk with one another about their new school, and the theme entered their play, illustrating Vygotsky's point that young children use play to explore real-world events that excite and confuse them.

The parents, too, were concerned about their young children's transition to elementary school, which would involve new activities such as reading and writing, making new friends, and so on. They approved and participated in the teachers' introduction of activities which anticipated the coming transition, and which gave the young children opportunities to prepare for what was to come and for the increased demands they would face.

2. LEARNING THROUGH PARTICIPATION AND APPRENTICESHIP

Children's learning can take place through specialized educational activities in a "formal" setting (though later we will question this label), or more directly through participation in everyday adult activities. This latter kind of learning sustains and reproduces traditional cultural practices, whereas schooling often introduces a curriculum that is foreign to the child and her community (Mead, 1943; Scribner & Cole, 1973). Learning through participation is education that merges the emotional and the intellectual, and the child who learns in this way often has a strong personal identification with the adults from whom she learns. School, in contrast, is organized around the impersonal roles of student and teacher (Dreeben, 1968).

In this section I will consider the education and learning that occurs through participation in adult activities, then the specific case of learning through apprenticeship. We will explore Rogoff's concept of learning as "guided participation." Then we consider the proposal that the conditions that caregivers establish for children create a feedback loop, so that fathers resemble their children. Finally, we will explore and question the distinction between formal and informal education.

2.1 LEARNING THROUGH PARTICIPATION

In many hunter-gather communities and agricultural societies even today children are prepared for adult life not by attending school but through **participation** in everyday activities. Rather than receiving deliberate instruction, children learn "on the job," by being included in adult activities in a way that gradually transfers responsibilities to them as their cognitive, social, and physical skills develop.

Even in cultures where children are not in school, then, middle childhood is a time for learning and practicing increasingly complex responsibilities. Less time is spent playing. A child's competence and intelligence are usually judged in terms of how successful she proves to be in accomplishing these responsibilities. In some African societies, for example, intelligence is defined as "to be able to be sent out"—that is, to run errands (Serpell, 1993). There is no way for a child to be judged as "smart" but lacking social competence as there is in the West. And it turns out that children who frequently take care of siblings do better in school exams if they also attend school (Weisner, 1996).

The fact that a child can start to assume responsibilities for some adult tasks amounts to an important increase in the resources available to her family. In many parts of the world a primary concern is how children can contribute to the social and economic well-being of the household. In middle childhood a child changes from being primarily a mouth to feed to someone who can really pull their own weight. The child can now first participate in, and then carry out unassisted, everyday tasks such as delivering a message, herding cattle, going to the store, or guarding the house. It is assumed now that the child can be taught, has common sense and an established personality, that she can take responsibility for wrongdoing, will show modesty, and that if she needs to be punished it can be by appealing to her sense of responsibility (Rogoff et al., 1975).

During middle childhood the degree of supervision of children steadily decreases. Adults in many cultures say that 8- to 10-year-old children are now useful and competent enough to perform tasks responsibly without supervision. Ethnographic studies of childhood in rural communities in Mexico and Guatemala confirm that a significant change occurs at this age. Although younger children are involved in household work, at 10 years of age there is an abrupt change in the responsibilities that are assigned. A combination of competence, independence, and reliability is required for most of the chores assigned to children of this age (Rogoff et al., 1980).

The same adult work task can be learned in different ways in communities that seem at first glance to be very similar. For example, among the Zinacanteco Maya in Chiapas, girls learn to weave by watching their mothers, then helping with simple tasks such as boiling the thread. Adults give a lot of explicit guidance, until by age 12 or 13 a girl has become a proficient weaver. In a Guatemalan Mayan community, in contrast, a girl learns to weave first on a child-sized loom, and then on her mother's loom but without explicit guidance. She learns by observation and by trial-and-error, without deliberate instruction or adult-defined procedures. In the first case, learning is intentional with explicit instruction by adults; in the second case, learning is incidental, through experimentation and observation.

Learning from observation in this way has been called **intent participation**. In this style of learning, knowledge is acquired through practice and demonstration, not through instruction and explanation (Rogoff et al., 2003). Anthropologists have noted that children learning in this way rarely ask "why?"; instead they pay careful attention to the activity and its context.

Weaving was the focus when Patricia Greenfield combined experimentation with ethnography in her research on processes of children's development in a Zinacantec Mayan community in Chiapas, Mexico (Greenfield et al., 2003; see also Greenfield, 2009). She first visited in 1969, and returned regularly for the next 20 years. She observed how girls in two generations learned the traditional practices of weaving cloth on a backstrap loom. (Boys do not learn to weave in this community, though weaving is men's work in some indigenous cultures.) She also conducted experiments designed to explore how the children represented patterns, like the ones they created when weaving.

When she observed the first generation of girls, their parents were emphasizing the reproduction of traditional patterns. During the 20 years that followed, the community made a transition from agriculture to a commercial economy, selling artisan products, and buying much of their food instead of growing it themselves. When she visited again, Greenfield found that parents now placed emphasis on independent learning and encouraged their children to invent new weaving patterns. In the pattern-construction task, the children in the second generation constructed more abstract patterns, while their parents had, when they had been children, used a more detailed, "thread-by-thread" approach.

Greenfield concluded that the trajectories and processes of development had changed historically, as the community in which the children were developing had undergone transformations.

The design of her research had several components. The *longitudinal* component was the comparison of the parenting practices of two different generations. The *naturalistic* observation component was her video-recording of the practices in which weaving was learned, which were then coded. The *experimental* component was the procedure in which children and adults were asked to represent striped woven patterns by placing colored wooden sticks in a frame.

Learning to weave through participation might seem very straightforward, merely technical, and even simplistic. In fact, though, it is far from being a simple imitation of what an adult does.

Knotting and weaving have been crucially important to human life for millennia, dating back at least 5,000 years to Neolithic Egypt. The Telefol people in central New Guinea have many uses for string bags, *bilum*, which they make from plant fibre. Children begin to learn how to make a *bilum* at an early age. The ethnographer who studied these people, Adrian Mackenzie, wrote that the children learned, and a traditional practice was handed down, through a process in which "observation is followed by internalization and then mimesis [copying]" (MacKenzie, 1990, p. 100; MacKenzie, 1991).

But is "internalization and copying" an adequate explanation of this kind of learning? Another anthropologist, Tim Ingold, disagrees:

> This is precisely where the standard model of the social learning of technical skills goes wrong. For in attributing the intergenerational conformity of movements to rules that are transmitted and internalised *in advance* of their practical application in mimesis, the model assumes that practice is a matter of executing identical, rule-governments over and over again, leading to gains in speed, efficiency and automation. (Ingold, 2000, p. 357)

Ingold argues that to successfully make a *bilum* the child has to learn how the movements of spinning the fibre and then looping it together feel like "from the inside," so as to effectively coordinate perception and action. At first the child will be clumsy, and improvement will come not only from observation but also from "the gradual attunement of movement and perception," so that the skilled bag maker is one "who has a feel for what she is doing … whose movement is continually and subtly responsive to the modulations of her relation with the material" (Ingold, 2000). These "ways of the hand" (Sudnow, 1974) are "acquired" not in the form of rules that can be handed down as a package, but as practical know-how that has to be picked up, in circumstances arranged by adult experts and often with their expert guidance. MacKenzie's own observations suggest that what happens is "a process of guided rediscovery" in which the role of experienced bilum-makers is to set up the contexts within which novices are enabled to gain proficiency for themselves, or in other words to "grow into the skills of spinning and looping" (Ingold, 2001, p. 24).

The absence of explicit instruction when a child learns about adult work by participating in it does not mean a lack of sophistication or complexity. Work by children is often viewed as scandalous, and certainly child workers can be as exploited as any kind of worker. However, in many communities if a child were to be segregated from adult work, this would prevent her from ever becoming a mature member of that community (Morelli et al., 2003).

For example, communities as different as the Efe foragers in the Congo and the Maya in Guatemala involve children as young as 5 in work activities, and if the Maya children attend school it is only for a few hours a day, and for a few years. The Maya, in fact, view school as a "foreign" institution, partly because the teaching is in Spanish, not in the Mayan language that is spoken at home, but also because what children learn in school seems not directly relevant to their lives, or to the ways of the community.

You will see during the course of this chapter and the chapter that follows that we can distinguish between institutionalized schooling that is largely System 2 focused and types of education that are focused primarily on System 1 (while not necessarily excluding System 2). The latter fosters practical agency in a way that is founded in interdependence, while the former seeks to foster autonomy and independence (collaboration is considered "cheating"), and in these respects is often at odds with community values.

Another example of the way in which children can learn by participating alongside adults and older children is provided by the Meriam people, who live on islands in the Torres Straits, between Australia and Papua New Guinea. These people grow their food and trade it, but they also fish and forage on the tidal reef, collecting edible mollusks such as conch and clams. The adults are reluctant to take younger children on the reef, but once a child turns 4 or 5 they are expected to accompany adults in order to retrieve seafood that the adult has spotted. At first they simply learn what is edible, and what dangers to avoid. But by around 6 they begin to forage in groups with older children, actively helping them and learning where to look for shellfish and which ones to select. Their foraging skills evolve in this collaboration with older children. Counts of the number and type of seafood that the children collect show that because they move more slowly than adults they encounter fewer of the most prized food items, and so their foraging is less selective and less efficient. But they still collect enough to contribute to the family meal at the end of the day (Bird & Bird, 2002).

As we noted in Chapter 10, another way in which children, especially girls, contribute to the social and economic well-being of their family is by taking care of infants and other young children. In that chapter we considered this from the perspective of the young child, but older children also benefit from being given these responsibilities. It amounts to a kind of apprenticeship in which the master is the older child. Still far too young to have children herself yet old enough to act responsibly, a girl in middle childhood can reduce her mother's burdens at a time when, without available contraception, the mother is likely to have given birth again. (The spacing of births varies with culture; for example, among the !Kung foragers, who live in an environment with limited resources, there is about a 50-month interval between births: Blurton-Jones, 1986.) The 5-year-old is just enough older than a newborn, and just enough younger than a teenager, to be especially useful around the house, and viewed in evolutionary terms this usefulness

Figure 11.2   Children at play in the Masig island of the Torres Straits

contributes not only to the child's own survival but also the survival of her relatives. She contributes to the well-being of her family, and so to the reproduction of the community.

During middle childhood, consequently, children are often assigned care-taking responsibilities for those younger than themselves. In industrialized countries it would be viewed as evidence of parental misconduct for a 6-year-old to be left at home with complete responsibility for younger siblings, but in many cultures this is standard practice.

For example, Zinacantán Maya children aged 3 to 11 teach their 2-year-old siblings how to do every-day household tasks such as cooking and washing. The older children's skills increase with practice in this guidance, and they become highly skilled at initiating teaching situations, explaining, giving manual demonstrations, and offering feedback (Maynard, 2002). Middle childhood, then, is not only a develop-mental stage for learning, it can also be a stage for teaching.

In middle childhood, in fact, children of different ages will often form a **chain of support**, in which one helps the next, and so on, often under the supervision of adult women. This kind of **shared-management family caretaking system** offers benefits to caregivers—who are freed to per-form other important tasks—and to the children, who now understand the tasks and roles assigned to them and enjoy fulfilling these.

However, this kind of family organization depends on the local circumstances. Families living in rural settings that have organized their childcare in this way lose this kind of chain if they move to the city, and their children are likely to become more disruptive and aggressive, less sociable, and likely to pester their mothers (Weisner, 1987).

There is a widespread tendency for girls more than boys to start caretaking and domestic activities at this age, though the precise character of what they do varies. In Kenya, for example, 90 percent of girls aged 5 to 9 take care of younger children, and 82 percent of boys, but by age 10 or 12 only

28 percent of boys continue to do so, while 82 percent of girls continue (Reynolds, 1991, cited in Weisner, 1996). At this point the mother provides only about 23 percent of all caretaking acts—her children provide the rest.

Indeed, boys and girls are often given very different responsibilities during middle childhood, in a way that reflects the gender distribution of the work that adults do in their community. Boys may at first participate in taking care of younger children, but as they grow older they will often leave the domestic sphere, perhaps herding animals on their own, or working alongside adult men. For example, in the Ngoni of Malawi in Central Africa boys must leave the protection of their home at age 6 and move into dormitories, where adult men from outside the family are in charge, and they begin to engage in at least rudimentary forms of adult work. This abrupt change is stressful for them: "From having been impudent, well fed, self-confident, and spoiled youngsters among the women many of them quickly became skinny, scruffy, subdued, and had a hunted expression" (Read, 1959, p. 49).

The separation between the genders that began in early childhood continues through middle childhood and into adolescence. In most cultures, even when they are not working, boys and girls are passing the time with same-sex peers, as adults expect them to.

2.2 LEARNING THROUGH APPRENTICESHIP

In many parts of the world, even today, the education of children in the specialized skills and knowledge for adult work takes the form of **apprenticeship**. An adult master will provide training to children by organizing their participation in productive labor, together with instruction and guidance.

We tend to take classroom teaching as the standard against which to judge and understand how children learn. But apprenticeship is a far older and more widespread kind of education. Apprenticeship illustrates clearly that learning involves not only new ways of knowing and acting, but also new forms of identity, and ways of being. Apprenticeship entails preliminary and provisional membership in a community of practitioners, and mastery of the ways of this community, through what has been called **legitimate peripheral participation** (Lave & Wenger, 1991).

For example, a midwife in a Mayan community is most likely herself the daughter of a midwife. As a child she would have observed her mother giving a massage to a woman about to give birth, run to get supplies, and heard stories about difficult cases (Jordan, 1989).

In many cultures middle childhood is the age when children become apprentices. They leave the confines of their family for the first time, some for a few hours each day, others permanently.

2.3 FORMAL VERSUS INFORMAL EDUCATION?

How best to conceptualize and understand these types of learning? Learning outside school has often been defined as education that occurs "in context" through participation in everyday activities, and considered **informal education**. Schooling, in contrast, is considered **formal education**. However, the formal/informal dichotomy is problematic, since it implies that simply because learning occurs outside a classroom it lacks "form," and that a classroom is not itself a context. It also conflates several dimensions of difference between school and non-school learning. A more informative approach would be to define kinds of education in terms of (1) whether learning is intentional or

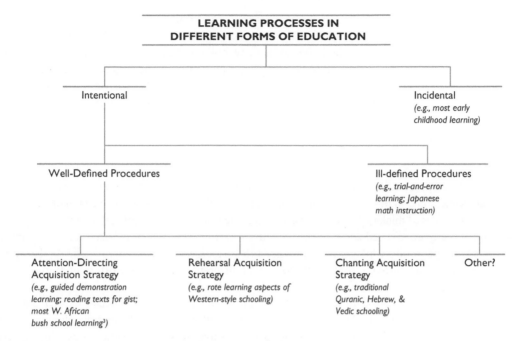

Figure 11.3 Forms of education arranged on the basis of the learning processes that are involved

Source: Strauss (1984)

incidental on the part of the learner, (2) whether or not its procedures are clearly defined, and (3) the specific learning strategies that are employed (see Figure 11.3) (Strauss, 1984).

Institutionalized schooling is a place of intentional learning, with clearly defined procedures, and specific strategies such as memorization, rehearsal, and testing.

However, learning through participation may also be intentional, with procedures, such as guided demonstration and even explicit instruction, that are designed and implemented by adults. Learning through observation is more likely to have ill-defined procedures, but it too can be intentional. When a community has no schools, it may still have deliberately organized education that occurs apart from everyday life.

Often, these organized and intentional forms of education are intended to teach attitudes and values as much as knowledge and skills. Initiation rites are a clear example—they involve a sequence of challenging activities that are intended to educate their young participants.

There has been very little research on this kind of education, in which children may be taught such things as military skills, music, the memorization of an oral tradition, and much more.

2.4 WHEN FATHERS RESEMBLE THEIR CHILDREN

The various kinds of arrangements that societies make for the education of their children—in particular, the kinds and degree of contact that occur between children and adults—obviously have an impact on those children. Less obviously, the arrangements also have an impact on the society, precisely because the children will themselves become adults and, in turn, have their own children. There is a positive feedback loop between childhood and adulthood, so that psychological characteristics developed in middle childhood, for example, will become amplified and distributed through the culture over time.

It has been suggested that this feedback loop can explain a difference between cultures that has fascinated social scientists for a long time, and been a topic of much hot debate and argument—the so-called "primitive" thinking that appears in some groups (Tuzin, 1990).

Freud proposed that adults in some cultures are "primitive" because they have not outgrown their childhood. Piaget proposed that young children show "primitive" thinking because they have not yet accommodated to reality. Both these psychologists viewed development as a movement from a "primitive" mentality to a "civilized" one, and saw it as a process that both individuals and societies go through, some making more progress than others. In this view, some individuals and some cultures may hold on to fantasies, to beliefs in magical causes, and to irrational modes of thinking that fail to acknowledge the realities of the empirical world.

We have already considered some of the objections to this view, which is based on the assumption that there is a single reality which is conceptualized in various ways, some more adequate than others. We have seen how the "ontological turn" proposes that different cultures have different ontologies, different cosmologies.

However, an additional possibility is that when adults seem childlike this is because of what and how they learned when they were children. If, as we now think, cultures define distinct developmental pathways from childhood to adulthood, some of those pathways may foster the psychological characteristics we call "primitive"—appeals to fantasy, an emphasis on imagination rather than logic, emotionality, and ways of thinking and relating that are conflict-laden and show sexual repression and hostility.

Non-literate societies, in particular, tend to rely less on deliberate adult–child instruction than do societies where children go to school. In some of these societies children will work alongside adults. In others, however, children may be largely excluded from adult affairs, and this can alter the conditions for their development.

Donald Tuzin was an anthropologist who conducted fieldwork among the Arapesh in New Guinea, a people who practice strict separation between adults and children (Tuzin, 1990). The Arapesh do not require their children to learn a specific work skill, but instead allow them to follow their own inclinations. A child can learn to weave, or to make bracelets, or can simply do nothing. What is more important, for the Arapesh, is that children learn to express their emotions. Once they reach middle childhood, girls spend their time involved in female activities with other girls and adult women. On the other hand, the boys, who are considered not yet physically strong enough to help the adult men when they hunt large animals, or build houses, or plant and harvest, are left to their own devices. The boys hang out together, roaming the village and its surroundings.

Tuzin argued that because of this separation between Arapesh boys and adult men, especially during middle childhood, the boys learn mainly from one another. This gives their understanding of the world a distinctive emotional and cognitive quality. Many topics the boys learn about together—topics such as sex and death—are ones which everyone in their culture views with anxiety and a degree of irrationality. In addition, middle childhood is a stage when boys are still struggling with the conflicts and stresses of their differentiation from the mother (see Chapter 10), and in consequence their thoughts and actions have an aggressive and sexual character.

Both social scientists and parents have tended to assume that there is a one-way process of influence that flows from adult to child, a process in which culture is something "out there" before the child was even born. They may call this process education, or socialization, or enculturation. However, we have seen that children are in fact both active learners and active teachers, and they actively make sense of what adults are up to. Tuzin identified how this establishes a positive feedback loop between childhood and adulthood. It works in the following manner.

Children who are in close contact with adults in middle childhood are likely to come to think in ways that more closely resemble the thinking of those adults. This kind of contact with adults occurs in cultures with schools, of course, but not only in these. As we saw in the previous sections, there are many cultures in which children learn from adults, or are taught by them, as apprentices. In such cases we would expect that children become more adult-like in their reasoning. As a result, when they are adults they will be less "childish."

Among the Arapesh, in contrast, the separation of boys from adults gives their psychology specific characteristics that persist into adulthood, because the children sustain these characteristics in their peer groups and teach them to other children. For example, Arapesh men are reluctant to accept domestic responsibilities until they are in their late 20s, and they tend to continue to view their gods as literal personifications.

When children learn with or from adults they come to resemble those adults. Then, when they become adults themselves, they will in turn teach the next generation of children, who will be even more adult-like. In contrast, when children learn mainly from other children, and teach other children their own age or a little younger, the adults they become will remain more like the children they once were in their beliefs and reasoning.

In short, two different cultural arrangements for the contact between adults and children produce quite distinct conditions for learning and development in middle childhood, with consequences that persist into adulthood. Adults the world over think and feel in ways that reflect the children they once were, but the kind of children they were depended on the contact they had with their elders.

This positive feedback implies that what has been called "primitive" thinking is not the consequence of slow development, or of arrested development, but is the result of a middle childhood lived largely outside adult

Figure 11.4 Boys among the Arapesh

supervision and guidance, with the consequence that qualities of imagination and sublimation, fears and ambitions, are preserved into adulthood.

In Chapter 12 I will consider another example of this positive feedback, the analysis by Nancy Chodorow of when mothers resemble their daughters.

3. UNDERSTANDING OTHER PEOPLE: MENTAL STATES AND INSTITUTIONS WITH ROLES AND RULES

Research on the ways that other people are understood during middle childhood has been much less extensive than the investigations focused on early childhood. It has often been assumed that once children pass false-belief tasks their achievement of theory of mind is completed. Research on children's understanding of normativity at this stage is also very limited—the research on this theme has been focused on toddlers and young children.

Consequently, in order to draw some conclusions about these capacities we will need to draw inferences indirectly, based upon an area that has been much studied in middle childhood, namely judgments about moral issues.

3.1 STUDIES OF MORAL JUDGMENT

Given our discussion in previous chapters of how toddlers can grasp intentions-in-action and customary practices, and the way young children can understand prior intentions and social conventions, it may seem odd to learn that for many years developmental psychologists have believed that children at 6 years of age judge the goodness and badness of actions merely in terms of their physical consequences, and simply do what powerful adults demand and reward (Kohlberg & Hersch, 1977).

As I mentioned in Chapter 10, Piaget observed that younger children judge an act in terms of its consequences, rather than in terms of the intentions of the wrongdoer. For example, a younger child considers it more harmful to break 10 plates accidentally than to break one plate on purpose. An older child, however, will judge the act on the basis of the intention to do harm. The younger children, apparently, have only a limited understanding of people's intentions.

In addition, based on his interviews with Swiss children of different ages playing the game of marbles, Piaget came to the conclusion that young children viewed the rules of the game as sacred and unchangeable, and as having in effect a moral force. As he wrote:

> We have had occasion to see during our analysis of the rules of a game that the [young] child begins by regarding these rules not only as obligatory, but also as inviolable and requiring to be kept to literally. We also showed that this attitude was the result of the constraint exercised by the older children on the younger and of the pressures of adults themselves, rules being thus identified with duties properly so called. (Piaget, 1965[1932], p. 109)

In other words, the younger children apparently didn't draw a distinction between social conventions and moral norms. They accepted the authority of their parents, and judged right and wrong on the basis of their respect for this authority.

We shall see in Chapter 12 that the games played in middle childhood involve explicit rules: games such as baseball, football, chess, and others in which the children invent their own rules. Piaget proposed that these rule-based games mark a significant change in children's understanding of right and wrong. It is the change from **heteronomous morality** to **autonomous morality**. Morality is "heteronomous" when it comes from outside: young children, in Piaget's view, understand right and wrong in terms of the evaluations of an authority, such as a parent. Morality becomes "autonomous" when children themselves become capable of deciding what is right and wrong, and Piaget considered games with rules to be evidence of such an ability.

In Piaget's view, the rules of games in middle childhood become the conditions for social relationships among the children, laws that govern the equilibrium of these relationships. Mutual respect and solidarity among the children are now the basis for their sense of justice. Feelings such as sympathy, gratitude, and vengeance have now taken on a logical form.

For Piaget, then:

> All morality consists in a system of rules, and the essence of all morality is to be sought for in the respect which an individual acquires for these rules. (Piaget, 1965[1932], p. 13)

You can see similarities with Tomasello's definition of morality:

> From an evolutionary perspective, morality is a form of cooperation ... Without attempting a complete definition, in our evolutionary perspective, moral interactions are a subset of cooperative interactions. Arguably, the main function of morality is to regulate an individual's social interactions with others in the general direction of cooperation, given that all individuals are at least somewhat selfish. (Tomasello & Vaish, 2013, pp. 231–232)

Inspired by Piaget's research, moral judgment—how right and wrong are understood—has become a widely studied aspect of children's conceptions of the world.

In research that became very influential, Lawrence Kohlberg interviewed boys aged 7 to 16 about hypothetical moral dilemmas. One of these, the well-known Heinz dilemma, is shown below. Kohlberg identified three major levels of development of moral judgment. These levels were (I) a premoral or preconventional morality, (II) a morality of conventional role-conformity, and (III) a morality of self-accepted moral principles. Each level was composed of two stages, defined by their general type of moral orientation.

At the first level, the preconventional level, cultural rules and labels of good and bad were interpreted in terms of physical consequences and physical power:

Type 1. **Punishment and obedience orientation**: The physical consequences of an action determine its goodness or badness. Good behavior consists of avoiding punishment and deferring to power.

Type 2. **Instrumental-relativist orientation**: Good behavior is what satisfies one's own needs. Fairness and reciprocity are interpreted in a physical, pragmatic way. The child judges that one should conform in order to obtain rewards and to have favors returned.

At the second level, the conventional level, what was judged moral is maintaining the expectations of the family, group, or nation, regardless of consequences. The social order should be maintained and justified:

Type 3. **Interpersonal concordance orientation**: One should conform in order to avoid the disapproval and dislike of other people. Moral conduct is what pleases or helps others and is approved by them: it is important to be a "good boy" or a "nice girl." Behavior is generally judged by whether the person's intention is to be nice or do well.

Type 4. **"Law and order" orientation**: One should conform in order to avoid censure by legitimate authorities, and to avoid feeling guilt. Moral conduct is doing one's duty, following the rules, respecting authority, and maintaining the social order.

At the third level, the postconventional level, there was an effort to define moral values and principles that have validity apart from the people or groups who adopt these principles:

Type 5. **Social-contract, legalistic orientation**: One should conform in order to maintain the respect of an impartial spectator, who judges actions in terms of their consequences for community welfare. Moral behavior is defined in terms of individual rights and standards. Procedures are necessary in order to reach consensus democratically. Laws can be changed when there are rational considerations to do so.

Type 6. **Universal-ethical-principle orientation**: One should conform in order to avoid self-condemnation. Behavior is moral when it follows from self-chosen ethical principles of justice, reciprocity, and equality. These principles are abstract, universal, and consistent.

Figure 11.5 shows the percentage of moral statements of each type at four ages, from 7 to 16 years of age. It shows how the simpler kinds of judgment are progressively replaced with more complex judgments.

In Kohlberg's view, these stages of moral judgment are "spontaneous products of the child's effort to make sense out of his experience in a complex social world," and they form a universal sequence, each stage arising from the earlier ones. You can see that Kohlberg proposed that the distinction an adult makes between what *is* the case and what *ought* to be the case is constructed gradually as a child develops. In the lower stages, children's judgments about moral issues confuse "is" and "ought," and make reference to personal and conventional concerns. As moral development progresses, what "ought" to be done is increasingly separated from what "is" done, and from existing laws, norms, and customs.

In particular, only at level III, which starts to appear at around 13 years of age, does the teenager draw a distinction between morality and convention. At level II the child is unable to recognize that, for example, a law may be immoral.

In Europe, a woman was near death from cancer. One drug might save her, a form of radium that a druggist in the same town had recently discovered. The druggist was charging $2,000, ten times what the drug cost him to make. The sick woman's husband, Heinz, went to everyone he knew to borrow the money, but he could get together only about half of what it cost. He told the druggist that his wife was dying and asked him to sell it cheaper or let him pay later. But the druggist said no. The husband got desperate and broke into the man's store to steal the drug for his wife. Should the husband have done that? Why?

Level	Orientation
I: Preconventional level	
Stage I	Punishment and obedience
Stage 2	Instrumental relativist
II: Conventional level	
Stage 3	Interpersonal concordance
Stage 4	"Law and order"
III: Postconventional level	
Stage 5	Social contract, legalistic
Stage 6	Universal ethical principle

Figure 11.5   The three levels and six stages of Kohlberg's theory of the development of moral judgment

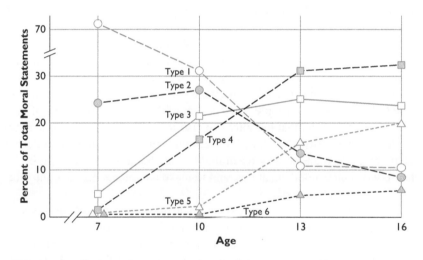

Figure 11.6   The percentage of moral statements of each of the six types of moral judgment at four ages

Source: Kohlberg (1964, p. 403)

It is worth pausing to reflect upon a significant difference between Kohlberg's findings and those of research with younger children. We saw in Chapter 10 that there is evidence that even young children around 4 years of age distinguish between moral transgressions (that do harm) and transgressions of social conventions (that maintain social order) in the preschool playground (Nucci & Turiel, 1978). Yet Kohlberg concluded that this distinction is not recognized until early adolescence!

One likely reason for this difference lies in the methodology of these studies. Research with young children has tended to take the form of observations of their activity in the home, in the playground, or in the laboratory. Studies in middle childhood, in contrast, have often taken advantage of the child's rapidly advancing verbal skills, and conducted interviews. In addition, these interviews have often presented questions based on stories about hypothetical situations and dilemmas.

It seems likely that these different techniques tap different kinds of knowledge: practical know-how (System 1) on the one hand, and reflective judgment (System 2) on the other. This may well account for at least some of the inconsistencies in findings—for example, the age and stage at which children start to pay attention to a person's intentions in judging their actions as moral or immoral. Young children, and even older toddlers, may have a practical grasp of other people's intentions, but it may not be until middle childhood that this grasp can be put into words and explained to an interviewer. In addition, only older children will be able to reason about a situation that is presented to them verbally, rather than one they have experienced directly.

Kohlberg's claim that no distinction is recognized in middle childhood between moral norms and social conventions was challenged by the work of Elliot Turiel. It was Turiel, with Larry Nucci, who studied young children's reactions to transgressions in the preschool playground, and Turiel insisted that in middle childhood a distinction is indeed drawn between moral matters and matters of social convention. These, Turiel proposed, are distinct **domains** of social knowledge (along with a third domain, that of personal matters) (Turiel, 1975).

The same distinction has been found outside school in children's play together (Nucci & Nucci, 1982), and in different cultures (Turiel, 1983). For Turiel and his colleagues, these domains "constitute separate developmental pathways" (Nucci & Turiel, 2009, p. 152).

This line of research, based on both clinical interviews and observations, suggests that young children consider it wrong to hurt or mistreat people, independent of the social conventions of their community, though they do not yet understand that morality can also involve issues of fairness and reciprocity. In addition, young children have difficulty taking into account in their moral judgments the needs of several people at the same time. By the time they reach middle childhood, however, children become able to understand relatively complex moral situations, and to make judgments that take into account both the moral and the nonmoral aspects of a situation.

The observation that children become able to coordinate the moral and nonmoral aspects of situations is an important one. Contrary to Kohlberg's claim that moral judgments become increasingly independent of factual considerations, it has become clear that every moral judgment is based on interpretation of the facts that are considered relevant. For example, the judgment that it is immoral to kill may be changed by knowledge that the person who dies had a painful, incurable illness, while the person who arranged their death was a doctor in a terminal care clinic.

One result of this dependence of moral judgments on factual information is that the content of children's moral judgments is not the same everywhere. Their understanding of morality operates against a background of their understanding of the world. Moral evaluations are made against a background of construals and interpretations about what are taken to be the relevant aspects of reality.

This means that what children consider immoral in one culture may be considered perfectly acceptable in another, where there are different beliefs about reality: "Take as an example the practice of putting one's elderly parents to death. This practice is presumed to be common in cultures where it is believed, as a matter of fact, that people continue to exist in the afterlife with the same condition of health they had at the time of death" (Wainryb, 2004, p. 7). In such a culture, it is generally accepted that there is a moral obligation to ensure one's parents' place in the afterlife. It is on the basis of such interpretations of reality—what we have called a cosmology—that people's intentions are inferred.

Once we recognize that people's moral judgments are based not only on their values but also on their beliefs, it becomes an interesting question to ask to what degree, and when, children take this into account. It also becomes clear that there may well be a connection between children's development in making moral judgments and their understanding of other people's beliefs, desires, and intentions (Chandler et al., 2000). It is becoming recognized that children's understanding of other people provides "a set of factual beliefs and understandings (for example, about how the mind in fact works) that inform and constrain in systematic ways children's moral judgments" (Wainryb, 2004, p. 14). Consequently, we can turn now to consider what is known about the way children in middle childhood understand other people's beliefs and desires.

3.2 THE MENTALISTIC STANCE

As I noted, there has been much less research on understanding of other people in middle childhood than in early childhood. Performance on first-order false-belief tasks is usually at a ceiling after 5 years of age; that is to say, children now pass these tasks and it is assumed that their acquisition of theory of mind is complete.

Nonetheless, important developments take place during the years from 6 to 11. Children come to understand a wider range of mental states, and their understanding of mental actions grows, as they learn how to control and regulate their own thoughts, beliefs, and feelings. They start to understand differences between kinds of belief, and the origins of people's beliefs (Miller, 2012).

Importantly, children come to understand second-order false beliefs—what one person knows or believes about another. For example, they can understand that "Tom believes that John thinks that it is raining outside." They now recognize that people can have beliefs not only about the material world but also about other people's "mental states"—not only their beliefs, but also their intentions and emotions. Second-order false-belief tasks involve reasoning about a person's mistaken beliefs about another person's beliefs. More complex reasoning will become possible in adolescence: for example, that "Ben thinks that Anna believes that he knows that Mum wants perfume for her birthday."

During the years of middle childhood, then, children become increasingly sophisticated in applying their understanding of other people to make sense of complex social situations. They grasp that people can have different interpretations of the same situation, that people with the same information can interpret it in different ways, and that facts are often ambiguous and open to various interpretations. Children begin "thinking about beliefs different from their own not as necessarily false or mistaken, but as alternative interpretations of reality" (Wainryb, 2004). This new ability has been called both a **representational theory of mind** (Wainryb & Brehl, 2006) and an **interpretive theory of mind** (Carpendale & Chandler, 1996).

Children now recognize that a person's moral decisions and actions are based on what that person believes to be true, although they might be mistaken. As a consequence they now tend to forgive a person who acted on the basis of false beliefs. For example, told a story about a society in which children are beaten with sticks because adults believe it is right to hurt children, they strongly disapprove. In contrast, when told a story about a society in which children who misbehave are beaten to drive out evil spirits, they disapprove less because they judge these people to be acting with good intentions (Wainryb, 2004).

The research on moral judgment that we considered in the previous section also illustrates how in middle childhood children have become able to talk about, and reason about, people's desires and beliefs. Together, these two strands of research suggest that it is now accurate to attribute to the child a "theory of mind" in the sense of System 2 abilities to discuss and reason explicitly about another person's beliefs, desires, and motives. Presumably this new ability does not replace the earlier System 1 ability to understand intentions that are visible in a person's actions, and then to grasp prior intentions. The capacity for judgements about mental states surely builds upon those earlier abilities.

Middle childhood, then, seems to be the age in which an understanding of other people's actions is achieved that is based not only on intention-in-action and prior intentions but also on the attribution of private and personal beliefs and desires, which are viewed as internal mental states. In this stage, children in Western culture accept the dominant folk psychology that interprets consciousness as inner and mental. Whereas younger children understand desirability, for example, as an objective property of situations (Perner, 1991), now children view desires as "subjective relations to reality" (Wainryb & Brehl, 2006, p. 140). Following Dennet (1978), I am calling this new way of understanding people the **mentalistic stance**. (See Figure 11.7.)

However, we must immediately add that more research is needed with children living in cultures with a different ethnopsychology (Lillard, 1998, 1999). In addition, we shall see in Chapter 14 that one consequence of this new grasp of beliefs as interpretations of reality can be a step into epistemological and ethical relativism, in which no distinction is drawn between knowledge and opinion.

Once again, however, this mentalistic stance is not the only way to understand another person's actions. Middle childhood is, in addition, the time of a growing ability to comprehend the ways that institutions define the roles that people can adopt, and so dictate their actions. In parallel with the emergence of the mentalistic stance is a new understanding of normativity, to which we now turn.

3.3 THE INSTITUTIONAL STANCE

The young child came to understand other people within a social context of characters, conventions, and scenarios that was grounded in the Great-We of infancy. In middle childhood, the child is now often involved in more than one social context. The family involves not only customary practices but also often rules and roles. The school, however, involves a different set of rules and roles. Each day the child moves from being a *daughter* to being a *student*, and back again. While this, too, is an area in which more research is needed, there is evidence that in middle childhood an understanding of other people can now take into account the institutional context in which they are acting, the role they occupy in that institution, and the rights and responsibilities that define that role. I shall call this understanding of the roles and rules that define what people do, and what they *must* do, the **institutional stance**.

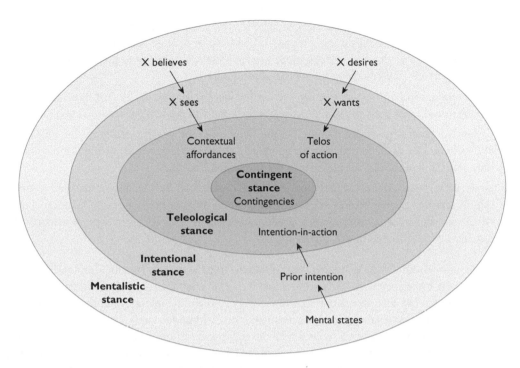

Figure 11.7 The mentalistic stance in middle childhood

Indeed, it seems likely that a child's understanding of beliefs and desires occurs *within* the framework of an institutional reality. For example, until the 1960s, punishment in British schools included being beaten with a cane by a teacher or a senior student. The intention-in-action would appear to be that of hurting the child. The prior intention would seem to be to punish. Yet this action was understood by people within the institution in terms of their belief that caning was a just penalty for wrongdoing, that it discouraged further misbehavior, and that it was in the best interests of the child. To understand the beliefs and desires of someone who is hitting a child with a stick one must be able to understand the institutional reality in which that person is participating.

In an institution, the relations, interactions and actions are impersonal and formal. What do we know about children's understanding of these characteristics? There was a burst of research in the 1970s and 1980s that centered on children's understanding of institutions such as banks, shops, and schools, though since then the question has largely been ignored.

For example, Hans Furth and colleagues conducted interviews with almost 200 children aged 5 to 11, in Southern England, about social institutions that the children knew firsthand, such as schools, stores, and transportation, and familiar roles such as teachers, doctors, and police, and entities such as money (Furth et al., 1976).

Furth and his colleagues distinguished four stages in the children's understanding of these social institutions:

(1) Minimal inference beyond the observed events. For example, a shop may be understood as providing food, and as also providing money in the form of change. Imaginative elaborations may be offered, such as that some of the money received by a store goes to the Queen. Nearly all the children aged 5 and 6 displayed this kind of reasoning.

(2) Basic recognition of social functions, such as the fact that payments by customers are made with money saved from their work. This kind of reasoning was typical of children aged 7 and 8.

(3) Expanded functional understanding, as the child starts to grasp general social functions and obligations. Just as customers pay for goods in a store, storekeepers must pay for the goods that they sell. This reasoning was shown by children aged 9 to 11.

(4) Grasp of some general rules pertaining to social institutions. For example, the head teacher of a school receives money from the government, which obtains funds through taxation. The child still lacks, however, a comprehensive understanding of societal structures. A minority of the older children reasoned in this manner.

It appears, then, that children's understanding of institutional roles advances from the simple view that someone occupies a role when they want to do so, and that their characteristics are individual and idiosyncratic, to the more complex view that occupation of a role depends on ability, interest, and training, and that role occupants have stereotypic characteristics. Increasingly, the child understands the "impersonal" character of institutional roles: that people act in accord with the rights and responsibilities of the roles they occupy, rather than from their personal preferences and desires, and that the rules that define these rights and responsibilities stem from abstract entities (the government, the economy) rather than from personal authority.

It is worth noting that Furth later came to have some doubts about his own conclusions, after he conducted research on young children's fantasy play. Furth, like Tomasello, came to believe that the work of constructing society begins in the pretense play of early childhood. He noted that:

> The societal features and the interactional use of pretend frames observed in the play of 4- to 5-year-old children show competencies that stand in sharp contrast to the ignorance and inconsistencies reported for much older children in the research reviewed at the beginning of this study. (Furth, 1996, p. 25)

Furth attributed this difference to two factors. The first parallels the point just made about the methodology of interviews versus observations. The older children whom Furth interviewed were talking reflectively about society, while the young children whom he observed were displaying their practical knowledge. In addition, second, the older children were talking about the world of grown-ups, while the young children were constructing their own pretend society.

Along a similar line, Anna Emilia Berti and Anna Silvia Bombi carried out a series of investigations into children's understanding of basic economic phenomena, such as the operation of banks (Berti & Bombi, 1988). They distinguished five increasingly sophisticated levels of understanding:

(1) Young children think that anyone can go to a bank and get money.

(2) From 6 or 7 to 9 or 10 years of age, children know that only people who have deposited money in a bank can request it.

(3) By age 9 or 10, children know a bank also lends money.

(4) Around age 11 or 12, children understand the relationship between deposits and loans, but do not understand interest.

(5) Adolescents grasp that the interest received on loans makes possible the interest paid on deposits.

(6) A few adolescents around age 14 to 16 recognize that interest received is higher than interest paid, so that banks make a profit.

At age 11 to 12, half of the children in this study were only at levels 2 and 3. Nonetheless, this research too indicates that middle childhood is a stage in which the impersonal rights and obligations of institutional roles become salient.

What about children's understanding of the school as a social institution? Interviews by Marta Laupa with children aged 7 through 11 about the authority of a teacher versus that of a peer found that the oldest children were least likely to accept that a teacher has authority to intervene in a conflict over use of a slide that is off school premises, though children at all ages accepted that a teacher can legitimately intervene in a fight between children outside school (Laupa & Turiel, 1986). Similar interviews about whether a school principal can direct behavior and make rules in a public park and in a child's home showed that the older children were least likely to accept that the principal had legitimate authority outside school (Laupa & Turiel, 1993).

Similarly, Nicholas Emler and colleagues interviewed children aged 6 to 12, from middle-class and working-class backgrounds, in Scotland and France (Emler et al., 1987). By 11 years of age, children

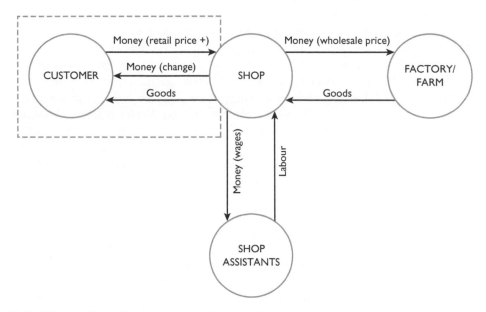

Figure 11.8   The shop lies at the intersection of three economic systems

Source: Jahoda (1984)

recognized that "there is a hierarchy of responsibility in school and that teachers are in their turn subject to the authority of persons, such as head teachers, above them in this hierarchy." The children insisted that teachers cannot change or ignore the rules, and should not act on the basis of personal preferences. The French children recognized the features of school bureaucracy somewhat earlier than the Scottish children, but at the same time they were more hostile towards it.

Studies such as these suggest that the roles and rules of a societal institution, such as a bank, a shop, and a school, become evident in middle childhood. A bank involves the roles of depositor, borrower, and lender. A shop involves staff, customers, and a manager. A school involves the roles of student, teacher, and head teacher. In each case, there are explicit rules and laws that govern the obligations and responsibilities of the people who occupy such roles. It seems that Arnold Gesell was correct when he wrote that in middle childhood the child becomes a small businessman, organizes gangs and clubs, and competes with his fellows.

In Chapter 3 we saw how humans, in response to the problems that followed from increasing population, constructed societal institutions to coordinate human activity and organize the use of technologies of increasing complexity. But what exactly is a societal institution? There is some debate over the answer to this question. A helpful definition can be found in the *Stanford Encyclopedia of Philosophy*: "Roughly speaking, an institution that is an organisation or system of organisations consists of an embodied (occupied by human persons) structure of differentiated roles. These roles are defined in terms of tasks, and rules regulating the performance of those tasks" (Miller, 2014).

Philosopher John Searle has proposed that the social world is an "institutional reality." Societal institutions play a key part, but so too do other kinds of social objects, processes, and events, all of which are, Searle argues, **institutional facts**. These institutional facts are "the glue" which enables "the construction of social reality" (Searle, 2005, p. 1).

Despite the name, an institutional fact is not an item of information, but an aspect of the reality in which people live. Money, presidents, and private property are institutional facts in many societies. Searle points out that these institutional facts share a common formal structure: "X counts as Y in context C" (Searle, 1995, 2006). For example, a plastic card counts as money in the context of a modern economy but not in a small hunter-gatherer group deep in the Amazon forest. A yellow line counts as a prohibition against parking on a city street but not in a Jackson Pollack painting. A specific person counts as president in the context of the US political system but not in Saudi Arabia. Some of these facts involve societal institutions in that they involve roles and rules. Others are simpler—for example, in the context of a friendship one person's words may count as a promise to the other, but not in the context of an encounter with a stranger. Or simpler still, a particular sequence of sounds may count as a word in the English language but not in Swahili.

In Searle's terms, then, human societies are constituted of societal institutions and related institutional facts. For Homo sapiens, unlike any other species, the construction of a complex niche of interlocking institutions and institutional facts has become a crucial aspect of survival and reproduction.

In order to explain the implications of the institutional character of human social life, we need to understand two additional technical terms. We have noted that institutional facts such as money, presidents, and promises constitute new kinds of objects. Searle calls this an **ontology**. He refers to institutional facts as a "huge invisible institutional ontology" that social scientists have generally taken for granted.

Institutional facts have another property: they define rights and responsibilities—a **deontology**. The terms "ontology" and "deontology" sound very similar, and they have similar Greek roots. Ontology is the study of what exists, from the Greek word for "being"; deontology is the study of duty and obligation, from the Greek words for "being necessary." The ontology is what something *counts as*, while the deontology is what one *can and cannot* do, *should and should not* do, with that something. For example, if an animal counts as a household pet, one should in general not eat it. However, in a time of widespread starvation, that pet might count as food.

The institutionalized character of the societal niches that humans have constructed consists in the new kinds of objects—clans, presidents, subprime loans—that humans recognize, and the new kinds of motives—duties, laws, rights, conventions—that humans acknowledge. Institutional facts open up new possibilities for action, and they close off other possibilities. For example, Americans can do things with a dollar bill that they cannot do with just any piece of paper, though their dollar may be worthless in another country. Among the Matsigenka in the Amazon, as another example, a man cannot marry the daughter of his uncle because she counts as his sister, but he can marry the daughter of his aunt (Johnson, 2003). These examples illustrate a key feature of institutional facts that Searle calls their **status function**—a function that can be performed by someone or something not because of intrinsic characteristics, but because it has a status that is collectively recognized.

Different societies, of course, are constituted of different institutional facts. One society may have a president, another a monarch. Two societies may both have money, but their coins will not be directly interchangeable. We saw in Chapter 9 that cultural anthropologists have been hotly debating what has become known as the "ontological turn"—the proposal that people in a different culture don't simply have different perceptions and conceptions of the world, they actually live in a different world, and that ethnography must aim to grasp its ontology (Kohn, 2015; Pedersen, 2012; Viveiros de Castro, 2012).

At first glance this proposal might sound fanciful, but viewed in terms of Searle's concept of institutional facts it is entirely reasonable. In the USA, people live in a world of senators, freeways, dollars, and hedge-fund managers. The Matsigenka, in contrast, live in a world of spirits, co-wives, cotton-spinning, and manioc beer. The two ontologies are quite different (not to mention the deontologies). This is not a matter of individual perceptions and conceptions, because institutional facts are created not by what individuals believe but by public practices (involving other institutional facts) that everyone participates in.

In middle childhood, then, children recognize the roles and rules of societal institutions. These institutions are institutional facts. Looking back on previous stages, we can now recognize that toddlers and young children recognize simpler kinds of institutional facts. Everyday artifacts are institutional facts, in the sense that what can be done with them is defined not only by their physical characteristics but also by custom. The characters in fantasy play are institutional facts: young children declare that "This stick counts as a horse in the context of our play." Children are, evidently, ascending the levels of complexity of the institutional facts of their society.

3.4 EMOTION REGULATION

Finally, societal institutions often prescribe the emotions that are acceptable, and how emotions should be controlled or managed. The work that someone does to induce or inhibit their feelings in order to

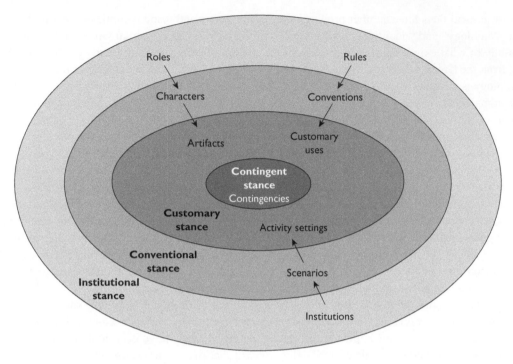

Figure 11.9 The institutional stance in middle childhood

make them appropriate to a situation is called **emotion work** (Hochschild, 1979). By the end of the 5-to-7 transition the child begins to regulate her emotions in simple ways, saying to her mother, for example, "I am going to be mad at you for a long time," adding, after a brief silence, "A whole two weeks" (Kravtsova, 2006). During middle childhood the regularities of communication and interaction with others in a variety of institutional settings—family, classroom, playground, and others—provide an additional resource for the child to endow emotions with new meaning so as to control them. At this age, children show **meta-emotion**—the ability to reflect on their own emotions and decide voluntarily what to do with them (Gottman et al., 1997). They gain greater ability to manage emotions, and the sense of self obtained as a result gives them satisfaction. This mastery of emotion is seen in the fact that children can now verbalize them.

The child now has the ability to follow emotional display rules, such as smiling and saying "thank you" for a present, even if it is not what she wanted. In middle childhood, children adopt and adapt these rules. Many studies have found that girls can mask negative emotions better than boys, and that they improve in this ability more rapidly than boys (Holodynski, 2009). Around 10 or 11 another gender difference appears: boys start to cry less than girls.

When someone learns to hide their emotions, the subjective feeling and the objective expression of emotion have become distinct. This has been called a **desomatization** of emotion (Malatesta &

Haviland, 1985). It is not clear whether what happens is a suppression of emotion, or its symbolization. Children at this stage show a **miniaturization** in the expression of emotions if they are alone, when presumably emotion serves only self-regulation. In general, emotional expression decreases during childhood. Emotions have now become inner, subjective feelings that are decoupled from action and overt speech (Damasio, 2003). There is a now a distinct difference between what the child experiences personally and what can be observed by another person. It is now possible for the child is engage in **emotional deception**, deliberately displaying an emotion that is not felt at all (Holodynski, 2004).

Our understanding of children's emotional development is still limited by the small number of studies that have involved children from cultures outside industrialized nations. One research project that explored the role of culture in children's understanding of appropriate emotional behavior involved interviews of school-aged children (2nd, 4th and 5th grade) in three societies: Brahman from India; the Tamang, who are indigenous inhabitants of the Himalayan regions of Nepal; and a farming community in the United States. The Brahmans were high-caste Hindus who had migrated to Nepal from northern India. They value group harmony and respect for authority, and require a high level of awareness and self-control in social interaction. The Tamang are a Buddhist rural people who probably originated in China. They downplay differences in luck or success, share what they have, and solve problems communally, taking all members' views into account. Like the Brahmans they also value interpersonal harmony and respect for authority, but they have a more communal and egalitarian approach to resolving conflict. They strive to become selfless and free from emotions and desires. The American children were from a rural northeastern farming community (Cole et al., 2002).

The children were told stories about both pleasant and difficult interpersonal situations, such as "You have a piece of candy. You are taking the paper off so that you can eat this great candy. Your friend is with you and she snatches the candy away from you. You say, 'Give it back!' but by that time your friend has eaten it." Then they were asked questions about how they would feel in this situation, whether they would want other people to know about their feelings, why, and what they would do.

The results provided evidence of culturally distinct patterns of appraising and acting on emotions in difficult interpersonal situations. The Tamang children were most likely to interpret the situations in terms of shame, while the Brahman and US children talked about anger. The Tamang Children did not talk about feeling anger, but about two possible emotions. They talked of feeling *thiken* ("okay") in difficult situations, and also talked of feeling shame. When asked why they would not be angry, they replied, "*Tilda bomo khaba?*" ("Why be angry?"), and explained that there was no value to being angry after the events had occurred.

The Brahman children were most likely not to want to communicate negative emotion. They described feeling angry, for example, but not showing their anger. They explained that it was wrong to show anger because "father gave me life" or "friends must cooperate" and that one should just "sit quietly." They did, however, feel entitled to experience anger, perhaps because they were proud of their high social status.

The US children appeared to be more problem focused and action oriented than children from the other two cultures. Their responses showed the American emphasis on self-expression and the importance of each individual asserting their rights. These children said that anger could be communicated in difficult situations. They showed both a higher tolerance for anger and a greater appreciation of the role of anger in resolving conflict. They were most likely to try to change the situation, rather than trying to change their emotional reaction to it.

It seems that the older children in all three cultures had developed ways of modifying their appraisal of situations to produce the emotions that their culture considered appropriate. Their ability to reflect on their own emotional responses and to manipulate them is typical of the degree of self-regulation of emotion that is achieved in middle childhood.

Middle childhood has often been seen as a time for mastering intellectual skills, using the cognitive tools of language and other material symbol systems. This mastery of one's own "inner space" (when this is what the culture emphasizes) is important. But middle childhood is also a time when the child's understanding of society, morals, ethics, and law changes, as she becomes more skilled with societal institutions. She comes to understand other people in more complex ways, and this enables changes in relationships with peers and with parents.

During middle childhood, children develop a sense of moral obligation within various institutions, and a sense of accomplishment that comes from fulfilling those obligations, or in contrast a feeling of guilt from failing to fulfill them. Increased self-control and an increased ability to plan and monitor their own activities means that children become able to complete the complex tasks that many social institutions require. They become able to anticipate and accept evaluation by authority figures—parents, teachers, elders—who inhabit institutional roles. Increasingly, what children *should* do is defined by the institutions they participate in, and they are expected to accept this.

Moral development is often regarded as a specific and separate "domain," but in fact it has a general psychological relevance. As Carol Gilligan suggests, moral actions and judgments provide a window into how children understand the social world:

> Moral development, in the work of Piaget and Kohlberg, refers specifically to the expanding conception of the social world as it is reflected in the understanding and resolution of the inevitable conflicts that arise in the relations between self and others. The moral judgment is a statement of priority, an attempt at rational resolution in a situation where, from a different point of view, the choice itself seems to do violence to justice. (Gilligan, 1977, p. 483)

In addition, understanding right and wrong is tied up with mastery of one's own behavior. The notion that it is "right" to do something, while it is "wrong" to do something else, is a way of understanding the actions, and increasingly the intentions and the beliefs and desires, of other people. But it is also a way of understanding, and increasingly directing, one's own behavior. And this, Vygotsky argued, is the key to higher psychological functions. These functions are higher principally because they are voluntary.

During middle childhood there is a growing understanding of who one is, both to oneself and in the eyes of others. At this stage, a child builds her sense of self in interactions not only with parents and siblings, but also with teachers and other students, or with community elders and leaders. This sense of self is usually called **self-concept.** There is also an *evaluation* of who one is: the child now can reflect upon her own successes and failures, as well as better understand the ways that other people view her. This is **self-esteem**—confidence and a sense of one's own value or abilities; a *generalized* sense of self, of the kind of person that one is. When things go well the child acquires a sense of being industrious, diligent, and hard-working that is based on her perception of these evaluations of her by significant other people. The consequence of a failure to resolve the challenges of this developmental stage is a negative self-evaluation. A child with low self-esteem is more vulnerable to depression and withdrawal, anger and aggression.

Morality, then, is at the core of the child's understanding of other people. It is also at the core of her self-understanding, and of her sense of her own agency.

CONCLUSION

Both Piaget and Freud viewed middle childhood as a quiet time before the challenges of adolescence and adulthood. We now know that many important changes take place during this stage. Reasoning skills increase, along with knowledge about how to learn: how to acquire new knowledge, how to use it, and how to create it. The child becomes more capable than before of establishing goals and planning how to attain these.

The years of middle childhood are an important time for mastering skills in preparation for adult work. In some cases this mastery is accomplished with the aid of adults, who immerse the child in systematic education of one kind or another. In cultures without schooling, preparation during middle childhood can take the form of instruction such as apprenticeship, in which the child learns from a master, by example and practice as well as from teaching. Many children, however, learn from working rather than from teaching. They learn "on the job," so to speak. Girls will often have tasks around the household, including taking care of younger children. Boys will often have tasks outside the household, working alongside adults, often adult men.

By the end of middle childhood, in many cultures the child is much closer to being a full member of her community. She is often, at the same time, much more individualized. She is now able to participate competently in a variety of social institutions, and she also has much more deliberate control of her thoughts, beliefs, and desires. Thinking and acting are now differentiated: the child can think before acting, and she can decide not to act. Whereas for the young child thinking, imagination, and will were carried out and developed in action, now, in middle childhood, thinking and imagining occur prior to and separate from action.

The way children learn or are educated obviously has consequences for the kinds of adult they will become. Less obvious is that a feedback loop operates—adults educate children, who become the adults who will educate the next generation of children. This is an important way in which each culture defines a distinct developmental pathway from childhood to adulthood. When children are kept apart from adults at this stage the character of their emotions and cognition is more likely to persist when they become adults.

Children now can understand the components of the institutional reality of the society in which they live. This provides the basis for moving from the intentional stance of understanding people on the basis of their goals and prior intentions to a *mentalistic stance* of inferring hidden beliefs and desires, along with an *institutional stance* of inferring the roles and rules that define what people are doing.

The child entered middle childhood with a new attitude towards herself, grounded in the discovery of her personal and private inner space. This attitude to self, this new self-awareness, led to a new attitude to others. She now appreciates that other people also have an inner space, that they too have private thoughts and feelings she cannot perceive directly. As a consequence she starts to rebuild her relationships with adults.

Social institutions define the positions that people can occupy and the perspectives they can adopt; they define the stereotypes that people use to simplify the task of understanding the world. They define what emotions are acceptable and how to manage them. The child can now grasp these aspects of her culture. She shows meta-emotion, the desomatization and miniaturization of emotion, and she can engage in emotional deception.

In consequence, skills develop in communication and negotiation with an increasingly wide range of other people, and with *kinds* of other people. The child has a growing understanding of others' perspectives, values, and systems of belief. She develops the ability to consciously employ strategies of communication and influence.

It is to these settings and practices that we turn in the next chapter.

Mentalistic stance	What the person belives (+ what they see + contextual affordances)	What the person desires (+ what the want + telos of action)	The person's mental states (+ prior intention + intention-in-action)
Institutional stance	The roles (+ characters + artifacts)	The rules for action (+ conventions + customary uses)	The institution (+ scenario + activity setting)

Figure 11.10 Two ways of understanding other people in middle childhood

SUMMARY

THE TRANSITION AT 5 TO 7 YEARS

- Between ages 5 and 7 there is a marked change in the attitude towards children in many cultures, perhaps all. They become viewed as having the capacity to be sensible and responsible, to contribute to the household in significant ways. As a consequence, children are now treated differently.

LEARNING THROUGH PARTICIPATION AND APPRENTICESHIP

- Despite this apparently universal transition, middle childhood is a stage at which the trajectories of development of children in different cultures diverge even more markedly than before. Most importantly, some are educated in institutions known as schools, while for many others their education takes place during work activities or in apprenticeships (so-called "informal" education).

- During middle childhood, the family remains an important context for development but other settings become increasingly important, settings such as school, after-school institutions, and the peer group. In many cultures, children are spending more time alongside adults.

- In this stage children are learning to control the "inner space" of their own private thoughts and feelings, guided by adults who are experts in the symbolic systems used in their culture to guide thinking, systems such as writing and mathematics. These symbol systems provide "simulations" of some aspect of reality. While notions of mental states of "belief" and "desire" are parts of a Western folk psychology, there is not yet much research on the ways children in communities with other kinds of folk psychology understand and master their own psychological processes of thinking, remembering and reasoning.

UNDERSTANDING OTHER PEOPLE: MENTAL STATES AND INSTITUTIONS WITH ROLES AND RULES

- Children also now recognize the way that social institutions define social roles, such as "student" and "teacher," or "social rank," position in a social hierarchy, that can also be said to operate "behind" behavior.

- Children become capable of forming a general sense of their own value and competence, based on a growing ability to reflect on what they do, and their increased understanding of the views that others have of them. The child will end this stage with a sense of her self-esteem or inferiority, judged against an "ideal self."

ONLINE RESOURCES

Read more: A program for street children in Bogotá. www.theguardian.com/journalismcompetition/street-children-bogota

CHAPTER 12

MIDDLE CHILDHOOD

(6–12 YEARS)

TOWARDS THE ACTUAL AND THE POSSIBLE

LEARNING OBJECTIVES

This chapter continues our examination of middle childhood:

- The school as a site for learning and development, and research on the psychological consequences of schooling.
- Research on the impact of schooling on concrete operational reasoning.
- We will consider Vygotsky's distinction between the lower psychological functions and higher psychological functions.
- The psychological and neurological consequences of learning to read and write.
- The question of what children do when they are outside school or outside work: in children's organizations, hanging out with peers, or playing games with rules.
- Factors contributing to peer reputation, also called sociometric status.
- The changing character of parenting at this stage of development, and the continuing process of forming an understanding of one's gender.

FRAMING QUESTIONS

- Can you estimate how many hours you have spent in a school or university classroom?
- In your view, how has attending school changed the way you think about the world?
- Are you in favor of children working instead of attending school? Explain your answer.

INTRODUCTION

In the previous chapter we considered how the stage of middle childhood is a time of assignment of increased responsibilities, and involvement in adult work which provides opportunities for learning various important work skills in a variety of ways, intentional and incidental, with well-defined or ill-defined processes. In this chapter we turn to examine a very different context for teaching and learning, that of the school classroom. The past few centuries have seen "a transformation unique in the history of our species: the spread of formal schooling and literacy around the world" (Weisner, 1984, p. 361). The institution of schooling has old roots, but for much of its existence it has been restricted to an elite—those children who need to master material systems of recording and manipulating symbols, often for economic purposes.

Increasingly, though, schooling has come to be expected of all children. In this chapter we explore what is known about the psychological consequences of schooling, and in particular the consequences of learning to read and write. Schools are so familiar to us that it might seem odd to say that we really do not understand how they work, or what impact they have on children's development, but this is indeed the case.

The psychological consequences of formal schooling have been studied extensively, but still there is much that we do not know. The cognitive consequences of schooling seem to include an increase in logico-mathematical abilities, together with learning a variety of skills that have value in the classroom, such as memorization techniques. Abilities such as conservation, which Piaget called infralogical, seem to be acquired whether a child goes to school or not. The precise logico-mathematical abilities that children acquire in school appear to be specific to the kinds of task they are introduced to in the classroom—that is, children master a particular kind of mathematics, and a particular form of logic: not ecological reasoning, for example, in the majority of cases.

This suggests that schooling has an influence on System 2, the conscious and voluntary psychological abilities that Vygotsky called the higher psychological functions. System 1 abilities, such as understanding the conservation of physical properties, develop independent of school. However, presumably changes in System 2 can lead in turn to changes in System 1, the lower psychological functions, as new System 2 abilities become automatized.

Meanwhile, outside school children participate in various organizations. They can now organize their activities without needing the help of adults, but adults don't always allow them to do this. The peer group becomes increasingly important, and children form enduring reputations and peer status, becoming recognized as popular, rejected, or isolated. Children now form relatively stable and enduring friendships, grounded in their improved ability to understand the personality of another person.

1. THE INSTITUTION OF SCHOOL

There [in school], with varying abruptness, play is transformed into work, game into competition and cooperation, and the freedom of imagination into the duty to perform with full attention to the techniques which make imagination communicable, accountable, and applicable to defined tasks. (Erikson, 1977, p. 104)

Each school defines a context outside the household in which the activities of children's learning are separated from everyday tasks, and in which children's development is given a specific direction. Schooling is part of a trend that began with industrialization, in which work became increasingly separated and divided from the household. The institution of school has close ties to the ways that adult work has become organized: "basic techniques are taught which are essential to the participation in the economic and technical system, whether it be predatory and/agricultural, mercantile and/or industrial, literary and/or scientific" (Erikson, 1977, p. 104).

Centrally, school is a place where children are taught the skills of material systems of formal representation: reading, writing, and arithmetic. **Literacy**—the ability to comprehend and produce written language—is a key skill in many cultures. It is also believed to have important psychological consequences, though the evidence for this is not clear cut, as we shall see in the next section.

In school the child opens books, and the accumulated wisdom of not only her own cultural group but also of many others becomes available to her. Books contain factual information, but they also contain their authors' thinking, crystallized in written form. They contain cultural works: poems, novels, philosophy, plays, commentaries, manuals, and textbooks. It has been estimated that since the invention of the printing press over 130 million different books have been published. And, of course, written language is not confined to books: it includes articles, newspapers, handwritten documents and diaries, and now the internet. Each text is a cultural archive, a repository of knowledge, a cache of scholarship, a chronicle of exploration. When she starts reading, the child enters a new mode of participation in the ways of thinking and seeing of current and previous generations of humankind.

We inherit our alphabet and our arithmetic from our ancestors and, consequently, when children learn in school this is an aspect of societal reproduction. The first arithmetic systems were invented around three thousand years ago. Systems of writing are about two thousand years older. The scribes of the ancient Greeks marked tablets of wet clay. Medieval monks scraped vellum and scratched illuminated manuscripts. These material systems are external aspects of cognition, and they enable not just the products but also the processes of reasoning to be handed from one person to another and passed down from one generation to the next.

These material systems may use alphabetic script, or hieroglyphs, or some other kind of inscription. They represent aspects of the material world in a way that permits manipulation of symbols in place of manipulation of what the symbols stand for:

> The symbols are manipulated by reference to their form only. We do not interpret the meanings of the symbols while they are being manipulated. The manipulation of the symbols results in some other symbolic expression. Finally, we may interpret a newly created string of symbols as meaning something about the world of phenomena. (Hutchins, 1995, pp. 359–360)

For example, instead of combining and counting two bags of apples we can "add" the symbols "5" and "6" to get the answer "11," which tells us how big the combined collection would be. We interpret the result of the symbolic manipulation as telling us about a possible action in the world (Hutchins, 1995).

A number of people have suggested that learning to use material representations leads the child to think and feel more deliberately. For example, to read a book can be to involve oneself with a machine for producing emotions—to find oneself moved by the words on the page. To follow a mathematical equation is to involve oneself with a calculating machine, and to begin to see the world in a new way. We will examine in the next section some of the evidence for and against this claim.

Vygotsky defined education at all ages as the social mastery of a natural process, in which "a human being as a specific biotype is transformed into a human being as a sociotype" (Vygotsky, 1993, p. 160). In many societies the school has become a key social institution in which this mastery and transformation take place.

1.1 THE HISTORICAL ROOTS OF SCHOOLING

Schooling has a long history, though in many respects its forms have not changed significantly over the centuries. The first schools were established around four thousand years ago to train scribes—professionals who could record transactions using soft clay pads and styli.

Schooling has been an important part of children's lives in many parts of the world, invented independently. For example, before there was any contact with Europe, children of the Aztec nobility in Mesoamerica entered the *calmécac* at age 5 or 6, to receive rigorous religious and military preparation, including instruction in song, ritual, reading, and writing, and the calendar. (They went on to formal military training at age 15.) They also learned history, science, astronomy, discipline, music, and how to paint codices: in short, everything they needed to become priests, judges, teachers, or rulers.

In contrast, girls were taught to be pious and warned not to listen to foolish gossip. And the children of commoners attended the *telpochcalli*, where they were trained in military arts. The *telpochcalli* taught history, religion, military techniques, and a trade or craft, such as agriculture or handicrafts. Its central purpose was to train young men to be warriors.

A generation after the Spanish conquest of Mexico, Bernardino de Sahagún conducted interviews with Aztec nobles, and one shared advice for boys that one might still hear today: "Speak calmly and quietly, or people will call you an imbecile, shameless, a yokel. Don't stare at people; and don't gossip – just listen. Don't be like those boys who go around jeering, being rude and clumsy, with their sandals flopping about the feet and the straps trailing along the ground" (James, 2009). In short, training in the material representations of codices—ancient illustrated manuscript texts—went hand in hand with instruction in how to behave and how to live.

However, the dominant form of schooling today is based on a European model, one that evolved in the nineteenth century and followed European armies into other parts of the world (LeVine et al., 2001; Serpell & Hatano, 1997). Over the past two hundred years Western-style schooling has become available and expected for many of the world's children. Worldwide, 90 percent of primary-school-age children are enrolled in this kind of school. There are still countries, particularly in sub-Saharan Africa and South Asia, where enrollment is lower, around 66 percent (UNICEF, 2012). In addition, most countries now admit girls and boys equally into primary education, though girls remain disadvantaged in many parts of Africa. These statistics hint at the transformative potential of schooling: changing the roles for girls and boys in the community, and consequently for men and women; drawing children away from their participation in family and community work and household tasks, and as a consequence transforming their community membership.

In many cultures, then, this is the age at which children are sequestered from the family for at least part of each day in order to be instructed, by adults who are not members of the family, in the specific techniques for the mastery of the psychological functions employed in that culture. In industrialized countries those techniques center around literacy—reading and writing in various ways.

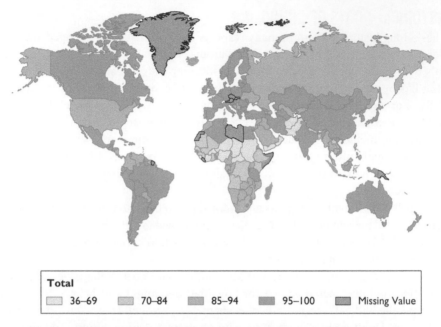

Total				
36–69	70–84	85–94	95–100	Missing Value

Figure 12.1   The percentage of children attending school in different areas of the world

Figure 12.2   One of the oldest writing systems, Proto-Elamite

1.2 PSYCHOLOGICAL CONSEQUENCES OF SCHOOLING

The fact that schooling is compulsory creates difficulties for developmental researchers, because it is very hard to distinguish the influence of school from the effect of other factors, including age itself. When all children go to school, no comparison of schooled and non-schooled is possible. Indeed, most of what psychologists take to be typical about the development of children in middle childhood has come from studying those who attend school, and it is entirely possible that what has been found are the results of schooling, and that children who do not attend school might have quite different patterns of development.

In particular, age and years of schooling are "confounded": the time a child has been in school is highly correlated with her age, making it difficult to separate the effects of these two variables.

In the 1970s psychologists began to explore ways to avoid these problems. It might seem obvious that the best solution would be to compare schooled and non-schooled children on various tasks. Much research has taken advantage of the fact that in cultures where schooling is not universal it is possible to compare those children who are attending school with those who are not. The difficulty here is that most psychological tasks are very similar to school tasks, so that they have very low **ecological validity** for children who don't attend school. Such children may do badly on a task simply because they are unfamiliar with the format of being asked odd questions by a strange adult.

Another difficulty with a comparison of schooled and non-schooled children is that there may be a **selection bias**. For example, it may be that the more advantaged children go to school, or stay in school longer. Pretests are sometimes used to rule out the first possibility, and in fact these have shown that parents often do indeed encourage their more academic children to attend school, or to start school earlier. Another approach is to attempt to eliminate possible **confounds** statistically. Analyses of the covariants of schooling have found that schooled children in general have more educated and literate parents, and also more books, toys, newspapers, and televisions in the home.

Differences such as these make it difficult to interpret the results of a simple comparison between schooled and non-schooled children. Nonetheless, this remains a popular research design.

However, there is another way to study the effects of schooling, even when it is compulsory. The **school cut-off design** compares two groups of children whose birthdays are very close to the "cut-off" date for school entrance. Those whose birthday occurs before this date are allowed to enroll in school, while those whose birthday falls after this date must wait for a year. Their ages are very similar, but their exposure to schooling will be different. These two groups can be compared by researchers while the first passes through first grade and the second stays in kindergarten. (We shall see an example of such a design later in this chapter.)

An alternative version of this research design is the **between-grade design**, where the children who are compared are in two different grades—one group just starting school, the other having completed their first year. We will see an example of this design in an interest investigation in section 3.3, below.

Research has been conducted using each of these designs, looking for consequences of schooling for a variety of psychological abilities and characteristics, such as perception, memory, IQ score, classification and use of concepts, and problem solving, as well as performance on Piagetian tests of level of cognitive development (Ceci, 1991; Rogoff, 1981). In this section I will briefly explore some of the findings on intelligence, and the formation of concepts.

1.2.1 SCHOOLING AND INTELLIGENCE

The **Intelligence Quotient** (IQ) is usually thought of as a measure of innate intellectual ability, but in fact there is a lot of evidence that attending schooling increases a child's IQ score. The more years a child spends in school, the higher her IQ score is likely to be. Drops in IQ score occur after summer vacation, or if the child's entry into school is delayed, or if she doesn't attend regularly, or if she drops out. IQ score is correlated with scores on achievement tests, which indicates that both achievement and intelligence are taught. In addition, there have been historical increases in average IQ, and these are correlated with the increase in the average number of years that children spend in school.

However, the association between IQ and schooling should not be surprising, because the psychologist who developed the first IQ test, Alfred Binet, did so by asking teachers to describe the types of questions that children with difficulty learning found hardest to answer in their classes. There is an inherent circularity in the concept of IQ: school success is explained as due to intelligence, but school success is the basis for the definition of intelligence. Equally, lower intelligence is defined as a lack of school success, but low IQ is viewed as the cause of poor performance in school.

Consequently, these changes in IQ score may not indicate an increase in intellectual ability. It is entirely possible that higher IQ scores reflect the child's increased familiarity with the types of questions used in the IQ exam and with the format of standardized testing, so that "schooling does nothing to alter the efficiency of an individual's cognitive processes but merely supplies them with a reservoir of IQ-relevant knowledge and shapes their style of responding" (Ceci, 1991, p. 717). Certainly, school provides children with the kind of knowledge that is needed on IQ tests. For example, the WISC-R intelligence tests has included the question, "Who wrote *Hamlet*?" In school, children may encounter for the first time discussion of hypothetical entities and situations, along with a formal kind of language, and IQ test questions will often employ one or both of these. In addition, schools also provide experience in being questioned and evaluated by an adult, as generally happens in an IQ test.

Furthermore, schools usually teach the kind of organization of categories that is valued on IQ tests. A distinction is often drawn between categorization that is **perceptual** (grouping on the basis of color, size, etc.), **functional** (grouping on the basis of use or function), and **taxonomic** (grouping on the basis of semantic class). (These last two are sometimes called **syntagmatic** and **paradigmatic** categorization, respectively.)

In **functional** categorization, words are related if the objects they refer to could be used together: for example, *wood-axe*. In **taxonomic** categorization words are related if one word could replace another in a sentence because it is in the same semantic category: for example, *red-black*; *dog-cat*.

When an IQ test includes a question such as "*How are an apple and an orange alike?*", a higher score is given for the answer "*Both are fruit*" (taxonomic) than for the answer "*Both can be eaten*" (functional) or "*Both are round*" (perceptual). Schools will often introduce children to the hierarchical organization of taxonomic categorization (Brown, 1977; Nelson, 1977).

1.2.2 SCHOOLING AND CONCEPT DEVELOPMENT

Indeed, the development of concepts has been studied mainly in terms of the organization that children impose on words, or pictures, or objects, in tasks such as free-association, or sorting objects (or pictures, or sometimes their names) into groups. Perceptual categorization is generally considered more "concrete" and less advanced, while taxonomic categorization is considered more "abstract" and advanced (Smiley & Brown, 1979). The fact that schooling tends to promote a movement from perceptual and functional categorization to taxonomic categorization has encouraged the idea that schools promote abstract thinking. A number of psychologists have suggested that attending school may alter a child's cognitive processes in a fundamental way by encouraging thinking that is more abstract or dis-embedded and by introducing the child to concepts that are less tied to personal experience. However, there is no strong evidence to support this suggestion.

For example, Vygotsky's colleague Alexander Luria conducted a series of studies in Central Asia in the early 1930s, when a reorganization of agriculture was changing the lifestyle of rural peasants and providing many of them with a school education for the first time. Luria found that people who attended school (many as young adults) were more likely to categorize objects taxonomically than functionally, while those who had never gone to school used functional categorization (Luria, 1933, 1976).

Luria interpreted these results as showing that a transformation in cognition had been provoked—that schooling had encouraged the development of more advanced conceptualization, and a movement towards a more abstract kind of reasoning.

However, the non-schooled participants' comments indicated that they simply viewed the taxonomic categorization as inappropriate and rather stupid. For example, one peasant was asked to explain which three items were similar: a hammer, a saw, a hatchet, and a log. The first three clearly fit into the category *tool*. However, viewed in terms of their function all four items can be grouped together. The peasant insisted on a functional grouping:

"They all fit here! The saw has to saw the log, the hammer has to hammer it, and the hatchet has to chop it. And if you want to chop the log up really good, you need the hammer. You can't take any of these things away. There isn't any you don't need."

Interviewer: "But one fellow … said that the saw, hammer, and hatchet are all alike in some way, while the log isn't."

"So what if they're not alike? They all work together and chop the log. Here everything works right, here everything's just fine."

Interviewer: "Look, you can use one word – tools – for these three but not for the log."

"What sense does it make to use one word for them all if they're not going to work together?" (Luria, 1976, p. 58)

Luria's research has been repeated in other places. However, the researchers who conducted the replication found that the non-schooled participants also had the vocabulary for taxonomic categories, and were able to use taxonomic categorization in a variety of experimental conditions. It seems entirely possible that the results that Luria obtained were a consequence of a difference not in reasoning ability between the schooled and non-schooled participants, but in their degree of familiarity with the kind of research task, and how they interpreted the task as a social situation (Cole et al., 1971).

An illustration of the danger of equating performance on an experimental task with general ability or competence can be found in an investigation in which members of the Kpelle people in the African country of Liberia participated in a task similar to that used by Luria. The participants consistently sorted 20 everyday objects into functional groups, and explained that this was how a wise man would do things. The researcher finally asked, in exasperation, "How would a fool do it?" Immediately the participants sorted the materials into "four neat piles with foods in one, tools in another, and so on" (Glick, 1975, p. 636)!

In Chapter 13, we shall explore Vygotsky's distinction between everyday concepts and scientific concepts, and the role of schooling in the transition from the former to the latter.

1.3 SCHOOLING AND CONCRETE OPERATIONAL REASONING

If we are interested in the consequences of schooling on a child's cognition, it would seem to make sense to conduct research using Piagetian tasks. Piaget had his own account of children's reasoning in middle childhood: it is what he called **concrete operational** reasoning. In his view, the child has now constructed organized systems of mental operations, and these are evident in reasoning tasks such as classification, serial ordering, and forming correspondences. That is, the child can successfully classify things into categories and subcategories. She can place things in the serial order of their properties, for example lining up pencils with increasing length. And she can understand relationships of correspondence between one class of things and another. She is now able to think about the consequences of a transformation, because she can mentally reverse the transformation. One result of this latter ability is that the child can now solve conservation tasks because, in Piaget's interpretation, she can now draw on her comprehension of the act of pouring the liquid, or squashing the Play-Doh, to conclude that it is logically necessary that the quantity of material remains the same.

The child is now able to distinguish between appearance and reality: between how something appears to the senses, and how it actually is. Reasoning is now "operational," since it has the logical properties that define a true operation: reversibility, identity, negation, and commutativity. (We first met these properties in our discussion of the practical logic of sensorimotor action, in Chapter 5. Commutativity is closely related to the associativity we defined there. Now, in middle childhood, in Piaget's view, the child's *mental* actions have these logical properties.) As a result, reasoning in middle childhood is more advanced, more organized and systematic, more logical, than the preoperational reasoning of the previous stage, early childhood.

For example, reasoning that "*fathers plus mothers equals parents*," or that "*5 plus 6 equals 11*," involves coordinating actions such as uniting and ordering in very general ways. These actions are **reversible** (we can separate *mothers* and *fathers* again into their original groups), and they can be **coordinated** into systems, such as a **system of classification**, or the system of the **number sequence**.

Moreover, in any system of operations some feature remains constant—it is "conserved" under transformation. When liquid is poured from container A into B or C, the young child saw that the liquid was higher in B than it was in A, and she concluded that there was now more liquid. The young child saw the pouring, but could not draw any conclusions from witnessing the transformation. The concrete operational child, in contrast, argues that the liquid could be poured back (*reversibility* by inversion), or that while the level of liquid is higher the container is narrower (*reversibility* by compensation). The states of the liquid are now less important than the transformation of pouring, and the child now understands that this transformation is reversible. Now she can reason about the transformation to explain both the apparent differences in the liquid in the two containers, and draw conclusions about what stays constant.

However, in Piaget's view there are still limitations to this kind of reasoning. Concrete operations are coordinated into structures, but these structures are weak. Mental operations remain limited, in that the child's reasoning moves from one partial link to the next, without relating that link to all the others.

Infancy 0–12 months	Sensory-motor stage	*Mental representations are dynamic, but restricted to concrete objects.*
Toddler 1–2.5 years	Sensory-motor stage	*Conservation tasks are solved (infralogical Early childhood 2.5–6 years Preoperational stage operations).*
Early childhood 2.5–6 years	Preoperational stage	*Appearance & reality are now distinguished.*
Middle childhood 6–12 years	**Concrete operational stage**	*Mental operations have properties of identity, reversibility, negation, and commutativity.*
Adolescence 12–	Formal operational stage	*Logico-mathematical operations: serial order, transitivity, classification.*

Figure 12.3   The key characteristics of concrete operational intelligence, according to Piaget

Only step-by-step reasoning is possible, not generalized conclusions. In addition, this kind of reasoning is called "concrete" because the operations still "relate directly to objects and not yet to verbally stated hypotheses" (Piaget & Inhelder, 2008[1966], p. 100). The operational child has not yet achieved the kind of reasoning of which adolescents are capable, which is, in Piaget's terms, **formal operational reasoning**. In the latter, as we shall see in Chapter 13, all possible combinations can be considered, without reference to the objects that actually exist, or to the actual state of affairs, and each partial link is grouped in relation to a "structured whole."

1.3.1 CONCRETE OPERATIONS AND CULTURE

Early in his career, Piaget believed that there would be large differences in cognitive development between technologically primitive and advanced cultures (Piaget, 1995[1928]). However, when he started to conduct research on cultural variation in cognitive development in the 1960s he assumed that the sequence of developmental stages that he had observed in Geneva was universal, and he focused only on factors that he thought might modify the speed at which children progressed through these stages, rather than exploring the possibility that different cultures might show different sequences (Piaget, 1964). The key factor, he proposed, was the amount of **operational exercise**, the interplay between assimilation and accommodation that could drive the cognitive system to higher, more adequate levels of equilibration. Some societies, he speculated, might provide more opportunities for operational exercise by helping children confront and think about their environment. He was dubious about the extent to which schooling might play a role, because he believed that the authority structure in the school classroom encourages accommodation rather than assimilation, and so hinders equilibration. For Piaget, schooling is no different from any other experience: in fact, since school removes children from the "real world," it might actually slow down their development (Goodnow & Bethon, 1966).

Although it would seem that cross-cultural comparisons of children who have and who have not been to school should be a relatively straightforward way to test Piaget's hypotheses, the history of such research illustrates the difficulties of cross-cultural research. To find children who do not attend school, researchers have needed to travel to countries where schooling is not compulsory. As we saw earlier, Africa is one place where this is the case. However, researchers conducting studies in poor communities in Africa have confronted many difficulties.

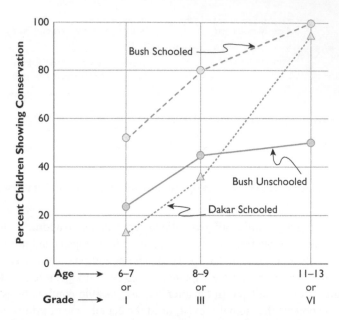

Figure 12.4 Performance on conservation tasks for children from different backgrounds, and schooled versus un-schooled.

Source: Greenfield (1966)

These difficulties are exemplified by studies with the Wolof people in rural Senegal, in West Africa. Early research seemed to show that children who attended school showed a steadily improving ability to solve conservation tasks, while only about half of *adults* who had not been educated in school were able to solve those tasks (Greenfield, 1966; Greenfield & Bruner, 1969). This led researchers to suggest that concrete operational thinking is simply impossible if one has not received a school education. This would mean that adults in non-literate societies, unable to read and non-schooled, would fail to develop in their reasoning abilities beyond preoperational thought. Their thinking would remain concrete and primitive (Hallpike, 1976, 1979). However, it is very hard to imagine that any kind of society would survive if its members were unable to understand such crucial properties of the physical world as the conservation of quantity, and other social scientists disagreed strongly with this conclusion (Jahoda, 1993).

The central problem with this kind of research is one we encountered in Chapter 7, in our discussion of the use of the Strange Situation to assess attachment. When a test or task that has been designed in one culture is used in another, how do we know that the participants have understood it in the same way? A Piagetian task requires a social interaction between the researcher and the child, and the interaction may be understood quite differently in one culture than it is in another. For example, in school a child will often be questioned by an adult who clearly already knows the answers to their questions. For a child who has not attended school, however, this situation may be unfamiliar and odd. Among the Wolof, for example, such questioning is interpreted as an aggressive challenge, or as a riddle which will likely have a trick answer (Irvine, 1978). Miscommunication is even more likely when not only is the test or task imported but the researcher also comes from a different culture. The assumption that the test measures the same capability in two different cultures becomes highly questionable.

Indeed, in at least some of the studies that have compared schooled and non-schooled children on Piagetian tasks, it seems that children failed the tasks because they simply did not understand how the problem was framed by the researcher. For example, in a follow-up to the research in Senegal the task was presented as an opportunity to instruct the ignorant researcher, rather than as a test of the child. With this reframing, both non-schooled children and adults said that although the water in one beaker was higher as a result of pouring, the amounts were the same, using the appropriate terms in their language (Irvine, 1978).

There is additional evidence to support the interpretation that when children from different cultures appear to differ in their degree of development of concrete operational thinking this is a result of differences in how they understand the Piagetian interview situation. For example, a study with young children in the USA between 4 and 6 years of age found that they interpreted a repeated question from an adult as a cue that they needed to change their answer. The children were skilled in the conventions of everyday conversation, but in a clinical interview these conventions are often deliberately put aside (Siegal, 1991).

In the original research with the Wolof there were indeed indications that the research situation influenced the children's conservation judgments. When the Wolof children poured the water themselves, instead of watching while the researcher poured, their performance in the conservation task improved markedly (see Figure 12.5). The researcher's interpretation was that in this case the children were less likely to attribute the results to "magic powers," but it is equally likely that they were less likely to be concerned with satisfying the foreign lady researcher.

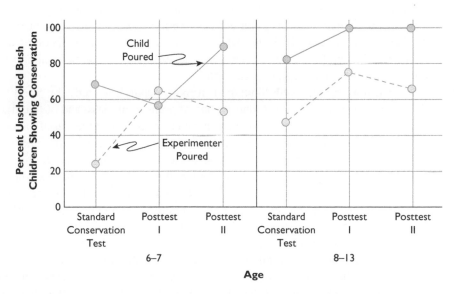

Figure 12.5 Performance on conservation tasks when researcher pours or child pours

Source: Greenfield (1966)

413

In addition, a number of studies have found no differences between the conservation performance of schooled and non-schooled children in developing countries when the person who conducted the research was a member of the same cultural group as the children (Kamara & Easley, 1977; Nyiti, 1976).

Overall, research looking for differences in conservation tasks between schooled and non-schooled participants has produced ambiguous results. Some investigations have found differences, and some have found none (Rogoff, 1981; Rogoff & Chavajay, 1995). The balance of opinion seems to be that conservation is universally acquired (just as Piaget thought), and that attending school does not have an influence on whether a child acquires an understanding of conservation, or on how quickly this acquisition occurs. On the other hand, a child's performance on specific Piagetian conservation tasks may be improved by attending school because school provides experience in testing situations. What seems to be influenced by schooling, then, is not the child's general cognitive ability (in Piagetian terms, at least, and as judged by conversation tasks in particular) but her ability to understand the language of testing and the presuppositions of the testing situation.

However, there is evidence that aspects of concrete operational reasoning other than conservation are influenced by schooling. Piaget in fact distinguished between two kinds of concrete operations, which he called **infralogical operations** and **logical-mathematical operations**. The infralogical operations are used to deal with continuous objects—like Play-Doh and liquids—and they are based on judgments of proximity and separation in space and time. Judgments of conservation are based on infralogical operations. In contrast, classification and counting are logical-mathematical operations, and they are applied to distinct objects—apples and oranges, fathers and mothers. Piaget explained that the former "are called 'infralogical' because they relate to another level of reality, and not because they develop earlier" (Piaget & Inhelder, 2008[1966], p. 106). If infralogical and logico-mathematical operations involve reasoning about different levels of reality, it is reasonable to inquire whether they respond differently to schooling.

Piaget believed that these two kinds of operations develop in parallel and in a synchronized way, at the same rate. However, a recent study indicates that performance on infralogical operational tasks simply improves with age, while performance on logico-mathematical operational tasks improves with the amount of schooling a child receives (Cahan et al., 2008).

This is a very interesting result, worth looking at in more detail. The study, by Sorel Cahan and colleagues, included three infralogical tasks (conservation of number, of mass, and of liquid), and three logico-mathematical tasks (classification, class inclusion, and transitivity). In the classification task each child was asked to arrange nine cards, four of which were square (two black and two white) and five of which were circular (all black), and to explain their classification. In the class inclusion task each child was shown the same cards arranged with the two white squares at the top, the two black squares underneath, and the five black circles at the bottom, and they were asked questions such as 'Are there more white cards or square cards?' (Class-inclusion is the way classes of objects relate to one another: for example, all sisters are children, but not all children are sisters, so the class of sisters is included within the class of children.)

In the "transitivity" task two objects were shown, for example two toy cars, and the child was told that one was faster than the other. The second car was replaced with a third, and again the child was told which was faster. Then the first and third cars were shown, and the child was asked to point out the faster one, a task which requires combining the pairs into an ordered series of three items. A relation is **transitive** when if it applies between successive members of a sequence, it must also apply between *any* two members. For instance, if A is larger than B, and B is larger than C, then A is larger than C. Transitivity is a logical property; understanding transitivity is believed to underly children's capacity for number and counting. (Not all relations are transitive: for example, if A is father to B, and B is father to C, A is not father to C, he is grandfather.)

The participants in this research were first and second grade students at five elementary schools in Israel, aged from 5 years 10 months to 7 years 10 months. The tests were carried out at the beginning of the school year, when the first graders were new to school and the second graders had completed a year of schooling and were also, of course, on average a year older, though both groups contained children with a range of ages. (This is the "between-grades" research design we discussed earlier.)

The analysis of the task scores used statistical techniques to separate the influence of time attending school from the influence of age. The results showed that the more *time in school* the children had, the better their performance on the logico-mathematical tasks. However, the *older* the children were, the better their performance on the infralogical tasks. Figure 12.6 shows one of each type of task: the transitivity task (logico-mathematical) and the conservation of liquid task (infralogical). You can see that in the transitivity task, performance improved only slightly with increasing age, but there was a big performance jump between the children who had just started first grade and those who had just started second grade. In the conservation task, performance improved steadily with age, and the move from kindergarten to first grade had almost no effect.

This pattern of results strongly suggests that logico-mathematical operations, such as classification and transitivity, were improved by attending school, even though these were not skills that were explicitly taught in the classroom. On the other hand, the infralogical abilities simply developed as the children grew older and had more experience, and attending school had no effect. This suggests that the acquisition of conservation, which is infralogical, is a universal process, the consequence of the child's interaction with the world around her whether she is in school or not. The acquisition of an understanding of properties such as class inclusion and transitivity, on the other hand, seems to require schooling.

However, since these logico-mathematical operations were not explicitly taught we are still faced with the question of how they were improved as a consequence of attending school. The researchers have two suggestions, and these will lead us away from Piaget's way of thinking about cognitive development towards (1) the neuroscience of human thinking and (2) Vygotsky's theory of the **higher psychological functions**.

1.4 SCHOOLING AND THE HIGHER PSYCHOLOGICAL FUNCTIONS

I have discussed several times the dual systems of human psychological functioning. The researchers who compared logico-mathematical operations with infralogical operations suggest that school improves children's performance on logico-mathematical tasks because it supports System 2 analytical processes:

> According to this hypothesis, schooling affects performance on these tasks not by teaching them, but rather by increasing children's awareness to the possibly faulty outputs produced by System 1 and their motivation and ability to use the effortful and deliberate analytical systems of reasoning (System 2) in order to correct it. (Cahan et al., 2008, p. 274)

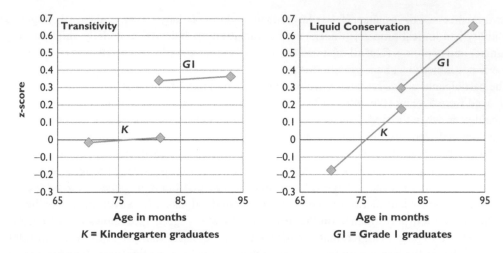

Figure 12.6 Performance on Piagetian tasks for children who had recently graduated from kindergarten and were starting first grade (K), and children who had just graduated from first grade and were starting second grade (G1). Both groups included children of a range of different ages. Transitivity is a logico-mathematical task; conservation of liquid is an infralogical task

Source: Cahan et al. (2008)

Cahan's suggestion is that school may increase children's use of deliberate, analytical strategies of reasoning (System 2) both directly, through practice with the rules of logical reasoning, and indirectly, by encouraging perseverance and motivation. System 1 processes, on the other hand, are able to develop without school instruction. This is not to say that school cannot influence System 1, simply that school is not necessary for its development. Judgments about conservation are unconscious and reflexive; they do not require schooling because there is enough everyday experience with this level of reality for every child, whether attending school or not, to come to understand it.

Furthermore, if school educates System 2 through daily practice in the material symbol systems of logic and arithmetic, presumably what the child learns may in time become automatized and part of System 1, though the researchers do not make this suggestion.

This way of thinking about the influence of schooling on logico-mathematical skills is very similar to a proposal made by Vygotsky. He devoted a chapter of his final work, *Thinking & Speaking*, to the topic of the relationships among teaching, learning, and development.

Vygotsky suggested that learning and development are not the same, but nor are they completely separate or independent. Russian has a word *obuchenie* which can be translated roughly as **instructed learning**; it is a term that combines both *teaching* and *learning*. Instructed learning, Vygotsky proposed, is "knotted" together with development. That is to say, these two have a complex, tangled connection.

As we have seen, Piaget tried to cut this knot. He believed that development occurs whether or not a child is taught. If the stages of development are universal, as he maintained, the most teaching can do is speed up development, accelerating the pace at which a child moves through the stages.

(Even here, Piaget said he was more interested in how *far* we can help children's intelligence grow than in how *fast* we can help it grow; he called this second preoccupation "the American question" [Cf. Piaget, 1971; see also Duckworth, 1979]). For Piaget, teaching is not necessary, because learning and development are disconnected. It is, consequently, ironical that many school curricula have been designed on the basis of his description of stages of cognition, because he himself was not very interested in schooling.

Other psychologists have assumed that teaching–learning and development are the same thing. These psychologists don't recognize the knot—they believe that all development is the consequence of the child being taught, implicitly or explicitly, by adults. Behaviorism is one example of this approach: all development was seen by behaviorists such as Watson and Skinner as following on from the way a child is shaped by other people. Many theories of "socialization" are similar: they assume that a child develops because adults teach her to behave in an acceptable way. School, from this perspective, is just another place where socialization occurs.

Vygotsky disagreed with both these positions. He did not believe that development is unaffected by teaching, but nor did he believe that all development is the result of adult instruction. He insisted that we have to study the way that teaching and development are knotted together. He proposed that teaching "can move ahead of development, pushing it further and eliciting new formations." What teaching can accomplish, he argued, is to enable a child to move from an unconscious, automatic level of psychological functioning to a voluntary, intentional, and conscious level. You can see that this distinction is very similar to the distinction between System 1 and System 2 modes of reasoning. Vygotsky referred to these two levels as the **lower psychological functions** and the **higher psychological functions**. The higher functions include deliberate remembering, voluntary attention, conceptual thinking, logical memory, categorical perception, creative imagination, the higher emotions, and foresight. In each case, an unconscious and automatic psychological function—memory, attention, inference, perception, imagination, emotion—has come under deliberate and conscious control.

1.4.1 LEARNING TO WRITE

An example of the movement from an unconscious level to a voluntary level is the process of learning to write. Written language is rarely simply a transcription of oral speech, it is usually something altogether more abstract. Writing not only abstracts from the sounds of speech, it also abstracts from the situation of spoken language. When a child *talks*, her use of language is regulated by the dynamics of the situation, and her speech is directed towards a specific other person or people. Speech, for the school-aged child, has become automatic, spontaneous, and unconscious. When the child *writes*, in contrast, this is communication without another person. We usually don't write about what is in front of us to someone who is actually present here and now. We write for a reader who we may not even know, who may read our words in circumstances that we cannot anticipate.

In learning to write, then, the school-age child learns a new kind of communication, one that is abstracted from the world around her: writing deals not with words, but with *representations* of words; it lacks the connections to the immediate context that speech usually has; it also lacks the music of speech, and the writer must make up for this by using various grammatical and rhetorical techniques. Writing is, for the child (and for many adults), a deliberate, conscious process, one that involves making careful, considered decisions. The child must develop voluntary control of the basic elements of syntax and semantics, whereas these elements in the child's everyday speech have been mastered and become unconscious, spontaneous, and automatic.

In short, learning how to write requires a new conscious awareness and voluntary control of language. It might seem that in order to teach writing to a child we would need to wait for these abilities to develop. But Vygotsky said no, these abilities develop *during* the process of learning to write—they have "an indissoluble internal link" with the teaching of writing. Learning to write, then, is not only an *example* of the transformation that, according to Vygotsky, is brought about by schooling—the transformation from an unconscious, automatic plane to a voluntary, intentional, and conscious plane—it is also a central *technique* by which this transformation is brought about. The teaching of writing, Vygotsky suggested, helps form the higher psychological functions, all of which have the property of conscious awareness and voluntary control. Together these functions form a new system, a new unified structure, that is the foundation for further development in adolescence and adulthood.

This is a provocative suggestion, which calls for further exploration in research. For example, it may be that it is not literacy per se that produces this psychological transformation but instead specific kinds of literacy, or perhaps it is a specific kind of instruction in how to read and write. In the next section we will explore further the psychological consequences of literacy.

The system of higher psychological functions, in Vygotsky's view, will not be completed in middle childhood, but its components begin to form during this stage. Various psychological functions start the transition from unconscious, automatic operation to conscious, deliberate operation at different times. In Vygotsky's view, the last psychological function to undergo this transition is thinking itself, which remains unconscious throughout middle childhood. As he put it in the passage quoted at the start of this chapter, the child's processes of thinking "flow with him just as actions flowed previously," and "only with the passage of years does the child learn to control the course of his thought" (Vygotsky, 1997a, p. 250). In his view, during middle childhood it is first perception and memory that come under conscious awareness and control.

There is no reason to think that school is the *only* social institution in which the higher psychological functions can develop, and we can imagine that in societies without schooling there are other opportunities for this development to take place. For Vygotsky, however, who worked with the Ministry of Education in Soviet Russia, understanding and improving school teaching and learning were of central importance.

His suggestion that schools encourage the development of higher-order reasoning that is conscious, deliberate, and voluntary—and that this then transforms lower-order reasoning that is intuitive, rapid, and unconscious—is a very interesting proposal. It is compatible with the discovery that schooling is not necessary for conservation (System 1), but does foster logico-mathematical reasoning (System 2). Much research remains to be done to explore the validity of Vygotsky's ideas, and to spell out the details, but he offered us a fresh way of thinking about schooling, and his approach is increasingly influential in educational psychology and teacher training.

1.4.2 THE ZONE OF PROXIMAL DEVELOPMENT

No discussion of Vygotsky's views on teaching and learning would be complete without mention of his concept of **the zone of proximal development**. This concept is perhaps the most widely known aspect of all of his work, but it should now be clear that it is merely a special case of Vygotsky's **general genetic law of cultural development**.

Vygotsky defined the zone of proximal development as "the distance between the actual developmental level as determined by independent problem solving and the level of potential development as determined through problem solving under adult guidance, or in collaboration with more capable peers" (Vygotsky, 1978, p. 86). He was pointing to the fact that a child can solve problems more successfully when working with another person, and suggesting that this shows us something important about her capabilities. He was not, however, proposing any specific approach to teaching or instruction. On the contrary, he suggested that there are different kinds of teaching at different stages of development.

However, it has often been assumed that Vygotsky was recommending that a teacher is an expert and figure of authority who functions at a level higher than their student and who provides assistance that is analogous to "scaffolding." This idea is often attributed to him, but he never used the term. The word "scaffolding" was first used in an article on tutoring that described it as the control of those elements of a task that are initially beyond a learner's capacity, so that the learner can concentrate on the elements that are within their competence (Wood et al., 1976). Parallels were then drawn between this proposal and Vygotsky's concept, but the problem with the scaffolding metaphor is that it may create the impression that the child is being passively constructed, like a building. Vygotsky himself might well have said that the scaffolding metaphor makes the child seem too passive (cf. Pea, 2004).

Vygotsky insisted not only that a child is always active, but also that social interaction and communication are of central importance to her development. As we have seen, language is a **mediator** of the child's interactions with other people, with profound psychological consequences. This is as true in the school as it was in the family. In fact, one might see Vygotsky as having placed emphasis on the need for parents and teachers to adjust to the changing level of a child's abilities. Developmental changes in children often require the adults to adjust, rather than the other way round (Maccoby, 1984b). When Vygotsky first introduced the concept of the zone of proximal development (Vygotsky, 1987, p. 209) he simply cited "the well known fact that with collaboration, direction, or some kind of help the child is always able to more and solve more difficult tasks than he can independently," and immediately added, "What we have here is only an example of this more general rule."

The "more general rule," of course, is the genetic law. We have seen that this law states that every psychological function appears twice, first as a social, "interpersonal" function between people, and second as an "intrapersonal" function for the individual. In this law, Vygotsky emphasized the social origins of an individual's intellectual, emotional, and conative (willful) abilities. Clearly, the zone of proximal development is only a particular case of the general genetic law of cultural development. It is another example of the fact that an activity occurs among people prior to becoming a personal activity.

1.5. THE PSYCHOLOGICAL CONSEQUENCES OF LITERACY

In the previous section I described Vygotsky's proposal that the teaching of writing helps form the higher psychological functions, whose characteristics are conscious awareness and voluntary control. So does the empirical evidence support his views about the important role of literacy in schooling? Other psychologists have also made grand claims about the psychological consequences of literacy. The vital question here, however, is whether empirical research bears this out. Does learning how to read and write make a child a better thinker? No less a figure than the Greek philosopher Plato suggested that if our reasoning is not to be clouded by emotion, it must be written down.

We tend to assume that writing is primarily a system for recording speech or recording thoughts, but this would be incorrect. Historical evidence shows that early scripts recorded things rather than words or concepts. These early notational systems would record "three goats" as three tokens, one for each goat, rather than as two, one for each word. It was not until between 1000 and 700 BC that writing systems were developed that recorded words, and then phonemes. Despite these differences and developments, strong general claims have been made for the transformative potential of writing.

Anthropologist Jack Goody has suggested, for example, that when the Greeks created the alphabet this enabled them to invent logic (Goody & Watt, 1963). His claim was based on the observation that in writing the relationship between a word and its referent is more general and more abstract, less connected to time and place, than is the case in speech. Could this have been the basis for the idea of logic, as a kind of immutable and impersonal mode of discourse? In addition, Goody suggests that when accounts of events could be written down this may have lead to a distinction between "myth" and "history," and to the past becoming distinct from the present, making historical thinking possible for the first time. This, in turn, could foster a healthy skepticism, not only about myths but also about all kinds of received ideas. The next step could be the building and testing of alternative explanations, out of which arose an intellectual tradition of logical, specialized, and cumulative reasoning.

It seems equally plausible, however, that the ancient Greeks' skills at reasoning developed orally, in the marketplace and the forum, where one had to think quickly, on one's feet. In fact, ancient Greek literacy took many forms and had a variety of functions, most of them linked to oral speech in one way or another.

When ethnographic studies of literacy across the world were collected and compared, no evidence could be found that the "consequences of literacy" that Goody predicted had actually occurred (Goody, 1968). He responded with the suggestion that these were only cases of "restricted literacy," which seems not entirely satisfactory.

Educational researcher and psychologist David Olson has proposed that writing provides a **metalinguistic vocabulary**—for talk about talk—and hence concepts that make possible the evolution of a new kind of thinking, one that is focused on form rather than content. His argument is that becoming literate enables someone to think about both spoken and written language in a new, more scientific way. This "metalanguage" enables children to differentiate between what someone *says* and what is *meant*: the distinction between **speaker meaning** and **sentence meaning** (Olson, 1996).

For example, children between 5 and 8 years of age were told a story in which two children went to a movie and bought and shared some popcorn. Kevin then complained to Susie: "You have more than me." When asked what Kevin had *said*, more than half of the kindergarten children replied "Give me some." By Grade 2, in contrast, the majority reported verbatim what had been said and, when asked, indicated that they knew what was *meant* as well.

This change may be a consequence of the way that writing turns language into an object, whereas speech is a process. To read, a child has to reconstruct what was meant from what is written, and in doing so she learns to draw a distinction between the two. She is aided in this by a new vocabulary about linguistic forms and speech acts. She realizes that linguistic form can be analyzed into constituent parts.

In fact, when a child learns the word "word," she first assumes that it refers to a unit of writing or print, rather than a unit of sound, or a unit of meaning (Francis, 1975). Non-literate cultures, it is true, appear to have few words that are used to describe aspects of language form.

1.5.1 NEW FUNCTIONAL SYSTEMS

As we saw in the previous section, researchers have compared children's functional and taxonomic categorization. Schooled and unschooled children perform equally well on tasks that involve functional categorization, but on tasks that require taxonomic categorization, schooled children generally perform better. Schooled children also perform better when a task requires specific intellectual techniques such as memorization. They also perform better on tasks where language is the topic—where there is talk about talk (Cole & D'Andrade, 1982; Cole et al., 1976).

Many psychologists have interpreted this pattern of experimental results as evidence that schooling has produced a fundamental restructuring in children's cognition, or at minimum a significant change in their verbal reasoning: a transition from prelogical to logical cognition, or from empirical reasoning to theoretical reasoning, or from concrete to abstract reasoning. However, there are several reasons not to jump to this conclusion.

First, people produce different kinds of associations to familiar words and unfamiliar words. They make concrete associations to familiar words ("sexy"; "many"), but abstract associations to unfamiliar words ("erotic"; "myriad") (Stolz & Tiffany, 1972). Most people can make *both* kinds of association. Perhaps what school does is introduce more unfamiliar words.

Second, when unfamiliar words are presented in sentences, unschooled people show evidence that they understand the taxonomic character of these words (Cole & D'Andrade, 1982). Apparently unschooled people do have the capacity to respond taxonomically—whether they do so or not depends primarily on the situation. School provides children with practice in the kind of situation that most tests involve, namely questions about words. Non-schooled participants aren't familiar with this situation, and when asked about *words*, they tend to respond by talking about *objects*.

This suggests that taxonomic categorization does not replace concrete, functional categorization, it works alongside it. School doesn't move a child to a new level of cognition that replaces the older level, it simply reorganizes existing psychological functions. What gets transformed is not cognition in general, but the kinds of mediated interaction a child can engage in with her environment.

School can be viewed, then, as a system of activities that rearranges the child's psychological functions into new cognitive systems by promoting some functions and demoting others. The functions that are promoted will have roles outside school—indeed, this is presumably why we have schools. But school itself is a place where people's interactions are mediated by words much more than by objects. In fact, language plays a double role in school: a theoretical role, in which words are manipulated, and a concrete role, in which communication is about assessment and evaluation. Outside school, activity is mediated by language in many different ways, few of which will resemble what happens in school. Activity outside school is mediated by objects as well as by words.

How does this conclusion relate to our discussion of schooling and concept formation and reasoning earlier in this section? School emphasizes written symbol systems, and the schoolchild comes to use written language deliberately and consciously. This is System 2 with regard to the use of language, and it acts back to transform the System 1—for example, increasing awareness of phonemes, transforming how words are linked. Certainly, "Access to the experience of schooling is access to a treasure trove of [linguistic] tools for dealing with our lives" (Cole & D'Andrade, 1982, p. 25).

It seems possible that the differences between schooled and non-schooled adults and children in taxonomic categorization and hypothetical reasoning tasks are due to the way that System 2 use of language is called for in these tasks. This is not at all to suggest that non-schooled people cannot reason deliberately and consciously, but simply that school *requires* children to think in this way *about the kinds of task that researchers typically use.* Outside school, however, the reasoning skills of a master plumber, for example, are no less deliberate and conscious. Here System 2 involves a form of reasoning that is as much spatial as it is verbal, but it is no less intelligent for that.

The occasions when non-schooled people use System 2 reasoning have largely been overlooked by researchers. Researchers have tended to equate intelligent reasoning with the manipulation of written language, rather than the manipulation of complex non-verbal artifacts. We need more research like the series of studies of workplace reasoning conducted by Silvia Scribner (Scribner, 1986). In order to acquire this kind of intelligent reasoning children often learn in institutions quite different from that of the Western school classroom.

The main problem when studying the issue of the cognitive consequences of literacy is that most people who learn to read and write do so in Western-type schools. This makes it very difficult to separate the effects of literacy from the effects of schooling, or from the effects of a specifically Western way of reading and writing. In the 1970s, Silvia Scribner and Michael Cole looked for an appropriate context to try to distinguish between the consequences of literacy and the consequences of schooling, and they found it in the Vai people of Liberia, a country in Western Africa (see Figure 12.7). The Vai have Western-style schools, teaching English literacy, and Islamic schools teaching Koranic reading

Figure 12.7   The country of Liberia

Figure 12.8 The Vai syllabary

in Arabic. They also have an indigenous syllabary (a set of written characters that represent syllables: see Figure 12.8) that is learned outside formal schooling. This situation offered the opportunity to separate the effects of learning to read and write from the effects of going to school. Thirty percent of adult Vai males are literate in one or more of these scripts. Each form of literacy—English, Arabic, and Vai—is learned and used in quite different contexts (Scribner & Cole, 1981).

Scribner and Cole compared groups of literate and non-literate individuals: people who were schooled and literate in English; people who had learned Koranic reading in Islamic schools; people who were unschooled but literate in the indigenous syllabic script of Vai; and individuals who had not been to school and could not read any script.

Each of the participants received cognitive tasks that assessed their logical reasoning, memory, abstract thinking, reflective language awareness, metalinguistic knowledge, and taxonomic categorization.

Overall, Scribner and Cole found that the literate and the non-literate groups showed no differences in their performance on these tasks. There were no significant differences in cognitive ability between the Vai literate and non-literate populations, nor were there were more advanced cognitive skills that distinguished the literate groups.

However, the group that was literate in Arabic had a better memory for written text. This was most probably because the Koranic school pedagogy depended on this type of memorization. In addition, the group literate in the Vai syllabary were more skilled in providing context when they were asked to write a letter to someone who was far away. This was probably because one of the main uses of Vai was to write letters.

There was, Scribner and Cole concluded, no evidence that becoming literate had improved general cognitive abilities. There was no evidence of a "cognitive restructuring" as a result of learning to read and write.

These conclusions "challenge just about every speculation about the psychological effects of literacy that has been proposed since Plato's time" (Frake, 1983).

Equally importantly, Scribner and Cole concluded that literacy is not a unitary phenomenon, but a flexible tool that can be used in a variety of ways to accomplish diverse ends. Literacy is not a single technology that transforms the thinking of its users in one distinct way. Their findings demonstrated that specific uses of reading and writing promoted specific skills. There is enormous cultural variation in the uses of writing, and Scribner and Cole recommended that it is necessary to study specific cultural practices of reading and writing, and not the nebulous (Western, academic) category of "literacy."

As an example of a cultural practice of literacy, among the Hanunóo people of the Philippines, in the mountains of Mindoro, almost all men and women have for hundreds of years learned a Indic syllabary (Conklin, 1949). There are no schools. This old and demographically widespread literacy is used not to keep records or for rituals, but almost exclusively for romance: one can only imagine what the psychological consequences might be!

Such findings throw cold water on the notion that simply learning to read and write dramatically transforms the mind. Schooling involves instruction in a few specific kinds of literacy. For example, it is probably not correct to say that the new technology of writing makes it necessary to draw a distinction between what is said and what is meant. Rather, writing makes it *possible* to draw this distinction, but school may or may not provide the means—the meta-vocabulary—to do so.

To understand the psychological consequences of Western-style schooling, then, we need to study the specific uses of reading and writing in classrooms. Schools may help children become aware of linguistic structures and functions that are implicit and unconscious in oral language. Equally, it has been suggested, they may help children become aware of the beliefs, wants, and desires that are implicit in intentional action by teaching the explicit names for speech acts such as asking, stating, ordering, and promising (Olson & Hildyard, 1981). But these would be specific consequences, not ones that are general to every child who becomes literate.

1.5.2 LITERACY AND THE BRAIN

Recent research has shown us that becoming literate has a significant impact on the brain. Researchers have studied the errors that adult readers make, compared with errors made by people with various kinds of damage to their brains, and they have used brain imaging to see which areas are involved.

For example, the part of the corpus callosum that connects the right and left posterior parietal cortices is larger in literate people. We saw earlier that schooled children and adults are more adept with two-dimensional representations. Studies show that non-literate adults have more difficulty naming two-dimensional representations of everyday objects than literate participants, though there is no difference when naming real objects: this suggests that learning to read changes the visual system, or the interaction between this system and the language systems. Learning to read also has an impact on the brain's systems for oral language (Reis et al., 2001). Such studies show that:

> learning to read has major, constructive effects on the neurocognitive system. It does not, of course, create a new system from scratch. Like other biological and cultural processes of adaptation, learning to read takes old parts and remodels them into a new system. The old parts are computational processes and cortical regions originally adapted, genetically and culturally, for object recognition and spoken language, but it is an ontogenetic, cultural process – literary training – that makes them into a new system specialized for cultural learning. (Heyes, 2012, p. 2182)

One of the mysteries about reading and writing is how children can do it at all! Writing systems were invented very recently in evolutionary terms, and there has been little time for the brain to adapt to their use. Presumably humans would not have invented a tool that no one could use, but it is nonetheless surprising that literacy is as widespread as it is today. Some children do struggle when learning to read and write, but the question is, how do children learn at all?

Research in cognitive neuroscience by Stanislas Dehaene has explored this issue. His principal finding is that learning to read "recycles" regions of the brain that evolved for other purposes. Reading acquisition invades and makes use of cortical circuits that are universal, and competes with their prior functions, which include visual recognition and face processing (Dehaene, 2009).

In general terms, becoming literate does three things to the brain (Dehaene et al., 2015). First, it boosts the visual cortex. The left occipito-temporal pathway starts to respond more strongly to written characters, and at the same time the response to faces shifts into the right hemisphere. Second, the network for processing speech in the left hemisphere becomes activated by print, as the functional and anatomical links between phonemic and graphemic representations are strengthened. Third, becoming literate improves the way that speech is processed: the neurological coding of phonemes is modified. Reading can become as efficient as speaking, even though reading is a very new ability for our species and speaking a very old one. However, there are costs: once we learn to read, our ability to recognize familiar faces becomes worse!

1.6 SCHOOL AS A SOCIETAL INSTITUTION

> [E]ducation is not *just* about conventional school matters like curriculum or standards or testing. What we resolve to do in school only makes sense when considered in the broader context of what the society intends to accomplish through its educational investment in the young. How one conceives of education, we have finally come to recognize, is a function of how one conceives of the culture and its aims, professed and otherwise. (Bruner, 1996, pp. ix–x)

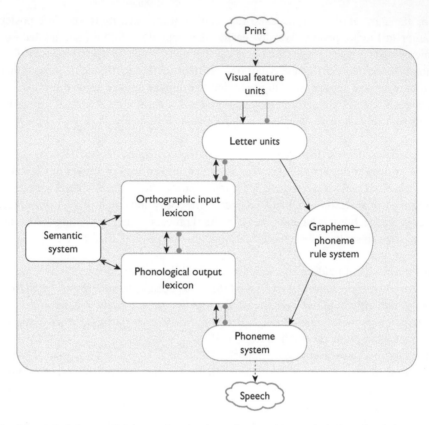

Figure 12.9 A model of the parallel routes for visual word recognition and reading aloud that are created in the brain as a result of learning to read

Source: Heyes (2012, p. 2183)

School, of course, is not just a site for teaching and learning, it is a complex societal institution. The research I have summarized, with its studies of the consequences of schooling, treats school as a black box whose inputs and outputs can be measured but whose "internal" processes remain mysterious. This research suffers from many of the same problems as cross-cultural investigations: they treat schooling merely as an independent variable.

However, some researchers have actually entered the "box" and conducted detailed ethnographic studies of everyday life in school classrooms. They have reported on the complex, negotiated character of what takes place. The classroom is a social setting where relationships are forged, emotion and morality are central, and social dynamics are subtle and complex. In particular, school is a place of continual comparison and competition (Packer, 2001).

The modern school exists within a complex, nested societal system, organized on multiple levels, with both direct and indirect chains of influence among people and resources, and school has an impact not only on children's cognition but also on their socioemotional and moral development. The transition to school can often seem abrupt and disruptive to the child: it is a completely new institution, separate from the family, with new and unfamiliar practices of evaluation and competition. A classroom, with students of the same age and a single adult in charge, may seem to offer none of the opportunities for practical and relevant learning that a child has outside school.

What and how a child learns in school follow not simply from what she is taught, nor from an interaction between instruction and her aptitudes; they are also a consequence of her understanding and evaluation of herself, as a person but especially in her new role as a student. The child is an active participant in her schooling, evaluating what happens in the classroom and making choices, based on her stage of development and her particular trajectory through that stage. Her learning in school depends on her need for self-esteem, her response to figures of authority, and her evaluation of the value and importance of the curriculum. Children in different cultural settings, and at different times in history, have understood their schooling in quite different ways, and in consequence have had very different motivations to study and learn, or not to do so (Modell, 1994).

For example, an ethnographic study of boys from working-class families in a British industrial town found that these boys—who called themselves "the lads"—rejected the opportunities that their high school offered, opportunities to improve economically and get middle-class jobs (Willis, 1977). They preferred to drop out of school in order to work in local factories. In the ethnographer's analysis, the boys' opposition and antagonism to formal education amounted to a "counter-school culture," and in this sense their active resistance to their teachers' efforts to enforce discipline in the classroom can be considered a process of **cultural production**. From their point of view, teachers offered their students only book knowledge, in exchange for an attitude of respect which they did not deserve. The result—that the boys dropped out or left school as soon as they could—was an unintended consequence of the fact that school is generally an institution that embodies middle-class values, and that teachers usually have a middle-class background. The boys actively opted out of school, choosing instead a life of tough manual labor which, although they could partially grasp its inequities, they considered to be genuinely masculine. Far from being simply a consequence of academic "failure," this outcome was a result of the boys' active resistance to the ideology of the school and to the system of institutionalized education as a whole.

Numerous studies have documented the ways that school systems impose greater challenges on children from poor and minority families. Reading materials often reflect a white, middle-class vocabulary and interests. Standardized tests involve settings and activities that are more familiar to children from wealthier families. Schooling, at least as it is currently organized, generally perpetuates social inequities. Children may recognize this and reject the legitimacy of their role as students.

1.6.1 SECOND-GENERATION EFFECTS

The character of school as a social institution can be seen in the fact that it has effects not only on the child who attends school but also on their children. Studies in Mexico, Nepal, Zambia, and Venezuela have shown that women who attend school have fewer pregnancies and lower infant death rates when they grow up, largely because they make better use of access to health services and contraceptive advice. Women educated in school also tend to marry later, and they take greater advantage of prenatal care (LeVine et al., 2004).

This research indicates that the key factor here is the literacy these women achieved in school. Women who can understand technical and bureaucratic language become better informed and better able to use community resources. Even a few years of schooling provides women with the skills with written and oral language that are necessary to interact with the bureaucracies of health care. This takes us to the theme of the next section, which focuses on the psychological consequences of literacy—of learning to read and write.

2. OUTSIDE SCHOOL AND WORK

Even in cultures where children attend formal schooling, they do other things as well. School takes up a good portion of each day, but not the whole of a child's waking hours.

Middle childhood is a time of greater responsibilities, but in a sense it is also a time of increased freedom. Studies of where children in Western societies spend time during the day show that during middle childhood they spend fewer hours with parents and more hours with teachers, coaches, and other adults, in a variety of settings such as camp, Sunday school, sports teams, classes in things such as music and ballet, boy scouts and girl scouts. Once children start school, they are with their parents less than half as much as before (Maccoby, 1984a).

In middle childhood, children also spend an increasing amount of time with other children the same age. Time spent in peer groups away from adult supervision and intervention provides them with new opportunities and new responsibilities. Of course, it is difficult for researchers to find out what children do when adults are not around. By definition, we cannot be with them to observe. When we ask them, they are likely to be selective in what they tell us. But the new abilities for deliberate thinking and planning, and for understanding the perspectives of others, become evident in children's relationships with peers.

2.1 ORGANIZATIONS FOR CHILDREN

Children's organizations outside school can be important contexts that foster development. For example, the Girl Scouts is an international organization for girls as young as 6 years of age. Its educational philosophy emphasizes the value of girls working together in small groups, managing and planning, and learning cooperation and citizenship.

One of the central activities of the Girl Scouts in the USA is raising funds by selling cookies. Rogoff and her colleagues studied the organization of this activity, and the learning opportunities it provided. Over 1 million girls sell cookies each year, assisted by 400,000 adults. Cookie Chairs are trained in each troop, then orders are gathered through phone calls and door-to-door sales. Six weeks later the cookies have been baked and must be delivered to the correct addresses. The girls must take orders, plan delivery routes, and transport the cookies to their purchasers. Doing all this requires skills of planning, imagination, and memorizing (Rogoff et al., 2002).

However, these psychological activities are not carried out by each girl scout individually. On the contrary, other scouts, their mothers, the scouting organization, the cookie company, and even the customers play significant roles in the cognition that is required. Various **cognitive tools** have a role, too. One of these is the cookie order form, developed over several generations of scouts. Rogoff describes a cognitive tool as a part of culture that has become "naturalized"—taken for granted by the people who inherit it. It is a social artifact that amplifies human activity, transforming and constraining it. It is a representation of people's solutions to similar problems in earlier times. The cookie order form is used to bring together the various people who have to solve the problems of how to purchase, distribute, and sell the cookies.

Participation in organizations such as the Girl Scouts and learning to use cognitive tools such as the cookie form provides girls with an education that takes place outside school walls.

2.2 THE PEER GROUP

A number of prominent psychologists, including Freud, Piaget, and Erikson, have argued that the **peer group** has an important influence during middle childhood. Peers are children the same age, not members of the family. Study of peer groups began in the 1930s (see Renshaw, 1981), and greatly increased in the 1970s and 1980s.

In the 1960s, animal studies conducted with rhesus monkey infants found that when they had no contact with peers they failed to develop normal social skills, even though they were raised by their mothers. It was also found that contact with peers could compensate for some of the negative consequences of being deprived of a mother (Harlow, 1969). This suggested that peer relations might be important for healthy development in humans. Around the same time, longitudinal studies of children found associations between poor relations with peers in childhood and later delinquency and psychopathology (Cowen et al., 1973).

In the 1970s and 1980s, researchers worked to identify components of children's **social competence** and relate them to **status** in the peer group, such as being popular, or at least accepted. Peer status was assessed using **sociometric** techniques, based on children's ratings of their peers, and sometimes also observation of, for example, school playground interactions.

2.2.1 SOCIOMETRIC TYPES

Types of Sociometric Status	
Popular children	Receive many nominations or high ratings, and very few negative nominations or low ratings
Rejected children	Receive few nominations or high ratings, and many negative nominations, or low ratings
Neglected or isolated children	Receive few nominations of either kind
Controversial children	Receive both high positive and high negative nominations, or both high and low ratings

Figure 12.10 Reputation among peers, called sociometric status, is usually assessed by asking children to rate or name those who they do and do not like to play with amongst their peers

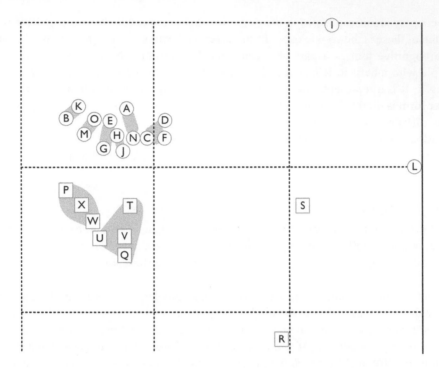

Figure 12.11 Sociometric status in a class of children. Circles are girls, squares are boys

Not too surprisingly, it was found that prosocial (helping) behavior leads to **peer acceptance**, while antisocial and disruptive acts lead to **peer rejection**. Children with social skills are more likely to form friendships. Experimental research—teaching children the necessary skills, such as being helpful and friendly, following rules, cooperating—supported this hypothesis that social skills are necessary for better relations with peers, while a deficit in skills leads to problematic relations, such rejection by peers and a lack of friends (Ladd, 1999).

Researchers then began to look for the origins of these skills. One line of investigation focused on children's thinking about interpersonal interactions and about themselves. It was found that children with poor skills are more likely to have **instrumental goals** or **self-focused goals** for their social interactions with peers, to follow ineffective or aggressive strategies to try to obtain these goals, and to believe, incorrectly, that these strategies will be effective. In addition, children who are aggressive tend to interpret the motives of other children as hostile. Children who are disliked are more likely to think of themselves as lower in competence than more popular children. In other words, social skills seem to be based at least in part on biased ways of reasoning about social situations.

Note, however, that this way of conceptualizing the problem sees social relations as following on from forms of cognition. One might argue that the opposite is the case: that cognition—thinking and reasoning—arises from the need to manage social relationships, interactions, and institutions.

There is also evidence that children are aggressive when they have difficulty **regulating** their emotions, or controlling the behaviors that are prompted by strong emotion. Differences in temperament and affective responses have been found between sociable and shy children. In other words, children accepted by their peers may be both less inclined to feel negative emotions and better able to regulate these emotions when they do arise. But there is also evidence suggesting that a child is better able to regulate their emotion when dealing with a peer whom they like than with one whom they dislike. This is important, because it shows that emotion regulation is not entirely a fixed characteristic of the individual child.

A second line of investigation explored how social skills with peers are learned in the family. Both direct influences—deliberate attempts by parents to influence their child's peer relations—and indirect influences—patterns of attachment and parenting styles—were explored. Studies of the direct influences found considerable variation across families, but in general that mothers are more involved than fathers, and that a mother's participation in her child's play with peers, for example, is associated with competence in young children but with deficits in older children. When parents arrange for their young child to have regular contact with peers this generally leads to better peer relations in the future: having the opportunity to meet and interact with other children from outside the family at an early age seems to benefit later peer relations.

Studies of the indirect influences, such as attachment and parenting styles, found that children with secure attachment have better peer relations, and are more responsive and less critical with other children. Warm and responsive parenting was found to be linked with a child's social competence. In contrast, harsh discipline seems to encourage aggression in children. Coercive parenting seems to lead to oppositional behavior, both towards parents and towards peers. Experience of parental divorce or depression often leads to poor social skills. On the other hand, parenting that is emotionally expressive, responsive, and supportive enables children to learn social skills that will lead to positive peer relations.

Researchers also began to distinguish among different types of relationships, and what each type provides a child. Friendship, defined as "a voluntary, dyadic form of relationship that often embodied a positive affective tie" (Ladd, 1999, p. 337), has been distinguished from simple membership in a group of peers. When young children talk about friendship they distinguish five aspects: validation, aid, disclosure of negative emotion, exclusivity, and conflict. In middle childhood, children add companionship, intimate exchange, and conflict resolution. At this stage, girls see friendship as involving intimate exchange, validation, and help more than boys do. Younger boys and girls do not differ on this aspect of friendship.

Disagreements between friends are more common and last longer than disagreements with non-friends, suggesting that friendship provides a safe space within which to express negative feelings.

Do these different kinds of peer relationship have different influences on a child's development? Studies of friendships over time suggest that they provide children with an opportunity to recognize another person's emotions, and consequently to learn how to coordinate activity and offer support. Validation and low conflict are characteristics of more stable friendships among children.

In addition, researchers began to explore the possibility that there is a two-way influence between peer acceptance and social skills, rather than only a one-way influence. For example, rejection by peers may lead to deviant behavior and vulnerability, rather than vice versa. Studies also began to distinguish among the consequences of different kinds of aggression. Instrumental aggression has been found to lead to rejection by peers throughout the school years, but angry-reactive aggression becomes more important when children are older. In contrast, aggression in rough play does not lead to rejection at any age.

Aggression is not the only route to isolation from peers; some children actively withdraw. This withdrawal, of course, limits opportunities to form relationships. Older children, moreover, often view withdrawal as deviant and this leads them to further rejection of a withdrawn peer.

Longitudinal investigations have found that rejection by peers is relatively stable over time, and that it predicts various problems during the school years, into middle school. The more severe and longer lasting the rejection, the greater the problems. However, neglect by peers (rather than rejection) is associated with higher achievement motivation. Friendship also predicts emotional well-being and adjustment through the school years. Victimization by peers—bullying and other kinds of abuse—is associated with anxiety, loneliness, depression, and poor adjustment to school. Friendship seems to offer a child different rewards from those that group membership provides, and consequently facilitates different outcomes.

An important question is whether acceptance and rejection become stable over time because a child develops a reputation in the eyes of peers, or because her interactions continually reproduce her status. The research suggests that her actions lead to a reputation among her peers, which then becomes self-perpetuating.

Children with a negative reputation among their peers tend to lack friends, or to have friendships that are less supportive. Aggressive children tend to have friendships with more jealousy, exclusivity, and hostility.

Gender differences have been somewhat neglected in this research. Early assumptions that boys are more aggressive than girls have been replaced by recognition that the genders express and handle hostility in different ways. Boys are more likely to confront, girls are more likely to try to harm a peer's reputation or her relationships. This kind of **relational aggression** is just as strongly related to later social maladjustment as is direct aggression. There is also evidence that rejection has different causes and consequences for girls.

As you can see, much of the research on peer relations during middle childhood has focused on the characteristics of individual children. The focus on individual differences has tended to overshadow describing and understanding trajectories of developmental change (Maccoby, 1984a). In addition, many of the measures used involve value judgments that might reflect the cultural and social background of the researcher. Little attention has been paid to the cultural customs and the social processes and practices in which children interact with peers. Only recently have researchers begun to pay attention to the cultural background of the children, and to the cultural context in which they are forming relationships with one another.

Since the 1990s there has been more effort to pay attention to children who are not white and middle class, though much work remains to be done. Not surprisingly, ethnically diverse friendships and peer groups are fostered when schools enroll children from diverse backgrounds. African-American children have been found to have more friendships, and more opposite-sex friendships, than Euro-American children. Cross-cultural studies have found that friendships are more stable in some cultures than in others, and that shyness is positively correlated with social competence and acceptance among Chinese children, but not among Canadian children, for example.

It seems unlikely that peer relationships make the same contribution to development in every culture, but we know very little about this important topic (Chen et al., 2006). Research is needed that will help us understand how children's peer relations both affect and are affected by the cultural structures and processes within which they are involved (Corsaro, 2006). As we saw in Chapter 9, children themselves *create* a culture, in the sense of a persisting pattern of practical activities.

One possibility is that children in every culture form a **peer system** but that the characteristics of this system vary, such as in the way helpfulness and aggression are practiced, for example. A second possibility is that because a culture defines specific developmental goals and objectives, the developmental consequences of experiences with peers will vary. A culture in which kinship ties are strong and multiple may place less emphasis on relations with peers outside the family. If this is the case, findings from research in one culture will have little relevance in another.

2.2.2 FRIENDSHIP

One important type of peer relationship is friendship. I have mentioned that researchers have defined **friendship** as a dyadic relationship that is entered into voluntarily and is based on emotional needs rather than instrumental needs. However, this may turn out to be a definition that reflects white, Western, middle-class experience.

Here too, studies of children's friendships have tended to take for granted the setting in which children meet. Usually it is the school, but this setting is organized for children by adults, who then supervize the children's interactions to a greater or lesser degree. Children rarely have the opportunity to form friendships outside adult influence, and this means that adult values shape the children's relationships.

Research in the USA has found that among boys, friendships tend to link into interconnected networks over time, while girls' friendships tend to remain dyadic. Rejected children may be more likely to try to form a friendship with a child of the opposite sex, and children with same-sex friends tend to have stronger social skills. Boys and girls seem to have different priorities in their friendships: girls are more concerned with connection, boys with status and competition.

Here too, much work remains to be done exploring the character of children's friendship in distinct cultures, and the impact of friendship on their development (Krappmann, 1998).

However, we do know that although friendship is found in all societies, it takes different forms. In general, friendship is considered to be voluntary, a relationship with reciprocal obligations, though the precise character of these obligations is very difficult to specify in advance. But friendships operate within a cultural frame that defines the parameters of the relationship. All languages have a word for a close relationship outside the family, but these words have different connotations. Some emphasize material assistance, while others emphasize emotional connection. For example, *tomo* in Japanese implies mutuality and affiliation among members of a group of friends.

It has been reported that in hunting and gathering societies groups of same-age juveniles do not form, probably because mixed-aged groups provide the opportunity for learning culturally important skills. In such societies friendships may not form until adulthood, at which point they may be so significant as to be defined as ceremonial kinship relations: blood brotherhood. One hypothesis is that the kind of adult friendship varies with the type of family organization within the culture: close friendships will form when alliances outside the clan are permitted. Casual friendships will form when there are loosely associated family groups. Expedient friendships will form in cultures where family bonds are weak. Evidence against this hypothesis, however, is the fact that each of these kinds of friendship can be found in Western cultures.

There has also been a suggestion that friendships are emotional where social structures assign each person a fixed place and specific resources, but friendships are more instrumental in societies where resources are more flexibly available. In some cultures, the peer group may take precedence over friendships, both in childhood and in adulthood.

2.3 GAMES WITH RULES

In many parts of the world, when children in middle childhood play together, their activity now often takes the form of **games with explicit rules**, especially for boys. Children now play baseball, or marbles, or make up their own games, but with explicit verbal agreements about how to play, and what counts as cheating. Children can now play without adult guidance, though adults don't always let them. A **rule** is a prior obligation or injunction: something one should or should not do. Following a rule means a kind of **self-regulation** that is agreed upon in advance. Where the toddler responded immediately to the affordances around her, and the preschooler responded principally to the imaginary situation she created, in middle childhood the child is able to do what she has been told to do by adults, or what she has agreed to do with peers, even when the demands of the situation call for something different. This is an extension of the self-control that was acquired in sociodramatic play, with the rules now explicit, agreed upon in advance, and self-imposed. As soon as activity is regulated by rules a whole range of possibilities for action is ruled out. As was the case with sociodramatic play, games with rules require and foster self-control. This kind of play is another aspect of the sense of responsibility that the child now shows.

Once again, we see that play is not simply about having fun, or satisfying one's desires in fantasy. On the contrary, in obeying rules children "follow the line of greatest resistance; for by subordinating themselves to rules, children renounce what they want, since subjection to rule and renunciation of spontaneous impulsive action constitute the path to maximum pleasure in play" (Vygotsky, 1966, p. 12). By following and obeying rules in play with other children the child is learning to create and follow personal and private rules. She becomes able to resists her impulses and act later, after taking time to think.

We can observe this in the fact that a child will have greater self-control in play than outside it. Following the rules brings pleasure, and so the child learns a new kind of desire—a desire that relates to her fictitious role in the game. In play with rules the child's willpower becomes stronger.

Sociodramatic play in early childhood involved an obvious imaginary situation and rules that were only implicit. If games in middle childhood have overt, explicit rules, what has happened to the imaginary situation? A game with rules like chess, or baseball, has a hidden, or concealed, imaginary situation. The participants act "as if" the chess piece has real powers, and "as if" the bases define a real pathway to victory. As adults, we tend not to notice the degree of imagination that our everyday social reality involves. In a game, the child has a fictitious "I." Games help the child to understand that she has a position in a **system of social relationships**. It is now that children become able to form

generalizations about the *relations* among people who inhabit institutional roles (roles such as "student" and "teacher"). This reflects their growing ability to participate in "imagined worlds."

Studies have found differences in the ways boys and girls play during middle childhood. We have already mentioned that boys are somewhat more involved in games with rules. Boys generally engage in more **aggressive play** and more **rough and tumble play** than girls, as well as more functional, solitary-dramatic and **exploratory** play. Boys tend to be involved more than girls in group play, whereas girls participate more in parallel and constructive play as well as in more conversations among peers. The fact that gender self-segregation is continued in this stage suggests that the children are still working out aspects of their gender identity in their play.

2.4 CARE-GIVING IN MIDDLE CHILDHOOD

Whereas parenting toddlers involved playing the role of an external ego, and with young children playing the role of an external superego, in middle childhood it is more a matter of being an alter ego: that is, an intimate and trusted equal. At this stage, parents can try to influence their child's actions with rational argument, appealing to her growing sense of reason and fairness.

We have seen that in middle childhood children enter a broader world, and this raises challenges for their parents, who must adjust to multiple, simultaneous changes. Parents can rely on the fact that their child has more self-control and autonomy, and a greater sense of responsibility. But they still also need to promote these abilities in their child, encouraging her self-control while at the same time regulating what she does, where, when, and with whom. This is a difficult balancing act. Increasingly, parents find themselves involved in their child's relationships with people outside the family—with teachers, other children, and other families (Collins et al., 2002).

In Western societies, parenting in middle childhood shifts away from satisfying the child's needs to focus on mutual and reciprocal responsibilities. Caregivers can now explain the reasons for their decisions to a child and expect to be understood, but they also must find ways to handle her expanding social networks. Children are now being guided and evaluated by other adults, not only their caregivers.

Theories of effective parenting suggest that parents of children in this developmental stage should be flexible, yet maintain clear core values and expectations. Effective parenting, to many psychologists, helps children further develop their self-regulation. Parents should monitor what their child is doing, and exert influence in a way that is sensitive to her needs and interests.

Research indicates that no dramatic changes occur in parents' style of childrearing in middle childhood, but new strategies for influencing the child's behavior are often introduced. Where parents of young children often distract and are physically assertive, in middle childhood parents are more likely to remind the child of her responsibilities, appeal to her self-esteem, induce guilt, or withhold privileges. Parental discipline works best when it focuses on the implications of what the child does, rather than when power is used to force compliance. Parents can assume that the child can and should control her own conduct, and also that misbehavior may be deliberate.

Some psychologists view this as a three-phase transfer of power, from **regulation** (parents in charge), to **co-regulation** (in which the parents have overall control but allow children some responsibility), and eventually to **self-regulation**, in adolescence and beyond (Maccoby, 1984b).

During the preschool years, children are learning to regulate their own affective states, and parents are contributing to this, partly through their direct dealings with the child's emotional outbursts, but also by regulating the rate at which she is exposed to new experiences. In this period, parents do a great deal of monitoring of the child's moment-to-moment activities and provide much direct feedback. During the school-aged years, the amount of direct contact between parent and child diminishes greatly—parental monitoring is more distal. In a sense, much of it involves monitoring her self-monitoring. She must now join the family system as a contributor, a cooperative interactor (Maccoby, 1984a, p. 324).

In some cultures, however, co-regulation rather than autonomy remains the norm as a child grows up, although the form of interdependence between child and adults will become more complex. In such cultures, as the child develops she will play an increasingly involved role in a system of reciprocity (Maccoby, 1992). In fact, the autonomy and independence that are valued in cultures in the USA are probably best viewed as a specific *kind* of interdependence. From this point of view, what happens in middle childhood is not a transfer of power and control but a reorganization of patterns of responsibility.

We tend to view child-centered parenting as crucial for children's development, but in fact it is a very culture-specific practice. Industrialized countries have separated the home from the workplace. In doing so, they have separated children from the world of work. The creation of specialized settings to educate children contributes to this segregation. Parenting has become transformed as a consequence. The modern parent must monitor at a distance what their child is doing at school, and must coordinate the increasing number of school-related and out-of-school activities and organizations in which she participates.

Authoritative parenting (see Chapter 10) continues to be related to various positive outcomes in middle childhood, such as acceptance by peers, success in school, and competence in various tasks. Outcomes are less positive when parents are preoccupied with their own needs and interests. Many children are starting to complain that their parents are tied up on the cell phone or in front of their computers, and have no time to talk or hang out with them (Turkle, 2012).

In middle childhood, parents and children generally show less overt affection to one another, and children have fewer emotional outbursts or tantrums. Parents need to resort to discipline less often. However, children this age are more likely than younger children to sulk, or avoid their parents, and be passively non-cooperative. Children now have different expectations of and attitudes towards their parents. They understand that their parents are doing things for them, that parents know more than they do, and that they have expectations of fairness. They are more likely to attribute conflicts with their parents to a lack of their help or attention, but they are likely to agree with their parents about where authority lies in the family. Children are now more accurate in their understanding of their parents' views of them.

Parenting a child who has started to attend school involves demands that are different from those when the child is contributing to work inside and outside the home. The relationship between parents and child often shifts from being focused on satisfying the child's needs to focusing on mutual and reciprocal responsibilities. Parents can now explain to their child the reasons for their decisions; in fact, they may now find that she demands such explanations.

Parents will also have to cope with the child's expanding social networks of friends and acquaintances. More time is now spent outside the family and away from parents. Children become concerned with their peer relationships, their social reputation and their popularity. The school peer culture becomes as important to them as their family, and parents have to find ways of monitoring influences that they cannot experience firsthand (Hartup, 1982). This also means that children are receiving social support from people outside the family. They become more skilled at managing and resolving conflict with peers, but their parents must still play a role at times.

Children now often spend more time out of the home in their local neighborhood, which can be a source of resources for play and exploration, but also may mean exposure to violence, drugs, and alcohol. Children cope better with the new stresses that middle childhood can bring when adults are available with whom they can discuss these matters.

Overall, parents continue to play a central role in the lives of children during middle childhood. But the new social situation of this developmental stage means that a child receives multiple, sometimes conflicting, sources of evaluation of what she does and who she is, not only from parents but also from other important adult figures and from peers. The child has to incorporate these multiple evaluations into her self-understanding, which becomes richer and more complex during this period of time.

Guidance during middle childhood often involves explicit training in the different roles and responsibilities of males and females. As we will see in the next section, in many societies boys now enter a hierarchy of males outside the family, while girls remain among family relationships. This contributes to the tendency for women's social position to be reproduced from one generation to the next.

2.5 GENDER ROLES IN MIDDLE CHILDHOOD

We saw in Chapter 10 that during early childhood an understanding of gender—a "gender personality"—formed though processes that were largely unconscious. Young children understand gender largely in terms of conventions: girls carry a purse and wear a skirt; boys wear trousers. In middle childhood, in contrast, children start to understand gender roles. They often receive explicit training in gender-related matters. As we have seen, in many cultures a girl remains with her mother and other female family members, while a boy receives training or schooling which takes him out of the family, and often breaks the boy's connection with both mother and father (Chodorow, 2001). Girls can continue to participate in household activity while boys are in something of a limbo—not yet ready for adult work but not expected to participate in household tasks.

Today many girls go to school, but at the same time there is often a subtle message that a girl should prepare to be a wife and mother as much as, if not more than, she should prepare for work. Even when she goes to school, there is more overall continuity to her home situation than there is for boys. Whether she is at home or at school, a girl is more likely to receive preparation for nurturance and responsibility, while a boy will receive preparation for achievement and self-reliance. Boys begin to enter a social hierarchy, while girls continue to be members of a system of family relationships. Girls are connected to adult women who are defined by their relations—as someone's wife, or daughter, or mother. Boys have contact with adult men who are defined by their status with respect to other men—as someone's boss, or employee—and they do not form strong emotional connections with these men.

Some psychologists have suggested that this difference leads to more flexible ego boundaries in girls, and an orientation more focused on the present than on the future, while in boys it gives rise to a more individualistic approach and a more analytic cognitive style. Some researchers have proposed that girls will mix analytic and relational styles, and that they will feel conflicted about this.

In Nancy Chodorow's analysis, the general consequence of these distinct arrangements for children of different genders is that in middle childhood a girl is forming a personality with a secure sense of what she calls "gender identity," based on relationships and connections, which prepares her to become a wife and mother who will foster the same kind of relationships with her own children. If so, this would explain why women's relatively disadvantaged social position tends to be reproduced from one generation to the next, and why this position is so common in many cultures of the world. It would also explain why many women experience difficulty differentiating from their mother and vice versa. As we saw in the previous chapter, these changes may lead adult men to be more anxious at connection, and adult women more anxious at separation.

This "reproduction of mothering" (Chodorow, 1999[1978]) is another example of a positive feedback loop operating in cultural reproduction, as the conditions that parents arrange for the education of their children influence the kinds of adults that those children become, and how they in turn relate to their own children.

During middle childhood, children are also working out their gender role in their relations with peers. This developmental stage continues to be a time of gender segregation in most cultures. Western elementary schools illustrate this: even though boys and girls may be in class together they will choose to be apart whenever they can, in the lunch room and the playground. There is less segregation when adults are supervising activities, but when left to their own devices children will spontaneously separate.

Research by Barry Thorne has explored this gender separation. She has aimed to move beyond individualistic explanations in terms of such factors as behavioral compatibility, psychoanalytic processes and cognitive dynamics, towards explanation in terms of "border work"—social interactions that strengthen the boundary between the gender groups—and activities of "crossing"—seeking access to groups and activities of the other gender.

Thorne found that boys tend to form larger and more visible groups, they are involved in activities that take up more space, with more physically aggressive play and fighting, and their relations with one another tend to be more hierarchical and competitive, with many direct insults and challenges. Even when they are not playing sports, boys often use sports metaphors, talking of "teams" and "captains." Dirty words—swear words or sexual terms—are often used, and transgression of rules in public seems to be exciting to boys, and to be a way of bonding among them. They also form larger groups, which provide transgressors with more anonymity (Thorne, 1994).

In contrast, girls form smaller groups, or pairs with shifting alliances. Their activities involve more turn-taking, and although they talk about cooperation they do experience conflict, though this tends to be more indirect than is the case for boys. In general, girls are more concerned with constructing emotionally intimate, one-to-one relationships in which they learn how to make and break connections. Girls focus on who is "nice," and who is "liked" or "disliked." Their play often involves stylized performances, such as dance steps and jumping rope. They make relaxed physical contact, stroke or comb each other's hair, and comment on physical appearance. Best friends disclose secrets; they display knowledge of interpersonal motivation and the complexities of relationships, knowledge which they say boys lack. Their talk is more about romance than dirty words.

Around age 10 and 11 children begin the transition from the gender system of childhood to that of adolescence (Thorne & Luria, 1986). At this time the complex relationships between sexuality and gender can cause much confusion. Different gender-specific contexts may provide quite different pathways to adolescent sexuality for girls and boys. Whereas in early childhood and the start of middle childhood boys frequently touched one another, hugging or holding hands, by fifth grade this has turned into mock violence and shoving gestures, and rituals like "giving five." For boys, patterns of masculinity include using homophobic labels as insults, and suspected crushes on girls are teased. Girls learn about the romantic and emotional before the sexual; for boys it is the reverse. It seems likely that when they start dating, each sex teaches the other what it expects.

Moreover, sexuality is not necessarily postponed until adolescence. Kissing, erotic touching, masturbation, and even intercourse have been documented in middle childhood, though the overtly sexual is mostly a matter of words and excited play—children's knowledge about sexuality is still fragmented. The two same-gender groups provide a starting place for couples, both real and imaginary. "Liking" someone of the opposite sex is a topic for teasing, messages are sent between the groups, and the boundaries between boys and girls are patrolled and policed. Boys threaten to kiss girls, but treat such contact as contaminating. Girls may threaten to kiss boys to make them run away. Teasing and play in middle childhood are evidently sexual, while at the same time they maintain the boundary between the genders.

By and large, then, during middle childhood the genders usually stay apart, though there is some contact and connection across the boundary. We shall see in Chapter 14 how in adolescence that boundary is torn down.

CONCLUSION

I opened Chapter 11 by noting that developmental researchers have very often studied only children who attend school. It will have become clear that this approach leaves out many children around the world, neglects other equally important settings for learning, and takes for granted a very particular institutional context. School classrooms foster individual and independent work, competition, self-control, and self-direction. Self-worth easily becomes based on comparison with others. However, in the shrinking number of societies that don't send their children to school, and in settings outside the classroom, it is shared work, interdependence, and compliance with figures of authority that are encouraged. Worth comes from being a productive member of the community.

School is of course all about the three Rs: reading, writing, and arithmetic. That is to say, students are introduced in school to material symbolic systems, both linguistic and mathematical. The proposal that schools encourage children's deliberate, conscious use of these material symbol systems seems a reasonable one, but it requires further exploration.

School seems to encourage a kind of thinking that is "abstract" in the sense of being about language itself, rather than about specific concrete contexts, even though this thinking occurs in the context of the classroom. Not surprisingly, within the framework of schooling this kind of thinking is assessed as being "more advanced." But it seems more accurate to consider it to be one specific kind of reorganization of thinking among many that we might imagine or discover.

Insofar as schools provide special experience with written texts, "access to the experience of schooling is access to a treasure trove of tools for dealing with our lives" (Cole & D'Andrade, 1982, p. 25). However, what a child is able to do with these tools depends a great deal on the resources available to her *outside* school.

There are criticisms of the narrow emphasis that schooling places on reading and writing. Some people say that this is just "book learning," detached from the real world, decontextualized, and with minimal relevance. Calls are regularly made for an education that is more practical, more relevant, more hands-on, more geared towards the skills and capacities of a specific vocation or profession.

Others argue that learning to read and write has a general significance, a relevance that goes beyond simply learning the content that is presented in textbooks. Vygotsky certainly thought so; however, as we have seen in this chapter, research does not support the claim that literacy inevitably transforms cognition.

Rather, it appears that the new forms of activity in which a child participates in school lead to some cognitive skills and techniques whose value is largely limited to settings similar to the classroom.

There is some evidence that schooling fosters general abilities, but we must be careful not to over-interpret these. Piaget believed that relations such as transitivity (if A > B and B > C, then A > C) and class-inclusion (all fathers are men, but not all men are fathers) are aspects of a universal logic. It would be more accurate to see them as aspects of a Western rationality (Lachterman, 1989). What children achieve in school, then, is mastery of specific intellectual tools, not some kind of timeless universal competence.

If this conclusion is correct, research on the psychological consequences of schooling teaches us something about specific cultural practices that should make us cautious about claiming that these practices are necessary, or that they are clearly beneficial to all children's development. The specific abilities that children acquire in school support a specific mode of life. Other ways of living are equally valid, and they will involve equally valuable practices and settings for development in middle childhood.

During middle childhood, a contradiction is building. We have seen that by the time they are 10 years old, children are considered sufficiently responsible to work unsupervised in many activities. Yet although they have adult responsibilities, they often do not have adult rights. The growing contraction towards the end of middle childhood is the conflict among biological, psychological, and cultural definitions of maturity.

In cultural settings where children have been participating with increased responsibility and independence in adult work-related activities, it is possible that once they pass through puberty they will be granted adult status. In the West, however, middle childhood is a time for school, a form of indirect preparation for adult life. Adolescence is not an end to schooling, because school attendance is compulsory in most Western nations until 16 years of age. A child of 11 or 12 years of age can be forgiven if she experiences frustration and confusion at her situation. Many years will seem to stretch out ahead before she becomes recognized as an adult.

The child's deliberate, conscious thinking leads her to an awareness of the possibilities of her circumstances, and to a differentiation between what is *actual* and what is *possible*. The sense of a gap between these two is an important aspect of the crisis in which the child becomes an adolescent. Her increasingly awareness of the gulf between how things are and how they could be is a source of both frustration and inspiration.

The transition to adolescence involves the biological changes of puberty, but it amounts to much more than this. By the end of middle childhood, the child has come to construct a sense of both who she is, and who she could be. She has a multifaceted sense of herself, and she has the intellectual power to imagine possibilities for herself that do not yet exist.

SUMMARY

THE INSTITUTION OF SCHOOL

- Schools have been an important institution in many societies, though principally for training an elite.
- Schooling seems to have some degree of influence on children's perception, memory, intelligence, and categorization, principally due to the character of academic tasks.
- The impact of school on concrete operational tasks such as conservation seems minimal.
- However, there is evidence that schooling improves infralogical aspects of reasoning.
- Vygotsky proposed that learning to write promotes development of the higher psychological functions, which are deliberate and conscious.
- Vygotsky's concept of the zone of proximal development is a special case of his general genetic law of cultural development.
- There is no evidence that literacy promotes a general transformation of thinking. Rather, specific techniques of reading and writing promote specific skills.
- Learning to read involves "recycling" brain regions dedicated to other, older functions.
- School is a societal institution, within which children may reject the legitimacy of their role as students.

OUTSIDE SCHOOL AND WORK

- During middle childhood, children spend more time outside the family. The peer group has an important influence.
- Play with peers now involves games with rules.
- Research on peer relations in middle childhood has focused on individual factors that predict sociometric status. Recently, attention has been paid to cultural background and cultural context.
- Middle childhood is a time for a growing understanding of gender roles.

CHAPTER 13

THE TEENAGE YEARS

(12 YEARS AND UP)
ADOLESCENT OR ADULT?

LEARNING OBJECTIVES

In this chapter we shall explore the teenage years, and consider:

- The many biological changes that mark the start of the second decade of life.
- The historical and cultural differences in the way teenagers have been treated in the past, and are treated today.
- Research on the ways that teenagers think and reason.

FRAMING QUESTIONS

- In your view, does adolescence always involve conflict with parents?
- How many ways can one throw a six with three dice?
- At what age do you consider a young woman is ready to marry? And at what age is a young man ready? If there is a difference between your two answers, explain why.
- Have you ever kept a diary? If so, at what age did you start?

INTRODUCTION

We hear and read so much about the character and challenges of adolescence that it is hard to imagine that this is not a universal stage of development. In fact, however, adolescence emerged very recently in human history, though perhaps not for the first time. Even today it is not present in all cultures. Those anthropologists who view adolescence as universal add the caveat that in some cultures it is no more than a very brief transition (e.g., Schlegel, 1995, 2009).

Adolescence was raised as a concern for educators and politicians at the start of the last century. It became a recognized topic of study in psychology when G. Stanley Hall published his two-volume book *Adolescence* in 1904 (Steinberg & Lerner, 2004). For Hall, adolescence spanned the ages from 14 to 25 years. Even today, for all our talk about adolescence there is still no clear agreement about when it begins and ends, or whether it should be thought of as a developmental stage or as a developmental transition.

It may seem odd to say these things, because in Chapter 3 I pointed to fossil evidence which suggested that adolescence had evolved by the time of earliest Homo sapiens. Anatomically speaking, it does seem to be the case that early Homo sapiens, unlike other hominins, had a **growth spurt**, an acceleration in the rate of growth in height and weight shortly after **puberty**. This was an important step in the evolution of the human life cycle.

However, what is made of this biological difference varies from one culture to another. In some cultures, once the **biological capacity for reproduction** is achieved **adult status** is granted and young people have children of their own. In others, many years must pass before a young person is considered (and considers herself) ready to raise children.

The gap between these two events—puberty and the biological capacity to reproduce on the one hand, and socially sanctioned procreation on the other—is what we call adolescence. The first event is biologically based and clearly marked, by physical changes and often by social celebration. The second event is culturally defined and often ambiguously so. Hence the variability in the duration and character of human adolescence.

1. BIOLOGICAL CHANGES IN THE TEENAGE YEARS

The biological changes early in the second decade of life include the dramatic events of puberty and developments in key regions of the brain. These biological changes are associated with new motivations and emotions, and a new ability for self-monitoring and self-control.

1.1 PUBERTY

Puberty is a sequence of physiological changes that has the outcome that the person becomes biologically capable of sexual reproduction. In humans the process lasts for three or four years and is accompanied, unlike in the case of other primates, by a growth spurt and a rapid increase in height and weight.

Puberty begins with events in the neuroendocrine systems in the brain. The main region of the brain that is involved is the **hypothalamus**. The size of a grape, in the center of the head just below the top of the spinal cord, this brain region formed early in vertebrate evolution. Puberty begins when a hormone (gonadotrophin releasing hormone: GnRH) is secreted by the hypothalamus. A **hormone** is a chemical released by a cell or gland that functions as a messenger, travelling to other parts of the body and altering the metabolism of other cells or whole organs. GnRH travels to the **pituitary gland**, signalling it to secrete in turn two hormones, called *luteinising hormone* (LH) and *follicle stimulating hormone* (FSH), that act on the gonads, the **ovaries** or **testes**, stimulating them to release yet more hormones, steroids that effect many other parts of the body. The main sex hormone in boys is an androgen called *testosterone*. In girls, it is an estrogen called *estradiol*. These hormones promote development in the ovaries and testes, so that these begin to produce the **sperm** and **egg** cells whose fusion can create an embryo, as we saw in Chapter 4 (see Figure 9.1). The testes and ovaries also produce "feedback" hormones that act back on the hypothalamus and pituitary to regulate the whole process.

In a boy, testosterone stimulates enlargement of the testicles, growth of the penis, growth of pubic hair and hair on the face, in the armpits and over the body, and growth of the muscles and heart. A consequence of beginning to produce spermatozoa is the first ejaculation, an event known as **semenarche**.

Puberty starts in girls on average a year earlier than it does in boys. In a girl, oestrogen stimulates are growth of the breasts, growth of pubic hair, maturation of the genitals, increased fatty tissue, further breast growth, and the start of the menstrual cycle. As a girl begins to ovulate and menstruate her first period is known as **menarche**. Regular ovulation does not begin until one or two years after menarche, and the pelvic outlet does not widen until around 18, so childbirth can be dangerous for young teenage girls. The charity Save the Children reports that the biggest killer of teenage girls worldwide is pregnancy. However, it may be that this is due to a lack of adequate health care rather than pregnancy itself.

As a result of this cascade of changes a teenage girl's body becomes ready to support the complex processes of prenatal development that we described in Chapter 4, and a teenage boy's body becomes ready to fertilize the egg and contribute to the embryo.

The changes in the genitals are known as **primary sexual characteristics**. The other changes such as facial hair in boys and a lower voice, and curves in girls due to body fat, are known as **secondary sexual characteristics**. The latter are readily observable by other people, and may serve to display publicly the young person's new biological potential for reproduction.

Puberty occurs in all mammals—what is unique to humans is the **growth spurt** that accompanies puberty. This is an *acceleration* in the rate of growth in height and weight, for both girls and boys. It is the third growth spurt in human development: the first was prenatal, while the second occurred during the 5-to-7 transition. Other primates gain weight rapidly after puberty, but none show the skeletal growth that humans undergo—an increase of 6 or 7 centimetres per year in height (Bogin, 1999). For example, whereas a 7-year-old chimp has 88 percent of its adult body size, an 11-year-old boy has only 81 percent of the size he will have as an adult (Smith & Tomkins, 1995). A teenage boy may grow 9 inches taller, while a teenage girl may grow 7 inches. Boys are on average 2 centimetres shorter than girls before puberty begins, but an adult man is on average 13 centimetres taller than an adult woman.

Why do humans have this growth spurt at puberty? Why does growth not simply continue in a linear manner? It may be that during middle childhood human children are suppressed in their growth compared with juvenile primates, and consequently an acceleration in growth is needed in order to catch up. This may be related to the fact that sexual maturity is prepared for by puberty, but in the case of females it will not be complete for several more years. Once puberty has occurred, at the beginning of the teenage years, girls will appear to be sexually mature but in fact they are not. Boys at the same age will appear to be sexually immature, due to their shorter height and smaller weight, but in fact they *are* now biologically capable of reproduction. Evolutionary biologists have argued that these arrangements—girls appearing fertile when they are not, boys appearing not to be fertile when they are—have evolutionary advantages for both genders. The smaller, shorter status of boys during the juvenile stage, for example, may function to elicit extended parental care, while providing more time for learning. However, one consequence is that accelerated growth is needed during the teen years to achieve an adult size and weight.

Another possible explanation for the growth spurt after puberty is that it represents a trade-off that has evolved in the human life cycle: growth of the body has been delayed in middle childhood to dedicate maximum resources to brain growth.

This growth spurt may continue for ten years in a teenage girl, and even longer in a boy. It starts in the lower parts of the body, so the legs grow before the chest and arms. The body also changes in shape, as teenage girls deposit fat in breasts and buttocks and their hips widen, and teenage boys' shoulders widen and their muscle mass increases, while body fat decreases. By the end of the growth spurt, boys are physically stronger than girls.

1.1.1 TIMING OF THE GROWTH SPURT

The growth spurt at puberty occurs in every human group that has been examined. However, its timing and duration vary considerably, depending on the circumstances in which people live, their level of nutrition, incidence of disease, and other environmental influences (Bogin et al., 1992).

For example, among the Quechua Indians, who live high in the Andes, the teenage growth spurt starts later and is more drawn out, continuing until 22 years of age or older. This seems to be due to the heavy work these people need to do, to a degree of malnutrition, and to the physical stress of low temperatures and oxygen deficiency at such an elevated altitude.

The timing of menarche also depends on environmental factors. As we have seen, the series of biological events of puberty starts when hypothalamic neurons are activated, and one important trigger of this activation seems to be the proportion of body fat. Teenage girls today who engage in lots of exercise, such as gymnastics and dance, experience a delayed start of puberty. The body seems to adjust to the nutritional resources available, so that if food is scarce, the capacity for procreation is postponed.

An example of this was seen in Bangladesh in the period 1971–1976, when malnutrition was common as a result of war, postwar inflation, floods, and famine. One consequence was a delay of menarche,

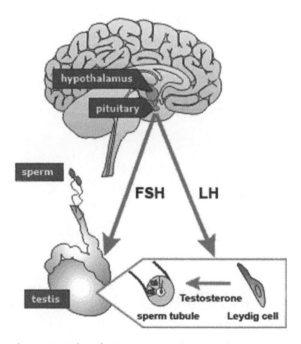

Figure 13.1 Hormonal pathways in male puberty

which went along with a shift towards later age at marriage (Chowdhury et al., 1977). Researchers also observed a seasonal trend in the onset of menarche, with a peak in the winter months when the annual rice harvest was collected, and so more food was available.

In fact, there has been a historical decrease in the average age at which menarche occurs. This change, known as the **secular trend**, amounts to a drop of around four months every ten years. It is most likely due to improving nutrition. In the past, hard work and a poorer diet meant less body fat, and menarche occurred later. In Northern European countries today the age at which menarche occurs is about three years earlier than it was a hundred years ago.

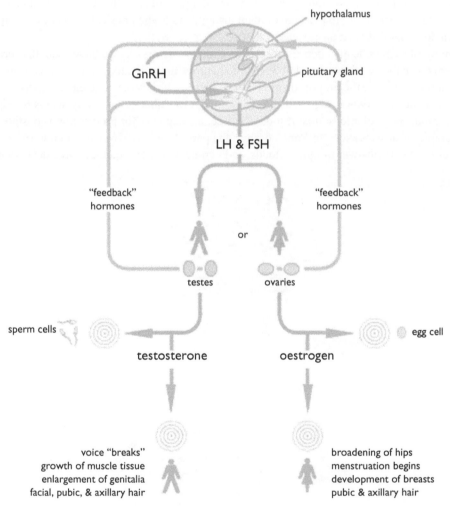

Figure 13.2 Normal hormonal control of puberty

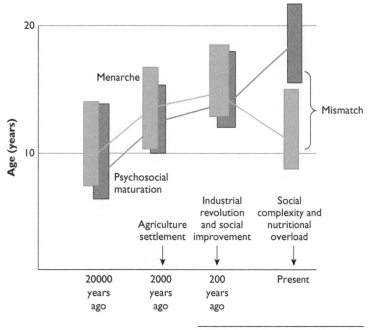

TRENDS in Endocrinology & Metabolism

Figure 13.3 The recent mismatch between reproductive maturity (menarche) and adult status (psychosocial maturation)

Source: Gluckman & Hanson (2006)

The secular trend is a significant change in a comparatively short time. It is probable that in Paleolithic times (about forty thousand years ago), human females would have experienced puberty when they were old enough to have been psychosocially mature. It would probably have been a significant disadvantage for a young woman in the Paleolithic to be able to reproduce before she had the necessary skills to be a mother. Today, in contrast, there is in many societies a significant gap or mismatch between the age at which a young woman becomes biologically capable of having a baby, and the age at which she has the skills, resources, and social status of an adult.

Reconstructions based on fossil evidence and primate data have led some researchers to conclude that this mismatch between reproductive maturity (menarche) and adult status appeared as recently as two hundred years ago—just yesterday in evolutionary terms (Gluckman & Hanson, 2006). (See Figure 9.2.) Limited nutritional resources and disease probably postponed menarche for much of human history. However, it is quite possible that earlier than two hundred years ago advanced civilizations were able to provide adequate nutrition for at least an elite in their young woman, who would have as a consequence passed through puberty while relatively young. If this was the case, the gap between reproductive maturity and adult status may have existed for a time in the past, only to subsequently disappear until it reappeared about two hundred years ago.

This mismatch between biological reproductive capability and socially defined adult status is a central topic of the rest of the chapter.

The biological processes of puberty bring about changes that are striking to the individual concerned, but are also evident to other people, who begin to treat that young person differently. Perhaps for this reason, puberty marks the start of a period of time during which there is increased vulnerability to mental health problems, including clinical depression. The incidence of depression rises after puberty in both sexes, and depression at this age is likely to last longer than depression in adults. Depression is more common in girls than boys, especially girls for whom puberty starts early. There is some evidence that adolescent depression is increasing, perhaps because puberty is starting at a younger age.

1.2 BRAIN DEVELOPMENT

The second decade of human brain development is as dynamic as the preceding one—the human brain continues to grow and change in both a structural and a functional sense (Paus, 2009, p. 111).

Recent neuroscience research has made the startling discovery that important structural and functional changes are taking place in key areas of the brain throughout the teenage years and even later (Rees, 2010, p. 155). It had been thought that such changes in the nervous system were completed in the first few years of life, but it appears that the hormones released during puberty stimulate gene expression, which leads to further significant brain development (Walker, 2002).

There are two changes in the overall character of the brain following puberty. First, while the overall volume of brain tissue stays the same there is an increase in myelin. This is evident as an increase in overall white matter. It is now recognized that myelin is an adaptable structure, not a static structure with fixed properties. Neuronal activity appears to promote changes in myelin, which in turn affect the neural circuitry by modulating electrical conduction (Bechler & ffrench-Constant, 2014). Second, there is first an increase and then a decrease in the density of synapses. This is evident in a curved change—first up, then down—in overall gray matter.

These changes take place principally in two specific brain regions: the **frontal cortex** and **prefrontal cortex**, and the **limbic system**.

1.2.1 FRONTAL AND PREFRONTAL CORTEX

In the adult human the frontal cortex makes up nearly a third of the area of the whole cortex. The *pre*frontal cortex is the region at the very front of the cortex. It is one of the cortical regions that has undergone the greatest expansion during human evolution, and it is one of the last brain regions to achieve its mature form, anatomically and functionally, during ontogenesis. During the teenage years, myelination and synaptic pruning occur in both the frontal and prefrontal cortex, and also for the axons that connect these regions to other regions. The waves of synaptic overproduction and subsequent pruning in the frontal and prefrontal cortex resemble what we saw in lower areas of the brain in infancy. Research using fMRI imaging shows frontal brain activity is increased in the teen years (Paus, 2009, 2010).

The prefrontal cortex plays a key role in the organization of action over time. Differences across animal species in their ability to control their behavior are correlated with the ratio of the size of their prefrontal cortex to the size of the rest of the brain. Overall, the prefrontal cortex seems to have the role of integrating experiences that have occurred at different times, in order to give a coherent structure to behavior in the present. To do this it draws on memory of past events, forms plans on the basis of interests and motivations, and then executes activity and monitors the consequences, including the rewards and costs that the action leads to.

All of this is clearly System 2 psychological functioning. It is what we have called the higher psychological functions. The biologically based research that shows where and how the teenage brain is changing fits well with cultural psychological theory, and also with research on teenage thinking and decision making, as we shall see later in this chapter.

1.2.2 LIMBIC SYSTEM

The second brain region that undergoes dramatic changes during and after puberty is the **limbic system** (Armstrong, 1991). As we saw in Chapter 4, this is a collection of structures at the base of the cerebrum below the cortex, including the thalamus, hypothalamus, amygdala, and hippocampus. These structures manage information about rewards and incentives and are associated with emotional reactions. They influence the endocrine system and the autonomic nervous system, and are closely connected to the brain region in the basal ganglia that has been called the "pleasure center" (Olds & Milner, 1954). Limbic system structures are part of System 1 (Lieberman, 2007).

During the teenage years, limbic structures increase in volume as new neurons form (Eriksson et al., 1998). These structures also undergo myelination and synaptic pruning, somewhat earlier than the same processes occur in the frontal and prefrontal cortex. In addition, links *between* the basal ganglia and the prefrontal cortex increase markedly during the teenage years and into adulthood.

In addition, the neurotransmission of *dopamine* and *oxytocin* alters around puberty, and this is believed to change the sensitivity of the limbic system. (Dopamine is an organic compound and oxytocin is a hormone. Both act as neuromodulators in the brain. Neuromodulation is a process in which one cell releases a chemical that influences many other cells, rather than influencing a single other cell as is the case in synaptic neurotransmission.) For example, the response in the *nucleus accumbens* to rewards becomes greater in the teenage years.

As a consequence of these changes, the balance between the limbic and prefrontal regions shifts. On the one hand, the subcortical limbic system produces heightened responses to rewards, incentives and emotional situations. On the other hand, the prefrontal cortex provides steadily increasing top-down monitoring and control. Many researchers see this shift in the balance between brain regions as the key to understanding teenage behavior:

> Adolescence is often a period of especially heightened vulnerability as a consequence of potential disjunctions between developing brain, behavioral and cognitive systems that mature along different timetables and under the control of both common and independent biological processes. Taken together, these developments reinforce the emerging understanding of adolescence as a critical or sensitive period for a reorganization of regulatory systems, a reorganization that is fraught with both risks and opportunities. (Steinberg, 2005, p. 70)

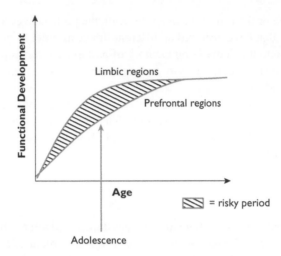

Figure 13.4 Development in the prefrontal cortex and in the limbic system are out of balance during much of adolescence

Source: Casey et al. (2008)

Some of the strengths and weaknesses of teenagers do make new sense in light of this recent brain research. As we shall see, the teenage years are considered a time both of increasingly sophisticated and complex reasoning and also of impulsivity and risky behavior. This apparent contradiction may reflect the lack of balance between the prefrontal cortex and the limbic system (see Figure 13.4). It is possible that at first the emotional responses of the limbic system are likely to predominate over the monitoring performed by the prefrontal cortex, so that a teenager will act on impulse even when she knows better (Casey et al., 2008).

However, it is important to remember that neurophysiology is very sensitive to influences from the environment, and this means that changes in the brain can be consequences as well as causes. We must always consider the interweaving of biology and culture, as the neuroscientist Tomáš Paus reminds us:

> Quite often, we view developmental changes in brain structure as (biological) prerequisites of a particular cognitive ability. For example, the common logic assumes that cognitive/executive control of behavior emerges in full only after the prefrontal cortex reaches the adult-like level of structural maturity. But given the role of experience in shaping the brain, it might also be that high demands on cognitive control faced, for example, by young adolescents assuming adult roles due to family circumstances may facilitate structural maturation of their prefrontal cortex. (Paus, 2009, p. 110)

The neurological changes I have just described certainly imply that education during the teenage years can be vitally important. The fact that the brain is still developing and adapting at this age suggests that it remains open to being shaped and directed by social influences. And this raises the question of the extent to which teenagers' behavior and cognition are products of the social circumstances in which they are placed. Since much of the research has been conducted in a very limited range of circumstances, it is difficult to know how general a picture we have of the psychology of the second decade of life.

2. CONSTITUTING ADOLESCENCE

The noun *adolescent* in English dates to the mid-fifteenth century, when it was used to mean a youth or a young man, and was taken from the Latin word *adolescentem* meaning "growing, near maturity, youthful." The use of the word *adolescent* as an adjective dates from the late eighteenth century.

2.1 ADOLESCENCE AND CULTURE

I have described the changes in body and brain that are associated with, or are direct consequences of, puberty. It might seem, then, that puberty marks the start of adolescence. However, biology alone does not define adolescence. It is what culture makes of these biological changes that defines whether a distinct developmental stage of adolescence exists, and if so how it is played out.

Although all cultures mark the distinction between childhood and adulthood, they do so at very different ages. Some cultures grant adult status when puberty occurs. Others don't consider the young person to be an adult for another decade or even later. In the former case, adolescence will be a relatively rapid transition, or perhaps it will not occur at all. In the latter case, there will be a prolonged period where the individual is neither child nor adult. In such a culture, adolescence is a distinct period of development, though whether it is a stage or a drawn-out transition is still a matter of debate.

One reason that both biology and culture play a role in defining adolescence is the undeniable fact that sexual reproduction is the only biological function that a human being cannot perform alone. This means that a partner must be selected before sexual reproduction can occur. In some cultures the selection of this partner is a matter of individual choice, but in many it is the business of extended families or wider social units, and here the selection of a sexual partner is not an individual choice but a social matter, decided by the family and community. Cultures differ in how they balance personal choice and social influence, but sexuality is an aspect of human life that is everywhere subject to intense cultural scrutiny and prohibition. Whether or not premarital sexuality is permitted or frowned upon, for example, will depend on whether what is considered desirable in a bride is virginity or sexual expertise, or whether having a large family is valued (as it has been in many royal and aristocratic families) or not. In many cultures, contact between the genders is severely regulated during the teenage years, and perhaps prohibited altogether. In others, marriages are arranged, and often carried out, in which a teenage (or even younger) girl is betrothed to a man, often older, who has been selected by her parents.

Clearly, the issue of who can marry who—which we first discussed in Chapter 4—has important economic and political implications, and this means that granting a young person the status of an adult, and hence as marriageable, cannot be based on biology alone. The specific ways of arranging these matters will determine whether or not the teenager spends a period of time with an ambiguous status—no longer a child but not yet an adult.

In addition, we need to remember that from early childhood through middle childhood the two genders have actively segregated themselves from one another. Teenage boys and girls need to come together before there can be any question of them forming emotional and sexual pair bonds. It is generally during the teenage years that this coming together takes place.

Adolescence, then, can be defined on the one hand as the gap or mismatch between the age at which the young person becomes biologically capable of reproduction—of having a baby—and on the other hand as the age at which adult status is achieved—when the young person is considered capable of contributing to the maintenance of their society, and so it is considered appropriate for them to become a parent. This gap varies in duration from one culture to another, to an extreme of not existing at all in some cultures. It has also varied in its duration (and existence) over the course of human history, as I explained in the first section of this chapter. In those cultures that do have some form of adolescence its "cultural structuring" varies greatly (Crockett, 1997), as do its onset and duration.

Western cultures today have an adolescence with an especially long duration, and this is in at least two respects a cultural phenomenon. First, puberty now starts at a younger age because of the rich diet that modern society makes available to at least some of its members. Second, entry into adulthood has been increasingly delayed because further education is considered necessary, and because financial independence takes a long time in modern economies.

In addition, in Western industrialized societies a differentiation of legal, educational, and religious systems of institutions, each with its own rules and roles, has led to the coexistence of multiple, ambiguous markers of adult status—for example, that there are different ages at which a teenager can take communion or celebrate bar mitzvah or bat mitzvah, can drive, purchase alcohol or cigarettes, get married, join the army, and so on.

Moreover, in these cultures a further stage of "youth" or "young adulthood" may follow adolescence, marking a further delaying of the achievement of adult status (Arnett, 2000; Schlegel, 2009).

One might assume that technologically advanced cultures have adolescence, while cultures with simpler technology do not. However, things are not that straightforward. For example, among the Abelam people who live in the tropical rain forest of Papua New Guinea (we met them in Chapter 11) boys are initiated into adulthood extremely slowly, and they are not expected to become fully adult until they are around 30 years of age. Most Abelam men, even when they are married and might be expected to have adult responsibilities, are unable to feed their own family without help from other people. Abelam teenage boys take on their adult responsibilities very slowly, in a cycle of ceremonies that takes at least 20 years. There is no explicit instruction in these ceremonies; instead, the boys are supposed to be motivated by undergoing ordeals such as being rubbed with stinging nettles (Forge, 1970, p. 278).

2.2 ADOLESCENCE AND HISTORY

The fact that adolescence is defined by both biology and culture becomes especially visible when historical changes transform the transition to adult status. If we look back in time to, for example, Tudor England, we find that at the time of Henry VIII (who reigned from 1509 to 1547), marriage regularly took place between a bride and groom aged perhaps 14 or younger. The average life expectancy was around 40, and everything happened faster and earlier than it does today. King Henry himself died when he was 56. In this period a child became an adult a few years after puberty, 14 was the age of legal responsibility, and a male of this age might find himself leading troops into battle. There was no mismatch between puberty and adult status—and hence no adolescence.

Towards the end of the nineteenth century, however, people in Western cultures started to identify a distinct period in the life cycle between puberty and adulthood. Many began to work outside the household in factories, and young people could not easily contribute to this work. As first even children were recruited as laborers, but as the work became more skilled laws were passed restricting child labor and making schooling compulsory. Teenagers who found themselves not yet working, yet no longer children, became an issue for society as a whole (Modell & Goodman, 1990).

Industrialization during the nineteenth century meant that preparation for adulthood became more complex. Increasingly, this preparation occurred in institutions in which teenagers were in contact with others their own age rather than with adults. Formal education was increasingly necessary, even for children from farming families. The middle-class family became a private place, cut off from the community and places of work. The child became viewed no longer as a helpful resource, but as a gift to be invested in. At the same time, movement from the country to the city meant that there was now a public world outside the family that teenagers needed to be protected from. Teenagers became completely economically dependent on their parents, as apprenticeship declined and work was postponed. Teenage sexuality—especially among boys—became viewed as threatening and dangerous, while teenage girls were supposed to control their appetite, for both sex and food.

By the end of the nineteenth century the public high school was the normative route to adulthood. It provided training for the skilled and educated workers that were now required. New part-time opportunities for clerical and office work demanded literacy and numeracy, along with honesty and a work ethic. High school expanded to hold teenagers who were no longer needed as workers, and to whom it promised opportunities for social mobility.

During most of the twentieth century, the age for leaving school and entering work increased in many Western countries, while the age of first marriage decreased, until the 1960s, when it reversed, probably due to the appearance of the new developmental stage of young adulthood. Although marriage was delayed, moving out of the family home occurred earlier. Adolescence in these countries now came to include a period of emotional and sexual exploration prior to marriage. At the same time, increased opportunities for part-time work while adolescents were still students weakened the control of the school, and enabled them to become consumers.

Other kinds of historical change in adolescence occurred outside Europe. Among the Inuit in the Canadian Arctic, for example, the transition to adult status was relatively smooth and rapid in the early twentieth century, for both males and females. More recently, however, as the Inuit's population grew, their economic security increased and they had more contact with the mainstream of North American culture, a prolonged adolescence emerged. Inuit teenagers came to have greater freedom and autonomy. They found it increasingly difficult to simply adopt the ways of their parents, and they had to create strategies to cope with a fundamentally different society (Condon, 1990). Definitions of adult male and female identity were now drawn not only from traditional sources but also from "southern" sources, including television, magazines, schooling, and travel.

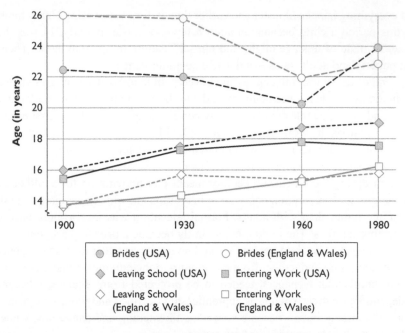

Figure 13.5 Transition from secondary school, entering work, and marriage

Source: Modell & Goodman (1990)

3. ADOLESCENT REASONING AND DECISION MAKING

Analogical reasoning	similarity to what has been successful in the past
Law-based reasoning	conforms to rules of logic or other epistemic laws
Dialectical reasoning	based on reflection and argumentation

Figure 13.6 Different kinds of reasoning

Source: Moshman (2004)

In general terms, the teenage years are marked by important and impressive changes in both intellectual ability and intellectual interests. Psychologists have long recognized that many teenagers become able to think systematically, logically, and hypothetically. Indeed, some teenagers have a concern, at times an obsession, with possibilities: with the way things could be, with worlds of fantasy and imagination, with possible universes. Many teenagers show an interest in fiction, art, and philosophy, and have a fascination with abstract ideas.

There has been much more research on cognition during early and middle childhood than during the teenage years (Kuhn, 2006, 2009). Perhaps the first thing to be noted about cognitive development during this period is its enormous individual variability. In part this is due to the different environments in which teenagers live, but it also follows from the fact that they are actively choosing what they do, based on their abilities and interests, and becoming to a greater degree than ever before "producers of their own development" (Kuhn, 2009, p. 152).

In particular, researchers on moral development see the teenage years as a time when the young person becomes able to recognize the conventionality of culture, and to think beyond the conventions of her specific culture. A distinction is now drawn between what is legal and what is ethical. This is known as **post-conventional reasoning**.

At the same time, many psychologists view teenagers as likely to make particularly bad decisions. Is this, then, a time of heightened intellectual ability? Or of impulsiveness and risky choices? Or both?

In this section I will first introduce Piaget's notion of formal operational reasoning, and then turn to research that has enthusiastically explored how the dual systems, 1 and 2, operate in the teenage years. This research tends to try to reduce the psychological developments to neuropsychological changes, but we can reinterpret them in terms more congenial to a cultural psychology. Next I will consider an approach that focuses on the positive abilities of teenagers and aims to foster these abilities. Then I will contrast these preceding approaches with Vygotsky's insistence that the higher form of intellectual activity is only one aspect of the psychological changes of adolescence.

It has to be noted that most of what we know about cognition and thinking during the teenage years comes from studies conducted in Western societies. As we have seen, adolescence is defined by both biology and culture, and there are strong indications in the research which I shall review in this section that adolescent cognition stems from the social situation in which a teenager finds herself as much as from her individual characteristics. Vygotsky convincingly defined this "age of transition" as the consequence of a separation of biological, sexual, and cultural maturity, even though he did not explore whether the psychological changes usually considered typical of this age would occur in other cultural settings.

As Vygotsky's colleague Aleksei Leontiev proposed, only in specific societal conditions is it possible to reason about "theoretical" objects:

> Only later, at relatively higher stages of development, can activity also appear in the form of truly 'ideal' activity, theoretically interrelating the child with 'a theoretical' object, for instance, in the form of abstract thought, far removed from practical action and from an immediate material object of activity. However, this separate internal activity remains only a special form of activity of a social man, a form that can develop only under historical conditions where the division of labor makes this separate activity vitally real as a result of the simple fact that in exchange for its theoretical product, man receives a material product of the practical activity of another man. (Leontiev, 2005, p. 24)

3.1 PIAGET AND FORMAL OPERATIONAL REASONING

A pizza parlor is offering five different kinds of pizza toppings: extra cheese, olives, sausages, green peppers, and mushrooms. Customers can order from one to five toppings on their pizza. How many different kinds of pizza does this restaurant offer?

This is a Piagetian task the solution to which requires, in Piaget's terms, formal operational reasoning. Can you solve the problem? To do so will almost certainly require pencil and paper.

Some of my students draw circles to represent pizzas. Others write down the names of the toppings, or they write abbreviations, such as EC, O, S, GP, M. Some simply write down numbers. For example:

123, 124, 125, 134, 135, 145, 234, 235, 245, 345.

Can you see or figure out what this list of numbers represents? The point here is that one does not solve this problem by handling actual pizzas or the toppings. (I once ordered pizzas for the class, but this didn't help anyone solve the problem!) Instead, one manipulates *representations* of the toppings. These representations could be words (the names of the toppings), or letters, or numbers. This isn't really a question about pizzas at all, it is a question about combinations and possibilities. How many possible ways are there to combine from one to five different things?

When we look at the way a child or young person goes about solving this task, then, we are less interested in whether or not they got the correct answer than we are in the kind of strategy they used. What kind of representations? Did they generate combinations in a particular order? Did they seem certain that they had the correct answer? Or certain that they did not? What strategy did they use for generating combinations? Did they display a sense of certainty in their answer?

[W]hen pre-school children reach correct conclusions, they don't even know they have made an inference, much less know anything about the nature, purpose, or justifiability of that inference … [W]hat develops beyond early childhood is not the basic ability to make logical inferences, but metalogical knowledge about the nature and justifiability of logical inferences, and metacognitive awareness, knowledge, and control of one's inferential processes. (Moshman, 2004, pp. 222–223)

According to Piaget, the final stage of cognitive development is **formal operational reasoning**, and this appears around 12 years of age and is consolidated during adolescence (Inhelder & Piaget, 1958). According to Piaget, what happens is not simply that the teenager knows more about the world but that her knowledge is organized in a different way, and is accessible in the form of a new kind of mental representation.

In Chapter 9 we defined reasoning as an advanced form of thinking that consciously follows accepted standards of rationality (Moshman, 2004). Reasoning, unlike the thinking (and the inference) on which it is based, involves a deliberate effort to follow what one believes to be justifiable epistemic norms. David Moshman argues that there are several kinds of reasoning, each with distinct norms. Analogical reasoning is based upon a similarity with what has been successful in the past. Law-based reasoning conforms to the rules of logic. Dialectical reasoning is based on reflection and argumentation. All of these develop during the teenage years.

In these terms, Piaget focused on law-based reasoning. In his account, it is during the teenage years that reasoning can reach the highest degree of equilibrium. The mental operations a teenager is now capable of are sufficiently flexible and powerful that she can solve complex theoretical problems. A central part of the power of her reasoning is that she can explore all the possibilities in a situation. Her reasoning is no longer tied to the properties of concrete objects and circumstances, and she can now consider **imaginary** scenarios. It is important, however, to add that for Piaget the capacity to explore possibilities is at root a result of a new kind of ability with logic, rather than the creative power of imagination.

This kind of reasoning is not completely detached from the real world, but the world is now known in such a way that **hypothetical** situations can be reasoned about. Piaget described this new ability to handle problems that go beyond immediate experience:

> [It] can be seen with the adolescent whose capacity to understand and even construct theories will create for him an entry into the society and ideology of adults; this is often, of course, accompanied by a desire to change that society and, if necessary (in his imagination) destroy the present one in order to elaborate better ones. (Piaget, 2008, p. 42)

As we saw in Chapter 2, in Piaget's theory of development the *form* of reasoning at one stage of cognition becomes the *content* at the next stage. The action schemas of sensorimotor intelligence became the mental images of preoperational thinking. The class membership relations that a child could organize using concrete operational reasoning now become the content that the teenager reasons about. What makes this stage of reasoning "formal" is the fact that, in Piaget's view, the adolescent is no longer reasoning about objects and their individual properties, she is reasoning about **statements** about objects, and about the relationships among those statements.

In mathematical terms, the statements are **propositions**. Formal operational reasoning consists of the manipulation and transformation of propositional statements that refer to classes of objects and the relations among these classes. The teenager can now understand and reason about propositions such as "*If it's a terrier, then it's a dog*," and she can transform these propositions in various ways, such as negating or combining them.

Piaget proposed that the operations in this final stage in the construction of knowledge about the world follow the laws of **propositional logic**. Propositional logic is a formal system in mathematics in which formulas represent propositions, and a system of axioms and inference rules is used to transform these formulas to arrive at new propositions, whose truth or falsity follows on logically.

Formal reasoning goes beyond concrete operational thinking in several ways. First, it includes the propositional operations of *implication* and *disjunction*. Formal operational reasoning also grasps the distinction between two forms of reversibility: undoing an effect (*negation*) and countering an effect with an opposite effect (*reciprocity*). Piaget considered this to be the kind of reasoning that scientists use. He wrote:

> the adolescent's logic is a complex but coherent system that is relatively different from the logic of the child, and that constitutes the essence of the logic of cultured adults and even provides the basis for elementary forms of scientific thought. (Piaget, 2008, p. 43)

On this basis of their new reasoning ability, teenagers can solve problems concerning matters such as proportions, probability, conservation of momentum in a frictionless medium, and mechanical equilibrium. They can solve problems that involve combinations of factors (such as the pizza problem), and proportions or ratios (such as the balance beam problem). They can systematically generate and explore all the logical possibilities (combinations or permutations) that are inherent in a situation.

The characteristics of formal operational reasoning permit several new kinds of thinking:

Hypothetical reasoning: thinking about what is not actually observed, such as theoretical or conjectural situations.

Counterfactual reasoning: the ability to handle propositions that run counter to the known facts ("*If the moon were made of cheese …*").

Reasoning beyond the conventional: thinking about what might be done, as distinct from what is usually done. This gives adolescent thinking its quality of idealism. Adolescents think about fundamental issues of ethics and morality, politics and philosophy.

Reasoning about the future: thinking that goes beyond what is immediately present, to anticipate future events and plan ahead.

Deductive reasoning: thinking that depends entirely on the form of the given problem, not on its content.

Metacognitive reasoning: thinking about thought itself, in complex, deliberate, and systematic ways. The adolescent can think more deeply and systematically about the thinking of other people, and about her own thinking.

In all these kinds of thinking, reality has become secondary to possibility. Because a teenager's thinking deals with propositions rather than with concrete objects and events it is not bound by what actually exists. She considers not only what she observes, but also what *might* be the case. What has *actually* occurred becomes merely a subset of what is logically *possible*. What *is* the case is less important than what *could* be the case.

Infancy 0–12 months	Sensory-motor stage	Hypothetical reasoning
Toddler 1–2.5 years	Sensory-motor stage	Counterfactual reasoning Reasoning beyond the conventional
Early childhood 2.5–6 years	Preoperational stage	Reasoning about the future
Middle childhood 6–12 years	Concrete operational stage	Deductive reasoning Metacognitive reasoning
Adolescence 12–	**Formal operational stage**	Operations on propositions

Figure 13.7 Characteristics of formal operation intelligence, according to Piaget

3.1.1 IS FORMAL OPERATIONAL REASONING UNIVERSAL?

As was the case with concrete operational reasoning, research has explored the universality of formal operational reasoning. It seems that formal operational reasoning does become possible only in the teenage years, for it can be found in very few children. However, it seems that not all teenagers, or all adults for that matter, become able to use formal operational reasoning. In fact, it has been proposed that "the reasoning of many individuals in so-called 'primitive' societies [may] not develop beyond the stage of concrete operations" (Dasen, 1972). The question that then arises is whether when adults appear not to use formal operational reasoning this is because they are incapable of using it, or because they have no need for it, or because psychologists have been looking for it in the wrong place.

As we know, however, the question of the universality of any of Piaget's stages is a complex one. Many of the issues we discussed in Chapter 12 concerning cross-cultural studies of concrete operational thinking apply here too. First, if no evidence is found for formal operational reasoning among some people, the fault could lie with the tasks the experimenters have used, or the way the experimental situation has been defined. Or it may be that Piaget's description of stages of cognitive development does not include all the ways that people can reason. Or people's reasoning may develop along the lines Piaget described but the content of the task may influence their thinking, even though Piaget maintained that formal operational reasoning is independent of the content of the propositions on which it operates (Carraher & Carraher, 1981).

Piaget himself discussed these issues (Piaget, 2008[1972]). His own research on this stage of cognitive development was conducted with students aged 11 to 15 in privileged schools in Geneva, but he acknowledged that other psychologists' research appeared to indicate that in some other populations "it is as though these subjects had stayed at the concrete operational level of thinking" (2008[1972], p. 43).

In an unusual departure from his general position that the stages of cognitive development are universal, Piaget considered three possible interpretations for this research finding (Kuhn, 2008). First, he suggested, there is the possibility that the *speed* of development varies, due to the stimulation and opportunities provided by different environments, so that formal operations might be slower to develop and will appear later in some environments.

Second, there is the possibility that individuals have different aptitudes for this kind of reasoning, and indeed that such differences might become increasingly marked during ontogenesis. This might have the consequence, Piaget suggested, rather provocatively, that teenagers who are more interested in literary, artistic, or practical activities might be incapable of developing formal operational reasoning.

Third, and in Piaget's opinion most likely, is the possibility that all people do in fact attain formal operational thought, but mainly in those activities for which they have both aptitude and interest. This implies that formal reasoning might be used in different ways by different people. Carpenters, locksmiths, and mechanics, for example, would almost certainly "know how to reason in a hypothetical manner in their speciality" (Piaget, 2008[1972], p. 46). However, when faced with a problem outside their area of expertise people in such occupations might appear to reason only at a concrete level.

Piaget's analysis suggests that a higher level of cognition might be revealed in those activities in which a teenager (or an adult) is interested and capable. Does the research evidence support this proposal? Very little research has been directly addressed to this question. Much of the research on the cognition of teenagers has simply been carried out with standardized tasks in school settings. There is a need for research outside school where teenagers are involved in activities they find interesting. In particular, research is needed that explores teenagers' cognitive abilities in cultures where school attendance is not the norm.

3.1.2 SCHOOLING AND FORMAL OPERATIONAL REASONING

What is the influence of schooling on formal operational reasoning? Here there have been many studies. In general, people who have not attended school often perform poorly in the Piagetian tasks that have been used to assess formal operational reasoning. However, even people who have attended school often perform badly (see Berry et al., 1992). In fact, studies have found that college students in the USA frequently fail such tasks! A study of 10,000 British school students between 9 and 14 years of age found that only one-fifth showed formal operational thinking on the tasks that were used (Shayer et al., 1976).

This kind of association between schooling and performance on formal operational reasoning tasks may be due to school having a general influence on cognitive development, but in light of our discussion in Chapter 13 it seems more likely that school encourage the formulation of problems in a propositional form, so that their form becomes more important than their content. It is also possible that school heightens the metacognitive capacities that are developing during these years, helping teenagers control their own processes of reasoning. This "thinking about thinking" would most likely improve their performance on Piagetian logico-mathematical tasks.

In Chapter 12 I described Alexander Luria's research in Central Asia. This research had a further component which I did not mention, but which has become well known: several studies of deductive reasoning. Luria found that the non-schooled people who participated in his research were reluctant to respond to a question posed in the form of a syllogism. A **syllogism** is a form of reasoning in which a conclusion is drawn from two given propositions:

> *In the Far North, where there is snow, all bears are white. Novaya Zemlyn is in the Far North and there is always snow there. What color are the bears there?*

> An illiterate peasant replied: "If there was someone who had a great deal of experience and had been everywhere, he would do well to answer that question."

> *But can you answer that question on the basis of my words?*

> "A person who had travelled a lot and been in cold countries and seen everything would answer; he would know what color the bears are."

Luria took this kind of response as evidence for the lack of a capacity for abstract, theoretical reasoning (Luria, 1976). He maintained that schooling, along with work in an industrial society, would encourage this kind of theoretical reasoning.

Subsequent investigation, however, suggests that the non-schooled people did not lack the capacity for logical reasoning, they were simply unwilling to apply logic to a question that they considered unreasonable. They refused to discuss topics that went beyond their personal experience, and they rejected the premises that they were given. They reasoned that they could not verify the truth of these premises, and so they responded on the basis of experience rather than on the basis of a logical coherence with the premises. This kind of response has been called an **empiric** mode, in contrast to a **theoretic** mode (Scribner, 1977). Even the non-schooled subjects responded in a theoretic mode to *some* of the syllogisms, showing that they were not incapable of this kind of reasoning, they were just uncomfortable with it.

It is not hard to understand how people might be unwilling to consider as "logical" a kind of reasoning that excludes, or even runs counter to, what they know from personal experience. It seems that we should view syllogisms as part of a specialized genre of language rather than as a purely formal logical structure. School is one place where children and adolescents learn this language genre. Scribner concluded that reasoning "on the basis of the words alone" is a particular (and peculiar) language genre that is central to standard schooling practices, but whose use outside of those circumstances is unclear.

A more recent research project with the same interest involved a detailed investigation in rural Yucatan with almost 400 Maya and Mestizo subjects, ranging in age from 10 to 56 years (Sharp et al., 1979). The researchers explored the influence of age and educational experience on the development of the cognitive skills needed for formal reasoning. The experimental tasks included the categorization and memorization of objects and words, and problem solving using verbal and non-verbal materials. The researchers also surveyed various demographic and economic factors that were associated with the amount of schooling people received, to rule out the possibility that these might be the source of differences.

The research results suggested that the participants with more schooling were more likely to engage in intellectual activities that were not rigidly predetermined by the structure of the tasks. Only a few years of educational experience were enough to encourage a person to treat the researchers' questions as a matter of reasoning from given premises to a conclusion, while those who were not schooled tended to base their conclusions on empirical facts

Here again, as we saw in Chapter 12, it seems that schooling encourages a kind of thinking—counterfactual, verbal, and theoretical rather than practical—that within Western culture is considered more advanced. It is necessary to recognize, however, that other ways of thinking may be equally valuable for other ways of living.

Some researchers have concluded that formal operations is a universal achievement but one that occurs within specific contexts in which there has been dense practice (Cole, 1990a). School may increase the range of contexts in which this kind of reasoning can be used. In other words, school may enable a teenager to attain formal thought in many activities, not only in those in which she is especially interested. Or, on the contrary, school may restrict the range of contexts in which teenagers gain experience in this kind of reasoning.

3.2 JUDGMENT AND DECISION MAKING

We revise our opinion [of the adolescent's cognitive maturity] when we turn from the examination of the adolescent's intellectual processes themselves to consider how they fit into the general picture of his life. We are surprised to discover that this fine intellectual performance makes little or no difference to his actual behavior. His empathy into the mental process of other people does not prevent him from displaying the most outrageous lack of consideration toward those nearest to him. (Anna Freud, 1966, cited in Selman, 2008).

Piaget's studies of cognition in adolescence were focused on the cool, analytical reasoning that we now know to be characteristic of System 2. Vygotsky, too, emphasized conscious thinking and deliberate control of the psychological functions. But what about System 1, the unconscious, rapid, and intuitive reasoning? Isn't the adolescent often considered—perhaps a little unfairly—to make decisions in a hasty and emotional way, without much reflection and with a lot of peer pressure? This sounds very much like the territory of System 1.

In fact, paying attention to the two systems has thrown light on aspects of adolescent reasoning and decision making that studies of formal operational reasoning did not explore. Over the past two decades there has been a growing amount of research on **judgment and decision making** (JDM) in the teenage years. This research has passed through several phases.

Until the mid-1990s, psychologists focused on the ways in which judgment, especially about risks, is poorer in adolescents than in adults. The motivation for this research was a concern that adolescents make risky decisions and engage in high-risk behavior such as driving under the influence of alcohol, smoking, and having casual sex. These are activities which can have long-term negative consequences, and so it is not obvious why anyone would act in such a way. The supposition was that adolescents lack the cognitive skills to reason about the risks involved. Perhaps an adolescent does not yet have the ability to see the risks, or she supposes that these are less probable than in fact they are. Or maybe she imagines that she is invulnerable, so that the risks don't apply to her.

However, this research found that in general adolescents are quite capable of anticipating risks, and they know when they are vulnerable. However, one finding has been that adolescents who have already engaged in an activity such as binge drinking, smoking, or unprotected sex without having suffered any negative consequences view these activities as less risky than those who have had no experience with them. This suggests that if we want to reduce such activities we should not over-emphasize their risks, because as adolescents gain experience they may come to distrust such advice. It is also the case that they perceive many of these activities to offer benefits, and may consider those benefits to outweigh the risks. As a consequence, researchers turned to explore adolescents' percep-tions not only of risks but also of benefits.

Researchers also started to explore not only adolescents' cold, analytic cognition but also their hot, intuitive cognition. The consensus now is that the balance between these two modes of reasoning shifts during the teen years. Research on the dual systems has found that adolescents show steady improvement in analytic abilities such as statistical reasoning and conditional reasoning, perhaps because their metacognitive abilities are increasing so they can better monitor and control their think-ing. At the same time, they seem to make more heuristic judgments that lead to errors. For example, if asked, *Is this perky, outgoing girl a cheerleader or a member of the band?* an adolescent is more likely to reason on the basis of stereotypes (cheerleaders are perky) than probability (more girls are band members than cheerleaders). When the questions are not about social topics (as this one is), she is more likely to reason correctly (Klaczynski, 2001).

Perhaps risky behavior, then, results from developmental changes in the balance between these two modes of reasoning—hot and cold, intuitive and reflective. There is evidence that young adolescents do not deliberately decide to engage in risky behavior, they make snap judgments. Older adolescents become better able to consciously and deliberately control such judgments. There is also evidence that intuitive, heuristic judgments improve as adolescents gain real-world experience, especially first-hand experience with the negative consequences of risky choices.

In this area of investigation, then, one hypothesis is that the adolescent uses System 1 until System 2 catches up. There has, however, also been the opposite suggestion, that younger adolescents make riskier decisions because they are relying too much on System 2—thinking things through too much—because System 1 has not yet caught up with System 2 (Reyna & Brainerd, 1995; Reyna & Farley, 2006; Rivers et al., 2008). An approach called **fuzzy trace theory** builds on the dual-process model to suggest that risky decision making occurs when an adolescent relies on analytic thinking because her heuristic thinking is underdeveloped (Chick & Reyna, 2012). Because she must consciously analyze the expected risks, she often gets the wrong answer, and the heightened sensitivity to rewards at this age magnifies this effect. With time, however, intuitive thinking advances so that it can help to guard against risk taking and facilitate cognitive control.

In either case—whether adolescents use System 2 too little or too much—the consensus is that the two modes of reasoning slowly becomes more balanced during the teenage years. Many psychologists today agree with a point that Vygotsky made—what is central to psychological development in adolescence is the achievement of more conscious and self-directed psychological functions (this has been called "the assembly of an advanced 'executive suite' of capabilities"; see Steinberg, 2005, p. 70).

Certainly, in the later teenage years self-regulation steadily increases, and continues to do so into early adulthood. Flexible rule use and strategic problem solving also improve. Cognition and emotion become more coordinated, and the teenager becomes better able to regulate the emotional and social influences that had pushed her to make hasty, intuitive judgments.

3.2.1 PEER INFLUENCE ON DECISIONS AND REASONING

A popular image of adolescence is that it is a time when peers have a negative impact on a teenager's choices and judgments. One hypothesis is that as a teenager becomes more focused on the future, more able to plan and delay gratification, she also becomes more able to resist the influence of her peers.

There is indeed some evidence that a young adolescent is more likely to make risky choices when she is with a group of friends. Why might this be? Is there simply more opportunity when she is with friends to do fun but risky things? Does an adolescent copy what her peers are doing? Or do adolescents who enjoy taking risks hang out together? For example, an experimental study in which adolescents played a computer-simulated driving task either alone or with two peers in the room found they made twice as many risky decisions when the peers were present, suggesting that merely having other teenagers there increased the tendency to take risks.

However, we know little about the influence of peers on adolescents' formal reasoning, or on their intuitive judgments, because most JDM research has simply asked individuals to solve verbal problems in a laboratory situation. What is needed is more research in real settings, seeing how adolescents reason when they are faced—alone and with peers—with everyday problems. However, it has been well documented that relations with peers are very important during the teenage years. I will explore the characteristics and functions of the peer group during adolescence in the next chapter.

In summary, the JDM research has been strongly influenced by dual-systems theory, and also by neurophysiological research on brain changes during the teenage years. The new attention given to Systems 1 and 2 has increased the frequency of biological explanations of adolescent psychology (Kuhn, 2006). Researchers have attributed the psychological characteristics of adolescents entirely to neurological changes—changes which they then assume are due to biological maturation.

However, as we have seen, neurological change can follow behavior as well as precede it. In cultures where adolescence exists, in the form of a gap or mismatch between biological reproductive capability and adult status, teenagers are placed in confusing and ambiguous circumstances. They need to make choices that will affect them for the rest of their lives, yet their parents may permit them scant opportunity to make their own decisions around the house. It seems very likely that this contradictory social situation influences the way an adolescent thinks about herself and her options; indeed, that it simply influences the way she thinks! It seems entirely possible, also, that the contradictory social situation has an impact on neurological development, perhaps stimulating development of the prefrontal cortex. In the next subsection I will turn to an approach to judgment and decision making in adolescence that takes seriously these social circumstances.

3.3 POSITIVE YOUTH DEVELOPMENT

An inescapable conflict is built into adolescence. Just when we become mature enough to want to make our own decisions, everyone starts telling us to work hard, plan ahead, not to drink, not to take drugs, and not to sleep with anyone. When teenagers then press their elders for the reasons for their advice, those reasons are rarely forthcoming (Bainbridge, 2009, p. 2).

Some researchers have argued that the common view of adolescence as a time of impulsive and risky behavior provides only a one-sided and incomplete picture (Larson, 2000; Lerner, 2005). The **positive youth development** (PYD) approach emphasizes that adolescents have many positive characteristics: they can be resilient and take the initiative, they can be creative and caring. This approach also stresses that we must understand adolescent behavior in context, and it recommends that psychologists adopt a systems-theory perspective from which they can promote positive outcomes rather than trying merely to prevent undesirable outcomes.

The positive youth development approach aims to study adolescence as a relational phenomenon, as an interaction between the teenager and her environment. It also insists that an adolescent exercises active agency in the course of her own development. It steps beyond disengaged research into the design of interventions that seek to change the character and trajectory of teenage development, in the form of policy and programs.

The principal assumption of the positive youth development approach is that many adolescents in the USA and Europe find themselves in social circumstances that provide little opportunity for them to develop their abilities, especially to become independent and responsible. Teenagers are surrounded by adults who make most of their decisions for them. Schools give them few opportunities to develop initiative, and boredom and alienation are often the result. For example, a study of young White adolescents, working class and middle class, sampled at random a remarkable 16,000 times over a week, found that they reported feeling bored on 27 percent of these occasions (Larson & Richards, 1991). Perhaps so-called risky, problem behavior stems not from poorly evaluated risks but from the lack of anything more interesting to do.

The development of initiative requires several things: first, **intrinsic motivation** (wanting to do an activity for its own sake, rather than for an external reward such as money or praise); second, engagement and constructive **concentrated attention**; that is, third, maintained over an **extended period** of time, in a project of activity than has to be planned, followed through, adjusted as necessary, and brought to fruition.

In a classroom, however, an adolescent's attention is under the control of adults, and she is extrinsically motivated by an adult-designed reward structure of grades and sanctions. Adolescents do indeed report that when in the school classroom they have to concentrate, but also that they have difficulty concentrating and they feel bored. They report having little intrinsic motivation for schoolwork, and 15-year-olds reported even less motivation than 10-year-olds, suggesting that the problem gets worse.

Outside school, things are not much better. Between 7 and 14 percent of an adolescent's waking hours are spent watching television. Adolescents do report high intrinsic motivation when they are with peers, but this is combined with low concentration and low challenge. Here too, with peers, there is little opportunity to develop initiative (Larson, 2000).

In an effort to counter this situation, various psychologists have developed after-school and community-based programs that have been designed to provide more opportunity for adolescents to develop what have been called "the Five Cs"—competence, confidence, character, connection, and caring. These programs aim to engage adolescents in mutually beneficial relations with adults and social institutions, and preliminary studies have shown they can be effective.

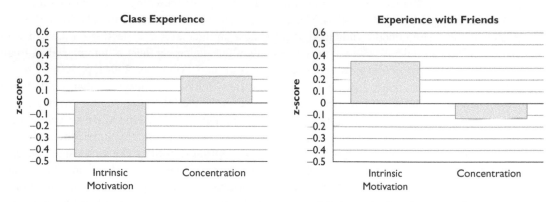

Figure 13.8 Adolescents' ratings of their motivation and concentration in the school classroom, and outside school with friends

Source: Larson (2000)

3.4 VYGOTSKY AND ADOLESCENT PSYCHOLOGICAL DEVELOPMENT

> What lies at the core of adolescent cognitive development is the attainment of a more fully conscious, self-directed and self-regulating mind. (Steinberg, 2005, p. 70)

Vygotsky, like Piaget, argued that in the teen years there is a transition to a higher form of intellectual activity. However, he insisted that although this change in cognition is centrally important, it is only one aspect of the psychological development of adolescence.

One might expect that Vygotsky would have described a crisis at age 13 followed by another stage, but instead he considered adolescence as a whole to be "the age of transition," a time of crisis. In his view, there is a basic contradiction to the whole age, because culture has broken down the biological harmony of maturation by separating **three peaks of development**: one organic, another sexual, and the third cultural. This implies that Vygotsky's account of adolescence would have to be specific to the time and place in which he wrote, unless he believed that *every* culture breaks down this harmony. However, Vygotsky does not seem to have acknowledged this implication of his analysis.

Adolescence is a step closer to the summit of Vygotsky's account of development: now the human being who was *"in herself"* becomes *"for herself,"* and in doing so becomes both logical and able to freely choose her actions. He wrote, "This is the conversion of the child from a man [a human being] in himself into an adolescent—a man for himself—and this makes up the principle content of the whole crisis of the adolescent age" (Vygotsky, 1998[1931], p. 149).

The conversion of the child into the adolescent, then, is a movement to a new level of self-consciousness. In Vygotsky's view the adolescent becomes conscious of her own psychological processes, including the complex world of her feelings, as a *particular* way to be. She is now aware not just of having a particular personality but also of *being* that personality, and she feels the need to embody the characteristics that she considers valuable.

Vygotsky wrote that "the adolescent is differentiated internally into the acting 'I' and into another 'I' – the reflecting 'I'" (Vygotsky, 2004a, p. 487). There is no longer simply an internal world of thoughts and feelings, as was the case in middle childhood, there is now an internal *self*, reflecting on the self who acts. At the same time, "In the structure of the personality of the adolescent there is nothing stable, final, and immovable. Everything in it is transition, everything is in flux" (Vygotsky, 2004a, p. 490).

Vygotsky's notion of an inner, reflecting "I" closely resembles the "ego identity" that psychologist Erik Erikson saw as central to adolescence, as I shall describe in the following chapter. In Vygotsky's account, this internal self, this "personality," participates in, and directs, all the higher psychological functions: as an agent who reasons, remembers, attends, and perceives voluntarily and deliberately.

The leading factor in all this, in Vygotsky's view, is **conceptual thinking**. Thinking using concepts "penetrates into the internal essence" of things, disclosing their "connections and relations" and their "movement" and "development." This disclosure occurs because "to develop a concept of some object means to disclose a series of connections and relations of that object with all the rest of reality, to include it in the complex system of phenomena" (Vygotsky, 2004a, p. 441).

As we have seen, some psychologists believe that even infants possess concepts. I have emphasized throughout these chapters that Vygotsky's view was very different: he argued that concepts are the products of a long and complex process of sociocultural development. Like Piaget, he insisted that infants know the world in practice, not in concepts. Toddlers begin to use words to categorize the world around them, but for Vygotsky, unlike Piaget, their most important accomplishment is not becoming able to form mental representations, but grasping and beginning to use the *material* representations of their culture. Intent on avoiding dualistic thinking, Vygotsky refused to accept that the mind works like a computer, constructing representations (models, theories, concepts) of the world. Indeed, as we saw in Chapter 10, Vygotsky insisted that "mind" is an appearance but not a reality: the neurological developments that enable us to speak without making any noise lead us to mistakenly assume that each of us has a mental space some-where "inside." For Vygotsky, to think is to reach out into the world and grasp it; thinking always arises from practical activity and returns to activity. To say that someone thinks "conceptually" is to say that she grasps the world in a specific, sophisticated way.

Conceptual thinking is like looking through a microscope to see a complex, inner structure. For Vygotsky a concept is not a thing but a process, a "system of acts of thinking" (2004a, p. 443). In concep-tual thinking, both the form and the content of thinking are qualitatively transformed. A concept provides "mediated knowledge" of objects, an "integral image" not a "dry, empty, gray abstraction." Thinking using concepts is itself a kind of action, action on oneself.

This new kind of action is evident in a new interest in abstract reasoning, with an emphasis on logic and proof. For an adolescent, this interest doesn't come from biology alone, but also from his-tory and culture: "The brain did not of itself generate logical thinking, but the brain assimilated the form of logical thinking in the process of the historical development of man" (Vygotsky, 1998[1931], p. 134). Moreover, the kind of logic that Vygotsky had in mind was not traditional formal logic but **dialectical logic**, in which "a concept includes not only the general, but also the individual and particular" (Vygotsky, 2004a, p. 441).

Vygotsky drew a distinction between **everyday concepts** and **scientific concepts**. The child arrives at school with a lot of knowledge about the world, but her knowledge is not systematic. Her everyday concepts are functional and unconscious. In school, the child—and then the adolescent—is taught con-cepts that are verbally defined and systematically organized. She becomes conscious of these scientific concepts, and this influences her everyday concepts, so those too become more systematically organized and conscious. This is part of the process we described in Chapter 12, in which, in Vygotsky's view, school encourages the movement to a deliberate, conscious level of psychological functioning.

At this point, concrete details become something of a burden for the adolescent. In Vygotsky's obser-vation, she now has less interest in school subjects such as natural history and zoology which focus on factual details, and becomes more interested in philosophical issues. She has less interest in concrete historical stories and in arts such as painting and drawing, and she instead pays more attention to music, "the most abstract art" (Vygotsky, 2004a, p. 431). Of course, these are sweeping generalizations, but they capture the flavor of his view of the psychology of adolescence.

Traditional views of adolescence have often placed **imagination** front and center, but Vygotsky argued that this is an error that comes from viewing fantasy "one-sidedly" as intrinsically emotional, and failing to see its link to intellectual activity. In adolescence, fantasy and thinking interact in new ways as imagination "breaks its links with real objects" (Vygotsky, 1998[1932–1934], p. 280). Imagination is linked closely with thinking in concepts, and now imagination too is intellectualized and begins to perform a new function. Where children's fantasy was passive and imitative, adolescent fantasy is active and creative. Adolescent fantasy is *less* intense and emotional than fantasy in childhood, but it is richer, more creative, and more productive; we can see this in the poems and diaries written by adolescents. Adult fantasy, however, will be even more productive, because it will include a degree of critical judgement that adolescents still lack.

In Vygotsky's view, the adolescent's creative imagination synthesizes the emotional and intellectual aspects of her behavior, combining desires and thoughts in complicated new ways. Imagination branches into two "channels." One channel brings emotional satisfaction to the moody, needy adolescent: it is an intensely private and subjective activity in which the adolescent fantasizes about personal experiences and conceals her fantasies. In this *subjective* imagination the adolescent discovers how to take charge of her emotional life and give it direction. The other channel is *objective* creativity, which helps the adolescent solve practical problems and contributes to her intellectual understanding. This is the kind of creativity behind literary works, scientific inventions, and technical achievements.

3.4.1 CONSCIOUS AWARENESS AND DELIBERATE CONTROL

Adolescence is characterized by an increased need to regulate affect and behavior in accordance with long-term goals and consequences, often at a distance from the adults who provided regulatory structure and guidance during childhood. (Steinberg, 2005, p. 69)

In Vygotsky's account, with the help of conceptual thinking the psychological functions are "intellectualized" and brought under conscious and deliberate control. The adolescence is now capable of categorical perception, logical memory, voluntary attention, creative imagination, the higher emotions, and foresight. Together these higher psychological functions form a new system, a new unified structure, that is the basis for a higher synthesis of personality and world view.

Perception, for example, is again transformed. A transformation of perception was achieved much earlier, as the toddler became skilled with oral language (see Chapter 6). But now the adolescent sees with "an ordered, categorical perception" (Vygotsky, 1998a[1931], p. 90): "The adolescent is not only conscious of and comprehends the reality that he perceives, but also comprehends it in concepts, that is, in the act of visual perception, abstract and concrete thinking are completely synthesized" (Vygotsky, 1998a[1931], pp. 89–90).

Memory is transformed too: now we have "logical memory developed on the basis of synthesis of intellect and [elementary] memory" (Vygotsky, 1998a[1931], p. 91). During the early school years, thinking was mainly a matter of remembering, and memory, imagination, and thinking were barely differentiated. The child's thinking depended on concrete images. In adolescence the relationship is inverted and memory becomes a function of intellect. The adolescent remembers what she perceived and comprehended logically, mastering her memory by using signs, in what Vygotsky calls "mediated remembering." The adolescent no longer depends on concrete visual images, and the material she memorizes is now systematically organized and arranged, often on the basis of internal speech, and using deliberate mnemonic techniques.

Attention, too, is now controlled by conceptual thinking, and becomes voluntary. Attention can now be deliberately focused first on one object, then on another. The field of things the adolescent can attend to is extended and reorganized. The child could include many objects and details in her attention, but the adolescent now has the ability to attend to all of the characteristics of an object in a hierarchical synthesis.

These new, intellectualized higher psychological functions are "the product of the historical development of humanity and its phylogenetic plan, but they also have their special ontogenic record." Vygotsky insists that we can see clearly here the "complicated dynamic synthesis" of historical development and biological evolution in the development of the adolescent.

It is important to understand that for Vygotsky, thinking using concepts is not an ability the individual can achieve alone. The adolescent must participate in particular kinds of social institution if she is to become capable of this kind of systematic reasoning. School was the institution that Vygotsky focused on, but presumably other institutions could also lead to conceptual thinking. It would be dangerous to conclude that adolescence, with its new insights and abilities, does not exist without schooling. On the other hand, Vygotsky (like Piaget) was studying and writing about a small group of privileged and educated teenagers, and we should take care before generalizing to other young people in other settings.

After all, Vygotsky himself insisted that thinking using concepts arises on the basis of the new tasks that the adolescent faces. This advanced kind of thinking is always in service of a goal, to solve a particular problem, and the adolescent's problems are thrown up by the society around her. They "are connected with the process of growing into the cultural, professional and social life of adults" (Vygotsky, 1998a[1931], p. 5). Vygotsky's own analysis implies that other cultures, in which adults live differently, might define different developmental tasks for the teenager, so that the character and contradictions of adolescence would be different, or may disappear altogether.

It may even be the case that conceptual thinking and formal reasoning are only needed when routine customary practices break down. In traditional cultures, to the degree that custom and ritual are reproduced without changing, such thinking may not be a necessary part of psychological development. Alternatively, conceptual thinking may be limited to those few individuals who are charged with solving those problems that do arise. These are rich themes for future research to explore.

CONCLUSION

We learned in Chapter 2 that archaeologists have identified the skeletal changes associated with puberty only in Homo sapiens. Only in our species of hominins is there a growth spurt associated with puberty. However, we have also learned that it would be a mistake to define adolescence entirely in terms of these biological markers. The way other people recognize and respond to these physical and physiological changes plays an important role in the definition of adolescence. The age at which the young person comes to adopt, or is required to adopt, adult roles and responsibilities does not always correspond with the age at which sexual maturity is achieved and it becomes appropriate to have children of one's own. Sometimes adult responsibilities come first: this is what happens today to child brides, and it is what occurred in Europe in the 1500s, when a child aged 7 or 8 would leave home to become a domestic servant in another household. In such cases, the start of a stage of the lifespan that has been called "youth" is defined not by biology, by puberty, but by when a child can make a contribution to their family by being part of a valued marriage bond, or by earning a living. More often today, at least in Western countries, adulthood is typically achieved some years after sexual maturity. This time is passed in a culturally defined moratorium in which new skills are learned and contact between the genders is monitored, in some cultures permitted or even encouraged while in other cultures prohibited. In some cases these adolescent years are largely free from contradictions and psychological conflict or confusion. In other cases, such as in the West during much of the twentieth century, contradiction and conflict seem to have been the norm.

Psychology discovered adolescence not long after modern industrialized society re-invented it, by creating institutions of secondary education that isolated teenagers from the world of work, demanded their obedience to the authority of teachers and parents, corralled them with their peers, and then interpreted any failure of conformity as rebellion and delinquency, calling for harsher authority, punishment, or treatment.

When contradictory demands are placed on any person, psychological conflict is the response. The picture psychologists have painted of the adolescent is one of several kinds of conflict: confusion over identity, conflicting social roles and responsibilities, and the conflict between sophisticated, deliberate reasoning and impulsive decisions.

Piaget's account of formal operational reasoning describes it as something separate from other aspects of the adolescent's psychology. In Vygotsky's account, in contrast, the new kind of thinking that becomes possible in adolescence is interwoven with changes in perception, memory, imagination, and emotion. More deeply still, Vygotsky saw conceptual thinking as key to a reorganization of the adolescent's personality. No longer simply "in herself," she becomes "for herself." There is a new differentiation, between the acting "I" and the reflecting "I." There is now a "personality" with the capacity to freely chose a life plan.

Of these two, it is the Vygotskian account that fits better with what many psychologists have seen as central to adolescence, the search for identity, a central theme of the next chapter. It also fits better with the proposal that thinking and decision making by adolescents ought to be studied and understood in their peculiar social context.

Indeed, it has become clear that adolescence cannot be properly understood without attention to the social institutions in which teenagers find themselves. Most contemporary research on adolescent psychology has failed to pay this attention. Instead, psychologists frequently revert to biological explanations of adolescent thinking and behavior, drawing inferences from the latest neuroscience research in ways that are not well-warranted.

The picture of adolescence painted by many social scientists is not very rosy: it is seen as a time of risk-taking, thrill-seeking, rebellion, and even delinquency. Some researchers see these characteristics, when they occur, as evidence for an over-reliance on System 1 intuitive judgments, while others interpret them as showing an over-reliance on System 2 deliberate reasoning. Some attribute them to the tension between the prefrontal cortex and the limbic system, and some propose that the risky behavior of adolescence may have evolved to support the dangerous process of going out into the world to make a new life outside the family, even outside the community, and to find a sexual partner. Others hold the environment responsible, arguing that adolescents have become trapped in classrooms they find boring, and in which all decisions are made for them by adults. Perhaps several of these explanations are valid: when an adolescent is expected to stay in school rather than to explore new lands, adults may consider her adventurous tendencies as inappropriate.

SUMMARY

BIOLOGICAL CHANGES IN THE TEENAGE YEARS

- Puberty is the sequence of physiological changes, trigged by the brain, which has the outcome that the person becomes biologically capable of sexual reproduction. Humans, unlike other primates, experience an acceleration in their growth.
- The timing of puberty varies across cultures and is changing historically.
- Developments in the prefrontal cortex and in the limbic system are out of balance during much of adolescence.

CONSTITUTING ADOLESCENCE

- The gap between puberty and adult status defines adolescence. Its duration varies, and in some cultures (and in the past) adolescence does not occur.

ADOLESCENT REASONING AND DECISION MAKING

- Teenagers often become capable of complex reasoning that is counterfactual, verbal, and theoretical. Piaget called this formal operational intelligence; Vygotsky called it the higher psychological functions.
- Formal operational reasoning appears to be based on a theoretic mode that is encouraged in school.
- Adolescents also often engage in risky judgments and decisions. One proposal is that this is due to an imbalance between two modes of reasoning, intuitive and reflective. The presence of peers also increases the likelihood of risky behavior.
- The Positive Youth Development approach sees adolescence as a relational phenomenon, an interaction between teenager and environment. It emphasizes the need to provide more engaging and challenging environments.
- For Vygotsky, adolescence is a transition during which the higher psychological functions are reorganized to form a personality, an inner "I" who reflects and evaluates. This "I" is the agent who directs all the higher psychological functions. Conceptual thinking makes possible a system of acts of thinking, evident in abstract reasoning.

CHAPTER 14

THE TEENAGE YEARS

(12 YEARS AND UP)
TOWARDS ADULTHOOD

Many social issues, like the death penalty, gun control, or medical care, are pretty much matters of personal opinion, and there is no basis for saying that one person's opinion is any better than another's. So there's not much point in people having discussions about these kinds of issues. Do you agree, somewhat agree, or disagree? (If disagree) What do you think? (Kuhn, 2009, p. 178)

Adolescence is a naturally occurring time of transition—a time when changes happen that affect the experience of self and relationships with others. Thus adolescence is a situation for epistemological crisis, an age when issues of interpretation come to the fore. The turbulence and indeterminacy of adolescence, long noted and often attributed to conflicts over sexuality and aggression, can also be traced to these interpretive problems. (Gilligan, 1987, p. 2)

INTRODUCTION

Who is the adolescent? This may seem an odd question to ask, but it is a question that preoccupies the adolescent herself. With good reason: this is a time for important changes in self-understanding, in the organization of personality, and in societal position and status. Many psychologists have suggested that adolescence is a time of preoccupation with **identity**.

The question of identity can become a new and pressing concern for a teenager as she becomes aware of who she might be as well as who she is, and as she compares her own view of herself with other people's views of her. Identity is a matter of self as self-conscious subject, self as known by self and by other people. The kind of self-awareness and self-control that emerges in the teenager involves a new psychological center, a new form and source of agency.

This chapter begins with a discussion of the task of identity, and we explore the ways that Erik Erikson considered culture and history to be central to this task. But "peer culture" is also an important contributor to identity, as well as an illustration of the adolescent's growing capacity for cultural production. Finally, research on moral judgments once again opens a window on the ways that adolescents understand other people.

1. WHO IS THE ADOLESCENT?

It seems to be the case that forming an identity today in Western culture is more difficult than it was in the past. For much of history each young person simply adopted prescribed roles, often ones that their parents occupied. For many a child, the kind of adult she was going to be was simply not an issue. Her religion, her occupation, and her social standing were laid out for her, and she had a duty and obligation to accept these and make them her own. Only as more complex divisions of labor developed and, at the same time, social systems became more fluid has it become possible, even necessary, for choices to be made. Today a teenager is faced with a vast variety of choices, from occupation and living-place to religion and nationality, extending to sexual preference and even gender identification and ethnicity. However, there are important questions about the degree to which this "choice-based" identity can be generalized to non-Western cultures (Côté, 2009).

1.1 THE TASK OF FORMING AN IDENTITY

The idea that identity formation is the principal psychological task of adolescence comes largely from the writings of Erik Erikson (Erikson, 1994a[1959]; 1994b[1968]). As we saw in Chapter 2, Erikson's "psychosocial" model of development expanded Freud's psychosexual model to include attention to the culture in which a child develops.

Erikson himself had personal reasons to be interested in identity. When Erik was born, his mother had not seen her husband for several years. All that we know of his biological father is that he was Danish (like his mother), and was probably named Erik. His mother remarried when her son was 3, and his stepfather adopted him a few years later. He knew nothing about the circumstances of his birth until he was an adolescent. Young Erik's surname changed several times, from Salomonsen to Homburger, until he named himself "Erikson." He was raised in the Jewish religion but was tall and blond and his family lived in Germany, so he was teased for looking Nordic and for being Jewish. One imagines that identity had great personal importance for him.

Erikson viewed the human life cycle as a process that passes through distinct stages. The crisis that is specific to adolescence (which Erikson considered to be a stage) centers around the formation of an **ego identity**. This idea has been very influential: Erikson has been called "Identity's Architect"

(Friedman, 1999). He considered identity to be the product of an unconscious striving for personal continuity and consistency, together with solidarity with a particular social group.

Freud had suggested that identity is formed during childhood as a result of identification with parents, and does not change significantly during adolescence or adulthood. Erikson, in contrast, proposed that after childhood ends there still remains the task of choosing and consolidating an adult identity. Adolescence is, and ought to be, a time for reworking childhood identity into a larger sense of one's ideals in important domains of life. A key part of becoming an adult, for Erikson, is self-knowledge.

The adolescent has to make commitments to adult tasks and responsibilities, while maintaining a sense of continuity within herself. Each of these two aspects of adult identity presents challenges; together they may be in conflict. To successfully manage this crisis a new view of self and of the world is necessary: a new worldview and identity. Adolescence amounts to a **moratorium** between childhood and adulthood, a postponing of needing to be an adult, a time during which teenagers are "concerned with what they appear to be in the eyes of others as compared with what they feel they are," and during which they engage in a "search for a new sense of continuity and sameness" (Erikson, 1994a[1959], p. 261).

The ego identity that is achieved during this moratorium is based on the psychological work of earlier stages of development, including the toddler's attachment to caregivers and the young child's identification with the same-sex caregiver, but it is also based on the new social roles that become available to the teenager. Erikson wrote about ego identity for the first time when he worked with shell-shocked soldiers during the Second World War. He wrote that "they were impaired in that central control over themselves for which, in the psychoanalytic scheme, only the 'inner agency' of the ego could be held responsible" (1994b[1968], p. 17). Later, he observed the same lack of agency in young people whose confusion was due to "a war within themselves." He interpreted these cases as illustrations of normal characteristics of the stage of adolescence that had taken an amplified form due to social setting and the roles available.

1.1.1 THE IDENTITY STATUS MODEL

Erikson recognized that the identity crisis of adolescence can take a number of forms, with varying duration and severity. He considered a severe crisis to be unusual. In many cultures, even today, teenagers simply take up the values of their parents, and any identity crisis is muted and brief. In traditional cultures, adults often arrange a **rite of passage** that guides the young person through a short transition from childhood into adulthood. As a consequence of his observations of these cultural differences in the process of forming of an adult identity, Erikson distinguished between two possible outcomes of the crisis: **identity achievement** and **identity diffusion**.

For almost 30 years, the study of identity centered around a model that was based on Erikson's original analysis. This **identity status model**, developed by James Marcia, distinguished not only the two possible outcomes that Erikson recognized, but in addition two others. The model proposes, then, four key identity statuses (Marcia, 1966, 2001). Although this model was based on Erikson's work, questions have been raised about whether it successfully operationalized the processes that he considered necessary for the formation of identity. I will return to this issue in a moment.

The identity status model proposes that as an adolescent deals with the issue of her identity in some *domain*—such as occupation, political affiliation, or religion—two factors can be present or absent:

Has a crisis been experienced?

		Yes	No
Has a commitment been made?	**Yes**	Identity achievement	Foreclosure
	No	Moratorium	Identity diffusion

Figure 14.1 The four identity statuses

exploration and **commitment**. *Exploration* (which was originally called "crisis") is a time in which the adolescent tries to choose among the alternatives that are meaningful to her. *Commitment* is a high degree of personal involvement in the alternative that is selected. In this model, a period of exploration of possibilities is necessary for the formation of identity, but so is the commitment to a specific possibility.

The four **identity statuses** are identified on the basis of the presence or absence of these two factors. An adolescent who has explored the options and made a commitment has the status of **identity achievement**. An adolescent who is currently exploring the options is in the status of **moratorium**. If this exploration becomes emotionally difficult, the status is one of **identity crisis**. An adolescent who has made a commitment without exploring the options has a status of **foreclosure**. If foreclosure occurs, this is often because the adolescent has simply adopted the worldview of her parents or of other authority figures without exploring alternatives. Finally, if an adolescent has not made a commitment and is not even exploring the options, her status is **identity diffusion**.

An example of *foreclosure* would be the medical student who comes from three generations of doctors, or the young man who steps into the family business just as soon as his father is ready to retire.

The statuses were originally identified through short interviews. For example, here is a sample question in the religious domain, followed by typical responses for each identity status:

Have you ever had any doubts about your religious beliefs?

[Identity achievement] Yeah, I even started wondering whether or not there was a god. I've pretty much resolved that now, though. The way it seems to me is ...

[Moratorium] Yes, I guess I'm going through that now. I just don't see how there can be a god and yet so much evil in the world or ...

[Foreclosure] No, not really, our family is pretty much in agreement on these things.

[Identity diffusion] Oh, I don't know. I guess so. Everyone goes through some sort of stage like that. But it really doesn't bother me much. I figure one's about as good as the other! (Marcia, 1966)

Subsequent research explored the psychological characteristics that seem to be associated with each identity status (Marcia, 2001). This research was conducted with college students, mainly in the USA, so its general validity is unknown, but the findings were as follows.

An adolescent who has *achieved* identity is generally able to resist efforts to raise or lower her self-esteem (in experimental settings), and she resists peer pressure. She also tends to think clearly in stressful circumstances, and is likely to have a family that accepts and acknowledges differences. She is also likely to have realistically high self-esteem and not place overly strong restrictions on herself.

An adolescent in *moratorium* also has relatively stable self-esteem and resists pressure to confirm. She also thinks effectively, but she may tend to oscillate between judging herself harshly and indulging herself. She probably has an ambivalent relationship with her parents, and is unlikely to support authoritarian values, perhaps because she is keen to differentiate herself from her family.

An adolescent in *foreclosure* is likely to be inflexible in her thinking and to support authoritarian values. She will either easily agree when other people have opinions that are different from her own, or she will stubbornly resist them. She will tend to describe her family in unrealistically positive terms.

An adolescent in *identity diffusion* has unstable self-esteem and her thinking becomes disorganized in stressful situations. She often feels quite distant from her parents, especially her mother, and feels she can't make them happy, or be like them. She is insecure in her romantic relationships (Marcia, 2001).

1.1.2 ARRIVING AT IDENTITY STATUS

Subsequent studies have gone beyond this classification of identity statuses to explore the processes through which an adolescent arrives at one of them.

One finding has been that a distinction should probably be made between positive and negative forms of moratorium (Crocetti et al., 2008). An adolescent in moratorium may be actively searching for and evaluating alternatives. This has been called **searching moratorium**. Alternatively, moratorium may indicate a coming identity crisis, when an adolescent is aware that she needs to make a choice but has no strong commitments. This second form of moratorium is linked to anxiety, depression, and loneliness.

Another contribution of more detailed investigation has been to show that an adolescent will often reconsider her identity commitment and perhaps revise her identity status.

Research has also distinguished among different styles of personal problem solving and decision making that contribute to the work of forming an identity. In the **identity style model** three such styles have been identified. Some adolescents actively explore alternatives and search for information: this is the **information orientation**. Others are more conformist and deferential to social conventions, and to the standards and expectations held by other people: they have a **normative orientation**. Finally, some adolescents avoid exploring and are unwilling to engage: they show a **diffuse orientation**. The first approach is more likely to lead to moratorium or achievement, the second to foreclosure, and the third to diffusion (Berzonsky, 1989, 1990).

In addition, new aspects of identity have been explored, including the phenomenon of **personal expressiveness**—finding purpose and meaning in a particular activity (Waterman, 1999)—and **existential** aspects of identity—choice within the opportunities that the culture offers, made with personal integrity and responsibility.

Findings such as these have given rise to a lot of debate over the question of whether the four identity statuses line up in a developmental sequence. It has been proposed that diffusion, foreclosure or moratorium, and achieving commitment form a logical developmental order, so that an adolescent will pass through these in sequence (e.g., Meeus et al., 1999). However, regression also seems to occur, which is something that the identity status model has trouble explaining (Berzonsky & Adams, 1999; Waterman, 1999). It has also been suggested that an adolescent may remain for a considerable time in a less mature identity status, or may move in various ways among the statuses (van Hoof, 1999).

There are also suggestions that the four identity statuses are more like enduring types of character than developmental stages (van Hoof, 1999).

1.2 THE CULTURAL SETTING OF IDENTITY

In the 1990s there was a return to Erikson's writings, and researchers began to propose expansions and extensions of identity status theory (Schwartz, 2001). In addition, more attention began to be paid to the cultural and historical context in which identity is formed. Various criticisms were levelled at the identity status model.

One criticism has been that the identity status model takes for granted a Western process of identity formation. In the USA today, the emphasis on choice and individuality means that adolescence is relatively long, that forming an identity requires conscious deliberation and culturally sanctioned experimentation, and that adolescence ends with commitments that remain provisional and open to revision. This **choice-based identity crisis** has been taken as the norm by many researchers, even though it occurs only in specific cultures, as Erikson certainly recognized.

A second criticism of the identity status model is that it leaves out aspects of adolescence that Erikson considered important (Côté, 2009). Within the identity status model, identity is defined as "a person's sense of continuity with the past that constitutes the foundation for a meaningful personal and social present, which, in turn, suggests directions for their future" (Marcia, 2001, p. 7159). This definition treats exploration and commitment as intrapsychic processes, and it remains unclear how they might be connected to the social circumstances in which an identity is formed (Côté & Schwartz, 2002). Researchers do often acknowledge that the formation of identity is a social as well as a psychological process, but their research has often not included the social dimensions of establishing an identity (Yoder, 2000).

This leads us to a third, related, criticism of the identity status model: that it pays no attention to the role of the adolescent's culture in identity formation. Its definition of identity makes no mention of the culture in which the adolescent is living, nor of historical changes in that culture. Erikson himself complained that much of the research on identity formation had taken for granted the "cultural conditions of a sedentary middle class" (Erikson, 1994b[1964], p. 24), and had assumed that the social world is unchanging. He noted that not only does the process of identity formation change as historical circumstances change, it is precisely the job of identity formation to match the person to the particular historical circumstances of their specific culture. To leave out the latter is surely to misunderstand the challenge that identity presents to an adolescent.

When we turn back to Erikson's texts we find that he emphasized how identity formation is a clear example of the interplay of ontogenesis and history. It is not simply a matter of self-concept on one side and role-ambiguity on the other. He wrote:

we cannot separate personal growth and communal change, nor can we separate … the identity crisis in individual life and contemporary crises in historical development because the two help to define each other and are truly relative to each other. (Erikson, 1994b[1968], p. 23)

Erikson argued that there are in fact three components of identity formation—personality, social relations, and culture—and he distinguished among **ego identity** (a subjective sense of continuity), **personal identity** (a person's particular goals and preferences), and **social identity** (the person's position and social roles in a culture) (Levine & Côté, 2002). Erikson insisted that these three components need to come together, in an interplay of the psychological, interpersonal, and cultural, for a secure identity to be achieved. When this does not happen not only will there be a subjective sense of confusion, there will also be disturbed behavior, and a lack of satisfaction with any of the available cultural roles.

Recently, researchers have begun to explore this role of cultural context in identity development, though this research has not gone much further than simply looking at the "influence" of "external factors" on the supposedly "internal" psychological processes of identity formation. The research has also focused on patterns of individual difference, rather than on processes of identity formation. I will consider some examples of this research before turning to evidence from other cultures.

1.2.1 FAMILY CONTEXT: PARENTING AND IDENTITY

One aspect of cultural context is, of course, the family. Research has begun to explore the influence of parents on the adolescent's identity formation. Most studies have used Baumrind's typology of parenting styles, or Maccoby and Martin's dimensional approach to parenting (see Chapter 10). This research suggests that, in general, both over-controlling authoritarian parenting and under-controlling permissive or neglectful parenting deny an adolescent the opportunity to explore opportunities in a supportive family environment, and so they place obstacles in the path of creating a stable identity.

However, parents and their adolescent children are of course in a constant process of interaction, and researchers have begun to explore how mutual influence in the relationship between adolescent and parents guides identity development, in what is known as **identity control theory** (Kerpelman et al., 1997).

For example, one study exploring the relationships between styles of identity formation and styles of parenting found that adolescents with an information-oriented style reported that their parents were supportive but also psychologically controlling. Adolescents with a normative identity style, in contrast, saw their parents as supportive but behaviorally controlling. Adolescents with a diffuse-avoidant identity style saw their parents as psychologically controlling (Smits et al., 2008). Study of changes over a year during late adolescence found, not surprisingly, that adolescents and parents influenced each other: specifically, supportive parenting led to broader exploration in identity alternatives, while the adolescents' evaluation of these alternatives was related to more supportive parenting (Beyers & Goossens, 2008).

1.2.2 ETHNIC CONTEXT AND ETHNIC IDENTITY

Another important context for formation of identity is that of one's ethnic group. Studies of **ethnic identity** have been carried out, though largely these studies have applied the identity status model, even though it has been acknowledged that ethnic identity is unusual in that everyone is a member of an ethnic group, so that ethnic identity is not so much something one chooses as it is something that one recognizes (Phinney, 1990).

In terms of ethnic identity, what corresponds to the identity status of diffusion (or foreclosure) is **unexamined ethnicity**. In this status, adolescents are likely to accept the attitude and values of the majority group, including negative stereotypes about themselves. This status has also been called *pre-encounter*, *white-identified*, and *conformity*. However, there may also be foreclosure in ethnic identity that simply takes the form of adopting one parents' ethnic identity; this can be difficult to distinguish from identity diffusion.

Corresponding to the status of moratorium is **ethnic identity search**. This status may be initiated by an event that challenges the adolescent's worldview, or by a growing dissonance: the awareness that dominant cultural values are harmful to an ethnic minority. This status has also been called *resistance* and *immersion*. It may be accompanied by anger and protest.

The final status is **ethnic identity achievement**. This status is said to be characterized by a clear, confident, and calm sense of one's ethnicity. Ethnic identity in this status is based on comparison both with other people in the same ethnic group and also with people from the majority group. The result may be *integration* (bi-cultural), *assimilation*, or *separatist/dissociative*. Some adolescents, however, end up feeling marginal to both majority and minority ethnic groups.

It has been suggested that these statuses form a sequence of stages, so that an ethnic minority adolescent will begin with rootedness and diffusion, and then progressively differentiate her identity from others, sometimes to a point where group identities are transcended and a sense of unity within diversity is achieved (Hutnik & Street, 2010).

Studies in the USA have found not only that a strong ethnic identity is related to higher self-esteem (Phinney & Alipuria, 1996), but also that adolescents in an ethnic minority may be more foreclosed.

A study of ethnic minority and majority adolescents in the Netherlands found that the former were more likely to be in moratorium, both positive and negative. The majority adolescents, in contrast, were more likely to be in foreclosure or diffusion. This difference may reflect that fact that a member of a minority group, especially from an immigrant family, has to consider both her cultural heritage and the culture in which she lives. There may be clashes between the two, such as a focus on collectivism versus individualism, or different expected roles for women. Adolescents may seek to integrate, to separate, or to maintain an ambivalent position. The latter approach seems likely to lead to an identity status of moratorium (Stevens et al., 2004).

We have seen that Erikson considered a transitional period, a moratorium, to be necessary for the adolescent to be able to form an identity. It helps if the environment is stable and supportive at this time, but for many adolescents this is not the case. Immigration is one situation in which the environment changes drastically. A study of Russian and Ukrainian adolescents whose families emigrated to Israel found that a few years later they had an inconsistent bicultural identity. These adolescents felt more positive towards their new culture than towards the old, but they also had less of a sense of belonging to the new culture than to the old (Tartakovsky, 2009).

The interplay of ethnic identity and **national identity** has also been a focus of attention. The relation between these two is a matter of culture and of history. For example, both Algeria and Vietnam were French colonies, but Algerians in France tend to adopt a monocultural identity, while Vietnamese in

France adopt a bicultural identity of acculturation (cultural assimilation) in an "invisible" way, in which they maintain strong cultural customs at home but try not to attract attention in public.

Ethnicity may be invisible and unquestioned, or it may become salient within a diverse society, for members of an ethnic minority or for immigrants. Difference, conflict, and discrimination heighten awareness of one's ethnicity. In addition, of course, national identity is likely to be affected when there is discrimination within a nation on the basis of ethnic identity.

Some researchers have assumed that ethnic and national identities are contradictory and mutually exclusive (Wissink et al., 2008). Others believe that the two are aspects of identity that can co-exist when an immigrant has a sense of belonging to two groups simultaneously (Berry & Sam, 1997; Rumbaut & Komaie, 2010). To some degree the relationship between these two aspects depends on the specific circumstances. For example, Mexican immigrants to the USA can have both an ethnic and national identity, while Jewish immigrants to the USA and Surinam immigrants to the Netherlands often do not (Phinney et al., 2001). We do not yet know the precise processes that lead to these differences.

1.2.3 IDENTITY ACROSS CULTURES

Cross-cultural research offers another way to explore the influence of social context in identity formation. As we have seen, cross-cultural researchers often draw a distinction between **individualistic** cultures and **collectivist** cultures. In addition, it is assumed that every culture offers its members various dimensions of self-evaluation, known as **self-construals**. The proposal has been made that individualistic cultures offer **independent** self-construals, while collectivist cultures offer **interdependent self-construals**. One example of the distinction is that individualistic cultures often provide strategies for their members to *enhance* self, elaborating positive aspects of their identity. Collectivist cultures, in contrast, often provide strategies to *efface* self, such as modesty and self-criticism. Self-effacing strategies might seem negative, but they can motivate self-improvement by focusing the person on the task of changing aspects of self.

We can see these differences in the fact that people in the USA tend to attribute their successes to themselves, and to blame failures on factors beyond their control. Perceived differences between the ideal self and the real self are less in the USA than in Japan, for example. For people in the USA, when differences are perceived between how one is and how one would like to be, this can lead to depression. For people in Japan, such differences are more likely to give rise to efforts to improve in order to achieve the ideal (Harter, 2012). In Japan the emphasis is on maintaining harmonious relationships and having a "quiet ego" (Wirtz & Chiu, 2008). Pride is considered an inappropriate response to success, and contradiction and ambiguity in identity are tolerated. Japanese adolescents seem comfortable with seemingly contradictory but co-existing aspects of self. They believe that all these aspects contribute to their true self. For Western adolescents, on the other hand, having multiple conflicting self-descriptions is a disturbing experience, and much effort is put into their trying to figure out the "real me" (Harter et al., 1997).

1.3 REMAINING QUESTIONS ABOUT IDENTITY FORMATION

Many issues and questions remain about the formation of identity during the teenage years, some of them empirical, others conceptual. One is the question we have just raised, whether it is truly healthier to have an integrated identity. It has been suggested that in the USA today we live in a culture of multiple identities, and that it would be healthier to celebrate the differences among these rather than trying to make them all fit together coherently. Some psychologists argue that what is optimal is a flexible ability to adapt one's identity to new experiences and new situations. This implies that the formation of identity during adolescence is just the start of maintaining a healthy adult identity.

Erikson himself certainly recognized the reality of multiple selves, although he maintained that a healthy personality pulls these together:

> consider the nude body self in the dark or suddenly exposed to the light; consider the clothed self among friends or in the company of higher-ups or lower-downs; consider the just awakened drowsy self or the one stepping refreshed from the surf or the one overcome by retching and fainting; the body self in sexual excitement or in rage. (Erikson, 1968, p. 217, cited in Levine and Côté, 2002, p. 106)

Of course, the forming of identity starts before adolescence. Already by middle childhood children are evaluating themselves differently in different contexts, and we might say that they are forming multidimensional selves. Adolescents describe themselves differently with friends, teachers, parents, and romantic partners. The identity that is formed during adolescence can certainly seem to be multifaceted. An adolescent can have a different identity with the various people in her life. She may be "depressed and sarcastic with parents, caring and rowdy with friends, curious and attentive as a student, and flirtatious but also self-conscious with someone in whom one is romantically interested" (Harter et al., 1997, p. 837). An unanswered question is to what extent it is healthier for these selves to be fitted together consistently.

Another issue is that the ways in which identity is conceptualized sometimes show an unwitting gender and culture bias. For example, the statement "Adolescents and adults with a strong sense of their own identity see themselves as separate, distinct individuals" (Conger & Galambos, 1997, p. 41) assumes an individualistic stance that is, speaking generally, more common for men than for women, and more common for Westerners than for people in Eastern cultures.

Identity formation was originally seen—by Freud, for example—as part of a process of individuation: of psychological separation from the parents. However, as we have seen, female gender identity in early childhood is not typically based on separation, and this suggests that the process of identity formation in adolescence may differ for the two genders. While an adolescent boy may be struggling for autonomy, adolescence for a girl may be a time of dialog and consolidation of her relations with her parents. This may be even more the case in cultures where matrilineal intergenerational links are strongly maintained.

A study of Pakistani Muslim immigrant families in Britain illustrated this last point. A teenage girl in such a family faces many challenges. Respectfulness to her parents may be interpreted by her Western friends as submissiveness or shyness. The protectiveness and support that the family consider important to provide to their daughter may be interpreted as oppression and patriarchy by her peers outside the family. These peers may view the modest clothing that she wears as an assertion of traditional values, as a hostile gesture to the host culture. In addition, fears of Muslim fundamentalism can lead to misunderstandings all around. An adolescent living in such circumstances may feel that she is caught between two cultures, and fits into neither (Hutnik & Street, 2010).

A related point is that if ego identity provides a sense of agency, as Erikson proposed, and if women are "less agentic" than men, as a number of psychologists have suggested, does this mean that women have less sense of identity than men? In many cultures, women are defined relationally: as someone's wife, mother or daughter, secretary (Chodorow, 1999[1978]). It has been suggested that women may be more relational while men are more analytic. If this is the case, how do these differences influence formation of identity during adolescence?

1.3.1 IDENTITY AND COGNITION

In addition, it is worth considering the fact that Erikson defined identity formation in a way that is strikingly similar to the way Piaget defined formal operational reasoning (Cole, 1990b):

> In psychological terms, identity formation employs a process of simultaneous reflection and observation, a process taking place on all levels of mental functioning, by which the individual judges himself in the light of what he perceives to be the way in which others judge him in comparison to themselves and to a typology significant to them; while he judges their way of judging him in the light of how he perceives himself in comparison to them and to types that have become relevant to him. (Erikson, 1994b[1968], pp. 22–23)

This definition of the process of forming an identity seems to point towards a relationship between identity formation and cognitive development. As we saw in the previous section, Vygotsky certainly maintained that these two are both aspects of the complex system of the higher psychological functions. However, little research has been conducted to explore the relationship.

1.3.2 WHAT IS IDENTITY?

Perhaps the most important unresolved question is, what is identity? Identity has been variously conceived of as a "structure," as a "theory of the self," and as "a conceptual structure composed of self-representational and self-regulatory constructs" (Berzonsky, 2004). However, if identity is a theory about the self, who holds the theory? What self is the theory about, if it is not the self that has been created by forming an identity?

The phenomenon I am drawing attention to here has been described in terms of the "I" and the "Me." The "Me" has been defined as the understanding (for some psychologists it is a concept or a theory) that a person has of themself. The "I" has been defined as the subject who forms that understanding. Certainly, a central aspect of adolescence is a new kind of self-consciousness. We saw in Chapter 11 that in middle childhood the child became conscious of an "inner world" of thoughts and feelings. Now, in adolescence, there is in addition a consciousness of an "inner self," a sense of being an agency in that inner world. Each developmental transition involves a differentiation, and in adolescence the division is between the self that acts, and the self that reflects. The adolescent not only acts deliberately and consciously in the world, she also actively and deliberately directs her own thinking and her imagination. This is what Vygotsky meant when he wrote that adolescence involves a change from the *for-oneself* to the *in-oneself*.

Certainly, identity in the sense of a self-concept or a theory about oneself is important. The adolescent can now form a conception or theory about who she is in contrast with who she could ideally be, or who she would like to be. In doing so, she will compare her own sense of who she is with other people's sense of who she is, as she perceives this. We see here the "knots" that existential psychiatrist Ronald Laing (1971) considered to be at the core of human identity—people tie themselves in knots thinking about what others think of them.

Younger adolescents in particular are intensely self-conscious, and are often said to have an unstable self-concept. The adolescent becomes aware of her conflicting attributes before she becomes able to resolve them. Relationships with different significant people may come into conflict: for example, her relations with her mother may clash with her relations with her father. The conflict between those attributes that the adolescent regards as true of herself and those that she considers false can be especially painful, and can set the stage for low self-esteem and depression.

Older adolescents become less self-critical and more sure of themselves. In late adolescence the adolescent begins to develop strategies to resolve the conflicts between her attributes. Having many identities may start to seem something that is desirable, rather than a problem. In part this is because it becomes possible for the older adolescent to weave these identities together into a coherent life story.

The ability for self-examination and self-knowledge is, then, an important achievement of adolescence, but what is equally important is an ability for self-determination: a new ability to actively make choices about life. Both Vygotsky and Erikson considered this to be the most significant psychological achievement of adolescence. It would seem that an adolescent's sense of being in charge of her life, of actively making choices, rests on a sense of some distance between herself and her circumstances. The immersion in the world of infancy and toddlerhood is now left far behind. The adolescent, with her sense of an inner self, may in fact experience a degree of distance from the social world in which she lives that becomes disorienting and alienating. At times, this alienation may become the motivation to participate in a shared **peer culture**, which is our next topic.

2. PEER CULTURE

In secondary education … we are beset by a peculiar paradox: in our complex industrial society there is increasingly more to learn, and formal education is ever more important in shaping one's life chances; at the same time, there is coming to be more and more an independent 'society of adolescents,' an adolescent culture which shows little interest in education and focuses the attention of teenagers on cars, dates, sports, popular music, and other matters just as unrelated to school. (Coleman, 1959)

Much has been made of the importance of **peer culture** during adolescence. Adolescents spend even more time with peers than children did in middle childhood, and there has been much theorization and research about the reasons for these peer groups, and their structure and function. The peer group certainly constitutes an important aspect of the social situation of adolescence.

It is important to bear in mind a point I made in the previous chapter, that much of the research on adolescent reasoning and cognition has focused on the individual, and has failed to take into account the undeniable fact that adolescents make decisions and choices within a group of influential friends and acquaintances. This section will begin to explore this aspect of the social context of adolescence.

To some degree, a teenager's involvement with peers should not surprise us. It is logical that she will be forming relationships with people outside the family; indeed, this is what family members expect. Much of the time, teenagers find that they are in institutions that segregate them from people who are either older or younger.

However, the consequence is that when we consider the social situation of development during adolescence, we need to consider not only the family (sibs and parents are still important) and the school (or an equivalent institution of education), but also a peer culture that is not only somewhat autonomous but oftentimes also somewhat rebellious and oppositional. What is going on here?

2.1 CLIQUES, CROWDS, AND ROMANCE

In the eyes of many adults, adolescents seem to have a passionate herding instinct. (Brown, 1990, p. 171)

We saw in Chapter 11 that groups of same-gender peers form in middle childhood, and these groups take on new importance in adolescence. High school students spend twice as much time with peers as with parents or other adults (30 percent versus 15 percent). Peers may form 40 percent of an adolescent's social network. It has been suggested that in Western cultures the peer group serves several functions. First, peer groups involve very little adult guidance or control, or even supervision: it seems that teenagers try to escape from adults in order to spend time with peers (we will explore the relationship between teenagers and parents in a later section of this chapter). Second, membership of a peer group can facilitate the search for identity, which we have seen is central to adolescence. Third, peers can be a source of emotional support and affirmation. In addition, the adolescent peer group provides a context within which contact begins to take place with members of the opposite gender.

The peer group is also a counterpoint to the way high schools are generally organized, with constant movement among classrooms each of which has different students. The high school is a complex and impersonal institutional structure, and this can create the need for an alternative source of personal and social support. The organization of school has been found to have a strong influence on peer group formation, in both middle childhood and adolescence. For example, the size of **cliques** varies with classroom size (Hallinan & Smith, 1989). Cliques form within academic tracks rather than across them, and the interactions of the members of high-track and low-track cliques have different characteristics (Schwartz, 2008). The emphasis the school places on academics, sport, drama, and so on seems to shape the types of clique that form.

Peer groups have been portrayed as homogeneous, enforcing conformity and narrow-mindedness. However, an adolescent may participate in multiple peer cultures, so in this regard they may foster diversity (Brown, 1990).

The opposition towards adult society sometimes shown by a peer group during adolescence has often been emphasized. Research has tended to pit peers against parents, assuming that they have opposite influences and trying to figure out which is more important: "In principle, every teenager is a delinquent" (Burlingame, 1970). However, both parents and peers are important to the typical teenager, and there is no definitive type of peer relationship (Giordano, 2003). Just as the family is a necessary context for development but can have beneficial or detrimental influences, so too does the adolescent peer group seem to play a necessary role in the development of many young people, though it receives the greatest amount of attention when its influence is detrimental (Ogbu, 1981).

Adolescent culture has been described as pleasure seeking, as valuing appearance over academic achievement in a ruthless pursuit of popularity, and as alienated from adult society. While in some cases physical appearance is the basis for peer group status, there are adolescent groups that value academics—popularized in the famous rivalry between *jocks* and *nerds*. The assumptions that peers always outweigh parents, that there is an unbridgeable "generation gap," and that peer influence inevitably leads to deviant activities, have not found much empirical support.

An influential investigation of the structure and function of adolescent peer culture was carried out by Dexter Dunphy in Sydney, Australia, at the end of the 1950s. Over 300 adolescents from 13 to 21 years of age participated, responding to questionnaires and interviews, or keeping diaries of their activities. Dunphy also studied "natural groups" of teenagers, which he contacted through youth clubs, and traced in detail for four to six months (Dunphy, 1963).

We have seen that children form "gangs" in middle childhood, and that these are generally single gender and sex categorized/stereotyped. This, then, is the kind of peer structure in which children enter adolescence.

Dunphy described five stages of transformation in this peer social organization. The single-gender "cliques" that were formed in middle childhood continued into early adolescence. In time, however, these single-gender cliques made connections with cliques made up of members of the opposite sex. These cliques formed a loose association that allowed more complex social activities. Dunphy named this loose association the "crowd." Towards the end of adolescence the crowd tended to dissipate into cliques again, but this time into cliques that were mixed gender. Among the adolescents that Dunphy studied, most became members of heterosexual groups. The crowd functioned, then, as a context within which to meet and pair with a member of the opposite sex.

Let me describe the stages in a little more detail.

At the beginning of the study, when the teenagers were aged 14 and 15, about 70 percent of the boys and 80 percent of the girls belonged to peer groups. Cliques were the smaller, and more clearly defined and cohesive, unit of adolescent social life. These cliques varied in size from three to nine members, and they were characterized by close relations among those members and strong cohesion. Members of a clique usually lived near to each other. Dunphy noted that the cliques were similar in size to the family, and he hypothesized that they served some of the same functions as an adolescent's family.

At stage 2, around mid-adolescence, the clique system was transformed. Many of the cliques came together to form a crowd. Each crowd was basically an association of cliques (from two to four of them). Crowds were the largest social unit that was observed in the study. Although people differed greatly when asked who belonged to their crowd and who did not, observations and interviews showed a high level of consensus about the boundaries. Each crowd had from 15 to 30 members. Not all cliques became part of a crowd, but clique membership seemed to be a requirement for joining a crowd. Members of one clique within a crowd considered other members of the same crowd who were not in the same clique as not "real buddies." Crowds differed in the age of their members, and they formed a hierarchy, with the crowds with older members higher in the hierarchy.

All of the crowds were of mixed gender. This was an age, Dunphy observed, when contact with the opposite sex was seen as daring, and it required the support and security of the other members of one's clique. Much of the interaction between the genders was apparently hostile.

For example, two crowds arranged a party. People arrived and left with other members of the same clique. During the party people socialized across clique boundaries, but the two crowds stayed largely apart: one spent most of their time in the kitchen, the other were in the lounge for most of the time.

In the third stage the first dating occurred, but within the context of a clique that now contained members of both genders. Adolescents usually kept a foot in their original clique too. The crowd—by

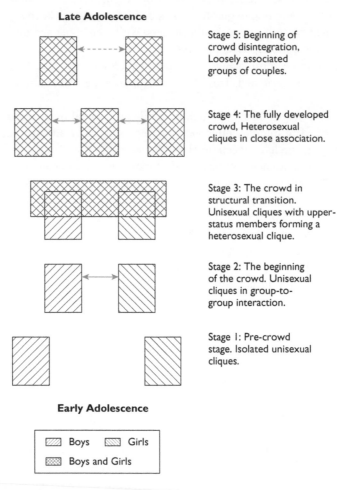

Late Adolescence

Stage 5: Beginning of crowd disintegration, Loosely associated groups of couples.

Stage 4: The fully developed crowd, Heterosexual cliques in close association.

Stage 3: The crowd in structural transition. Unisexual cliques with upper-status members forming a heterosexual clique.

Stage 2: The beginning of the crowd. Unisexual cliques in group-to-group interaction.

Stage 1: Pre-crowd stage. Isolated unisexual cliques.

Early Adolescence

Boys   Girls

Boys and Girls

Figure 14.2 Stages of group development in adolescence

Source: Dunphy (1963)

now an extended mixed-gender peer group—seemed to play a central role in the process of bringing the two genders together

At stage 4, an extensive reorganization took place and mixed-gender cliques came to predominate, associated together within the crowd.

In the final stage, the crowd dissolved and what was left were cliques made up of loosely associated couples, who were either dating or were engaged to be married.

Dunphy's research was carried out in a specific time and place—Sydney, Australia, in the late 1950s. Little similar research has been carried out since, so it is hard to know how general his findings are. His research is an example of what have been called **dating-stage theories**, which propose that there is a single pathway towards an adult sexual relationship, with stages along the way. However, it seems likely that there is more than one pathway, and that the cultural context defines the routes.

Certainly, the romantic relationships that emerge in adolescents are something completely new, both for the social scientist and for the adolescents themselves. And for adolescents in Western countries today dating does often occur in unsupervised mixed-gender groups, which is very different from the dating patterns of their parents. Observers—and sometimes the participants themselves—often have difficulty distinguishing between opposite-sex friends and romantic partners (Connolly & Goldberg, 1999).

In social circumstances such as these, it is the high-status members of the social crowd who are the first to initiate heterosexual contact. However, by late adolescence most of the members will be participating in an ongoing romantic relationship (Collins, 2003). Commitment to a partner leads many adolescents to transform what they at first viewed as a voluntary relationship into one that is more obligatory and more permanent (Laursen & Jensen-Campbell, 1999).

The peer social system provides opportunities to meet potential romantic partners, to practice the social skills necessary for forming and maintaining a relationship, while at the same time having a boyfriend or girlfriend provides status within the peer group. Friends provide support for and prototypes of dating behavior. Romantic relationships typically are more intense than other kinds of relationship in adolescence, and are marked by expressions of affection and by either sexual behavior or its anticipation.

However, we know that the institutional setting plays a role. A single-sex school will provide less opportunity for a mixed-gender group to form.

In addition, in many cultures around the world the family and community continue to be closely involved in the relationships that adolescents have with each other. Cultural background is evident in parents' expectations and values: for example, parents of Asian descent generally think that dating should occur later than do parents with a European background. Parents monitor these relationships, and they often play an active role in deciding who their adolescent child may or may not interact with. Both Latina and African American girls in early adolescence in the USA tell researchers that they keep their boyfriends secret from members of the family, especially their mother, for fear of being forced to end the relationship (O'Sullivan & Meyer-Bahlburg, 2003).

One study that explored the relevance of Dunphy's research today was conducted with adolescents aged 9 to 14 in either mixed or single-sex Canadian public schools. Over the course of a year, questionnaires were given to young Canadian adolescents of Asian, European, and Caribbean backgrounds—675 boys and 700 girls, in grades 5 through 8. Some of the questions are shown in Figure 14.4 below (Connolly et al., 2004).

On the basis of their answers, each student was coded as being in one of four possible romantic stages: *same sex*, *affiliative*, *dating*, and *romantic dyad*. The data that were then collected supported the distinctions among these stages: in particular, the incidence of the later stages increased with age (see "Table 3" below). The ways in which the adolescents moved from one stage to another were explored by calculating the "conditional probability" of each possible movement, as shown in "Table 4" below. We can see that passage through the stages generally followed a sequential order. Adolescents were more likely to move forward than backward. However, there was also evidence that adolescents in the middle stages—*affiliative* or *dating*—were more likely to stay in that stage than to move forward. Dating seemed to complement activities with the group or with a friend, rather than replace them.

The research also found some differences among the adolescents with different ethnic backgrounds. Those from Asian-Canadian families were more likely to report same-gender friendships, were less interested in romantic relationships, and were less likely to participate in any romantic activity than those from other family backgrounds. However, the Asian-Canadian adolescents moved through the stages in a similar manner to the others—they simply started to move when they were older.

Surprisingly, there was little difference between adolescents in same-sex schools and those who attended mixed schools. However, the romantic activities of the girls in the single-sex schools did not increase during the year, while those of the boys did. This suggests that it is the boys who initiate a dating relationship, and that without access to a mixed-gender group not very much happens in the dating scene.

I.   Boys and girls can spend time together in many ways. Answer True or False in the boxes beside each of the sentences below to describe the types of way you spend time together with girls (boys) after school and on weekends:

- I only spend time with other boys (girls)   T   F
- I hang around with both boys and girls   T   F
- I go to dances or parties where both boys and girls are there   T   F
- I go to clubs, groups or sports activities where both boys and girls are   T   F
- I meet a group of boys and girls at night   T   F
- I go out with a another boy (girl) and a couple of girls (boys)   T   F
- I go on dates with a girl (boy), but with a group   T   F
- I go on dates with a girl (boy), just the two of us   T   F

An item from the questionnaire

Source: Connelly et al. (2004)

It should be added that there is still not much research on adolescents with a same-gender sexual preference. It seems that even among adolescents who identity themselves as being heterosexual, the gender of the people who they find attractive can be quite fluid over time, especially for adolescent girls. Estimates of homosexuality in adolescents range from 1 percent to 21 percent, indicating that it is something that is hard to define, both for young people and for researchers (Collins et al., 2009).

		Affiliative Activities	*Dating Activities*
Grade 5	Fall	1.71 (1.12)	0.36 (0.85)
	Spring	1.83 (1.10)	0.47 (0.91)
Grade 6	Fall	2.00 (1.04)	0.59 (1.00)
	Spring	2.16 (1.01)	0.64 (1.07)
Grade 7	Fall	2.38 (0.92)	1.15 (1.33)
	Spring	2.54 (0.83)	1.48 (1.44)
Grade 8	Fall	2.57 (0.76)	1.39 (1.38)
	Spring	2.64 (0.69)	1.57 (1.43)

Figure 14.3 Affiliation and dating in different grades

Source: Connelly (2004)

Note: Affiliative score range = 0 to 3; dating score range = 0 to 4. *N* = 1,220 at both times with complete data.

	Spring Romantic Stage				
	Same-Sex	*Affiliative*	*Dating*	*Dyad*	*Total N (Fall)*
Fall romantic stage					
Same sex	.43	.55	.02	.00	93
Affiliative	.04	.68	.22	.06	557
Dating	.00	.17	.58	.25	370
Romantic dyad	.00	.10	.24	.66	258
Total *N* (spring)	62	523	402	291	1,278

Figure 14.4 Probability of making the transition from one stage in the fall to another stage the following spring

Source: Connelly (2004)

2.2 ARRANGING CONTACT BETWEEN THE GENDERS

In many cultures, adults will make arrangements for—or place restrictions on—contact between the genders during the teenage years. In pastoral societies, for example, teenage boys work alongside men, but when the work is done they are excluded from the adults and hang out together (Schlegel, 1995). Teenage girls work with other females, and spend leisure time with them. In such cultures there is very little non-sexual friendship between teenage boys and girls. However, there is often sexual activity among them, though the degree and form of this vary across cultures. In cultures where children are a valued resource, premarital adolescent sex is likely to be accepted. In cultures where virginity is valued (usually because the girl brings property to her marriage, and will pass it to her children), premarital adolescent sexuality is frowned upon. Both adults and peers will monitor what is going on.

One example of the former is found in various tribes in India. The community arranges adolescent dormitories, called *ghotul*, in which the head girl and boy arrange that partners change regularly (Elwin, 1947). The dormitory "assumes the role of a mixed youth club" (von Fürer-Haimendorf, 1950, p. 121). The *ghotul* is where teenagers "dance and dine together for marital selection and understanding of mates" (Singh, 2004, p. 680). Within the dormitory "Sexual intercourse between the unmarried is allowed … and it is strictly taboo for dormitory members to disclose to adults the happenings in the dormitory. Offenders against this rule are fined three rupees, a large sum for a youngster" (von Fürer-Haimendorf, 1950, p. 124). Exclusive dyadic sexual relations are discouraged. If a teenage girl becomes pregnant, however, she is expected to marry the father. Many tribal cultures arrange marriage during the teenage years, with girls marrying between 13 and 17, and boys between 16 to 20. Those involved may select their partner by mutual consent, or by the boy paying a brideprice to the girl's father.

This might seem odd or even shocking to us. But one anthropologist described the arrangement in these terms:

> The message of the *ghotul*—that youth must be served, that freedom and happiness are more to be treasured than any material gain, that friendliness and sympathy, hospitality and unity are of the first importance, and above all that human love—and its physical expression—is beautiful, clean and precious, is typically Indian. (Elwin, 1947, p. 272)

2.3 PARENTING IN ADOLESCENCE

Anna Freud, Sigmund's daughter, viewed the psychological task of adolescence as being a "detachment" from the parents after a period of inevitable conflict. In this view, the upsurge of sexual impulses at the end of the latency period led to regression and hostility (Freud, 1958). Subsequent theories in clinical psychology emphasized "individuation" rather than detachment: individuation was defined as the achievement of a distinct sense of self as autonomous and competent. Achieving individuation, according to these theories, involves challenging the parents' values and beliefs rather than overt rebellion or rejection. Whatever the details of the various theories, the relationship with parents has been seen as a key component to the creation of a healthy identity, and ultimately a healthy life (Steinberg & Silk, 2002).

More recent models of adolescent development do not view conflict as inherent in the relationship between parents and adolescent. Individuation is still considered important, but this is thought to be possible within a close parenting relationship. This relationship is transformed, rather than broken. Responsibility, competence and independence are considered to be the healthy outcomes of a process in which parents actively foster their adolescent's autonomy within an emotionally close and affectionate relationship.

Individuation is thought to allow the adolescent to develop an identity that is independent of the parents, while remaining connected to them as important sources of advice and support. There is a transformation in adolescents' perceptions of parents. In childhood parents are generally seen as "all knowing" and "all powerful." In adolescence, parents are first de-idealised, and then become appreciated as persons themselves (Smollar & Youniss, 1989). The balance of power shifts: parents are no longer authority figures (whether it be authoritative or authoritarian), they now engage their child in cooperative negotiation.

This sounds like a tough balancing act. It also sounds very middle class. What does it involve? Once again, most of the research has been conducted in Western urban families. Certainly, parents must adjust to rapid and striking changes in their child—changes that are physical, emotional, and intellectual. The sexual maturation at puberty will usually require some adjustment on the part of parents. The changes she is going through are going to alter the way the new adolescent relates to her parents. Hormonal changes may increase adolescent moodiness, though not as much as parents have usually been led to believe. In many families more conflict occurs, and there is less support and enjoyment, as parents and offspring each feel that they have become more distant from the other (Steinberg & Silk, 2002).

We have seen that adolescents are becoming capable of reasoning and making decisions in new ways, and this has several consequences for their relations within the family. The adolescent may directly challenge the way her parents make decisions and arrange the family's daily life. At the least, she will bring a fresh perspective to family decisions. She will probably expect to be listened to and taken more seriously. Parents may respond to this in different ways. Some will welcome the adolescent's new role, while others will push back and resist the change.

We have seen that adolescents can now recognize the conventional character of social norms and roles. We shall see in the next section that they start to question societal conventions and ethical values. These changes too can lead to conflicts with parents. To the adolescent, parental authority may well no longer be sufficient justification for rules about the clothing she may wear, or the hour at which she should be home each evening. She is likely now to view these as matters of personal taste rather than right or wrong. To some parents this attitude may seem a challenge to these values, to others it may seem a rejection of their worth. The feeling that one has lost respect in the eyes of one's child is not easy to accept.

The task of finding an identity during adolescence in a situation that has many contradictions can also lead to changed relations with parents. We have seen that identity can be achieved by adopting parental values and choices without questioning them, but it can also be achieved through opposition, by challenging and rejecting the parents' choices and values. Peer culture provides a vehicle and an impetus for the latter option. In addition, parents may wish, consciously or unconsciously, to preserve the dependence and acquiescence of their child. At the same time, an adolescent may demand independence and autonomy while still being entirely economically dependent on her parents, and while still taking for granted their material and emotional support.

As the peer group becomes increasingly important to an adolescent, and as she spends more time with peers and less time with her family, parents may feel excluded. They may try to control who the adolescent spends time with, but she is likely to resent such restrictions and find ways to circumvent them. And when an adolescent makes rash judgments, parents need to find ways of having an influence while respecting her autonomy.

All these changes lead to a renegotiation of the family relationships, whether or not the participants consciously want this. The parents of an adolescent may find that they too need to create a new identity.

The time when a child enters adolescence is generally also the time when her parents enter middle age (around 40 years of age), and this is often a point when parents experience low levels of satisfaction, and are at increased risk of divorce (Gottman & Levinson, 2000). Parents are often feeling less attractive just as their teenage child is entering the period that is often considered the most physically and sexually attractive. The adolescent is thinking about future possibilities, and at the same time feeling invincible and immortal, while her parents are seeing their own parents aging and are reminded of their own mortality. The parents may find themselves having to take care of an elderly and infirm grandparent and meeting the new demands and challenges of their adolescent child at the same time. They may feel that their child now has opportunities they once had, or never had, and this can lead to envy or competition.

Western psychologists tend to assume that the healthy outcome of these developmental challenges for both child and parents is for the adolescent to establish a firm sense of individuality within family relations that are not so distant as to be isolating, but not so close as to be stifling.

Autonomy is a term that has been used in different ways, and it has several components. Emotional autonomy includes the de-idealization of parents, which sometimes leads to the adolescent pointing out her parents' failings. It also involves the adolescent not sharing all her emotions with her parents. Behavioral autonomy is a matter of the adolescent making her own decisions and acting on them. However this can be a cause of conflict. Parents may respond with psychological control—attempting to influence their adolescent child's thoughts and feelings—or with behavioral control, attempting to influence her behavior and activities. These seem to have different consequences for adolescent adjustment.

However, this focus on autonomy ignores the emphasis on values of respect for elders and family obligation in many cultures. It also ignores the key role that adolescents continue to play in many families, such as families of immigrants. In such a family the adolescent may be needed to translate between parents and the outside community. Her family cannot afford to grant her autonomy—she is needed as a language broker (Dorner et al., 2008).

The adolescent in Western culture spends more time in "leisure activities" than her time at school and at work combined (Larson, 2000). Much of this time is unsupervised by adults. Parents must resort to their cell phone to try to monitor their adolescent's activity and whereabouts. Schools now are less likely to report to parents on the academic progress of their adolescent child.

3. UNDERSTANDING OTHER PEOPLE: ETHICAL AND EPISTEMOLOGICAL RELATIVISM

We turn now to explore what is known, and what is not, about the ways adolescents understand other people. Once again there are two aspects to this. First, adolescents' judgments about moral behavior, principally when they are asked to reason about someone (usually fictional) who is faced with a dilemma, provide a window on how they understand the social reality in which they live. Second, research on adolescents' views about the nature of knowledge, their "epistemological understanding," provides a window on how they understand their own and other people's "minds."

In Chapter 11 we considered Kohlberg's account of the development of moral judgement through three levels and six stages. We saw how at level III, which is a kind of judgment that in most cases does not occur before 13 years of age, a distinction becomes drawn between what is moral and what is conventional. We also saw that Kohlberg's conclusions were challenged by Turiel and colleagues, who obtained evidence that even in early childhood a distinction between moral and conventional transgressions is made in practice on the preschool playground.

Further explorations using Kohlberg's methodology concluded that stage 6 was so rare that it was dropped from further consideration. In addition, longitudinal research provided evidence that suggested the existence of a stage that was transitional between conventional moral reasoning (stage 4) and post-conventional (stage 5) moral reasoning. This transitional stage was called stage 4½.

The kind of reasoning in stage 4½ was characterized as "relativism." Young people who are considered to be in this stage argue that norms are moral only within a particular society. Since societies have different norms, morality is no more than a matter of what seems right to a person, in her particular context.

For example, one 19-year-old explained:

I think I am now less sure of things than before. I am more sure—this is perhaps a paradox— I am *more* sure of myself because I am *less* sure of things: meaning that is a very big burden to carry around to know every goddamn thing in the world and be correct all the time. (Tappan, 1989, p. 307)

Researchers have offered a variety of explanations for this phenomenon of "values relativism" in adolescence, which appears at least for a time and at least among the groups that have been studied. Before we consider these explanations, it will be helpful to consider another aspect of adolescent relativism.

3.1 EPISTEMOLOGICAL RELATIVISM

The relativism that characterizes reasoning in adolescence involves not only morality but also epistemology—that is, many adolescents express relativistic views not only about people's values but also about people's knowledge, including their own.

To illustrate this, consider again the question that was posed at the start of this chapter:

Many social issues, like the death penalty, gun control, or medical care, are pretty much matters of personal opinion, and there is no basis for saying that one person's opinion is any better than another's. So there's not much point in people having discussions about these kinds of issues. Do you agree, somewhat agree, or disagree? (If disagree) What do you think? (Kuhn, 2009, p. 178).

Diana Kuhn asked this question of middle-school and high-school students (13 and 17 years old respectively) and their mothers, in three subcultures in the northeastern USA: upper-middle class, suburban Caucasians; middle-class, urban Chinese-Americans; and middle-class, urban Korean-Americans.

Kuhn and her colleague Seung-Ho Park evaluated the responses to this question, and others, in terms of the theoretical framework shown in Figure 14.5. They drew a distinction among four ways of understanding knowledge. The first, a *realist* understanding, sees knowledge as a copy of external reality.

Level	Assertions	Knowledge	Critical Thinking
Realist	Assertions are *Copies* of an external reality.	Knowledge comes from an external source and is certain.	Critical thinking is unnecessary.
Absolutist	Assertions are *Facts* that are correct or incorrect in their representation of reality.	Knowledge comes from an external source and is certain but not directly accessible, producing false beliefs.	Critical thinking is a vehicle for comparing assertions to reality and determining their truth or falsehood.
Relativist	Assertions are *Opinions* freely chosen by and accountable only to their owners.	Knowledge is generated by human minds and therefore uncertain.	Critical thinking is irrelevant.
Evaluativist	Assertions are *Judgments* that can be evaluated and compared according to criteria of argument and evidence.	Knowledge is generated by human minds and is uncertain but susceptible to evaluation.	Critical thinking is valued as a vehicle that promotes sound assertions and enhances understanding.

Figure 14.5   Levels of epistemological understanding

Source: Kuhn & Park (2005)

The second, an *absolutist* understanding, sees knowledge as correct or incorrect representations of reality. The third, a *relativist* understanding (also called "multiplist"), sees knowledge as opinions, constructed by individuals, and considers each opinion to be equally valid. The fourth, an *evaluative* understanding, sees knowledge as individual judgments that can be evaluated and compared through argument and evidence.

You will see that this framework fits well with what we have learned in previous chapters. We have seen that young children assume that experience corresponds with reality. By the start of middle childhood, however, they have come to accept that people hold beliefs, and that these can be incorrect. The pendulum has swung from an objective view of knowledge to a subjective view of knowledge.

In adolescence, according to Kuhn, the pendulum moves again, as the adolescent tries to coordinate what is subjective with what is objective. The relativist way of understanding now sees knowledge as a matter of individual and personal opinion, and at the same time assumes that every opinion is valid. As a consequence, there is nothing to be gained from debate or discussion. This, then, is "epistemological relativism." Only with the move to an evaluative understanding of knowledge is there a recognition that opinions can be evaluated through argument and the presentation of evidence.

Kuhn and Park found that the relativist stance was the most common amongst the adolescents they studied, and also their mothers. Although 90 percent of the Caucasian mothers showed an evaluative stance, only 45 percent of the Korean-American mothers did so, and only 19 percent of the Chinese-American mothers. The majority showed absolutist or relativist thinking. Among their children, there was no difference between the 13- and 17-year-olds, and only 60 percent of the Caucasian-Americans showed an evaluative stance, only 54 percent of the Korean-Americans, and only 36 percent of the Chinese-Americans. There was no association between parental performance and the performance of their child.

For Kuhn, this was a disconcerting pattern of results. In her view, it is important that adolescents are educated in scientific reasoning, but for an adolescent who adopts the relativist stance, and for whom all knowledge is opinion and all opinions are valid, there is no point to logical argument or empirical evidence, both of which are at the core of scientific reasoning. As Kuhn and Park wrote:

> By adolescence typically comes the likelihood of a radical change in epistemological under-standing. In a word, everyone now becomes right. The discovery that reasonable people—even experts—disagree is the likely source of recognizing the uncertain, subjective aspect of knowing … Adolescents typically fall into 'a poisoned well of doubt' … and they fall hard and deep. (Kuhn & Park, 2005, p. 113)

What is going on here? We saw in Chapter 11 that during middle childhood, children come to understand beliefs as alternative interpretations of reality. It is as though, having achieved this understanding, ado-lescents now treat all interpretations as equal.

Research in this area of "epistemological understanding" owes a lot to the work of William Perry (1970), who described a trajectory of movement among university undergraduates in their understanding of the knowledge they were learning in their classes. Their journey began with a "dualistic" conception of knowledge (as either right and wrong), moved to a "multiplistic" stance (that one opinion is as good as another), then to "relativism" (an understanding that knowledge is contingent and contextual), and finally to "commitment within relativism" (an affirmation of one specific position).

Writing of an adolescent in the relativistic position, Perry illustrated this way of understanding knowledge:

> He 'realizes' that the world, instead of being divided between right and wrong, is divided between those things about which right/wrong can be determined and those about which not even Authority knows. In this new domain of indeterminacy, where 'Everyone has a right to his own opinion,' he feels a new freedom. In this domain no one can be called wrong because the right is unknown. By implication all opinions are equally valid. This broad tolerance provides for peace in the dor-mitory before dawn. At the same time it means that [he] will feel outraged when you question his opinion, especially if you asked for it. (Perry, 1985, p. 5)

Relativism was, in Perry's view, the consequence of a new self-consciousness on the part of the ado-lescent: a consciousness of being active in the construction of knowledge. The adolescent had come to recognize that every act of knowing involves taking a point of view. But then, surely every point of view has its own validity?

In other words, the adolescent becomes aware of something that we have emphasized throughout this book: that people actively construct their knowledge of the world in which they live. Strikingly, this awareness has a somewhat traumatic character to it.

The phenomenon of adolescent epistemological relativism has been studied by Michael Chandler. Chandler concludes that most normal adolescents pass through a stage of relativism. He has found that relativism occurs for adolescents who are capable of formal operational reasoning, but not for those who are still reasoning on the concrete operational level. His research indicates that relativism is more com-mon among adolescents who have achieved a more mature ego-identity status (Chandler et al., 1990).

Chandler also suggests that formal operational reasoning leads to an "epistemic loneliness," a sense of isolation and estrangement, to which some adolescents respond with cliquishness and conformity (Chandler, 1975).

It was quickly noted that Perry's research had been conducted almost exclusively with young men. Mary Belenky, Blyth Clinchy, and colleagues set out to explore "women's ways of knowing." They conducted long interviews with more than 100 young women, not only college students but also women who were seeking help from human service agencies. In the responses they identified five epistemological perspectives, which they described in terms of "voice" (Belenky et al., 1986; Hofer & Pintrich, 1997):

1. *A position of silence.* Knowledge is obtained by listening passively to figures of authority.
2. *A position of received knowledge.* Knowledge comes from outside the self, and there is only one truth. This truth can be spoken of, although young women with this perspective tend not to align with the authority they are voicing.
3. *A position of subjective knowledge.* The source of true knowledge is within the self. Truth is seen as an intuitive reaction, personally experienced, rather than an "opinion." Everyone can be right. Everyone can be right. The most trustworthy knowledge comes from personal experience.
4. *A position of procedural knowledge.* True knowledge comes from reasoned reflection and systematic analysis. This knowledge can take either of two forms:

    (a) *Connected knowledge* emerges through care and empathy. This mode of knowing emphasizes understanding over judgment.
    (b) *Separate knowledge* is impersonal and detached. This mode of knowledge is emphasized in traditional university education. Anyone may be wrong.

5. *A position of constructed knowledge.* There is an integration of subjective and objective aspects of knowledge. Knowledge is seen as constructed, and the knower is part of the known. Knowledge is contextual, and depends on the knower's frame of reference.

For Perry, commitment to relativism was an intellectual achievement, an appreciation that not only one's knowledge but also one's relationships, careers, values, and even identity depend upon making a commitment. Belenky and her colleagues proposed, however, that what Perry had discovered was "the way in which a relatively homogeneous group of people are socialized into and make sense of a system of values, standards, and objectives" (p. 15). Their own study, which ventured into various contexts, disclosed not a universal sequence but a series of voices among which young women might move.

One of these voices — that of separate procedural knowledge — resembles what young men told Perry. The other kind of procedural approach, however, while also moving beyond a subjective approach to knowledge, does not abandon subjectivity. It is a step towards involvement and acceptance rather than detachment and analysis. As one young woman explained:

When I have an idea about something, and it differs from the way another person is thinking about it, I'll usually try to look at it from that person's point of view, see how they could say that, why they think that they're right, why it makes sense. (p. 100)

The work of Belenky and her colleagues is valuable in showing that the epistemological and ethical need not be separated, and that young women, in particular, become aware of this. The notion of "care" involves both knowledge and value, because "ideas and values, like children, must be nurtured, cared for, placed in environments that help them grow" (p. 152).

3.2 ETHICAL RELATIVISM: DANGER OR ACHIEVEMENT?

Let us step away from epistemological relativism and return to the ethical relativism that many adolescents arrive at. There have been different interpretations of what this ethical relativism amounts to. Is it a danger? Or is it an achievement?

Kohlberg suggested that ethical relativism is a transitional step beyond understanding society as a system of conventions, with justice and fairness viewed in terms of what is socially acceptable (stage 4), in the direction of a "postconventional" position, in which justice and fairness become understood as principled and independent of the conventions of a particular society (stage 5). In this transitional step, social conventions are rejected because they are considered to be based only on what appears moral in a particular situation. Kohlberg proposed that relativism is a danger and a trap, but one that it is necessary for the adolescent to pass through in order to arrive at a postconventional understanding.

In contrast, Perry proposed that relativism is an *achievement* of adolescence. Relativism, he suggested, is more realistic, more adequate to the complexity of real moral dilemmas. Relativism amounts to a discovery of the problems and dangers in any attempt to base moral judgments on abstract principles.

Larry Nucci, following Turiel, has suggested that relativism during adolescence follows on from a deepening understanding of social conventions, and a growing understanding of societal organization. In their view, relativism is not a danger so much as a necessary step towards a mature understanding of society as built from interactions that are coordinated by conventions.

Figure 14.6 shows the stages that Nucci and Turiel propose characterize understanding of social convention and society from age 5 onward. You will see that this description of stages does not include all the distinctions that in previous chapters we have seen are important: customary practices, verbally agreed conventions, institutional roles defined by rules. It is based on clinical interviews about conventions such as forms of address (calling teachers by their first names), modes of dress (dressing casually in a business office), gender and occupation (a boy wants to become a nurse caring for children), living arrangements (fathers living apart from the family), and modes of eating (with hands or knife and fork). These are largely customs and agreements rather than rules or laws. I will focus on stages 5, 6, and 7.

Nucci and Turiel's stage 5 (which emerges in middle to late adolescence, around 14 to 17 years), involves "understandings in the conventional domain that social norms are constituent elements of social systems" (Nucci, 2001, p. 82). The adolescent now starts to have a systematic conception of society, seeing it not as defined by authorities and their rules, but as a system of organization that controls and guides the interactions of its members. A society has fixed roles, in a hierarchical organization of social positions. Previously, conventions were seen as imposed by authority, and rejected when that authority seemed corrupt or illegitimate. Now, social conventions are seen as regulated and institutionalized within the framework of society. They are normative and binding within a social system; violating a convention can disrupt society, and the moral consequences of this are now evident:

> Informally, you just call any of your friends by their first names, but you really don't have that relation with a teacher. (Turiel, 1983, p. 110)

Next, there occurs the transition to values relativism. This is Nucci and Turiel's stage 6 (corresponding to Kohlberg's stage 4½, at around 17 to 20). There is greater reflection on the societal functions that social conventions serve, and they are increasingly questioned. Conventions are now seen as codified standards of a society, but the necessity of such standards is questioned. Conventions do not in fact serve the functions they are claimed to serve; they have become habitual and unquestioned and are merely perpetuated by tradition.

Finally, with Nucci and Turiel's stage 7 (in adulthood, corresponding to Kohlberg's stage 5), the understanding of conventions changes again. Society is now seen as dependent upon, and constituted by, the interactions among its members. Conventions become viewed as uniformities whose function it is to coordinate these interactions. Conventions amount to knowledge that is shared and agreed-upon by members of a social group, and this shared knowledge enables them to do the everyday work of keeping their society running:

> Conventions make things move along smoothly and also—are most consistently understandable communication. (Turiel, 1998, p. 112)

Nucci explains that these changing conceptions of society and its conventions have consequences for the way someone is scored in Kohlberg's scheme, because the Kohlbergian dilemmas involve both moral and nonmoral concerns. In the case of ethical relativism, the adolescent appears to reason that if morality is based on the conventions—the norms and laws—of a specific society, and these conventions are themselves arbitrary, then morality can be no more than what seems right to a person in a specific situation in society. Ethical relativism stems from the fact that there is not yet any sense of morality being "prior" to society. It is a consequence of the negation of conventions, which itself follows on from a specific understanding of society, as not in fact served by its conventions.

Yet another interpretation of relativism has been offered by Carol Gilligan, who became concerned that Kohlberg's stage theory had unquestioningly adopted the questionable assumption that the endpoint of psychological development is to be independent and separate. As she put it, it valued "an autonomous life of work" over "the interdependence of love and care" (Gilligan, 1977, p. 482). Evidence began to emerge that men and women diverge in their moral development, and that the transition from Stage 3 to Stage 4 is especially problematic for young women. This transition involves a change from understanding morality in terms of interpersonal relations to understanding it in terms of societal laws and rules.

For instance, in a study of high-school students, more girls scored at Stage 3 while more boys scored at Stage 4. Figure 14.6, from Holstein (1976), illustrates young adolescent boys obtaining

1. **Convention as descriptive of social uniformity (5–7 years)** *Stage 1*	Conventions are "reified" as descriptions of empirical regularities. "Women wear dresses, so women ought to wear dresses."
2. **Negation of 1 (8–10 years)** *Stage 2*	Exceptions to conventions are taken as evidence that they are arbitrary. The mere existence of a norm is not sufficient basis for compliance. "Not all women wear dresses."
3. **Convention as affirmations of role system (10–12 years)** *Stage 3*	*Early concrete conception of a social system.* Conventions maintain order. "Drive on the left." Social authorities make rules, which can be changed and vary by context.
4. **Negation of 3 (12–14 years)** *Stage 3B*	Conventions are rejected as "nothing but" social expectations. Since conventions are arbitrary they do not have the force of rules.
5. **Convention as mediated by social system (14–17 years)** *Stage 4*	*Emergence of systematic concepts of social structure.* Conventions are normative and binding within a social system with fixed roles, and a static hierarchy.
6. **Negation of 5 (17–20 years)** *Stage 4½*	Conventions are rejected as "nothing but" societal standards codified through habitual use. They are arbitrary and have no function.
7. **Convention as coordination of social interactions (Adulthood)** *Stage 5*	*Systematic concepts of society.* Conventions are uniformities that are functional in coordinating social interactions. Knowledge of conventions shared by members of social groups facilitates interaction and operation of the system.

Figure 14.6 Stages of understanding of social conventions and society. Kohlberg's stages are indicated in italics in the first column

Source: Author, based on Turiel (1983) & Nucci (2001)

higher scores than adolescent girls, the higher incidence of stage 3 among the girls, and their apparent tendency not to progress to stage 4. Girls and young women apparently did not pass beyond stage 3, or they even "regressed" from stage 4 to stage 3. As Constance Holstein pointed out, however, the definition of stage 3 contains some strikingly stereotypically female characteristics:

> One of the hallmarks of stage 3 reasoning is a stress on compassion, sympathy, or love as a reason for moral action. Another hallmark of stage 3 is a concern for the approval of others, especially those in the primary group [i.e. the family]. (Holstein, 1976, p. 60)

Could it really be that adolescent females are less advanced than adolescent males in their moral judgments? For Gilligan, this pattern of evidence raised the "possibility of a 'sex-related bias' in Kohlberg's scoring system" (Gilligan, 1977, p. 489). Explicitly linking her concerns to Nancy Chodorow's proposals about the child-rearing experiences typical for young girls and young boys (we considered these in Chapters 10 and 12), Gilligan began to explore whether women might have a different perspective on moral problems, and whether they might speak of such problems "in a different voice" (Gilligan, 1977, 1982).

Gilligan interviewed women who had considered or decided upon an abortion, so only some of the participants were adolescents. Nevertheless, her findings help us understand the changes that take place during adolescence in how self and society are understood.

In the responses that her research participants gave to her interviews, which were about real-life moral dilemmas rather than hypothetical ones, Gilligan did see a progression from a preconventional to a conventional and finally to a postconventional moral perspective, but "the conventions that shape women's moral judgments differ from those that apply to men" (1977, p. 492). The young women spoke of selfishness and responsibility, of an obligation to care and not to hurt. Gilligan described the three levels in these terms:

1. *Preconventional*: An initial focus on the self, and on individual survival. For example, "An eighteen-year-old, asked what she thought when she found herself pregnant, replies: 'I really didn't think anything except that I didn't want it. [Why was that?] I didn't want it, I wasn't ready for it, and next year will be my last year and I want to go to school'" (1977, p. 492).

2. *Conventional*: The concept of responsibility now provides the basis for an equilibrium between self and others; the emphasis is now on protection of those who are dependent. The good is caring for other people. The earlier focus on self is now seen as selfishness. For example, "I came to this decision that I was going to have an abortion [because] I realized how much responsibility goes with having a child" (1977, p. 494).

3. *Postconventional*: A moral principle of non-violence becomes central, and the previous focus on caring is now seen as self-sacrifice. For example, a 25-year-old woman explained: "I have a responsibility to myself, and you know, for once I am beginning to realize that that really matters to me … instead of doing what I want for myself and feeling guilty over how selfish I am, you realize that that is a very usual way for people to live … doing what you want to do because you feel that your wants and your needs are important, if to no one else, then to you, and that's reason enough to do something that you want to do" (1977, p. 506).

Gilligan concluded that these considerations of care and intimacy represented a moral voice and perspective that were distinct from the emphasis on autonomous judgment that Kohlberg had seen at the core of morality, and that, as we have seen, has often been placed at the center of theories of children's psychological development. She suggested that it would be too simplistic to assume that the care voice is female, while the judgment voice is male: both males and females have access to both moral perspectives.

This last point is illustrated by a study that used one of Aesop's fables, about a porcupine and a family of moles (see the box below). This implied that the girls and young women who appeared to "regress" from stage 4 to stage 3, were actually progressing:

Results indicate that the Kohlberg regressors are progressors when evaluated against a standard of commitment in relativism instead of absolute principles of justice. Real-life data on the same subjects suggest that this progression is related to actual experiences of moral conflict and choice which lead to the restructuring of moral judgment to a more dialectical mode. (Murphy & Gilligan, 1980, p. 77)

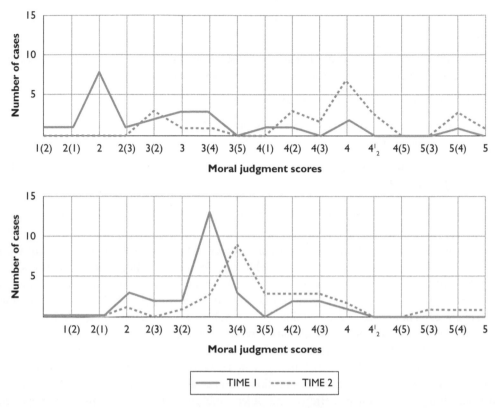

Figure 14.7 Moral judgment scores over a three-year test–retest interval for adolescent males (above) and females (below)

Source: Holstein (1976)

THE FABLE OF THE PORCUPINE AND THE MOLES

It was growing cold and a Porcupine was looking for a home. He found a most desirable cave, but saw it was occupied by a family of Moles.

"Would you mind if I shared your home for the winter?" the Porcupine asked the Moles.

The generous Moles consented, and the Porcupine moved in. But the cave was small, and every time the Moles moved around they were scratched by the Porcupine's sharp quills. The Moles endured

(Continued)

(Continued)

this discomfort as long as they could. Then at last they gathered courage to approach their visitor. "Pray leave," they said, "and let us have our cave to ourselves once again."

"Oh no!" said the Porcupine. "This place suits me very well."

What is the problem? That the porcupine won't leave? Or that there is a disagreement between the porcupine and the moles?

What is the solution? Find a way to get the porcupine out? Or find a way to resolve the conflict so that all involved are happy?

Sixty 11- and 15-year-olds from two schools in a typical middle-class suburb were told this story, and asked to explain the problem and then solve it (Johnston, 1994). The justice perspective offers a way of defining the problem as that the porcupine won't leave, so that the solution would be to find a way to get the porcupine out. The care perspective, in contrast, offers a way of defining the problem as being that there is a disagreement between the porcupine and the moles, so that the solution would be to find a way to resolve the conflict which meant that all those involved were happy.

The majority of the children and adolescents framed the problem in one of these two ways. But when given the opportunity about half (more of the 15- than the 11-year-olds) changed perspective and solved the problem in the other mode. Others did so following a cue about the form a change might take.

Gilligan, along with Lyn Mikel Brown and other colleagues at Harvard University, conducted an intensive study of girls aged from 7 to 16 years of age at a private school in New York State (Brown & Gilligan, 1992). They documented a "moment of resistance" at around 11 years of age, when the girls showed a peak of self-confidence and clarity about their roles and responsibilities in the world. These girls were outspoken and honest.

By age 16, however, the girls' resistance had gone underground. They had become apologetic and hesitant, uncertain of who they were and what they were doing. What had happened, Gilligan and Brown proposed, was that these adolescent young women had begun to experience the dangers of being an outspoken woman in a patriarchal and sexist society. They had learned to hide themselves, out of self-protection. They had learned that silence was safer than speaking out.

3.3 RECONSIDERING ADOLESCENCE

What lessons can we draw from these explorations of adolescent relativism? Carol Gilligan has proposed that developmental researchers ought to reconsider adolescence (Gilligan, 1987). At the start of this chapter I quoted one of her observations:

Thus adolescence is a situation for epistemological crisis, an age when issues of interpretation come to the fore. The turbulence and indeterminacy of adolescence, long noted and often attributed to conflicts over sexuality and aggression, can also be traced to these interpretive problems. (Gilligan, 1987, p. 2)

We saw in Chapter 11 that children in middle childhood grasp that people's beliefs are interpretations of reality. This might seem a step forward, and indeed it is, but it leads to interesting consequences for the way knowledge is understood. What is interpretation? Is it no more than forming an opinion? Does an interpretation reflect a particular point of view? A specific context? A position within society? Can interpretations be questioned and defended? Should they be listened to and tolerated?

These are the kinds of questions that adolescents agonize over. They are at the root of the epistemological crisis of adolescence, and of epistemological relativism, as well as the moral crisis of adolescence with its ethical relativism. For much of adolescence, no distinction appears to be drawn between knowledge and opinion. Knowledge is understood as no more than an individual interpretation of the world, no more than an opinion. As a result, discussion and debate are considered fruitless, because they can never move beyond statements of opinion.

Gilligan has proposed that adolescents feel keenly the involvements with, and commitments to, other people that are at the core of adult life, of adult identity, and of participation in a society. Adolescents are aware of their changing relationship with their parents, and at the same time their relationships with peers and partners are changeable and troubling. How could they not be preoccupied with issues of connection and responsibility?

Yet psychologists have judged the development of these young people in a way that predominantly values detachment, autonomy, and separation. This tendency "encourages a way of speaking in which the interdependence of human life and the reliance of people on one another becomes largely unrepresented or tacit" (Gilligan, 1987, p. 4).

The web of attachments and responsibilities in which we all live presses equally upon male and female adolescents. But, as Gilligan pointed out, "it is women's elaboration of care considerations that reveals the coherence of a care ethic as a framework for decision—its premises as a world view or way of constructing social reality, its logic as a problem-solving strategy, and its significance as a focal point for evaluating actions and thinking about choice" (1987, p. 6). The justice ethic that male adolescents tend to adopt, which insists that everyone be treated equally, tends to render this web invisible.

Furthermore, from a care perspective, what counts as moral conduct is by no means obvious, the nature of moral maturity is not self-evident, and the pathway to moral development is not clear. This lack of clarity suggests an alternative interpretation of the twin phenomena of ethical and epistemological relativism in adolescence. These could be seen as consequences of adopting a critical perspective that challenges the prevailing worldview.

What do I mean by this? In every society, people in disadvantaged positions become more aware of injustice and inequity than those people who occupy positions of power and influence. As Turiel has noted, "people in subordinate positions regularly challenge cultural practices of inequality and unfair restrictions on their personal choices and autonomy" (Turiel, 2012, p. 17).

The adolescents who have been participants in the research investigations described in this section have generally been from advantaged backgrounds. However, adolescents often feel disadvantaged when faced with adult authorities, including researchers who are often also university professors. Could their ethical and epistemological relativism be an appeal, in the face of adult authority, to the importance of listening to all views, all opinions, all voices, all people? Could it be a form of resistance to the adult authority that still prevails in their lives?

Making and sustaining connections with other people requires paying attention to differences in interpretation. This attention is not simply a matter of the logic of formal operations, of reasoning and acting consistently and without contradiction, not simply a matter of argument and evidence, as Kuhn assumes. It is also a matter of perspective, of point of view, and of listening to different voices and sustaining connection. It is about commitment. Adolescent relativism has been to a great degree dismissed. But it may be an attempt to insist on the value of the views of the less powerful, in the face of figures of power and authority. For adolescents are "able to see through false claims to authority at the same time as they yearn for right answers or for someone who will tell them how they should live and what they should do" (Gilligan, 1987, p. 10).

In this section, we have once again used research on moral judgment as a window onto the ways that other people are understood. By late adolescence there is generally an advanced level of reflective and discursive competence: a capability for self-reflection and self-report. This ability to reflect on, and talk about, oneself and one's past is essential for the ability to forge an identity, in the sense of a project for the future, for "It is out of retrospection that a project, an approximation toward desired ends, can be revealed. The shape that emerges out of the past extends itself into the future" (Freeman, 1984, p. 17,

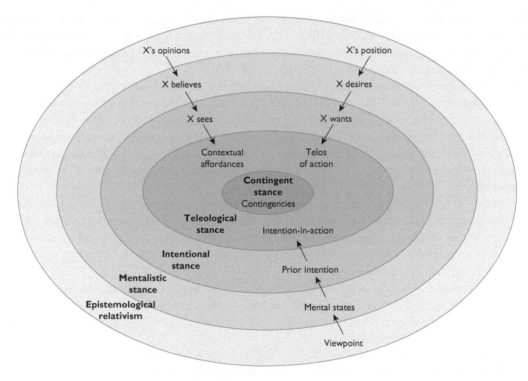

Figure 14.8 The sequence of stances regarding mind

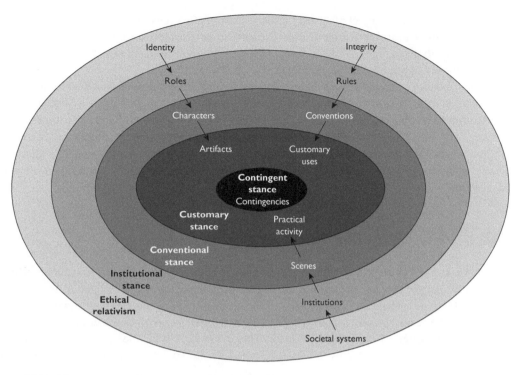

Figure 14.9   The sequence of stances regarding normativity

cited in Tappan, 1989, p. 313). Gilligan has made a similar point, that "In adolescence, when thinking becomes more reflective and more self-conscious, moral orientation may become closely entwined with self-definition, so that the sense of self or feelings of personal integrity become aligned with a particular way of seeing or speaking" (Gilligan, 1987, p. 8).

There are linkages, then, between the considerations in an adolescent's moral judgments and her understanding of her own identity. It is very likely, though there has been no direct research, that there is also a linkage to the terms in which she understands other people. The adolescent can now understand and judge other people's personal integrity, or what she perceives as their insincerity.

However, Gilligan suggests that adolescence is also a time "when the interpretive schemes of the culture, including the system of social norms, values, and roles, impinge more directly on percep-tion and judgment, defining within the framework of a given society what is 'the right way' to see and to feel and to think—the way 'we' think. Thus adolescence is the age when thinking becomes conventional" (1987, p. 8). In earlier stages we have seen action become conventional; now in adolescence thinking can become conventional. Schools teach conventions of interpretation. As Gilligan points out, scores on Kohlberg's scheme of moral judgement are correlated with education, social class and IQ (e.g., Colby et al., 1983). This should give us reason to pause: are poorer people less advanced in their moral judgments? This correlation suggests that Kohlberg's scheme is measuring something that is taught. And the fact that a care orientation does not show this correlation suggests that it may challenge the predominant worldview.

The ethical relativism of adolescence reflects a way of understanding society. Adolescent epistemological relativism reflects a way of understanding other people. Once again, there is a normative stance and a stance for understanding mind. Although there has been little attempt to directly explore the relations between the two, it appears that ethical relativism reflects the adolescent's attention to identity and integrity within societal systems, while epistemological relativism reflects the adolescent's attention to individuals' opinions, understood as following on from the viewpoint given by a position within those societal systems.

4. AND ON TO ADULTHOOD ...

A strong case could be made that this book should have considered the entire human lifespan. Developmental researchers have tended to assume that the endpoint of development is the start of adulthood, and that development is the process of the child achieving adult status. However, it should now be clear to the reader that human psychological development involves the entire span of human life, the cycle of ontogenesis from birth to death. This cycle should be understood not only in terms of the individual who lives and dies, but also in terms of the social relations of reproduction in a community.

There has been an unprecedented increase in life expectancy (see Figure 14.10), and this book has told only part of the story of the human life cycle. As young people become parents and then grandparents, or as they become teachers, coaches, or recognized community figures, their lives intersect and interact with those of children, both their own and those of other people. The stages from infant to adolescent are not separate and distinct from later stages of the life cycle. We have seen that parents and caregivers play a crucial role in a young child's development. Even death has an intimate connection to birth: human life truly is a cycle, albeit one that extends as a helix through time.

Viewed this way, the human life cycle is a process in which:

> persons are formed and dissolved, move between dependent impotence and independent authority, divide and multiply their being through relations with others, know more and less about the world, and acquire and lose the capacity to change it. (Robertson, 1996, p. 591)

It is worth emphasizing one more time that nature and culture are not opposed but operate together, and we can see this in the fact that the human lifespan is longer today than at many times in the past, and in many parts of the world it is growing even longer, probably because nutrition and health care are postponing the senescence programmed into our genes. As a result, many infants will interact not only with parents but also with grandparents and even great-grandparents as never before in human existence.

This intergenerational contact and interaction creates opportunities for a variety of influences on the child, including mentorship, advice, alliances, and a richer density of social relations.

Not only does psychological development not end at age 20, but during the rest of her life a person can also contribute in a variety of ways to the development of the children who are at the various stages that we have considered in this book. There are many things one might say about psychological development during the adult years, given the rich variety of ways that adults live on our planet. I will merely mention briefly some of the ways that adults remain woven into the lives of children and influence their development.

Most obviously, an adult may become a parent and/or caregiver. We have mentioned caregivers frequently in previous chapters, and discussed the developmental consequences of a toddler's attachment to caregivers, and of the different styles of parenting in early and middle childhood. We have talked about the way a caregiver must be an external ego for their child, and then an external superego. In time, too, an adult may also become a grandparent. This is possible, of course, only when longevity has increased to the point where an adult can live for double the length of time it takes to reach reproductive maturity (defined both biologically and culturally). For Homo erectus, this point was reached around age 15, and so if an individual became a parent at 16, they might become a grandparent at age 30 or so. Today in the USA about one-third of adults are grandparents, and the average age at which they become a grandparent is 48.

In addition to contributing as a grandparent to the development of children in one's own family, many adults contribute to children to whom they are not related. Some become teachers, for example. An adult may work in a variety of professions that make a contribution to the lives of children, such as the health professions, law, or social services. Adults can also influence children in less direct ways, by writing books that are read by young people. To pick just one familiar recent example, J. K. Rowling, the author of the *Harry Potter* books, has touched the lives of many children. Other adults work to create the movies and television programs that entertain and educate children, such as the Children's Television Workshop, responsible for *Sesame Street*.

While elderly statespeople may be physically weaker than their younger contemporaries they can be psychologically superior to them in important ways. In many societies it is not an accident that it is the aging and weak who are in charge, not the strong, energetic youth. It is the aged who are often centrally concerned with the formal definition of their culture and understand that it should be imparted to children and young adults. The human lifespan includes a time for learning and a time for teaching, and it is the old who tell stories to the young more than vice versa. The old guide the young, though they also learn from them. The productive life of each and every adult was made possible by their development as a child, but it is equally true that the development of children would not occur in the absence of the parenting, guidance, education, and support that adults provide.

Finally, there is a real sense in which the ultimate contribution an adult can make to the lives of future generations of children is by dying! Odd as this sounds, this last stage in the human life cycle is just as necessary as any other. If human beings did not die, the population of this planet would have become unsustainable a long time ago. There truly is a cycle in which birth and death are closely linked and equally necessary. We cannot understand one without the other.

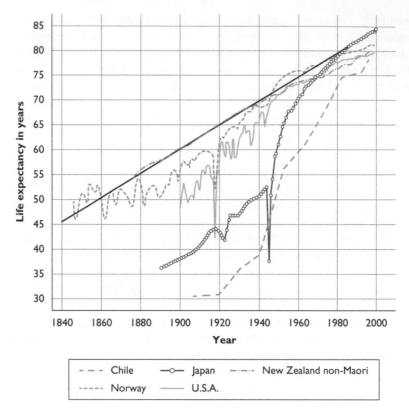

Figure 14.10 Historical change in female life expectancy in selected countries

Source: Oeppen (2002)

CONCLUSION

It is important to recognize that in this chapter we have talked very little about teenagers in societies where adolescence does not exist. In fact, we have talked very little about adolescents who live outside the few societies that have been studied. The predominant focus of research has been middle-class adolescents in the USA. One researcher active in the area of epistemological understanding notes that:

> We know very little about how these schemes replicate in other cultures, whether the developmental trajectory is consistent, or whether higher levels of the schemes in particular are grounded in Western education … and are unlikely to appear in the same sequence elsewhere. (Hofer, 2008, p. 6)

Second, even within this narrow focus there is a great deal of individual variation. As Kuhn has pointed out, this is an age when more than ever before the child has become the driver of her own development. One consequence is that the divergence amongst developmental trajectories becomes even larger.

Adolescence is often viewed as a time during which the primary task is that of forming an identity. Erikson's writings have inspired much research, but only recently has attention been paid to the contributions of social relationships and culture, even though Erikson himself considered these central. Identity involves a new level of self-awareness and a sense of an inner agency, but it also depends on historical and cultural circumstances. The psychological demands that are placed on adolescents today to juggle multiple, often contradictory, social roles surely create confusion and disorder.

An identity is best thought of as a dynamic process that continues throughout life (Beyers & Cok, 2008). It is when identity is challenged that its formation and maintenance become visible. We have seen that at each transition in the course of development the child is transformed, and a differentiation takes place. What makes adolescence such a challenging time is the clash between definitions of who the young person is. Biological, cultural, and psychological kinds of maturity must somehow be reconciled, or at least their divergence must be managed.

We have traced human development from its prenatal beginnings through birth and infancy, toddlerhood and early childhood, through middle childhood, to a point now in the teen years where the growing child has acquired the ability to have children of their own. The fact that often this new capacity is not immediately put into practice only adds to the complexity of the topic of this chapter. Is adolescence a stage? Or is it best thought of as a drawn-out transition and crisis?

Adolescence, then, provides a very clear illustration of the way that culture and biology together define the trajectories and milestones of human development. The end of adolescence is not the end of ontogenesis, of psychological development. Far from it. Instead, what we can see at this point are the contradictions and preoccupations that for most of us define our adult lives. We are capable of sophisticated and complex thinking and creative imagination. We are also capable of impulsive and thoughtless behavior, acts of both kindness and cruelty. We remain concerned to define and discover who we are, in ways that cannot be captured by measures of "commitment" on a questionnaire or statements in an interview. Truly becoming somebody requires more than stating who one wishes to be—it requires dedicated study and hard work. At the end of adolescence the developing human being has still only just begun.

SUMMARY

WHO IS THE ADOLESCENT?

- A primary psychological task of adolescence is defining one's identity.
- In one model, the adolescent passes through a series of identity statuses.
- Erik Erikson insisted that we should not separate identity crisis in individual life and crises in historical development.

(Continued)

(Continued)

- Ethnicity is a key aspect of one's identity.
- There is still debate over whether or not identity is a concept one has about oneself.

PEER CULTURE

- In Western society, it is in the crowds and cliques of peer culture that adolescents begin to form intimate, romantic relationships.
- In many cultures, adults arrange the circumstances of contact between the genders in the teenage years.

UNDERSTANDING OTHER PEOPLE: ETHICAL AND EPISTEMOLOGICAL RELATIVISM

- Often adolescence involves both ethical relativism and epistemological relativism.
- In ethical relativism, values are taken to be a matter of a person's position in society.
- In epistemological relativism, knowledge is viewed as a matter of individual opinion. All opinions should be listened to, but debate is not productive.

ON TO ADULTHOOD ...

- Adulthood is not the end of psychological development. Psychological development is an aspect of the human life cycle.
- Adults contribute centrally to the psychological development of children, not only as caregivers but also as teachers, coaches, and community figures.

CHAPTER 15

SUMMING UP

Humans are massive constructors of developmental environments. By modifying the world, human niche construction creates artefacts and other externally inherited resources that not only act as sources of biological selection on human genes but shape the learning opportunities and developmental trajectories of recipient organisms. (Flynn et al., 2013, p. 299)

INTRODUCTION

In this book I have sought to offer the reader an introduction to a cultural perspective on children's development. As we have seen, this is a perspective which acknowledges that children live, grow, and develop within a community, a society, that is essential for their survival. A society is an environmental niche that a community has constructed in order to live, survive, and reproduce. In this final chapter I will review the central phenomena that have become visible from adopting this cultural perspective on children's development.

We have seen that cultural psychology is not simply a specialized area within psychology, it is a fresh approach to all areas of psychology, whether developmental, cognitive, clinical, or even neurological. A cultural psychology pays attention to the undeniable fact that human beings are cultural animals. We live in culture, we create culture, and we are created by culture. This is not to say that biology plays no part—on the contrary, we have seen in every chapter that culture and biology are woven together so tightly that it is difficult to distinguish one from the other.

We have also seen that a cultural perspective on children's development means thinking about culture not as a causal variable, or as a factor that simply has an influence on psychological processes and that consequently produces differences among children who grow up in different cultures, but instead as having a *constitutive* role in children's development: culture (along with biology, of course) is what *makes possible* the complexity and sophistication of human psychological functioning.

For example, one proposal in cultural psychology has been that humans live and work in "cognitive ecosystems" in which material representations enable us to carry out the processes that have traditionally been attributed to the inner workings of the human mind (Hutchins, 1995). The navigational maps of the Polynesians are one example of such material representations. A modern computer is another. In this way of thinking, cognition is "dispersed" over a person (often several people) and a system of artifacts. Moreover, if the psychological functions work together as a dynamic system there seems to be no reason to restrict this way of thinking only to human cognition. It must be equally true of human emotion, motivation, and perception.

The mind, in this way of thinking, is a "user illusion" (Norretranders, 1991)—merely one way of talking about, and consequently perceiving, our own relationship to the world. A cultural perspective on children's development means avoiding the ontological dualism of mind and matter, mind and body, or mind and world.

The cultural perspective is, then, a fresh approach that helps us understand how human children develop uniquely human abilities without drawing a rigid boundary between ourselves and other animals (by claiming that humans have unique biologically based capacities, for example), and without dividing research in two (insisting that neurobiology has nothing to say to the study of culture and social interactions, for example). What has started to emerge over the past decade or so is an interdisciplinary approach to the study of children's development in context, in diverse contexts, that does not restrict itself to the limited techniques of traditional experimental research design. The fruits of this approach, and this way of thinking, are what I have shared in the chapters of this book.

It has become evident that while cognitive developmental psychology and Piagetian constructivism view the child as developing though the individual construction of knowledge—concepts for the former, schemas for the latter—the cultural perspective views knowledge as only part of the story. The child herself is transformed in the course of her development. This transformation, this constitution, is not an individual process, it is a social process. At the same time, it involves a progressive differentiation from other people, and we have seen the series of transitions of this differentiation that define the stages of development. In the first section I review and summarize these transitions and stages.

At the same time, stages and transitions cannot be separated from the overall trajectory of a child's psychological development. In general terms, this trajectory is always towards the ability to contribute to the reproduction of the community over time. This ability may take the form of parenting the next generation of children, or teaching these children, or other kinds of productivity within the institutions of a society. The precise character of this ability will vary from culture to culture, and we have reviewed some of the attempts to relate developmental trajectories to the form of life of the community—whether its members forage or farm; whether they value independence or interdependence. In the first section, then, I will also review and summarize what we know about trajectories.

We have seen that a human society is composed of institutional facts that define an ontology (which has also been called a cosmology) and a deontology. The culture of a society is made up of this ontology and deontology, and it is crucial for the developing child that she comes to understand these aspects of her society. We have traced, in the chapters of this book, the various steps in the acquisition of this "normative stance," and considered the proposal that it is more fundamental than, and perhaps provides the basis for, "theory of mind." In the section below I summarize and review the stages in development of these two stances, the "normative stance" and "theory of mind," and propose that they are both forms of semiosis.

We humans are not separate from the world in which we live. We are in, and of this world. We are animals, biological organisms, who eat, breathe, and sleep, as well as think, feel, and dream. Psychology makes a mistake if it fails to recognize the embodied and embedded character of human existence. In the third section I review the ways we have seen that children's development has a practical basis, a cycle of perception-and-action that grows in complexity and sophistication. Psychological development is embodied, embedded and distributed.

These three sections are summarized in Figure 15.1.

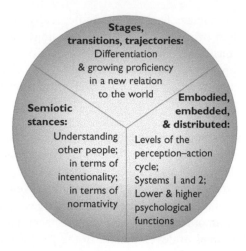

Figure 15.1   The three sections of Chapter 15

1. STAGES, TRANSITIONS, AND TRAJECTORIES

This book has been organized chronologically, as a sequence of stages and transitions. The reader might ask why I would arrange the book in this way if I am trying to break away from the assumption of universal developmental stages. After all, it is common to organize developmental psychology textbooks around a series of stages in a way that combines common-sense divisions of childhood—infant, toddler, preschooler, school-age child, and adolescent—with theoretically grounded distinctions, such as Piaget's famous definitions of sensorimotor, preoperational, concrete operational, and formal operational cognition. The problem with this approach is that these common-sense stages are so everyday and the Piagetian stages are so abstract that together they lose completely the diverse, concrete circumstances in which children live and develop. Piaget's research was conducted for the most part with a very select sample of the children of middle-class Genevans, but even then he abstracted from the concrete circumstances of their lives.

Ideally, I would have presented the reader with a series of portraits of children's stages of development in diverse cultural settings. The state of the research literature is not yet at that point, in my opinion. We have seen how researchers have begun to conceptualize the way different cultures create distinct developmental trajectories. It remains an open question, and a pressing research priority, to what extent these trajectories define sequences of stages that differ from those I have presented in this book.

Today, developmental researchers simply don't yet know enough to describe even one developmental trajectory in detail. The sequence of stages that we have often taken to be universal is that of middle-class families, predominantly white, living in technologically advanced societies. We still can't adequately characterize the development of even those children, let alone do so for children from less well-known circumstances.

Nonetheless, a review of over 1,000 ethnographic reports about children from hundreds of cultures concluded that the majority of those cultures recognize six life phases (Grove & Lancy, 2016). The first phase includes birth, the newborn, and infancy. The second phase begins when caregivers are confident that their child will survive: often the transition from crawling like an animal to walking is recognized as an indication of this. The toddler is then introduced to the community, usually with ceremonies such as a first haircut or naming. Phase three pushes the young child towards independence from caregivers with weaning and toilet training. The young child typically participates more with peers in this phase. The fourth phase entails useful work: children are assigned chores, girls largely within the domestic sphere while boys work more often outside the home. The fifth phase is that of adolescence, which is recognized in variable and flexible ways both within and across cultures. Often adolescence is short, ending when young people begin to live together. When adolescence is longer there is often intergenerational conflict. The sixth phase begins with marriage or the equivalent, and is defined primarily by the successful bearing and raising of children.

These phases correspond sufficiently well with Western definitions of infancy, toddlerhood, early childhood, middle childhood, and adolescence, respectively, to make me reasonably confident that this way of organizing the book has not been unduly insensitive to cultural difference. At least we can now begin to place this sequence in its proper cultural context, and this is what I have tried to do. In each chapter I have compared children in different parts of the world, or in different economic circumstances in the same location, to illustrate the different pathways.

We have seen, then, that in children's development there are periods of relative stability that are interrupted by times of abrupt change. The periods of stability we call **stages**, and the periods of rapid change we call **transitions**. Children's development is an alternation of stages and transitions. Stages are qualitatively distinct from one another, not only in the form of intelligence that the child employs (as Piaget noted), but also in the child's way of being in the world. Each stage involves a specific way of relating to the world and relating to self, and as a result of this a new way of experiencing and understanding.

Transitions are those times when new properties rapidly emerge. A transition is a point of inflection, a crisis. In a transition there is a dramatic change in the child's way of being in the world, so that she discovers new possibilities in that world and gains a new sense of herself—of her abilities and capacities. During the stage that follows, the child progressively masters this new way of living in the world. These transitions are truly changes not only in the child but also in the whole child-caregiver-niche system of which she is a component:

> Anthropologists have long recognized another feature of cultural transitions: They are potentially dangerous as well as hopeful. They represent changes in the social order, in social relationships, and in personal identity, changes in which many in the community have a stake. They are often, therefore, marked through rituals, initiations, ceremonies, and special, culturally marked events. (Weisner, 1996, p. 296)

In addition, cultures define distinct **trajectories** for children's development. A trajectory is the path or route followed by an object, often something that has been thrown. A developmental trajectory is the progression or line of development that is typical for a child in a specific cultural setting. As we shall see, the age at which developmental transitions occur can vary widely across different cultures.

The characteristics of each stage can also vary. The stage of adolescence does not exist in some cultures. We have seen that researchers are paying increasing attention to these different developmental trajectories.

In addition, we have seen that a central aspect of each of the transitions is that they involve **differentiation** and **reintegration** on a higher level. With each new transition the child becomes both more differentiated from the other components of the system in which she lives and at the same time is reintegrated with those other components in a new way, and on a higher level (see Figure 15.2). The preceding chapters can be summarized in these terms.

Prenatal development and birth: These processes of differentiation and reintegration can be seen already in prenatal development and birth (the topics of Chapter 4). Prenatal development, embryogenesis, is a kind of assisted self-assembly. The ovum contains DNA and the sub-cellular mechanisms for transcription and assembly necessary for cell growth, division, and differentiation. The uterus is an environment that provides nutrients and protection.

Researchers are still seeking to answer the question of how together the genetic information in the fertilized egg and the environment of the uterus enable the construction of the complex structure of the human body. In particular, during this process a first distinction appears between developmental

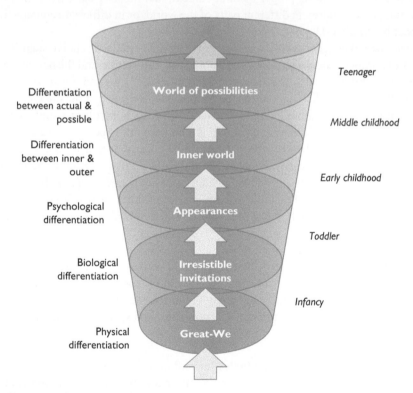

Figure 15.2 Overview of stages and transitions

trajectories: those of the two genders. The placenta is the first ontogenetic niche, constructed to enable the zygote to develop by drawing upon resources provided by the mother's body while still becoming sufficiently independent to permit the separation that will take place at birth.

A central concern during this stage of human development is who gets to have a baby with whom? All societies have customs, rules, and often laws that regulate marriage, conception, and pregnancy. The event of conception, of fertilization, can be explored not only in terms of its biological aspects, but also in terms of its social and cultural aspects. As we have seen repeatedly through the developmental stages, these two are thoroughly interwoven.

We saw how at birth the neonate and her mother become physically separated, though the newborn remains completely dependent on other people and must continue to interact biologically with them (obtaining milk or a substitute food). Birth, then, is a physical differentiation from the mother's body. Newborn and caregiver must then reintegrate in a new way: for example, food is provided by nursing rather than through the umbilical cord. The newborn has inherited the genes to build (with the help of her mother) a body (with a brain) whose design has evolved over millennia. She has also inherited the accumulated artifacts of her community, which she must learn how to use.

Infancy: Chapter 5 explored infancy, the developmental stage from birth to around one year of age, and described how the infant lives within an undifferentiated sociality—the "Great-We." A central theoretical issue here was whether we should think of the infant as knowing the world around her in the form of concepts and theories, or whether it makes more sense to think of her knowledge as a practical and intuitive know-how.

The distinction between these two types of knowledge has been important throughout this book. We considered the growing evidence, both psychological and neurological, for the operation of two different modes of psychological functioning. One is fast, automatic, and operates largely outside of conscious awareness; the other is slower, deliberate, and we are conscious of its operation. Research with children is still scarce, but the available evidence supports the view that infants understand the world around them using the first mode, and that with development the second mode plays a role that grows in importance. In particular, infants seem sensitive to the contingencies of their interaction with the world around them, including with other people.

In addition, an infant's understanding is not differentiated between what is social and what is cognitive, or what is social and what is emotional. Emotionality, as an unreflective evaluation of events, is central, but adults play a central part in this because the infant's abilities to respond are so limited. However, a practical concern at this age is whether or not caregivers should form an emotional connection with their infant. Psychological research has come to place great emphasis on the attachment relationship and its roots during infancy in attentive and responsive parenting. In many societies, however, infant mortality is high and adults avoid forming emotional bonds with their infant children until their survival seems likely. In many societies, ceremonies celebrate the infant "becoming a person," at around 5 or 7 months of age, or even later.

The infant, then, is already learning to master the world of the Great-We, in participation with, and with the aid of, caregivers and members of her family and community. The end of infancy is marked by the first steps, the first words, and a new independence that also carries with it a new sense of vulnerability. It is a biological differentiation from the mother.

Toddlerhood: Becoming able to move independently dramatically changes the infant's way of inhabiting the world, and she becomes a toddler. We considered three aspects of this transition which occurs at an age that varies widely around the world, for walking too is influenced by the caregivers and community, who may encourage and facilitate it, or discourage and restrict it. Her first steps will transform the way the toddler knows the world: her practical intelligence becomes increasingly powerful. Her first words also transform how she interacts with her family. These transformations define a transition that amounts to a biological differentiation, in which the toddler becomes less dependent on other people—since she no longer requires that they move her or hand over what interests her—but in which she seems to become more aware of her continued dependence. The various phenomena of the attachment relationship—fear of strangers, anxiety at separation—raise complex questions about the character of the toddler's bond with caregivers and, once again, the degree to which autonomy or interdependence is the goal of caregiving. A universal concern, however, is when and how to wean the toddler.

Chapter 8 explored how language starts to transform the toddler's relationship to the world. At first the toddler is unable to resist the invitations her environment offers her. Caregivers have to guide her steps and monitor her closely. However, the words of her community's language offer names for things, people, and events that define general categories and draw her attention to shapes. The world becomes composed of permanent objects. At first, she treats these words as part of the things they are used to name, but increasingly she masters the pragmatic and mathetic functions of spoken language (though not yet combining them).

As the toddler participates in a widening range of activities, guided by caregivers, she observes how things are done in her family, and she understands this as how things ought to be done. She begins to recognize the tacit social norms and customs that her family lives by, and she shows a growing ability to understand intention-in-action. She begins to hold other people, and then herself, accountable to these customs: her grasp of normativity is underway.

Towards the end of this stage, the toddler shows a growing ability to understand material representations such as pictures and models. In Chapter 8 we reviewed the debate over whether this means the toddler is now forming mental representations, or whether this semiotic ability is of a different kind. Along with this comes a new consciousness of self: a psychological differentiation takes place.

Early Childhood: The chapters on early childhood—from roughly 3 to 6 years of age—explored how the young child starts to *create* material representations in her pretend play with other children. She is now capable of exploiting the power of words: giving something or someone a new name to change what it counts as being. She turns one thing into another, exercises her imagination in practice, and develops initiative and self-control. Now in her speech she is able to combine the interpersonal and ideational, talking both to influence people and to share her opinions. She starts to go beyond the appearances of the objects and people around her, to grasp a reality that amounts to the cosmology of her community. She is no longer so swayed in her thinking by the way things appear. In addition, speech provides the basis for a new verbal kind of thinking, the result of an "internalization" that involves physiological changes in the brain.

Piaget considered the young child to be inherently egocentric and self-centered, so that development called for socialization. Vygotsky disagreed, proposing that the young child is inherently social and that her development is a matter of *individualization*. Certainly, during this stage the young child starts to understand the intentions that people form prior to acting, and also the conventional scenarios within which people act. She seems to see people now as "characters," kinds of person like the characters in a book. As a consequence she understands more clearly that she too is a kind of person, such as a "sister," or a "girl."

Once again, the discussion of caregiving for young children has centered around the question of whether the goal is always emancipation (as Baumrind proposed) or may also be interdependence (as Kağitcibaşi proposed).

Middle Childhood: The transition between 5 and 7 years of age involves a differentiation within the child. She now hears her own thoughts as inner speech, words "in her mind," and she also applies the distinction between appearance and reality to herself. She starts to learn how to control an "inner space" of private feelings, memories, and thoughts, and she becomes more responsible, more self-controlled, and deliberate, and more able to assume tasks alongside adults.

In many communities, this is how the child will acquire the skills and knowledge she will need as an adult, through the assignment of chores and responsibilities, either in the home or where adults are working in her community. In some cultures this learning takes the form of apprenticeship, where the child learns from a master or mentor. In an increasing number of cultures around the world, the acquisition of skills and knowledge takes place in the institution called *school*. Schools are institutions in which assessment and achievement—usually defined through competition—are central. Outside school, cooperation and interdependence are likely to be more useful and successful. In this regard, the trajectories of development diverge even more markedly than before.

Chapters 11 and 12 explored some of what we know about the psychological consequences of schooling. Schooling appears to have an influence upon one aspect of concrete operational reasoning, logico-mathematical operations, but not upon infralogical operations. Children at this age are guided by their teachers to learn to master the symbolic systems that their culture uses to "simulate" aspects of reality. It is these specialized skills, seemingly, that require a special institution. Learning to read and write is a profound new ability, even if the empirical research doesn't support the claim that doing so guarantees a transformation in one's mode of thinking. It turns out that what is important are the specific practices in which texts are produced and used. Once again, a general cultural tool—in this case the written or printed word—has various implementations, with variable consequences. Vygotsky may have overstated the role of learning to write in the formation of the higher psychological functions. Nonetheless, learning to use this tool requires "recycling" brain circuits that were previously dedicated to older functions.

Children are now able to recognize the ways societal institutions define roles, such as "student" and "teacher," that can be said to operate behind people's behavior. In a similar way the child can also now infer the beliefs and desires that underlie a person's actions, at least according to the folk psychology of Western culture.

There are tremendous opportunities for research with children in the stage of middle childhood. Most of what we know comes only from studying children who attend school, often while they are in school. In addition, much of the research has involved clinical interviews that solicit judgments from the child, in place of observing what they actually do. One consequence is that it is difficult to connect our knowledge of middle childhood with what is known about early childhood, where naturalistic methods have more often been used.

It also should be added that the differentiation between "inner" and "outer" may be characteristic only of cultures for which "mind" belongs to the cosmology. I quoted philosopher Charles Taylor at the start of Chapter 11: this notion of interiority is "a historically limited mode of self interpretation, one which has become dominant in the modern West" (Taylor, 1989, p. 111). There has not yet been research exploring what occurs in middle childhood in cultures with a different mode of self-interpretation.

Adolescence: In many communities, at the end of middle childhood aged around 11 years, the child becomes an adult. Adolescence as a distinct developmental stage has emerged very recently and it not universal across cultures. The dramatic biological changes of puberty mark the acquisition of the biological capacity for reproduction, but like conception (to which it is obviously related) this is also a cultural event, handled energetically but differently by adults in communities around the world. The transition from childhood to adulthood involves both the emergence of the biological capacity for sexual reproduction and the cultural recognition of adult status. In some cultures these two coincide, and the teenager becomes an adult at puberty or only a short time later, in a transition often marked by ceremonies of initiation. In other cultures there is a gap or mismatch between these two: between the biological changes of puberty and the ability and opportunity to take on adult responsibilities. In such cases, adolescence exists as a distinct stage of psychological development—something that has occurred recently in human history (though probably not for the first time).

The world of the adolescent is one of possibilities; indeed one can say that possibility has become more important than reality, or that reality has become just one among many possibilities. The differentiation here is between what is actual and what is possible. This is a stage in which the higher psychological functions become paramount, when an adult identity is formed, and when young people become highly sensitive to what they perceive as the authenticity or insincerity of adults.

Chapters 13 and 14 explored the biological changes of puberty, the historical and cultural character of the definition of adolescence, and some of the psychological tasks that confront an adolescent. We saw how adolescence is a time for exploring possibilities, and also often a time for rejecting the social conventions of society as "mere conventions," in a relativism that is both ethical and epistemological.

Adulthood: There are many ways to be an adult. Whereas Piaget's account of development assumed a single *telos* to development, the achievement of scientific rationality, characterized by what Piaget called formal operational reasoning, there is growing evidence that adults in different cultures not only live in different ways, they also think, perceive, and feel in different ways. They use different kinds of tools, speak different languages, and work in different kinds of social institutions. These diverse adulthoods are stages in the cycle of life, and are both endpoints to ontogenesis and contributions to ontogenesis.

In addition, we have seen how cultures define distinct developmental trajectories for children's development. Researchers are paying increasing attention to these trajectories. A trajectory is the path or route followed by an object, often something that has been thrown. A developmental trajectory is the progression or line of development that is typical for a child in a specific cultural setting. As we have seen, the age at which developmental transitions occur can vary widely across different cultures. In addition, the characteristics of each stage can vary.

For example, attachment theorists assume that the goal of caregiving is to foster autonomy and independence in the child. However, as we saw in Chapter 5, researchers have identified distinct styles of interaction between caregiver and infant, which they have named proximal and distal styles. These styles involve different patterns of contingencies, in which infants are encouraged to become the kind of person that is valued in their community.

Traditional farming communities, for example, generally value interdependence and obedience, and caregivers interact with infants and toddlers with the proximal style. The family model encourages compliance and tends to lead to a heteronomous-related self.

Urban families, in contrast, tend to value autonomy and independence. So too do nomadic pastorals, such as the Fulani. Caregivers practice the distal style of interaction with infants and toddlers. This style encourages self-sufficiency and an autonomous-separate kind of self. The family model here is one that values independence.

We also saw that other values characterize families that move from the countryside to urban settings. Here the family model of psychological interdependence encourages control, order, and autonomy along with continued connection, and tends to lead to an autonomous-related self—a child and young person who can make their own decisions but also maintain close bonds with their family. No clear style of interaction with infants has been indentified in such families: I will assume that it is a "mixed" style.

These are distinct trajectories of development, grounded in the family's relationship to ecological circumstances and to the economic system of their society. The social-biofeedback in these different styles quickly leads to developmental differences, such as the presence or absence of social smiling from 2 months of age.

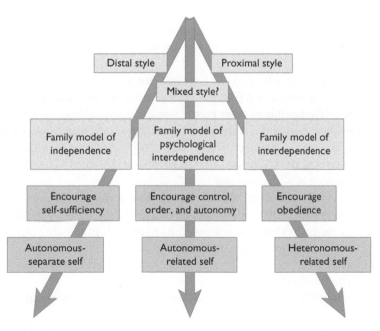

Figure 15.3 Developmental trajectories

2. SEMIOTIC STANCES

I want now to focus on one aspect of the stages that we have studied, namely the sequence of interpretive stances that children adopt as they learn to understand the other people with whom they live. The societies that humans have created—the niches we have constructed—are complex and sophisticated. Even a hunter-gather society, such as that of the !Kung, is composed of customs, verbal agreements, laws (oral rather than written but still with compelling force), and institutions such as the kinship group. Every society involves a way of living on and in the community's territory, and this generally entails transformation of the land.

To survive in her society, a child needs to become able to recognize its institutional facts, and to manage and create them. We have seen that children adopt two sequences of stances in which they understand other people both in terms of their intentions, beliefs and desires, and in terms of the normativity of their society. These two sequences are summarized in the Figure 15.4 and 15.5.

Theory of Mind: We have seen how an infant adopts a *contingent stance*, recognizing the contingencies between one action or event and another. As a toddler she then adopts a *teleological stance*, understanding other people in terms of their *intention in action*. The toddler does not focus on consequences and overlook intentions, as is often proposed, she intuits the teleology of an action from its character and its consequences, within the affordances of the local context. This is how even 3-year-olds can distinguish between accidental and deliberate actions.

We saw next how the young child begins to adopt an *intentional stance*, understanding other people in terms of *prior intentions*. We also saw that researchers have often not recognized the distinction between mental states and prior intentions, with the consequence that they have conflated the intentional stance and the mentalistic stance. Prior intentions are identified on the basis of what a person sees, and what they want.

By middle childhood, a child will generally have adopted a *mentalistic stance*, understanding other people by attributing to them private and personal *mental states* of belief and desire.

In adolescence, the understanding of other people deepens again, as both beliefs and values are seen as products of interpretation, and in this sense are viewed as opinions that follow on from adopting the viewpoint from a specific position in society. This means adopting, at least for a time, a stance of *epistemological relativism*, a critical attitude towards the authorities of the society in which they live, in which they insist that every opinion is worth listening to.

Normative Stance: At the same time, the developing child is paying attention to the normativity of her society. We have seen in the preceding chapters that there is growing evidence that children's understanding of normativity passes systematically through a sequence of important stances.

In infancy, it is, once again, *contingency* that is paid attention to.

Then, in what I have called the *customary stance*, the toddler starts to recognize the *customary uses* of simple artifacts in practical activity.

The young child adopts the *conventional stance*, attending to the conventional actions of characters in familiar scenes.

Around 6 years of age she starts to understand the *roles and responsibilities* that are defined by the rules of social institutions, adopting the *institutional stance*.

In her teenage years, with a deepening understanding of societal systems of institutions, she adopts a stance of *ethical relativism*, in which she pays attention to the identities that people construct within society, as well as their integrity or insincerity.

In short, to live in a society involves recognizing (1) natural features of the environment, (2) implements with customary functions and uses, (3) the purposeful actions that are performed in conventional social interactions, (4) the roles and statuses that are defined by social institutions, and (5) the societal systems within which people make a commitment to a particular identity. Cultural psychologists have tended to focus on customary activities with implements—tools and signs—but the other levels are equally important.

These two sequences of stances indicate children's growing ability to understand and interpret the various levels at which their culture is organized. Clearly the two types of stance are interrelated. As they develop, children move beyond the prereflective interactions of infancy and toddlerhood, in which they simply acted spontaneously in routine and repetitive interactive sequences. As toddlers they are able to navigate the social matrix in which they find themselves using embodied skills, with the ability to perceive intentions-in-action but no need to understand other people's beliefs or reasons for acting. By early childhood, language has become a resource for young children to discuss, recollect, and imagine their divergent interests and concerns. In middle childhood, children become able to understand a person's role within an institution such as school, or the Scouts, or a baseball team. This understanding is still embodied, but it is imaginatively freed from the immediate concrete context. It is based on active participation rather than the construction of theories of mind (Martin et al., 2008). This is now a reflective intersubjectivity, where multiple perspectives can be grasped simultaneously within intersubjective transactions.

Dennet defined a stance as a cognitive-perceptual filter or bias that influences how a person interprets events. But one could equally say that a stance is a specific manner of interpretation, a form of semiosis.

This semiosis is guided by the deontology of a culture. For example, at the most basic level there are simply the contingencies of what goes together, of what works practically. On the second level, artifacts are used as implements whose functions are governed by social norms or customs. One eats with a spoon by holding the handle in a particular way. These norms or customs are implicit and usually unspoken. On the third level, routine social interactions in recognizable situations involve conventions that define appropriate actions, such as how to greet someone when meeting them. On the fourth level, institutions employ explicit rules and laws that define the responsibilities and powers of people who occupy roles within the institution. At the fifth and most complex level of semiosis, the societal systems of a community define what constitutes a worthwhile way to live.

Children's psychological development involves not only physical growth and biological change, but also increasingly sophisticated ways of thinking, not to mention emotional relationships with significant other people, and changing roles and responsibilities in family and community. In order to understand the complex interconnections among these various aspects of the developmental process it is tremendously helpful to recognize the child's changing semiotic abilities. The way a child understands and interprets the world she lives in is key to how she thinks, feels, and acts.

In this book I have described ontogenesis, the development of children, as a movement through this series of levels of semiosis. At each stage new aspects of the social world become evident, and there is also a new and deeper understanding of the rights and wrongs that every culture defines. Every society, with its culture, can be understood on a series of levels of semiosis, of increasing complexity and sophistication. At each level of semiosis, a different kind of entity is perceived: objects, tools, situations, institutions, traditions. At each level, specific kinds of obligations and responsibilities are also recognized: contingencies, customs, conventions, rules and laws, traditions. The child, as she develops, learns to understand and grasp the artifacts of her culture and employ them in terms of these obligations and responsibilities. However, we currently know very little about variations in this sequence from one culture to another; important and interesting research will be done here.

	"Theory of Mind"		Normative Stance	
Infancy 0–12 months	Contingent stance	Contingencies	Contingent stance	Contingencies
Toddler 1–2.5 years	Teleological stance	Intention-in-action Telos of action Contextual affordances	Customary stance	Artifacts Customary uses Practical activity
Early childhood 2.5–6 years	Intentional stance	Prior intention X wants X sees	Conventional stance	Scenes Conventions Characters
Middle childhood 6–12 years	Mentalistic stance	Mental states X desires X believes	Institutional stance	Institutions Rules Roles
Adolescence 12–	Epistemo-logical relativism	X's opinions X's position Viewpoint	Ethical relativism	Societal systems Identity Integrity

Figure 15.4 The two sequences of stances summarized

3. EMBODIED, EMBEDDED, AND DISTRIBUTED

Classic theories of cognition … regard the human brain as an information processing machine operating on mental representations in the form of amodal encapsulated entities independent from the perceptions and actions of the agent interacting with the world. … As such, symbolic theories of knowledge representation postulate a separation between world, body, and mind.

Non-symbolic theories of cognition are significantly different from this classic view. They draw the focus away from the mind as a universal Turing Machine, with the body as its mere input–output interface, toward the view that cognition relies on the experiences of the whole organism in its constant interactions with the environment. Crucially, according to this view, it takes both the body and the world to form, integrate, and retrieve knowledge. (Myachykov et al., 2013, pp. 1–2)

When psychology was first emerging as a scientific discipline, many of its central figures recognized the role and importance of culture in human life. There was a general view that what distinguishes us from other animals is culture, and that while we share the "lower psychological functions" with our animal relatives, so that these abilities can be studied using the techniques of the natural sciences, the "higher psychological functions" call for a special kind of study. Wilhelm Wundt (1832–1920), the man often considered the "father" of experimental psychology, called this study "cultural psychology." Language, works of art, myths, and customs are, in Wundt's view, beyond the reach of experimentation. Cultural products such as these, he believed, are "spiritual" in character. Between 1900 and 1910, Wundt published ten volumes on *Volkerpsychologie*, "An investigation of the laws of the development of language, myth, and custom" (Wundt, 1910).

This recognition of our human ability to create works that no other animal is capable of was important, and it seems often to have been forgotten in psychology since then. However, it had the effect of separating psychology into two branches. This division was strongly opposed by Lev Vygotsky, the Russian psychologist of the early twentieth century whose work has had a strong influence on cultural psychology today. We have seen that Vygotsky diagnosed the psychology of his time as suffering from a disease that he called dualism, and the line that Wundt drew between experimental psychology and cultural psychology was an example of dualism.

Today, cultural psychology does not reject experimentation, nor does it view the biological aspect of human functioning as somehow inferior. As we have seen, it studies *both* the lower psychological functions and the higher psychological functions.

In the chapters of this book we have come across these distinct levels in the guise of various different conceptualizations. They have been described in terms of levels of the perception–action cycle, as System 1 and System 2, as infralogical and logico-mathematical processes, and as lower psychological functions and higher psychological functions.

In this book I have followed Vygotsky's advice and sought to offer an account of child development that rests upon a non-dualistic ontology (Packer & Goicoechea, 2000). It is undeniable that human beings are material organisms living in a material world, and it is surely an undeniable fact that humans have consciousness. It would be a mistake, however, to assume that consciousness somehow exists "in the mind." Instead, the logical way to view consciousness is that it is an aspect of the way a human being lives in the world. The experience of "having a mind" is, I have suggested, something that appears at a certain age and not before, and it is the product of a particular ethnopsychology or folk psychology—a particular way of interpreting other people's behavior and one's own experience that is not found in every culture.

It must be acknowledged, however, that in psychology there is currently a fierce debate over whether or not mental states and mental representations exist. The assumption that psychology is the study of mental states has been at the core of the discipline since cognitive psychology battled behaviorism in the 1950s, but today more and more people are questioning this assumption. I have tried to describe fairly the debate taking place today, but I have argued for the position that I consider to be the logical consequence of following Vygotsky's advice to eliminate dualism.

The model of brain functioning that we adopt has significant implications for the ways we then think about human knowledge, about human psychology, and about children's development. If the brain is like a digital computer, processing formal representations, it follows that human knowledge about the world is made up of these representations: as we've seen, these are usually referred to as "models," "concepts," and even "theories." And then it is only a small step to assume that our experience is made up of "mental states" in which we are conscious of these formal representations. In other words, the *computational view of the brain* is linked to a *representational view of knowledge* and a *mental state view of consciousness*. This has been the **cognitive developmental model of brain and mind**.

On the other hand, if the embodied brain and the environment form a unified system, and the brain functions as one component within this system, then at least one kind of human knowledge about the world would seem to be practical know-how—the skilled capability to get around in specific environments without needing to form representations. And it will seem more likely that human experience is not composed of mental states, instead, it is the way we become conscious of our embodied involvement and interaction with the world. In other words, the *embodied view of the brain* is linked to a *non-representational view of knowledge* and an *emergent view of consciousness*. This is the **cultural developmental model of brain and mind**.

These alternative views of the brain and their linkages (see Figure 15.5) have important implications for the study of children's development, which we have explored in detail in the preceding chapters. There is increasing empirical evidence and conceptual analysis in support of the second of these views, and one reason for writing this book has been to explore the degree to which we can now construct a compelling account of children's development in terms of this cultural developmental model.

The weight of evidence supports the view that the embodied brain functions as a semiotic device, recognizing and reading signs, and responding appropriately. As we have seen, this semiosis occurs on a series of levels, and with various degrees of awareness (unconscious, conscious, and self-conscious). A child becomes able to unconsciously and unthinkingly interpret the signs within perceptual input so as to experience a stable world of enduring entities. She becomes able to recognize, among these entities, the characteristics that define the function of an artifact that make it a tool. She becomes able to grasp the purpose of a controlled behavior that defines it as a conventional social action: a greeting, for example. She becomes able to interpret the social standing of a person who is enacting a specific role. Each of these abilities is a way of interpreting aspects

Cognitive Perspective	Cultural Perspective
The brain operates as a digital computer	The brain is a component of the body-environment system, the perception–action cycle: embodied and embedded
Knowledge is formal representation (models, concepts, theories) of an external world	Knowledge is grounded in practical know-how
Experience is composed of mental states	Experience is emergent: we become conscious of aspects of our living in the world

Figure 15.5 Two contrasting perspectives on the brain, knowledge, and human experience

of the world, and each is a kind of semiosis. These developments have been a central theme in each of the chapters in this book.

These processes of interpretation, then, are evident as a series of semiotic stances, in which a child understands people in terms of both intentionality and in terms of normativity, and these stances are important aspects of the larger movements through stages and transitions that define a child's psychological development. These interpretive processes are, as we have seen, embodied and embedded. They depend upon the fact that a child's brain and body are directly involved in the environment in which she lives—an environment which her community has constructed.

In addition, these processes are distributed: they depend on the fact that every child lives with and depends upon other people. We have seen this most clearly in the case of emotion, but it is surely also true of the other psychological functions. In our discussion of infancy we saw how the components of each emotion—physiological changes, evaluation, feeling, behavior—are distributed between infant and adults. The infant is operating with system 1 components (the lower psychological functions), but caregivers are able to provide the system 2 components (the higher psychological functions). The balance of this distribution of abilities between infant and caregivers shifts over time, as the child becomes more aware and deliberate in her emotions. But without the adult's contribution, this growth in abilities on the part of the child would not be possible.

CONCLUSION

Theories of children's development have generally been a-cultural, assuming that development is the same the world over. The value of studying children's development in various societies is not simply that this gives us a glimpse of how other people live. Cross-cultural research also serves to help us recognize that the way children develop in our own culture is not "natural," it is based on specific shared goals for how children should behave and develop (Gaskins, 2006).

A cultural perspective seeks to understand the interrelationship between culture and children's psychological functioning. Some social scientists have argued that culture is built on the foundation of fundamental psychological characteristics, so that it is simply a product of human nature (e.g., Schaller & Crandall, 2012). For example, it has been suggested that adult culture depends on children's culture and children's psychology:

> Many adult cultural beliefs, I suggest, are sustained precisely because of the way the child's mind is organized and the way children organize their own cultural environments. Many cultural forms are stable and widely distributed just because children find them easy to think and easy to learn … Pursuing this argument affords an informative yet unappreciated perspective on the relationship between individual psychological phenomena and their role in the constitution of cultural forms. (Hirschfeld, 2002, p. 611)

There is certainly some truth to the proposal that children's psychology places constraints on the possible form any culture can take. But it is equally true to say that what children find easy to learn depends on the culture in which they live. Individual psychological phenomena play a role in the constitution of culture, but at the same time culture plays a role in the constitution of human psychological phenomena. For example, we have seen that the higher psychological functions—deliberate memorization, for example—are consequences of a child's participation in culture. At the same time, functions such as this make possible the reproduction of culture.

There is every reason to think that the process through which children become adults is open-ended and changing (Toren, 1993). Children will become adults tomorrow who are different from adults today. Furthermore, human history truly extends back to the first creatures called Homo sapiens, even though written historical records date back only a few thousand years.

As one historian has put it, "The 'upward' link from developing individual to the evolving 'context' is just as important as (if more elusive than) the 'downward' link from evolving context to developing individual" (Modell, 2000, p. 102). In the chapters that make up this book I have tried to capture this dynamic interaction between the developing child and her changing context: child and family, child and peer group, child and school, and so on. At each stage of development the child is herself is a growing, dynamic organism. But as this organism adapts to the environment at the same time there is "exaptation" of that environment (exaptation is the process in which features acquire functions for which they were not originally adapted or selected), and what I mean is that the developing child is able to discover new possibilities in her environment, possibilities of which adults are unaware. Any adequate developmental psychology textbook must pay attention to this two-way interaction.

Furthermore, this is not simply a matter of paying attention to context. What is required is more than a description of the child plus a description of the context, that gives a particular kind of attention to the relationship between the two, and explores "how changing contexts affect what children appropriate from them and how children's appropriations modify the very contexts that guide development" (Modell, 2000, p. 83). The choices that face a child are defined by her context (including, of course, the other people in her life), but at the same time her choices transform that context.

Children's psychological development is important not only for the children themselves but for all of us. It is a critical aspect of the reproduction that is essential to the continued existence of human beings—like any other species. And because humans can only live together in a society with a culture, collaborating and cooperating, the psychological development of human children is a complex and extended process.

Living in society is much more than cognition, than reasoning, than logic. It is all these things, but at the same time it is coming to recognize the complex institutional facts, the cosmology, the culture that the society has formed—its particular ontology and deontology. Children learn to reason, and they also learn what to reason about: the things of their society. They reason about mental states and social statuses, and the complex social relationships in which they participate. They reason about mathematical entities and physical processes. They progressively make sense of the contingencies they find themselves involved in, identifying causes, customs, permanence, convention, and laws (both physical and societal).

A child must acquire the capacity for reproduction, and the human capacity for reproduction has both a biological side and a cultural side. We have seen the tensions that come when these two do not coincide: it is called adolescence. The acquisition of this capacity itself has a biological side and a cultural side, in which it would be pointless to try to distinguish nature from nurture. Human nature is constituted. It is human nature to be social, to live in society, to live in culture.

Cultures lead to differences in children's development. But at the same time culture is universal. The cultural perspective on human development pays attention to the differences, the various trajectories that open up for children in different societies around the world. But equally importantly culture, especially language, plays a constitutive role in children's development. The cultural perspective discloses the essential involvement of culture in children's psychological development.

REFERENCES

Adolph, K. E., Vereijken, B., & Shrout, P. E. (2003). What changes in infant walking and why. *Child Development*, *74*(2), 475–497.

Aichhorn, M., Perner, J., Kronbichler, M., Staffen, W., & Ladurner, G. (2006). Do visual perspective tasks need theory of mind? *Neuroimage*, *30*(3), 1059–1068.

Ainsworth, M. D. S. (1967). *Infancy in Uganda: Infant Care and the Growth of Love*. Baltimore, MD: Johns Hopkins University Press.

Ainsworth, M. D. S. (1969). Object relations, dependency, and attachment: A theoretical review of the infant–mother relationship. *Child Development*, *40*(4), 969–1025.

Ainsworth, M. D. S., & Bell, S. M. (1970). Attachment, exploration, and separation: Illustrated by the behavior of one-year-olds in a strange situation. *Child Development*, *41*(1), 49–67.

Ainsworth, M. D. S., Bell, S. M., & Stayton, D. (1974). Infant–mother attachment and social development: Socialization as a product of reciprocal responsiveness to signals. In M. P. M. Richards (ed.), *The Integration of a Child into a Social World* (pp. 99–135). Cambridge: Cambridge University Press.

Ainsworth, M. D. S., Blehar, M. C., Waters, E., & Wall, S. (1978). *Patterns of Attachment: A Psychological Study of the Strange Situation*. Mahwah, NJ: Erlbaum.

Albino, R. C., & Thompson, V. (1956). The effects of sudden weaning on Zulu children. *British Journal of Medical Psychology*, *29*, 177–210.

Allport, S. (2002). Women who eat dirt. *Gastronomica*, *2*(2), 28–37.

Als, H., Tronick, E., Lester, B. M., & Brazelton, T. B. (1977). The Brazelton neonatal behavioral assessment scale (BNBAS). *Journal of Abnormal Child Psychology*, *5*(3), 215–229.

Alvarez-Buylla, A., & García-Verdugo, J. M. (2002). Neurogenesis in adult subventricular zone. *Journal of Neuroscience*, *22*(3), 629–634.

Ambert, A.-M. (1994). An international perspective on parenting: Social change and social constructs. *Journal of Marriage and the Family*, *56*(3), 529–543.

Anscombe, G. E. M. (1957). *Intention*. Cambridge, MA: Harvard University Press.

Apgar, V. (1966). The newborn (Apgar) scoring system. *Pediatric Clinics of North America*, *13*(3), 645–650.

Aptekar, L. (1988). Street children of Colombia. *Journal of Early Adolescence*, *8*(3), 225–241.

Aptekar, L. (1990). Family structure and adolescence: The case of the Colombian street children. *Journal of Adolescent Research*, *5*(1), 67–81.

Ardila, A. (2008). On the evolutionary origins of executive functions. *Brain and Cognition*, *68*(1), 92–99.

Aries, P. (1962). *Centuries of Childhood: A Social History of Family Life*. New York: Vintage.

Armstrong, E. (1991). The limbic system and culture: An allometric analysis of the neocortex and limbic nuclei. *Human Nature*, *2*(2), 117–136.

Arnett, J. J. (2000). Emerging adulthood: A theory of development from the late teens through the twenties. *American Psychologist*, *55*(5), 469–480.

Atkinson, Q. D. (2011). Phonemic diversity supports a serial founder effect model of language expansion from Africa. *Science*, *332*, 346–349.

Atran, S., Medin, D., & Ross, N. (2004). Evolution and devolution of knowledge: A tale of two biologies. *Journal of the Royal Anthropological Institute*, *10*(2), 395–421.

Atran, S. (1998). Folk biology and the anthropology of science: Cognitive universals and cultural particulars. *Behavioral and Brain Sciences*, *21*(04), 547–569.

Atran, S., Medin, D., Lynch, E., Vapnarsky, V., Ek', E. U., & Sousa, P. (2001). Folkbiology doesn't come from folkpsychology: Evidence from Yukatek Maya in cross-cultural perspective. *Journal of Cognition and Culture*, *1*(1), 3–42.

Atran, S., Medin, D., & Ross, N. O. (2005). The cultural mind: Environmental decision making and cultural modeling within and across populations. *Psychological Review*, *112*(4), 744–776.

Austin, J. L. (1975). *How to Do Things with Words* (2nd edn). Cambridge, MA: Harvard University Press.

Avis, J., & Harris, P. L. (1991). Belief-desire reasoning among Baka children: Evidence for a universal conception of mind. *Child Development*, *62*(3), 460–467.

Azevedo, F. A., Carvalho, L. R., Grinberg, L. T., Farfel, J. M., Ferretti, R. E., Leite, R. E. et al. (2009). Equal numbers of neuronal and nonneuronal cells make the human brain an isometrically scaled-up primate brain. *Journal of Comparative Neurology*, *513*(5), 532–541.

Baillargeon, R. (1993). The object concept revisited: New directions in the investigation of infants' physical knowledge. In C. Granrud (ed.), *Visual Perception and Cognition in Infancy* (pp. 265–315). Hillsdale, NJ: Erlbaum.

Baillargeon, R. (2004). Infants reasoning about hidden objects: Evidence for event-general and event-specific expectations. *Developmental Science*, *7*(4), 391–414.

Bainbridge, D. (2009). *Teenagers: A Natural History*. Vancouver: Greystone Books.

Baldwin, D. A., & Moses, L. J. (1996). The ontogeny of social information gathering. *Child Development*, *67*(5), 1915–1939.

Balter, M. (2012). Did Neandertals truly bury their dead? *Science*, *337*, 1443–1444.

Baltes, P. B., Reuter-Lorenz, P. A., & Rösler, F. (2006). *Lifespan Development and the Brain: The Perspective of Biocultural Co-constructivism*. Cambridge: Cambridge University Press.

Bamford, S. C., & Leach, J. (eds). (2009). *Kinship and Beyond: The Genealogical Model Reconsidered*. New York: Berghahn Books.

Bandura, A. (1973). *Aggression: A Social Learning Analysis*. Englewood Cliffs, NJ: Prentice-Hall.

Bandura, A. (1986). *Social Foundations of Thought and Action: A Social Cognitive Theory*. Englewood Cliffs, NJ: Prentice-Hall.

Bandura, A., & McClelland, D. C. (1977). *Social Learning Theory*. Englewood Cliffs, NJ: Prentice-Hall.

Bargh, J. A., & Chartrand, T. L. (1999). The unbearable automaticity of being. *American Psychologist*, *54*(7), 462.

Barry, H., Child, I. L., & Bacon, M. K. (1959). Relation of child training to subsistence economy. *American Anthropologist*, *61*(1), 51–63.

Barsalou, L. W. (2008). Grounded cognition. *Annual Review of Psychology*, *59*, 617–645.

Bates, E., Benigni, L., Bretherton, I., Camaioni, L., & Volterra, V. (1977). From gesture to the first word: On cognitive and social prerequisites. In M. Lewis & L. A. Rosenblum (eds), *Interaction, Conversation, and the Development of Language* (pp. 247–307). New York: Wiley.

Bates, E., Camaioni, L., & Volterra, V. (1979). The acquisition of performatives prior to speech. In E. Ochs & B. B. Schieffelin (eds), *Developmental Pragmatics* (pp. 111–129). New York: Academic.

Bateson, P., Gluckman, P., & Hanson, M. (2014). The biology of developmental plasticity and the Predictive Adaptive Response hypothesis. *Journal of Physiology, 592*(11), 2357–2368.

Baumrind, D. (1966). Effects of authoritative parental control on child behavior. *Child Development, 37*(4), 887–907.

Baumrind, D. (1991). The influence of parenting style on adolescent competence and substance use. *Journal of Early Adolescence, 11*(1), 56–95.

Bayertz, K., & Roughley, N. (eds), *The Normative Animal? On the Anthropological Significance of Social, Moral and Linguistic Norms.* Oxford: Oxford University Press.

Baynes, K., & Gazzaniga, M. S. (2000). Consciousness, introspection, and the split-brain: The two minds/one body problem. *The New Cognitive Neurosciences, 2*, 1355–1368.

Bechler, M. E., & ffrench-Constant, C. (2014). A new wrap for neuronal activity? *Science, 344*(6183), 480–481.

Behne, T., Carpenter, M., Call, J., & Tomasello, M. (2005). Unwilling versus unable: Infants' understanding of intentional action. *Developmental Psychology, 41*(2), 328–337.

Behne, T., Carpenter, M., Gräfenhain, M., Liebal, K., Liszkowski, U., Moll, H., et al. (2008). Cultural learning and cultural creation. In U. Müller, J. I. M. Carpendale, N. Budwig, & B. Sokol (eds), *Social Life and Social Knowledge: Toward a Process Account of Development* (pp. 65–103). New York: Erlbaum.

Behrens, K. Y., Hesse, E., & Main, M. (2007). Mothers' attachment status as determined by the Adult Attachment Interview predicts their 6-year-olds' reunion responses: A study conducted in Japan. *Developmental Psychology, 43*(6), 1553–1567.

Belenky, M. F., Clinchy, B. M., Goldberger, N. R., & Tarule, J. M. (1986). *Women's Ways of Knowing: The Development of Self, Voice, and Mind.* New York: Basic Books.

Bell, S. M., & Ainsworth, M. D. (1972). Infant crying and maternal responsiveness. *Child Development, 43*(4), 1171–1190.

Belsky, J., Steinberg, L., & Draper, P. (1991). Childhood experience, interpersonal development, and reproductive strategy: An evolutionary theory of socialization. *Child Development, 62*(4), 647–670.

Belsky, J., Woodworth, S., & Crnic, K. (1996). Trouble in the second year: Three questions about family interaction. *Child Development, 67*(2), 556–578.

Bem, S. L. (1989). Genital knowledge and gender constancy in preschool children. *Child Development, 60*, 649–662.

Berry, J. W., & Sam, D. (1997). Acculturation and adaptation. In J. W. Berry, M. H. Segall, & C. Kagitcibasi (eds), *Handbook of Cross-cultural Psychology. Volume 3: Social Behavior and Applications* (pp. 291–326). Boston, MA: Allyn & Bacon.

Berry, J. W., Poortinga, Y. H., Segall, M. H., & Dasen, P. R. (1992). *Cross-cultural Psychology: Research and Applications.* New York: Cambridge University Press.

Berti, A. E., & Bombi, A. S. (1988). *The Child's Construction of Economics.* New York: Cambridge University Press.

Bertin, E., & Striano, T. (2006). The still-face response in newborn, 1.5-, and 3-month-old infants. *Infant Behavioral Development, 29*(2), 294–297.

Berzonsky, M. D. (1989). Identity style conceptualization and measurement. *Journal of Adolescent Research, 4*(3), 268–282.

Berzonsky, M. D. (1990). Self-construction over the life-span: A process perspective on identity formation. *Advances in Personal Construct Psychology, 1*, 155–186.

Berzonsky, M. D. (2004). Identity processing style, self-construction, and personal epistemic assumptions: A social-cognitive perspective. *European Journal of Developmental Psychology, 1*(4), 303–315.

Berzonsky, M. D., & Adams, G. R. (1999). Reevaluating the identity status paradigm: Still useful after 35 years. *Developmental Review, 19*(4), 557–590.

Beyers, W., & Cok, F. (2008). Adolescent self and identity development in context. *Journal of Adolescence, 31*(2), 147–150.

Beyers, W., & Goossens, L. (2008). Dynamics of perceived parenting and identity formation in late adolescence. *Journal of Adolescence, 31*(2), 165–184.

Biemiller, A. (2005). Size and sequence in vocabulary development: Implications for choosing words for primary grade vocabulary instruction. In E. H. Hiebert & M. L. Kamil (eds), *Teaching and Learning Vocabulary: Bringing Research to Practice* (pp. 223–242). Mahwah, NJ: Erlbaum.

Bird, D. W., & Bird, R. B. (2002). Children on the reef: Slow learning or strategic foraging? *Human Nature, 13*(2), 269–297.

Biringen, Z., Emde, R. N., Campos, J. J., & Appelbaum, M. I. (1995). Affective reorganization in the infant, the mother, and the dyad: The role of upright locomotion and its timing. *Child Development, 66*(2), 499–514.

Bischof-Kohler, D. (2012). Empathy and self-recognition in phylogenetic and ontogenetic perspective. *Emotion Review, 4*(1), 40–48.

Bixler, R. H. (1982). Sibling incest in the royal families of Egypt, Peru, and Hawaii. *Journal of Sex Research, 18*(3), 264–281.

Black, R. E., Morris, S. S., & Bryce, J. (2003). Where and why are 10 million children dying every year? *The Lancet, 361*(9376), 2226–2234.

Bloch, M. (2008). Why religion is nothing special but is central. *Philosophical Transactions of The Royal Society B: Biological Sciences, 363*(1499), 2055–2061.

Bloom, L. (1991). *Language Development from Two to Three.* New York: Cambridge University Press.

Bloom, L. (1998). Language acquisition in its developmental context. In D. Kuhn & R. Siegler (eds), *Handbook of Child Psychology. Volume 2: Cognition, Perception and Language* (pp. 309–370). New York: Wiley.

Bloom, P., & German, T. P. (2000). Two reasons to abandon the false belief task as a test of theory of mind. *Cognition, 77*(1), B25–31.

Blurton Jones, N. (1972). Comparative aspects of mother–child contact. In N. Blurton Jones (ed.), *Ethological Studies of Child Behaviour* (pp. 305–328). Cambridge: Cambridge University Press.

Blurton-Jones, N. (1986). Bushman birth spacing: A test for optimal interbirth intervals. *Ethology and Sociobiology, 7*(2), 91–105.

Bogin, B. (1999). Evolutionary perspective on human growth. *Annual Review of Anthropology, 28*, 109–153.

Bogin, B., & Smith, B. H. (2000). Evolution of the human life cycle. In S. Stinson, B. Bogin, R. Huss-Ashmore, & D. O'Rourke (eds), *Human Biology: An Evolutionary Perspective* (pp. 377–424). New York: Wiley-Liss.

Bogin, B., Wall, M., & MacVean, R. B. (1992). Longitudinal analysis of adolescent growth of *Ladino* and Mayan school children in Guatemala: Effects of environment and sex. *American Journal of Physical Anthropology, 89*(4), 447–457.

Bolhuis, J. J., Brown, G. R., Richardson, R. C., & Laland, K. N. (2011). Darwin in mind: New opportunities for evolutionary psychology. *PLoS Biology, 9*(7), e1001109.

Bornstein, M. H. (2002). Parenting infants. In M. H. Bornstein (ed.), *Handbook of Parenting: Volume 1: Children and Parenting* (pp. 3–44). Mahwah, NJ: Erlbaum.

Bornstein, M. H. (ed.). (2010). *Handbook of Cultural Developmental Science* (2nd edn). New York: Taylor & Francis.

Boroditsky, L. (2011). How language shapes thought. *Scientific American, 304*(2), 62–65.

Bowlby, J. (1951). Maternal care and mental health. *Bulletin of the World Health Organization, 3*(3), whole number, 355–533.

Bowlby, J. (1958). The nature of the child's tie to his mother. *International Journal of Psycho-Analysis, 39*, 350–373.

Bowlby, J. (1969). *Attachment and Loss. Volume 1: Attachment.* London: Hogarth.

Bowlby, J. (1980). *Attachment and Loss. Volume 3: Loss, Sadness and Depression.* New York: Basic.

Bowlby, J. (1982). Attachment and loss: Retrospect and prospect. *American Journal of Orthopsychiatry, 52*(4), 664–678.

Boysen, S. T., Berntson, G. G., Hannan, M. B., & Cacioppo, J. T. (1996). Quantity-based interference and symbolic representations in chimpanzees (*Pan troglodytes*). *Journal of Experimental Psychology: Animal Behavior Processes, 22*(1), 76.

Boysen, S. T., Mukobi, K. L., & Berntson, G. G. (1999). Overcoming response bias using symbolic representations of number by chimpanzees (*Pan troglodytes*). *Animal Learning & Behavior, 27*(2), 229–235.

Brady, K. W., & Goodman, J. C. (2014). The type, but not the amount, of information available influences toddlers' fast mapping and retention of new words. *American Journal of Speech-Language Pathology, 23*(2), 120–133.

Braine, M. D. S. (1963). The ontogeny of English phrase structure: The first phase. *Language: Journal of the Linguistic Society of America, 39*(1), 1–13.

Branco, T., & Häusser, M. (2010). The single dendritic branch as a fundamental functional unit in the nervous system. *Current Opinion in Neurobiology, 20*(4), 494–502.

Brazelton, T. B., & Nugent, J. K. (1995). *Neonatal Behavioral Assessment Scale* (3rd edn). Vol. 137. London: Mac Keith Press.

Bretherton, I. (1992). The origins of attachment theory: John Bowlby and Mary Ainsworth. *Developmental Psychology, 28*(5), 759–775.

Broch, H. B. (1990). *Growing up Agreeably: Bonerate Childhood Observed.* Honolulu: University of Hawaii Press.

Bronfenbrenner, U. (1977). Toward an experimental ecology of human development. *American Psychologist, 32*(7), 513–531.

Bronfenbrenner, U. (1970). *Two Worlds of Childhood: U.S. and U.S.S.R.* New York: Russell Sage Foundation.

Bronfenbrenner, U., Kessel, F., Kessen, W., & White, S. (1986). Toward a critical social history of developmental psychology: A propaedeutic discussion. *American Psychologist, 41*(11), 1218–1230.

Brown, A. L. (1977). Development, schooling and the acquisition of knowledge about knowledge. In R. C. Anderson, R. J. Spiro, & W. E. Montague (eds), *Schooling and the Acquisition of Knowledge* (pp. 241–253). Hillsdale, NJ: Erlbaum.

Brown, B. B. (1990). Peer groups and peer cultures. In S. S. Feldman & G. R. Elliott (eds), *At the Threshold: The Developing Adolescent* (pp. 171–196). Cambridge, MA: Harvard University Press.

Brown, L. M., & Gilligan, C. (1992). *Meeting at the Crossroads: Women's Psychology and Girls' Development.* Cambridge, MA: Harvard University Press.

Brown, R. (1970). *Psycholinguistics: Selected Papers by Roger Brown.* New York: The Free Press.

Brown, R. (1973). *A First Language: The Early Stages.* Cambridge, MA: Harvard University Press.

Brown, R., & Fraser, C. (1964). The acquisition of syntax. *Monographs of the Society for Research in Child Development, 29*, 43–79.

Bruner, J. S. (1964). The course of cognitive growth. *American Psychologist*, *19*(1), 1–15.

Bruner, J. S. (1990). *Acts of Meaning*. Cambridge, MA: Harvard University Press.

Bruner, J. S. (1997). Celebrating divergence: Piaget and Vygotsky. *Human Development*, *40*, 63–73.

Bruner, J. S. (1996). *The Culture of Education*. Cambridge, MA: Harvard University Press.

Bunce, L., & Harris, P. L. (2014). Is it real? The development of judgments about authenticity and ontological status. *Cognitive Development*, *32*, 110–119.

Buchler, J. (ed.) (1955). *Philosophical Writings of Peirce*. New York: Dover.

Burlingame, W. V. (1970). The youth culture. In E. D. Evans (ed.), *Adolescents: Readings in Behavior and Development* (pp. 131–149). Hinsdale, IL: Dryden.

Byrnes, J. P. (1988). Formal operations: A systematic reformulation. *Developmental Review*, *8*(1), 66–87.

Byrnes, J. P. (1992). Meaningful logic: Developmental perspectives. In H. Beilin & P. Pufall (eds), *Piaget's Theory: Prospects and Possibilities* (pp. 163–184). Hillsdale, NJ: Erlbaum.

Cahan, S., Greenbaum, C., Artman, L., Deluya, N., & Gappel-Gilon, Y. (2008). The differential effects of age and first grade schooling on the development of infralogical and logico-mathematical concrete operations. *Cognitive Development*, *23*(2), 258–277.

Callaghan, T., Moll, H., Rakoczy, H., Warneken, F., Liszkowski, U., Behne, T., et al. (2011). Early social cognition in three cultural contexts. *Monographs for the Society for Research in Child Development*, *76*(2), whole number.

Callaghan, T., Rochat, P., Lillard, A., Claux, M. L., Odden, H., Itakura, S., et al. (2005). Synchrony in the onset of mental-state reasoning: Evidence from five cultures. *Psychological Science*, *16*(5), 378–384.

Callaway, E. (2014). Bone technique redrafts prehistory. *Nature*, *512*, 242.

Campos, J. J., Anderson, D. I., Barbu-Roth, M. A., Hubbard, E. M., Hertenstein, M. J., & Witherington, D. (2000). Travel broadens the mind. *Infancy*, *1*(2), 149–219.

Campos, J. J., Mumme, D. L., Kermoian, R., & Campos, R. G. (1994). A functionalist perspective on the nature of emotion. *Monographs of the Society for Research in Child Development*, *59*(2–3), 284–303.

Camras, L. A., & Shutter, J. M. (2010). Emotional facial expressions in infancy. *Emotion Review*, *2*(2), 120–129.

Carlson, S. M., Mandell, D. J., & Williams, L. (2004). Executive function and theory of mind: Stability and prediction from ages 2 to 3. *Developmental Psychology*, *40*(6), 1105.

Carpendale, J. I., & Chandler, M. J. (1996). On the distinction between false belief understanding and subscribing to an interpretive theory of mind. *Child Development*, *67*(4), 1686–1706.

Carpendale, J. I., & Lewis, C. (2004). Constructing an understanding of mind: The development of children's social understanding within social interaction. *Behavioral and Brain Sciences*, *27*(1), 79–96.

Carraher, T. N., & Carraher, D. W. (1981). Do Piagetian stages describe the reasoning of unschooled adults? *The Quarterly Newsletter of the Laboratory of Comparative Human Cognition*, *3*(4), 61–68.

Casey, B. J., Jones, R. M., & Hare, T. A. (2008). The adolescent brain. *Annals of the New York Academy of Sciences*, *1124*(1), 111–126.

Caspari, R., & Lee, S.-H. (2004). Older age becomes common late in human evolution. *Proceedings of the National Academy of Sciences*, *101*(30), 10895–10900.

Caspari, R., & Lee, S.-H. (2006). Is human longevity a consequence of cultural change or modern biology? *American Journal of Physical Anthropology*, *129*(4), 512–517.

Cassidy, J., & Berlin, L. J. (1994). The insecure/ambivalent pattern of attachment: Theory and research. *Child Development*, *65*(4), 971–991.

Cassidy, J., & Shaver, P. R. (2008). *Handbook of Attachment: Theory, Research, and Clinical Applications* (2nd edn). New York: Guilford.

Caudill, W., & Plath, D. W. (1966). Who sleeps by whom? Parent–child involvement in urban Japanese families. *Psychiatry: Interpersonal and Biological Processes*, *29*(4), 344–366.

Ceci, S. J. (1991). How much does schooling influence general intelligence and its cognitive components? A reassessment of the evidence. *Developmental Psychology*, *27*(5), 703.

Cetina, K. K., Schatzki, T. R., & Von Savigny, E. (2005). *The Practice Turn in Contemporary Theory*. London: Routledge.

Chandler, M. J. (1975). Relativism and the problem of epistemological loneliness. *Human Development*, *18*(3), 171–180.

Chandler, M., Boyes, M., & Ball, L. (1990). Relativism and stations of epistemic doubt. *Journal of Experimental Child Psychology*, *50*(3), 370–395.

Chandler, M., Sokol, B. W., & Wainryb, C. (2000). Beliefs about truth and beliefs about rightness. *Child Development*, *71*(1), 91–97.

Chen, X., French, D. C., & Schneider, B. H. (2006). *Peer Relationships in Cultural Context*. Cambridge: Cambridge University Press.

Chen, X., Hastings, P. D., Rubin, K. H., Chen, H., Cen, G., & Stewart, S. L. (1998). Child-rearing attitudes and behavioral inhibition in Chinese and Canadian toddlers: A cross-cultural study. *Developmental Psychology*, *34*(4), 677–686.

Chick, C. F., & Reyna, V. F. (2012). A fuzzy trace theory of adolescent risk taking: Beyond self-control and sensation seeking. In V. F. Reyna, S. B. Chapman, M. R. Dougherty, & J. Confrey (eds), *The Adolescent Brain: Learning, Reasoning, and Decision Making* (pp. 379–428). Washington, DC: American Psychological Association.

Chisholm, J. S. (1980). Development and adaptation in infancy. *New Directions for Child and Adolescent Development*, *1980*(8), 15–30.

Chisholm, J. S. (1993). Death, hope, and sex: Life-history theory and the development of reproductive strategies. *Current Anthropology*, *34*(1), 1–24.

Chisholm, J. S. (2009). *Navajo Infancy: An Ethological Study of Child Development*. Piscataway, NJ: Aldine Transaction. (Original work published 1983.)

Chodorow, N. (1999). *The Reproduction of Mothering: Psychoanalysis and the Sociology of Gender*. Berkeley, CA: University of California Press. (Original work published 1978.)

Chodorow, N. (2001). Family structure and feminine personality. In D. M. Juschka (ed.), *Feminism in the Study of Religion: A Reader* (pp. 43–66). London: Continuum.

Choi, S., & Gopnik, A. (1995). Early acquisition of verbs in Korean: A cross-linguistic study. *Journal of Child Language*, *22*(03), 497–529.

Chomsky, N. (1956). Three models for the description of language. *IRE Transactions on Information Theory*, *2*(3), 113–124.

Chomsky, N. (1957). *Syntactic Structures*. The Hague: Mouton.

Chomsky, N. (1965). *Aspects of the Theory of Syntax*. Cambridge, MA: MIT Press.

Chomsky, N. (1984). *Modular Approaches to the Study of the Mind*. San Diego, CA: San Diego State University Press.

Chowdhury, A. K. M. A., Huffman, S. L., & Curlin, G. T. (1977). Malnutrition, menarche, and marriage in rural Bangladesh. *Biodemography and Social Biology*, *24*(4), 316–325.

Chudek, M., & Henrich, J. (2011). Culture–gene coevolution, norm-psychology and the emergence of human prosociality. *Trends in Cognitive Sciences*, *15*(5), 218–226.

Clark, A. (2006). Material symbols. *Philosophical Psychology*, *19*(3), 1–17.

Clark, A. (1998). *Being There: Putting Brain, Body, and World Together Again*. Cambridge, MA: MIT Press.

Clark, A. (2006). Language, embodiment, and the cognitive niche. *Trends in Cognitive Sciences, 10*(8), 370–374.

Clément, F., Bernard, S., & Kaufmann, L. (2011). Social cognition is not reducible to theory of mind: When children use deontic rules to predict the behaviour of others. *British Journal of Developmental Psychology, 29*(Pt 4), 910–928.

Colby, A., Kohlberg, L., Gibbs, J., Lieberman, M., Fischer, K., & Saltzstein, H. D. (1983). A longitudinal study of moral judgment. *Monographs of the Society for Research in Child Development, 48*(1/2), 1–124.

Cole, M. (1990a). Cognitive development and formal schooling: The evidence from cross-cultural research. In L. Moll (ed.), *Vygotsky and Education: Instructional Implications and Applications of Sociohistorical Psychology* (pp. 89–110). Cambridge: Cambridge University Press.

Cole, M. (1990b). Cultural psychology: A once and future discipline? In J. J. Berman (ed.), *Nebraksa Symposium on Motivation 1989*. Lincoln, NE: University of Nebraska Press.

Cole, M. (1991). A cultural theory of development: What does it imply about the application of scientific research? *Learning and Instruction, 1*(3), 187–200.

Cole, M. (1995). The supra-individual envelope of development: Activity and practice, situation and context. *New Directions for Child Development, 67*(Spring), 105–118.

Cole, M. (1996). *Cultural Psychology: A Once and Future Discipline*. Cambridge, MA: Harvard University Press.

Cole, M. (2007). Phylogeny and cultural history in ontogeny. *Journal of Physiology Paris, 101*(4–6), 236–246.

Cole, M., & D'Andrade, R. (1982). The influence of schooling on concept formation: Some preliminary conclusions. *The Quarterly Newsletter of the Laboratory of Comparative Human Cognition, 4*(2), 19–26.

Cole, M., Gay, J., Glick, J. A., & Sharp, D. W. (1971). *The Cultural Context of Learning and Thinking*. New York: Basic.

Cole, M., & Packer, M. (2016). Design-based intervention research as the science of the doubly artificial. *Journal of the Learning Sciences, 25*(4), 503–530.

Cole, M., & Scribner, S. (1977). Cross-cultural studies of memory and cognition. In R. V. Kail & J. W. Hagen (eds), *Perspectives on the Development of Memory and Cognition* (pp. 239–271). Hillsdale, NJ: Erlbaum.

Cole, M., Sharp, D. W., & Lave, C. (1976). The cognitive consequences of education: Some empirical evidence and theoretical misgivings. *The Urban Review, 9*(4), 218–233.

Cole, M., & Wertsch, J. V. (2011). Freedom and constraint in human action. *Journal of Russian and East European Psychology, 49*(4), 5–30.

Cole, P. M., Bruschi, C. J., & Tamang, B. L. (2002). Cultural differences in children's emotional reactions to difficult situations. *Child Development, 73*(3), 983–986.

Cole, P. M., Walker, A. R., & Lama-Tamang, M. S. (2006). Emotional aspects of peer relations among children in rural Nepal. In X. Chen, D. C. French, & B. H. Schneider (eds), *Peer Relationships in Cultural Context* (pp. 148–169). Cambridge: Cambridge University Press.

Coleman, J. S. (1959). Academic achievement and the structure of competition. *Harvard Educational Review, 29*(4), 330–351.

Coley, J. D. (1995). Emerging differentiation of folkbiology and folkpsychology: Attributions of biological and psychological properties to living things. *Child Development, 66*(6), 1856–1874.

Collins, W. A. (2003). More than myth: The developmental significance of romantic relationships during adolescence. *Journal of Research on Adolescence, 13*(1), 1–24.

Collins, W. A., Madsen, S. D., & Susman-Stillman, A. (2002). Parenting during middle childhood. In M. Bornstein (ed.), *Handbook of Parenting: Volume 1: Children and Parenting* (pp. 73–102). Mahwah, NJ: Erlbaum.

Collins, W. A., Welsh, D. P., & Furman, W. (2009). Adolescent romantic relationships. *Annual Review of Psychology*, *60*, 631–652.

Colunga, E., Smith, L. B., & Gasser, M. (2009). Correlation versus prediction in children's word learning: Cross-linguistic evidence and simulations. *Language and Cognition*, *1*(2), 197–217.

Condon, R. G. (1990). The rise of adolescence: Social change and life stage dilemmas in the central Canadian arctic. *Human Organization*, *49*(3), 266–278.

Condon, R. G., & Scaglion, R. (1982). The ecology of human birth seasonally. *Human Ecology*, *10*(4), 495–511.

Conger, J. J., & Galambos, N. L. (1997). *Adolescence and Youth: Psychological Development in a Changing World* (5th edn). Harlow: Longman.

Conklin, H. (1949). Bamboo literacy on Mindoro. *Pacific Discovery*, *2*(4), 4–11.

Connolly, J., Craig, W., Goldberg, A., & Pepler, D. (2004). Mixed-gender groups, dating, and romantic relationships in early adolescence. *Journal of Research on Adolescence*, *14*(2), 185–207.

Connolly, J., & Goldberg, A. (1999). Romantic relationships in adolescence: The role of friends and peers in their emergence and development. In W. Furman, B. B. Brown, & C. Feiring (eds), *The Development of Romantic Relationships in Adolescence* (pp. 266–290). Cambridge: Cambridge University Press.

Corkum, V., & Moore, C. (1998). The origins of joint visual attention in infants. *Developmental Psychology*, *34*(1), 28–38.

Corsaro, W. (1979). Young children's conception of status and role. *Sociology of Education*, *52*(1), 46–59.

Corsaro, W. (2006). Qualitative research on children's peer relations in cultural context. In X. Chen, D. C. French, & B. H. Schneider (eds), *Peer Relationships in Cultural Context* (pp. 96–122). Cambridge: Cambridge University Press.

Corsaro, W., & Eder, D. (1990). Children's peer cultures. *Annual Review of Sociology*, *16*, 197–220.

Corsaro, W., & Molinari, L. (2000). Priming events and Italian children's transition from preschool to elementary school: Representations and action. *Social Psychology Quarterly*, *63*(1), 16–33.

Corsaro, W., & Nelson, E. (2003). Children's collective activities and peer culture in early literacy in American and Italian preschools. *Sociology of Education*, *76*(3), 209–227.

Cosmides, L., & Tooby, J. (1997). The modular nature of human intelligence. In A. B. Scheibel & J. W. Schopf (eds), *The Origin and Evolution of Intelligence* (pp. 71–101). Burlington, MA: Jones & Bartlett Publishers.

Côté, J. E. (2009). Identity formation and self-development in adolescence. In R. M. Lerner & L. Steinberg (eds), *Handbook of Adolescent Psychology. Vol 1: Individual Bases of Adolescent Development* (pp. 266–304). Hoboken, NJ: Wiley.

Côté, J. E., & Schwartz, S. J. (2002). Comparing psychological and sociological approaches to identity: Identity status, identity capital, and the individualization process. *Journal of Adolescence*, *25*(6), 571–586.

Cowen, E. L., Pederson, A., Babigian, H., Izzo, L. D., & Trost, M. A. (1973). Long-term follow-up of early detected vulnerable children. *Journal of Consulting and Clinical Psychology*, *41*, 438–446.

Crocetti, E., Rubini, M., Luyckx, K., & Meeus, W. (2008). Identity formation in early and middle adolescents from various ethnic groups: From three dimensions to five statuses. *Journal of Youth and Adolescence*, *37*(8), 983–996.

Crockett, L. J. (1997). Cultural, historical, and subcultural contexts of adolescence: Implications for health and development. In J. Schulenberg, J. L. Maggs, & K. Hurrelmann (eds), *Health Risks and Developmental Transitions During Adolescence* (pp. 23–53). Cambridge: Cambridge University Press.

Dalgleish, T. (2004). The emotional brain. *Nature Reviews: Neuroscience*, *5*(7), 583–589.

Damasio, A. (2003). Feelings of emotion and the self. *Annals of the New York Academy of Sciences*, *1001*(1), 253–261.

Darling, N., & Steinberg, L. (1993). Parenting style as context: An integrative model. *Psychological Bulletin*, *113*(3), 487.

Darwin, C. (2002). *The Expression of the Emotions in Man and Animals*. New York: Oxford University Press. (Original work published 1872.)

Dasen, P. R. (1972). Cross-cultural Piagetian research: A summary. *Journal of Cross-Cultural Psychology*, *3*(1), 23–40.

Davis, N. Z. (2008). Women on top. In J. B. Collins & K. L. Taylor (eds), *Early Modern Europe: Issues and Interpretations* (pp. 398–411). Oxford: Blackwell.

De Neys, W. (2006). Dual processing in reasoning: Two systems but one reasoner. *Psychological Science*, *17*(5), 428–433.

De Saussure, F. (1915). *Course in General Linguistics*. New York: Philosophical Library.

de Wolff, M. S., & van IJzendoorn, M. H. (1997). Sensitivity and attachment: A meta-analysis on parental antecedents of infant attachment. *Child Development*, *68*(4), 571–591.

Dediu, D., & Levinson, S. C. (2013). On the antiquity of language: The reinterpretation of Neandertal linguistic capacities and its consequences. *Frontiers in Psychology*, *4*, 1–17.

Dehaene, S. (2009). *Reading in the Brain: The New Science of How We Read*. Harmondsworth: Penguin.

Dehaene, S., & Cohen, L. (2007). Cultural recycling of cortical maps. *Neuron*, *56*(2), 384–398.

Dehaene, S., Cohen, L., Morais, J., & Kolinsky, R. (2015). Illiterate to literate: Behavioural and cerebral changes induced by reading acquisition. *Nature Reviews Neuroscience*, *16*(4), 234–244.

DeLoache, J. S. (2004). Becoming symbol-minded. *Trends in Cognitive Sciences*, *8*(2), 66–70.

DeLoache, J. S. (2011). Early development of the understanding and use of symbolic artifacts. In U. Goswami (ed.), *The Wiley-Blackwell Handbook of Childhood Cognitive Development* (pp. 312–336). Oxford:Wiley.

DeLoache, J. S., Pierroutsakos, S. L., Uttal, D. H., Rosengren, K. S., & Gottlieb, A. (1998). Grasping the nature of pictures. *Psychological Science*, *9*(3), 205–210.

Dennett, D. C. (1978). Three kinds of intentional psychology. In R. J. Stainton (ed.), *Perspectives in the Philosophy of Language: A Concise Anthology* (pp. 163–186). Peterborough, ON: Broadview Press

Dennett, D. C. (1989). *The Intentional Stance*. Cambridge, MA: MIT Press.

Dettwyler, K. A. (2004). When to wean: Biological versus cultural perspectives. *Clinical Obstetrics and Gynecology*, *47*(3), 712–723.

Diamond, A. (1985). Development of the ability to use recall to guide action, as indicated by infants' performance on A˘B. *Child Development*, *56*(4), 868–883.

Diamond, A. (2000). Close interrelation of motor development and cognitive development and of the cerebellum and prefrontal cortex. *Child Development*, *71*(1), 44–56.

Dixon, J. C. (1957). Development of self recognition. *Journal of Genetic Psychology*, *91*(2), 251–256.

Dor, D., & Jablonka, E. (2010). Plasticity and canalization in the evolution of linguistic communication: An evolutionary developmental approach. In R. K. Larson, V. Deprez, & H. Yamakido (eds), *The Evolution of Human Language: Biolinguistic Perspectives* (pp. 135–147). Cambridge: Cambridge University Press.

Dorner, L. M., Orellana, M. F., & Jimenez, R. (2008). 'It's one of those things that you do to help the family': Language brokering and the development of immigrant adolescents. *Journal of Adolescent Research*, *23*(5), 515–543.

Dreeben, R. (1968). *On What is Learned in School*. Reading, MA: Addison-Wesley.

Duckworth, E. (1979). Either we're too early and they can't learn it or we're too late and they know it already: The dilemma of 'Applying Piaget'. *Harvard Educational Review*, *49*(3), 297–312.

Dunn, J. (1990). The beginnings of moral understanding: Development in the second year. In J. Kagan & S. Lamb (eds), *The Emergence of Morality in Young Children* (pp. 91–112). Chicago: University of Chicago Press.

Dunn, J., Brown, J., Slomkowski, C., Tesla, C., & Youngblade, L. (1991). Young children's understanding of other people's feelings and beliefs: Individual differences and their antecedents. *Child Development*, *62*(6), 1352–1366.

Dunn, J., & Munn, P. (1985). Becoming a family member: Family conflict and the development of social understanding in the second year. *Child Development*, *56*(2), 480–492.

Dunphy, D. C. (1963). The social structure of urban adolescent peer groups. *Sociometry*, *26*(2), 230–246.

Duranti, A. (2008). Further reflections on reading other minds. *Anthropological Quarterly*, *81*(2), 483–494.

Durkheim, E. (1895). *The Rules of Sociological Method*. New York: Free Press.

Durrett, M. E., Otaki, M., & Richards, P. (1984). Attachment and the mother's perception of support from the father. *International Journal of Behavioral Development*, *7*(2), 167–176.

Edmond, K. M., Zandoh, C., Quigley, M. A., Amenga-Etego, S., Owusu-Agyei, S., & Kirkwood, B. R. (2006). Delayed breastfeeding initiation increases risk of neonatal mortality. *Pediatrics*, *117*(3), e380–e386.

Edwards, C. P., & Liu, W.-L. (2002). Parenting toddlers. In M. H. Bornstein (ed.), *Handbook of Parenting: Volume 1: Children and Parenting* (pp. 45–71). Mahwah, NJ: Erlbaum.

Edwards, C. P., & Whiting, B. B. (1993). 'Mother, older sibling, and me': The overlapping roles of caregivers and companions in the social world of two-to three-year-olds in Ngeca, Kenya. In K. MacDonald (ed.), *Parent–Child Play: Descriptions and Implications* (pp. 305–329). New York: SUNY.

Eimas, P. D. (1985). The perception of speech in early infancy. *Scientific American*, *252*(1), 34–40.

Ekman, P. (1980). Explaining emotions. In A. Rorty (ed.), *Biological and Cultural Contributions to Body and Facial Movement in the Expression of Emotions*. Berkeley, CA: University of California Press.

Ekman, P. (1994). All emotions are basic. In P. Ekman & R. Davidson (eds), *The Nature of Emotion: Fundamental Questions* (pp. 15–19). Oxford: Oxford University Press.

Ellis, N. C. (1998). Emergentism, connectionism and language learning. *Language Learning*, *48*(4), 631–664.

Ellis, N. C., Römer, U., & O'Donnell, M. B. (2016). Usage-based approaches to language acquisition and processing: Cognitive and corpus investigations of construction grammar. *Language Learning Monograph Series*, *66*(sup 1), 23–352.

Elwin, V. (1947). *The Muria and Their Ghotul*. London: Oxford University Press.

Emde, R. N., Biringen, Z., Clyman, R. B., & Oppenheim, D. (1991). The moral self of infancy: Affective core and procedural knowledge. *Developmental Review*, *11*(3), 251–270.

Emler, N., Ohana, J., & Moscovici, S. (1987). Children's beliefs about institutional roles: A cross-national study of representations of the teacher's role. *British Journal of Educational Psychology*, *57*(1), 26–37.

Engelen, E.-M., Markowitsch, H. J., Scheve, C., Röttger-Rössler, B., Stephan, A., Holodynski, M., et al. (2009). Emotions as bio-cultural processes: Disciplinary debates and an interdisciplinary outlook. In B. Röttger-Rössler & H. J. Markowitsch (eds), *Emotions as Bio-cultural Processes* (pp. 23–53). New York: Springer.

Epstein, S. (1984). Controversial issues in emotion theory. *Review of Personality & Social Psychology*, *5*, 64–88.

Ergazaki, M., & Andriotou, E. (2010). From 'forest fires' and 'hunting' to disturbing 'habitats' and 'food chains': Do young children come up with any ecological interpretations of human interventions within a forest? *Research in Science Education*, *40*(2), 187–201.

Erikson, E. H. (1950). *Childhood and Society* (2nd edn). New York: Norton.

Erikson, E. H. (1977). *Toys and Reason: Stages in the Ritualization of Experience*. New York: Norton.

Erikson, E. H. (1994). *Identity and the Life Cycle*. New York: Norton. (Original work published 1959.)

Erikson, E. H. (1994). *Identity: Youth and Crisis*. New York: Norton. (Original work published 1968.)

Eriksson, P. S., Perfilieva, E., Björk-Eriksson, T., Alborn, A. M., Nordborg, C., Peterson, D. A., et al. (1998). Neurogenesis in the adult human hippocampus. *Nature Medicine, 4*(11), 1313–1317.

Erlhagen, W., & Schöner, G. (2002). Dynamic field theory of movement preparation. *Psychological Review, 109*(3), 545–572.

Evans, C. A., & Porter, C. L. (2009). The emergence of mother-infant co-regulation during the first year: Links to infants' developmental status and attachment. *Infant Behavioral Development, 32*(2), 147–158.

Evans, J. S. B. T. (2008). Dual-processing accounts of reasoning, judgment, and social cognition. *Annual Review of Psychology, 59*, 255–278.

Fabricius, W. V., Boyer, T. W., Weimer, A. A., & Carroll, K. (2010). True or false: Do 5-year-olds understand belief? *Developmental Psychology, 46*(6), 1402.

Fair, D. A., Cohen, A. L., Power, J. D., Dosenbach, N. U., Church, J. A., Miezin, F. M., et al. (2009). Functional brain networks develop from a local to distributed organization. *PLoS Computational Biology, 5*(5), 1–14.

Fajans, S., & Lewin, K. (1933). Erfolg, ausdauer und aktivität beim säugling und kleinkind. *Psychologische Forschung, 17*(1), 268–305.

Fausto-Sterling, A. (1993). The five sexes: Why male and female are not enough. *The Sciences, 33*(2), 20–24.

Fausto-Sterling, A. (2000). *Sexing the Body: Gender Politics and the Construction of Sexuality*. New York: Basic.

Fausto-Sterling, A. (2012). *Sex/Gender: Biology in a Social World*. Abingdon: Routledge.

Fein, G. G. (1981). Pretend play in childhood: An integrative review. *Child Development, 52*(4), 1095–1118.

Feldman, M. W., & Laland, K. N. (1996). Gene-culture coevolutionary theory. *Trends in Ecology & Evolution, 11*(11), 453–457.

Fenson, L., Kagan, J., Kearsley, R. B., & Zelazo, P. R. (1976). The developmental progression of manipulative play in the first two years. *Child Development*, 232–236.

Fernald, A., & Morikawa, H. (1993). Common themes and cultural variations in Japanese and American mothers' speech to infants. *Child Development, 64*(3), 637–656.

Field, T. M., & Walden, T. A. (1982). Production and discrimination of facial expressions by preschool children. *Child Development, 53*(5), 1299–1311.

Fiese, B. H. (1990). Playful relationships: A contextual analysis of mother-toddler interaction and symbolic play. *Child Development, 61*(5), 1648–1656.

Fiske, J. (1909). *The Meaning of Infancy*. Boston, MA: Houghton Mifflin. (Original work published 1871.)

Flavell, J. H., Everett, B. A., Croft, K., & Flavell, E. R. (1981). Young children's knowledge about visual perception: Further evidence for the level 1-level 2 distinction. *Developmental Psychology, 17*(1), 99–103.

Flavell, J. H., Flavell, E. R., & Green, F. L. (1987). Young children's knowledge about the apparent–real and pretend–real distinctions. *Developmental Psychology, 23*(6), 816.

Flynn, E. G., Laland, K. N., Kendal, R. L., & Kendal, J. R. (2013). Developmental niche construction. *Developmental Science, 16*(2), 296–313.

Fodor, J. A. (1985). Fodor's guide to mental representation: The intelligent auntie's vade-mecum. *Mind: A Quarterly Review of Philosophy, 94*(373), 76.

Fogel, A., & Garvey, A. (2007). Alive communication. *Infant Behavior & Development, 30*(2), 251–257.

Forge, A. (1970). Learning to see in New Guinea. In P. Mayer (ed.), *Socialization: The Approach from Social Anthropology* (pp. 269–291). London: Tavistock.

Forrester, L. W., Phillips, S. J., & Clark, J. E. (1993). Locomotor coordination in infancy: The transition from walking to running. In G. J. P. Savelsbergh (ed.), *The Development of Coordination in Infancy* (pp. 359–422). Amsterdam: North-Holland.

Fouts, H. N., & Lamb, M. E. (2005). Weanling emotional patterns among the Bofi foragers of Central Africa: The role of maternal availability and sensitivity. In B. S. Hewlett & M. E. Lamb (eds), *Hunter-gatherer Childhoods: Evolutionary, Developmental, and Cultural Perspectives* (pp. 309–321). New Brunswick, NJ: Aldine.

Frake, C. O. (1983). Did literacy cause the great cognitive divide? *American Ethnologist, 10*(2), 368–371.

Francis, H. (1975). *Language in Childhood: Form and Function in Language Learning.* New York: St. Martin's Press.

Freud, S. (1933). *New Introductory Lectures on Psychoanalysis.* London: Penguin.

Freud, A. (1958). Adolescence in the psychoanalytic theory. *The Psychoanalytic Study of the Child, 13*, 255–278.

Friedman, L. J. (1999). *Identity's Architect: A Biography of Erik H. Erikson.* New York: Scribner.

Furth, H. G. (1996). *Desire for Society: Children's Knowledge as Social Imagination.* New York: Springer.

Furth, H. G., Baur, M., & Smith, J. E. (1976). Children's conception of social institutions: A Piagetian framework. *Human Development, 19*(6), 351–374.

Fuster, J. M. (2002). Frontal lobe and cognitive development. *Journal of Neurocytology, 31*(3–5), 373–385.

Fuster, J. M. (2005). *Cortex and Mind: Unifying Cognition.* Oxford: Oxford University Press.

Fuster, J. M. (2006). The cognit: A network model of cortical representation. *International Journal of Psychophysiology, 60*(2), 125–132.

Gallese, V., & Lakoff, G. (2005). The brain's concepts: The role of the sensory-motor system in conceptual knowledge. *Cognitive Neuropsychology, 22*(3), 455–479.

Gallup, G. G. (1970). Chimpanzees: Self-recognition. *Science, 167*(3914), 86–87.

Gardner, H. (1985). *The Mind's New Science: A History of the Cognitive Revolution.* New York: Basic.

Gaskins, S. (2006). The cultural organization of Yucatec Mayan children's social interaction. In X. Chen, D. C. French, & B. H. Schneider (eds), *Peer Relationships in Cultural Context* (pp. 283–309). Cambridge: Cambridge University Press.

Gaskins, S., & Goncu, A. (1992). Cultural variation in play: A challenge to Piaget and Vygotsky. *The Quarterly Newsletter of the Laboratory of Comparative Human Cognition, 14*(2), 31–35.

Gaskins, S., & Miller, P. J. (2009). The cultural roles of emotions in pretend play. In C. D. Clark (ed.), *Transactions at Play* (pp. 5–21). Lanham, MD: University Press of America.

Geertz, C. (1973). *The Interpretation of Cultures.* New York: Harper & Row.

Geertz, H. (1959). The vocabulary of emotion: A study of Javanese socialization processes. *Psychiatry: Interpersonal and Biological Processes, 22*, 225–237.

Gelman, S. A., & Markman, E. M. (1987). Young children's inductions from natural kinds: The role of categories and appearances. *Child Development, 58*(6), 1532–1541.

Gelman, S. A., & Tardif, T. Z. (1998). Generic noun phrases in English and Mandarin: An examination of child-directed speech. *Cognition, 66*, 215–248.

George, C., & Solomon, J. (1996). Representational models of relationships: Links between caregiving and attachment. *Infant Mental Health Journal, 17*(3), 198–216.

George, C., & Solomon, J. (2008). The caregiving system: A behavioral systems approach to parenting. In J. Cassidy & P. R. Shaver (eds), *Handbook of Attachment: Theory, Research, and Clinical Applications* (2nd edn), (pp. 833–856). New York: Guilford.

Gergely, G., Bekkering, H., & Király, I. (2002). Rational imitation in preverbal infants. *Nature, 415*(6873), 755–755.

Gergely, G., & Csibra, G. (2003). Teleological reasoning in infancy: The naïve theory of rational action. *Trends in Cognitive Sciences, 7*(7), 287–292.

Gergely, G., Nádasdy, Z., Csibra, G., & Bíró, S. (1995). Taking the intentional stance at 12 months of age. *Cognition, 56*(2), 165–193.

Gergely, G., & Watson, J. S. (1996). The social biofeedback theory of parental affect-mirroring: The development of emotional self-awareness and self-control in infancy. *International Journal of Psycho-Analysis*, *77*, 1181–1212.

Gergely, G., & Watson, J. S. (1999). Early socio-emotional development: Contingency perception and the social-biofeedback model. In P. Rochat (ed.), *Early Social Cognition: Understanding Others in the First Months of Life* (pp. 101–136). Mahwah, NJ: Erlbaum.

Gesell, A. (1930). Child psychology. In E. R. A. Seligman & A. Johnson (eds), *Encyclopedia of the Social Sciences* (pp. 391–393). New York: Macmillan.

Gesell, A. (1932). How science studies the child. *The Scientific Monthly*, *34*, 265–267.

Gesell, A. (1934). *An Atlas of Infant Behavior: A Systematic Delineation of the Forms and Early Growth of Human Behavior Patterns*. New Haven, CT: Yale University Press.

Gesell, A. (1940). *The First Five Years of Life: A Guide to the Study of the Pre-school Child, from the Yale Clinic of Child Development*. New York: Harper & Row.

Gesell, A. (1945). *The Embryology of Behavior*. New York: Harper & Row.

Gesell, A., Ilg, F. L., Learned, J., & Ames, L. B. (1943). *Infant and Child in the Culture of Today: The Guidance of Development in Home and Nursery School*. New York & London: Harper & Brothers.

Gibson, J. J. (1966). *The Senses Considered as Perceptual Systems*. Boston, MA: Houghton Mifflin.

Gilbert, M. (1990). Walking together: A paradigmatic social phenomenon. *Midwest Studies in Philosophy*, *15*(1), 1–14.

Gilligan, C. (1977). In a different voice: Women's conception of the self and of morality. *Harvard Educational Review*, *47*(4), 481–517.

Gilligan, C. (1987). Adolescent development reconsidered. *New Directions for Child and Adolescent Development*, *1987*(37), 63–92.

Gillis, J. R. (1974). *Youth and History: Tradition and Change in European Age Relations, 1770–present*. New York: Academic.

Giordano, P. C. (2003). Relationships in adolescence. *Annual Review of Sociology*, *29*(1), 257–281.

Glick, J. (1975). Cognitive development in cross-cultural perspective. *Review of Child Development Research*, *4*, 595–654.

Gluckman, P. D., & Hanson, M. A. (2006). Evolution, development and timing of puberty. *Trends in Endocrinology and Metabolism*, *17*(1), 7–12.

Goldberg, E., Podell, K., & Lovell, M. (1994). Lateralization of frontal lobe functions and cognitive novelty. *Journal of Neuropsychiatry*, *6*(4), 371–378.

Goldin-Meadow, S. (2007). Pointing sets the stage for learning language and creating language. *Child Development*, *78*(3), 741–745.

Goldin-Meadow, S., Butcher, C., Mylander, C., & Dodge, M. (1994). Nouns and verbs in a self-styled gesture system: What's in a name? *Cognitive Psychology*, *27*(3), 259–319.

Goldin-Meadow, S., & Mylander, C. (1998). Spontaneous sign systems created by deaf children in two cultures. *Nature*, *391*(6664), 279–281.

Goldschmidt, W. (1975). Absent eyes and idle hands. *Ethos*, *3*(2), 157–163.

Goodenough, W. H. (1994). Toward a working theory of culture. In R. Borofsky (ed.), *Assessing Cultural Anthropology* (pp. 262–273). New York: McGraw-Hill.

Goodnow, J. J., & Bethon, G. (1966). Piaget's tasks: The effects of schooling and intelligence. *Child Development*, *37*(3), 573–582.

Goody, J. (1968). *Literacy in Traditional Societies*. Cambridge: Cambridge University Press.

Goody, J., & Watt, I. (1963). The consequences of literacy. *Comparative Studies in Society and History*, *5*(3), 304–345.

Gopnik, A. (2012). Scientific thinking in young children: Theoretical advances, empirical research, and policy implications. *Science*, *337*(6102), 1623–1627.

Gopnik, A., & Wellman, H. M. (1992). Why the child's theory of mind really is a theory. *Mind & Language*, *7*(1–2), 145–171.

Gottlieb, A. (2015). *The Afterlife is Where We Come From*. Chicago, IL: University of Chicago Press.

Gottman, J. M. (1983). How children become friends. *Monographs of the Society for Research in Child Development*, *48*(3, Serial No. 201).

Gottman, J. M., Katz, L. F., & Hooven, C. (1997). *Meta-emotion: How Families Communicate Emotionally*. Englewood Cliffs, NJ: Erlbaum.

Gottman, J. M., & Levenson, R. W. (2000). The timing of divorce: Predicting when a couple will divorce over a 14 year period. *Journal of Marriage and Family*, *62*(3), 737–745.

Gräfenhain, M., Behne, T., Carpenter, M., & Tomasello, M. (2009). One-year-olds' understanding of nonverbal gestures directed to a third person. *Cognitive Development*, *24*(1), 23–33.

Graves, R. R., Lupo, A. C., McCarthy, R. C., Wescott, D. J., & Cunningham, D. L. (2010). Just how strapping was KNM-WT 15000? *Journal of Human Evolution*, *59*(5), 542–554.

Green, R. E., Krause, J., Briggs, A. W., Maricic, T., Stenzel, U., Kircher, M., et al. (2010). A draft sequence of the Neandertal genome. *Science*, *328*(5979), 710–722.

Greenfield, P. M. (1966). On culture and conservation. In J. S. Bruner, R. P. Oliver, & P. M. Greenfield (eds), *Studies in Cognitive Growth* (pp. 225–256). New York: Wiley.

Greenfield, P. M. (2009). Linking social change and developmental change: Shifting pathways of human development. *Developmental Psychology*, *45*(2), 401–418.

Greenfield, P. M. (2010). Particular forms of independence and interdependence are adapted to particular kinds of sociodemographic environment: Commentary on 'independence and interdependence in children's developmental experiences'. *Child Development Perspectives*, *4*(1), 37–39.

Greenfield, P. M., & Bruner, J. S. (1969). Culture and cognitive growth. In D. A. Goslin (ed.), *Handbook of Socialization Theory and Research* (pp. 633–657). New York: Rand McNally.

Greenfield, P. M., Maynard, A. E., & Childs, C. P. (2003). Historical change, cultural learning, and cognitive representation in Zinacantec Maya children. *Cognitive Development*, *18*(4), 455–487.

Greenough, W. T., Black, J. E., & Wallace, C. S. (1987). Experience and brain development. *Child Development*, *58*(3), 539–559.

Gross, C. G. (2002). Genealogy of the "grandmother cell". *The Neuroscientist*, *8*(5), 512–518.

Grossmann, K., Grossmann, K. E., Spangler, G., Suess, G., & Unzner, L. (1985). Maternal sensitivity and newborns' orientation responses as related to quality of attachment in northern Germany. *Monographs of the Society for Research in Child Development*, *50*(1–2 Serial No. 209), 233–256.

Grossmann, K. E. (2000). The evolution and history of attachment research and theory. In S. Goldberg, R. Muir, & J. Kerr (eds), *Attachment Theory: Social, Developmental, and Clinical Perspectives* (pp. 85–121). Hillsdale, NJ: Analytic.

Grossmann, K. E., & Grossmann, K. (2005). Universality of human social attachment as an adaptive process. In C. S. Carter, L. Ahnert, K. E. Grossmann, S. B. Hardy, M. E. Lamb, S. W. Porges, et al. (eds), *Attachment and Bonding: A New Synthesis*. Dahlem workshop report (Vol. 92, pp. 199–228). Cambridge, MA: MIT Press.

Grossmann, K. E., Grossmann, K., & Keppler, A. (2006). Universal and culture-specific aspects of human behavior: The case of attachment. In W. Friedlmeier, P. Chakkarath, & B. Schwarz (eds), *Culture and Human Development: The Importance of Cross-cultural Research to the Social Sciences* (pp. 75–97). Abingdon: Psychology.

Grossmann, T. (2013). Mapping prefrontal cortex functions in human infancy. *Infancy, 18*(3), 303–324.

Grove, M. A., & Lancy, D. F. (2016). Cultural models of stages in child development. In U. P. Gielen & J. L. Roopnarine (eds), *Childhood and Adolescence: Cross-cultural Perspectives and Applications* (pp. 47–62). Santa Barbara, CA: Praeger.

Gussler, J. D., & Briesemeister, L. H. (1980). The insufficient milk syndrome: A biocultural explanation. *Medical Anthropology, 4*(2), 145–174.

Hacking, I. (2007). Natural kinds: Rosy dawn, scholastic twilight. *Royal Institute of Philosophy Supplement, 61*(1), 203–239.

Hagmann, P., Cammoun, L., Gigandet, X., Meuli, R., Honey, C. J., Wedeen, V. J., et al. (2008). Mapping the structural core of human cerebral cortex. *PLoS Biology, 6*(7), e159.

Haight, W. L., & Miller, P. J. (1993). *Pretending at Home: Early Development in Sociocultural Context*. Albany, NY: SUNY.

Haith, M. M., & Campos, J. J. (1977). Human infancy. *Annual Review of Psychology, 28*(1), 251–293.

Hall, G. S. (1904). *Adolescence: Its Psychology and its Relations to Physiology, Anthropology, Sociology, Sex, Crime, Religion and Education*. New York: Appleton.

Halliday, M. A. K. (1975). Learning how to mean. In E. H. Lenneberg & E. Lenneberg (eds), *Foundations of Language Development: A Multidisciplinary Approach* (Vol. 1, pp. 239–265). Paris: UNESCO.

Halliday, M. A. K. (1975). *Learning How to Mean*. London: Edward Arnold.

Halliday, M. A. K. (1993). Towards a language-based theory of learning. *Linguistics and Education, 5*(2), 93–116.

Hallinan, M. T., & Smith, S. S. (1989). Classroom characteristics and student friendship cliques. *Social Forces, 67*(4), 898–919.

Hallpike, C. R. (1976). Is there a primitive mentality? *Man, 11*(2), 253–270.

Hallpike, C. R. (1979). *The Foundations of Primitive Thought*. Oxford: Clarendon.

Hardy, K., Buckley, S., Collins, M., Estalrrich, A., Brothwell, D., Copeland, L., et al. (2012). Neanderthal medics? Evidence for food, cooking, and medicinal plants entrapped in dental calculus. *Naturwissenschaften, 99*(8), 1–10.

Harkness, S., & Super, C. M. (2002). Culture and parenting. In M. H. Bornstein (ed.), *Handbook of Parenting: Volume 2: Biology and Ecology of Parenting* (pp. 253–280). Mahwah, NJ: Erlbaum.

Harkness, S., & Super, C. M. (1994). The developmental niche: A theoretical framework for analyzing the household production of health. *Social Science & Medicine, 38*(2), 217–226.

Harlow, H. F. (1958). The nature of love. *American Psychologist, 13*, 673–685.

Harlow, H. F. (1969). Age-mate or peer affectional system. In D. S. Lehrman (ed.), *Advances in the Study of Behavior, Volume 2* (pp. 333–384). Cambridge, MA: Academic.

Harlow, H. F., & Harlow, M. K. (1965). The affectional systems. In A. M. Schrier, H. F. Harlow, & F. Stollnitz (eds), *Behavior of Nonhuman Primates: Modern Research Trends* (Vol. 2, pp. 287–334). New York: Academic.

Harper, L. V. (1975). The scope of offspring effects: From caregiver to culture. *Psychological Bulletin, 82*(5), 784.

Harris, P. L. (2000). *The Work of the Imagination*. Oxford: Wiley-Blackwell.

Harris, P. L., Núñez, M., & Brett, C. (2001). Let's swap: Early understanding of social exchange by British and Nepali children. *Memory & Cognition, 29*(5), 757–764.

Harter, S. (2012). *Construction of the Self: Developmental and Sociocultural Foundations* (2nd edn). New York: Guilford.

Harter, S., Bresnick, S., Bouchey, H., & Whitesell, N. R. (1997). The development of multiple role-related selves during adolescence. *Development and Psychopathology*, *9*, 835–853.

Hartup, W. W. (1982). Two social worlds: Family relations and peer relations. In M. Rutter (ed.), *Scientific Foundations of Developmental Psychiatry*. London: Heinemann.

Harvey, G. (2006). *Animism: Respecting the Living World*. New York: Columbia University Press.

Havighurst, R. J. (1972). *Developmental Tasks and Education*. New York: David McKay.

Hawkes, K. (2003). Grandmothers and the evolution of human longevity. *American Journal of Human Biology*, *15*(3), 380–400.

Hawkes, K. (2004). The grandmother effect. *Nature*, *428*(6979), 128–129.

Hawkins, J., Pea, R. D., Glick, J., & Scribner, S. (1984). 'Merds that laugh don't like mushrooms': Evidence for deductive reasoning by preschoolers. *Developmental Psychology*, *20*(4), 584–594.

Hawks, J., Hunley, K., Lee, S.-H., & Wolpoff, M. (2000). Population bottlenecks and Pleistocene human evolution. *Molecular Biology and Evolution*, *17*(1), 2–22.

Heath, S. B. (1983). *Ways with Words: Language, Life and Work in Communities and Classrooms*. Cambridge: Cambridge University Press.

Hedger, J. A., & Fabricius, W. V. (2011). True belief belies false belief: Recent findings of competence in infants and limitations in 5-year-olds, and implications for theory of mind development. *Review of Philosophy and Psychology*, *2*(3), 429–447.

Henning, A., Striano, T., & Lieven, E. V. M. (2005). Maternal speech to infants at 1 and 3 months of age. *Infant Behavior and Development*, *28*(4), 519–536.

Herskovits, M. J. (1955). *Cultural Anthropology*. New York: Knopf.

Hesse, E., & Main, M. (2000). Disorganized infant, child, and adult attachment: Collapse in behavioral and attentional strategies. *Journal of the American Psychoanalytic Association*, *48*(4), 1097–1127; discussion 1175.

Hewlett, B. S., Lamb, M. E., Shannon, D., Leyendecker, B., & Schölmerich, A. (1998). Culture and early infancy among central African foragers and farmers. *Developmental Psychology*, *34*(4), 653–661.

Heyes, C. M. (1998). Theory of mind in nonhuman primates. *Behavioral and Brain Sciences*, *21*(1), 101–114.

Heyes, C. (2001). Causes and consequences of imitation. *Trends in Cognitive Sciences*, *5*(6), 253–261.

Heyes, C. (2012). Grist and mills: On the cultural origins of cultural learning. *Philosophical Transactions of the Royal Society of London: B Biological Sciences*, *367*(1599), 2181–2191.

Hildebrand-Nilshon, M., & Seeger, F. (2006). *Sign and Triangulation: From Vygotsky to Peirce and Back*. Proceedings from First International Symposium of Cultural-Historical Activity Theory and Cultural-Historical Psychology.

Hill, K., & Hurtado, A. M. (1996). *Aché Life History: The Ecology and Demography of a Foraging People*. New York: Aldine de Gruyter.

Hinde, K., & Lewis, Z. T. (2015). Mother's littlest helpers. *Science*, *348*(6242), 1427–1428.

Hirschfeld, L. A. (2002). Why don't anthropologists like children? *American Anthropologist*, *104*(2), 611–627.

Hirschfeld, L. A. (2013). The myth of mentalizing and the primacy of folk sociology. In M. R. Banaji & S. A. Gelman (eds), *Navigating the Social World: What Infants, Children, and Other Species Can Teach Us* (pp. 101–106). Oxford: Oxford University Press.

Hobson, P. (2002). *The Cradle of Thought*. London: Pan Macmillan.

Hochberg, Z., Feil, R., Constancia, M., Fraga, M., Junien, C., Carel, J.-C., et al. (2010). Child health, developmental plasticity, and epigenetic programming. *Endocrine Reviews*, *32*(2), 159–224.

Hochschild, A. R. (1979). Emotion work, feeling rules, and social structure. *American Journal of Sociology*, *85*(3), 551–575.

Hofer, B. K. (2008). Personal epistemology and culture. In M. S. Khine (ed.), *Knowing, Knowledge and Beliefs: Epistemological Studies across Diverse Cultures* (pp. 3–22). New York: Springer.

Hofer, B. K., & Pintrich, P. R. (1997). The development of epistemological theories: Beliefs about knowledge and knowing and their relation to learning. *Review of Educational Research*, *67*(1), 88–140.

Hoffman, L. W., Gandelman, R. J., & Schiffman, H. R. (1982). Preface. In L. W. Hoffman, R. J. Gandelman, & H. R. Schiffman (eds), *Parenting: Its Causes and Consequences* (pp. vi–viii). Hillsdale, NJ: Erlbaum.

Holmberg, A. R. (1969). *Nomads of the Long Bow: The Siriono of Eastern Bolivia*. Garden City, NY: Natural History Press.

Holodynski, M. (2004). The miniaturization of expression in the development of emotional self-regulation. *Developmental Psychology*, *40*(1), 16–28.

Holodynski, M. (2009). Milestones and mechanisms of emotional development. In B. Röttger-Rössler & H. J. Markowitsch (eds), *Emotions as Bio-cultural Processes* (pp. 139–163). New York: Springer.

Holodynski, M. (2013). The internalization theory of emotions: A cultural historical approach to the development of emotions. *Mind, Culture, and Activity*, *20*(1), 4–38.

Holodynski, M., & Friedlmeier, W. (2006). *Development of Emotions and Emotion Regulation*. New York: Springer.

Holstein, C. B. (1976). Irreversible, stepwise sequence in the development of moral judgment: A longitudinal study of males and females. *Child Development*, *47*, 51–61.

Howell, S. (1981). Rules not words. In P. Heelas & A. Locke (eds), *Indigenous Psychologies: The Anthropology of the Self* (pp. 133–143). New York: Academic.

Hrdy, S. B. (1999). *Mother Nature: A History of Mothers, Infants, and Natural Selection*. New York: Pantheon.

Hrdy, S. B. (2009). *Mothers and Others: The Evolutionary Origins of Mutual Understanding*. Cambridge, MA: Harvard University Press.

Hua, J. Y., & Smith, S. J. (2004). Neural activity and the dynamics of central nervous system development. *Nature Neuroscience*, *7*(4), 327–332.

Hubel, D. H., & Wiesel, T. N. (1972). Laminar and columnar distribution of geniculo-cortical fibers in the macaque monkey. *Journal of Comparative Neurology*, *146*(4), 421–450.

Huizinga, J. (1955). *Homo Ludens: A Study of the Play Element in Culture*. Abingdon: Routledge & Kegan Paul.

Hutchins, E. (1995). *Cognition in the Wild*. Cambridge, MA: MIT Press.

Hutchins, E. (2008). The role of cultural practices in the emergence of modern human intelligence. *Philosophical Transactions of the Royal Society B: Biological Sciences*, *363*(1499), 2011–2019.

Hutnik, N., & Street, R. C. (2010). Profiles of British Muslim identity: Adolescent girls in Birmingham. *Journal of Adolescence*, *33*(1), 33–42.

Huttenlocher, P. R. (1979). Synaptic density in human frontal cortex: Developmental changes and effects of aging. *Brain Research*, *163*(2), 195–205.

Hutto, D. (2011). Understanding fictional minds without theory of mind! *Style*, *45*(2), 276–282.

Inagaki, K. (1990). The effects of raising animals on children's biological knowledge. *British Journal of Developmental Psychology*, *8*(2), 119–129.

Inagaki, K., & Hatano, G. (1993). Young children's understanding of the mind–body distinction. *Child Development*, *64*(5), 1534–1549.

Inagaki, K., & Hatano, G. (2006). Young children's conception of the biological world. *Current Directions in Psychological Science*, *15*(4), 177–181.

Ingold, T. (2000). *The Perception of the Environment: Essays in Livelihood, Dwelling and Skill*. London: Routledge.

Ingold, T. (2001). Beyond art and technology: The anthropology of skill. In M. B. Schiffer (ed.), *Anthropological Perspectives on Technology* (pp. 17–32). Dragoon, AZ: Amerind Foundation.

Ingold, T. (2004). Beyond biology and culture: The meaning of evolution in a relational world. *Social Anthropology, 12*(2), 209–221.

Ingold, T. (2008). Relational thinking: Capacity for culture. *Anthropology Today, 24*(3), 25.

Ingram, D. (1971). Transitivity in child language. *Language: Journal of the Linguistic Society of America, 47*, 888–910.

Inhelder, B., & Piaget, J. (1958). *The Growth of Logical Thinking from Childhood to Adolescence*. New York: Basic.

Irvine, J. T. (1978). Wolof "magical thinking": Culture and conservation revisited. *Journal of Cross-Cultural Psychology, 9*(3), 300–310.

Ittelson, W. H. (1996). Visual perception of markings. *Psychonomic Bulletin & Review, 3*(2), 171–187.

Izard, C. E. (1992). Basic emotions, relations among emotions, and emotion-cognition relations. *Psychological Review, 99*(3), 561–565.

Izard, C. E. (1993). Four systems for emotion activation: Cognitive and noncognitive processes. *Psychological Review, 100*(1), 68–90.

Jablonka, E., & Raz, G. (2009). Transgenerational epigenetic inheritance: Prevalence, mechanisms, and implications for the study of heredity and evolution. *Quarterly Review of Biology, 84*(2), 131–176.

Jahoda, G. (1984). The development of thinking about socio-economic systems. In H. Tajfel, C. Fraser, J. Maria, & F. Jaspars (eds), *The Social Dimension (European Developments in Social Psychology): Volume 1: Social Psychology* (pp. 69–88). Cambridge: Cambridge University Press.

Jahoda, G. (1993). *Crossroads between Culture and Mind: Continuities and Change in Theories of Human Nature*. Cambridge, MA: Harvard University Press.

James, N. (2009). *Aztec Manners*. Available at: www.mexicolore.co.uk/aztecs/home/aztec-manners/kids (last accessed 6 October 2016).

Jeans, P. C., Smith, M., & Stearns, G. (1955). Dietary habits of pregnant women of low income in Iowa. *Journal of the American Dietary Association, 31*, 576.

Jeffree, D. M., & McConkey, R. (1976). An observation scheme for recording children's imaginative doll play. *Journal of Child Psychology and Psychiatry, 17*(3), 189–197.

Jenni, O. G., & O'Connor, B. B. (2005). Children's sleep: An interplay between culture and biology. *Pediatrics, 115*(1 Suppl), 204–216.

Johnson, A. (2003). *Families of the Forest: The Matsigenka Indians of the Peruvian Amazon*. Berkeley, CA: University of California Press.

Johnson, A. W., & Earle, T. (2000). *The Evolution of Human Societies: From Foraging Group to Agrarian State* (2nd edn). Palo Alto, CA: Stanford University Press.

Johnson, M. H., & De Haan, M. (2011). *Developmental Cognitive Neuroscience* (3rd edn). Chichester: Wiley-Blackwell.

Johnson-Hanks, J. (2002). On the limits of life stages in ethnography: Toward a theory of vital conjunctures. *American Anthropologist, 104*(3), 865–880.

Jones, H. E. (1938). The California adolescent growth study. *Journal of Educational Research, 31*(8), 561–567.

Jones, S. S., & Smith, L. B. (1993). The place of perception in children's concepts. *Cognitive Development, 8*(2), 113–139.

Jordan, B. (1989). Cosmopolitical obstetrics: Some insights from the training of traditional midwives. *Social Science & Medicine*, *28*(9), 925–937.

Kagan, J. (1981). *The Second Year*. Cambridge, MA: Harvard University Press.

Kagan, J. (2005). Human morality and temperament. In G. Carlo & C. P. Edward (eds), *Moral Motivation Through the Lifespan* (pp. 1–32). Lincoln, NE: University of Nebraska Press.

Kagan, J., Lapidus, D. R., & Moore, M. (1978). Infant antecedents of cognitive functioning: A longitudinal study. *Child Development*, *49*(4), 1005–1023.

Kağitcibaşi, C. (1997). Individualism and collectivism. In J. W. Berry, M. H. Segall, & C. Kagitcibasi (eds), *Handbook of Cross-cultural Psychology. Volume 3: Social Behavior and Applications* (pp. 1–49). Boston, MA: Allyn and Bacon.

Kağitcibaşi, C. (2005). Autonomy and relatedness in cultural context. *Journal of Cross-Cultural Psychology*, *36*(4), 403.

Kahneman, D. (2011). *Thinking, Fast and Slow*. New York: Farrar, Straus and Giroux.

Kaiser, J. (2014). Gearing up for a closer look at the human placenta. *Science*, *344*(6188), 1073.

Kalish, C. W. (2012). Generalizing norms and preferences within social categories and individuals. *Developmental Psychology*, *48*(4), 1133–1143.

Kalish, C. W., & Shiverick, S. M. (2004). Children's reasoning about norms and traits as motives for behavior. *Cognitive Development*, *19*(3), 401–416.

Kamara, A. I., & A, E. J. (1977). Is the rate of cognitive development uniform across cultures? A methodological critique with new evidence from Theme children. In P. R. Dasen (ed.), *Piagetian Psychology: Cross-cultural Contributions*. New York: Gardner.

Kamei, N. (2005). Play among Baka children in Cameroon. In B. S. Hewlett & M. E. Lamb (eds), *Hunter-gatherer Childhoods: Evolutionary, Developmental, and Cultural Perspectives* (pp. 343–359). New Brunswick, NJ: Aldine Transaction.

Kaplan, B. J. (1972). Malnutrition and mental deficiency. *Psychological Bulletin*, *78*(5), 321.

Karpova, S. N., & Petrushina, L. G. (1982). Significance of games involving a plot and role-playing for the development of moral behavior. *Journal of Russian and East European Psychology*, *21*(1), 18–31.

Kärtner, J. (2015). The autonomous developmental pathway: The primacy of subjective mental states for human behavior and experience. *Child Development*, *86*(4), 1298–1309.

Kärtner, J., Holodynski, M., & Wörmann, V. (2013). Parental ethnotheories, social practice and the culture-specific development of social smiling in infants. *Mind, Culture, and Activity*, *20*(1), 79–95.

Kaufmann, L., & Clément, F. (2014). Wired for society: Cognizing pathways to society and culture. *Topoi*, 1–17.

Ke, J., & Holland, J. H. (2006). Language origin from an emergentist perspective. *Applied Linguistics*, *27*(4), 691–716.

Keenan, J. P., Gallup, G. C., & Falk, D. (2003). *The Face in the Mirror: The Search for the Origins of Consciousness*. London: HarperCollins.

Keenan, J. P., Wheeler, M. A., Gallup, G. G., & Pascual-Leone, A. (2000). Self-recognition and the right prefrontal cortex. *Trends in Cognitive Sciences*, *4*(9), 338–344.

Keller, H. (2013). Attachment and culture. *Journal of Cross-Cultural Psychology*, *44*(2), 175–194.

Keller, H., & Kärtner, J. (2013). Development: The cultural solution of universal developmental tasks. In M. J. Gelfand, C. Chiu, & Y. Hong (eds), *Advances in Culture and Psychology. Volume 3* (pp. 63–116). New York: Oxford University Press.

Keller, H., Yovsi, R., Borke, J., Kärtner, J., Jensen, H., & Papaligoura, Z. (2004). Developmental consequences of early parenting experiences: Self-recognition and self-regulation in three cultural communities. *Child Development, 75*(6), 1745–1760.

Kelley, H. H. (2000). The proper study of social psychology. *Social Psychology Quarterly, 63*(1), 3–15.

Kelley, S. A., Brownell, C. A., & Campbell, S. B. (2000). Mastery motivation and self-evaluative affect in toddlers: Longitudinal relations with maternal behavior. *Child Development, 71*(4), 1061–1071.

Kerpelman, J. L., Pittman, J. F., & Lamke, L. K. (1997). Toward a microprocess perspective on adolescent identity development: An identity control theory approach. *Journal of Adolescent Research, 12*(3), 325–346.

Kincaid, H., & Mckitrick, J. (2007). *Establishing Medical Reality: Essays in the Metaphysics and Epistemology of Biomedical Science.* New York: Springer.

Kisilevsky, B. S., Hains, S. M. J., Brown, C. A., Lee, C. T., Cowperthwaite, B., Stutzman, S. S., et al. (2009). Fetal sensitivity to properties of maternal speech and language. *Infant Behavior & Development, 32*(1), 59–71.

Klaczynski, P. A. (2001). Framing effects on adolescent task representations, analytic and heuristic processing, and decision making: Implications for the normative/descriptive gap. *Journal of Applied Developmental Psychology, 22*(3), 289–309.

Klahr, D. (1982). Non-monotone assessment of monotone development: An information processing analysis. In S. Strauss & R. Stavy (eds), *U-shaped Behavioral Growth* (pp. 63–86). New York: Academic.

Klaus, M. H., & Kennell, J. H. (1976). *The Impact of Early Separation or Loss on Family Development.* Saint Louis, IL: Mosby.

Klein, G., & Jarosz, A. (2011). A naturalistic study of insight. *Journal of Cognitive Engineering and Decision Making, 5*(4), 335–351.

Kockelman, P. (2005). The semiotic stance. *Semiotica, 2005*(157), 233–304.

Kockelman, P. (2006a). Representations of the world: Memories, perceptions, beliefs, intentions, and plans. *Semiotica, 2006*(162), 73–125.

Kockelman, P. (2006b). Residence in the world: Affordances, instruments, actions, roles, and identities. *Semiotica, 2006*(162), 19–71.

Kockelman, P. (2013). *Agent, Person, Subject, Self: A Theory of Ontology, Interaction, and Infrastructure.* New York: Oxford University Press.

Kohlberg, L., & Hersh, R. H. (1977). Moral development: A review of the theory. *Theory into Practice, 16*(2), 53–59.

Kohlberg, L. A. (1966). A cognitive–developmental analysis of children's sex role concepts and attitudes. In E. E. Maccoby (ed.), *The Development of Sex Differences* (pp. 82–173). Stanford, CA: Stanford University Press.

Kohn, E. (2015). Anthropology of ontologies. *Annual Review of Anthropology, 44*, 311–327.

Konner, M., & Shostak, M. (1987). Timing and management of birth among the !Kung: Biocultural interaction in reproductive adaptation. *Cultural Anthropology, 2*(1), 11–28.

Krappmann, L. (1998). Amicitia, drujba, shin-yu, philia, freundschaft, friendship: On the cultural diversity of a human relationship. In W. M. Bukowski, A. F. Newcomb, & W. W. Hartup (eds), *The Company They Keep: Friendship in Childhood and Adolescence* (pp. 19–40). Cambridge: Cambridge University Press.

Kravtsova, E. E. (2006). The concept of age-specific new psychological formations in contemporary developmental psychology. *Journal of Russian and East European Psychology, 44*(6), 6–18.

Kretch, K. S., & Adolph, K. E. (2012). Cliff or step? Posture-specific learning at the edge of a drop-off. *Child Development, 84*, 226–240.

Kristeva, J. (1992). *Black Sun: Depression and Melancholia*. New York: Columbia University Press.

Kuhn, D. (2006). Do cognitive changes accompany developments in the adolescent brain? *Perspectives on Psychological Science*, *1*(1), 59–67.

Kuhn, D. (2008). Formal operations from a twenty-first century perspective. *Human Development*, *51*(1), 48–55.

Kuhn, D. (2009). Adolescent thinking. In R. M. Lerner & L. Steinberg (eds), *Handbook of Adolescent Psychology. Vol 1.: Individual Bases of Adolescent Development* (3rd edn). Oxford: Wiley.

Kuhn, D., & Park, S.-H. (2005). Epistemological understanding and the development of intellectual values. *International Journal of Educational Research*, *43*(3), 111–124.

Lacan, J. (1956). *The Language of the Self: The Function of Language in Psychoanalysis*. New York: Delta.

Lachterman, D. R. (1989). *The Ethics of Geometry: A Genealogy of Modernity*. New York: Routledge.

Ladd, G. W. (1999). Peer relationships and social competence during early and middle childhood. *Annual Review of Psychology*, *50*(1), 333–359.

Lagercrantz, H., & Changeux, J.-P. (2009). The emergence of human consciousness: From fetal to neonatal life. *Pediatric Research*, *65*(3), 255–260.

Lagercrantz, H., & Changeux, J.-P. (2010). Basic consciousness of the newborn. *Seminars in Perinatology*, *34*(3), 201–206.

Laing, R. D. (1971). *Knots*. New York: Vintage.

Laitman, J. T., Reidenberg, J. S., Gannon, P. J., Johansson, B., Landahl, K., & Lieberman, P. (1990). The Kebara hyoid: What can it tell us about the evolution of the hominid vocal-tract? *American Journal of Physical Anthropology*, *81*(2), 254–264.

Lakoff, G., & Johnson, M. (1999). *Philosophy in the Flesh: The Embodied Mind and its Challenge to Western Thought*. New York: Basic.

Laland, K. N., Odling-Smee, J., & Myles, S. (2010). How culture shaped the human genome: Bringing genetics and the human sciences together. *Nature Reviews: Genetics*, *11*(2), 137–148.

Laland, K. N., & Sterelny, K. (2006). Seven reasons (not) to neglect niche construction. *Evolution*, *60*(9), 1751–1762.

Lamb, M. E., & Lewis, C. (2011). The role of parent–child relationships in child development. In M. H. Bornstein & M. E. Lamb (eds), *Developmental Psychology: An Advanced Textbook* (6th edn, pp. 469–517). Mahwah, NJ: Erlbaum.

Lancy, D. F. (2008). *The Anthropology of Childhood: Cherubs, Chattel, Changelings*. Cambridge: Cambridge University Press.

Lancy, D. F. (2013). "Babies aren't persons": A survey of delayed personhood. In H. Keller & O. Hiltrud (eds), *Different Faces of Attachment: Cultural Variations of a Universal Human Need* (pp. 66–109). Cambridge: Cambridge University Press.

Lancy, D. F., & Grove, M. A. (2011). Getting noticed: Middle childhood in cross-cultural perspective. *Human Nature*, *22*(3), 281–302.

Laqueur, T. (1990). *Making Sex: Body and Fender from the Greeks to Freud*. Cambridge: Harvard University Press.

Larson, R. W. (2000). Toward a psychology of Positive Youth Development. *American Psychologist*, *55*(1), 170–183.

Larson, R. W., & Richards, M. H. (1991). Boredom in the middle school years: Blaming schools versus blaming students. *American Journal of Education*, *99*(4), 418–443.

Latour, B. (2005). *Reassembling the Social: An Introduction to Actor-Network-Theory*. Oxford: Clarendon.

Latour, B. (2013). *An Inquiry into Modes of Existence: An Anthropology of the Moderns* (C. Porter, Trans.). Cambridge, MA: Harvard University Press.

Laupa, M., & Turiel, E. (1986). Children's conceptions of adult and peer authority. *Child Development, 57*, 405–412.

Laupa, M., & Turiel, E. (1993). Children's concepts of authority and social contexts. *Journal of Educational Psychology, 85*(1), 191–197.

Laursen, B., & Jensen-Campbell, L. A. (1999). The nature and functions of social exchange in adolescent romantic relationships. In W. Furman, B. B. Brown, & C. Feiring (eds), *The Development of Romantic Relationships in Adolescence* (pp. 50–74). New York: Cambridge: Cambridge University Press.

Lave, J. (1991). Situating learning in communities of practice. In L. B. Resnick, J. M. Levine, & S. D. Teasely (eds), *Perspectives on Socially Shared Cognition* (pp. 63–82). Washington, DC: American Psychological Association.

Lave, J., & Wenger, E. (1991). *Situated Learning: Legitimate Peripheral Participation*. New York: Cambridge University Press.

Lavelli, M., & Poli, M. (1998). Early mother–infant interaction during breast- and bottle-feeding. *Infant Behavior and Development, 21*(4), 667–683.

LeDoux, J. (2012). Rethinking the emotional brain. *Neuron, 73*(4), 653–676.

Leekam, S., Perner, J., Healey, L., & Sewell, C. (2008). False signs and the non-specificity of theory of mind: Evidence that preschoolers have general difficulties in understanding representations. *British Journal of Developmental Psychology, 26*(4), 485–497.

Lieberman, M. D. (2000). Intuition: A social cognitive neuroscience approach. *Psychological Bulletin, 126*(1), 109–137.

Leiderman, P. H., Tulkin, S. R., & Rosenfeld, A. (eds) (1977). *Culture and Infancy: Variations in the Human Experience*. New York: Academic.

Leighton, D. C., & Kluckhohn, C. (1969). *Children of the People: The Navaho Individual and His Development*. Cambridge, MA: Harvard University Press. (Original work published 1947.)

Lenroot, R. K., & Giedd, J. N. (2006). Brain development in children and adolescents: Insights from anatomical magnetic resonance imaging. *Neuroscience & Biobehavioral Review, 30*(6), 718–729.

Leontiev, A. N. (1978). *Marxism and Psychological Science: Activity, Consciousness and Personality*.

Leontiev, A. N. (1981[1931]) The development of higher forms of memory. In A.N. Leontiev (ed.), *Problems of the Development of the Mind* (pp. 327–365). Moscow: Progress.

Leontiev, A. N. (2005). Study of the environment in the pedological works of L. S. Vygotsky: A critical study. *Journal of Russian and East European Psychology, 43*(4), 8–28.

Lerner, R. M. (2005). Positive Youth Development: A view of the issues. *Journal of Early Adolescence, 25*(1), 10–16.

Lévi-Strauss, C. (1971[1949]). *Elementary Structures of Kinship*. Boston, MA: Beacon.

Levine, C. G., & Côté, J. E. (2002). *Identity, Formation, Agency, and Culture: A Social Psychological Synthesis*. Englewood Cliffs, NJ: Erlbaum.

LeVine, R. A. (1988). Human parental care: Universal goals, cultural strategies, individual behavior. *New Directions for Child and Adolescent Development, 1988*(40), 3–12.

LeVine, R. A. (2010). The six cultures study: Prologue to a history of a landmark project. *Journal of Cross-Cultural Psychology, 41*(4), 513–521.

LeVine, R. A., Dixon, S., LeVine, S., Richman, A., Keefer, C., Liederman, P. H., et al. (2008). The comparative study of patenting. In R. A. Levine & R. S. New (eds), *Anthropology and Child Development: A Cross-cultural Reader* (pp. 55–65). Malden, MA: Blackwell.

LeVine, R. A., & LeVine, S. E. (1988). Parental strategies among the Gusii of Kenya. *New Directions for Child and Adolescent Development, 1988*(40), 27–35.

LeVine, R. A., LeVine, S. E., Rowe, M. L., & Schnell-Anzola, B. (2004). Maternal literacy and health behavior: A Nepalese case study. *Social Science & Medicine, 58*(4), 863–877.

LeVine, R. A., LeVine, S. E., & Schnell, B. (2001). 'Improve the women': Mass schooling, female literacy and worldwide social change. *Harvard Educational Review, 71*(1), 1–50.

LeVine, R. A., & New, R. S. (eds) (2008). *Anthropology and Child Development: A Cross-cultural Reader*. Malden, MA: Blackwell.

LeVine, R. A., & Norman, K. (2001). The infant's acquisition of culture: Early attachment reexamined in anthropological perspective. In C. C. Moore & H. F. Mathews (eds), *The Psychology of Cultural Experience* (pp. 83–104). Cambridge: Cambridge University Press.

LeVine, R. A., & White, M. (1987). Parenthood in social transformation. In J. B. Lancaster, J. Altmann, A. S. Rossi, & L. R. Sherrod (eds), *Parenting Across the Life Span: Biosocial Dimensions* (pp. 271–293). New York: Aldine de Gruyter.

Lewis, M. (1997). The self in self-conscious emotions. *Annals of the New York Academy of Sciences, 818*(1), 119–142.

Lewis, M. (1995a). Self-conscious emotions. *American Scientist, 83*(1), 68–78.

Lewis, M. (1995b). *Shame: The Exposed Self*. Simon & Schuster.

Lewis, M. (1998). Altering fate: Why the past does not predict the future. *Psychological Inquiry, 9*(2), 105–108.

Lewis, M. (1999). Contextualism and the issue of continuity. *Infant Behavior and Development, 22*(4), 431–444.

Lewis, M., Sullivan, M. W., Stanger, C., & Weiss, M. (1989). Self development and self-conscious emotions. *Child Development, 60*(1), 146–156.

Leypey, F., & Fomine, M. (2009). Food taboos in precolonial and contemporary Cameroon: A historical perspective. *Gastronomica, 9*(4), 43–52.

Li, S.-C. (2003). Biocultural orchestration of developmental plasticity across levels: The interplay of biology and culture in shaping the mind and behavior across the life span. *Psychological Bulletin, 129*(2), 171–194.

Lieberman, M. D. (2000). Intuition: A social cognitive neuroscience approach. *Psychological Bulletin, 126*(1), 109–137.

Lieberman, M. D. (2007). Social cognitive neuroscience: A review of core processes. *Annual Review of Psychology, 58*, 259–289.

Lieberman, M. D., Gaunt, R., Gilbert, D. T., & Trope, Y. (2002). Reflexion and reflection: A social cognitive neuroscience approach to attributional inference. *Advances in Experimental Social Psychology, 34*, 199–249.

Lillard, A. (1993). Pretend play skills and the child's theory of mind. *Child Development, 64*(2), 348–371.

Lillard, A. (1998). Ethnopsychologies: Cultural variations in theories of mind. *Psychological Bulletin, 123*(1), 3–32.

Lillard, A. (1999). Developing a cultural theory of mind. *Current Directions in Psychological Science, 8*(2), 57–61.

Lillard, A., & Skibbe, L. (2005). Theory of mind: Conscious attribution and spontaneous trait inferences. In R. Hassin, J. Uleman, & J. Bargh (eds), *The New Unconscious* (pp. 277–305). Oxford: Oxford University Press.

Lillard, A. S., Lerner, M. D., Hopkins, E. J., Dore, R. A., Smith, E. D., & Palmquist, C. M. (2013). The impact of pretend play on children's development: A review of the evidence. *Psychological Bulletin, 139*(1), 1–34.

Lillard, A., Skibbe, L., Zeljo, A., & Harlan, D. (2001). 'Developing explanations for behavior in different communities and cultures'. Unpublished manuscript, University of Virginia.

Lindqvist, G. (2001). When small children play: How adults dramatise and children create meaning. *Early Years, 21*(1), 7–14.

Liu, D., Wellman, H. M., Tardif, T., & Sabbagh, M. A. (2008). Theory of mind development in Chinese children: A meta-analysis of false-belief understanding across cultures and languages. *Developmental Psychology*, *44*(2), 523–531.

Lock, A. E. (1978). *Action, Gesture and Symbol: The Emergence of Language*. Cambridge, MA: Academic.

Locke, J. L. (1983). *Phonological Acquisition and Change*. Cambridge, MA: Academic.

Locke, J. L., & Bogin, B. (2006). Language and life history: A new perspective on the development and evolution of human language. *Behavioral and Brain Sciences*, *29*(3), 259–280.

Lockman, J. J. (2000). A perception–action perspective on tool use development. *Child Development*, *71*(1), 137–144.

Lodygensky, G. A., Vasung, L., Sizonenko, S. V., & Hüppi, P. S. (2010). Neuroimaging of cortical development and brain connectivity in human newborns and animal models. *Journal of Anatomy*, *217*(4), 418–428.

Longo, L. D., & Reynolds, L. P. (2010). Some historical aspects of understanding placental development, structure and function. *International Journal of Developmental Biology*, *54*(2–3), 237–255.

Lucy, J. A. (1992). *Language Diversity and Thought: A Reformulation of the Linguistic Relativity Hypothesis*. Cambridge: Cambridge University Press.

Lupyan, G., Rakison, D. H., & McClelland, J. L. (2007). Language is not just for talking: Redundant labels facilitate learning of novel categories. *Psychological Science*, *18*(12), 1077–1083.

Luria, A. (1933). The second psychological expedition to central Asia. *Science*, *78*(2018), 191–192.

Luria, A. R. (1972). *The Man with a Shattered World: The History of a Brain Wound*. Cambridge, MA: Harvard University Press.

Luria, A. R. (1973). *The Working Brain: An Introduction to Neuropsychology*. New York: Basic.

Luria, A. R. (1976). *Cognitive Development: Its Cultural and Social Foundations*. Cambridge, MA: Harvard University Press.

Luria, A. R. (1987). *The Mind of a Mnemonist: A Little Book about a Vast Memory*. Cambridge, MA: Harvard University Press.

Luria, A. R. (2002). L. S. Vygotsky and the problem of functional localization. *Journal of Russian and East European Psychology*, *40*(1), 17–25.

Lutz, C. (1987). Goals, events, and understanding in Ifaluk emotion theory. In D. Holland & N. Quinn (eds), *Cultural Models in Language and Thought* (pp. 290–312). New York: Cambridge University Press.

Ma, J. (2014). The synergy of Peirce and Vygotsky as an analytical approach to the multimodality of semiotic mediation. *Mind, Culture, and Activity*, *21*(4), 374–389.

Maccoby, E. E. (1984a). Middle childhood in the context of the family. In W. A. Collins (ed.), *Development During Middle Childhood: The Years from Six to Twelve* (pp. 184–239). Washington, DC: National Academy.

Maccoby, E. E. (1984b). Socialization and developmental change. *Child Development*, *55*(2), 317–328.

Maccoby, E. E. (1992). The role of parents in the socialization of children: An historical overview. *Developmental Psychology*, *28*(6), 1006–1017.

Maccoby, E. E., & Martin, J. A. (1983). Socialization in the context of the family: Parent–child interaction. In P. H. Mussen & M. Hetherington (eds), *Handbook of Child Psychology: Vol. 4. Socialization, Personality, and Social Development* (Vol. 4, pp. 1–101). New York: Wiley.

Macfarlane, A. (1977). *The Psychology of Childbirth*. Cambridge, MA: Harvard University Press.

MacKenzie, M. (1990). The Telefol string bag: a cultural object with androgynous forms. In C. Barry & D. Hyndman (eds), *Children of Afek: Tradition and Change among the Mountain-Ok of Central New Guinea* (Vol. 40, pp. 88–108). Sydney: University of Sydney Press.

MacKenzie, M. A. (1991). *Androgynous Objects: String Bags and Gender in Central New Guinea*. Chur, Switzerland: Harwood.

MacNeilage, P. F., Rogers, L. J., & Vallortigara, G. (2009). Origins of the left & right brain. *Scientific American*, *301*(1), 60–67.

MacWhinney, B. (2006). Emergentism: Use often and with care. *Applied Linguistics*, *27*(4), 729–740.

Mahler, M. S., Pine, F., & Bergman, A. (1975). *The Psychological Birth of the Infant*. New York: Basic.

Main, M. (2000). The organized categories of infant, child, and adult attachment: Flexible vs. Inflexible attention under attachment-related stress. *Journal of the American Psychoanalytic Association*, *48*(4), 1055–1096.

Main, M., & Cassidy, J. (1988). Categories of response to reunion with the parent at age 6: Predictable from infant attachment classifications and stable over a 1-month period. *Developmental Psychology*, *24*(3), 415–426.

Main, M., Goldwyn, R., & Hesse, E. (2002). 'Adult attachment scoring and classification system'. Unpublished manuscript, University of California, Berkeley.

Main, M., & Solomon, J. (1990). Procedures for identifying infants as disorganized/disoriented during the Ainsworth Strange Situation. In M. T. Greenberg, D. Cicchetti, & E. M. Cummings (eds), *Attachment in the Preschool Years: Theory, Research, and Intervention* (pp. 121–160). Chicago, IL: University of Chicago Press.

Majid, A., Bowerman, M., Kita, S., Haun, D., & Levinson, S. C. (2004). Can language restructure cognition? The case for space. *Trends in Cognitive Sciences*, *8*(3), 108–114.

Malatesta, C. Z., & Haviland, J. M. (1985). Signals, symbols, and socialization: The modification of emotional expression in human development. In M. Lewis & C. Saari (eds), *The Socialization of Emotions* (pp. 89–116). New York: Plenum.

Mandler, J. M., Scribner, S., Cole, M., & DeForest, M. (1980). Cross-cultural invariance in story recall. *Child Development*, *51*(1), 19–26.

Marcia, J. E. (1966). Development and validation of ego identity status. *Journal of Personality and Social Psychology*, *3*(5), 551–558.

Marcia, J. E. (2001). Identity in childhood and adolescence. *International Encyclopedia of the Social & Behavioral Sciences*, 7159–7163.

Mareschal, D., & Johnson, M. H. (2003). The what and where of object representations in infancy. *Cognition*, *88*(3), 259–276.

Markman, E. M. (1991). *Categorization and Naming in Children: Problems of Induction*. Cambridge, MA: The MIT Press.

Martin, J., Sokol, B. W., & Elfers, T. (2008). Taking and coordinating perspectives: From prereflective interactivity, through reflective intersubjectivity, to metareflective sociality. *Human Development*, *51*(5–6), 294–317.

Mastropieri, D., & Turkewitz, G. (1999). Prenatal experience and neonatal responsiveness to vocal expressions of emotion. *Developmental Psychobiology*, *35*(3), 204–214.

Matsuzawa, J., Matsui, M., Konishi, T., Noguchi, K., Gur, R. C., Bilker, W., et al. (2001). Age-related volumetric changes of brain gray and white matter in healthy infants and children. *Cerebral Cortex*, *11*(4), 335–342.

Mauss, M. (1973). Techniques of the body. *Economy and Society*, *2*(1), 70–88.

Maynard, A. E. (2002). Cultural teaching: The development of teaching skills in Maya sibling interactions. *Child Development*, *73*(3), 969–982.

McGrew, W. C. (2004). *The Cultured Chimpanzee: Reflections on Cultural Primatology*. Cambridge: Cambridge University Press.

Mead, M. (1932). An investigation of the thought of primitive children, with special reference to animism. *Journal of the Anthropological Institute of Great Britain and Ireland*, *62*, 173–190.

Mead, M. (1943). Our educational emphases in primitive perspective. *American Journal of Sociology*, *48*(6), 633–639.

Mead, M. (2008). The ethnography of childhood. In R. LeVine & R. S. New (eds), *Anthropology and Child Development: A Cross-cultural Reader* (pp. 22–27). Malden, MA: Blackwell.

Mead, M., & Macgregor, F. C. (1951). *Growth and Culture: A Photographic Study of Balinese Childhood.* New York: Putnam.

Meaney, M. J., & Szyf, M. (2005). Environmental programming of stress responses through DNA methylation: Life at the interface between a dynamic environment and a fixed genome. *Dialogues in Clinical Neuroscience*, *7*(2), 103–123.

Medin, D., Ross, N., Cox, D., & Atran, S. (2007). Why folkbiology matters: Resource conflict despite shared goals and knowledge. *Human Ecology*, *35*(3), 315–329.

Meeus, W., Iedema, J., & Vollebergh, W. (1999). Identity formation re-revisited: A rejoinder to Waterman on developmental and cross-cultural issues. *Developmental Review*, *19*(4), 480–496.

Merleau-Ponty, M. (1964). *The Primacy of Perception.* Evanston, IL: Northwestern University Press.

Meyer, J. S., Novak, M. A., Bowman, R. E., & Harlow, H. F. (1975). Behavioral and hormonal effects of attachment object separation in surrogate-peer-reared and mother-reared infant rhesus monkeys. *Developmental Psychobiology*, *8*(5), 425–435.

Miller, G. A. (2003). The cognitive revolution: A historical perspective. *Trends in Cognitive Sciences*, *7*(3), 141–144.

Miller, J. G. (1984). Culture and development of everyday social explanation. *Journal of Personality and Social Psychology*, *46*(5), 961–978.

Miller, P., & Sperry, L. L. (1987). The socialization of anger and aggression. *Merrill-Palmer Quarterly: Journal of Developmental Psychology*, *33*(1), 1–31.

Miller, P. J., & Goodnow, J. J. (1995). Cultural practices: Toward an integration of culture and development. *New Directions for Child Development*, *1995*(67), 5–16.

Miller, S. (2012). *Theory of Mind: Beyond the Preschool Years.* Abingdon: Psychology.

Miller, S. (2014). Social institutions. *The Stanford Encyclopedia of Philosophy* (edited by N. Z. Edward). Available at: http://plato.stanford.edu/archives/win2014/entries/social-institutions/ (last accessed 6 October 2016).

Mintz, S. (2004). *Huck's Raft: A History of American Childhood.* Cambridge, MA: Belknap.

Mithen, S. J. (2005). *The Singing Neanderthals: The Origins of Music, Language, Mind, and Body.* Cambridge, MA: Harvard University Press.

Miyake, K., Chen, S.-J., & Campos, J. J. (1985). Infant temperament, mother's mode of interaction, and attachment in Japan: An interim report. *Monographs of the Society for Research in Child Development*, *50*(1–2), 276–297.

Modell, J. (1994). The developing schoolchild as historical actor. *Comparative Education Review*, *38*(1), 1–9.

Modell, J. (2000). How may children's development be seen historically? *Childhood*, *7*(1), 81–106.

Modell, J., & Goodman, M. (1990). Historical perspectives. In S. S. Feldman & G. R. Elliott (eds), *At the Threshold: The Developing Adolescent* (pp. 93–122). Cambridge, MA: Harvard University Press.

Morelli, G., Rogoff, B., & Angelillo, C. (2003). Cultural variation in young children's access to work or involvement in specialised child-focused activities. *International Journal of Behavioral Development*, *27*(3), 264–274.

Morelli, G., Rogoff, B., Oppenheim, D., & Goldsmith, D. (1992). Cultural variation in infants' sleeping arrangements: Questions of independence. *Developmental Psychology*, *28*(4), 604–613.

Morrison, F. J., Smith, L., & Dow-Ehrensberger, M. (1995). Education and cognitive development: A natural experiment. *Developmental Psychology*, *31*(5), 789.

Moses, L. J., Baldwin, D. A., Rosicky, J. G., & Tidball, G. (2001). Evidence for referential understanding in the emotions domain at twelve and eighteen months. *Child Development*, *72*(3), 718–735.

Moshman, D. (1998). Cognitive development beyond childhood. In D. Kuhn & R. Siegler (eds), *Handbook of Child Psychology* (5th edn, pp. 947–978). New York: Wiley.

Moshman, D. (2004). From inference to reasoning: The construction of rationality. *Thinking & Reasoning, 10*(2), 221–239.

Mosier, C. E., & Rogoff, B. (2003). Privileged treatment of toddlers: Cultural aspects of individual choice and responsibility. *Developmental Psychology, 39*(6), 1047–1060.

Mulder, E. J. H., Robles de Medina, P. G., Huizink, A. C., Van den Bergh, B. R. H., Buitelaar, J. K., & Visser, G. H. A. (2002). Prenatal maternal stress: Effects on pregnancy and the (unborn) child. *Early Human Development, 70*(1), 3–14.

Murphy, J. M., & Gilligan, C. (1980). Moral development in late adolescence and adulthood: A critique and reconstruction of Kohlberg's theory. *Human Development, 23*, 77–104.

Murray, L., & Trevarthen, C. (1985). Emotional regulation of interactions between two-month-olds and their mothers. *Social Perception in Infants*, 177–197.

Myachykov, A., Scheepers, C., Fischer, M. H., & Kessler, K. (2013). TEST: A Tropic, Embodied, and Situated Theory of Cognition. *Topics in Cognitive Science* (2013), 1–19.

Nakagawa, M., Lamb, M. E., & Miyake, K. (1989). Psychological experiences of Japanese infants in the Strange Situation. *Hokkaido University Research & Clinical Center for Child Development Annual Report, 11*, 13–24.

National Institute of Child Health and Development (NICHD). (2003a). Does quality of child care affect child outcomes at age 4 1/2? *Developmental Psychology, 39*(3), 451–469.

National Institute of Child Health and Development (NICHD). (2003b). Modeling the impacts of child care quality on children's preschool cognitive development. *Child Development, 74*(5), 1454–1475.

Naumova, O. Y., Lee, M., Rychkov, S. Y., Vlasova, N. V., & Grigorenko, E. L. (2013). Gene expression in the human brain: The current state of the study of specificity and spatiotemporal dynamics. *Child Development, 84*(1), 76–88.

Neisser, U. (1991). Two perceptually given aspects of the self and their development. *Developmental Review, 11*(3), 197–209.

Nelson, C. A. (1987). The recognition of facial expressions in the first two years of life: Mechanisms of development. *Child Development, 58*(4), 889–909.

Nelson, K. (1977). Cognitive development and the acquisition of concepts. In R. C. Anderson, R. J. Spiro, & W. E. Montague (eds), *Schooling and the Acquisition of Knowledge* (pp. 215–240). Hillsdale, NJ: Erlbaum.

Newell, A., & Simon, H. A. (1972). *Human Problem Solving*. Englewood Cliffs, NJ: Prentice-Hall.

Ninio, A., & Snow, C. (1999). The development of pragmatics: Learning to use language appropriately. In W. C. Ritchie & T. K. Bhatia (eds), *Handbook of Child Language Acquisition*. San Diego, CA: Academic.

Norretranders, T. (1991). *The User Illusion: Cutting Consciousness Down to Size*. New York: Viking.

Nucci, L. P. (2001). *Education in the Moral Domain*. Cambridge: Cambridge University Press.

Nucci, L., & Nucci, M. S. (1982). Children's responses to moral and social conventional transgressions in free-play settings. *Child Development, 53*, 1337–1342.

Nucci, L., & Turiel, E. (1978). Social interactions and the development of social concepts in preschool children. *Child Development, 49*, 400–407.

Nucci, L., & Turiel, E. (2009). Capturing the complexity of moral development and education. *Mind, Brain, and Education, 3*, 151–159.

Núñez, M., & Harris, P. L. (1998). Psychological and deontic concepts: Separate domains or intimate connection. *Mind & Language, 13*(2), 153–170.

Nyiti, R. M. (1976). The development of conservation in the Meru children of Tanzania. *Child Development*, *47*(6), 1122–1129.

O'Donnell, J. M. (1985). *The Origins of Behaviorism: American Psychology, 1870–1920*. New York: New York University Press.

O'Sullivan, L. F., & Meyer-Bahlburg, H. F. L. (2003). African-American and Latina inner-city girls' reports of romantic and sexual development. *Journal of Social and Personal Relationships*, *20*(2), 221–238.

Ochs, E., & Schiefflin, B. B. (1984). Language acquisition and socialization: Three developmental stories and their implications. In R. Shweder & R. LeVine (eds), *Culture Theory: Essays on Mind, Self, and Emotion* (pp. 276–320). Cambridge: Cambridge University Press.

Ogbu, J. U. (1981). Origins of human competence: A cultural-ecological perspective. *Child Development*, *52*(2), 413–429.

Ogushi, S., Palmieri, C., Fulka, H., Saitou, M., Miyano, T., & Fulka, J. (2008). The maternal nucleolus is essential for early embryonic development in mammals. *Science*, *319*(5863), 613–616.

Olds, J., & Milner, P. (1954). Positive reinforcement produced by electrical stimulation of septal area and other regions of rat brain. *Journal of Comparative and Physiological Psychology*, *47*(6), 419–427.

Oller, D. K., Eilers, R. E., Urbano, R., & Cobo-Lewis, A. B. (1997). Development of precursors to speech in infants exposed to two languages. *Journal of Child Language*, *24*(2), 407–425.

Olson, D. R. (1994). *The World on Paper: The Conceptual and Cognitive Implications of Writing and Reading*. Cambridge: Cambridge University Press.

Olson, D. R. (1996). Literate mentalities: Literacy, consciousness of language, and modes of thought. In D. R. Olson & N. Torrance (eds), *Modes of Thought: Explorations in Culture and Cognition* (pp. 141–151). Cambridge: Cambridge University Press.

Olson, D. R., & Hildyard, A. (1981). Assent and compliance in children's language: Knowing vs. doing. In P. Dickson (ed.), *Children's Oral Communication Skills* (pp. 313–335). New York: Academic.

Packer, M. J. (2001). *Changing Classes: School Reform and the New Economy*. New York: Cambridge University Press.

Packer, M. J. (2011). *The Science of Qualitative Research*. New York: Cambridge University Press.

Packer, M. J., & Goicoechea, J. (2000). Sociocultural and constructivist theories of learning: Ontology, not just epistemology. *Educational Psychologist*, *35*(4), 227–241.

Palmer, D. K. (2004). On the organism-environment distinction in psychology. *Behavior and Philosophy*, 317–347.

Papalia, D. E., Olds, S. W., & Feldman, R. D. (2004). *A Child's World: Infancy through Adolescence* (9th edn). New York: McGraw-Hill.

Papousek, H., & Papousek, M. (2002). Intuitive parenting. In M. H. Bornstein (ed.), *Handbook of Parenting: Volume 2, Biology and Ecology of Parenting* (pp. 183–206).

Papousek, M. (2007). Communication in early infancy: An arena of intersubjective learning. *Infant Behavior & Development*, *30*(2), 258–266.

Parker, L. N. (1991). Adrenarche. *Endocrinology Metabolism Clinics of North America*, *20*(1), 71–83.

Paul, L., & Paul, B. D. (1975). The Maya midwife as sacred specialist: A Guatemalan case. *American Ethnologist*, *2*(4), 707–726.

Paul, R. A. (1995). Act and intention in Sherpa culture and society. In L. Rosen (ed.), *Other Intentions: Cultural Contexts and the Attribution of Inner States* (pp. 15–45). Santa Fe, NM: School of American Research Press.

Paus, T. (2009). Brain development. In R. M. Lerner & L. Steinberg (eds), *Handbook of Adolescent Psychology* (pp. 95–115). Wiley Online Library.

Paus, T. (2010). Growth of white matter in the adolescent brain: Myelin or axon? *Brain and Cognition*, *72*(1), 26–35.

Paus, T., Zijdenbos, A., Worsley, K., Collins, D. L., Blumenthal, J., Giedd, J. N., et al. (1999). Structural maturation of neural pathways in children and adolescents: In vivo study. *Science*, *283*(5409), 1908–1911.

Pea, R. D. (2004). The social and technological dimensions of scaffolding and related theoretical concepts for learning, education, and human activity. *Journal of the Learning Sciences*, *13*(3), 423–451.

Pedersen, E. (2012). Common nonsense: A review of certain recent reviews of the 'ontological turn'. *Anthropology of This Century*, available at http://aotcpress.com/articles/common_nonsense/.

Pelto, G. H., Zhang, Y., & Habicht, J.-P. (2010). Premastication: The second arm of infant and young child feeding for health and survival? *Maternal & Child Nutrition*, *6*(1), 4–18.

Pembrey, M. E., Bygren, L. O., Kaati, G., Edvinsson, S., Northstone, K., Sjöström, M., et al. (2005). Sex-specific, male-line transgenerational responses in humans. *European Journal of Human Genetics*, *14*(2), 159–166.

Pereira, A. F., Smith, L. B., & Yu, C. (2008). Social coordination in toddlers' word learning: Interacting systems of perception and action. *Connection Science*, *20*(2–3), 73–89.

Perinat, A., & Sadurní, M. (1999). The ontogenesis of meaning: An interactional approach. *Mind, Culture, and Activity*, *6*(1), 53–76.

Perner, J. (1991). *Understanding the Representational Mind*. Cambridge, MA: The MIT Press.

Perner, J., & Roessler, J. (2012). From infants' to children's appreciation of belief. *Trends in Cognitive Sciences*, *16*(10), 519–525.

Perner, J., Ruffman, T., & Leekam, S. R. (1994). Theory of mind is contagious: You catch it from your sibs. *Child Development*, *65*(4), 1228–1238.

Perry, G. H., & Dominy, N. J. (2009). Evolution of the human pygmy phenotype. *Trends in Ecology & Evolution*, *24*(4), 218–225.

Perry, W. G. (1970). *Forms of Intellectual Development in the College Years*. New York: Holt.

Perry, W. G. (1985). Different worlds in the same classroom: Students' evolution in their vision of knowledge and their expectations of teachers. *On Teaching and Learning*, *1*(1), 1–17.

Petitto, L. A. (2005). How the brain begets language. In J. McGilvray (ed.), *The Cambridge Companion to Chomsky* (pp. 84–101). Cambridge: Cambridge University Press.

Phinney, J. S. (1990). Ethnic identity in adolescents and adults: Review of research. *Psychological Bulletin*, *108*(3), 499–514.

Phinney, J. S., & Alipuria, L. L. (1996). At the interface of cultures: Multiethnic/multiracial high school and college students. *Journal of Social Psychology*, *136*(2), 139–158.

Phinney, J. S., Horenczyk, G., Liebkind, K., & Vedder, P. (2001). Ethnic identity, immigration, and well-being: An interactional perspective. *Journal of Social Issues*, *57*(3), 493–510.

Piaget, J. (1924). Les traits principaux de la logique de l'enfant. *Journal de Psychologie*, *21*, 48–101.

Piaget, J. (1926). *La représentation du monde chez l'enfant*. Presses Universitaires de France.

Piaget, J. (1927). *La causalité physique chez l'enfant*. Librairie Félix Alcan.

Piaget, J. (1951). *Play, Dreams and Imitation in Childhood*. London: Routledge. (Original work published 1945.)

Piaget, J. (1952a). *The Origins of Intelligence in Children*. New York: International Universities Press. (Original work published 1936.)

Piaget, J. (1952b). Jean Piaget. In E. Boring, H. Langfeld, H. Werner, & R. Yerkes (eds), *A History of Psychology in Autobiography* (pp. 237–256). Worcester, MA: Clark University Press.

Piaget, J. (1954). *The Construction of Reality in the Child*. New York: Basic. (Original work published 1937.)

Piaget, J. (1955). *The Child's Construction of Reality*. London: Routledge & Kegan Paul. (Original work published 1937.)

Piaget, J. (1960). *The Child's Conception of the World*. London: Routledge & Kegan Paul. (Original work published 1929.)

Piaget, J. (1964). Development and learning. In R. E. Ripple & V. N. Rockcastle (eds), *Piaget Rediscovered* (pp. 7–20). Ithaca, NY: Cornell University Press.

Piaget, J. (1965). *The Moral Judgment of the Child*. New York: Free. (Original work published 1932.)

Piaget, J. (1971). *Science of Education and the Psychology of the Child*. London: Longman.

Piaget, J. (1988). *Structuralism*. New York: Harper & Row. (Original work published 1970.)

Piaget, J. (1995). Genetic logic and sociology. In L. Smith (ed.), *Sociological Studies: Jean Piaget* (pp. 184–214). New York: Routledge. (Original work published 1928.)

Piaget, J. (2008). Intellectual evolution from adolescence to adulthood. *Human Development*, *51*(1), 40–47. (Original work published 1972.)

Piaget, J., & Inhelder, B. (2008). *The Psychology of the Child*. New York: Basic. (Original work published 1966.)

Piattelli-Palmarini, M. (1980). *Language and Learning: The Debate between Jean Piaget and Noam Chomsky*. Cambridge, MA: Harvard University Press.

Piattelli-Palmarini, M. (1994). Ever since language and learning: Afterthoughts on the Piaget–Chomsky debate. *Cognition*, *50*(1), 315–346.

Pijnenborg, R., Vercruysse, L., & Hanssens, M. (2008). Fetal-maternal conflict, trophoblast invasion, preeclampsia, and the Red Queen. *Hypertension in Pregnancy*, *27*(2), 183–196.

Pinker, S. (1988). Learnability theory and the acquisition of a first language. In F. Kessel (ed.), *The Development of Language and Language Researchers: Essays in Honor of Roger Brown* (pp. 97–119). Hillsdale, NJ: Erlbaum.

Pinker, S. (1998). *How the Mind Works*. London: Penguin.

Pinker, S. (2000). *Words and Rules: The Ingredients of Language*. New York: Harper Perennial.

Podell, K., Lovell, M., & Goldberg, E. (2001). Lateralization of frontal lobe functions. In S. P. Salloway, P. F. Malloy, & J. D. Duffy (eds), *The Frontal Lobes and Neuropsychiatric Illness* (pp. 83–100). Arlington, VA: American Psychiatric Publishing.

Pollitt, E., Saco-Pollitt, C., Jahari, A., Husaini, M. A., Huang, J., & Schürch, B. (2000). Effects of an energy and micronutrient supplement on mental development and behavior under natural conditions in undernourished children in Indonesia. *European Journal of Clinical Nutrition*, *54*(supp 2), S80–S90.

Prasad, R. (1991). The Vygotskian perspective on education [Review of 'Vygotsky and Education,' by L. Moll]. *Social Scientist*, *19*(8/9), 85–89.

Preissler, M. A., & Carey, S. (2004). Do both pictures and words function as symbols for 18- and 24-month old children? *Journal of Cognition and Development*, *5*(2), 185–212.

Pylyshyn, Z. W. (1984). *Computation and Cognition*. Cambridge, MA: MIT Press.

Quartz, S. R., & Sejnowski, T. J. (1997). The neural basis of cognitive development: A constructivist manifesto. *Behavioral and Brain Sciences*, *20*(4), 537–556.

Quartz, S. R., & Sejnowski, T. J. (2002). *Liars, Lovers, and Heroes: What the New Brain Science Reveals about How We Become Who We Are*. New York: Morrow.

Quinlan, R. J., & Quinlan, M. B. (2008). Human lactation, pair-bonds, and alloparents. *Human Nature*, *19*(1), 87–102.

Quinn, P. J., O'Callaghan, M., Williams, G. M., Najman, J. M., Andersen, M. J., & Bor, W. (2001). The effect of breastfeeding on child development at 5 years: A cohort study. *Journal of Paediatrics and Child Health*, *37*(5), 465–469.

Raeff, C. (2010). Independence and interdependence in children's developmental experiences. *Child Development Perspectives*, *4*(1), 31–36.

Rakoczy, H. (2010). From thought to language to thought: Towards a dialectical picture of the development of thinking and speaking. *Grazer Philosophische Studien, 81*(1), 77–103.

Rakoczy, H., & Schmidt, M. F. H. (2013). The early ontogeny of social norms. *Child Development Perspectives, 7*(1), 17–21.

Rakoczy, H., & Tomasello, M. (2007). The ontogeny of social ontology: Steps to shared intentionality and status functions. In S. L. Tsohatzidis (ed.), *Intentional Acts and Institutional Facts: Essays on John Searle's Social Ontology* (pp. 113–137). Berlin: Springer Verlag.

Rakoczy, H., Tomasello, M., & Striano, T. (2005). How children turn objects into symbols: A cultural learning account. In L. Namy (ed.), *Symbol Use and Symbol Representation* (pp. 67–97). New York: Erlbaum.

Read, M. (1959). *Children of their Fathers: Growing Up Among the Ngoni of Nyasaland.* New York: Holt, Rinehart & Winston.

Rees, T. (2010). Being neurologically human today: Life and science and adult cerebral plasticity (an ethical analysis). *American Ethnologist, 37*(1), 150–166.

Regier, T., & Kay, P. (2009). Language, thought, and color: Whorf was half right. *Trends in Cognitive Science, 13*(10), 439–446.

Reines, M. F., & Prinz, J. (2009). Reviving Whorf: The return of Linguistic Relativity. *Philosophy Compass, 4*(6), 1022–1032.

Reis, A., Petersson, K. M., Castro-Caldas, A., & Ingvar, M. (2001). Formal schooling influences two- but not three-dimensional naming skills. *Brain and Cognition, 47*(3), 397–411.

Renshaw, P. D. (1981). The roots of peer interaction research: A historical analysis of the 1930s. In S. R. Asher & J. M. Gottman (eds), *The Development of Children's Friendships* (pp. 1–25). Cambridge: Cambridge University Press.

Reyna, V. F., & Brainerd, C. J. (1995). Fuzzy-trace theory: An interim synthesis. *Learning and Individual Differences, 7*(1), 1–75.

Reyna, V. F., & Farley, F. (2006). Risk and rationality in adolescent decision making: Implications for theory, practice, and public policy. *Psychological Science in the Public Interest, 7*(1), 1–44.

Rindfuss, R. R., Swicegood, C. G., & Rosenfeld, R. A. (1987). Disorder in the life course: How common and does it matter? *American Sociological Review, 52*(6), 785–801.

Rivers, S. E., Reyna, V. F., & Mills, B. (2008). Risk taking under the influence: A fuzzy-trace theory of emotion in adolescence. *Developmental Review, 28*(1), 107–144.

Roberts, R. G. (2015). Intractable tangles in the bird family tree. *PLoS Biology, 13*(8), e1002225.

Robertson, A. F. (1996). The development of meaning: Ontogeny and culture. *Journal of the Royal Anthropological Institute, 2*(4), 591–610.

Rochat, P., & Zahavi, D. (2011). The uncanny mirror: A re-framing of mirror self-experience. *Consciousness and Cognition, 20*(2), 204–213.

Rogoff, B. (1981). Schooling and the development of cognitive skills. In H. C. Triandis & A. Heron (eds), *Handbook of Cross-cultural Psychology* (Vol. 4, pp. 233–294). Boston, MA: Allyn & Bacon.

Rogoff, B. (1990). *Apprenticeship in Thinking: Cognitive Development in Social Context.* New York: Oxford University Press.

Rogoff, B. (2008). Observing sociocultural activity on three planes: Participatory appropriation, guided participation, and apprenticeship. In *Pedagogy and Practice: Culture and Identities* (pp. 58–74). Thousand Oaks, CA: Sage.

Rogoff, B. (2011). *Developing Destinies: A Mayan Midwife and Town.* New York: Oxford University Press.

Rogoff, B., & Chavajay, P. (1995). What's become of research on the cultural basis of cognitive development? *American Psychologist, 50*(10), 859–877.

Rogoff, B., Malkin, C., & Gilbride, K. (1984). Interaction with babies as guidance in development. *New Directions for Child and Adolescent Development, 1984*(23), 31–44.

Rogoff, B., Mistry, J., Göncü, A., Mosier, C., Chavajay, P., & Heath, S. B. (1993). *Guided Participation in Cultural Activity by Toddlers and Caregivers*. Monographs of the Society for Research in Child Development.

Rogoff, B., Newcombe, N., Fox, N., & Ellis, S. (1980). Transitions in children's roles and capabilities. *International Journal of Psychology, 15*(1–4), 181–200.

Rogoff, B., Paradise, R., Arauz, R. M., Correa-Chavez, M., & Angelillo, C. (2003). Firsthand learning through intent participation. *Annual Review of Psychology, 54*, 175–203.

Rogoff, B., Sellers, M. J., Pirrotta, S., Fox, N., & White, S. H. (1975). Age of assignment of roles and responsibilities to children: A cross-cultural survey. *Human Development, 18*, 353–369.

Rogoff, B., Topping, K., Baker-Sennett, J., & Lacasa, P. (2002). Mutual contributions of individuals, partners, and institutions: Planning to remember in girl scout cookie sales. *Social Development, 11*(2), 266–289.

Rogoff, B., & Waddell, K. J. (1982). Memory for information organized in a scene by children from two cultures. *Child Development, 53*(5), 1224–1228.

Roopnarine, J. (2010). Cultural variations in beliefs about play, parent–child play, and children's play: Meaning for childhood development. In A. D. Pellegrini (ed.), *The Oxford Handbook of the Development of Play* (pp. 19–40). Oxford: Oxford University Press.

Roopnarine, J., & Krishnakumar, A. (2006). Parent–child and child–child play in diverse cultural contexts. In D. Pronin Fromberg & D. Bergen (eds), *Play from Birth to Twelve: Contexts, Perspectives and Meanings* (pp. 275–288). New York: Routledge.

Roscoe, W. (1992). *The Zuni Man-Woman*. Albuquerque, NM: University of New Mexico Press.

Rosenfeld, C. S., & Roberts, R. M. (2004). Maternal diet and other factors affecting offspring sex ratio: A review. *Biology of Reproduction, 71*(4), 1063–1070.

Rothbaum, F., Pott, M., Azuma, H., Miyake, K., & Weisz, J. (2000). The development of close relationships in Japan and the United States: Paths of symbiotic harmony and generative tension. *Child Development, 71*(5), 1121–1142.

Rothbaum, F., Weisz, J., Pott, M., Miyake, K., & Morelli, G. (2000). Attachment and culture: Security in the United States and Japan. *American Psychologist, 55*(10), 1093–1104.

Röttger-Rössler, B., & Markowitsch, H. J. (eds) (2009). *Emotions as Bio-cultural Processes*. New York: Springer.

Rubin, J. Z., Provenzano, F. J., & Luria, Z. (1974). The eye of the beholder: Parents' views on sex of newborns. *American Journal of Orthopsychiatry, 44*(4), 512–519.

Ruffman, T., Perner, J., Naito, M., Parkin, L., & Clements, W. A. (1998). Older (but not younger) siblings facilitate false belief understanding. *Developmental Psychology, 34*(1), 161–174.

Ruffman, T., Perner, J., & Parkin, L. (1999). How parenting style affects false belief understanding. *Social Development, 8*(3), 395–411.

Ruffman, T., Slade, L., & Crowe, E. (2002). The relation between children's and mothers' mental state language and theory-of-mind understanding. *Child Development, 73*(3), 734–751.

Ruffman, T., Slade, L., Devitt, K., & Crowe, E. (2006). What mothers say and what they do: The relation between parenting, theory of mind, language and conflict/cooperation. *British Journal of Developmental Psychology, 24*(1), 105–124.

Rumbaut, R. G., & Komaie, G. (2010). Immigration and adult transitions. *The Future of Children, 20*(1), 43–66.

Sagi, A., van IJzendoorn, M. H., Aviezer, O., Donnell, F., Koren-Karie, N., Joels, T., et al. (1995). Attachments in a multiple-caregiver and multiple-infant environment: The case of the Israeli kibbutzim. *Monographs of the Society for Research in Child Development, 60*(2/3), 71–91.

Sagi, A., van IJzendoorn, M. H., Aviezer, O., Donnell, F., & Mayseless, O. (1994). Sleeping out of home in a kibbutz communal arrangement: It makes a difference for infant–mother attachment. *Child Development, 65*(4), 992–1004.

Sahlins, M. (2011). What kinship is (part one). *Journal of the Royal Anthropological Institute, 17*(1), 2–19.

Sameroff, A. (ed.). (2009). *The Transactional Model.* Washington, DC: American Psychological Association.

Samuelson, L. K., Smith, L. B., Perry, L. K., & Spencer, J. P. (2011). Grounding word learning in space. *PLoS One, 6*(12), 1–13.

Scaglion, R., & Condon, R. G. (1979). Abelam yam beliefs and sociorhythmicity: A study in chronoanthropology. *Journal of Biosocial Science, 11*(01), 17–25.

Schaller, M., & Crandall, C. S. (eds) (2012). *The Psychological Foundations of Culture.* Mahwah, NJ: Erlbaum.

Scherer, K. R., Clark-Polner, E., & Mortillaro, M. (2011). In the eye of the beholder? Universality and cultural specificity in the expression and perception of emotion. *International Journal of Psychology, 46*(6), 401–435.

Schlegel, A. (1995). A cross-cultural approach to adolescence. *Ethos, 23*(1), 15–32.

Schlegel, A. (2009). Cross-cultural issues in the study of adolescent development. In R. M. Lerner & L. Steinberg (eds), *Handbook of Adolescent Psychology. Vol 2: Contextual Influences on Adolescent Development* (pp. 570–589). Hoboken, NJ: Wiley.

Schmidt, M., Perc, M., & Sommerville, J. A. (2011). Fairness expectations and altruistic sharing in 15-month-old human infants. *PLoS ONE, 6*(10), e23223.

Schmidt, M., Rakoczy, H., Mietzsch, T., & Tomasello, M. (forthcoming). Young children understand the role of agreement in establishing arbitrary norms-but unanimity is key. *Child Development.*

Schroeder, S. (2009). A tale of two problems: Wittgenstein's discussion of aspect perception. In J. Cottingham & P. Hacker (eds), *Mind, Method, and Morality: Essays in Honour of Anthony Kenny* (pp. 352–372). Oxford: Oxford University Press.

Schultz, E. (2009). Resolving the anti antievolutionism dilemma: A brief for relational evolutionary thinking in anthropology. *American Anthropologist, 111*(2), 224–237.

Schwartz, S. J. (2001). The evolution of Eriksonian and neo-Eriksonian identity theory and research: A review and integration. *Identity: An International Journal of Theory and Research, 1*(1), 7–58.

Schwartz, S. J. (2008). Self and identity in early adolescence: Some reflections and an introduction to the special issue. *Journal of Early Adolescence, 28*(1), 5–15.

Scollon, R. (1976). *Conversations with a One Year Old: A Case Study of the Developmental Foundation of Syntax.* Honolulu, HI: University Press of Hawaii.

Scott, A. O. (2010). Voyage to the bottom of the day care center [Review of *Toy Story 3*], *The New York Times,* 17 June.

Scribner, S. (1977). Modes of thinking and ways of speaking: Culture and logic reconsidered. In P. C. Johnson-Laird & P. C. Wason (eds), *Thinking: Readings in Cognitive Science* (pp. 483–500). New York: Cambridge University Press.

Scribner, S. (1986). Thinking in action: Some characteristics of practical thought. In R. J. Sternberg & R. K. Wagner (eds), *Practical Intelligence: Nature and Origins of Competence in the Everyday World* (pp. 13–28). Cambridge: Cambridge University Press.

Scribner, S., & Cole, M. (1973). Cognitive consequences of formal and informal education. *Science, 182*(4112), 553–559.

Scribner, S., & Cole, M. (1981). *The Psychology of Literacy*. Cambridge, MA: Harvard University Press.

Searle, J. (1969). *Speech Acts: An Essay in the Philosophy of Language*. New York: Cambridge University Press.

Searle, J. (1972). Chomsky's revolution in linguistics. *New York Review of Books, 18*(12), 16–24.

Searle, J. R. (1980). The intentionality of intention and action. *Cognitive Science, 4*(1), 47–70.

Searle, J. R. (1995). *The Construction of Social Reality*. New York: Simon & Schuster.

Searle, J. R. (2005). What is an institution? *Journal of Institutional Economics, 1*(1), 1–22.

Searle, J. R. (2006). Social ontology: Some basic principles. *Anthropological Theory, 6*(1), 12–29.

Seki, T. (2011). *Neurogenesis in the Adult Brain. Vol. I: Neurobiology*. New York: Springer.

Selby, J. M., & Bradley, B. S. (2003). Infants in groups: A paradigm for the study of early social experience. *Human Development, 46*(4), 197–221.

Sellen, D. W. (2007). Evolution of infant and young child feeding: Implications for contemporary public health. *Annual Review of Nutrition, 27*, 123–148.

Selman, R. L. (2008). Through thick and thin. *Human Development, 51*(5–6), 318–325.

Senghas, A., Kita, S., & Ozyürek, A. (2004). Children creating core properties of language: Evidence from an emerging sign language in Nicaragua. *Science, 305*(5691), 1779–1782.

Serpell, R. (1993). Interface between sociocultural and psychological aspects of cognition. In E. A. Forman, N. Minick, & C. A. Stone (eds), *Contexts for Learning: Sociocultural Dynamics in Children's Development* (pp. 357–368). New York: Oxford University Press.

Serpell, R., & Hatano, G. (1997). Education, schooling, and literacy. In J. W. Berry, P. R. Dasen, & T. S. Saraswarthi (eds), *Handbook of Cross-cultural Psychology. Vol. 2: Basic processes and Human Development* (2nd edn, pp. 339–376). Boston, MA: Allyn & Bacon.

Shaham, S. (2005). Glia-neuron interactions in nervous system function and development. *Current Topics in Developmental Biology, 69*, 39–66.

Sharp, D., Cole, M., & Lave, C. (1979). Education and cognitive development: The evidence from experimental research. *Monographs of the Society for Research in Child Development, 44*(1/2), 1–112.

Shayer, M., Küchemann, D. E., & Wylam, H. (1976). The distribution of Piagetian stages of thinking in British middle and secondary school children. *British Journal of Educational Psychology, 46*(2), 164–173.

Shenkin, J. D., Broffitt, B., Levy, S. M., & Warren, J. J. (2004). The association between environmental tobacco smoke and primary tooth caries. *Journal of Public Health Dentistry, 64*(3), 184–186.

Shostak, M. (1981). *Nisa: The Life and Words of a !Kung Woman*. Cambridge, MA: Harvard University Press.

Shweder, R. A. (1999). Why cultural psychology? *Ethos, 27*(1), 62–73.

Shweder, R. A., & Jensen, A. (1985). Who sleeps by whom. *New Directions for Child Development, 67*, 98–121.

Shweder, R. A., Jensen, L. A., & Goldstein, W. M. (1995). Who sleeps by whom revisited: A method for extracting the moral goods implicit in practice. *New Directions for Child Development, 67*, 17–39.

Siegal, M. (1991). A clash of conversational worlds: Interpreting cognitive development through communication. In J. M. Levine & L. B. Resnick (eds), *Socially Shared Cognition*. Washington, DC: American Psychological Association.

Siegal, M., & Peterson, C. C. (1998). Preschoolers' understanding of lies and innocent and negligent mistakes. *Developmental Psychology, 34*(2), 332–341.

Simmons, W. K., & Barsalou, L. W. (2003). The similarity-in-topography principle: Reconciling theories of conceptual deficits. *Cognitive Neuropsychology, 20*(3–6), 451–486.

Singh, K.S. (2004). *People of India: Maharashtra* (edited by B.V. Vahnu). Mumbai: Popular Prakashan.

Sinha, C. (2006). Epigenetics, semiotics, and the mysteries of the organism. *Biological Theory, 1*(2), 112–115.

Sinha, C. (2009). Language as a biocultural niche and social institution. In V. Evans & S. Pourcel (eds), *New Directions in Cognitive Linguistics* (pp. 289–310). Amsterdam: John Benjamins.

Skinner Buzan, D. (2004). 'I was not a lab rat', *Guardian,* 3 March.

Skinner, B. F. (1953). *Science and Human Behavior.* New York: The Free Press/Collier-Macmillan.

Skinner, B. F. (1957). *Verbal Behavior.* New York: Appleton-Century-Crofts.

Smiley, S. S., & Brown, A. L. (1979). Conceptual preference for thematic or taxonomic relations: A nonmonotonic age trend from preschool to old age. *Journal of Experimental Child Psychology, 28*(2), 249–257.

Smith, B. H., & Tompkins, R. L. (1995). Toward a life history of the Hominidae. *Annual Review of Anthropology, 24,* 257–279.

Smith, L. B. (2005). Cognition as a dynamic system: Principles from embodiment. *Developmental Review, 25*(3–4), 278–298.

Smith, L. B., & Jones, S. S. (2011). Symbolic play connects to language through visual object recognition. *Developmental Science, 14*(5), 1142–1149.

Smith, L. B., & Pereira, A. F. (2010). Shape, action, symbolic play, and words: Overlapping loops of cause and consequence in developmental process. In S. P. Johnson (ed.), *Neoconstructivism: The New Science of Cognitive Development* (pp. 109–131). Oxford: Oxford University Press.

Smith, L. B., Thelen, E., Titzer, R., & McLin, D. (1999). Knowing in the context of acting: The task dynamics of the A-not-B error. *Psychological Review, 106*(2), 235–260.

Smith, L. B., & Yu, C. (2008). Infants rapidly learn word-referent mappings via cross-situational statistics. *Artificial Life, 106*(3), 1558–1568.

Smith, L. B., Yu, C., & Pereira, A. F. (2011). Not your mother's view: The dynamics of toddler visual experience. *Developmental Science, 14*(1), 9–17.

Smits, I., Soenens, B., Luyckx, K., Duriez, B., Berzonsky, M., & Goossens, L. (2008). Perceived parenting dimensions and identity styles: Exploring the socialization of adolescents' processing of identity-relevant information. *Journal of Adolescence, 31*(2), 151–164.

Smollar, J., & Youniss, J. (1989). Transformations in adolescents' perceptions of parents. *International Journal of Behavioral Development, 12*(1), 71–84.

Soltis, J. (2004). The signal functions of early infant crying. *The Behavioral and Brain Sciences, 27*(4), 443–490.

Son, J. Y., Smith, L. B., & Goldstone, R. L. (2008). Simplicity and generalization: Short-cutting abstraction in children's object categorizations. *Cognition, 108*(3), 626–638.

Spitz, R. A. (1965). *The First Year of Life: A Psychoanalytic Study of Normal and Deviant Development of Object Relations.* Oxford: International Universities Press.

Sroufe, L. A. (1997). *Emotional Development: The Organization of Emotional Life in the Early Years.* Cambridge: Cambridge University Press.

Sroufe, L. A., Carlson, E. A., Levy, A. K., & Egeland, B. (1999). Implications of attachment theory for developmental psychopathology. *Development and Psychopathology, 11*(1), 1–13.

Stapel, D. A., & Semin, G. R. (2007). The magic spell of language: Linguistic categories and their perceptual consequences. *Journal of Personality and Social Psychology, 93*(1), 23.

Steffen, W., Crutzen, P. J., & McNeill, J. R. (2007). The anthropocene: Are humans now overwhelming the great forces of nature? *AMBIO: A Journal of the Human Environment, 36*(8), 614–621.

Steinberg, L. (2005). Cognitive and affective development in adolescence. *Trends in Cognitive Sciences, 9*(2), 69–74.

Steinberg, L., & Lerner, R. M. (2004). The scientific study of adolescence: A brief history. *Journal of Early Adolescence, 24*(1), 45–54.

Steinberg, L., & Silk, J. S. (2002). Parenting adolescents. In M. Bornstein (ed.), *Handbook of Parenting. Volume 1: Children and Parenting* (pp. 103–133). Mawah, NJ: Erlbaum.

Stern, D. N. (1977). *The First Relationship: Infant and Mother*. New York: Fontana/Basic.

Stern, D. N. (1985). *The Interpersonal World of the Infant: A View from Psychoanalysis and Developmental Psychology*. New York: Basic.

Stevens, G. W. J. M., Pels, T. V. M., Vollebergh, W. A. M., & Crijnen, A. A. M. (2004). Patterns of psychological acculturation in adult and adolescent Moroccan immigrants living in the Netherlands. *Journal of Cross-Cultural Psychology*, *35*(6), 689–704.

Stigler, J. W., Schweder, R. A., & Herdt, G. (1990). *Cultural Psychology: Essays on Comparative Human Development*. Cambridge: Cambridge University Press.

Stiles, J., & Jernigan, T. L. (2010). The basics of brain development. *Neuropsychology Review*, *20*, 1–22.

Stolz, W. S., & Tiffany, J. (1972). The production of 'child-like' word associations by adults to unfamiliar adjectives. *Journal of Verbal Learning and Verbal Behavior*, *11*(1), 38–46.

Stone, J. E., Carpendale, J. I. M., Sugarman, J., & Martin, J. (2012). A Meadian account of social understanding: taking a non-mentalistic approach to infant and verbal false belief understanding. *New Ideas in Psychology*, *30*(2), 166–178.

Strauss, A., & Corbin, J. (1990). *Basics of Qualitative Research: Grounded Theory Procedures and Techniques* (1st edn). Newbury Park, CA: Sage.

Strauss, C. (1984). Beyond "formal" versus "informal" education: Uses of psychological theory in anthropological research. *Ethos*, *12*(3), 195–222.

Strong, A. K. (2005). Incest laws and absent taboos in Roman Egypt. *Ancient History Bulletin*, *19*(1–2), 31–41.

Subbotsky, E. (2014). The mind of an individual as a system of realities: The computational revolution and spirit in exile. *Reason & Science*, 1–33.

Sudnow, D. (1974). *Ways of the Hand: The Organization of Improvised Conduct*. Cambridge, MA: Harvard University Press.

Sugarman, S. (2011). *Children's Early Thought: Developments in Classification*. Cambridge: Cambridge University Press.

Super, C. M. (1987). The role of culture in developmental disorder: Introduction. In C. M. Super (ed.), *The Role of Culture in Developmental Disorder* (pp. 1–8). New York: Academic.

Super, C. M., & Harkness, S. (1982). The infant's niche in rural Kenya and metropolitan America. In L. L. Adler (ed.), *Cross-cultural Research at Issue* (pp. 47–55). New York: Academic.

Super, C. M., & Harkness, S. (1986). The developmental niche: A conceptualization at the interface of child and culture. *International Journal of Behavioral Development*, *9*(4), 545–569.

Super, C. M., & Harkness, S. (2002). Culture structures the environment for development. *Human Development*, *45*(4), 270–274.

Sutton-Smith, B. (1986). *Toys as Culture*. New York: Gardner.

Svetlova, M., Nichols, S. R., & Brownell, C. A. (2010). Toddlers' prosocial behavior: From instrumental to empathic to altruistic helping. *Child Development*, *81*(6), 1814–1827.

Swain, J. E., Lorberbaum, J. P., Kose, S., & Strathearn, L. (2007). Brain basis of early parent–infant interactions: Psychology, physiology, and in vivo functional neuroimaging studies. *Journal of Child Psychology and Psychiatry*, *48*(3–4), 262–287.

Synofzik, M., Vosgerau, G., & Newen, A. (2008). Beyond the comparator model: A multifactorial two-step account of agency. *Consciousness and Cognition*, *17*(1), 219–239.

Szabo-Rogers, H. L., Geetha-Loganathan, P., Whiting, C. J., Nimmagadda, S., Fu, K., & Richman, J. M. (2009). Novel skeletogenic patterning roles for the olfactory pit. *Development*, *136*(2), 219–229.

Tamis-LeMonda, C. S., & Adolph, K. E. (2005). Social referencing in infant motor action. In B. D. Homer & C. S. Tamis-LeMonda (eds), *The Development of Social Cognition and Communication* (pp. 145–164). Mahwah, NJ: Erlbaum.

Tamis-LeMonda, C. S., Adolph, K. E., Dimitropoulou, K. A., & Zack, E. (2007). No! Don't! Stop!: Mothers' words for impending danger. *Parenting: Science and Practice, 7*(1), 1–25.

Tappan, M. B. (1989). Stories lived and stories told: The narrative structure of late adolescent moral development. *Human Development, 32,* 300–315.

Tardif, T. (1996). Nouns are not always learned before verbs: Evidence from Mandarin speakers' early vocabularies. *Developmental Psychology, 32*(3), 492.

Tardif, T. (2006). But are they really verbs? Chinese words for action. In K. Hirsh-Pasek & R. M. Golinkoff (eds), *Action Meets Word: How Children Learn Verbs* (p. 477). New York: Oxford University Press.

Tardif, T., Shatz, M., & Naigles, L. (1997). Caregiver speech and children's use of nouns versus verbs: A comparison of English, Italian, and Mandarin. *Journal of Child Language, 24*(3), 535–565.

Tartakovsky, E. (2009). Cultural identities of adolescent immigrants: A three-year longitudinal study including the pre-migration period. *Journal of Youth and Adolescence, 38*(5), 654–671.

Taumoepeau, M., & Ruffman, T. (2006). Mother and infant talk about mental states relates to desire language and emotion understanding. *Child Development, 77*(2), 465–481.

Taumoepeau, M., & Ruffman, T. (2008). Stepping stones to others' minds: Maternal talk relates to child mental state language and emotion understanding at 15, 24, and 33 months. *Child Development, 79*(2), 284–302.

Taylor, C. (1971). Interpretation and the sciences of man. *Review of Metaphysics, 25*(1), 3–34, 45.

Taylor, C. (1989). *Sources of the Self: The Making of the Modern Identity.* Cambridge, MA: Harvard University Press.

Thelen, E. (1995). Motor development: A new synthesis. *American Psychologist, 50*(2), 79–95.

Thelen, E., & Fisher, D. M. (1982). Newborn stepping: An explanation for a "disappearing" reflex. *Developmental Psychology, 18*(5), 760–775.

Thelen, E., Schöner, G., Scheier, C., & Smith, L. B. (2001). The dynamics of embodiment: A field theory of infant perseverative reaching. *Behavioral and Brain Sciences, 24*(1), 1–34; discussion 34.

Thompson, R. A., & Nelson, C. A. (2001). Developmental science and the media: Early brain development. *American Psychologist, 56*(1), 5–15.

Thorne, B., & Luria, Z. (1986). Sexuality and gender in children's daily worlds. *Social Problems, 33*(3), 176–190.

Thorne, B. (1994). *Gender Play: Girls and Boys in School.* New Brunswick, NJ: Rutgers University Press.

Tobin, J., Hsueh, Y., & Karasawa, M. (2009). *Preschool in Three Cultures Revisited: China, Japan, and the United States.* Chicago: University of Chicago Press.

Tobin, J., Wu, D. Y. H., & Davodson, D. H. (1989). *Preschool in Three Cultures: Japan, China, and the United States.* New Haven, CT: Yale University Press.

Tomasello, M. (2001). First steps toward a usage-based theory of language acquisition. *Cognitive Linguistics, 11*(1–2), 61–82.

Tomasello, M. (2003). *Constructing a Language: A Usage-based Theory of Language Acquisition.* Cambridge, MA: Harvard University Press.

Tomasello, M. (2006). Why don't apes point? In N. J. Enfield & S. C. Levinson (eds), *Roots of Human Sociality: Culture, Cognition and Interaction* (pp. 506–524). Oxford: Berg.

Tomasello, M. (2011). Language development. In U. Goswami (ed.), *The Wiley-Blackwell Handbook of Childhood Cognitive Development* (pp. 239–257). Oxford: Wiley.

Tomasello, M. (2016). Precís of a natural history of human thinking. *Journal of Social Ontology*, *2*(1), 59–64.

Tomasello, M., & Carpenter, M. (2007). Shared intentionality. *Developmental Science*, *10*(1), 121–125.

Tomasello, M., Carpenter, M., Call, J., Behne, T., & Moll, H. (2005). Understanding and sharing intentions: The origins of cultural cognition. *Behavioral and Brain Sciences*, *28*(5), 675–691.

Tomasello, M., Carpenter, M., & Liszkowski, U. (2007). A new look at infant pointing. *Child Development*, *78*(3), 705–722.

Tomasello, M., & Vaish, A. (2013). Origins of human cooperation and morality. *Annual Review of Psychology*, *64*, 231–255.

Tooby, J., & Cosmides, L. (1992). The psychological foundations of culture. In J. Barkow, J. Cosmides, & J. Tooby (eds), *The Adapted Mind: Evolutionary Psychology and the Generation of Culture* (pp. 19–136). New York: Oxford University Press.

Topál, J., Gergely, G., Miklósi, A., Erdöhegyi, A., & Csibra, G. (2008). Infants' perseverative search errors are induced by pragmatic misinterpretation. *Science*, *321*(5897), 1831–1834.

Toren, C. (1993). Making history: The significance of childhood cognition for a comparative anthropology of mind. *Man*, *28*(3), 461–478.

Trevarthen, C. (1974). Conversations with a two-month-old. *New Scientist*, *62*(896), 230–235.

Trevarthen, C. (1979). Communication and cooperation in early infancy: A description of primary intersubjectivity. In M. Bullowa (ed.), *Before Speech: The Beginning of Interpersonal Communication* (pp. 321–347).

Trevarthen, C. (1998). The concept and foundations of infant intersubjectivity. In S. Bråten (ed.), *Intersubjective Communication and Emotion in Early Ontogeny* (pp. 15–46). Cambridge: Cambridge University Press.

Trevarthen, C. (2004). How infants learn how to mean. In M. Tokoro & L. Steels (eds), *A Learning Zone of One's Own: Sharing Representations and Flow in Collaborative Learning Environments*. Amsterdam: Ios.

Trevarthen, C. (2005). First things first: Infants make good use of the sympathetic rhythm of imitation, without reason or language. *Journal of Child Psychotherapy*, *31*(1), 91–113.

Trevarthen, C., & Aitken, K. J. (2001). Infant intersubjectivity: Research, theory, and clinical applications. *Journal of Child Psychology and Psychiatry and Allied Disciplines*, *42*(01), 3–48.

Tronick, E. Z. (1989). Emotions and emotional communication in infants. *American Psychologist*, *44*(2), 112–119.

Tronick, E. Z., Morelli, G. A., & Ivey, P. K. (1992). The Efe forager infant and toddler's pattern of social relationships: Multiple and simultaneous. *Developmental Psychology*, *28*(4), 568–577.

Tronick, E. Z., Thomas, R. B., & Daltabuit, M. (1994). The Quechua manta pouch: A caretaking practice for buffering the Peruvian infant against the multiple stressors of high altitude. *Child Development*, *65*(4), 1005–1013.

Tulving, E. (1983). *Elements of Episodic Memory*. Oxford: Clarendon.

Turiel, E. (1975). The development of social concepts: Mores, customs, and conventions. In J. M. Foley & D. J. DePalma (eds), *Moral Development: Current Theory and Research*. Hillsdale, NJ: Erlbaum.

Turiel, E. (1983). *The Development of Social Knowledge: Morality and Convention*. Cambridge: Cambridge University Press.

Turiel, E. (2012). Moral reasoning, cultural practices and social inequalities. *Innovación Educativa*, *12*(59), 17–32.

Turkle, S. (2012). *Alone Together: Why We Expect More from Technology and Less from Each Other*. New York: Basic.

Turner, J. S. (2009). *The Extended Organism: The Physiology of Animal-built Structures*. Cambridge, MA: Harvard University Press.

Tuzin, D. F. (1990). Of the resemblance of fathers to their children: The roots of primitivism in middle-childhood enculturation. In L. B. Boyer & S. A. Grolnick (eds), *Psychoanalytic Study of Society: Essays in Honor of Melford E. Spiro* (Vol. 15, pp. 69–103). New York: International Universities.

Tversky, A., & Kahneman, D. (1974). Judgment under uncertainty: Heuristics and biases. *Science, 185*(4157), 1124–1131.

Underwood, E. (2015). Lifelong memories may reside in nets around brain cells. *Science, 350*(6260), 491–492.

United Nations Children's Fund (2012). *Children in an Urban World: The State of the World's Children 2012.* New York: UNICEF.

Van Gelder, T. (1995). What might cognition be, if not computation? *Journal of Philosophy, 92*(7), 345–381.

van Hoof, A. (1999). The identity status field re-reviewed: An update of unresolved and neglected issues with a view on some alternative approaches. *Developmental Review, 19*(4), 497–556.

van IJzendoorn, M. H., Bakermans-Kranenburg, M. J., & Sagi-Schwartz, A. (2006). Attachment across diverse sociocultural contexts: The limits of universality. In K. H. Rubin & O. B. Chung (eds), *Parenting Beliefs, Behaviors, and Parent-child Relations: A Cross-cultural Perspective* (pp. 107–142). New York: Taylor & Francis.

van IJzendoorn, M. H., & Sagi, A. (1999). Cross-cultural patterns of attachment: Universal and contextual dimensions. In J. Cassidy & P. R. Shaver (eds), *Handbook of Attachment: Theory, Research and Clinical Applications* (1st edn). New York: Guilford.

Varela, F. J., Thompson, E., & Rosch, E. (1992). *The Embodied Mind: Cognitive Science and Human Experience.* Cambridge, MA: MIT Press.

Ventura, P., Pattamadilok, C., Fernandes, T., Klein, O., Morais, J., & Kolinsky, R. (2008). Schooling in western culture promotes context-free processing. *Journal of Experimental Child Psychology, 100*(2), 79–88.

Vereijken, B., & Adolph, K. E. (1999). Transitions in the development of locomotion. In G. J. P. Savelsbergh, H. L. J. van der Maas, & P. C. L. van Geert (eds), *Non-linear Analyses of Developmental Processes* (pp. 137–149). Amsterdam: Elsevier.

Vicedo, M. (2011). The social nature of the mother's tie to her child: John Bowlby's theory of attachment in post-war America. *British Journal for the History of Science, 44*(3), 401–426.

Vihman, M. M. (1992). Early syllables and the construction of phonology. In C. A. Ferguson, L. Menn, & C. Stoel-Gammon (eds), *Phonological Development: Models, Research, Implications* (pp. 393–422). Tominium, MD: York.

Vinden, P. G. (1996). Junín Quechua children's understanding of mind. *Child Development, 67*(4), 1707–1716.

Vinden, P. G. (1998). Imagination and true belief: A cross-cultural perspective. In J. de Rivera & T. R. Sarbin (eds), *Believed-in Imaginings: The Narrative Construction of Reality* (pp. 73–85). Washington, DC: American Psychological Association.

Vinden, P. G. (1999). Children's understanding of mind and emotion: A multi-culture study. *Cognition & Emotion, 13*(1), 19–48.

Vinden, P. G. (2002). Understanding minds and evidence for belief: A study of Mofu children in Cameroon. *International Journal of Behavioral Development, 26*(5), 445–452.

Visalberghi, E., & Fragaszy, D. M. (1994). Do monkeys ape? In S. T. Parker & K. R. Gibson (eds), *'Language' and Intelligence in Monkeys and Apes: Comparative Developmental Perspectives* (pp. 247–273). Cambridge: Cambridge University Press.

Viveiros de Castro, E. (2012). Cosmologies: Perspectivism. In *Cosmological Perspectivism in Amazonia and Elsewhere* (pp. 45–168). Manchester: HAU Network of Ethnographic Theory.

von Fürer-Haimendorf, C. (1950). Youth-dormitories and community houses in India: A restatement and a review. *Anthropos: International Review of Ethnology and Linguistics, 45*(1/3), 119–144.

Vygotsky, L. S. (1966a). Play and its role in the mental development of the child. *Voprosy Psikhologii, 12*(6), 62–76. (Original work published 1933.)

Vygotsky, L. S. (1966b). Play and its role in the mental development of the child. *Soviet Psychology*, *5*(3), 6–18.

Vygotsky, L. S. (1978). *Mind in Society: The Development of Higher Psychological Processes*. Cambridge, MA: Harvard University Press.

Vygotsky, L. S. (1987). Thinking and speech. In R. W. Rieber & A. S. Carton (eds), *The Collected Works of L. S. Vygotsky. Volume 1: Problems of General Psychology* (pp. 39–285). New York: Plenum.

Vygotsky, L. S. (1989). Concrete human psychology. *Journal of Russian and East European Psychology*, *27*(2), 53–77.

Vygotsky, L. S. (1993). The dynamics of child character (J. E. Know & C. B. Stevens, Trans.). In R. W. Rieber & A. S. Carton (eds), *The Collected works of L. S. Vygotsky. Vol. 2: The Fundamentals of Defectology* (pp. 153–163). New York: Plenum.

Vygotsky, L. S. (1997a). The history of the development of higher mental functions. In R. W. Rieber & A. S. Carton (eds), *The Collected Works of L. S. Vygotsky. Vol. 4: The History of the Development of Higher Mental Functions* (pp. 1–252). New York: Plenum.

Vygotsky, L. S. (1997b). *Educational Psychology*. Boca Raton, FL: St. Lucie. (Original work published 1926.)

Vygotsky, L. S. (1998a). Pedology of the adolescent. In R. W. Rieber (ed.), *The Collected Works of L. S. Vygotsky. Vol. 5: Child Psychology* (pp. 31–184). New York: Plenum. (Original work published 1931.)

Vygotsky, L. S. (1998b). The problem of age. In R. W. Rieber (ed.), *The Collected Works of L. S. Vygotsky. Vol. 5: Child Psychology* (pp. 187–205).

Vygotsky, L. S. (1998c). Lectures on child psychology. In R. W. Rieber (ed.), *The Collected Works of L. S. Vygotsky. Vol. 5: Child Psychology* (pp. 207–296). New York: Kluwer Academic/Plenum Publishers. (Original work published 1932–1934.)

Vygotsky, L. S. (2004a). Dynamics and structure of the adolescent's personality. In R. W. Rieber & D. K. Robinson (eds), *The Essential Vygotsky* (pp. 471–490). New York: Kluwer Academic/Plenum.

Vygotsky, L. S. (2004b). The historical meaning of the crisis in psychology: A methodological investigation. In R. W. Rieber & D. K. Robinson (eds), *The Essential Vygotsky* (pp. 227–357). New York: Kluwer Academic/Plenum Publishers. (Original work published 1927.)

Waddington, C. H. (1940). *Organisers and Genes*. Cambridge: Cambridge University Press.

Wagner, D. A. (1981). Culture and memory development. In D. A. Wagner, H. C. Triandis, & A. Heron (eds), *Handbook of Cross-cultural Psychology* (Vol. 4, pp. 187–232). Boston, MA: Allyn & Bacon.

Wainryb, C. (2004). 'Is' and 'ought': Moral judgments about the world as understood. *New Directions for Child and Adolescent Development*, *2004*(103), 3–18.

Wainryb, C., & Brehl, B. A. (2006). 'I thought she knew that would hurt my feelings': Developing psychological knowledge and moral thinking. *Advances in Child Development and Behavior*, *34*, 131–171.

Walker, E. F. (2002). Adolescent neurodevelopment and psychopathology. *Current Directions in Psychological Science*, *11*(1), 24–28.

Walker-Andrews, A. S., Krogh-Jespersen, S., Mayhew, E. M. Y., & Coffield, C. N. (2011). Young infants' generalization of emotional expressions: Effects of familiarity. *Emotion*, *11*(4), 842–851.

Waterman, A. S. (1999). Identity, the identity statuses, and identity status development: A contemporary statement. *Developmental Review*, *19*(4), 591–621.

Waters, E., Hamilton, C. E., & Weinfield, N. S. (2000). The stability of attachment security from infancy to adolescence and early adulthood: General introduction. *Child Development*, *71*(3), 678–683.

Waters, E., Merrick, S., Treboux, D., Crowell, J., & Albersheim, L. (2000). Attachment security in infancy and early adulthood: A twenty-year longitudinal study. *Child Development*, *71*(3), 684–689.

Watson, J. B. (1913). Psychology as the behaviorist views it. *Psychological Review, 20*(2), 158.

Watson, J. B. (1916). The place of the conditioned-reflex in psychology. *Psychological Review, 23*(2), 89.

Watson, J. B. (1925). *Behaviorism*. New York: The People's Institute.

Watson, J. B. (1928). *Psychological Care of Infant and Child*. New York: Arno Press & The New York Times.

Watson, J. S. (2005a). The elementary nature of purposive behavior: Evolving minimal neural structures that display intrinsic intentionality. *Evolutionary Psychology, 3*, 24–48.

Watson, J. S. (2005b). *Causal Logic and the Intentional Stance*. Proceedings from international web conference on causality.

Watson-Gegeo, K. A. (2001). Fantasy and reality: The dialectic of work and play in Kwara'ae children's lives. *Ethos, 29*(2), 138–158.

Waxman, S. R., & Booth, A. E. (2001). Seeing pink elephants: Fourteen-month-olds' interpretations of novel nouns and adjectives. *Cognitive Psychology, 43*(3), 217–242.

Way, N. (2006). The cultural practice of close friendships among urban adolescents in the United States. In X. Chen, D. C. French, & B. H. Schneider (eds), *Peer Relationships in Cultural Context* (pp. 403–425). Cambridge: Cambridge University Press.

Weisner, T. S. (1984). Ecocultural niches of middle childhood: A cross-cultural perspective. In W. A. Collins (ed.), *Development During Middle Childhood: The Years from Six to Twelve* (pp. 335–369).

Weisner, T. S. (1987). Socialization for parenthood in sibling caretaking societies. In J. B. Lancaster, J. Altmann, A. S. Rossi, & L. R. Sherrod (eds), *Parenting Across the Life Span: Biosocial Dimensions* (pp. 237–270). Hawthorne, NY: Aldine de Gruyter.

Weisner, T. S. (1989). Comparing sibling relationships across cultures. In P. G. Zukow (ed.), *Sibling Interaction Across Cultures: Theoretical and Methodological Issues* (pp. 11–25). New York: Springer.

Weisner, T. S. (1996). The 5 to 7 transition as an ecocultural project. In A. Sameroff & M. M. Haith (eds), *The Five to Seven Year Shift: The Age of Reason and Responsibility* (pp. 295–326). Chicago, IL: University of Chicago Press.

Weisner, T. S., & Gallimore, R. (1977). My brother's keeper: Child and sibling caretaking. *Current Anthropology, 18*(2), 169–190.

Welles-Nystrom, B. (2005). Co-sleeping as a window into Swedish culture: Considerations of gender and health care. *Scandinavian Journal of Caring Sciences, 19*(4), 354–360.

Welles-Nystrom, B. (2006). Parenthood and infancy in Sweden. *New Directions for Child and Adolescent Development, 1988*(40), 75–80.

Wellman, H. M. (2011). Developing a theory of mind. In U. Goswami (ed.), *The Wiley-Blackwell Handbook of Childhood Cognitive Development* (2nd edn, pp. 258–284). New York: Wiley.

Wellman, H. M. (2014). *Making Minds: How Theory of Mind Develops*. Oxford: Oxford University Press.

Wellman, H. M., Cross, D., & Watson, J. (2001). Meta-analysis of theory-of-mind development: The truth about false belief. *Child Development, 72*(3), 655–684.

Wellman, H. M., & Miller, J. G. (2008). Including deontic reasoning as fundamental to theory of mind. *Human Development, 51*(2), 105–135.

Werner, E. E., & Gilliam, J. F. (1984). The ontogenetic niche and species interactions in size-structured populations. *Annual Review of Ecology and Systematics, 15*, 393–425.

Westermann, G., Mareschal, D., Johnson, M. H., Sirois, S., Spratling, M. W., & Thomas, M. S. C. (2007). Neuroconstructivism. *Developmental Science, 10*(1), 75–83.

Westermarck, E. (2003). *The History of Human Marriage*. London: Macmillan. (Original work published 1921.)

Whitehead, A. N. (2011). *Science and the Modern World*. Cambridge: Cambridge University Press. (Original work published 1926.)

Whiting, B. B. (1963). *Six Cultures: Studies of Child Rearing*. New York: Wiley.

Whiting, J. (1977). A model for psychocultural research. In P. H. Leiderman, S. R. Tulkin, & A. Rosenfeld (eds), *Culture and Infancy: Variations in the Human Experience* (pp. 29–48). New York: Academic.

Wiener, N. (1965). *Cybernetics or Control and Communication in the Animal and the Machine*. Cambridge, MA: MIT Press. (Original work published 1948.)

Williams, R. (1983). *Keywords: A Vocabulary of Culture and Society* (revised edn). New York: Oxford University Press.

Willis, P. (1977). *Learning to Labor: How Working Class Kids get Working Class Jobs*. New York: Columbia University Press.

Wilson, A. (1990). The ceremony of childbirth and its interpretation. In V. Fildes (ed.), *Women as Mothers in Pre-industrial England: Essays in Memory of Dorothy McLaren* (pp. 68–107). London: Routledge.

Wilson, P. J. (1988). *The Domestication of the Human Species*. New Haven, CT: Yale University Press.

Winsler, A., & Naglieri, J. (2003). Overt and covert verbal problem-solving strategies: Developmental trends in use, awareness, and relations with task performance in children aged 5 to 17. *Child Development, 74*(3), 659–678.

Wirtz, D., & Chiu, C. (2008). Perspectives on the self in the East and the West: Searching for the quiet ego. In H. Wayment & J. Bauer (eds), *Transcending Self-interest: Psychological Explorations of the Quiet Ego*. Washington, DC: American Psychological Association.

Wissink, I. B., Dekovic, M., Yagmur, S., Stams, G. J., & de Haan, M. (2008). Ethnic identity, externalizing problem behaviour and the mediating role of self-esteem among Dutch, Turkish-Dutch and Moroccan-Dutch adolescents. *Journal of Adolescence, 31*(2), 223–240.

Wolff, P., & Medin, D. L. (2001). Measuring the evolution and devolution of folkbiological knowledge. In L. Maffi (ed.), *On Biocultural Diversity: Linking Language Knowledge and the Environment* (pp. 212–227). Washington, DC: Smithsonian Institution.

Wood, D., Bruner, J. S., & Ross, G. (1976). The role of tutoring in problem solving. *Journal of Child Psychology and Psychiatry, 17*, 89–100.

Worthman, C. M., & Melby, M. K. (2002). Toward a comparative developmental ecology of human sleep. In M. A. Carskadon (ed.), *Adolescent Sleep Patterns: Biological, Social, and Psychological Influences* (pp. 69–117). New York: Cambridge University Press.

Wundt, W. (1910). *Volkerpsychologie: Eine Untersuchung der Entwicklungsgesetze von Sprache, Mythus, und Sitte*. Leipzig: Engelmann.

Wynn, T. (1979). The intelligence of later Acheulean hominids. *Man, 14*(3), 371–391.

Wynn, T. (1981). The intelligence of Oldowan hominids. *Journal of Human Evolution, 10*(7), 529–541.

Yoder, A. E. (2000). Barriers to ego identity status formation: A contextual qualification of Marcia's identity status paradigm. *Journal of Adolescence, 23*(1), 95–106.

Youngblade, L. M., & Dunn, J. (1995). Individual differences in young children's pretend play with mother and sibling: Links to relationships and understanding of other people's feelings and beliefs. *Child Development, 66*(5), 1472–1492.

Yovsi, R. D., & Keller, H. (2003). Breastfeeding: An adaptive process. *Ethos, 31*(2), 147–171.

Zahn-Waxler, C., Radke-Yarrow, N., & King, R. A. (1979). Child-rearing and children's prosocial initiations towards victims of distress. *Child Development, 50*, 319–330.

INDEX

Note: Page numbers in *italics* indicate figures and tables.